PHILOSOPHICAL INTERVENTIONS

# Philosophical Interventions

REVIEWS

1986–2011

Martha C. Nussbaum

OXFORD

UNIVERSITY PRESS

# OXFORD
### UNIVERSITY PRESS

Oxford University Press, Inc., publishes works that further
Oxford University's objective of excellence
in research, scholarship, and education.

Oxford   New York
Auckland   Cape Town   Dar es Salaam   Hong Kong   Karachi
Kuala Lumpur   Madrid   Melbourne   Mexico City   Nairobi
New Delhi   Shanghai   Taipei   Toronto

With offices in
Argentina   Austria   Brazil   Chile   Czech Republic   France   Greece
Guatemala   Hungary   Italy   Japan   Poland   Portugal   Singapore
South Korea   Switzerland   Thailand   Turkey   Ukraine   Vietnam

Copyright (c) 2012 Oxford University Press

Published by Oxford University Press, Inc.
198 Madison Avenue, New York, New York 10016
www.oup.com

Library of Congress Cataloging-in-Publication Data
Nussbaum, Martha Craven, 1947–
Philosophical interventions: reviews, 1986–2011/
Martha Nussbaum.
p. cm.
Includes bibliographical references and index.
ISBN 978–0-19–977785-3 (alk. paper)
1. Books—Reviews. 2. Nussbaum, Martha Craven, 1947—Books and
reading. I. Title.
Z1003.N93   2012
028.1—dc22      2011012606

3 5 7 9 8 6 4 2

Printed in the United States of America
on acid-free paper

*To Leon, who made so much of this possible*

# Contents

CONTENTS

CONTENTS

# CONTENTS

# CONTENTS

# CONTENTS

# Acknowledgments

I am very grateful to Peter Ohlin of Oxford University Press for suggesting the idea of this collection and for being so helpful throughout the process. I owe thanks to *The New York Review of Books*, *The New Republic*, *The Times Literary Supplement*, *The Nation*, and *The London Review of Books* for permission to reprint my essays—and of course, as the Introduction records, for their participation in generating the reviews in the first place and editing them. For research assistance I am most grateful to Ryan Long, and for comments on the Introduction to Brian Leiter, Richard Posner, and Saul Levmore.

# Complete List of Reviews to Date

1. Pierre Louis, *Aristote: Marche des animaux, Mouvement des animaux*, in *Journal of Hellenic Studies*, 1975.
2. H.-J. Newiger, *Untersuchungen zu Gorgias' Shrift über das Nichtseiende*, in *Journal of Hellenic Studies*, 1976.
3. S. Clark, *Aristotle's Man*, in *The Philosophical Review*, 1976.
4. Hazel Barnes, *The Meddling Gods*, in *Philosophy and Literature*, 1977–78 (review-article).
5. Iris Murdoch, *The Fire and the Sun: Why Plato Banished the Artists*, in *Philosophy and Literature*, 1978–79.
6. Edwin Hartman, *Substance, Body, and Soul: Aristotelian Investigations*, in *The Journal of Philosophy*, June 1980 (review-article).
7. Rudolph Kassel, *Der Text der aristotelischen Rhetorik* and *Aristotelis Ars Rhetorica*, in *Archiv für Geschichte des Philosophie*, 1981.
8. Marilyn French, *Beyond Power: of Women, Men, and Morals*, in *The Boston Globe*, July 21, 1985.
9. Michel Foucault, *The Use of Pleasure*, in *The New York Times Book Review*, November 10, 1985. Reply to letters, December 15.
10. Jane Roland Martin, *Reclaiming a Conversation: The Ideal of the Educated Woman*, in *The New York Review of Books*, January 30, 1986.
11. Iris Murdoch, *Acastos: Two Platonic Dialogues*, in *The Times Literary Supplement*, August 15, 1986.
12. Roger Scruton, *Sexual Desire*, in *The New York Review of Books*, December 18, 1986.
13. Michael Stokes, *Plato's Socratic Conversations*; Charles Griswold, *Self-Knowledge in Plato's Phaedrus;* and Christopher Rowe, *Plato: Phaedrus*, in *The Times Literary Supplement*, June 1987.
14. Allan Bloom, *The Closing of the American Mind*, in *The New York Review of Books*, November 5, 1987.
15. Wayne Booth, *The Company We Keep: An Ethics of Fiction*, in *Yale Journal of Law and Humanities* 1 (1988) (review-article).

16. Alasdair MacIntyre, *Whose Justice? Which Rationality?* in *The New York Review of Books*, December 7, 1989.

17. Phillip Mitsis, *Epicurus' Ethical Theory*, in *Philosophy and Phenomenological Research* 51(1991).

18. Anthony Price, *Love and Friendship in Plato and Aristotle*, in *The Times Literary Supplement*, February 1990.

19. David Halperin, *One Hundred Years of Homosexuality and Other Essays on Greek Love;* John J. Winkler, *The Constraints of Desire: The Anthropology of Sex and Gender in Greece*, in *The Times Literary Supplement*, June 1990.

20. Charles Taylor, *Sources of the Self: The Making of Modern Identity*, in *The New Republic*, April 1990.

21. Judith Shklar, *The Faces of Injustice*, in *The New Republic*, November 1990.

22. Gregory Vlastos, *Socrates: Ironist and Philosopher*, in *The New Republic*, September 15, 1991.

23. Richard A. Posner, *Sex and Reason*, in *The New Republic*, April 1992.

24. Andrea Dworkin, *Mercy*, in *The Boston Review*, April 1992. Replies to letters, September 1992.

25. Susan Moller Okin, *Justice, Gender, and the Family*, in *The New York Review of Books*, October 8, 1992.E

26. "'Only Grey Matter'? Richard Posner's Cost-Benefit Analysis of Sex," in *The University of Chicago Law Review* 59 (1992).

27. William Bennett, *The Book of Virtues*, in *The New Republic*, December 1993.

28. Anne Hollander, *Sex and Suits* (with two other books), in *The New Republic*, January 2, 1995.

29. Louise Antony and Charlotte Witt, eds., *A Mind of One's Own: Feminist Essays on Reason and Objectivity*, in *The New York Review of Books*, October 20, 1994. Reply to letters, March 1995.

30. Kenneth Dover, *Marginal Comment: An Autobiography*, in *Arion* 4 (1997).

31. Richard Sorabji, *Animal Minds, Human Morals*, in *The Philosophical Review* 105 (1996).

32. Kristen Monroe, *The Heart of Altruism;* and Tvetan Todorov, *Facing the Extreme*, in *The New Republic*, October 28, 1996.

33. Bernard Williams, *Making Sense of Humanity*, in *Ethics*, 1997.

34. Gregory Vlastos, *Socratic Studies*, in *The Journal of Philosophy* 94 (1997).

35. Andrea Dworkin, *Life and Death*, in *The New Republic*, August 11/18, 1997.

36. William Miller, *The Anatomy of Disgust*, in *The New Republic*, November 17, 1997.

37. Peter Unger, *Living High and Letting Die*, in *The London Review of Books*, September 4, 1997. Reply to letters, October 30, 1997.

38. A. Reath, B. Herman, and C. Korsgaard, eds., *Reclaiming the History of Ethics: Essays for John Rawls*, in *Ethics* 109 (January 1999).

39. Alexander Nehamas, *The Art of Living*, in *The New Republic*, January 4/11, 1999.

40. Judith Butler, four books, in *The New Republic*, February 22, 1999. Replies to letters, April 19, 1999. German translation in *Leviathan* 27 (1999). French translation in *Raisons politiques* 12 (2003). Italian version in *Il bello del relativismo*, ed. Elisabetta Ambrosi (Venice: Reset, 2005).

41. Michael Warner, *The Trouble with Normal*, in *The New Republic*, January 3, 2000.

42. Allen Buchanan, Dan W. Brock, Norman Daniels, and Daniel Wikler, *From Chance to Choice: Genetics and Justice*, in *The New Republic*, December 4, 2000.

43. Eva Feder Kittay, *Love's Labor: Essays on Women, Equality, and Dependency*; Michael Bérubé, *Life As We Know It: A Father, a Family, and an Exceptional Child*; Joan Williams, *Unbending Gender: Why Family and Work Conflict and What to Do About It*, in *The New York Review of Books*, January 11, 2001. In Italian as "La via delle persone disabili: Chi se ne prende cura?," *Il Mulino* 5 (2001).

44. Edward Said, *Reflections on Exile*, in *New York Times Book Review*, February 18, 2001.

45. Steven Wise, *Rattling the Cage: Toward Legal Rights for Animals*, in *Harvard Law Review* 114 (2001).

46. Peter Conradi, *Iris Murdoch: A Life*, in *The New Republic*, December 31, 2001, and January 7, 2002.

47. F. Robert Rodman, *Winnicott: Life and Work*, in *The New Republic*, October 27, 2003.

48. Mary Kinzie, *Drift*, in *Poetry*, 183 (January 2004).

49. Judith Brown, *Nehru: A Political Life*; Shashi Tharoor, *Nehru*, in *The New Republic*, February 14, 2005.

50. Bart Schultz, *Henry Sidgwick: The Eye of the Universe*, in *The Nation*, June 6, 2005.

51. Vivian Gornick, *The Solitude of Self: Thinking About Elizabeth Cady Stanton*, in *The Nation*, February 27, 2006.

52. Kenji Yoshino, *Covering: The Hidden Assault on Our Civil Rights*, in *The New Republic*, March 20/27, 2006.

53. Harvey Mansfield, *Manliness*, in *The New Republic*, June 26, 2006.

54. Harry Lewis, *Excellence Without a Soul: How a Great University Forgot Education*, in *Times Literary Supplement*, July 15, 2006.

55. Catharine A. MacKinnon, *Are Women Human?* in *The Nation*, July 31/August 7, 2006.

56. Philip Zimbardo, *The Lucifer Effect: How Good People Turn Evil*, in *Times Literary Supplement*, October 19, 2007. Polish translation in *Dziennik* 44 (2007).

57. T. N. Madan, *Images of the World: Essays on Religion, Secularism, and Culture*, in *Economic and Political Weekly* (India), December 8–14, 2007.

58. A. D. Nuttall, *Shakespeare the Thinker*; Colin McGinn, *Shakespeare's Philosophy*; Tzachi Zamir, *Double Vision: Moral Philosophy and Shakespearean Drama*, in *The New Republic*, May 7, 2008.

59. Nicholas Kristof and Sheryl WuDunn, *Half the Sky: Turning Oppression into Opportunity for Women*, in *The New York Times*, September 9, 2009.

60. Cristina Nehring, *A Vindication of Love*, in *The New Republic*, September 23, 2009.

61. Nicola Lacey, *Women, Crime, and Character: From Moll Flanders to Tess of the D'Urbervilles*, in *Times Literary Supplement*, September 18, 2009.

62. Astra Taylor, *The Examined Life* (film), in *The Point*, 2 (winter 2010).

63. Christine Stansell, *The Feminist Promise: 1792 to the Present*, in *The Nation*, October 25, 2010.

PHILOSOPHICAL INTERVENTIONS

# Introduction

This book began, perhaps, with a conversation with John Rawls in Bartley's Burger Cottage in Cambridge, in those far-away days when I still loved burgers. It is thus, inevitably, a record both of ongoing commitment and of personal change. I don't even remember the year of the conversation or the book we were discussing, but the conversation itself made a lasting impression on me. I had just been invited to review a book for some relatively public journal, and I sought Rawls's advice about whether I should spend my time in this way. I expected him to say no, that writing books and philosophical articles was the important thing: after all, that was how he had spent his life. But he surprised me. He told me that he knew that he himself did not have the ability to speak or write as a public intellectual (thinking, no doubt, of the stammer that always afflicted him, but perhaps also of his dense literary style). If, however, one has those abilities, he said to me, then one has a duty to use them for the public good. I never forgot that, and it has led not only to a side career as a book reviewer but also to the production of some books addressing public issues for a general public, books that I think of as a form of public service owed in gratitude for a life of remarkable happiness and self-indulgence, talking and writing about whatever I love most. Those books include *Cultivating Humanity: A Classical Defense of Reform in Liberal Education* (1997) (written after the Gifford Lectures that eventually became *Upheavals of Thought*, representing ten years of wanton self-indulgence on topics so lovely to struggle with); *The Clash Within: Democracy, Religious Violence, and India's Future* (2007); *From Disgust to Humanity: Sexual Orientation and Constitutional Law* (2009); *Not For Profit: Why Democracy Needs the Humanities* (2010); and this year, *Creating Capabilities: The Human Development Approach* (2011) (after the intellectual pleasure of pondering all the nuances of a philosophical position in two specialized books, a book explaining it very clearly to the general public). All these books, produced in the interstices of more scholarly and detailed investigations, are a type of public intervention, and thus the book reviews collected here represent just one part of my attempt to answer John Rawls's challenge.

This volume, then, is the record of twenty-five years of engagement with political and cultural issues from the vantage point of philosophy and through the genre of the book review. The reviews reprinted here constitute "interventions" in ongoing public debates, which attempt in some manner to change the course of those debates, though in some cases rather indirectly. Omitted are reviews that are of interest primarily to specialists in philosophy and classical studies—even when these include pieces on figures of major cultural interest, such as Bernard Williams, John Rawls, and Iris Murdoch. (A complete list of my reviews appears at the end of this Introduction.) Also omitted are reviews so brief that there is little opportunity to develop a sustained line of argument—even though these include discussions of major cultural figures such as Michel Foucault and Edward Said. Finally, some reviews that would otherwise fit well with the aims of the collection have been omitted because they have already been reprinted in other collections of mine: a review of Wayne Booth in *Love's Knowledge*, and reviews of Kenneth Dover, Andrea Dworkin, and Richard Posner in *Sex and Social Justice*. In the case of the Posner book, I have reproduced the general-audience review published in *The New Republic*, but not the more technical review published in a law journal; the version in *Sex and Social Justice* is an amalgam of the two.

The pieces reproduced here are all addressed to a general public audience and contain enough sustained argument to count, I hope, as philosophical interventions. Sometimes, of course, the argument is more up front and sometimes more indirect—as is also the case with my books and other essays. I have included a review of a volume of poetry by Mary Kinzie, because her work concerns issues of gender, violence, and the body that lie at the heart of my philosophical work, and because meditating on poetic images has always been, for me, one way of getting access to the human meaning of a philosophical position. Philosophers don't often get invited to review poetry, and this rare opportunity was both an honor and a pleasure.

When a philosopher speaks as a public intellectual, some aspects of professional style must be left behind. These include some lamentable tics of professional writing that I try to leave behind always, such as excessive use of acronyms, letters, and numbers; the unnecessary formalization of arguments where a simple prose statement would have been at least as clear; and the (often accompanying) unnecessary use of logical notation. They also, however, include some virtuous professional habits, such as due references to one's predecessors and contemporaries, the analysis of an argument into numbered steps where this actually advances clarity, and a rich sense of the history of a problem. What I do as a teacher and as a more specialized writer uses all of these techniques, and I believe they are immensely valuable in their own contexts. The prose of the public intellectual, however, must find a way of being lucid without footnotes or numbered steps, which are likely to repel the reader. That such a philosophical style has often been achieved in the past, by philosophers ranging from Plato and Seneca to John Stuart Mill and Henry Sidgwick, gives one confidence that it is possible to write in this way—clear and rigorous but without scholarly paraphernalia—if only one's care with language is sufficient. But it is not simply a matter of subtraction: doing justice to the dimensions of a philosophical problem for the general public requires additional virtues that are frequently absent from more specialized philosophical prose. These include human responsiveness, a sense of life that is both experienced and humble, the ability to dramatize an important problem, a sense of life's complexity, and a sense of humor. Philosophers writing for a wide public can combine insight and warmth with philosophical argument—as some great philosophers, including Seneca, Rousseau, Hume, and Mill, have in their different ways demonstrated.

Despite not being written primarily for professional philosophers, the pieces in this collection are all philosophical, as I understand that activity. My view of philosophy is Socratic and democratic. As I observe in my review of Astra Taylor's film *The Examined Life*, that understanding is opposed to some others that are popular, and, above all, to the image of the philosopher as spiritual guru and solitary thinker of profound thoughts. To me, philosophy is a contribution to a democratic conversation, most fully exemplified when there really is conversation and response, but the imagined conversation with an author can at times attain that sense of lively interaction, at the same time conducting a similar conversation with the reader. If the philosopher is to engage the reader in such a Socratic conversation, she must define the problem or problems in question, clarify the alternatives on offer, and present a sequence of reflections with sufficient articulation and clarity that the reader will know where she may leap in and say, "Wait a minute! Where did that premise come from?" Or, "I don't see how that follows." Or, "That term you are bandying about is actually multivocal, and you'd better get clear about its meaning." By making such objections to the authors I am reviewing, I invite similar critical activity on the part of the reader, and am never more happy than when I receive it. A lot of this responsive activity will go on outside of my awareness, as readers respond to a review and discuss it with their friends. Sometimes, though, it becomes possible for me to have a more direct exchange with readers—through letters to the editor, or personal e-mails. Indeed, since nobody publishes letters to authors, and since the e-mail addresses of authors are usually pretty inaccessible, the reviewer becomes an important intermediary, opening the door for lay readers to discuss, publicly or on e-mail, an author's contribution. (All too often, however—sadly—letters to the editor are disappointing in that regard: so often they are ill-argued, or intemperate, or given to griping rather than engagement. The exception stands out, such as a splendidly challenging letter written by Drucilla Cornell apropos of my Judith Butler review, which made me see similarities between Michel Foucault and Catharine MacKinnon that I have been pondering ever since.)

Our public culture, given to sound bites, macho denigration, and hysterical invective, badly needs the clarity philosophy can provide. It also needs the sense of mutual respect embodied in the commitment to engage with another person, not as an enemy to be humiliated, but as a rational being with a structure of argument to be patiently analyzed. I aspire to that Socratic respect, albeit with a greater commitment to the depths of the human emotions and the complexity of human psychology than Plato's early dialogues impute to the figure of Socrates. As I record in the recent review of Collini, maintaining that climate of respect, in a world of wide political, disciplinary, and other differences, requires the virtue of civility, a careful attention to tone and manner of argumentation that imposes particularly exigent demands when a member of a more powerful group is addressing traditionally marginalized minorities, whom it has been customary to dismiss as not full participants in intellectual debate.

Why the book review? First, it is an interactive medium that invites the sustained exchange of arguments (if one has enough words to play with), and thus it is particularly well suited to the type of public intervention a Socratic philosopher seeks to provide. It is also, perhaps more importantly, the only popular medium in which an academic in the United States has a real chance to engage with the public on a regular basis. Our cultural media rarely invite or even admit essays containing philosophical arguments on issues of the day. *Dissent*, *The Nation*, and *The Boston Review* are exceptions, and I have regularly written for them, but one can reach a wider audience— and on a far wider range of issues—by reviewing. In reviews one can address issues of love and friendship, for example, which the three journals named would not easily encompass. And one can reflect about the careers of prominent figures of the past by reviewing biographies, whereas writing an essay on, say, Henry Sidgwick, one would not be very likely to find publication in a general-interest journal.

In other countries it is—or at least was until the rapid decline of print journalism that has taken place during the past few years—easier than it is in the United States to write an article on a public issue and then have that article appear in a major newspaper or a general-interest magazine. Even an op-ed—a form so brief that it is not ideal for philosophizing—is far easier for a philosopher to publish in Holland or India or Sweden than in the United States—even for me, who lives and works here. So reviews are the best hope of establishing a reliable connection with the general public, particularly if one manages to have an ongoing relationship with one or more editors of quality who will regularly propose topics and to whom one might occasionally propose a topic of one's own. I therefore have been lucky to have established good working relationships with a series of review editors at *The Nation* and the *Times Literary Supplement*, with Robert Silvers at *The New York*

*Review of Books* (a connection that somehow came to a stop around ten years ago), and, above all, with Leon Wieseltier at *The New Republic*, who is a prince among editors, because he has terrific ideas for pairing authors with books, combined with a wide-ranging cultural and human intelligence that immediately seizes the point of an argument or a suggestion. Although Leon has definite views of his own, and sometimes urges me at least to discuss a particular type of objection, he never tries to slant my review, even when my own slant greatly surprises him, as my favorable treatment of Bennett's *The Book of Virtues* did. As a technical editor, he is interventionist enough to improve a piece greatly, but not so interventionist as to be dictatorial. He is also prompt and responsive, replying in a reasonable length of time with a plausible set of deadlines. Such is not always the case. Hence, my dedication of this collection to a person who has done as much, in his capacity as editor, to improve the quality of public discourse as anyone living.

Perhaps we are heading into a future in which even the book review will no longer serve as a device through which a public intellectual may find her public. The recent decline in print journalism has meant a sharp decline in the number of pages journals and newspapers devote to reviews, and also in the quality and depth of those that they do print. In my copy of Bernard Williams's *Ethics and the Limits of Philosophy*, a major philosophical book with much to offer a wider public, is a yellowed copy of a review from the *New York Times Book Review*, written by Ronald De Sousa, a first-rate philosopher, but hardly a household name. Today that book would not be reviewed there—very little serious nonfiction is—and if any book of philosophy were perchance to be reviewed there, it would not be reviewed by a first-rate philosopher. The *Los Angeles Times*, which had a very fine book review section to which such excellent philosophers as the late Richard Wollheim contributed, has dropped that section altogether—although the *Wall Street Journal* has recently added one, somewhat surprisingly. Silvers and Wieseltier are fighting a rear-guard action (although the *NYRB* apparently remains profitable), and it remains unclear how long even they can hold out. The book review is a fine genre for the public intellectual, and we can only hope that it continues to be so.

The Internet offers new opportunities for public intellectuals to engage with issues, but we should carefully weigh its promise against its liabilities, trying to avoid the latter as much as possible while we avail ourselves of the former. Its reach is extraordinary; on the other hand, its audience is often balkanized, thus often making it less, rather than more, likely that the public intellectual will reach a broad and diverse public. Again, it offers unparalleled opportunities for Socratic exchange with the public: one really can converse with anyone at all, and go into detail in responding to an individual's argument. On the other hand, the anonymity it offers is frequently abused, so that Socratic exchange (which thrives on personal accountability) degenerates into invective and even abuse. I myself have had a policy of not reading or writing for blogs, simply because I have calculated that the cost in terms of lost writing time would not be offset by the likely benefits. I think, however, that this is a questionable choice, given the prominence of the Internet in the future of public discourse, and I applaud public intellectuals who manage to use its potential creatively. Recently, I greatly enjoyed an opportunity to participate in a series of philosophical essays in the *New York Times* "Opinionator" blog, and to engage directly with the public in the discussion that followed my essay on religious toleration, apropos of European bans of the burqa. It was really lovely to have 5000 words or more to speak directly with one's critics, and in that case I really did feel that the blog had promoted a Socratic conversation. Even though many of the anonymous responses were just invective, there were enough that were thoughtful so that I felt exhilarated by the opportunity to respond person by person. Perhaps a good solution for the future will be that certain well-known Internet sites—for example, the blog sections of major newspapers—will become sites of public exchange, and book reviews themselves may appear in this online form. At any rate, as media change we must all think hard about how the virtues of the book review can be perpetuated in other forms.

How are reviews generated? I've encountered considerable misunderstanding on this score—often from authors who want me to review their books or to make sure that they get reviewed. Usually, the initial suggestion comes from the editor, who simply mails me a book. Then, the discussion is about whether I want to review it or not. At that point, I sometimes suggest a slight alteration: for example, it was I who proposed adding Tzachi Zamir's book on Shakespeare and philosophy (which was still in press) to the other two books by better-known authors. But the editor is usually firmly in the driver's seat, and this brings with it some limitation but, more often, surprise and opportunity. My reviews of Martin, Scruton, Bloom, MacIntyre, Halperin/Winkler, Taylor, Vlastos, Posner, Bennett, Hollander, Monroe/Todorov, Miller, Unger, Butler, Buchanan/Brock/Daniels/Wikler, Conradi, Kinzie, the two Nehru books, Schultz, Yoshino, Mansfield, MacKinnon, Zimbardo, Nuttall/McGinn, Lacey, and Stansell were all editor-initiated. I proposed only Okin, Antony/Witt, Warner, Kittay/Bérubé/Williams, the Winnicott biography, the group of books on widows and the related film, Nehring, and the Astra Taylor film. (As one can see from the unpublished widow piece, such self-generated projects, even when encouraged by an editor, as this one was, do not always end up in print.) I have also frequently said no to proposals, and at times, having said yes, have not gotten around to writing my review, if the pressure of other work and teaching has proved too much for me, or if the book ultimately fails to engage me sufficiently. When I have suggested a review to an editor, it is often because the book is one that deserves attention but is not likely to get it, because the author is little known, or young, or a feminist, or all three. Sometimes an editor becomes convinced that an entire field deserves further exploration: thus, after I had reviewed Martin's book at Bob Silvers's suggestion, he allowed me to initiate reviews of Okin, Antony/Witt, and Kittay, which brought feminist work to greater public attention. A couple of other attempts to review feminist work, however, didn't pan out. One, a review of Christina Hoff Sommers's *Who Stole Feminism*, suggested by Silvers, eventually ended up, much altered, as a chapter in my book *Sex and Social Justice*, because by the time I received comments from Silvers the book was already being remaindered, and its moment (since it was a slight book) had passed. Another, on a series of feminist books on care, never appeared, because we simply could not agree on the revisions proposed. The piece on widows in India, planned by me with Silvers's encouragement, never appeared anywhere (after he simply failed to send me any comments on it, presumably because he did not find it sufficiently interesting), and is printed here for the first time. Warner, Zamir, and Rodman were other authors whose work, though important, was not getting the attention it deserved. I suggested Nehring's book for a different reason: although I found the book flawed, it raised such fascinating questions that I really wanted to talk about it. Finally, my review of Astra Taylor's film, which appeared in a new Chicago cultural journal started by some students of mine, was written at my suggestion: I was getting invited to speak about the film, since I was in it, and I believed that my objections to it deserved a wider audience.

Readers should be aware that all reviews in general-interest periodicals are rather heavily edited by the editors in question. The versions printed here are drawn directly from the print version; in most cases I have no reliable electronic version, because changes are made up until the final moments. Occasionally I myself am surprised by what I see in print, although that experience represents a lapse and ought to be avoided by better communications. I typically have the opportunity to discuss and/or reject proposed edits, but a good relationship requires seeing the editor's point of view and accepting suggestions that are reasonable, even if one is not yet convinced that they are ideal. Usually the editor's eye is invaluable, spotting unclarities or ambiguities that a general reader will find bothersome. Sometimes I may continue to feel that my original version was slightly better, but I accept a proposal in the spirit of collegiality; if I feel that my version is a lot better, I dig in.

The titles that appear above the reviews are all created by the journal (sometimes by the editor, sometimes by someone else), and I am not consulted. Sometimes, indeed, I am rather surprised.

Should one review books by people one knows well? It is inevitable, when one has spent a long time in the academy, that one will know a lot of the people in one's own field, but I typically avoid reviewing books by people I know extremely well, or who have been my graduate students. In two cases where the person was a colleague at my own institution (Catharine MacKinnon, Christine Stansell), I showed each of them a draft of the review in order to give them an opportunity to correct any misstatements, but in neither case did this result in significant change. David Halperin is now a close friend, but I did not know him so well at the time of my review. One exception to this rule is my friend Richard Posner, whose book I reviewed after he was already becoming a friend, and about whose work I have since written with even more unbridled critical energy (in criticizing his Holmes Lectures in the *Harvard Law Review*). Here all I can say is that in the case of this particular friendship, frank speech and sparring are at its heart, and pulling one's punches in any way would be treachery. (Once when we were teaching together, a student evaluation, under the good points of the class, mentioned "the wonderful entertainment of watching the professors fight.") Of course a delight in sparring can lead to distortion just as can a delight in pleasing, so the reader is urged to watch out.

What makes a review responsible? Of course, this is not a question one poses to oneself as such, in the abstract; but some general principles evolve as one works in this genre. First, it is crucial to read the entire book, to read it carefully and often more than once, and to take copious notes. Many reviewers don't do this, and indeed many scholars don't, either, as one soon discovers if one writes long books. (My own personal favorite is the fact that quite a few reputable philosophers describe my position on the emotions as the position I outline in chapter 1 of *Upheavals of Thought*, even though I explicitly say there that the chapter presents a crude outline sketch, to be revised and modified by the inquiries in the subsequent three chapters. Apparently many people can't be bothered to read the other chapters, in an admittedly lengthy book; but they also didn't read chapter 1 carefully, since they missed my explicit account of its role.)

Having read the book carefully, the reviewer then has a duty to talk about the book, not to indulge herself by talking about whatever happens to interest her. This duty is complex, because sometimes the main interest of a book is that it does raise some general issues of interest, even when the book itself is comparatively thin; with such a book one may have a little more latitude. With a biography one has a duty to talk about the book and also about its subject, since the reader needs to know what the treatment of a figure contributes to our thought about that figure. My reviews of the biographies of Nehru, Murdoch, Winnicott, and Sidgwick are illustrations of the way I understand this divided duty.

The next duty is to be explicit, supporting claims by quotations if possible and page references. (Some journals print page references and some—for example, *The New Republic*—do not, but all my drafts contain dozens of such references, and the editor uses them to check the piece for accuracy.) A related duty of explicitness pertains to the construction of one's own argument: it's important to put one's cards on the table, trying to make any assumptions evident and in general to show the reader where the criticisms are coming from. Thus, the Socratic picture of philosophizing that I describe in detail in reviewing Astra Taylor is also made evident as background to my critique of Butler.

Another type of accountability is accountability to a field. If one criticizes a member of a subfield, then I think one has a responsibility to make clear whether this criticism applies to the entirety of that subfield or only to the author. Sometimes one can do this within a single review, and sometimes it emerges from a sequence of reviews, which may be self-chosen to at least some degree. Thus, my critiques of Allan Bloom and Harvey Mansfield, two students of Leo Strauss, was balanced by a more favorable treatment of Bennett, another Strauss-influenced thinker, though the project in question was not particularly Straussian. I did not initiate the Bennett review, but I agreed to it (having looked at the book) in part because it gave me a chance to indicate that I do not find all conservative writings on virtue objectionable. Again, the negative review of Butler was immediately juxtaposed by a favorable review of Michael Warner, another leading queer theorist, but one who writes with a type of clarity and rigor that I had found lacking in Butler. I initiated the Warner review, as much to illustrate my view of the field as to recognize Warner's under-noticed work.

A distinction that is very important for a reviewer to make, but one that too often gets obscured, is that between truth (as one sees it) and quality. Of course, often falsity is the result of a failure of quality: sloppy factual work, bad argument. But in complex matters where it is likely that nobody has the final truth, quality and truth-as-per-the-reviewer come apart to at least some extent. A book may be very slight and yet be on to something important (as Nehring's is). A book may also be myopic, or even perverse, and yet be illuminating—in exactly the way that books of philosophy may be wonderfully illuminating despite, or even on account of, their challenge to what one takes to be a reasonable view of human existence. (Thus, Plato and Bentham are indispensable, though not the sanest guides to life.) I usually have some parochial disagreements with all the books I review—after all, what would be the point of writing only to echo or summarize? But often I am in substantial agreement with the author, despite having such criticisms. At other times, however, even when I feel that a book is first rate and illuminating, I also have very deep and pervasive disagreements with it: William Miller's book on disgust is a case in point, as is Christine Stansell's *The Feminist Promise*. Sometimes my reservations concern the subject of a book rather than its author: thus Winnicott and Nehru, two of my personal heroes, also had very large flaws; about the wonderful philosopher and novelist Iris Murdoch, I remain profoundly ambivalent, personally and professionally. I hope that I have succeeded in conveying the message that a book is of lasting worth, when it is, even though I may disagree with it; for of course the reader may prefer the views on offer in the book to the views I express. In other cases, however (Bloom, Butler), I believe both that the views are wrong-headed and that the books are weak: someone who wants to investigate the type of view in question would be better off consulting a different book.

Finally, reviews ought to be accountable to the ongoing public debate on issues that the books raise. And this means that, where possible, they must both respond to an immediate situation and ponder more enduring issues— at times drawing on the history of philosophy to show how those issues have unfolded. Some of the reviews reprinted here are quite topical, in the sense that a particular public controversy was their occasion. My hope was and is, however, that while such a review does engage with a particular moment, it also raises issues that are more enduring. It's just not worth writing about something that is a mere will-o'-the-wisp. Even the slightest and least lasting of the books considered here—for example, Harvey Mansfield's *Manliness* and Cristina Nehring's *A Vindication of Love*, concern human issues of deep and abiding significance. Sometimes the issues are, in a sense, new arrivals—as the issue of justice for people with disabilities was new at the time I wrote the Kittay review. But none of the pieces raises issues that are merely transient, and surely the issues Kittay raises ought to have been recognized long before, although they weren't.

When one engages with a controversial issue, letters are frequently the result, and this, as I've said, produces a welcome continuation of the interactive Socratic process of reviewing. Not all letters to the editor are published, and some journals print very few of the letters they receive. Not all, moreover, give the author of the original review a chance to respond. I have reproduced here three exchanges of letters that seem of particular interest. One (Unger) involves a response from the author of the book under review, an important species of Socratic interaction—as well as involving the participation of Peter Singer, a philosopher of major significance. The Antony/ Witt letter exchange clarified some of the issues that divide feminists into factions, and one of the letters was from one of the authors discussed in the review of this multi-author collection. The Butler exchange, which involved some well-known philosophers, showed that sometimes people speak to the issue and sometimes not. My own policy, when I reply to letters (as in the reviews themselves), is always to speak to the issues and not to write ad hominem. I am delighted if a letter raises a substantial issue, as Cornell's did, giving occasion for the sort of clear and responsible public debate that I think philosophy ought to provide.

The reviews that appear here fall into a number of distinct categories. One obvious category is the review of a book of major significance that changes the state of debate in ethical or political thought. Such are my reviews of Charles Taylor's *Sources of the Self* and Gregory Vlastos's *Socrates: Ironist and Philosopher*. But I'd put some others in that category as well— certainly Okin's *Justice, Gender, and the Family*, Kittay's *Love's Labor*, and MacKinnon's *Are Women Human?*, all of which challenge conventional ways of seeing a given domain and reorient thought within it in a way that seems likely to endure.

Another genre might be called the "discovery review." Here, I try to bring valuable work that would otherwise go unrecognized to the attention of a broad general public. Feeling that good feminist work in philosophy and new scholarship on sexual orientation were often ill-covered, I've been particularly eager to tell people about it, and in these cases (Martin, Okin, Halperin/Winkler, Kittay, Antony/Witt, Warner, the never-published review of Chen) one can assume that I singled out the books (either initiating the review or agreeing to an editor's proposal) because I already found something valuable in them, and found that the work was not receiving the attention it deserved. The same is true of Zamir's Shakespeare book, which reenergized my interest in the topic, after it had been languishing because the two books by better-known authors (Nuttall, McGinn) did little to engage my imagination.

Then there is the deflationary review, and I'm afraid that these make a particularly deep impression on people, so that I am too often identified with this type of writing. Actually, only the pieces on Bloom, MacIntyre, Butler, Mansfield, and the part of the unpublished widow review that concerns Deepa Mehta's film fall into this category: all assail an allegedly overblown reputation and claim that the work is simply not good work. Indeed, the MacIntyre piece is only partly in this category, since I consider MacIntyre a major philosopher. Deflationary reviews are fun to read for people who dislike the ideas or influence of the target, but they are difficult to write, and they need to be written with unusual care and sobriety. It would be all too easy to be cheaply dismissive of others, and that tendency should be utterly repudiated. Therefore, in the pieces in question I make more than my usual effort to read and reread and to show the reader that I have done so. The only piece in which I allow myself some sarcasm and humor is the Mansfield piece, in part because the book is too slight as argument to merit the sort of serious engagement that I give the other three, in part because Mansfield's own approach to his topic verges on camp. (There is also humor in the review of Nehring, but that one is not really deflationary, since nobody was praising that book.) On the whole, though, I believe I have honored my commitment both to care in argument and to civility, in the sense of respectful confrontation. I agree with Collini that one can write very strong criticism of another person's views while still being fully respectful of the other person.

Why would one write a deflationary review in the first place, given the dangers of the genre? One should certainly not write too many, lest one get seduced into habits of disdain and flippancy. The only reason, I think, is to warn of a danger. If something is being widely praised and is exerting a great deal of influence, but on the basis of bad work (inaccurate facts, sloppy argumentation, some deep incoherence), then one ought to speak up, lest that influence do real damage. In part because of Bloom's personal charm and charisma, his broadside against new curricular thinking on campuses, inaccurate and full of half-baked claims to authority, was exerting a widespread influence on parents, trustees, and others with influence over the direction of higher education. Bloom's rhetorical strategy was to claim to be speaking on behalf of a wide range of great thinkers of the West, from Socrates onward. It was potentially useful, then, to point out that he had not done his homework and gave a very unconvincing portrayal of the thinkers on whom he based an argument that, in any case, was weak, diffuse, and riddled with contradiction. MacIntyre had achieved such cultural eminence with *After Virtue*, a much better book, that when he announced that liberalism was doomed to incoherence and that only authority-based moralities had historical authenticity and human weight, he was likely to convince a lot of people who might simply accept the historical claims in his book. People are all too ready to defer to authority anyway, and when some serious thinker tells them they have no choice they may feel relieved, because liberal democracy is difficult. Once again, showing that his arguments were based on inadequate textual work could potentially perform a public service. Mansfield's book, though lightweight by comparison, was another broadside against the equality of women and other liberal positions, and it was absurdly full of inaccuracy and bad argument. Attacking that one, I almost had a feeling of excess, but the widespread public acclaim given to his ideas (including the prestigious Jefferson Lecture of the National Endowment for the Humanities) convinced me that someone needed to speak up and say that this emperor has no clothes. With Deepa Mehta's film, the danger was of a different sort: that an American or European audience might take her portrayal of the situation of India's widows as factual, thus missing something of importance about women's resourcefulness and agency.

Butler is a figure of a very different sort ("left" rather than "right," "radical" rather than "conservative"), but she has more in common with Bloom and MacIntyre than one might at first blush suppose. She, too, practices philosophy in a way that subordinates reason to personal authority, and she, too, refrains from the sort of Socratic explicitness and vulnerability that is, to me, the hallmark of respectable philosophy, and of what philosophy can contribute to the public culture of a democracy. (That she shares these traits with some revered continental figures who were prominent in her education—Heidegger comes especially to mind—does not exactly offer a defense, though it may offer a partial explanation.) It often turns out that writing that is all dressed up in some sort of jargon looks lofty because of the jargon but poor and bare once it is translated into a publicly sharable language, and that, I tried to show, was the case with Butler. Although she had a couple of new ideas, many were common currency in feminism and gay studies before her, and there was a lot of obfuscation that simply got in the way of good thought. That is not to say that there is never any reason to write in an unusual way: as I have long tried to argue, Henry James and Marcel Proust contribute ingredients for our thought about ourselves and our relationship to the world that no plainer style could have captured. The two write in very different ways; Proust's style is much more direct. But both explore psychological nuance and complexity by dwelling at length on small movements of thought and desire. Butler's style, however, did not seem to me to be at all similar to what these wonderful novelists (or, indeed, a poet like Mary Kinzie) supply to our reflections. The jargon spun like wheels, and its only function was to reinforce deference to Butler and to discourage people from critical thinking.

I was hoping that my longstanding championing of gay studies, and of such authors as Halperin and Winkler, would make clear that my critique of Butler was just that—a critique of Butler; but just to make sure of that, I followed up that review with an admiring review of Michael Warner's *The Trouble with Normal*, which shows that you can express what is valuable in the germs of ideas like Butler's in clear, well-argued prose.

I also tried to show that Butler's ideas, once they were translated into a shared public language, were actually not so "left" or "radical"—that they had a great deal in common with right-wing libertarian thought. Once one holds that the appropriate reaction to political norms is a stance of parody or subversion, it requires some work to show why the stance that greets conservative sexual norms should not greet, as well, the norms of tax compliance or the requirements of national health insurance. Had the Tea Party been on the scene already, I could have made this point even more vividly. Political thought needs norms, and norms are not inherently repressive: only the ones that repress important human liberties are repressive, so one must begin by arguing about what those major areas of liberty are. None of this work is done by Butler, and she repudiates the whole inquiry as inherently repressive, which it isn't.

For better or for worse, my reviews of Bloom and Butler have garnered more attention than any other reviews in this collection, and the Butler piece has been translated several times. I don't like to be known for something negative, since I have spent most of my career offering constructive views on a variety of topics, and most of my career as a reviewer discovering praiseworthy work and showing my esteem for other good work already discovered. Still, I think those reviews performed a useful function.

One persistent misunderstanding needs to be firmly extinguished: I am sometimes paraphrased as having said that Butler and her work are "evil." If I had said that, it would certainly have been hyperbolic and uncivil. Read the review, however, and you will see that what it says is that she and her work—her "response" to the problems of injustice in our world—"collaborates with evil," the evils in question being sexism, violence against women, and discrimination against minority sexualities. The context makes plain that my point is that Butler, by encouraging a hip defeatism and quietism, allows these forces to have a sway they might not otherwise have in human life. If talented young intellectuals follow Butler, they will be drawn away from theorizing in a manner that contributes to the pursuit of social justice. (This was no mere hypothetical: the type of feminism that put sexual harassment on the map of the law, that won crucial changes in rape law, that produced a fruitful reexamination of conceptions of the family and care labor, was being gradually replaced, at that time, by a more hermetic and quietistic type of feminist scholarship.) For that reason my review calls for a more activist type of theory, a theory that gives useful direction for political action and encourages one to suppose that this action may be productive. (Of course, the fact that Butler may personally engage in valuable activism is neither here nor there. I am reviewing her books, and discussing the instructions they give to their reader.) "Feminism demands more and women deserve better," my review concludes. I believe that this strong criticism was civil and supported by argument, and that objecting to it on the grounds that it is likely to offend its target would be mistaken, in just the way discussed in Collini's useful book.

How are book reviews connected to the substance of one's philosophical work? It would be horrible if one's major contribution were in this genre, because, first of all, sustained philosophical thought needs a more capacious medium; and, second, one would not even be a good reviewer unless one were doing a good deal of other work, because the perceptions that lead to good reviewing are usually cultivated and sharpened elsewhere. On occasion, however, a review assignment can greatly enrich one's other work, or lead to new directions in it. Such was the case with my review of the group of books on disability. I was already thinking about that topic, and about the limitations of the social contract tradition in that respect. Working on those three valuable books, however, gave new traction to the thoughts and led to a far more radical critique of the contract tradition than I had previously been contemplating. My 2006 book *Frontiers of Justice* owes a great deal to the review. A catalyst of a different sort was my review of Miller's *The Anatomy of Disgust*. I had already written most of *Upheavals of Thought*, and had worked out a pretty detailed account of the cognitive structure of central emotions, which I had by then applied to a range of specific emotions, including grief, anger, love, and compassion. I had not, however, considered disgust. Miller's brilliant treatment—which also acquainted me with the wonderful empirical research of Paul Rozin and his colleagues—made me feel that this emotion had to figure in the revised version of that book, as it now does. But at the same time it started me on a new path. Miller, though a law professor, had virtually nothing to say about the role that disgust can and should play in the law, although this theme is prominent in legal theory since Lord Devlin's *The Enforcement of Morals*. I had a hunch that one could use the insights of the Rozin research and Miller's additions to it—albeit in a very different spirit from Miller's—to undertake a reexamination of the role of disgust in lawmaking. The book *Hiding From Humanity* (2004) was the result. More recently, I have returned to the theme in *From Disgust to Humanity: Sexual Orientation and Constitutional Law* (2009). So that one book review generated two books and a large chunk of another.

The reviews are all presented without rewriting of any kind, thus without cultural updating or second thoughts. Would I change any of my judgments? I think I might possibly emphasize more than I did the fact that

Allan Bloom and I share some extremely important commitments. We share a conviction that the humanities are educationally central and that they make an important contribution to democracy. We also share a belief in the depth and human importance of some philosophical classics standardly included in lists of "great books," such as the works of Plato, Aristotle, and Rousseau. I saw no need to emphasize those shared commitments in 1986, because no prominent figure in the United States was questioning them—although Margaret Thatcher's profit-oriented model of education had already put humanists on the defensive by that time in Britain, and classics departments were already producing desperate memos about how the classics produce efficient managers for industry. Bloom and I (and William Bennett, too) would have been utterly united in rejecting that impoverished profit-oriented model. Today, the terrain that American liberals and conservatives once shared is no longer common ground. The opposition to my educational ideal is now not a humanistic convervatism but a neo-Thatcherism that assesses all contributions in terms of economic growth and short-term profit for industry. I feel a nostalgia for my old conservative opponents: for although we had many and serious differences, we were united against the cheapening of learning into a set of useful skills for financial enrichment.

The shift toward agreement with Bloom that I have just described is not a change of position, but a shift of emphasis brought about by changing circumstances. But I think I have also shifted more toward Bloom in a way that involves a partial change in my own views: I now have far less objection than I once did to the idea of a liberal arts curriculum based on a list of Great Books. I still see the dangers of that approach: excessive deference to intellectual authority, excessive parochialism (such as the focus on European culture that Bloom recommended), and insufficient attentiveness to the activation of the student's own critical powers. Nonetheless, these pitfalls can be avoided by good teaching and by wise updating of the core lists themselves, as has by now been done at both Columbia and my own university. Such a core does something that is very good in this era of video games and social networking: it makes sure that people are actually reading big, complicated books. Times have changed, and it seems likely that the only way to make sure that undergraduates actually read a novel of George Eliot, a dialogue of Plato, or a treatise of Rousseau or Hume is to put it on a list— though one would be well advised to supplement any such list of "classics" with more recent works that engage undergraduates, and with works from a variety of cultural traditions. So, while I do not retract any of the specific criticisms of Bloom's own scholarship and argumentation that I made in that piece, and while I think he was utterly misguided in seeing women's studies and the study of race as cheapening the intellectual endeavor, I now see him as a potential ally who had some important things to say.

What about changes in me, those Proustian discontinuities I mentioned at the outset? Although some very general problems continue to obsess me, now as then—the nature of the emotions, the precariousness of human life, the aspiration to social justice—I have turned my attention to some problems that I did not appreciate earlier, particularly to issues of disability, animal rights, and global justice—the three "frontiers" that are the subject of my book *Frontiers of Justice*. In the case of disability, it was writing the Kittay review itself, and the indelible impact of Kittay's powerful analysis and description (as well as that of Bérubé's remarkable narrative), that turned me to that set of issues. And of course, going back further, issues of gender justice and sexual orientation were not part of my philosophical agenda when I first got my degree, although they were by that time a part of my political life; so even earlier, the problems that are my focus have shifted.

Apart from new problems, though, I don't think I've been changed very much by the passage of time—apart from thinking better of the idea of prolonging life, a topic that does not come up in the present collection. I find in this record of the years a continued stubborn optimism about personal love and friendship, about the possibility of justice, and about the power of theory to do some good in the world.

These commitments are not precisely philosophical, in the sense that no justification is offered for them, and perhaps none could be offered. Still, as Kant observed, when experience does not show our hopes for good things to be utterly impossible, it's a good thing to adopt hope as our "practical postulate," in order to motivate ourselves to "do something useful for the common good." Kant did not intend to include the hope for love and friendship within the scope of his injunction, but what wonderful part of human life is more in need of the sustenance of hope, or more richly rewards its exercise?

# CHAPTER ONE

# Women's Lot

JANE ROLAND MARTIN (1985), Reclaiming a Conversation:
The Ideal of the Educated Woman

Three Spartan women were being sold as slaves. Their captors asked them what they had learned to do. The first replied, "How to manage a household well." The second said, "How to be loyal." The third said, "How to be free."[1]

This ancient story, retold by Plutarch (in which Sparta serves as the proverbial example of a city that gives its women unusual latitude), poses some perennial questions about the education of women. If women are to be seriously educated, what sort of education should it be, and what will they become as a result? Will (and should) they become experts at dealing with a separate women's sphere, the sphere of the household? Will they still love and care for their husbands and children as before? Or will (and should) they become free and autonomous citizens, just like men? It is probably no accident that the anxiety generated by these questions is neutralized by their fictional context: since Plutarch's Spartan women are slaves anyway, it hardly matters if they have learned to be free. (As his story ends, the third woman manages to commit suicide.)

These questions are the subject of Martin's fascinating book. Philosophers have frequently discussed education. They have far less often addressed themselves to the special problems connected with the education of women. The philosophical discussions that have taken place are seldom consulted by contemporary theorists. The result, Martin claims, is that public debate on this issue is impoverished. Important public figures repeatedly make assumptions that have been successfully challenged centuries ago by major thinkers. If we doubt this, we might consider the assumptions behind Mr. Donald Regan's idea of what (educated) women would and would not comprehend about the Geneva summit.

Martin wants to correct this situation by calling our attention to several complex and well-argued philosophical accounts of women's education from which we can learn as we make our own choices. Instead of writing a continuous history of such views, she has decided (wisely, I think) to study five accounts in detail, offering her own comparative commentaries on them. She chooses Plato's account of the education of female guardians in the *Republic*; Rousseau's portrait of Sophie, Emile's "other half" (1762); Mary Wollstonecraft's vindication of women's equality (1792); Catharine Beecher's account of a professional domestic science (1842); and Charlotte Perkins Gilman's utopian novel about an all-female society, *Herland* (1915). The views are selected both because of their intrinsic interest and because of the ways in which they complement and reflect one another. The later writers have usually read the earlier ones and often either criticize or further develop their ideas. Even where this is not so, the juxtaposition of views, together with Martin's critical comparisons, illuminates each account by showing us what alternatives it has rejected or ignored.

We begin with Plato's female guardians, who will be given, from birth, an education identical to that proposed for men. Education for Plato is designed to develop and test each individual's natural abilities; and it is expected that the capacity for rulership and intellectual achievement will be found in both sexes, once the artificial barriers to women's development that exist in all actual cities are removed. Martin shows how this conception is connected with Plato's idea of citizenship as "doing one's own," that is, contributing whatever one is suited to contribute to the public good. She is disturbed, however, by the fact that in giving women the *same* education as men, Plato has omitted from the education of both sexes many functions traditionally assigned to women, such as child rearing and the management of the household; indeed, he has also neglected the emotions of love and care that are associated with these functions.

In Plato's ideal city, female guardians will not educate, love, or even know their own children; they will not care for a household; they will feel no emotional tie to their state-assigned sexual partners. If they pass the test for rulership, their lives will be coolly intellectual, devoted to learning and the contemplation of truth. Troubled by neither grief nor pity, neither passionate love nor jealousy, they will feel themselves to be stable and complete, in need of nothing outside their own reason. Martin suspects that while apparently offering women equality, Plato is imposing upon them a picture of goodness that comes from male experience and neglects female experience. This life, if equal, seems to her incomplete.

In search of a view that values what Plato omits, Martin turns to Rousseau's account of the education of Sophie, Emile's future wife. Unlike Plato's emotionless dialecticians, little Sophie is immediately recognizable as a woman—or, at least, as a common male stereotype of a woman. Charming, affectionate, vain, she loves to adorn herself and to delight others. She loves learning to sew because she enjoys dressing her doll in fancy clothes. Indeed, says Rousseau, her entire education is a preparation for "the moment when she will be her own doll"—dressing herself up as a living toy for her male owner.

Little Emile learns to exercise his reason independently and fearlessly, to look to nobody but himself for guidance. Sophie, by contrast, learns the arts of pleasing and helping; she will use her mind only to serve her husband. Emile will think and act independently all day, then come home to a wife who supports him in his public life by managing his household, loving and caring for his children, cleverly anticipating his every want. He will make all the decisions; but, since she does what he cannot do, he will depend upon her and regard her as his "other half."

Rousseau, Martin argues, does not believe that the natural differences between men and women are so great that these two different lives are simply natural developments of the different potentialities of each. His system of education promotes some abilities in each and blunts others. But Rousseau argues that if domestic and civic harmony is to be achieved, the best man and woman *must* be very unlike each other. If we cultivated, in each partner, the intellectual abilities as well as the abilities required in caring for the home, we would, he believes, have an "eternal discord"— both, apparently, within each individual and between them in their domestic relationship. But educated differently, so as to complement each other, Sophie and Emile become a single harmonious "moral person." This harmony is a necessary foundation for public order.

Martin's next two chapters consider doubts about this picture of the happy home. Mary Wollstonecraft's *A Vindication of the Rights of Woman* argues against Rousseau that Sophie, who has not been trained to reason independently, and who has been given no liberty to make her own moral and political choices, cannot do well even in the domestic role to which Rousseau assigns her. It is no accident that Sophie is manipulative and coquettish; this is what we must expect if we deny her an education similar to Emile's. The moral firmness and administrative competence that we need in wives and mothers cannot be achieved without both political liberty and the training of reason—training that Wollstonecraft tried to prescribe.

Though Martin sympathizes with these criticisms, she notices that Wollstonecraft's morally instructed wives, like Plato's guardians, become rational and dependable at the cost of suppressing their emotions. Most women, Wollstonecraft argues, live in a condition of moral weakness. Their senses and emotions overexcited, their reason undernourished, they are "blown about by every momentary gust of feeling." Education must aim above all at the suppression of these feelings. Passionate erotic love, especially, must be discouraged lest it endanger the home. Martin suspects that Wollstonecraft, like Plato, has adopted a conception of rational self-control that is based upon male aspirations and experience, too quickly discarding emotions that Wollstonecraft herself sees as important in women's actual lives.

These doubts are supported by Martin's reading of Catharine Beecher's *A Treatise on Domestic Economy*. Here (in addition to Beecher's argument that households cannot be well run unless the housewife has a great deal of scientific training) Martin discovers a conception of practical reason that emphasizes the value of intuitive and emotional responses for making good choices in concrete situations, such as planning meals or the living space in a house. If good practical judgment is not a matter of following abstract rules of duty (as Wollstonecraft seems to assume), but more a matter of perceiving, intuitively, what those particular situations are, in all their complexity, then suppressing the emotions—which frequently aid us in this sort of perceiving—might actually damage reason itself.

Martin's last group of educated women are the inhabitants of a strangely happy country called Herland, which has been discovered (in Gilman's novel) by three male adventurers. For three thousand years this land has been inhabited only by women; babies are born by asexual reproduction. The women of Herland, like Plato's guardians, have no experience of private property or nuclear families; they raise all children in common and distribute among themselves, according to ability, the tasks of citizenship. But unlike Plato's guardians they carefully cultivate love for and in their daughters. Maternal love is, in fact, the fundamental motive for all public planning. It has produced a culture that has more or less eliminated war, poverty, and disease. And yet, as we read on, we discover that this emotion has undergone a transformation in order to become a harmonious part of Gilman's idea of rationality. Since all children are held in common, a birth or a death matters far less than it does when the child is all you have, and all your own. Love becomes a kind of tranquil concern, hardly an emotion at all. As Martin summarizes, "No intense delight for the mothers of Herland, no shocks of joy, no sickening anxiety." Furthermore, like both Plato and Wollstonecraft, Gilman has entirely eliminated erotic love. *Herland* values the serenity achieved by these eliminations. In the end all three of the women who are the chief characters in the novel marry the male invaders; two of the three couples depart from Herland. So the utopia ironically comments upon its own possible incompleteness.

Here Martin misses a chance to dig deeper into a central ethical issue. She criticizes Plato, Wollstonecraft, and Gilman for neglecting the cultivation of the emotions. She claims that Plato (I shall confine myself to this example) has unthinkingly imposed upon his female guardians a norm of cool rationality that was the public ideal for males in his culture, failing to consider the possibility that the strong emotions linked in his society with "womanish" behavior (love, fear, grief) might have their own contribution to make to his new universal norm. I think she fails to see the depth and consistency of Plato's position; and she thereby misses a chance to make a deeper criticism of Plato. To see this we must understand the connection between Plato's repudiation of the emotions and his interest in human self-sufficiency.

Plato (along with most ancient Greek ethical thinkers) correctly sees that the central emotions (e.g., love, anger, fear, pity, grief) are not simply visceral feelings, distinguished from one another only by their felt quality. They are complexes of feeling and belief; they rest on and are in part made up of beliefs about the world, in such a way that removal of the relevant belief will remove not only the reason for the emotion but also the emotion itself. Anger, for example, is a composite of painful feeling and the belief that one has been wronged. The two elements are not incidentally linked: the belief is the ground of the feeling. If I discover that an apparent slight did not in fact take place, I can expect my painful angry feelings to go away. Or if they persist, I will not think of them as anger—but, say, as residual irrational irritation. This account implies that emotions may be assessed as rational or irrational, and also as true or false, depending upon the character of the beliefs that compose them. If I become angry because I hastily and uncritically believe a false story about an injury done to me, my anger may be criticized as both irrational and false.

Plato and the later Greek Stoics built their repudiation of the emotions on a deep insight: that the beliefs that are the bases of all the strong emotions involve a high evaluation of objects or persons over which I do not have full control. Fear, for example, requires the belief that my life can be significantly damaged by future events that I have no power to prevent. Pity requires the belief that someone else has been seriously hurt by an event that was not his or her fault. Passionate love requires that a unique (or at least not readily replaceable) value be ascribed to a person who is not under our control; jealousy and grief are its natural companions. (The Stoics work this out systematically, showing how anxiety is the other face of intense joy; how what in good times is gratitude will be anger in bad; and so forth.) In short: emotional life presupposes and rests upon a picture of the good life that makes it vulnerable, not self-sufficient, and subject in many ways to the vicissitudes of fortune.

Plato argues that such a life is intolerably unstable and disorderly; the evaluative beliefs on which it is based may be both pernicious and false. The true view of what is worthwhile in life teaches us that "the good person cannot be harmed," that what is of supreme value is virtue, an internal condition that is unaffected by the world. But this means that the emotions are false through and through, and do not belong in a good person's life. It would be both wrong and inconsistent, on Plato's view, to supplement the education of the guardians by encouraging the cultivation of the emotions; this would be like supplementing a true belief with its contradiction.

Greek men were in fact by no means "stoical" and unemotional. Their literature shows intense and frequently violent emotional feeling; the philosophers' obsessive emphasis on the therapy of emotion confirms this. (The zeal of Stoic writing on this subject would have no point, say, in contemporary England.) Plato wishes to change all this, for both women and men, by preventing citizens from developing the beliefs about the world on which the emotions are based. A child who has been farmed out to interchangeable wet nurses, who thinks that all older citizens are equally its parents, will never, Plato thinks, learn the intense love that is usually found in families: for this love requires the belief that one set of people is special. Later in life this same child will never know the torments of erotic passion or jealousy, because the state, which prevents intimate personal knowledge, will contrive to make sexual partners, too, seem similar and interchangeable. The intellectual life of the guardians will be a life of stable and unwavering devotion to truth, purified of the violent upheavals and disorders that characterize our ordinary lives. Thinking is always in our power, he argues, no matter what happens in the world; thus a life that ascribes supreme value to thinking contains no reasons for grief, or anger, or fear.

It is important to see that in the view of Plato and the Stoics it is this life, not the emotional life in which particular objects and persons are cherished, that is the life of gentleness and civic friendliness; for it is only when ethical beliefs are thus rearranged that we can have a politics of gentleness, rather than a politics of rage and jealousy. The Stoic philosopher Epictetus observes that if Menelaus had correctly understood that Helen was just one woman like all the others, "gone would have been the *Iliad*, and the *Odyssey* as well." One evaluative belief, one love, caused so much suffering for so many. Medea, he continues, would have lived a life free of guilt if only she had understood that Jason was not special. Murderous rage is a disease of reason.

All this means that if we are going to criticize Plato's attitude to the emotions we must radically criticize his conception of the human good as self-sufficient and unaffected by the workings of fortune. We must articulate and defend a conception of value that shows the worth of external attachments and commitments, arguing that a life that lacks deep personal love, commitment to particular children, etc., is impoverished by comparison with one that includes them. We cannot simply say, "Three cheers for love and caring." If we cherish these values (as, with Martin, I do), we must also confront Plato's hard questions: in what ways can people not be self-sufficient and yet have reasonably stable personal and civic lives? What degree and type of emotional attachment is compatible with gentleness, both private and public? How can we make room for the value of deep love, and its vulnerabilities, while protecting private and public life from destructive angers and jealousies?

Another issue of fortune and self-sufficiency confronts Martin's reader at this point. This is the issue of conflict of values. Given our finite power and resources, given the way the world is, can we in fact combine in a single life (and therefore appropriately teach in a single scheme of education) all the values, traditionally linked with either the male or the female, that have been defended by the thinkers she discusses? Those thinkers who defend an ideal in which male and female qualities complement one another have usually done so, she says, out of the belief that there are two discrete sets of human virtues, both needed for a flourishing community, that cannot be cultivated side by side in the same person—either because they are in

some way incompatible or because some division of ethical labor is necessary in order that people should not be perpetually torn by conflicting
demands.

The first type of argument is central to Rousseau's account of Sophie,
who can (he claims) be gentle and loving only if she does not learn to think
for herself. We are told by Rousseau that if women take on public rights and
responsibilities similar to those of men they will lose certain characteristic
virtues that a community as a whole requires for its continued health.
Women must be confined to the home because the home is a bastion of
gentleness that would be defiled by too much freedom. (Spartan woman
number 3 can no longer give the answers to numbers 1 and 2.)

One of the great merits of Martin's book is her acute demonstration of
the defects in this reasoning. She does not deny that some accounts of
female freedom and female citizenship sacrifice apparent virtues that the
rather repulsive Sophie does possess; indeed she stresses this point. But she
argues well that both Sophie and Emile (in addition to having impoverished
and one-sided lives) will fall short at their respective social tasks because
each is cut off from the other's virtues. Sophie, who has never learned to rely
on herself or to use reason to organize her life, will not manage a household
with the intelligence of Wollstonecraft's rationally educated woman or
Beecher's domestic scientist. And devoid of self-respect, taught to get her
way by flattery, she will not be the sort of loyal and understanding wife
who could best support Emile and raise his children. Emile, trained to see
himself as an isolated being who needs nothing from anyone, will have
difficulty becoming the attentive husband that Rousseau requires him to
be, dependent upon Sophie, her "other half." But if he cannot be a satisfactory husband and father, there are grave doubts whether he will have the
right sort of concern for the community. Martin argues persuasively that to
sever the development of intellect, judgment, and the sense of personal
worth from the development of abilities to love and care for a family is not
only not necessary, but is actually pernicious—*even* given the view of human
ends and social roles that governs a society such as Rousseau's. (The third
Spartan woman is in the *best* position to give, as well, the answers of the first
and second.)

There remains the second sort of conflict. Even if the two spheres of
virtue can be linked, isn't it impossible for any one person to do and to be all
of these things? Won't a person who tries to combine the best of both Sophie
and Emile be continually torn by the conflicting demands of these different
spheres? One advantage of assigning to each sex only half of the total number
of commitments that are recognized to be important is that there is a greater
chance, then, that nobody's life will turn out to be tragic. But we must now
ask: *is* that an advantage, if everyone's life is impoverished? (And impoverished, as Martin shows, even by the standards of its own proper virtues?)
Of course a person who cares about and pursues many valuable things will
encounter conflicts more frequently than someone who cares about only

one thing. That is the price one pays for having a fuller life. Well-known philosophers have often maintained that there are no genuine conflicts of obligation. Even those who acknowledge that there are such conflicts (this position is, fortunately, gaining ground)[2] often say that public planning should work toward their elimination.

It is not clear to me that, so simply put, this view is either possible or wise. Virtually any woman or man who both works and raises children is bound to face many conflicts between work and family; many times this person will have no choice but to neglect something that he or she values doing, and would have done had the world arranged things differently. Many of these conflicts could indeed be removed by a juster and more rational public culture (by more equity in salaries, by better schemes of child care). But they will not all be removed this way. For the only way to guarantee that the demands of a child's love never encroach upon one's professional life is to deny the child's love—to arrange for it to be raised, and loved, by someone else. This is what many men have frequently done. And it seems important to stress that these conflicts are present as much for men as for women—though until now fewer men have acknowledged that (for example) in spending little time caring for their children they are missing something of intrinsic value. There is a cost in recognizing how many things are valuable: it is that one also sees how often the world makes it impossible to do everything that is good.

One central question here is surely the future of the nuclear family. For, as Martin argues, we can imagine lives in which we bring up children and care for others and yet are free of many divisive conflicts if, as Plato and Gilman suggest, we assign the responsibility of child rearing to the community or state. Martin makes no final judgment on this issue. But, with Beecher, she asks some questions about the nature of practical judgment that suggest one reason, among others, to reject Plato's idea. If the sort of ethical knowledge that is most important for making good judgments as a parent is, or requires, a particular knowledge of each child's concrete history and personality, an ability to perceive and respond to that child as a person unlike any other, and if, as seems likely, one cannot have that concrete knowledge without intimacy, time, and also love, then we do away with the nuclear family at our peril.

So Aristotle argues against Plato: in an education based on the family, with its greater "precision of particularity," "each one will be more likely to get what is fitting."[3] Such arguments do not establish the superiority of what a notorious recent *Boston Globe* editorial rejecting foster parenting by gay couples was pleased to call the "normal family," namely a heterosexual couple, the woman a housewife. Many nontraditional parents, including single adults and homosexual couples, male or female, could provide a satisfactory family life. But any commitment to the raising of a particular child or children as one's very own will bring with it a potential for conflict with the claims of work and citizenship that was absent from Plato's city.

If we choose this value, we will have to learn to think wisely about these conflicts.

Martin's discussion leaves us, then, with the delicate and difficult task of combining all these commitments in a single life. (For we have said that they *are* all valuable; and that if they conflict in some particular situations, they are more often mutually supportive, and indeed frequently mutually necessary.) Where in the philosophical tradition is there a portrait of such a rich and complete existence? Each of the writers Martin discusses describes a life lacking in something that the discussion of them taken together shows to be of serious value. Those who emphasize freedom, intellect, and citizenship neglect or deny the household and/or the emotions; those (such as Rousseau and Beecher) who portray the value of household activity slight women's intellectual work and public freedom; all the writers alike seem to deny the value of erotic love (unless we imagine that Sophie and Emile will have an exhilarating relationship).

If we look beyond Martin's book to the ethical tradition more generally, the ideas we find are only a little better. Aristotle, for example, purports to describe a "complete" good life for a human being, one that will include every activity that is of intrinsic human worth. And his life does indeed include much that other parts of the tradition neglect: it includes personal friendship alongside justice, social and convivial excellences alongside intellectual pursuits. And yet he excludes from intrinsic value both erotic love and household work, together with close daily caring for children—believing that these are activities belonging to or requiring cooperation with inferior female beings. To a reader of Martin's discussion this life, too, must seem not "complete" but incomplete.

Martin's book ends with questions, not solutions. This, I think, is appropriate—for it has become plain in her discussion that the conclusions suggested by her criticisms are not to be found in the philosophical tradition at all. The tradition can help us see the issue more clearly; but a new, normative chapter remains to be written. And, as her contemporary references suggest, Martin thinks it is being "written" right now by women and men who are trying to live in the fuller way she proposes. Her open-ended conclusion invites us to realize that if the aspiration to completeness is expressed anywhere at all, it may be in our own muddled daily lives—as, in a way unprecedented in history, many women and men are now trying to express, in their sometimes bewildered confrontation with particular choices: a commitment to work, to citizenship and social justice, to personal love, to the care and raising of children, to the household, to friendship and hospitality, to other values as well. All this, many hope, without the compromises and failures of recognition that have characterized so many centuries in which the lives of men and women were separated. As they do this they sometimes encounter painful conflicts (conflicts, for example, between obligations to care for children and the demands of a career for uninterrupted time and thought; between either of these and the intensity of attention that personal love requires). It sometimes will turn out, too, that the quality of some activity is impaired by a commitment to balancing so many heterogeneous concerns.

This life can feel overcrowded—as if the small number of values that sat comfortably side by side in Aristotle's gentlemanly scheme of the good life were suddenly being asked to move over to make a place for as many more importunate newcomers. It is certainly not the life of the leisured Athenian gentleman. It is frequently hectic, breathless, lacking in grace and ease. And yet women and men who try to live such lives frequently discover that these many values support and illuminate one another when all are respected— that citizenship can be instructed by the experience of knowing and intimately caring for one's children; that personal love can be richer and more interesting when both partners care about and seriously pursue some form of work; that children can be better educated if they see that the adults who love and care for them also love and work for other valuable things.

It is too soon to see this new view of life clearly or to assess it; right now it is not a view at all, but a plurality of different lives. But ethical views, if they are to be of any use, *are* stories or summaries of particular lives. And it is in these lives, not in the study, that valuable new ethical conceptions are constructed. Martin ends with a plea that any future theory of women's education should bring itself "into tune with the full range of people's lives"— reminding us that it is in their daily choices, if anywhere, that men and women will succeed in constructing a new and fuller meaning for that venerable philosophical expression, "the complete human life." Like Martin, I find this idea remarkably exciting.

NOTES

1. Paraphrased from Plutarch, *Sayings of Spartan Women*, 242 CD. (This story is my contribution and is not discussed in Martin's book.)

2. See, for example, Bernard Williams's essay "Ethical Consistency," in *Problems of the Self* (Cambridge, UK: Cambridge University Press, 1972).

3. Aristotle, *Nicomachean Ethics* X.9, 1180b11–13 (my translation).

# CHAPTER TWO

# Sex in the Head

ROGER SCRUTON (1986), Sexual Desire: A Moral Philosophy of the Erotic

Roger Scruton is a Wagnerian romantic and a Thatcherite conservative; a tentative, questioning philosopher who is enamored of dogmatic political conclusions; a subtle writer on cultural diversity who is also drawn to making sweeping biological claims about human nature. These are some of the contradictions that inhabit his uneven, exasperating, yet never trivial new book. Scruton's career displays this complexity. A Reader in philosophy at Birkbeck College, London, he has written valuable books and articles on aesthetics, the imagination, the significance of culture. At the same time, he has written conservative journalism of a rather narrow and polemical type and served enthusiastically as an adviser to the Thatcher government.

This book suffers from this double commitment. As a philosopher, Scruton wants to help us reflect on a highly complex topic on which it is unlikely that any good work of philosophy would reach simple conclusions. Yet he also wants to advocate a simple, practical program that is critical of feminism and homosexuality, supportive of state religion and the institution of marriage. The program does not follow in any obvious way from the reflections to which his philosophical investigation leads him.

Scruton's central purpose is to attack the idea that sexual desire is simply an animal appetite, a blind physical urge that has no intimate connection with our thoughts and conceptions. He argues, instead, that desire is a part of our characteristically human "intentionality"—that is, it is connected with the way we take a perspective on the world and react to things as we interpret them. Desire does not simply push toward its object; it conceives of the object, and its own internal movements are highly sensitive to changes in conception and belief. Intrinsic to sexual desire is a conception of its object as another "first-person perspective," a living, interpreting self. The aim of desire, like that of conversation, involves the mutual awareness of an intention to communicate with another self, and a mutual responsiveness to that mutual awareness.[1]

From this starting point, Scruton goes on to argue that sexual desire is directed at an object that it sees as irreplaceably individual; and that its aim is some sort of spiritual union with the other person, insofar as the other expresses or manifests him or herself[2] through bodily signs. This being so, the true or natural aim of sexual desire is only fully satisfied in deep erotic love. And since love is closely linked to esteem, and cannot coexist with the belief that its object is profoundly unworthy, the aim of love is itself, in turn, satisfied only in a stable relationship that is based on moral approval, in which the partners come to share their central goals and aims. In a concluding political section, Scruton argues that this stable love can itself be best achieved and maintained within the institution of marriage; and that this institution can best be protected in a conservative society with a state religion. (He advances criticisms of feminism and homosexuality to which I shall turn later.) Thus, a straight path (apparently) leads from the true nature of sexual desire to Mrs. Thatcher's Britain.

A book on this most personal of subjects cannot fail to be shaped by the author's own sense of life. So we may begin by pointing out two features of Scruton's attitude that surface throughout the book, shaping both its arguments and its failures to argue. One is his distaste for the flesh—for animals and for the animal in human life. If Scruton defends the importance of thought and a specifically human form of awareness in sexual experience, it is in part because he finds the sexuality of animals so disgusting. He repeatedly speaks of the body as if, without human thought to animate it, it is something inert and repellent. In a revealing section on original sin, he argues that our complex self-conscious sexuality is a hard-won spiritual victory over the "original slime" of a life that is "no more than flesh." He earlier recalls an anecdote from Aubrey's *Brief Lives* about the Countess of Pembroke, who, preparing to meet a lover, excited herself by watching two horses mating. And Scruton cannot understand this except as the result of a perverted desire to "degrade" herself by divesting herself (in imagination) of all that is human. He altogether lacks the sense that the body of a stallion is beautiful, an object of wonder. It is no surprise, then, that he views with distaste any human lover who delights in the animal energy and exuberance of the sexual act, who sees this as one of its marvelous features, rather than as a constraint to be overcome. Sex, for him, is a heroic labor against the body, rather than an expression of joy in it.

Connected with this is the complete absence, in this long book, of any sense of play. Scruton has many serious things to say about sex; what he never says is that it is fun. His favorite writers on the topic seem to be Sartre and Wagner, neither one famous for a light touch. And his own humorless prose gives no hint of many aspects of sexual delight. Consider this passage, about the moments following intercourse:

Suddenly everything seems flat, arbitrary and mundane; what was for a moment a glowing body, offered and accepted as an individual life, is now only a piece of human flesh, to be rewrapped and set aside for another occasion. At no point does a woman feel cheaper or more expendable than at this one, and hence, out of shame, she will wish to lie still with her lover, naked, talking out of her nakedness, until it becomes accepted again as her.

Doesn't Scruton know that it is fun to talk in bed? Not out of shame, but out of simple delight in the relaxed and playful talk that is possible at that moment—and in the perceived similarity between the responsiveness of lovemaking and the responsiveness of good conversation? Delight, too, in the complete absence of shame and constraint, in the improvisatory freedom of the body. Scruton needs to listen less to *Parsifal* and more to Billie Holiday—an antidote that Nietzsche would surely have suggested, had he known of her.

Scruton's central thesis is actually at least four different theses, and he slides back and forth among them as he discusses the idea that desire's object is another "individual." I shall call them the Intentionality Thesis, the Particularity Thesis, the Romantic Thesis, and the Character Thesis. They differ in accordance with the different ways in which Scruton thinks of individuality.

The first and most pervasive thesis is that of Intentionality, according to which sexual desire (like the desire to engage in conversation) is directed at the other person as a "first-person perspective"; it aims at a conversational relationship characterized by a mutual awareness of intentions. The very same responses and movements will cease to be objects of desire if they are known to come from a machine, or even from a less than fully human form of life. This is persuasively argued; and on this basis Scruton makes effective criticisms of reductionist pseudosciences of sex that have severed desire from its personal and subjective aspects. But this thesis does not imply, clearly, that desire is naturally highly selective, or aimed at lasting union. To "converse" well with a partner requires attention to him or her as a separate life, as long as that relationship is in progress. But this sort of attention seems to be compatible with a sequence of affairs, and perhaps even with several simultaneous involvements. Scruton sees this point when he admits that Don Juan is a perfectly good case of sexual desire in this sense.

From the Intentionality Thesis and its conception of the individual object, Scruton accordingly, and unclearly, slides over to the Particularity Thesis and a different conception of the individual. Sexual desire treats its object as irreducibly unique and particular, attending to and cherishing all of its perceptible properties (apparently as elements in the object's "individuality"). Scruton defends this claim by an interesting comparison between sexual attention and the attention we give to works of art. But even this thesis and this analogy yield neither a very strong conception of the irreplaceability of the person desired nor a very "inner" conception of individuality. For the analogy implies, first, that anyone who shares all the same "external" perceptible characteristics should be acceptable as a replacement for the object of desire. And it also clearly suggests that there is nothing inappropriate in turning rather rapidly from one object of desire to another, as different perceptible features are found pleasing. When I look at Turner's *Regulus* in the Tate Gallery, I am not attending to it well unless I am examining all of its particular features with care. It could be said that a person who was unable to discriminate between *Regulus* and Turner's *The Angel Standing in the Sun*—a picture somewhat similar in composition that is hung nearby—and whose attention does not include the features that distinguish the two paintings, had not fulfilled an aim that is intrinsic to the structure of aesthetic desire and aesthetic attention. But surely it is no perversion of aesthetic values to turn from *Regulus* to *The Angel* after five minutes or so; and the suggestion that the natural aim of the desire to look at *Regulus* is the formation of a lasting inner union with that work seems absurd, if not perverse. Don Juan can satisfy the Particularity Thesis too.

To move further toward love, Scruton shifts (at times, and inconstantly) to talking about the desired person as a unique and irreplaceable spiritual being, characterized by a distinctive inner life that merely manifests itself on the surface of the body. And here we get the Romantic Thesis: desire's aim is to establish union with that ineffable spirit, through contact with its embodied traces. Scruton sometimes speaks as if this is just the same as the Intentionality Thesis, since that thesis too insists that the other person is seen as a distinct living being with its own inner life. But it is one thing to say that I desire a distinct life (I wouldn't make love with something I knew to be a machine), quite another to say that I desire this very distinct life and no other, that desire is superficial and second-rate if it does not aim at a lasting and deep relationship that involves the entire spiritual being of both parties.

Like many a romantic, I find this claim deeply appealing. I have the same difficulty Scruton evidently does in separating sex from erotic love; and I am tempted to believe that sexual experiences that stop short of deep love are, even as sex, deficient. But Scruton's argument (unlike his argument for the Intentionality Thesis) does not persuade me to think of these intuitions as more than pieces of my idiosyncratic history—not rare, perhaps, but surely not necessary, brought about, perhaps, by seeing too many operas at an impressionable age. I am sure we should hesitate to condemn people whose experience of desire is different from this; and Scruton gives us no reason at all to cast off that hesitation.

Finally, in his very interesting chapter on friendship and love, we get the Character Thesis, which lays the groundwork for Scruton's praise of marriage. Love is love of the other person's entire self. But it is plausible to think that some of the deepest aspects of selves are their traits of character: their moral commitments, their patterns of aspiration and evaluation. If the person I love changes in appearance, or health, or even occupation, there is no difficulty in believing that he or she is still the same person as before. But if from having been a just person, he or she becomes unjust, or if he or she changes in some other radical way with respect to basic values, then questions of identity are indeed raised. Thus, Scruton concludes that romantic love aims naturally at love of, and sharing in, such patterns of aspiration and evaluation. This is one reason for supposing that its natural home is in a shared way of life, therefore in some institution like marriage.

Again, I find this appealing. For like many readers of romantic stories (at least since the Greek romances)[3], I am drawn to the idea that desire, love, and lifelong marriage just naturally go together. I would accept hardly any evidence to the contrary. And in fact the Character Thesis seems to offer us a far more rich and appealing account of love than Scruton's earlier, more Wagnerian remarks about ineffable union. Still, I know that this is just one (powerfully appealing) account of love, and hardly a universal truth. None of it, surely, follows from the far more generally persuasive intentionality argument with which the book began. If it expresses some readers' intuitions, all very well. But those who find that their own experience of desire is plausibly captured by the Intentionality Thesis, but not by the Romantic and Character theses, need not think that any effective argument in this book has shown that a commitment to the first implies a commitment to the others.

Scruton now employs these arguments to criticize various forms of sexual activity that have been thought to be perversions. It is easy to see how an emphasis on mutual intentionality leads to a rejection of bestiality and necrophilia—though even here Scruton is remarkably lacking in curiosity about what these activities are actually like for those who engage in them. On sadomasochism he is much more imaginative, and offers an interesting vindication of these practices wherever they are performed with consent and involve pain rather than humiliation. But it becomes obvious to him at this point that nothing in his argument so far implies two conservative conclusions that he would very much like to reach: a rejection of female equality, and a condemnation of homosexuality. He reaches these positions through a further "argument" about the concept of gender, which needs to be scrutinized lest anyone think that there is really a substantial argument here.

Scruton concedes that gender is a human construct, though based on a natural biological difference, and that it is conceived in many different ways in different societies. And yet, he asserts, some such distinction is omnipresent and cannot be avoided, since it does have a natural basis. We can see the depth that gender has in human life from the fact that people commit suicide when they are confused about it. This shows us, he concludes, that gender is "morally significant," and that any feminist position that insists on ignoring gender differences altogether and treating all of us simply as "persons" is morally defective.

This "argument," besides being silly (for people become depressed over lots of morally insignificant things), does nothing at all to vindicate the traditional conception of gender difference to which Scruton is attached, according to which the female is passive and devoted to the home, the male roving and outward reaching. So Scruton here turns to sociobiology, which he has criticized eloquently in an earlier chapter, arguing that this traditional conception of women and men is rooted in the natural reality of the ways by which organisms strive to perpetuate their genetic material. The argument is simplistic and weakly stated. Even Scruton expresses grave doubts about it—though, oddly, this does not prevent him from asserting its conclusion in subsequent chapters as if it had been established by a sound argument. Since this part of the book is too obviously thin to have any political effect, I shall spend no more time on it.

The discussion of homosexuality has more specious plausibility and might actually have an influence—so it is worth criticizing it in detail. Gender, Scruton asserts again, is a morally significant feature of human beings, and especially significant because of its biological underpinnings. Someone who makes love with a person of the same sex is communicating with another world that is, with respect to this important feature, the same as his or her own. Thus, "his discovery of his partner's sexual nature is the discovery of what he knows." The heterosexual, on the other hand, ventures "beyond the divide which separates the world of men from the world of women." This means that there is an element of mystery and risk in heterosexual intercourse that is absent in the homosexual case. Scruton concludes that heterosexuality is a more courageous and morally valuable way of life; homosexuality is cowardly and borders on narcissism.

The argument is peculiar for several reasons. First, if it proves anything, it proves more than Scruton intends to prove: for to venture toward a person qualitatively different from oneself will then be superior in other cases as well, at least wherever the relevant differences have the same sort of cultural and biological depth that gender has been said to have. Race, for example, will surely have to be admitted as another such concept, since it, too, is constructed by social convention over a base of "natural" physiological difference. And, to be consistent, Scruton will have to grant that it is morally superior to have sexual relations with people who lie on the far side of the divide that separates the world of the white person from the world of the black person; and that any person who evinces a settled preference for partners of his or her own race is guilty of moral cowardice and narcissism. Heterosexual interracial unions will enjoy a double moral dignity. It is not clear that a politician with Scruton's commitments can happily accept that moral conclusion. Mrs. Thatcher might not be amused.

But none of this argument is very persuasive anyway. Scruton does not think that moral differences, or differences in physical health or attractiveness, make sexual relationships better. So why should he suppose this to be true of gender and other similar properties? The conception of individuality that he uses in his main argument offers a far deeper account of the risk and adventure that are involved in sexual experience: it is the experience of contact with another separate life, another viewpoint on the world, whose depths I can never inhabit as my lover does, though I can sense and respond to every perceptible sign. And with this hidden reality I engage, through perceptible signs, my own inner life, aiming not at some impossible fusion, but at attunement and responsiveness.

Scruton insists that the goal of both sexual desire and erotic love is a "union" or "fusion" of what was previously separate. This leads him, I think, to mislocate the risk of sexual experience, making it depend on qualitative difference. He does not consider that because union is not possible, risk is a necessary part of any intimate personal relationship. And union, even if possible, would be neither necessary nor sufficient for the happy responsiveness that sexual intimacy does achieve. Not necessary, because I can respond to a partner as another person, without denying that we must always remain apart. (And respond better, in fact, if I do not deny our fundamental separateness.) Not sufficient, because taking the partner's desires into my own awareness would not be to respond to them as his, to seek to please him as someone with a separate life. It is this sense of hiddenness and otherness that makes sex always a risk and a mystery; and with this sort of otherness qualitative similarity and dissimilarity have nothing much to do.

Behind Scruton's failure to say anything persuasive about homosexuality is a deeper failure: the failure to see that there is no one thing, "homosexual experience," about which persuasive remarks can be made. Scruton has elsewhere written very well about the deep ways that cultural and historical factors affect human values.[4] In this book, though he draws examples from many times and places, he has remarkably little real curiosity about history, about the ways in which the distinctions he discusses are differently constructed by different societies. And even in the case of a single society, a writer this committed to "individuality" in all its forms should not have forgotten that we are dealing with a complex plurality of individual lives, not a single abstract unity.

It is easy for advocates both of repression and of the liberal opposition to it to indulge in this sort of generalizing. When I was starting this review, I asked a homosexual friend of mine—a daring and brilliant scholar—to suggest some reading on homosexual experience that I could mention in dealing with Scruton's claim that homosexuals are afraid of difference. He looked at me for a long time; and then quietly said, with an expression I could not read, "You're the same person. One day you discover, or you admit to yourself, that you are gay, and still, you are the same person."

I thought about this for a long while, wondering how on earth it was an answer to my question. And I eventually saw that it was a deep, if gentle, rebuke, addressed both to me and to Scruton. Talk as we will of individuality, neither of us (neither the judgmental conservative nor the well-intentioned liberal) could quite make the step into perceiving that it is individual people who have homosexual relationships, men and women as different from one another as any heterosexuals are, living each one a unique life. Some may be fearful, some adventurous, some narcissistic, some capable of love. Whatever is true, they don't one day stop being themselves and turn into homosexuals, subjects of a single "homosexual experience." (Would he have asked me for a reading list on "heterosexual experience"?)

Most active homosexuals, to be sure, face common social problems and common medical risks in this society. And because of these problems it is sometimes useful to make generic statements. Homosexual students with whom I have talked while I was a member of a committee dealing with this issue in my university do feel a need to define themselves as a member of a single class, and to study homosexuality academically as if it is a single subject with its own distinct identity. Heterosexual students, for obvious reasons, do not feel a precisely similar need. But the goal of political generalizing that aims to make progress on behalf of minority groups should be, I think, to reach a point where everyone will be able to be respected as an individual, not herded into a class. And it is a lack of this respect for and imaginative attention to the individual that seems to me to be, throughout, the deepest failure of Scruton's book.

Does this imply that a good work of philosophy cannot be written on the subject of sexual experience? For philosophy has traditionally been committed to an "ascent" from the perception of particulars to the intellectual grasp of universals. It seems to me that good philosophy will always have a place in the investigation of any matter of deep human importance, because of its commitment to clarity, to carefully drawn distinctions, to calm argument rather than to prejudice and dogmatic assertion. But if philosophy is to illuminate sexual experience (or, indeed, any deep and intimate aspect of people's lives), it must, I think, become more attentive to particular histories, more explicit about the personal and cultural origins of its own statements, more tentative and suggestive, more humble before the mystery and complexity of living, than Scruton's philosophy is, and than contemporary philosophy (in both the Anglo-American and the Continental traditions) has usually been. It must, as the best works of philosophy on this topic, Plato's *Symposium* and *Phaedrus*, have done, find a language that retains philosophy's commitment to clarity and to explanation, while also expressing a respect for particularity and complexity.

Philosophy must recognize as well that sometimes there can be more precision of the relevant kind in a complex novelistic description than in the abstract and simplified terms of theoretical discourse; more accuracy sometimes in indefiniteness (where reality is itself bewildering and unclear) than in a false decisiveness of statement. Describing the novelist's art, Henry James spoke in his preface to *The Golden Bowl* of an "immense array of terms, perceptional and expressional, that . . . simply looked over the heads of the standing terms—or perhaps rather, like alert winged creatures, perched on those diminished summits and aspired to a clearer air." If philosophy is to become sufficiently alert on Scruton's topic, it needs to borrow those wings—or, rather, to discover them, as Plato's *Phaedrus* recommends, within its own soul.

### NOTES

1. Here Scruton's views have been anticipated by Thomas Nagel, "Sexual Perversion," in his *Mortal Questions* (Cambridge, UK: Cambridge University Press, 1979).

2. The pronouns are mine and not Scruton's; he defends the use of the masculine as "stylistically correct."

3. See John J. Winkler, "The Invention of Romance," *Laetaberis* (Journal of the California Classical Association, Northern Section) 1 (1983), pp. 1–26.

4. "The Significance of Common Culture," in *Philosophy* (1979), reprinted in revised form as "Emotion, Practical Knowledge, and the Common Culture," in *Explaining Emotions*, ed. Amelie O. Rorty (Berkeley, CA: University of California Press, 1980), pp. 519–36.

# CHAPTER THREE

# Undemocratic Vistas

ALLAN BLOOM (1987), The Closing of the American Mind: How Higher Education Has Failed Democracy and Impoverished the Souls of Today's Students

I

Asked whether women as well as men should study philosophy, the distinguished Roman Stoic philosopher Musonius Rufus, teacher of Epictetus, replied as follows:

> Women have received from the god the same rational faculty as men, the faculty that we use in communicating with one another and in reasoning about each matter, as to whether it is a good thing or a bad. Similarly, the female has the same faculties of sense perception as the male: seeing, hearing, smelling, and the rest. Similarly, they both have the same number of bodily parts, and neither has any more parts than the other. Furthermore, desire and natural orientation towards excellence belong not only to men, but also to women; for not less than men they are naturally pleased by fine and just deeds and repelled by the contrary. Since things are this way, why on earth should it be fitting for men to examine and inquire into how one should live well—which is what it is to do philosophy—and for women not?[1]

This passage states a conception of "higher education," and the place of philosophy in that education, that can be found not only in Stoic texts but also in the writings of many of the greatest philosophers of the Greek and Roman world. This conception of philosophy has three elements, closely connected, and all traced by Stoics to Socrates, their model and hero:

1. Philosophical education is *practical*. It is the rational search for the best human life. Its subject is, above all, the study of moral and social conceptions, and its purpose (as Musonius later makes plain)

is, through reflection, the amelioration both of the individual
student's life and, through the choices of educated individuals, of
the surrounding society.

2. In philosophical education the pupil is *active*. It is not the passive
reception of external truths, but the following out of paths of rational
and critical argument—indeed, the enlivening and developing of
the pupil's rational soul. (For this reason, Musonius later stresses, it
must be closely tailored, in each case, to the needs of the particular
student, like the prescriptions of a good doctor.)

3. Philosophical education should be *broadly distributed*. It is
appropriate to all who are by nature rational beings, that is, beings
capable of practical and ethical reasoning. (Epictetus was a slave
when he attended Musonius' lectures. Later he became a free
man and a distinguished philosopher.)

These three elements are connected. It is because philosophy's practical
content is so important for human life, both individual and communal, that
making it widely available is so important; fulfills, indeed, a basic human
need. And it is central to Stoicism's conception of philosophy's practical
purpose and of the reasons for its broad distribution to insist that philosophical education is not abstruse contemplation but the development of
each human being's capacities for active practical reasoning.

This picture of philosophy opposes itself, on the one hand, to conceptions of education that do not take philosophy seriously as a subject for
human study. On the other hand, it also sets itself against all conceptions of
philosophy that make of philosophy a purely theoretical and contemplative
discipline and (usually for reasons closely connected with this conception of
its function) limit its pursuit to a narrow favored elite. Philosophy is the
critical reflection about human life; and this reflection is essential to the full
health of all human beings and of society in general.

Allan Bloom, like Musonius, has written a book that defends the central
role of philosophy in higher education, and defends it as essential for the
health of human souls and human society. Like Musonius again, he initially
presents the philosophical activity he praises as a search, through active
critical argument, for the best human life; he praises as the founder of his
ideal university Socrates, the paradigm of tireless rational searching to whom
Stoics also appeal. But in Bloom's book the Socratic conception is in conflict
with another very different idea of philosophy: the idea of a study that is
open only to a chosen few specially suited by nature (and to some extent
also by wealth and social position) for its pursuit; the idea of a philosophy
that is concerned more with revealing fixed eternal truths than with active
critical argument; of a philosophy that not only does not aim at justice and
practical wisdom, individual and/or communal, but actually despises the
search for social justice and beckons chosen souls away from social pursuits
to a contemplative theoretical life.

To understand these contradictions, and their relation to Bloom's practical proposals for a reform of the university curriculum, we must begin with his diagnosis of contemporary American culture, for whose diseases philosophy is supposed to provide the cure. As Bloom sees it, the central problem in higher education today, and in American society more generally, is widespread relativism. Both teachers and students have been taught that all conceptions of the good human life are equally valid, and that it is not possible to find an objective viewpoint from which to make rational criticisms of any tradition or any study, however apparently trivial or even base. The most any such criticism can be, according to this prevalent view, as Bloom reports it, is an expression of unenlightened prejudice.

In education, however, so goes the prevalent view, we should refrain from such expressions of prejudice and cultivate "openness," which really means, Bloom concludes, a suspension of critical judgment and a laissez-faire attitude to all pursuits and all kinds of knowledge. The expression of relativism in the college curriculum, as Bloom sees it, is the removal of core requirements, whose absence encourages students to believe that no studies are more central to human life than others. As a result of this ethos of openness (which, Bloom argues, is really a kind of closing of the mind, incompatible with a true Socratic openness to reasoned arguments about the good), students have abandoned the idea on which the university (which Bloom traces to Socrates) was founded: the idea of a rational search for the best human life.

In support of this argument, Bloom constructs a colorful and highly rhetorical portrait of today's university students, who by his account seem to be pathetic characters indeed. Cut off from the nourishment of old religious and even secular traditions, their souls made small by the view that anything is as good as anything else, these students are rootless and enervated. Their personal relationships, devoid of lasting commitment, are further undermined, Bloom claims, by the excesses of feminism, one of his central targets, which he accuses of using "force" against "nature." Unable to pursue anything with passionate devotion, these students seem to live only for the "premature ecstasy" of rock music. Empty and selfish, "they can be anything they want to be, but they have no reason to be anything in particular."

Bloom now offers a historical argument that attempts to explain how the relativism he deplores became such a pervasive influence on American society. It is an idiosyncratic account, based almost exclusively on influences from the high intellectual tradition of nineteenth-century continental Europe. (Bloom, surprisingly, is silent about the influence of utilitarianism on American cultural and economic life—an influence that surely has a part in explaining why many Americans believe that all satisfactions are equally valid.) The account examines several key terms that the American social vocabulary has inherited from the continental tradition—terms like "the self," "culture," and "values," showing us both their original philosophical use by writers such as Nietzsche and Max Weber and how they have been democratized by American relativists. Now, he argues, this vocabulary corrupts students' perceptions of the world to such an extent that they cannot make sense of the ancient idea of a rational search for the best way of living. They speak of "my values," thinking of them as expressions of subjective preference that cannot be criticized with reference to any objective norm. They prefer the radical individualism of the term "self," with its emphasis on the subjective and idiosyncratic, to the ancient idea that human beings have a "nature" that can be objectively specified.

In order to give us a clearer idea of the ancient conception of education from which the modern university has allegedly fallen away, Bloom now offers a history of the university that traces its foundation to Socrates', and in general ancient Greek philosophy's, questioning about the best life. He then gives his own strangely un-Socratic account of the university: the university exists within democracy to call chosen "natures" away from the corrupt judgments of "the many" and teach them the superior value of the contemplative life. Bloom then tries to show us how the university, as he conceives of it, has been corrupted by contemporary democratic demands for equality, with the consequent erosion of intellectual standards. There follows a bitter account of the student movement of the Sixties, during which Bloom, lonely opponent of corruption, attempted to stop various changes that he deemed pernicious, such as the changing of curriculum requirements and even of faculty appointment procedures in response to student demands. To this time of timidity and lowering of standards he traces today's rootlessness and narcissism.

A survey of today's university departments yields, Bloom now argues, the conclusion that only the natural sciences are healthy—respected by all and flourishing in their research activities. The humanities, on the other hand, are, as he sees it, very badly off. Humanistic research lacks passion, quality, and focus; and, partly in consequence, humanities professors do not inspire respect either in their students or in society generally. Particularly weak and neglected, according to Bloom, is philosophy, which really ought to be leading the university, on account of its dedication to the deepest questions about how human beings should live. Philosophy must, he argues, be returned to its proper place as the leading force in the university. Universities should seek a remedy for their diseases in the establishment of required (and apparently uniform) core curricula based upon the Great Books of the Western tradition and principally on the central works of Western philosophy, and in particular ancient Greek philosophy, in which Bloom finds the antidote to the relativism that infects today's students.

We shall later see what he expects these curricula to accomplish, and for whom. And we can see by now some of the elements that explain his book's enormous appeal—its assault on cultural confusion and the lowering of standards, its defense of an education that will, allegedly, be a source of community and vitality, and its opposition to a narrow pre-professional specialization that cuts students off from one another and many ideas of lasting value. But in the very singleness and simplicity of Bloom's solution, so uninterested in the needs of different souls, and in the dogmatic complacency with which it is announced, so far removed from the Socratic demand for ceaseless self-questioning, we begin to sense the tension between Bloom's official allegiance to Socrates and the more dogmatic and religious conception of philosophy to which he is deeply drawn. Such simple prescriptions need careful scrutiny.

## II

Bloom delivers a blistering indictment of contemporary society and recommends a cure. The indictment is based upon his experience, the cure upon his understanding of the texts of ancient Greek philosophy and of the nature of the philosophical life. So we are invited to assess the quality of his observations of life, his readings of ancient texts, and his philosophical contribution. Bloom himself praises precision of description as an essential philosophical virtue:

> Concreteness, not abstractness, is the hallmark of philosophy. All interesting generalizations must proceed from the richest awareness of what is to be explained, but the tendency to abstractness leads to simplifying the phenomena in order more easily to deal with them.

This precision is, indeed, both an important philosophical virtue and, we might add, an essential component of the Socratic (and more generally ancient Greek) conception of moral argument. But if Bloom has this sort of rich awareness of the lives of American university students, it does not emerge in this book, which is written, almost throughout, in unqualified universals. "Students...," "The humanities scholar..."—such are, throughout, the subjects of his sentences, sentences that do not even suggest that they might not cover all the cases or that they might be in some other way imperfect. Bloom knows that he knows. Socrates knew that he didn't.

We have reason for unease from the very beginning, when Bloom describes his "sample" in this study:

> It consists of thousands of students of comparatively high intelligence, materially and spiritually free to do pretty much what they want with the few years of college they are privileged to have—in short, the kind of young persons who populate the twenty or thirty best universities. There are other kinds of students whom circumstances of one sort or another prevent from having the freedom required to pursue a liberal education. They have their own needs and may very well have very different

characters from those I describe here. My sample, whatever its limits, has the advantage of concentrating on those who are most likely to take advantage of a liberal education and to have the greatest moral and intellectual effect on the nation. It is sometimes said that these advantaged youths have less need of our attention and resources, that they already have enough. But they, above all, most need education, inasmuch as the greatest talents are most difficult to perfect, and the more complex the nature the more susceptible it is to perversion.

Here students who are materially well off and academically successful enough to go to a small number of elite universities and to pursue their studies there without the distraction of holding a job are equated with those having "the greatest talents" and the "more complex" natures. They are said to be the people who are "most likely to take advantage of a liberal education," and to be the ones who "most need education." It would seem that the disadvantaged, as Bloom imagines them, also have comparatively smaller talents, simpler natures, and fewer needs. But Bloom never argues that they do. He simply has no interest in the students whom he does not regard as the elite—an elite defined, he makes plain, by wealth and good fortune as much as by qualities of mind that have deeper human value.

The population of American universities has changed rapidly and dramatically since the 1950s (the time to which Bloom nostalgically refers as a time of greatness). Since 1950, enrollment in undergraduate higher education in the United States has increased by almost 400 percent, while the number of institutions of higher education has increased by 60 percent. (In the period between 1870 and 1940, the number of students increased by 3000 percent.) These changes, about which Bloom is utterly silent, reflect a judgment in our society that higher education is an important human need, and that it should be made available to anyone who can take advantage of it. Many capable and highly motivated students cannot attend elite universities such as the ones Bloom describes. Some, for example, must hold a job and attend school part time, something that the schools in Bloom's sample on the whole discourage; others must live at home and have no such school in their region.

Nationwide, 40 percent of undergraduates in colleges and universities are over twenty-five years old; fewer than 60 percent study full time. The comparable statistics from Harvard, to take one representative example of a university in Bloom's sample, are .03 percent and .03 percent, respectively.[2] And even at elite universities, many students fail to fit Bloom's description, since they hold one or even several jobs. Bloom's indifference to the situation of all but a few highly atypical students should make us wonder about all general statements about "students" and about American culture in this book.

Now let us turn to classical philosophy. For Bloom presents himself as someone whose insights come from a lifetime spent studying the texts of the ancient Greek philosophers, in whose writings he finds a view of human nature that is the antidote to contemporary relativisim about the good human life. "The substance of my being," he writes, "has been informed by the books I learned to care for. They accompany me every minute of every day of my life." His special love for these books has certainly prevented him from attending to works of literature and philosophy that lie outside the tradition they began. For he makes the remarkable claim that "only in the Western nations, that is, those influenced by Greek philosophy, is there some willingness to doubt the identification of the good with one's own way." This statement shows a startling ignorance of the critical and rationalist tradition in classical Indian thought,[3] of the arguments of classical Chinese thinkers,[4] and, beyond this, of countless examples of philosophical and nonphilosophical self-criticism from many parts of the world. (Bloom usually forgets that nonphilosophers can also be rational.) It shows as well a most un-Socratic unwillingness to suspect one's own ignorance. I have rarely seen such a cogent, though inadvert, argument for making the study of non-Western civilizations an important part of the university curriculum.

How does Bloom treat the books that he does read? Usually, it must be said, in a vague and offhand way. We find many statements about "the ancients." We find frequent appeals to their authority—something that is extremely odd in view of the insistence of every great ancient philosopher on the priority of rational argument to traditional authority. We find, as well, a few statements about particular writers, such as Plato, Aristotle, Cicero, and Plutarch, and, on rare occasions, a remark about a specific work. But there are almost never quotations or references to passages, and never an effort to discover the structure of an extended pattern of argument. Nor is there ever any indication that these texts are difficult to interpret, that scholars differ about their meaning. Bloom always knows what they mean, and so authoritatively that he does not need to support his statements with arguments or even precise references. In short, there is no indication that in practice Bloom accepts his own dictum that "learning must and can be both synoptic and precise."

This is all the more remarkable since in the one case, Plato's *Republic*, in which Bloom does advance a definite interpretation of a text at comparative length (which is to say, about a page and a half), he presents (following his teacher, Leo Strauss) an interpretation that is both bizarre and not accepted by any major non-Straussian interpreter of the text, beginning with Aristotle. He alleges that the *Republic* does not seriously propose the ideal city, the rule of philosophers, or the equal education of women. The *Republic*, he writes, ironically undercuts itself, and actually teaches to those in the know the impossibility of what it seems to advocate.[5] Why doesn't Bloom think it important to defend such controversial textual claims with arguments? Not to do so seems curiously lacking in respect for the text that one loves, and also for the readers with whom one is trying to converse.

Where Bloom makes authoritative claims about "the ancients" in support of his central moral and political conclusions, his argument contains extraordinary gaps and errors, of which I will mention only a few examples. In an important passage on the function of moral education, Bloom represents Aristotle's *Poetics* as saying that the fall of tragic heroes is due to "a flaw in their characters"—a mistaken Renaissance interpretation of Aristotle's concept of *hamartia* ("error," "mistake") that has been vigorously rejected by modern scholars with a remarkable degree of consensus. Aristotle, in fact, explicitly distinguishes such "mistakes" from flaws in character.

More prominent still in Bloom's central argument is his claim about ancient views of emotion. The modern feminist attempts to encourage men to be less "macho" and aggressive are criticized on the grounds that "the psychology of the ancients" shows the futility of this "nasty" attempt:

> Machismo—the polemical description of maleness or spiritedness, which was the central *natural* passion in men's souls in the psychology of the ancients, the passion of attachment and loyalty—was the villain, the source of difference between the sexes. . . . A host of Dustin Hoffman and Meryl Streep types invade the schools . . . and it is indeed possible to soften men. But to make them "care" is another thing, and the project must inevitably fail. . . . It must fail because in an age of individualism persons of either sex cannot be forced to be public-spirited, particularly by those who are becoming less so.

Here, as so often, one senses an absence of philosophical argument. The appeal to the authority of "the ancients" is no substitute. But if in fact Plato, Aristotle, and the major Hellenistic philosophers, Epicurean, Skeptic, and Stoic (Hellenistic philosophy is explicitly included in the category "ancients" by Bloom's numerous references to Cicero and Plutarch), *had* all arrived, by agreement, at Bloom's conclusion about the moderation of "spiritedness," this would be an interesting fact, and would call for reflection.

Do they? Not in the least. All major Greek thinkers about the passions of the soul—including Plato, Aristotle, Epicureans, Stoics, and Skeptics— agree that beliefs that are learned, and are not "natural," are important elements in the formation of passions such as anger, fear, and grief. For this reason, the passions can be modified by a modification of belief. Furthermore, all hold that the grief, fear, anger (etc.) that most people feel are based, to one or another extent, on beliefs that are *false*, and that the passions, therefore, *should* be modified by a modification of belief. "Spiritedness" is Bloom's translation of Plato's words *thumos* and *to thumoeides*; these are generic words for the part of the soul that is the seat of the emotions, as opposed to the appetites—of, for example, anger, pity, grief, fear, as opposed to hunger and thirst. These words are also used to refer in particular to one of the soul's passions, the passion of anger. Plato shows in *Republic* II–III how the modification of beliefs can transform both men's and women's experiences of many kinds of *thumos*—especially of fear and grief. He does allow certain members of the city (there is no reason to think them all male) to retain the capacity for anger—this is the part of Plato's view that I suppose Bloom is alluding to in his talk of "spiritedness." They retain that passion for military purposes.

All Greek thinkers after Plato, however, agree that this angry and reactive aspect of the soul (which they find in both men and women) is one of the central dangers in human life. Aristotle and his Peripatetic successors urge that it be retained but moderated, by cultivating correct beliefs about what is really an insult or damage, and what is not. They praise the virtue of "mildness of temper." The three Hellenistic schools denounce the passion far more strongly, as part of a general condemnation of the passions, treating all of them as artificial creations of corrupt society and obsessively reflecting on devices to bring about their complete elimination.

A thinker who truly loves ancient Greek and Roman philosophy, whose "substance" has been "informed" by its greatest books, could not fail to be aware of Cicero's *Tusculan Disputations*, Philodemus' *On Anger*, Plutarch's *On Being Without Anger*, Seneca's *On Anger* and *On Mercy*, Diogenes Laertius' *Lives* of Pyrrho, Zeno, and Chrysippus, and the fragments of Chrysippus' *On the Passions*. These works argue with commitment and precision against Bloom's view of the passion of "spiritedness," denying both its naturalness and its value. Such a thinker would surely remember Seneca's *Letter* 22, in which the voice of nature herself speaks, telling the reader that she is not responsible for the passions, which she calls "plagues" infecting human life. Such a thinker would be aware that Diogenes' *Life of Pyrrho* makes explicit the connections between eliminating the passions and altering some of the ways men and women conventionally behave. The philosopher Pyrrho, in his improved and "mild" state, is praised for helping his sister with the dusting and marketing. These are not out-of-the-way texts. They are well known and central. But Bloom, while claiming to be a lover of the ancients, simply ignores all texts that contradict his thesis.

The same question arises in connection with Bloom's more general assault on feminism as contrary to nature. Bloom tells us that feminism is "not founded on nature," and that it ends "in forgetting nature and using force to refashion human beings to secure that justice." Here again he refers to the ancient Greek tradition: not to Aristotle, who would have subscribed to this view, but whose supporting arguments about female biology are too evidently false to support a contemporary claim. Instead he appeals to the ancient tradition in general and especially to Plato, arguing in his characteristic fashion that the explicit proposals of Socrates defending the equal education of women in the *Republic* conceal Plato's real meaning, which is actually to attack, as impossible and bad, the idea that females might "have the same education, live the same lives and do the same jobs as men."

Bloom does not mention here the evidence of Aristotle, who, after having lived and talked with Plato for twenty years, takes these proposals absolutely seriously and argues against them. He is silent about the actual lives of Spartan women, who exemplify certain of these freedoms, and are criticized by Aristotle on this account. He does not mention the well-known evidence of Oxyrynchus Papyrus 3656, which establishes firmly that Plato took the radical step (for Athens) of teaching women in his philosophical school—a fact that surely sheds light on the *Republic*'s intentions.[6]

In his general discussion of "the ancients" on this topic he is entirely silent about Epicurus' support for the teaching of women; and, above all, about prominent Stoic arguments concerning women's nature, well summarized in the passage of Musonius Rufus that I have already cited. Musonius argues that nature actually *requires* that both men and women pursue philosophy, and pursue it in a way that connects it to practical and social activities. When Bloom is silent about evidence such as this, evidence that is not obscure, but is well known and essential, what are we to think of his attitude toward his readers, and toward the books with which he claims to live?

Still, it is not Socratic to rely on the authority of texts. If Bloom's own philosophical reasoning were precise and cogent, we could forgive him these historical failures—even though he himself rests his case on appeals to historical authority. How good a philosopher, then, is Allan Bloom? The answer is, we cannot say, and we are given no reason to think him one at all. His book is long on rhetoric, painfully short on argument. Central terms such as "relativism" go undefined and unanalyzed, in a way that would have caused Socrates to ask many irritating questions. "Relativism," Bloom writes, "has extinguished the real motive of education, the search for a good life." Yet nowhere does Bloom bother to describe the many distinct varieties of relativism that have been defended and criticized by philosophers. The contemporary philosophical scene in America (which, Bloom alleges, is largely "bleak") is in fact rich in arguments on exactly this question, among many others. And the analytic philosophers who, according to Bloom, "simply would not and could not talk about anything important" are addressing this very problem with arguments of considerable depth and complexity, since any good defense of or attack on conceptual relativism must deal not only with ethical questions but also with questions in the philosophy of science and of language.

Bloom has presumably studied the works of W. V. O. Quine, Nelson Goodman, Donald Davidson, Hilary Putnam, and the many other serious writers on these problems; for he claims to tell us what is going on in contemporary American philosophy, and to be a lover of "knowledge and certitude." How could he make such negative judgments without knowing the arguments he attacks? It would have been a public service if a book on philosophy and on relativism had explained these difficult debates for the general reader, letting the reader assess their significance. Bloom, once again, is silent. He does not even give us his own arguments for his anti-relativist position—except by linking relativism, somewhat obscurely, to practical consequences that seem to him self-evidently deplorable. But surely we cannot assess Bloom's contribution to philosophy—to the rational search for truth about the good life—until we have those arguments before us.

III

But if we approach Bloom's book expecting it to be a work of Socratic philosophy, answering the Socratic demand for definitions, explanations, and rational arguments, we may be mistaking its purpose. Portions of the book, especially in its early chapters, do indeed seem to defend a conception of philosophy much like that shared by Socrates and the Stoics, according to which philosophy is each individual person's search for the good through active reasoning and critical argument. On this view of philosophy's role in human life, we would expect the claim that philosophy should be at the heart of the university in American democracy to be a claim that in this democracy each and every person ought to have both the opportunity and the incentive to engage in studies that awaken the rational search for a good life. But in the later chapters of Bloom's book, in which Bloom turns from negative argument to the statement of his own position, a very different conception emerges both of philosophy and of the university as teacher of philosophy in a democracy. This conception, which is the one Bloom seems most deeply drawn to when speaking in his own voice, is of a philosophy that is not practical, alive, and broadly distributed, but contemplative and quasi-religious, removed from ethical and social concerns, and the preserve of a narrow elite.

This shift is prepared for earlier, since from the opening of the book, Bloom presents himself to us as a profoundly religious man, who deplores the decline of revealed religion and of the Bible's authority in American society. He speaks with nostalgia of "the gripping inner life vouchsafed those who were nurtured by the Bible." He praises the life of his grandparents as a life "based on the Book"; and for him "a life based on the Book is closer to the truth" and "provides the material for deeper research in and access to the real nature of things." He approves of the old idea that the highest aspiration one might have for one's children "is for them to be wise—as priests, prophets or philosophers are wise"—not suggesting that there is any salient difference between the philosopher and the other two. For his own description of "the philosophic use of reason" he cites Maimonides:

> This then will be a key permitting one to enter places the gates to which were locked. And when these gates are opened and these places are entered into, the soul will find rest therein, the eyes will be delighted, and the bodies will be eased of their toil and of their labor.

This is a conception of philosophy quite alien to the Socrates of the *Apology* and the *Euthyphro*—and, indeed, to very many of the greatest philosophers in the Western tradition, for whom the essence of philosophy is not mystical wisdom but careful reasoning, and for whom there is no rest and no ease so long as any intellectual or moral challenge remains, as it always does for human beings, to be seriously examined.

The Socratic conception of philosophy naturally led, in the practice of the Greek Stoics, to the conclusion that each and every human being can have and ought to have the chance to have a philosophical education. For Socratic philosophizing is based on nothing more specialized than the active use of practical reason, which seems to be the common and universal possession of all humans. And if, as Socrates said, "the unexamined life is not worth living for a human being," it might seem to follow that a society dedicated to securing, for its members, the conditions of a full and worthwhile life would have a duty to make sure that they could get this higher education.

The pressure for degrees and credentials has many sources in our society. But it is this Socratic idea, I believe, that gives fundamental legitimacy to democratizing higher education in America. It is an idea deeply connected with democracy's respect for each person's rational powers. Bloom's final rejection of democracy, and of the democratization of philosophy, are connected, I believe, with his very different conception of philosophy's nature and role. Because philosophy is not the active development of each person's own practical reason, but a specialized search, carried on through esoteric books, for a contemplative theoretical wisdom, it is, according to Bloom, open only to a few specially equipped "natures" and cannot be democratized without loss of standards. And because it cannot be democratized, and because its protection is, Bloom argues, the essential function of the university, he concludes that the university, in its essential nature, is, though within democracy, an undemocratic and even an anti-democratic institution.

Early in his book Bloom criticizes today's students by citing Plato's description of the democratic man from *Republic* VIII; later on, he makes Plato's attack on the democratic soul apply to modern democratic society in general. "The deepest intellectual weakness of democracy is its lack of taste or gift for the theoretical life," he writes; and he concludes that the function of the university in a democracy is to create a living alternative to democratic leveling and debasement, making it possible for "the rarest talents" to turn to the best way of life, the philosophical life (also called "the highest life"). The Bloomian university does not see itself as having any practical social aim, even the aim of educating citizens so that they will govern their own ethical lives better and more reflectively. For according to Bloom the aim of the "highest life" is to depart from the ethical and social life altogether, to find a permanent "wisdom" and to "find rest" in it.

Furthermore, Bloom derives from his idiosyncratic reading of "the ancients" the tragic moral that the relationship between the true philosopher and the "many" in a democracy must be hostile; and it must be hostile by "nature," since the "many" always fear death and therefore seek only "vulgar" satisfactions. The philosopher alone is above such fears. Being above them, he is also, says Bloom, above the moral and political life, and will seek to live apart from the people. "Changing the character of his relationship to them is impossible because the disproportion between him and them is firmly rooted in nature. Thus, he has no expectation of essential progress."

Bloom's contemplative conception of philosophy seems remarkably empty of content, since his account of philosophical activity evinces no interest in the traditional subjects of "the contemplative life," such as metaphysics, cosmology, and mathematics. Nonetheless, in the name of the contemplative, his conception teaches the would-be philosopher to look down on ethical concerns and the search for social justice. Universities, standing in the midst of corrupt and hostile democracies, must not, Bloom argues, seek to improve them—even, apparently, by training citizens to be more ethically reflective or by searching for better moral or political or economic theories. They must simply protect the nonethical life of wisdom, as Bloom understands it, making sure that the few specially chosen "natures" who are suited for this life will be able to lead it. Thus, Bloom is really proposing that the function of the entire American university system should be to perfect and then protect a few contemplative souls, whose main subject matter will, apparently, be the superiority of their own contemplative life to the moral and political life. Now we see why Bloom talked only about the elite from the beginning: because his "highest" goal has nothing to do with the good life of anyone else, and, indeed, nothing to do with morality and justice.

Bloom's proposals can be criticized on many fronts. But above all it is important to see plainly what he intends the university to be. Those who believe that the highest search for the truth does not turn away from concern for the quality of moral and social life and that the universities of America should exist for the sake of all its citizens, not only for the sake of a few, must find themselves opposed to Bloom's conception. In defending their position, they will find, contrary to Bloom's claims, strong support from the arguments of the ancient Greek thinkers, and especially of the Stoics, who spoke so eloquently of practical reason as a universal human possession, whose cultivation is a central human need.

And what of the curriculum? The Stoics saw that, in order to extend the benefits of higher education to all human beings, teaching would have to be responsive to the needs of many different types of human beings. This is why they held that a good teacher is like a good doctor, flexible and responsive to individuality. Bloom is concerned with only one narrow group of students; even in discussing this group he does not seem interested in their individuality. Thus, it is easy for him to believe that a single simple solution will suffice for college teaching.

Even for the narrow group described, it is not at all obvious that the best way to induce genuine reflection is to make a list of the Great Books of the Western tradition and to require their study of all students. There are many evident problems with that approach, even apart from the special aristocratic use to which Bloom himself wishes to put it.[7] The study of great works of philosophy can indeed enliven the mind. But required lists of Great Books encourage passivity and reverence, rather than active critical reflection; they inevitably select certain texts over others of equal intrinsic worth for reasons having to do with fashion and prejudice, and then tend to tell the student that these are the really "Great" ones, and all that he or she centrally needs to know. (This is the way to Bloom's contemptuous ignorance of non-Western traditions.)

Such courses, furthermore, are likely to be taught without sufficient grounding in the historical setting and even the languages of the texts studied. (For even if one shares Bloom's opposition to relativism and historicism, as I do, one needs to know a great deal of history to know what a text of an ancient author is actually asserting.) The advantages of the Great Books approach in encouraging cohesiveness and community among students who will share knowledge of central texts—advantages which are genuine enough—may be offset by these disadvantages. Perhaps they can be overcome; but Bloom does not show us how.

But the real problem with Bloom's advice on curriculum is the problem of the book as a whole: that it is not informed by concern for the diverse needs of diverse groups of American students. If we follow, in place of Bloom's aristocratic argument, the Stoic argument I have described, we will surely require a quite different approach to teaching. Such an approach, combining a universal and nonrelative account of human needs with a refined sensitivity to students' actual social situations, can be found, I suggest, in the wise and humane book, *General Education in a Free Society*, written at Harvard in 1945 by a committee including Paul Buck, John H. Finley Jr., I. A. Richards, George Wald, and others.[8] This book invites comparison with Bloom's because of its praise of ancient Greek models and its rejection of an education based on narrow specialization in favor of one that is "preparation for life in the broad sense of completeness as a human being." But it is miles away from Bloom's in its evident affection for the entire country of diverse people whose education it proposes to discuss, and in the tentative subtlety with which it investigates the problem of creating a program of general education in college and university curricula for this diverse population.

The report opens with the affirmation of a statement by the then president of Harvard, James Bryant Conant: "The primary concern of American education today is not the development of the appreciation of the 'good life' in young gentlemen born to the purple. It is the infusion of the liberal and humane tradition into our entire educational system." And the authors describe their conception of education's central purpose in a way that both explicitly refers to the Socratic-Stoic tradition and links that tradition, plausibly, with the American democratic belief in the equality of citizens and in the equal need of all for rational education:

> The task of modern democracy is to preserve the ancient ideal of liberal education and to extend it as far as possible to all the members of the community. . . . To believe in the equality of human beings is to believe that the good life, and the education which trains the citizen for the good life, are equally the privilege of all. And these are the touchstones of the liberated man: first, is he free; that is to say, is he able to judge and plan for himself, so that he can truly govern himself? In order to do this, his must be a mind capable of self-criticism; he must lead that self-examined life which according to Socrates is alone worthy of a free man. Thus he will possess inner freedom, as well as social freedom. Second, is he universal in his motives and sympathies? For the civilized man is a citizen of the entire universe; he has overcome provincialism, he is objective, and is a "spectator of all time and all existence." Surely these two are the very aims of democracy itself.

But this application of the Socratic-Stoic tradition leads the authors to reject a single curricular solution, as insufficiently attentive to the needs of different groups of students. Instead, they describe several essential human capacities that education ought to develop, and the sorts of knowledge that, in general, will be suited to the development of these abilities in various parts of life. Then they sketch tentatively a variety of ways in which curricula might, in different circumstances, approach this common task, speaking in detail only about the special case of Harvard, whose students' needs are not alleged to be either the same as or any more important than those of any other group.

An important difference between their curricular proposals and Bloom's is their insistence on the importance of history, both as a subject of study in its own right, and as a component in the study of philosophical and literary texts. Bloom gives history little place in the curriculum—apparently because he believes that it will distract students from the realization that the greatest truths are timeless. The Harvard authors plausibly insist that we cannot see how to bring timeless standards of goodness to our own society unless we have understood what possibilities historical change have made available to human beings at different times and in different places. Thus, the Stoic goal of becoming a citizen of the entire universe not only does not undermine but actually promotes the claim of history to a central place in the curriculum.

There are difficulties with the Harvard report's approach; there is much vagueness. And in the authors' silence about the education of women they do not follow well the Stoic thinkers whose views about rational self-government they so eloquently invoke. But the report should be revived for our close study, as an example of genuinely democratic thought about higher education in its relationship to human diversity and human need. And its hopeful humility, in the face of the complexity of this problem, should provide a counterpoise to Bloom's stridently confident pessimism, as well as encouragement to those of us who do not accept Bloom's conclusion that real philosophical education must be at odds with democratic values.

According to Bloom's dark vision, the Muse who inspired the Great Books of the ancient Greek world would be horrified at the chaos of contemporary America. She would surely flee for comfort, if she could, behind the walls of a privileged elite university, there to talk about hidden truths with a few chosen souls. Walt Whitman, a different sort of admirer of ancient Greek traditions, imagined the ancient Greek Muse actually choosing America as her home, on account of its active vitality and its commitment to the worth of each human being's self-development. In his poem "Song of the Exposition," he imagines this Muse migrating and settling down, not deterred from her inspirational role by the presence of rough conditions, creating, like this democracy, in the midst of labor and alongside laboring men and women. We see her

vigorously clearing a path for herself, striding through the confusion,
By thud of machinery and shrill steam-whistle undismay'd,
Bluff'd not a bit by drain-pipe, gasometers, artificial fertilizers,
Smiling and pleas'd with palpable intent to stay.

This is democratic romanticism. That does not make it either false or impossible. It expresses a noble wish for a country in which the souls of all citizens would flourish, each in its own setting, and find respect. We might consider it as an antidote to Bloom's apocalypse, and as the opening to a genuinely democratic discussion of democratic education.

### NOTES

1. C. Musonius Rufus, *Should Women Too Do Philosophy?*, edited by O. Hense (Leipzig: Teubner, 1905); see also C. E. Lutz, "The Roman Socrates," *Yale Classical Studies* 10 (New Haven: Yale University Press, 1947), p. 3ff.

2. For the national statistics, my sources are *Involvement in Learning: Realizing the Potential of American Higher Education*, Report of the Study Group on the Conditions of Excellence in American Higher Education, sponsored by the National Institute of Education, October 1984; and *General Education in a Free Society: Report of the Harvard Committee* (Cambridge, Mass.: Harvard University Press, 1945); the particular statistics about universities in Bloom's "sample" have been obtained from admissions offices and/or dean's offices.

3. See Martha Nussbaum and Amartya K. Sen, "Internal Criticism and Indian Rationalist Traditions," a Working Paper of the World Institute for Development Economics Research, Helsinki, published in *Relativism*, edited by M. Krausz (Notre Dame, Ind.: University of Notre Dame Press, 1988); also Bimal K. Matilal, *Perception* (Oxford, UK: Oxford University Press, 1985).

4. See especially Benjamin Schwartz, *The World of Thought in Ancient China* (Cambridge, Mass.: Harvard University Press, 1985).

5. The same view is asserted in Bloom's notes to his translation of the *Republic* (Basic Books, 1968), without any more satisfactory argument than what is presented here.

6. For this and other related evidence, and a discussion, see Mary R. Lefkowitz, *Women in Greek Myth* (Baltimore, Md.: Johns Hopkins University Press, 1986), p. 144.

7. A different and genuinely democratic approach to core requirements (at the level of elementary and secondary, not university, education) is carefully argued for in E. D. Hirsch Jr., *Cultural Literacy: What Every American Needs to Know* (Boston: Houghton Mifflin, 1987).

8. See reference above, note 2. The committee that prepared the report was chaired by Paul H. Buck; John H. Finley Jr. was vice-chairman. Its members were Raphael Demos, Leigh Hoadley, Byron S. Hollinshead, Wilbur K. Jordan, I. A. Richards, Phillip J. Rulon, Arthur M. Schlesinger, Robert Ulich, George Wald, and Benjamin F. Wright.

# CHAPTER FOUR

# Recoiling from Reason

ALASDAIR MACINTYRE (1989), Whose Justice?
Which Rationality?

In the second book of the *Politics*, Aristotle asks whether it is a good thing to encourage changes in society. Should people be offered rewards for inventing some change in the traditional laws? No, he writes, because this would lead to instability and unnecessary tampering with what is working well. Should we, on the other hand, listen to those who wish to keep ancestral traditions fixed and immune from criticism? No again—for if we reason well we can make progress in lawmaking, just as we do in other arts and sciences. Aristotle illustrates his point with examples drawn both from his own society and from the city of Cyme, in Asia Minor:

> The customs of former times might be said to be too simple and barbaric. For Greeks used to go around armed with swords; and they used to buy wives from one another; and there are surely other ancient customs that are extremely stupid. (For example, in Cyme there is a law about homicide, that if a man prosecuting a charge can produce a certain number of witnesses from among his own relations, the defendant will automatically be convicted of murder.) In general, all human beings seek not the way of their ancestors, but the good.

Aristotle's conclusion, here and elsewhere, is that change should not be too easy. Traditions embody many years of many people's effort and thought; and it is likely that no deeply held view will have failed to get something right. Traditions (both popular and philosophical) should, he believed, be the philosopher's starting point, and should be sensitively examined as guides to ethical truth.

On the other hand, law should also allow some latitude for people to criticize and make changes when they decide on reflection that change is called for. Sometimes these modifications will apply an existing principle to a new and unforeseen circumstance—as when a government takes account of its existing obligations to provide food for all its citizens in order to grapple with the special challenge posed by a famine or a migration of new settlers.[1] Sometimes the principles themselves may be modified, in the light of reflection about concrete experiences and other principles—as would happen if the citizens of Cyme gave up their homicide law after deciding that it relied too much on bad evidence and did not fit well with other principles they held concerning justice and the good human life.

Aristotle's reflections about justice and legal change expose a deep and pervasive problem, which is central to Alasdair MacIntyre's recent book. It is difficult, now as then, to think clearly about the tensions between tradition and critical reasoning that arise within a single society—as when Cymeans argue about the merits of their ancient legal code—and even more difficult to think clearly about issues of justice that arise in conflicts between different and opposed traditions. When one does try to reason on such questions, Aristotle's problem arises: How can one recognize the value of traditional thought and still be able to say, as he says: "This custom is barbaric"; "This law is extremely stupid"? The problem is made no simpler if one recognizes, as Aristotle does, that in any society the standards of practical reasoning—reasoning about what to do and how to choose—are themselves taught within a tradition, and are often closely linked to the tradition's other evaluations.

The problem is made vastly more complex if one acknowledges, as Aristotle did not, that traditions are embodied in languages and conceptual schemes that cannot be neatly translated into one another, that each tradition carves up the world of human experience in a somewhat different way. For example, the ancient Greeks (before and including Aristotle) had no concept exactly corresponding to the Christian concept of the "will." They analyzed human action by referring to various different types of reasoning, perceiving, and desiring. This makes it difficult to compare Greek and Christian thought on many ethical issues in which such conceptual differences arise.

Moral philosophy has sometimes dealt with the variety of ethical traditions shown us by history and anthropology simply by ignoring them, and by seeking, as some Kantians and utilitarians have done, principles of such high generality that they do not seem to be linked to any tradition whatever. But recently there has been increasing dissatisfaction with this approach among philosophers, on the grounds that it is simply too remote from concrete human experience. And there has been increasing interest in investigating, once again, the ancient Greek notion of virtue, which seems to promise the basis for an ethical view that will, like Aristotle's, show respect for history and for people's concrete experience, whether of friendship, or fear, or social and civic life, while still making room for critical rational argument. A number of contemporary moral philosophers, including Philippa

Foot and Bernard Williams, have contributed to this renewal of interest in the Aristotelian approach to ethics.[2] But one of the most widely influential defenders of the ancient approach has been Alasdair MacIntyre.

In his influential book *After Virtue* (1981), MacIntyre argued that the language of contemporary ethical debate is in hopeless disorder. Lacking the firm guidance of shared agreements about moral standards, lacking even a common moral language, we argue past one another, MacIntyre claimed, hurling at our opponents uprooted fragments of once vital ethical traditions. We believe that we can make some progress in arguments about which actions are "just" or "reasonable." But we do not realize that our arguments, and the terms we use to make them, are rootless, lacking connection to traditional beliefs and stories (such as, for example, Homeric stories about the justice and injustice of the gods) that alone give the moral terms a society uses a definite point and application. And because our arguments are rootless in this way, they are doomed to incoherence and to failure.

MacIntyre then vividly contrasted the contemporary cacophony with a portrait of the ethics of virtue in ancient Athens, where very often there was, according to MacIntyre, no need for ethical questioning, since shared agreements had made many moral choices as obvious as the choice of a next move in a game played according to well-defined rules. When questions did arise, the presence of a bedrock of agreement made the ensuing debate limited, well defined, and capable of producing a clear solution.

Could the contemporary world return to the ethical situation of the Greeks, as MacIntyre understood it? That was the question with which *After Virtue* ended. It was evident that MacIntyre saw in such a return the only hope for ethical order; and yet it was equally evident that he had at that time no clear view of how such a return might take place. He called for "the construction of local forms of community within which civility and the intellectual and moral life can be sustained through the new dark ages which are already upon us." And his last sentence declares, obscurely, "We are waiting not for a Godot, but for another—doubtless very different— St. Benedict." But this left a number of questions unanswered. In particular, would the new norms he called for be simply local in each case, and valid only relatively to local traditions, or would there also be standards of rational justification that we could use as reasons for preferring some local traditions to others?

The reader of *After Virtue* might easily have concluded from MacIntyre's references to local communities that the solution he favored would lie in some form of cultural relativism, in which the only appropriate standards for resolving ethical questions would derive their validity from local traditions and practices, and no appeal across or beyond the differing practices would be possible. MacIntyre's new book shows us that such a conclusion would have been a serious error. He now announces his deep opposition to cultural relativism and his determination to follow the example of Aristotle by providing a historically sensitive account of the way in which people should go about justifying their ethical ideas, especially their ideas of justice. And he gives his reader, in no uncertain terms, answers to the questions left over from *After Virtue*. The "new St. Benedict" is none other than St. Thomas Aquinas, who, according to MacIntyre, rationally justified Augustinian Catholicism by incorporating within it responses to the challenges presented by Aristotle's ethical views.

For MacIntyre, the norms of Thomist Catholicism derive their status from their ability to withstand dialectical examination through the ages. A major task of his book is to provide an account of how one tradition of thought challenges another, and how the rational superiority of one competing view over another can be established. But Catholic norms, as MacIntyre's account unfolds, also derive their status from the political authority of the Church, which imposes agreement concerning basic principles, subduing the disobedient human will. And MacIntyre clearly approves of the inculcation of such agreements through a system of education controlled by religious authority. He announces that he is now an "Augustinian Christian," and speaks favorably of religious tests for university appointments. (He himself has recently resigned his appointment at Vanderbilt University, a secular institution, to take up a chair at Notre Dame, an institution whose position on the relationship between orthodoxy and education is probably a good deal more liberal than the position taken in MacIntyre's book.)

To understand the relationship between MacIntyre's defense of reasoned argument and his sympathy with Church authority, and to discover how he strikes the balance between them, are evidently important tasks for any reader of *Whose Justice? Which Rationality?* But since MacIntyre develops his general ideas through a close study of four traditions, this task must begin with an understanding of that historical account.

MacIntyre identifies four traditions as especially important in the history of Western ethical thought. (He tells us that his project is incomplete because it does not include a study of either non-Western traditions or of the Jewish tradition.) The four are: the tradition of ancient Greek thought about virtue that began with Homer and culminated in Aristotle; the tradition of Christian thought, as exemplified in Augustine, and as modified by St. Thomas Aquinas to make room for the insights of Aristotle; the moral tradition of the Scottish Enlightenment, including such obscure thinkers as James Stair and Andrew Fletcher, in which MacIntyre finds a close Protestant relative of Aquinas's view; and, finally, the traitor to these three venerable and promising traditions, the tradition of modern liberalism, as begun in the work of David Hume, for whose life and thought MacIntyre has undisguised contempt.

We begin in the ancient Greek world, a world, according to MacIntyre, of clearly demarcated social roles, in which citizens do not need to deliberate over which principles to follow, since the proper behavior for each role is so well defined. According to MacIntyre, "classical Greeks, like Greeks of the archaic period, for the most part understood the forms and structures of their communities as exemplifying the order of *dike*," or justice; "and what gave literary expression to that understanding above all else was the recitation and the hearing and the reading of the Homeric poems." The notion of justice used by the ancient Greeks, he argues, "presupposed that the universe had a single fundamental order, an order structuring both nature and society, so that the distinction which *we* mark by contrasting the natural and the social cannot as yet be expressed." Zeus and the human kings he empowers to enforce justice preside over an order that is made up of "hierarchically ordered social rules. To know what is required of you is to know what your place is within that structure and to do what your role requires."

Within the system inherited from Homer, however, tensions arise: in particular, a troublesome tension between the pursuit of the "goods of effectiveness" (instrumental goods such as money and property, it would seem) and the "goods of excellence" (the forms of virtuous activity, such as acting in a just or moderate way). MacIntyre describes various attempts to resolve these tensions, giving highest praise to Aristotle for his convincing arguments against the vice of acquisitiveness. He argues that according to Aristotle practical wisdom presupposes a correct understanding of the ultimate ends of human life. A person who is merely clever at pursuing self-interest will not be wise, because he will lack such understanding. But for a person who has the correct understanding of ends, MacIntyre argues, reasoning will have something like the simplicity of the Homeric model.

According to MacIntyre, whose account here is unfortunately oversimple,[3] we can find such admirable simplicity in Aristotle's doctrine of the "practical syllogism," a form of deductive reasoning that immediately precedes action and also terminates in action. For example (to rely, for a moment, on MacIntyre's reconstruction), in considering whether or not to eat a certain light and nutritious salad that is put before me, I would start with a premise stating what particular good is at stake: "Eating light and nutritious food at lunchtime is good for everyone." I would then, as a second premise, note that a certain situation is at hand that bears on the good in question: "It is now lunchtime, and this salad that has just been placed before me offers light and nutritious food." The "conclusion" drawn takes the form of an action: I eat the salad.[4] MacIntyre contends that the conclusion of such syllogisms—always an action, according to Aristotle—will follow without any great difficulty once a person has the correct overall view of human ends and perceives the concrete situation he is in. So, more or less all human action in a well-run polis will have this easy and automatic character, and prolonged deliberation will be unnecessary.

MacIntyre's next chapters examine the response of Augustinian Christianity to the challenge presented by this Aristotelian view. Augustine, in effect, denied that Aristotelian practical reason could deal adequately with the central questions facing human beings: only faith in God could do so. For MacIntyre, Thomas Aquinas took one of the most important steps in the progress of rational thought when he incorporated Aristotelian elements into an essentially Christian scheme of belief inherited from Saint Augustine. In this section, to which I will return, MacIntyre's interpretation of Aquinas places heavy emphasis on the limits of human reason and the central importance of divine grace.

We turn next to a fascinating account of the moral teaching of the Scottish Enlightenment. MacIntyre says little about the debate between the Catholic and the Scottish traditions. Instead, in defending such little-known Scottish thinkers as Stair and Fletcher, he seems to find in the Scottish views a tradition whose achievements parallel, within Protestantism, the achievements of Aquinas within Catholicism. In particular, the Scottish tradition insists on the importance of rational debate (reacting against forms of Calvinism that denied this); but it insists, too, that rational debate must be carried on within a setting of religious homogeneity. Like the Aristotelian and the Thomist traditions, it defines practical rationality according to its account of what is good, and does so in such a way that the unlimited pursuit of self-interest could not count as rational. And like Aquinas, but unlike Aristotle, the Scottish teachers insisted on religious orthodoxy as a necessary condition of practical wisdom. They denied university appointments in philosophy—central in their idea of moral education—to those who did not share their basic religious agreements—and MacIntyre insists, discussing Hume's failure to get the chair in Edinburgh, that they were entirely right to do so.

Indeed, MacIntyre attacks Hume as a traitor to the Scottish cause who deserted to the corrupt ways of English culture—which, in MacIntyre's scathing portrait, included above all a defense of the unlimited pursuit of self-interest. According to MacIntyre, Hume believes that reasoning cannot make us initiate actions; the ultimate moving force in any action is some desire or passion. Nor for Hume does reasoning have a role to play in answering the question, "What ends shall I pursue? What will count for me as the elements of a good life?" Such questions are, in effect, answered already by the desires I happen to have. So Hume's views of rationality and virtue are defective, according to MacIntyre, because he does not see that practical wisdom must include the wise selection of ends, and cannot be independent of that process.

This mistake by Hume, MacIntyre claims, is the source of a similar error in modern liberalism generally. Without giving any serious attention to Kant or the German tradition, MacIntyre accuses virtually all of modern liberalism of the faults he imputes to Hume. He claims that all liberal thinkers define rational behavior as behavior tending to "maximize" self-interest, understood as the satisfaction of desires. This is the thinnest part of the book. Its failure to look seriously at the influence of Kant's very different conception of reason on liberal thinkers such as John Rawls makes it largely useless as an account of current moral philosophy. And the account of English thought suffers by comparison with the account in *After Virtue*.

MacIntyre's hostility to English thought and social life is now so bitter that Jane Austen, one of the heroines of *After Virtue*, no longer has a place in his argument.

MacIntyre ends with a detailed account of traditions and of the languages in which they are embedded. Here, in keeping with his new emphasis on divine grace and on self-evident first principles, MacIntyre quietly drops *After Virtue*'s interesting account of the importance of story-telling in giving moral terms their meaning. This was a particularly attractive feature of the earlier book, even for many readers who did not accept *After Virtue*'s pessimistic conclusions. Nothing of comparable power has replaced it. MacIntyre concludes by showing in detail how a confrontation between different traditions takes place. This account is meant to buttress the claim, which he reasserts, that the Augustinian Christian tradition, as modified by Aquinas, has established its rational superiority.

*Whose Justice? Which Rationality?* is a difficult book to read. Muddy and overlong, it lacks *After Virtue*'s crisp prose, and it is far less clearly argued. It is very difficult to extract from the text a clear account of its central concepts, such as the nature of 'rational justification,' the relationship between argument and authority, and the value of local, rather than universal, norms. In part this is because the book is full of maddening inconsistencies. MacIntyre attacks England for attempting to influence the local traditions of Scotland, but he praises the Pope for exercising moral authority over the recalcitrant bishops of Ireland. Hume is a traitor because he left his native Scottish traditions behind and moved to London, but no account is taken of the local traditions of Thrace, which Aristotle left to come to Athens; or those of Northern Africa, which Augustine left to come to Rome; or those of Southern Italy, which Aquinas left (much against the will of his family, who tried to kidnap him) to join the Dominicans in Paris.

No moral system has exterminated local traditions more relentlessly and more successfully than Christianity, especially in its Roman Catholic version. And yet, even while continuing to defend the integrity and authority of local traditions, MacIntyre gives his allegiance to Catholic Christianity. Again, he dismisses the English language as a rootless, traditionless, "internationalized" language, because it is used to translate from and to so many local languages; but the Latin of the Church receives no similar criticism. Furthermore, the same criteria that supposedly show liberalism to be an ignominious failure are taken, where Aquinas's view is concerned, as evidence that it is a tradition as yet "incomplete" and evolving.

But on one issue it seems important to try to pin MacIntyre down. For if, as I have suggested, a central task for contemporary moral theory is to construct an account of the way in which moral beliefs can be justified, an account that would be attentive to history while still retaining the capacity to criticize local traditions, then there is reason to believe that close study of MacIntyre's book will repay the effort. For the book sets out to develop just such an account, emphasizing the fundamental importance of traditions embodied in history while making a case against cultural relativism.[5] How, then, does MacIntyre combine his view that all argument takes place inside traditions with his claim to be able to justify a single tradition, the Catholic tradition, as rationally superior to others?

MacIntyre insists that people cannot successfully justify their moral beliefs in detachment from actual ways of life, as embodied in ethical traditions. When we compare different standards of justice, for example, we must bear in mind that each belongs to a complex cultural tradition that embodies, as well, an account of what is reasonable and what good reasoning is. We cannot understand how the Greeks thought about justice, for example, without seeing how their conception is linked to their understanding of the relationship between reason and desire. Hume's very different account of reason helps to explain why he adopts a very different view of justice. Since any argument about justice must employ some view of what reasoning is like, it would appear that there is no neutral standard by which this conflict, and others like it, can be adjudicated.

And yet, MacIntyre argues, people can and do rationally justify their beliefs—particularly when the partisans of two traditions challenge one another. When such a confrontation takes place, he argues, one view will frequently succeed in establishing itself as superior to the other and will win acceptance from the partisans of the other view. The triumphant view does this by explaining how to solve problems that had arisen within the other view, and showing at the same time that it can incorporate virtually everything in the rival view that does survive dialectical scrutiny. The point can be illustrated by a scientific example. The scientific tradition based upon the Copernican heliocentric view of the universe demonstrated its superiority to Aristotelian physics by showing how it could solve problems left unsolved in geocentric thinking. At the same time, it was able to incorporate and preserve elements in the Aristotelian tradition that did survive scrutiny: much of Aristotle's biology, for example, could be retained. MacIntyre's claim is that ethical debate can evolve in much the same way.

For MacIntyre, traditions are worthy of our respect and allegiance only when they display a respect for this sort of argument, or this sort of contest between differing arguments. A good tradition is "more than a coherent movement of thought": it must display self-awareness in its confrontation with challenges both from those who are adherents of the tradition and from those who are outside it, as its members seek "a rational way through or around (its) encounters with radically different traditions." So if Aquinas's view has won out over its rivals, as MacIntyre alleges, this should mean that it has identified deficiencies in its rivals' views—deficiencies that were to some extent perceived as such within the rival views—and shown how it can do better, using good arguments. MacIntyre does believe that each tradition will to some extent go by its own idea of what counts as a good argument—for example, Aristotle and Hume, as he presents them, have very different views of what reasoning is like and what it can establish.

But he also plainly believes that a successful argument for the superiority of one tradition over another must be persuasive not only to those already convinced, but to adherents of the rival tradition as well. In so arguing MacIntyre clearly has respect for standards in argument, such as logical consistency, that are not as such tied to any one tradition.

On the other hand, alongside this serious commitment to self-awareness and to dialectical argument, we also find, in MacIntyre's account of tradition, an equally deep and equally explicit interest in ethical certainty—in having certain fixed rules and agreements that make the choice of what to do an automatic matter, for which explicit reasoning is not necessary. The ancient Greek conception of justice appeals to him because it is (so he says) "an expression of some unitary order informing and structuring human life." And the Greek polis seems to him vastly superior to modern states because it is (again, so he says) "already provided with an ordering of goods, goods to be achieved by excellence within specific and systematic forms of activity, integrated into an overall rank-order." MacIntyre's admiration for such a hierarchy of values and activities leads him to argue that it is only within a fixed system of agreements of this kind that rational questioning about the good life can coherently go on. In perhaps the most revealing metaphor in his book, he compares the well-run ethical community to a hockey game:

> A hockey player in the closing seconds of a crucial game has an opportunity to pass to another member of his or her team better placed to score a needed goal. Necessarily, we may say, if he or she has perceived and judged the situation accurately, he or she must immediately pass. What is the force of this "necessarily" and this "must"? It exhibits the connection between the good of that person *qua* hockey player and member of that particular team and the action of passing, a connection such that were such a player not to pass, he or she must *either* have falsely denied that passing was for their good *qua* hockey player *or* have been guilty of inconsistency *or* have acted as one not caring for his or her good *qua* hockey player and member of that particular team. That is to say, we recognize the necessity and immediacy of rational action by someone inhabiting a structured role in a context in which the goods of some systematic form of practice are unambiguously ordered. And in so doing we apply to one part of our social life a conception which Aristotle applies to rational social life as such.

Here, as in *After Virtue*,[6] MacIntyre wishes to recover for the contemporary world the certainty of such an order; and clearly for him the promise of doing so is a great part of the appeal of "the universal Church," which he calls an "order in which each human being has his or her own allotted place and his or her own allotted duties."

On the one hand, then, we see a genuine respect in MacIntyre's book for rational argument; on the other, there's a wish not to have argument about the basic structure of the ethical community. How are we to put the two aspects of his thought together? The answer to this question emerges, I believe, from the sections of the book dealing with Aquinas and with the Scottish Enlightenment. Here, although the details of the positions differ, the two accounts are remarkably similar with respect to the values that MacIntyre finds commendable. Both of these traditions insist on the importance of rational philosophical argument; both develop in opposition to thinkers (Augustinian and Calvinist) who seek to minimize the role of reason in human life. Yet both also insist on starting from fixed first principles. Both have a strong commitment to distinguishing orthodoxy from heresy, and they do so in a way that severely limits the direction any rational argument may take.

The Scottish thinkers hold that their first principles are self-evident to reason; but this notion of the self-evident turns out to involve an appeal to religious authority. For the people to whom first principles must be self-evident are the professors of philosophy in Scottish universities; and these professors must be certified as orthodox in religious belief in order to win appointment. In the case of Aquinas, MacIntyre attacks interpreters who argue that the natural law can be known by reason alone. Without God's grace and revelation, natural law would lack authority; at the same time, for natural law to be accepted, the Church must use its authority to set bounds to rational debate.

Nonetheless, MacIntyre holds that the tradition that culminates in Aquinas's thought has demonstrated its rational superiority over other traditions. If this claim is to be made consistent with his general account of the way in which a position shows its superiority to its rivals, then dialectical reasoning ought to be able to scrutinize the theorists' system as a whole and to compare it favorably to its rivals, and to do so with self-awareness and an awareness of alternatives. Such reasoning ought to be able to show to people who hold different views the superior value of Aquinas's position for human life, and to do so with convincing arguments. In order to see to what extent this promise is fulfilled in MacIntyre's account, we must, then, try to understand on what grounds he believes the view of Aquinas to be superior to the traditions that both preceded and followed it.

How, then, does MacIntyre's Aquinas—described as a follower of Augustine who has incorporated into Augustinian Christianity certain elements of Aristotelianism—demonstrate the rational superiority of his position to that of Aristotle? The astonishing fact is that, in this lengthy book about Aristotelianism and rational justification, this question is never seriously asked. MacIntyre gives an interesting account of why Aristotle's thought was rationally superior to that of his predecessors in the Greek tradition. He gives reasons an Augustinianism modified by an infusion of Aristotelian dialectic is superior to Augustinianism alone. But how do we get from Aristotle to Augustine? The book is silent. We are simply transported into the Christian era, and, as if we are Christians already, we are asked to imagine the challenges the Christian position faces from its pagan adversaries.

It is no small task to show someone who finds Aristotle's account of human society persuasive that the Augustinian view is superior. For, as MacIntyre describes it, the Augustinian view takes as its central premise the doctrine of original sin: the view that the fundamental relation of the human will to the moral law is one of disobedience, and that sexual desire is the basic form of that disobedience. (MacIntyre does not emphasize the sexual aspect of original sin, but he tells us that he endorses Augustine's account of the doctrine; and condemnation of sexual desire is integral to Augustine's account.)

To an Aristotelian, this entire idea would seem crazy. In fact, Aristotle says that a person who did not find sexual relations pleasant would be "far from being a human being"; and this is not meant to be a compliment. To be lacking in the desires for food, drink, and sexual relations, or in the corresponding activities, is held by Aristotle to be an ethical defect. Indeed, he also holds that human beings are naturally drawn toward virtue rather than vice, love more than repudiation—and that, given sufficient education, material support, and personal effort, most people will be able to make good and reasonable lives for themselves. How do you convince someone who thinks this way that belief in original sin represents progress in rationality?

MacIntyre, remarkably enough, never argues these questions. And yet we can find at least elements of an answer within his account of the Christian view. From the beginning of his book, MacIntyre has often suggested that the rational strength of an argument depends on its ability to secure actual agreement from most of the parties involved. This is nowhere implied in his philosophical account of how beliefs are justified, nor does it even seem to be consistent with it. But it is an important feature of many of the judgments he makes about particular cases in which people attempt to justify their views. His account of the failure of the Enlightenment, for example, assumes that a successfully justified belief is one that can "unite conviction and rational justification"—something the Enlightenment, as he sees it, could not do.

This interest in the power to secure agreement on one view or another is natural enough, given MacIntyre's interest in forms of community in which choice will be automatic and will not require deep reflection. In his chapters on Christian belief, he implies that only an institution such as the Catholic Church, which combines reasoning with the authority to define orthodoxy and to suppress dissent, can actually bring about the desired agreement. "Men need control and restraint," he writes, "if any measure of justice or peace is to be attained and preserved."[7]

So only an institution such as the Church—and not some mere reasoner like Aristotle, sitting disenfranchised and powerless as a resident alien in Athens—could succeed in rationally justifying a set of beliefs as MacIntyre finally understands that task. It is not enough to bring forward good arguments. "Political acknowledgment" of the arguments is also required: that is to say, acknowledgment (as Aquinas writes, with MacIntyre's approval) that "Secular power is subject to spiritual power as the body is subject to the soul." Or, in MacIntyre's own words, "the Pope has legitimate authority over secular rulers." And clearly the doctrine of original sin had an important part in gaining for the Church the requisite acknowledgment of its political power. In this way, original sin seems to be "rationally justified," according to this complex account of justification, rather different from the one that MacIntyre originally endorsed.

But what does all this have to do with reason? Why is a view justified only if its backers can beat dissenters into line? The answer seems to be: because of the fact of original sin. Political authority, MacIntyre tells us on Augustine's behalf, is "the necessary, and in the Christian conception the divine, remedy for sin." And "the central human experience of morality" is that "of our inability to live by it." MacIntyre concludes that the way in which Augustine shows Aristotle's view to be "radically defective" is by pointing to a "radical defectiveness in the natural human order." In other words, the Catholic view, by combining the doctrine of original sin with the view that the political authority of the Church is necessary for order, is seen to be preferable because original sin is, in fact, our "central human experience."

For the secular Aristotelian the circularity of this argument is breathtaking. And if readers consider the fact, brilliantly argued (for example) in Elaine Pagels's recent book,[8] that original sin did not seem even to Christians to be a "central experience" until the Church used it as a rationale for the exercise of Church authority, then they may begin to suspect that MacIntyre is in the grip of a world view promulgated by authority rather than by reason. They may suspect as well that he is using this view to justify perpetuating authority at the heart of human life and, indeed, at the heart of human reason. An Aristotelian would have to repudiate this way of thinking, since Aristotle insists on a strong distinction between persuasion and manipulation, reason and force. And Aristotle, in an abrupt departure from Greek cultural conventions, did not even include piety within his long list of the virtues. This probably indicates his interest in separating practical reason from religious authority, and in keeping reason, rather than such authorities, in control of the most important matters.

And yet, one might ask, isn't MacIntyre on to something fundamental when he tells us that reason, undirected by authority, cannot construct a debate that is orderly enough to be productive? He has claimed that the only alternative to the authority he recommends is chaos, a Babel of unrelated and greedy voices. One might reply, they will at least be our own voices. And yet we would reply far more strongly if we could show that MacIntyre's pessimism about reason is not justified, that people from different traditions could, through secular, rational debate, make progress toward a convincing picture of the good life without relying on the virtue of piety to keep the debate in order, and that such a debate could attend to and respect local traditions, in each case, while criticizing tradition in the name of the good.

We can, I believe, find a promising example of such a debate in Aristotle himself—though in aspects of Aristotle's thought that do not figure in MacIntyre's account. First, Aristotle did not characterize the situation of the Greek polis as MacIntyre does. He did not, that is, believe that the rational debate in which he took part was based on a set of fundamental agreements. Indeed, he tells us at the outset of the *Nicomachean Ethics* that, although all human beings say their goal is *eudaimonia* (which we might render "the good life for a human being"), they agree on nothing beyond the mere name. "As to what *eudaimonia* is, they are at odds"—both one person with another, it emerges, and also each person with himself. The unanimity imagined by MacIntyre never existed, so far as Aristotle can see. But he believed it is possible to provide a reasoned justification for convictions without it.

Second, Aristotle does not believe that people need to seek arguments to justify their beliefs only from within each single local tradition. He considers ideas from Persia and Sparta, from Cyme and Athens, all in an attempt to construct an account of the good human life for any and every human being. His list of virtues is intended to be international, based upon experiences that all human beings share.

Third, Aristotle never expects universal agreement. People who are ill-educated, or unloved, or hungry, or unhealthy, or subjects of tyranny, and so on—and at any time this is likely to include a large proportion of the world's people—may not be able to listen to argument at all, much less to accept good arguments when they come forward. Aristotle's remedy for that is not to prefer views that are capable of bringing them into line; it is to demand of politics that it supply them with what they need for the good life—with food, clean water, family love, above all an education. Rationality has a material and institutional basis; the cause of ethical defects is not inherent evil, but bad politics.

Among those who take part in rational arguments, the task of describing human virtues begins, Aristotle believes, by giving an account of the general circumstances that all human beings, as such, share, and within which their choices are all made. In the *Nicomachean Ethics*, the description of each virtue begins by characterizing some sphere of shared human experience. Even before we get a very precise account of it, the virtue in question—courage, for example—is provisionally defined as a stable trait of character (involving patterns of desire and thought) that is productive of good choices and responses in that sphere. One can then go on to ask more specifically what good choices in that sphere would be, and to argue about other accounts, and thus to get a more precise account of the virtue. For example, all human beings are aware of their mortality, and all experience, at some time, the fear of death. The virtue of courage will be the trait of character that enables a person stably to act and react well (however that is more precisely defined) with regard to that fear.

Again, human beings all have bodily appetites and find it at times difficult to keep them under control. The virtue of moderation can be defined as the stable trait that makes it possible for someone to do that well. Thus, even if there is still much disagreement about what the best account of good choice, and therefore the virtuous trait, is, we will have a coherently ordered debate, and we will know that we are talking about the same thing.

Going through each of the spheres of human activity in this way, Aristotle gives a general account of what it is to live as a human being with both limitations and abilities. The story he tells should, he thinks, be intelligible to any human being who hears it, despite differences of language and culture. "One can see in one's travels to distant countries," he writes, "the experiences of recognition and affiliation that link every human being to every other human being." And it is on this basis that he holds out hope for a persuasive inquiry into the good that is not exclusively tied to one culture or another.

Aristotle's idea of a persuasive story of human life is only a starting point, one that is closely linked to the myths and stories people tell themselves when they ask themselves what it is to be a human being, and neither beast nor a god. But if it is possible to tell a general story in which we can all, as human beings using our imaginations, see ourselves, then MacIntyre's pessimism about open reasoned debate is not justified.

When one considers these aspects of Aristotle's account, one realizes, too, how silent MacIntyre has been about them—how silent, in general, about the fact that human beings have many common problems wherever they live, and also many shared capacities—humor, friendship, love, logic, a thirst for understanding. All of these are to some extent understood differently by different societies; but the fact that we can understand a Homeric hero's fear of death, or share Euripides' perplexity about the beauty and destructive power of erotic passion, or be struck by the insights of ancient Indian thought about the nature of perception, shows us that it is not foolish to suppose that there is common ground from which secular rational inquiry into the human good can begin.

This is not to minimize the difficulties of going beyond recognition of common experiences and problems to construct common norms. At each step such an inquiry should balance the concrete experience of particular groups with an interest in what is common to all. How one might do this remains an immensely challenging question, but I see no reason to suppose that it cannot be done.[9] If the doctrine of original sin, as MacIntyre interprets it, were true, the obstacles in the way of carrying out such a project would be formidable, since presumably original sin impedes the reasoning of each reasoner, as well as making it difficult for a reasoned view to win acceptance. But MacIntyre has given us no good reason to believe that doctrine is true. And unless and until we accept some such idea, we do not have reason to relax our demand for good reasons, deferring to authority.

Pursuing the Aristotelian quest I have described without relying on piety is a difficult matter, but it was always likely that it would be, since human beings are on their own in a harsh and complex world. The difficulty, and the frequent loneliness, of such a search need not, and should not, cause us to long nostalgically for a unanimity that human life has never really had, or to sink for comfort into the embrace of an authority, whether religious or secular, that will give us order at the price of reason.

## NOTES

1. Aristotle mentions special circumstances in *Politics* VII.1; he discusses nutrition and the membership of the poor in the "common meals" in II.10 and VII.11.

2. Philippa Foot, *Virtues and Vices* (Berkeley: University of California Press, 1985); Bernard Williams, *Ethics and the Limits of Philosophy* (Cambridge, Mass.: Harvard University Press, 1985); a representative sample of recent work on virtue is *Midwest Studies in Philosophy* (Notre Dame, Ind.: University of Notre Dame Press, 1988) devoted to that topic.

3. MacIntyre defends his account of the "practical syllogism" (since his own examination of the relevant texts is brief) by appealing to the work of several scholars, especially John Cooper, *Reason and Human Good in Aristotle* (Cambridge, Mass.: Harvard University Press, 1975), who did indeed argue for an account of the "practical syllogism" similar to the one MacIntyre presents. But Cooper concluded that the practical syllogism, just because of its trivial and automatic character, played no role in Aristotle's account of rational *deliberation*; it simply showed how the results of deliberation were applied in concrete circumstances. And Cooper held that, according to Aristotle, people do deliberate reflectively about what to do, both in selecting means to an end already established and in reflecting about the best specification of general ends themselves (looking, for example, for the best account of what courage and justice are). MacIntyre ignores this important distinction between syllogism and deliberation, presenting the syllogism as a complete account of all the deliberating an agent does. Nor does he deal effectively with the positions of philosophers as, for example, David Wiggins, in "Deliberation and Practical Reason," now in his *Needs, Values, and Truth* (Oxford: Basil Blackwell, 1987), who, interpreting Aristotle, gives deliberation an even larger role, holding that it can ask about the most ultimate ends of human life—asking, for example, whether friendship should or should not count as a part of the good human life.

4. There are obviously a number of logical problems about how alternatives are rejected. These and other difficulties have led some scholars, including David Wiggins (note 3 above) and myself (*Aristotle's De Motu Animalium* [Princeton, N.J.: Princeton University Press, 1978]) to argue, relying to some extent on the different accounts of the "syllogism" in the *De Motu Animalium*, that Aristotle's interest in the "syllogism" is not an interest in fitting practical reasoning into a deductive model.

5. MacIntyre is by no means the only contemporary philosopher to pursue this project. One might compare Charles Taylor, *Philosophy and the Human Sciences: Philosophical Papers* 2 (Cambridge, UK: Cambridge University Press, 1985); Hilary Putnam, *Reason, Truth, and History* (Cambridge, UK: Cambridge University Press, 1981), and *The Many Faces of Realism* (LaSalle, Ill.: Open Court Publishing Company, 1987).

6. *After Virtue* made this same point using a chess match as the example; now, apparently, MacIntyre does not want that much cogitation.

7. MacIntyre is here quoting, with explicit approval, from A. J. Carlyle's *A History of Medieval Political Theory in the West*, Vol. III (New York: Barnes and Noble, [1928] 1970), p. 97.

8. Elaine Pagels, *Adam, Eve, and the Serpent* (New York: Random House, 1988); see also "The Politics of Paradise," *The New York Review of Books*, May 12, 1988.

9. I give a somewhat longer account of this Aristotelian approach, and answer some objections, in "Non-Relative Virtues: An Aristotelian Approach," in *Midwest Studies in Philosophy* (above note 2).

# CHAPTER FIVE

# The Bondage and Freedom of Eros

JOHN J. WINKLER (1990), The Constraints of Desire:
The Anthropology of Sex and Gender in Ancient Greece;
DAVID M. HALPERIN (1990), One Hundred Years
of Homosexuality and Other Essays on Greek Love

The ancient Greeks, like most people who now study them, tended to think, and teach, that where sex is concerned some things are natural and other things are not, some things are up for grabs as expressions of personal taste and preference and others ruled out (or in) by our universal animal nature itself. Like many civilizations, they had strong views about what "nature" was here, and they were prepared to argue for these views using examples from the animal kingdom. Consider the following passage from Philo's *On Animals*—a typical example drawn from John J. Winkler's brilliant book, *The Constraints of Desire*—in which Philo "proves" the naturalness of having sexual relations only for reproductive purposes, and "proves," too, the naturalness of male self-restraint, which subdues female greediness:

> Not only among animals domesticated and reared by us but also among the other species there are those which appear to have self-restraint. When the Egyptian crocodile . . . is inclined to copulate, be diverts the female to the bank and turns her over, it being natural to approach her (when she is) lying on her back. After copulating, he turns her over with his forearms. But when she senses the copulation and the impregnation, she becomes malicious in purpose and pretends to desire copulation once more, displaying a harlot-like affection and assuming the usual position for copulation. So he immediately comes to ascertain, either by scent or by other means, whether the invitation is genuine or merely pretense. By nature he is alert to hidden things. When the intent of the action is truly established by their looking into each other's eyes, he claws her guts and consumes them, for they are tender. And unhindered by armored skin or hard and pointed spines, he tears her flesh apart. But enough about self-restraint.

As Winkler observes, there is a lot of culture packed into this *exemplum* from nature: male initiative and control, one "natural" position for intercourse ("did the crocodile learn it from missionaries or vice versa," he wonders), female seductiveness and wantonness (she wants more, even after she knows she is pregnant), grim patriarchal punishment. We can see the cultural origins of Philo's picture of nature more clearly, presumably, than could his original readers, since we stand at a certain distance from them and inhabit a somewhat different (though not altogether different) set of categories. Our response to the crocodile story might make us more sceptical, then, about our own society's appeals to nature and the natural, asking whether sexual activity and experience are not more profoundly shaped by historical and social context than we usually believe.

The central thesis of these two important collections is that both sexual activity and the experience of sexual desire itself are structured at a deep level by historical and cultural forces, and vary considerably from society to society. The categories in which a society articulates such experience shape the way its members see the world, and themselves, as desiring subjects. This is not a new idea; it was, in one form, the thesis of Foucault's *History of Sexuality*; and both Winkler and David M. Halperin, in *One Hundred Years of Homosexuality and Other Essays on Greek Love*, concentrate on the case of ancient Greece, which Foucault also made a focus of his argument. But both authors are judicious and discriminating classical scholars whose mastery of the relevant types of evidence (texts philosophical, literary and historical, papyri containing magic spells and curses, vase paintings, and much more) ranges well beyond that of Foucault. They are therefore able to produce a more complete and compelling picture of the organization of sex and gender in ancient Greek society—and, in this way, to advance our understanding of the more general question of the role, in sexual experience, of social forces. Both books are meticulous and reliable in scholarship, clear in argument, fully accessible to the general reader, and enormous fun to read, prompting repeatedly the kind of laughter that cuts through complacency and promotes self-understanding.

Winkler approaches the ancient world with the delicate touch of an especially alert anthropologist, determined not to read the Greek world as more like modern Europe and North America than the evidence warrants, and determined, too, to reconstruct a picture of Greek attitudes to sex and gender not simply from well-known authors but from a wide variety of little-known sources—including popular dream-interpreters, erotic love charms and a huge range of texts, many of them post-classical. The connecting themes of this varied collection are the way in which appeals to "nature" serve the purposes of culture, and the complex relationship between the cultural categories that constrain agents and the surprising variety and resourcefulness of their actual behaviour. Winkler reads texts with an exemplary subtlety, always alert to possibilities of irony and bluffing, aware that normative public statements have no simple relation to personal behaviour.

Critical of historians of ideas for not capturing the practices of real people, and of structuralists for missing "the contest and conflict of a society with multiple centers of authority and a high sense of bluff and the uncertain," he is subservient to no particular school, but with great originality forges standards of interpretation that set a new standard for the study of these central human concerns in their social context.

The volume begins with a section devoted to the sexual lives of males, especially in relationship to the perpetual Greek concern with power, status, and security. A remarkable essay on the dream manual of Artemidorus (second century AD)—more illuminating, I think, than Foucault's treatment of the same material—shows that, unlike most modern Westerners, who tend to interpret dreams about other matters as having a hidden sexual meaning, ancient Greeks tended to interpret all dreams, sexual ones included, as having a "real" significance connected with security or status. ("Having intercourse with one's male or female slave is good, for slaves are the dreamer's possessions and therefore signify that he will take pleasure in his own possessions as they increase in number and value.") The main things to watch for in the dream-image are dominance, profit, invasion, injury; and these, in the sexual sphere, are read as metaphors for the rise and fall of the dreamer's fortunes in public life. From a comprehensive study of this material, Winkler reconstructs certain aspects of ancient sexual experience that differ markedly from our own: sexual experience is on the whole understood (at least officially) as non-mutual, and as focused on issues of status and authority. (I shall return to these issues in discussing Halperin.)

A related essay, "Laying Down the Law," moves back to the fourth century BC to study the rhetoric of the public scrutiny of male behaviour in Athens, focusing on the "scare-figure" of the *kinaidos*, the shamelessly promiscuous male who hires himself out to be penetrated by another. Here, as before, Winkler insists that real life is usually far more complex and varied than public pronouncements: public images of discipline and uniformity that are put forward seriously in some contexts can be grumbled against, joked about, played with in others. But from the rhetoric emerges a power-ful public ideal: "the image of the stout-hearted citizen, who can be trusted to exercise his military duties and to control the pressure he may feel from his dependents, his circumstances, or from his own needs." Manliness requires this sort of self-containment and self-sufficiency; and sex is correctly managed if it is managed in accordance with that norm.

The collection's title essay, a study of erotic magical spells, begins to examine the impact of these social protocols on the lives of women. And it is in this area that the book makes its most surprising and original contribu-tions. It is valuable enough to have before one, analysed in such an elegant and accessible way, the technically difficult material contained in the magical papyri (in which people put down wishes for various torments and constraints that will serve to bring their loved one to their bed). What is more valuable still is Winkler's sensitive study of how these spells—often sadistic in content and apparently altogether misogynistic—could sometimes be exploited by women themselves, with or without the complicity of men, for the end of achieving their own autonomy and pleasure. The wish that the loved woman feel the bondage of Eros is, paradoxically, "a discourse (of sorts) about female desire"; and female desire as arising from within, not enforced by the choice of a parent or guardian. "May she come melting with *eros* and affection and intercourse, fully desiring intercourse with Apalos." "May she accomplish her own sexuality (*ta aphrodisiaka heautes*)." "Bring her loving me with lust and longing and cherishing and intercourse and a manic *eros*." In such spells, men recognize women as subjects of desire, not simply objects of familial and social constraint. And, Winkler shows, men and women could resourcefully exploit the language of desire's constraining power to help the woman evade the watchfulness of her family. A bride on the way to her new husband's house (reports the physiognomist Polemo in the second century AD) is kidnapped by a young man who shows all the signs of love's overwhelming constraint. "I later learned from people discussing the event," he remarks, "that it had happened with her consent."

A stunning essay on Longus' pastoral romance *Daphnis and Chloe* reflects further on the violence inherent in many male attitudes toward women. Winkler delicately shows how the initial symmetry and mutuality of the young couple's desiring love is darkened, as the novel goes on, by increasing awareness of the many possibilities of violence that await a woman in this male-centered world: rape, and indeed the violence and blood associated with intercourse itself. Winkler tentatively suggests that this reading is not merely a projection of modern concerns, but that the novel as a whole may be structured so as to invite critical and self-critical reflection about male force.

The second half of *The Constraints of Desire* is devoted to women's lives, real and fictional, and to the subtle stratagems by which they play with, move within, laugh at the constraints that males impose on them. "Penelope's Cunning and Homer's" finds in the *Odyssey* a subtlety of design that not every reader will believe in. At first I did not; and yet, by the end of the argument Winkler had convinced me that the events of the plot are carefully crafted in order to reveal Penelope's cunning practical wisdom and manipulative skill. Though constrained in countless ways, she none the less dictates, again and again, the shape of the plot. "Double Consciousness in Sappho's Lyrics" provides a detailed and compelling attempt to describe the sexual element in Sappho's poetry—and, to establish, against the scepticism of scholars, that much of this poetry is indeed about female homoerotic desire. Once again, some sceptics will remain; for the evidence is very fragmentary, and susceptible of multiple interpretations. But the grace and ingenuity of Winkler's readings compel respect and reflection; and such reading, as he says, "can enhance our own sense of this womanly beauty *as subject and as object* by helping us to un-learn our denials of it."

Finally, in "The Laughter of the Oppressed," Winkler argues that most previous interpretations of the Athenian religious festivals managed and attended by women—the Thesmophoria, Haloa, Adonia and Stenia—have asked about the function of these festivals from the point of view of male interests, never getting at the experience and interests of the women themselves. Criticizing Marcel Detienne for seeing the point of these festivals in terms of "good male agriculture" instead of "bad female sexiness," he uncovers a wealth of sexual humour (mostly at males' expense) and laughing self-assertion, in which women offer a comic commentary on male arrogance and insufficiency. Women led very enclosed lives: and yet, because they were not deluded, as many men were, into supposing that they and their vision were the entirely of the world, their vision could actually be more complete: "Behind the facade of public docility women had lives of their own and, arguably, a more comprehensive understanding of men than men had of women."

Halperin, in *One Hundred Years of Homosexuality*, focuses on the experience of male desire in Athens of the fifth and fourth centuries BC. More explicitly philosophical than Winkler's work, his book carries out, with careful scholarly arguments and a judicious, wide-ranging use of the evidence, the project Foucault mapped out in the second volume of his *History of Sexuality*: to shed light on the historical contingency and the non-naturalness of our current categories of sexual experience by confronting them with a detailed picture of a very different organization of sexual desire and activity. Clear and incisive, these essays are probably the best available introduction for the general reader to the issues raised by Foucault's work.

The volume's title essay—which alludes to the fact that "homosexuality," according to the *OED*, was first used in 1892—argues cogently that ancient categories of sexual experience differed considerably from our own, and that this affected the way desire itself was experienced. The central distinction in sexual morality was the distinction between active and passive roles. The gender of the object—as Halperin shows from a much wider range of evidence than that used by Foucault—is not in itself morally problematic. Boys and women are very often treated interchangeably as objects of desire. What is socially important is to penetrate rather than to be penetrated. Sex is understood fundamentally not as interaction but as a doing of something to someone; and the passive recipient is marked by that fact as of lower social status. Nor do we find evidence of anything like our modern idea that each person's identity is subtly organized and individuated at a deep level by a "sexuality," an inner orientation of desire that "holds the key to unlocking the deepest mysteries of the human personality." The Greeks were as far from categorizing people by such a "sexuality" as we are from organizing people in accordance with a "dieticity" or "edility"—a deep inner orientation to prefer certain sorts of food:

> it would never occur to us to refer a person's dietary object choice to some innate, characterological disposition or to see in his or her strongly expressed and even unvarying preference for the white meat of chicken the symptom of a profound psychophysical orientation, leading us to identify him or her in contexts quite removed from that of the eating of food as, say . . . a "pectoriphage" or a "stethovore."

So with the Greeks, where sexual object choice is concerned.

A related essay, "The Democratic Body," studies prostitution in classical Athens as a clue to the communal understanding of sexual activity in its relation to citizenship. Halperin argues that a manly control over one's bodily boundaries and over the appropriate use of sexual activities was considered to be an essential requirement of democratic citizenship. Thus, while both male and female prostitution flourished unchecked, and while no penalty attached to the patron of a prostitute, a citizen who once sold his own body for others to use as they pleased would thereby forfeit political privileges. This was so, Halperin convincingly argues, because such a person indicated by this gesture "that his autonomy was for sale to whoever wished to buy it." On the other hand, not to have access to any sexual outlet was also considered to be a diminution of one's manly control. This is how Halperin explains the surprising evidence that Solon was believed to have instituted a system of subsidized public brothels, within the price-range of even the poorest citizen, where women, stationed as "common possessions for all," ensured "that there would always be a category of persons for every citizen to dominate, both socially and sexually." This is an exciting and, on the whole, convincing argument, showing that for Athenians sex was, rather than a part of the "private" as opposed to the "public" sphere, an aspect of one's participation in the life of the city.

The central philosophical discussion of the volume is unfortunately brief. It takes the form of an exchange between Halperin and the editor of a newsletter at Harvard, on the topic of whether sexual experience is or is not a social construct. Here, Halperin clarifies some aspects of current debates in a useful way; but the compression imposed by the interview format makes it impossible for him to give his views the extended philosophical exploration and defense they warrant. For example, his analysis never distinguishes two explananda: (1) the categories that demarcate sexual assessment and experience in a given society, and (2) the placement of individuals within these categories. If social factors explain (1), it is also clear that they do not provide a complete explanation for (2). They do not, for example, explain how or why an individual brought up in the dominant class in a society comes to experience himself as a part of a less favoured group. Some further explanation—for example, a psychoanalytical account making reference to specific features of that individual's history—seems to be required to make sense of this. It is clear that only this further account will give, for example, a middle-class gay man in America the comprehensive self-understanding he is seeking. And yet Halperin (in criticizing biological "explanations" that themselves confuse the two explananda) sometimes speaks as if by appealing to social factors and their history we would have the answer to every important question about individuals.

Moreover, Halperin ends up, I think, taking a rather unclear position on the Nietzschean question of the "revaluation of values." Once we notice that our current distinctions between "homosexuality" and "heterosexuality" are of recent and somewhat arbitrary origin, and, at the same time, express the project of dominating and marginalizing certain classes of individuals, shouldn't this make us more sceptical of using these distinctions to organize our own experience in future? Noticing that the label "black" was invented in close connection with the institution of slavery, and served to group together people of heterogeneous linguistic and national origins as subjects of domination, might well make those so labelled seek, ultimately, to define themselves in ways that did not submit to that history, and which better reveal the variety and richness of their origins (though, clearly, a transitional period in which the formerly pejorative label is affirmed may be of enormous political value). Isn't the same thing true in the sexual sphere? Halperin does not deny that some labels may be less arbitrary than others, better suited to advance other aims human beings have for themselves. So what is to prevent us from doing away with those that seem inseparable from contempt or self-contempt, or to be especially stupid as modes of organization? He correctly notes that these categories lie very deep in our experience. But this just means it is a long matter to learn to think differently, a matter of patient inner work rather than snap decision. Halperin's further point seems to be that such categories create possibilities for desire, as well as imposing limits and constraints. But if in some concrete case the possibilities seem inseparable from self-contempt or contempt for others, shouldn't this make one cherish them rather less? Nietzsche thought that "genealogy" was the first step in a project of normative assessment, in which we would ask what these categories whose contingency we have demonstrated *do for us*, and in which we would attempt to create, within the constraints of history, a space for human freedom and creation. This more affirmative conception of genealogy is briefly mentioned elsewhere in the volume, in connection with Halperin's description of Foucault's last writing, but is never clearly linked with Halperin's account of his own views. It is a possibility, I think, that he needs to examine more seriously.

The rest of the collection is uneven. A dual review of Harald Patzer's book on Greek pederasty and Foucault's *History* makes many good points about each of the books; but its general methodological conclusions, rather critical of traditional philological methods, seem not to be fully justified by the arguments presented. A rather thin essay on heroic friendship and an extensive discussion of the figure of Diotima in Plato's *Symposium* complete the volume. The Plato piece is one of a group of five articles on Plato's theory of love that Halperin has written over the past several years. It is not, I think, by any means as convincing as the others, which are valuable contributions; and, isolated here, it lacks the further elucidation that their presence would have provided. Seeking to explain why Plato entrusted the most important lessons about *eros* to a female character, Halperin argues that Diotima's femaleness serves to remind the reader of two well-known features of male-female erotic relations that male-male experience lacked: erotic reciprocity, and a connection between *eros* and reproduction. The latter point, and its connection with Diotima's theory that love involves "giving birth in the beautiful," is not new; the former is highly controversial. Certainly it is the case that female-male sexual relations were understood by the Greeks to contain mutual pleasure in a way that pederastic relations did not (though most of the evidence on this point comes from centuries later than the Platonic dialogue). And Halperin has argued well elsewhere that the reciprocity of desire in the *Phaedrus* is a deliberate Platonic refashioning of male-male norms. But the *Symposium's* theory of desire contains no such reciprocity. So Plato would be introducing Diotima in order to allude to a theory that he does not state until a number of years later, and putting in her mouth a view that in a number of ways contradicts that later view.

Halperin then shifts focus: this use of women's experience, he now says, does not show that Plato really learns from women, acknowledges them, or wishes them to speak (this in spite of the evidence, which he produces, that Plato took the radical step of educating women in his school). It shows, instead, that Plato wishes to colonize and appropriate for male use that experience, turning it into a mere metaphor for (male) philosophizing. And then, with the reflexive turn by now obligatory in fashionable literary circles, he applies this structure to his own arguments: as a male speaking of and for women, he is probably just trying to avail himself of an opportunity to pursue questions about and of interest to men. It is not clear why any of this follows, unless it is to be a tacit premise of literary interpretation that human beings are incapable of generosity or understanding.

Although these two books have obvious links in content and methodology, and although each author acknowledges the other as a major source of advice and support, the worlds they reconstruct are, in the end, surprisingly different. Halperin's ancient world, rather like Foucault's, is a world of unsmiling constraint and uniformity, a world in which some penetrate and others are penetrated, and nobody seems to have much occasion for laughter; in which words are used to bind others, or to express one's own bondage; in which—in a rather Proustian fashion—each apparent gesture of compassion, altruism, or acknowledgement is bound to get unmasked somewhere along the line as a cover-up for some stratagem of domination. Halperin's ancient Greeks—and his modern Americans—seem to be thoroughly hemmed in by the distinctions society imposes on them, passive, lacking in resources, both unkind and amazingly gullible.

Winkler's ancient world, by contrast, is a world of exuberant variety and unexpected freedom, in which the people who hold the power don't always take it very seriously, and nobody regards the categories of public discourse as altogether binding on personal thought and behaviour. Each man, in this world, nods at the conventions of male dominance, "sagely and silently, with his fingers crossed behind his back." And the women discover in the very conditions of their oppression occasions for cunning, freedom and pleasure. The oppressed, indeed, often have the last laugh, because they see the structures of power more clearly, and so can the more cleverly evade them. And with all this power and cunning, there is room, as well, for such un-Foucauldian items as kindness, love, and self-criticism. Halperin thinks kindness is a mask worn by power; Winkler shows that power can also, sometimes, be a mask ironically worn by kindness. Their second thoughts about texts move, correspondingly, in opposite directions—Halperin deciding that, on further inspection, Plato's apparent acknowledgement of the female is actually colonization and expropriation, Winkler judging that what at first might seem merely exploitative and even sadistic in male erotic spells may sometimes serve as an occasion for female autonomy. Even their attitudes to their own writing are different. Halperin is forced by the logic of his cynicism to subject even his own feminist writing to suspicious scrutiny; Winkler sees no problem in simply asserting his alliance with feminist scholars who seek a more comprehensive understanding of women's resourcefulness.

It is not that Winkler's account of human life is naive or sunny; he just sees more possibilities, more variety in it, sees people as devious as well as passive, self-critical as well as domineering, capable of both aggression and love. His essay on Homer ends with a discussion of the remarkable simile in which Odysseus and Penelope embrace, sharing the same thoughts and feelings. On Halperin's usual way of reading, one can imagine that this moment would have been mistrustfully dissected as evidence that men (Odysseus? the author?) want always to invade and possess the thoughts of the women they desire. Winkler lets the moment stand, evidence of a rare intimacy, wrested from the constraints of language: "It is not easy to say in the cultural language of that highly stratified society that men and women are in any sense equal. But the author of the *Odyssey* has succeeded in doing so."

Each reader of these books must judge, ultimately, which picture of the ancient world seems more complete as an account of the evidence they present, and more compelling as a view of what possibilities a world of human beings is likely to contain. Both books are very impressive—resourceful and incisive in scholarship, clearly and delightfully written. And Winkler's is something more—a work, I think, of extraordinary originality and insight, amazingly beautiful, a work that will over the years stand comparison, one imagines, with the best writings of Nietzsche, as an exploration of what the Greeks have to show us about "jokes, cunning, revenge"—and, also, freedom.

John J. Winkler died on April 26, 1990, at the age of forty-six, of complications arising from AIDS, in Stanford, California.

# CHAPTER SIX

# Our Pasts, Ourselves

CHARLES TAYLOR (1989), Sources of the Self: The Making
of the Modern Identity

When we borrow the language of philosophy and social theory to talk about
ourselves, we often talk in an impoverished way. Trying to say what we care
about, what makes sense of ourselves and our lives, we find ourselves using
large abstract terms, such as "the good," "the right," "utility." The relation
of these terms to the actual fabric of our lives, to our strivings and our commitments, is puzzling. Sometimes the terms seem too vague to connect with
anything that really matters when we make judgments in ordinary life. This
lofty vagueness has been among the standing targets of Anglo-American
analytic philosophy, as in J. L. Austin's remark, "If only we could forget
for a while about the beautiful and get down instead to the dainty and
the dumpy." (Even within the analytic tradition, though, this call to
concreteness has not always been heeded.) And sometimes the discrepancy
lies deeper: not just in an abstractness that might be fleshed out, but in a
deliberately reductive strategy, in a style of thinking that seeks to deny or to
repudiate the diversity of the goods that people recognize in their lives, and
the specific quality of their commitments to those goods.

Such reductive strategies play a part in many areas of social thought.
They take a variety of forms, but common to most of them is the claim to
have provided a more "scientific" view of the human being than is available
in what is sometimes pejoratively called "folk psychology." One common
strategy is naturalistic: the observer assumes a detached perspective and
attempts to describe the human being as just one more part of the physical
world of nature, using no language that would not be used to explain
the behavior of other physical objects. Some such enterprises involve
the reduction of all psychological and mental language to physiological language. Others continue to use psychological language, but in a mechanistic
way, treating the human subject as a thing that is activated by stimuli
in specifiable ways. In both cases, the view that human subjects have of

themselves—which usually includes the notion that they are committed to certain ends as higher and more valuable than others, and that they love and cherish what deserves and claims their love—all this is treated as a sort of subjective illusion, or at best as a projection onto the "real world." From the scientific perspective, ethical value is not a part of the world of nature.

Some forms of utilitarianism in economics and public policy (and in the simpler philosophical accounts) are reductionist in a similar way. They hold that all our preferences are merely subjective, and so there is no reasonable way to make qualitative distinctions among them. Thus, the only notion of good that a science of economics can sensibly employ is one that refers to a simple aggregation of actual preferences or satisfactions of desire. In ordinary life, however, people usually consider that some things are so important, so claim our love and commitment, that they ought to be loved whether we currently love them or not; not to love them is a sign of obtuseness or callousness. And, conversely, people are usually aware that many of their desires are unreliable indices of real goodness, and would not stand up to critical examination. But the simpler utilitarianisms make no such distinctions. They consider that all evaluation is similarly unscientific.

There is, finally, a rather different type of reductionism, which has become popular in the humanities and the social sciences. This form uses the idea of "power" as its central notion and holds that all the ethical evaluations in which people ordinarily engage are simply the result of a dominant group's exercise of social control. Appealing usually to Nietzsche and to Foucault, proponents of such views insist that our experience of loving what deserves love, respecting what commands respect, is based on political illusion: when we attend to such norms we only repeat the slogans that have been set down for us by authority. Once again our ordinary distinctions between well-founded preferences and arbitrary ones, between what we ought to love and what we happen to desire, go by the boards. True scientific insight teaches us to jettison these distinctions as relics of our unsophisticated past. All apparent ethical persuasion is really political manipulation.

In his important and impressive book, Charles Taylor criticizes all these forms of reduction and simplification, arguing that they simply do not succeed in making sense of the ways in which human beings actually live and strive after what they love. He argues that we need to recover a sense of the qualitative distinctions that we make among our commitments, and a more complex picture of the diversity of the goods to which we are implicitly committed, if we are to understand ourselves well enough to confront the problems that face us.

Taylor describes his project as "an attempt to articulate and write a history of the modern identity"—that is, of "the ensemble of (largely unarticulated) understandings of what it is to be a human agent" that finds itself "at home in the modern West." He argues that we cannot even comprehend our unity and identity as subjects or selves without coming to grips with the complex set of goods to which we are committed. These commitments (such as political justice, the relief of suffering, the love of family and friends) are fundamental to our sense of who we are and what makes our lives hang together. By adopting forms of "scientific" social discourse that obscure or conceal all this, we become strangers to ourselves, we even mutilate ourselves. But a "close and patient articulation" of these goods makes their claim on us more evident, clarifying the nature of the choices currently before us.

Taylor focuses on three areas of ethical commitment and self-definition that are central to the western European tradition: on the development through history of a sense of "inwardness," the sense that we are beings with inner depths and spaces, and the connection of this with our emerging notions of individuality and selfhood; on what Taylor calls "the affirmation of ordinary life," or the development of the idea that personal relations, work, the household are spheres of deep spiritual meaning and engagement; and on the Romantic idea of nature as a source for the self. Taylor's aim is to articulate the history of each of these ethical ideas in a way that reveals their power for us today, their highly complex interrelationships, and the tensions to which these relationships give rise.

It is no surprise that Taylor has undertaken this massive project of retrieval and articulation, or that he has succeeded in carrying it through. During the past twenty-five years Taylor has been developing a distinctive position in political and social philosophy, a position that has fruitfully combined respect for reason and rigorous argument with attention to the richness of our discourse and history. Taylor has been an unusual figure in contemporary philosophy. He bridges the gap between the Continental and the Anglo-American traditions, so often mutually hostile and uncompre-hending. He combines the latter's insistence on rigor, plain speech, and a close attention to the everyday with the former's respect for history and the history of thought. And, as he repeatedly shows, it is a natural combination: we need plain speech and good arguments to make sense of our history, but we will have poor arguments, and a deficient sense of the everyday, if we do not see to what extent our imagination and our language are the products of the complexities of history. Retrieving the historical context in which our ideas have evolved makes the nature of their claim on us clearer, and clarifies the alternatives.

Taylor has always insisted that we can describe ourselves as subjects of political and social action in ways that are more complexly human, more fruitfully connected to the ways that we actually make sense of our lives, than the languages of the social sciences are when they closely emulate the natural sciences. And he has shown that we can do this without relaxing the demand for rationality and good argument characteristic of the natural science tradition at its best. *The Explanation of Behaviour* (1964), a meticu-lous and devastating critique of behaviorist psychology and its impoverished descriptive language, was followed by *Hegel* (1975), an impressive account of that then neglected thinker, which did an enormous amount to make Hegelian ideas available to the philosophical community.

These books were unified by Taylor's philosophical clarity, and by his interest in the self-interpretations of human beings in history. Two volumes of collected papers (*Human Agency and Language* and *Philosophy and the Human Sciences*, 1985) developed Taylor's account of self-interpretation and its role in the construction of an adequate discourse for the human sciences. Taylor insists that the attempt to describe the world of human life from a detached scientific point of view, disregarding the ways in which human beings themselves describe their lives and what has meaning in them, is both incomplete and incoherent: incomplete, because it omits so much of great importance; incoherent, because its conception of scientific rationality is not itself a feature of the universe as it is in itself, apart from human life, but a deep part of human life, whose claim to respect derives from its role within human history. It cannot provide us, therefore, with a detached external standard that can be used as a basis for repudiating other elements of our lives that have equal depth.

Taylor writes with forthrightness and clarity; most of his work is fully accessible to a non-professional audience. His work has a close relationship to that of several other political philosophers, such as Bernard Williams and Michael Walzer, who have defended a more "context-sensitive" and historically informed approach to problems of justice. But his anti-relativist position sets him apart from their (qualified) relativisms; and his insistence on deriving his positive conclusions from a close examination of history makes his work methodologically distinctive. Indeed, Taylor's thought should be far better known than it is, in fields such as literature, anthropology, the law, public policy, and economics, where philosophers distinctly inferior to Taylor are sometimes in vogue.

Taylor never offers simple solutions to complex problems; it is always difficult to summarize what he has said. His current book is *about* complexity; and its strength lies in its concrete illuminations, in the sureness with which, again and again, it brings to light unnoticed connections and deftly articulates the claim of norms too seldom acknowledged. The measure of its power is the exhilaration with which one recognizes, repeatedly, parts of one's own self that had been buried from view.

The first part of *Sources of the Self* contains the general philosophical arguments that motivate and justify Taylor's project. Here, he argues cogently that a complex account of our goods and commitments is necessary not only for an adequate moral theory, but even for an understanding of the ways in which we move through time as continuous subjects. For human beings move through the world orienting themselves toward various goals; the movement and direction of their lives cannot be adequately understood without grasping the depth of those loves and commitments. "In order to make minimal sense of our lives, in order to have an identity, we need an orientation to the good . . . [and] this sense of the good has to be woven into

my understanding of my life as an unfolding story." The artist orients herself around her striving after expressive fulfillment; the member of a family
around the "rich joys of family love" and to efforts, over time, to fulfill the
commitments exacted by that love; and most real people take their bearings
from some complex combination of such aims and efforts. An adequate
account of their identity cannot be given without telling how they are placed
on the way to these goals.

Next, Taylor argues that such projects and commitments need not be
merely subjective. The most common forms of relativism and subjectivism
have failed to establish that we cannot reason, and reason well, about what
is worth loving, about what is higher. Such reasons certainly cannot be found
outside human lives and human practices; but that was always the wrong
place to search for them. Human life and human history give standards of
assessment that we can draw on to show that the goods we value are real
and objective enough. "What better measure of reality do we have in human
affairs," he plausibly asks, "than those terms which on critical reflection
and after correction of the errors we can detect make the best sense of our
lives?" Against the naturalist, who holds that all moral evaluation is mere
subjective projection, Taylor objects that the contrast between the internal
human viewpoint and the viewpoint of scientific detachment has not
been adequately made out. The detached perspective has whatever merit
it has as *part* of the internal human viewpoint. If it really were totally
detached from human history, it would have no relevance to that history.
But then it is not clear how the scientific point of view is in a position to
call these other central parts of our experience into question. In general,
the question that scientific explanation should be answering is, "what
properties or entities or features our best account of things has to invoke."
When we ask this question, however, ethical commitment will not be
eliminated.

Utilitarianism is then criticized in similar ways, by showing that the
cost of its abandonment of qualitative distinctions, and of the notion of commitment to the good, amounts to an inability to make sense of human practices. Taylor does not grapple here with the more subtle forms of recent
philosophical utilitarianism (with, for example, the work of R. M. Hare,
R. B. Brandt, or James Griffin, all of whom make distinctions among types
of desires and preferences, and provide for various types of evaluation and
correction); thus the utilitarian philosopher will be bound to remain unsatis-
fied with Taylor's discussion. But against the simpler utilitarian views prevalent in economics and public policy, his criticisms are effective.

To the cultural relativist, who holds that all evaluation is either projection
or in some other way bounded by local traditions, Taylor replies that the
ethical outlook of traditional communities is itself, in almost all cases, inherently critical. Good history and good anthropology show that people do not
cherish what they cherish because tradition or authority tells them to do so.
They understand themselves, rather, to be striving after what is really good;

and this is what explains the debate and the self-scrutiny that exist in every developed ethical tradition.

To the followers of Foucault and Nietzsche, and to the related views of Derrida, Taylor objects that the fact that some goods can serve power does not show that all must serve power: the case has simply not been made. The ethical nihilism of such views leaves us, moreover, with a world stripped bare of meaningful commitment, a world that could not possibly make sense of the way we view ourselves and our lives:

> Derrida doesn't have the saving inconsistency of Nietzsche, for whom there emerged, out of the uncompromising recognition of the flux, something which deserved unconditional affirmation, yea-saying. For Derrida there is nothing but deconstruction, which swallows up the old hierarchical distinctions between philosophy and literature, and between men and women, but just as readily could swallow up equal/unequal, community/discord, uncoerced/constrained dialogue, and the like. Nothing emerges from his flux worth affirming, and so what in fact comes to be celebrated is the deconstructing power itself, the prodigious power of subjectivity to undo all the potential allegiances which might bind it; pure untrammeled freedom.

But this, Taylor concludes, is an impoverished world, in which life is not worth living.

If it is difficult to give a summary sense of the richness of Taylor's general arguments, doing justice to the 400 pages of historical articulation that follow is impossible. Taylor's historical discussions are clear and economical, and based on remarkable scholarship. On Plato, on Locke, on the rise of the modern novel, on modernist poetry and painting, *Sources of the Self* concisely says original and penetrating things. It is rare to find this sort of philosophical history written so lucidly, without vanity or jargon.

Taylor begins his historical narrative by looking at the development, from Plato through Augustine and on to Descartes and Montaigne, of the sense that the self is constituted by inner space and depth, that it has a special sort of access to itself through inner reflection. He shows how this idea develops into the idea of radical reflexivity and self-consciousness. And, very revealingly, he shows how this emphasis on a special sort of subjectivity is intimately and unexpectedly related to the development of a conception of the person as the detached object of scientific study, and the related growth of political individualism.

Then Taylor traces the development, from the Reformation onward, of the idea that ordinary life has deep moral worth. He shows how the changing sense of the role of the divine in human life during the eighteenth and nineteenth centuries transforms the sense of how and why ordinary life has moral importance, and where the sources of its value reside. The passions became not heuristic, but normative; and this, in turn, transformed political thought. The third major strand in Taylor's narrative is an examination of Romantic ideas about nature as source for the self—and of the connection between this idea and the further development of conceptions of individuality and sympathy in social discourse. Taylor shows that both Kantian autonomy and Romantic views of nature involve a critical reaction against the standard Enlightenment view of the subject: one involving a radical break with nature, one seeking the self in and through nature.

As an example of Taylor's historical work, it is useful to consider his arguments concerning "the affirmation of everyday life." In antiquity, and in most respects through the Middle Ages, the prevailing view was that activities of daily life, such as housework, child-rearing, work in a craft or a profession, even much of marital companionship, had no moral worth in their own right, were no part of what gave life its meaning and importance. At best, their role was to support the really important activities of politics and contemplation. At worst, they rendered the person who spent too much time in them unfit for such higher pursuits. Aristotle argues, for example, that neither farmers nor craftsmen should be permitted to be citizens in his ideal city—for, lacking the leisure for education and social conversation, they will lack the civic virtues.

Drawing on a rich variety of sources—historical, religious, philosophical, literary, and artistic—Taylor traces the rise, from the Reformation through the nineteenth century, of a different idea of the ordinary: the idea that the whole of life is "hallowed" and that "the substance of life" resides in the ways we serve God in a calling and in domestic life. (Elsewhere he also investigates the rather different origins of these views in Judaism.) Once this idea is widely accepted, in a religious or a secular form, it gives rise to a new political egalitarianism, which Taylor connects with the rise of the modern novel. Narrating ordinary lives in such a way that their daily particularities take on a rich significance, the novel provides a basis for viewing all human lives on the same footing.

Together with this idea, there develops a "growing idealization of marriage, based on affection, true companionship between husband and wife, and devoted concern for the children." And this leads, in turn, to a greater emphasis on the personal choice of a spouse, and in some cases to a greater tolerance for divorce. A fascinating account of the organization of domestic space in the eighteenth and nineteenth centuries shows how this new ideal of the nuclear family generates a demand for domestic privacy, and a greater distancing of the nuclear unit from more remote kin and from neighbors.

Particularly revealing is Taylor's account of the subtle shift in the moral weight attached to the care and the rearing of children. It is not, he says, that people in other times and other places have not loved or cared for children. What changed, rather, was the sense of the importance of this relation for one's identity, and for the meaning of life; and the sense of the essential role of the nuclear family—as opposed to other relatives and neighbors—in fulfilling this moral imperative. Taylor argues that this sense of an absolute and unshirkable moral demand to care for children in this intimate way is something we have come to feel as a result of a particular Western history. We should not expect others who have not had this history to define their identity in precisely the same way, to have the very same attitudes to children and to domestic privacy—or the same agonizing moral dilemmas in connection with separation and divorce. Taylor holds that these social arrangements have enriched our lives morally; that we would not choose to discard them, whatever the tensions they generate; that we could plausibly argue—to an ancient Greek or to a contemporary person whose cultural traditions contain no analogous norm—that there may be something missing from their lives, something that we are right to affirm as among the "central human fulfillments."

In a sense this is familiar material; these changes have been investigated by historians of the family, and such historians will probably find little new information here. And yet, in the way that history and moral reflection are combined, Taylor's discussion is surprising, precisely because its material is so mundane in our lives. One recognizes oneself—and one is astonished that one did not see, before, how one was actually making sense of one's life, and how easily things might be otherwise.

In his final chapters, Taylor traces the legacy of this complex history in contemporary political and social debates. Owing to the diversity of the goods for which compelling claims can be made, debate—about, for example, tensions between ecological values and technological progress—is a complex and delicate matter. It is no use, Taylor argues, to ignore these tensions, or to pretend that only one of the two contending goods is important, or that all goods can be easily reduced to a single good. These tensions are sometimes tragic: sometimes any choice will involve a violation of something important. But turning away from them conceals the motives we have for doing justice to all the things we love, insofar as we possibly can. To deprive ourselves in this way is "to incur a huge self-inflicted wound."

In particular, we need to see more clearly the concrete tensions we face between the claims of universal benevolence and justice and the claims of individual self-expression, for these tensions color every facet of our lives. Taylor's history has shown that until recently benevolence was shored up by religious love and aspiration. He is not certain that it will be possible, without the belief in God, to sustain a basis for extending help to those who do not appeal to us, or to help our personal projects. *Sources of the Self* ends with a highly tentative move toward the recovery of religious sources of value—not in the sense of church authority curbing disobedience, as in Alasdair MacIntyre's recent work, but in the very different sense of a love of that which is "incomparably higher." For Taylor, this love gives point and motivation to other loves. He tells the reader that he has no arguments here, only "hunches"; and he leaves the reader with the question whether a secular humanistic morality can succeed in motivating benevolence and a universal respect for human dignity without "any religious dimension or radical hope."

What prompts these hunches? Taylor observes that secular humanistic visions of justice have not prevented the spread of a sense of meaninglessness and purposelessness in human life. He also notes that such visions frequently seem insufficiently rich to sustain our love, since they derive their affirmations through a negation of the religious morality that preceded them. But the second criticism does not seem to apply equally to all secular ethical views: it does not apply, for example, to Kantian ethics, or to an Aristotelian morality based on ideas of virtue. It seems unfair, moreover, to blame secularism for the meaninglessness experienced by people who have ceased to believe in God. Surely Nietzsche is right that this despair is a pernicious legacy of that dependency.

Taylor's other hunch is that we now understand too much about what he calls "the murkier depths of human motivation" to have Aristotle's confidence that people who are raised with love, with material support, and with good education will be capable of virtue. But, once again, objections come to mind. Have those happy conditions ever been realized on a large scale? And what sort of evidence should we require before concluding that the human heart is radically defective, that it is insufficient to its own highest hopes? My own hunch is that the best work on the "murkier depths" of the human heart shows something rather different: that love proves to be, in the end, a more powerful source of motivation than hatred, and that even ugly childhood feelings of aggression, and guilt at one's own aggression, can frequently become powerful promptings toward benevolent action in adult life. (Such views have been powerfully defended in the work of Melanie Klein and Richard Wollheim.) Certainly Taylor has (as he says) no arguments against such views. So the discussion has barely begun. And one might ask, moreover, whether it is actually possible to turn to religious sources of motivation without also going in for religious authority, and putting that authority ahead of reason. The low likelihood of such an outcome, given our cultural arrangements, is yet another motive one might have for choosing the secular view, even if all else were equal.

Many questions are bound to be raised about Taylor's procedure. Most will concern, very properly, the concrete details of his history, which I have not adequately described. But there are general questions that must also be raised. Taylor devotes considerable attention to the absence of the history of political and economic structures from his history of our selfhood. Aware that he could easily be charged with offering an "idealist" account that subordinates these factors to intellectual ones, he plausibly replies that, although economic factors are indeed important, and are themselves essential to a more complete self-understanding, ideas do have their own power in history, shaping practices as they are shaped by them. He claims to offer not a complete historical explanation of what produced the modern sense of identity, but something more modest, an articulation of various visions of the good and their appeal.

Unfortunately, there are other objections that are less squarely faced in the text. One concerns the restriction of his account to the history of Western conceptions. Taylor articulates so much so brilliantly that it seems mean-spirited to suggest that his account is narrow. Still, if we want to know who and where we are—say, in the United States—an account of Western traditions will not suffice. The articulation of who "we" are and what "our" history is had better involve, for the purposes of moral and political reflection, some understanding of African, Asian, and Latino traditions. (The last is in some sense Western, but it is not included in Taylor's picture.)

There are three reasons for this. First, these traditions have in various ways made important contributions to the formation of the sense of self of most Americans and many Europeans. Take the example of the arts: this book, which devotes so much attention to the shaping role of literature and the other arts, describing figures such as Defoe, Trollope, Pound, Eliot, and Kandinsky as central actors, contains no reference to the blues or to jazz—which are surely, in Taylor's own sense, "moral sources" of enormous depth and power. How many of his readers, when they think about love or pain, owe as much to Trollope or Eliot or Holderlin as they do to Bessie Smith or Billie Holiday? And is the vision of suffering, joy, endurance—and justice—that unfolds in the searing, broken cadences of Holiday's last recordings any less worthy of close philosophical scrutiny than the forms of art and literature that Taylor does discuss, if what we are seeking is an articulation of the visions of goodness that have made us who we are? Related points could be made about other non-Western traditions.

Second, the fact is that a large number of our fellow citizens are members of non-Western traditions and define their identity even more centrally in terms of those traditions. Any account of a "we" in any modern Western nation had better show respect for "our" real complexity, and seek a broader understanding. I suspect that Taylor's careful attention to Voltaire and Rousseau would not satisfy even his own French-speaking fellow citizens in Quebec as a sufficient articulation of their identity.

Third, an inquiry broader than Taylor's would have value well beyond the boundaries of domestic politics. For many political problems to which the accounts of identity in this book have relevance—problems of global ecology, of hunger and poverty, of education, of gender justice—are increasingly being confronted in an international and multicultural way. Even if "we" North Americans *were* shaped only by Western ethical sources, and even if domestic social justice did not require any larger understanding, we would still need to do more to understand the larger "we" who will be deliberating about such matters.

In many ways, the self-recognitions engendered by this book do indeed promote that larger understanding. For only when we can grasp and articulate the specific contingencies that have fashioned our deep conceptions of the meaning of family life, or of romantic companionship, or of political freedom, will we be in a position to recognize that people from different traditions might not share exactly those conceptions. We will be likely to be less clumsy in dealing with them, more appreciative of, and less bewildered by, the evidence of their differences. Self-understanding is an essential prerequisite for sympathy and for justice. Still, Taylor might have done more to prepare the reader for the larger interpretive task that awaits her—and to have shown how its completion would enrich, in the ways I have described, both our understanding of others and our grasp of ourselves.

Taylor's account has another, related limitation. By confining his account to philosophy, to mainstream European religion, and to high culture, Taylor tends to omit, at many important points, the voices of the powerless and the marginalized, those cut off by gender or class or race from these forms of cultural expression. This is reasonable enough, up to a point: for the project is to study the ideas that have shaped us, not those that failed to have an impact. I am fully in agreement with Taylor that these intellectual traditions cannot be dismissed by asserting that they are merely systems of domination. They are much more than that, and obviously worthy of close scrutiny as valuable moral sources; to deny them this role is to impoverish our own possibilities. But there are other sources, too. They are less easily accessible to a historian with Taylor's text-centered methods, but they are powerful and deep: oral tradition, myths, stories, the self-understandings of women and oppressed people, insofar as these resourcefully reacted against and affected the cultures in which they lived.

Taylor would not deny this, I am sure. A compassion for the oppressed and a passion for justice are evident in every chapter of his book. But his methods do not permit him to reach very deeply into such lives. To take just one example: a story of the conception of the self in ancient Greece that bases itself on Plato and the philosophers cannot pick up much of what even an ordinary male Greek citizen thought and said—and hardly anything of what Greek women had to say about themselves and their identities.

Again, this simply means that Taylor has not told the entire story. It does not mean that his book is undermined, or exposed as a record of mere power-grabbing. His sort of Western-centeredness is altogether different from the unreflective ethnocentrism of the traditional undergraduate curriculum, and also from the militant ethnocentrism of Allan Bloom, because Taylor's account aims to show how traditional views can justify themselves through careful argument, and because all visions of goodness, in principle, are of interest to him, wherever they touch upon and shape human lives. In the current academic climate, where there is so much strident and ill-argued debunking of famous books and authors by appealing to ideas of power, it is refreshing to see a philosopher with Taylor's historical sensitivity, social compassion, and philosophical acumen argue against what is excessive in such approaches, and defend the practice of mining the dominant intellectual tradition for moral insight.

Still, such reflections lead to a deeper philosophical question about Taylor's narrative: to a question about justification. Once we recognize that our sense of self is made up of the complex and heterogeneous strands that Taylor's narrative disengages, where do we go from there? How, precisely, do we move from understanding to endorsement? There are really two questions here, closely related. First, how do we decide to reject a part of our current view of the good—say, one that is in tension with another part— if to do so will incur the self-mutilation that Taylor fears? Second, how do we deal with challenges to our own complex conceptions that come from other traditions of thought?

Taylor makes us suspicious of large general solutions to these problems. And yet he appears to commit himself to the view that at least some elements in the conception of good that he discusses can be defended as best for human life generally. He argues, for example, that the idea of universal respect for human dignity is no mere accident of our local history, but a way of seeing the world that can be shown to be good for human beings the world over, a necessary mark of any "higher" civilization. And in his early theoretical remarks he suggests a general view of how we should justify a conception of the good. The core of Taylor's account (he has given it more fully in a recent essay) is as follows. To show that an ethical view is a good and reasonable one for us to hold, we do not need to provide the sort of argument that Western philosophers ever since Aristotle have tended to favor as their paradigm of rational argumentation: that is, a deductive argument proceeding from premises that are true, necessary, and external to all history. The belief that only such an argument can validate an ethical conclusion, Taylor argues, is an error that has been at the bottom of many forms of skepticism and extreme cultural relativism in ethics. For many thinkers, when they find that such arguments do not appear to be available there, have too quickly concluded that no good arguments are available, that all ethical argument is a matter of mere power.

But, Taylor continues, there are good arguments of a different sort available in the ethical sphere: practical explanations of a view's merits that are fully internal to human history, non-deductive in structure, seeking coherence and fit between theory and our deepest and most indispensable beliefs about ourselves. (Here Taylor comes close to John Rawls's idea of "reflective equilibrium" as the desired outcome of a process of ethical reasoning.) In particular, Taylor argues, it is possible to show that a new view, B, is superior to an earlier view, A, by showing how B responds to tensions and problems in A and helps us understand why A got into difficulty— all this in a way that signals a genuine gain in understanding, not simply a transition from one authority to the next.

The test for this is found through historical narration. If B is really superior to A, it will be possible to tell a compelling story of the transition from A to B, an account showing progress in understanding; but it will not be possible to tell an equally compelling story in which the transition is reversed, going from B to A. Once all the relevant material is brought to light and articulated, the decisive considerations should be such that both sides will recognize their validity; and the movement from A to B is thus a move to preserve a deep part of what is common to both A and B, by removing a dissonance.

Taylor's book provides many compelling examples of such narration. He convinces the reader, for instance, that the progression from ancient Greek aristocratic conceptions of politics to a universal respect for human dignity is a progress in understanding that was generated by tensions within the ancient conceptions themselves (with their unarticulated acknowledgments of the humanness of women and slaves), and one that could not be reversed. "Once you grasp this possibility," he writes, "it can't help but seem prima facie right." Still, the general philosophical issue seems to me to need more extended and explicit discussion than he has given it. Granted that there is a real and urgent difference between progress in understanding and the imposition of political or cultural power, it is still not easy to tell the difference in particular cases. For power frequently masquerades as illumination. What criteria should we look for, whose lives, whose intuitions, whose interests should we consult, when we ask whether a new conception is a gain in understanding? Taylor's narrative tells us little about how to unmask pretenders.

Let A be the Aristotelian view that the "natural" situation of the human being combines capability with limitedness and vulnerability. Let B be the Augustinian view that our fundamental situation is one of sinfulness. To me, it seems most illuminating to narrate the story going not from A to B, but from B to A: people at some time come to realize that their basic situation is not original culpability, but capable finitude, and this is a gain in understanding. One can even describe such a development as prompted by tensions internal to the Christian view, since many early Christian views placed the stress on human helplessness and human freedom. Yet many Christians would find the actual historical transition, from A to B, the truly illuminating one—generated (as in Taylor's arguments for religion) by a sense that the Aristotelian view cannot explain all the ways in which life goes badly. I may strongly suspect that church power played the driving role here; but my opponent will reply that in this case power supported the truth. There are many ways to adjudicate this situation; the enterprise of justification does not need to collapse. But I do not see exactly which way Taylor favors, and how the developmental emphasis of his account of rationality will work in such cases.

Only a more extended account, moreover, will tell us how to assess tensions in our current set of ends, how to decide which are fruitful, which are the result of arbitrary and dispensable elements. And this becomes more urgent still if we wish to take in the entire human world. Taylor's account applies only to views that succeed one another within a continuous history. But many confrontations between views do not have this form. When members of two different traditions encounter one another, with subtly different ideas of freedom, of the meaning of family life, of nature, what structure can the conversation have, and what outcomes count as progress in understanding?

That more remains to be done is no surprise. For Taylor has taken on the most delicate and exacting of philosophical questions, the question of who we are and how we should live. He has shown the importance of the history of our ideas and conceptions for the sort of complicated self-articulation that we need in the further pursuit of the question. And he has made this an adventure of self-discovery for his reader. To have accomplished so much is an important philosophical achievement, which will considerably enhance the contribution made by contemporary philosophy to private and public life.

# CHAPTER SEVEN

# The Chill of Virtue

GREGORY VLASTOS (1991), Socrates, Ironist, and Moral Philosopher

He summons to virtue with a composed and lofty countenance, as in David's famous portrait, ready to drink the hemlock, finger pointing upward. But he arouses anger too, with his ugly snub nose and his irritating questions, jesting, mocking, riddling, with his incessant logical interrogations and his uncanny lack of affect. He is a maddening gadfly on the back of the Athenian democracy, and yet he is also "of all the people of his time whom we have known, the best and wisest and most just." He is like the satyr Marsyas, outrageous, erotic, a seductive charmer, and yet when you open him up you discover treasures of virtue and moderation.

Socrates, in short, is strange. Alcibiades, charmed and humiliated, concludes that his most remarkable trait is to be "similar to no human being, past or present. . . . This man is so strange, he and his speeches too, that you could search and search and find nobody near him." Socrates' strangeness has been avoided in various ways. Sometimes he is portrayed as a saintly moral hero who could be found irritating only by hypocrites and fools. Such reverential portraits tend to treat his knotty and precise logical arguments as peripheral, rather than as the core of what he was. And sometimes, by contrast, irritation altogether displaces reverence, as in I. F. Stone's recent assault, which displayed such exasperation with the methods and the content of Socrates' philosophical inquiries that it could offer little illumination about the achievements that make Socrates a pivotal figure in the history of Western ethics. Once again the arguments were shortchanged, as Stone treated Socrates' interest in logical precision and the clear definition of terms as an abstruse metaphysical predilection, without relevance for the conduct of life. And even when the arguments do take center stage, as they do in much contemporary philosophical scholarship, something is too often missing still: the man himself, the point and the motivation of his inquiries, the oddness of his mission to humanity.

Gregory Vlastos's new book begins from the conviction that Socrates' strangeness is "the key to his philosophy." It is a marvelous book, in which no major aspect of Socrates' career is eclipsed. The rigor of his arguments, the depth of his moral commitment and understanding, his complex relationship to Athenian ethical traditions, his rational religion: all this comes to life in writing whose vigor and lucidity put the challenge of Socrates squarely before the reader, and whose exacting scholarship will satisfy the most meticulous expert without burdening the common reader.

The book is the fruit of almost forty years of work on Socrates, spanning a career in which Vlastos, now in his 80s, has also given us seminal work on Plato and the Pre-Socratics, and has, with an exacting generosity, trained more than one generation of young scholars, immeasurably raising standards of rigor, scholarship, and insight in the study of ancient Greek philosophy. But this is Vlastos's finest work to date. Like his subject, Vlastos invites the reader to argue with him, even to refute him—and those who know Vlastos's freedom from vanity know that this is no joke. This is a book that loves virtue and truth more than honor, again like its subject. Still, since Vlastos seems to agree with Socrates that honor is valuable if bestowed on genuine virtue, I must not hesitate to say that his book deserves as much honor as any work of scholarship in Greek philosophy in this century.

Socrates wrote nothing. Any account of his career, therefore, must piece it together from sources that are bewildering in their heterogeneity. The comic playwright Aristophanes (c. 457–385 BC) lampooned Socrates in both the *Frogs* (405 BC) and, especially, the *Clouds* (423 BC). Though his portrait contains, I think, some deep critical understanding, it is a very unreliable source, on account of its vagueness and its parodic purpose—and it is too far removed from Socrates' trial and death in 399 BC to show us an overview of his career. The military leader, historian, and biographer Xenophon (c. 428–c. 354 BC) knew Socrates personally and portrayed him in a number of works, with the announced intent of vindicating him. These works are valuable sources, and yet they, too, are far from trustworthy. Xenophon's Socrates is an unoriginal moralist, without paradox or irony, who could neither have provoked the rage that Socrates provoked in Athens nor have altered the course of Western ethical thought. Aristotle (384–322 BC), from his later vantage point, provides some brief but valuable information, above all about the difference between Socrates and Plato. And a few other contemporaries or near-contemporaries give further aid.

But it is above all in the dialogues of Plato (429–347 BC) that we must search for Socrates, for it is only there that Socrates' brilliance and strangeness emerge undiminished. And this means that we have a further problem on our hands. For Plato was a great philosopher in his own right, whose philosophical career spanned around fifty years. In most of his dialogues, Socrates appears as a character; but it seems impossible that the aim can always have been to reconstruct with historical fidelity the views of his teacher. There are too many fundamental differences and inconsistencies among the various dialogues, and they are too suspiciously correlated with what we can figure out from other evidence about the chronology of the dialogues themselves.

In a group of dialogues that seem, on independent grounds, to be early works (in alphabetical order, *Apology, Charmides, Crito, Euthyphro, Gorgias, Hippias Minor, Ion, Laches, Protagoras*) we find a figure who bears a reasonable resemblance to other portraits of the historical Socrates. These are also often called the "elenctic" dialogues, since they portray Socrates as searching by question and answer, using the method of scrutiny-by-cross-examination that is known as the elenchus. But in the major works of Plato's middle period (*Republic, Phaedo, Cratylus, Symposium, Phaedrus, Parmenides, Theaetetus*) we find a very different Socrates, whose views tally with independent reports about Plato's mature philosophical views. (I give Vlastos's groupings; some scholars would dispute this one or that one, but there is pretty broad agreement. He calls "transitional dialogues" another group that includes *Euthydemus Hippias Major, Lysis, Menexenus, Meno*.)

Vlastos provides the most convincing account we have yet had of this complicated situation, arguing for a series of ten major differences between what he calls Socrates-E (early) and Socrates-M (middle, that is, Plato's mature views). Socrates-E is exclusively a moral philosopher; Socrates-M is also passionately interested in science, metaphysics, epistemology, and much else. Socrates-M has a metaphysical theory of "separately existing" Forms and of an immortal soul that learns by "recollecting"; Socrates-E has no such theories. Socrates-E seeks knowledge by questioning and denies that he has knowledge; Socrates-M seeks demonstrative (quasi-mathematical) knowledge and is confident that it can be attained. Socrates-M has an account of the soul as tripartite; Socrates-E has no such account, nor could he accept it consistently with his denial that people who have knowledge of the better ever do the worse. Socrates-M is fascinated about mathematics and shows a sophisticated mastery of current developments; Socrates-E has no such interest or expertise. Socrates-E is a philosophical populist, questioning anyone and everyone he meets; Socrates-M is a philosophical elitist, restricting this teaching to a few. Socrates-E pursues truth by questioning and refuting; Socrates-M expounds truth didactically to relatively passive interlocutors. Socrates-E, though critical of the Athenian democracy, prefers Athens to any other state; Socrates-M has a developed political theory that ranks democracy very low and defends the rule of a philosophical elite. Both Socrates are interested in eros, especially of a homoerotic kind; but Socrates-M is alone in praising "madness," and in grounding eros in a metaphysical search for the transcendent form of beauty. (Here, I think, Vlastos's contrast too simple: it is only in the relatively late *Phaedrus* that "madness" is praised, and this in conjunction with the adoption of a non-mathematical, non-deductive, experiential, and language-centered conception of the dialectic.) Finally, both Socrates are religious;

but Socrates-E has an ethical, action-oriented religion, while the religion of Socrates-M is mystical, and prefers contemplation.

Vlastos argues for this picture in two stages. First, he sets out the evidence that these differences do in fact exist within the Platonic corpus, and are in fact well correlated with (to some extent) independently established chronological sequences. Second, by comparing Socrates-E with the evidence of Xenophon and Aristotle, he argues that "in those essential respects in which Socrates-E's philosophy differs from that of Socrates-M, it is that of the historical Socrates, re-created by Plato in invented conversations which explore its content and exhibit its method." Vlastos thinks that Plato ascribed to the character Socrates only that which he himself at the time believed. But his own views developed and changed, from a close allegiance to the thought and the methodology of his teacher, to a very different conception of the method and the content of philosophy.

In partial explanation of this shift, Vlastos points to Plato's mathematical studies with the Pythagorean thinker Archytas of Tarentum. From this point on, he argues, Plato's mathematical interests and expertise grew rapidly, as geometry profoundly impressed him by its beauty, its elegance, its promise of epistemic certainty. The Socratic elenchus, by contrast, which attempted to derive truth simply from the cross-examination of each interlocutor's own beliefs, now seemed to him a fragile and unreliable instrument. Socrates had to assume that within the beliefs of each and every interlocutor the truth was there to be discovered—and that once it was elicited, it would prevail over those false beliefs with which it was shown to be in contradiction. Plato, more elitist than his teacher, more disdainful of democratic education and the beliefs of the "many," is unwilling to rest the search for knowledge on any such shaky foundation. And so, from the *Meno* on, he replaces the elenchus with the hypothetical method, to bring the certainty of geometry into ethics and politics.

This is historical detective work at its best, set out with elegance, logic, and evidential clarity. Vlastos's method of setting out in full the texts on which his argument relies makes the reader a partner in the inquiry, actively unraveling the puzzles rather than deferring passively to the verdicts of scholarly authority. On this basis, once established, Vlastos then constructs accounts of several of the central elements in Socrates' teaching. And here is my one serious complaint about the book: its scope. Vlastos has chosen here to omit some of his most important research on Socrates during the past decade: a groundbreaking analysis of the method of the elenchus; an exploration of Socrates' disavowals of knowledge, paradoxical in conjunction with his claims to know various things; and, finally, an account of Socrates' relationship to the Athenian democracy.

Those pieces are promised for a future collection of Vlastos's miscellaneous papers on Socrates; but they would have filled gaps in this book. The first two are crucial to Vlastos's arguments about Socratic irony and about the relationship between Socrates and Plato; though he summarizes their conclusions here, that is no substitute for giving the reader the close look at the evidence that the fuller versions would have afforded. And the third would have been of enormous benefit to the reader, who will look in vain here for any biographical or historical discussion.

His argument elsewhere is that, although Socrates was often accused of being a foe of democracy and a friend of oligarchy, there is no substance to such charges. Socrates was sharply critical of much of democratic practice, and wished to arouse sluggish citizens to a keener awareness of themselves and their goals; and he also probably preferred an indirect democracy, with room for expert wisdom, to the direct democracy that prevailed at Athens. Still, he insisted that democracy was the best system that he found, and he showed a very deep respect for its laws. Moreover, his unbroken friendships with leading democrats such as Lysias, after the overthrow of the oligarchy, showed that they did not suspect him of partisanship with their opponents. Vlastos's powerful portrait of the elenchus shows, moreover, how democratic structures are built into the entire Socratic enterprise. Each and every person is to search for truth within himself (or herself: Socrates announced his intention of questioning women in the afterlife, when no social restrictions would prevent him). Deference to external authority has no place in the search for wisdom.

Vlastos's discussion of Socratic irony, with which his book opens, carefully disentangles two very different meanings of the Greek ancestor of our word "irony": "deception" and "saying the opposite of what the hearer is to understand." Irony in the second sense is never deceptive, though it may be riddling, for it relies for its success on the hearer's awareness of a non-literal meaning. Vlastos argues that Socrates' famous irony is not deception at all, as some have claimed, but a riddling way of leading the pupil to insights that are not conveyed by the literal meaning of his words. Thus Socrates' irony is also totally unlike the seductive and nihilistic sort of irony occasionally praised in recent philosophy and literary theory: it is always morally serious, and its goals are truth and self-knowledge.

Sometimes a pupil may fail to get the point—if, like Alcibiades, he is too vain and self-centered to listen well. If he fails, Socrates will not bail him out. This, however, is not because of indifference to the pupil. It is because Socrates values one thing more than the pupil's grasp of truth: that the pupil should come to see it for himself. Thus a concept of moral autonomy is, in Vlastos's account, at the heart of Socrates' practice of teaching.

Socrates, Vlastos argues further, never cheats his interlocutors. Examining cases that have been thought to involve deliberate fallacy on Socrates' part, he explains them either as honest perplexity or as not fallacious at all (but merely compressed or elliptical). Here it is hard not to feel that Socrates' concern for the autonomy of his pupil sometimes leads to oddly casual treatment—as when, to explicate an argument in the *Gorgias*, Vlastos has to extrapolate well beyond anything Socrates actually says to Polus, filling in an account of desire and its objects that is nowhere stated in the dialogue.

I think that Vlastos is basically right about the argument, but I am less convinced that this is a way of respecting the interlocutor. Certainly it is very far from the way that Vlastos has written this book, which makes its every move transparently clear. This clarity enables Vlastos's reader to be fully autonomous; but Socrates, by contrast, gives Polus pretty murky and incomplete material.

And that is not an isolated case. Euthyphro, too, is tripped up with some arguments that are far from crystal clear; nor are all the ironies directed his way perspicuous or helpful to him, though they may be to later readers. Socrates' attention to the particularity of his interlocutors, then, is not consistent. Some of them he treats with sensitivity and gentleness, giving them at each stage only what they can absorb, while others are tripped up and tied in knots, partly on account of the elliptical and rapid nature of the argument. There might be a therapeutic purpose even in that: the *Meno* reports that the experience of being stung by Socrates (as by an electric ray) helps the numbed person to discard false confidence and to begin in earnest the search for understanding. But I'm not sure that Vlastos has shown this always to be the case.

A fine chapter on Socrates' religion argues that Socrates does indeed believe in supernatural deities and divine signs, but that his deities are required to meet the stringent standards of his ethical views. His gods must do no wrong and tell no lies. This entails, of course, a radical transformation in traditional Olympian religion. It is in this sense that Socrates did destroy old gods and make up new ones, as his accusers charged. And piety is reconstrued in an equally radical way, as "doing god's work to benefit human beings." Thus Socrates completely jettisoned the quasi-magical tradition in Greek religion, according to which pious ritual acts induce the gods to grant wishes. God and man, instead of bargaining with one another, the self-interest of each uppermost, join as ethical beings in an enterprise that seeks the good. What, then, does religion add to the Socratic ethical life? It adds, Vlastos speculates, a solid basis for concern with the good of others that is not present in Socratic eudaemonism alone. This is right, I think, but it shows something disturbing about Socrates' moral views, to which I shall return.

Two further chapters complete Vlastos's account. Vlastos argues that Socrates was the first Greek thinker to reject retaliation as unjust in all circumstances. And finally, in his book's climactic chapter, he addresses the relationship between virtue and *eudaimonia* in Socrates' moral theory. Vlastos follows the common practice of translating *eudaimonia* as "happiness." Here I cannot follow him. Although I agree that there is no good one-word substitute (hence my transliteration), I believe that "happiness" designates, to most contemporary readers, a state of the person (of satisfaction or pleasure or well-being), whereas for the Greeks *eudaimonia* may have been a state, or something else, such as a complex form of activity. (In Aristotle's conception, its parts include virtuous activities *and* relations of friendship and love.)

What people who talk about *eudaimonia* agree on is that it is the end of all desires, the final reason why we do whatever we do; and it is thus inclusive of everything that has intrinsic worth, lacking in nothing that would make a life more valuable or more complete.

Vlastos begins from the obvious fact that Socrates connects *eudaimonia* very closely with virtue. He then proposes three ways in which we might understand that relation, all exemplified somewhere in ancient Greek ethics: (1) The relation is purely instrumental; virtue is desirable only as a means to *eudaimonia*. (2) The relation is constitutive, but only partly; virtue is one of the things that make up *eudaimonia*, but not the only one. (3) The relation is one of identity; virtue is the only constituent of *eudaimonia*.

Vlastos argues that Socrates, like Plato and Aristotle, holds a version of (2), but (unlike Aristotle) a very strong version, according to which virtue is also sufficient for *eudaimonia*. When virtue is present, then *eudaimonia* can be made somewhat greater by the addition of other goods, such as money, health, and honor, which can be constitutive of *eudaimonia* when they are combined with virtue. Without virtue, however, these things have no intrinsic value. A virtuous person who lacks them utterly is still *eudaimon*, if in a somewhat lesser degree.

Vlastos demonstrates that the texts rule out the merely instrumental relation and the weaker forms of constituent relation (in which virtue is only necessary, but not sufficient, for *eudaimonia*). Matters are far less clear, however, when it comes to the choice between the Sufficiency Thesis and the Identity Thesis. Vlastos's primary argument against Identity (given that the texts are pretty unclear) is that it would leave Socrates with no way of choosing between two courses of action that are both compatible with virtue, but different in the other goods that they offer (between virtuous starving and virtuous eating, and so on). But this is not obvious, certainly not for the later Stoics, who do hold the Identity thesis and have a very elaborate account of how such choices will be made (referring to our natural adaptation to such goods, as beings of a certain sort). The main point, however, is plain: Socrates believes that so long as courage, moderation, justice, piety, and wisdom are present, a person's life is fully *eudaimon*, no matter what the world around him is doing.

Let us be clear about what this means. It means that virtue all by itself is sufficient—not just for feeling satisfied, but for having a life that is good, complete, choiceworthy, lacking in nothing. Other things, if present, can make the life a little better, but they are worth nothing without virtue, and they are no big deal if virtue is present, since full-fledged *eudaimonia* is already at hand. Now, this is relatively easy to swallow if we considered things like money, honor, and good birth (though we must remember, too, that some of these might be essential in order to *act* on one's virtue, a point stressed by Aristotle); but harder if we consider things like health and freedom from pain and political freedom, which seem so intimately connected to all our feeling and acting that it is hard to think of a life as complete without them; and hardest of all if we think of ties to children, friends, loved ones—"the greatest of the external goods," as Aristotle perceptively observed. What we have to believe, to agree with Socrates, is not just that the loss of a fortune has no serious significance, but also that the loss of a child or a parent, the departure or the death of a spouse or lover, a betrayal by a friend—that all these are no big deal, either. It is better, of course, to have children, friends, loved ones; but if chance should take them, or if they should prove false, Socrates will still judge himself *eudaimon*.

There is no room in this moral outlook, in other words, for the tragic emotions of fear and pity. For these (as Aristotle said, making explicit a central part of ancient Greek morality) involve the ascription of high importance to external things that may be damaged by fortune. We don't fear what won't be seriously bad when it comes. And we pity others only when we judge that what has befallen them is not their fault and not importantly bad. It is no surprise, then, that Socrates, who believes that he is securely in control of his virtue, of his *eudaimonia*, repudiates pity, as he does in the *Apology*, holding that to appeal to pity is unworthy of a free man. It is no surprise, either, that in the *Crito* and the narrative portions of the *Phaedo* (which may be used with caution to imagine Socrates' death) he turns an event that has all the makings of a tragedy—the unjust execution of a good man, mourned by friends—into an occasion for calm discussion. The friends say they expected to feel pity, but did not, for Socrates does not treat his death as a seriously bad thing. We are well on the way here to the Stoic Epictetus's denunciation of tragedy as "what happens when chance events befall fools."

In this picture, moreover, it is no heroic achievement to be rid of the desire for revenge and retaliation. For if the things that others can do to us don't matter very much, if they can't ever take away our *eudaimonia*, what reasons do we have for wanting to strike back? To control revenge, however, while allowing the events of life to cut deeply: that is an achievement that Socrates did not, and could not, attempt. Shall I take revenge if someone rapes my daughter? No, says Socrates, because revenge is unjust. But remember, too, that the rape of a child is no big deal, and is still compatible with your perfect *eudaimonia*.

It would have been possible, of course, for Socrates to insist on the absolute necessity of virtue for *eudaimonia*, but to deny it sufficiency, thus allowing attachments to the world and to others to play a deeper role. This was Aristotle's position. He held that you certainly could not be *eudaimon* without virtue, but he added that you need "external goods" as well—in the case of health and money, for example, not because they are good in themselves, but because they are necessary in order for people to be in a position to act on their virtue (a distinction that Socrates seems to ignore). In the case of friends and loved ones, however, Aristotle's view is much stronger: those very relations of mutual love and aid are major constituents of *eudaimonia*, without which "nobody would choose to live, even though he had all the other good things."

Socrates' picture of happiness, says Vlastos persuasively, is not a monochrome, but a "polychrome, most of it painted blue [standing for virtue], but flecked out with a multitude of other colors, each of those specks making some tiny but appreciable contribution to the design." But Aristotle's picture is a much more complex polychrome, with large swatches, say of blue (virtue and virtuous action), several different reds (family, friends, and other related loves), yellow (contemplation and intellectual work)— and each of these coloring the others in subtle and complex ways. (All our activities, he holds, are better performed with and toward others.)

Does not the strangeness of Socrates lie, then, in this single-mindedness about virtue that does not allow love of others to count as more than a "fleck"? In an essay written in 1971 and dedicated to the memory of his wife, Vlastos observed that "the best insight in this essay—that Socrates' ultimate failure is a failure in love—grew out of what I learned about love from her." In the present book, he softens his assessment. I think he was right the first time. For Socrates' conception *is* incompatible with any really deep love of persons—erotic, familial, or friendly.

Deep love opens the self to loss of its own highest good, should things go badly. Seneca, in his *Medea*, imagines Jason saying about his children, "Sooner would I part with breath, with limbs, with the light." His vindictive wife observes, "That's how he loves his children? Good. He is caught. There's a space wide open for a wound." That, indeed, is what it is to love another person deeply: to be wide open to the wounds of anger, betrayal, desertion, death. And I don't think that this is true only of individual love. It is also the sort of love that Jesus is depicted as having for all humanity. He could not have had such love without a willingness to suffer, to become an object of pity.

In his 1971 essay, Vlastos himself made that criticism, contrasting Jesus' grief with Socrates' "frigidity." In Socrates, there are no gaping holes. He is a solid piece of self-sufficient virtue, like a big gold Easter egg, with health and friendship painted on the surface as decorations. Again, we are not far from the Stoics—from Cicero's story of a father who, hearing the news of his son's death, says, "I was already aware that I had begotten a mortal." Maybe this is why Socrates sometimes notices his interlocutor's needs and sometimes not: they are all external, none gets beneath his skin.

What about society? Vlastos stresses the radical consequences of Socrates' rejection of retaliation for Greek social life. But surely his rejection of pity brings with it consequences no less radical and far more disturbing. In the Greek tradition, from Homer onward, pity is connected with fellow feeling and beneficence. Typically, the appeal for pity is accompanied by a reminder of the common weakness and neediness of humanity, for pity requires putting yourself on a footing with the sufferer, acknowledging your own similar vulnerability. The result of this reminder of neediness, when it works, is to make proud and inflexible people more responsive, more generous to the weak.

Achilles, recalling that he, too, has an aged father who may be suffering, weeps with Priam and returns the corpse of Hektor. When the suitor Antinoos spurns a similar appeal from the beggar Odysseus, who speaks of the vicissitudes to which all humans are subject, the reader knows that a grave offense has been committed, and harshly judges his lack of fellow feeling. How would Socrates treat beggars, hungry children, bereaved friends? We really cannot say: as Vlastos stresses, it is only by his religion that the connection of his virtue to the good of others is anchored, and it is unclear what acts of material beneficence, or even of friendship, that religion (based on the sufficiency of virtue) requires. What we do know, however, is that Socrates must lack the motive for beneficence that comes through pity and fellow feeling, for he has to believe that such losses of material and personal goods, for another as for himself, are of no serious consequence.

And here we find ourselves at the beginning of a debate that has continued for thousands of years in the history of Western philosophy. Is society best held together by an awareness of shared human weakness, neediness, and finitude, or by the aspiration to self-sufficiency and completeness? One might combine these approaches, as Aristotle did; but on the whole one or the other has prevailed. Either pity has been made a basic source of social cohesion or it has been dismissed as unworthy of our dignity as moral and rational beings. On the one side we have the Greek tragedians (especially Sophocles), Aristotle, most of Christian ethics, Rousseau, and Marx; on the other side we have Socrates, Plato, the Greek and Roman Stoics, Spinoza, Kant, and (in his own way) Nietzsche.

The debate is fascinating and complicated, but it turns finally on the answer to one simple question. Is virtue sufficient, or is it only necessary, for a complete good life? Socrates' radical adoption of the sufficiency thesis, closing the spaces for wounds, gave a clear and certain answer to that question. Vlastos sums it all up: unlike Achilles, Alcestis, and Antigone, Socrates "can't lose." He can't lose, because he does not care so deeply for the things that are subject to risk that their loss would be a serious loss for him. *There* is his strangeness, awe-inspiring and alarming. And it leaves a question: Is this a good way for human beings to live?

# CHAPTER EIGHT

# Venus in Robes

RICHARD POSNER (1992), Sex and Reason

THE STATUE: My experience is that one's pleasures don't bear thinking
        about.
DON JUAN: That is why intellect is so unpopular.
                         —Shaw, *Don Juan in Hell*

Sex is ubiquitous in American courts, as it is in American life. Judges must deal with it in civil, criminal, and constitutional cases of many kinds; they are called upon to concern themselves with topics such as prostitution, homosexuality, contraception, nudity, child abuse, and erotic art. And yet, as Richard Posner rightly observes, judges often know very little about such topics. Proceeding on the assumption that sexual matters are ahistorical and "natural," and therefore sufficiently understood by simply consulting one's own intuitions, they approach these matters, all too often, with little historical or scientific learning, and with a personal experience that is likely, as Posner notes, to be somewhat narrow and uniform, given the effectiveness with which the background checking of judges weeds out members of sexual minorities. Thus, in deeply important human matters, we all too often find opinions that combine naïveté with the puritanism and the moralism that are such a large part of the American cultural heritage.

Consider, for example, the opinions in *Bowers v. Hardwick* (1986), the case in which the Supreme Court denied that a gay man, arrested in his own bedroom while having oral sex with another man, could legitimately claim that the Georgia sodomy law under which he was arrested violated a fundamental personal liberty, in connection with the due process clause of the Fourteenth Amendment. The case bore, on its surface, a very close relationship to other privacy cases (dealing with contraception, abortion, and the use of pornographic materials in the home) in which the Supreme Court had upheld the rights of individuals to regulate their sexual conduct by their own choice.

It also invited comparison to earlier cases in which laws forbidding miscegenation had been struck down as violations of both the due process clause and the equal protection clause: for miscegenation in the South a few decades ago, like homosexual conduct in Georgia today, was highly unpopular, and not likely to seem to most citizens the sort of thing to which individuals had a fundamental right "implicit in the concept of ordered liberty." And yet the Court had ruled that the Lovings (the remarkably named interracial couple) did in fact have such a right. For, the ruling held, miscegenation was a species of a genus—choice of one's own marital partner—that was protected, as a genus, by the Constitution, whether one liked all of its species or not. The same could have been said for homosexual sex acts in *Bowers*. It was not.

One would have expected the judges deciding such a complex and delicate case to have investigated the phenomenon of homosexuality very thoroughly, finding out what history and science have to say about it, and considering in some depth the lives of homosexuals in American society. None of this happened. The justices spoke in vague and highly inaccurate terms of a general condemnation of homosexual conduct stretching back to "ancient roots." But in fact their scanty references to the ancient pagan world were largely inaccurate, and even their picture of the history of Christian views on the topic was highly misleading. Nor did they do better when thinking about the way of life of a gay man in America—for they managed to dismiss without argument the notion that what was at stake for Michael Hardwick in choosing a sexual partner bore any relation at all to any of the Court's previous cases. Thus, as Justice Blackmun observed in his eloquent dissenting opinion, they all too quickly avoided asking whether there was not indeed a generic right to sexual choice that Hardwick, as much as "straight" Americans, enjoyed; nor did they even reach the point of asking whether the case could be construed as having an equal protection aspect, as Blackmun suggested it did.

The opinions in *Bowers* have drawn a lot of criticism, but the ignorance that they display is not unusual. One could also cite, for example, the opinion of Judge Robert Bork in the case of *Dronenberg v. Zeck*, involving homosexuals in the military. Again without any argument at all, and without any evidence of interest in learning and research, Bork simply asserted that the presence of gays in the services will lead to problems of sexual harassment in the workplace—never pausing to wonder whether this problem does not obtain similarly between males and females as well, whether gays are any more likely to harass their fellow workers than straights, whether all such problems could not best be dealt with by effective regulations governing sexual harassment, rather than by the exclusion of an entire class of qualified persons from the services. And one could also cite the recent District Court ruling by Judge Oliver Gasch in *Steffan v. Cheney*, the case of the talented midshipman at the U.S. Naval Academy who was forced to withdraw shortly before graduation because he admitted to a homosexual orientation (though not to homosexual conduct). Without citing any of the pertinent literature on the topic, Gasch simply asserted that homosexual orientation is a mutable behavioral choice and that homosexuals are not disadvantaged with respect to political power in American society—all this in order to establish that homosexuals do not constitute a "suspect class" for the purposes of the equal protection clause.

I have focused on cases involving homosexuality since these are a rich repository of judicial bias and ignorance; but one could find many similarly unargued and insubstantial opinions in cases pertaining to other sexual matters. Prejudice, a lack of curiosity, flawed logic: all of these are depressingly common when judges confront the complexities of sex.

Posner wishes to alter this situation. A judge on the U.S. Court of Appeals for the Seventh Circuit, as well as one of the most distinguished and prolific legal thinkers of his generation, he is well known for opinions that combine broad erudition with clear argument and eloquent, pungent writing. Where sexual matters are concerned, these virtues are combined, in the opinions he has written to date, with a refreshing lack of cant and a passionate concern for artistic liberty of expression.

His most important opinion—recently overturned by the Supreme Court—held unconstitutional, on First Amendment grounds, an Indiana statute that banned nude dancing. Defending the right of the striptease dancers of the Kitty Kat Lounge to keep their nipples uncovered, Posner wrote a learned (and witty) disquisition on the expressive properties of the dance, on the role of the erotic in the history of dance, on expression in the verbal and non-verbal artistic media, on the relationship between "high" and popular culture, and on the limitations of American moralism. He concludes:

> The true reason I think for wanting to exclude striptease dancing from the protection of the First Amendment is not any of the lawyers' classification games that I have been discussing. . . . It is a feeling that the proposition, "the First Amendment forbids the State of Indiana to require striptease dancers to cover their nipples," is ridiculous. It strikes judges as ridiculous in part because most of us are either middle-aged or elderly men, in part because we tend to be snooty about popular culture . . . in part because we are Americans—which means that we have been raised in a culture in which puritanism, philistinism, and promiscuity are complexly and often incongruously interwoven. . . . But the element of the ridiculous is not all on one side. Censorship of erotica is pretty ridiculous too. What kind of people make a career of checking to see whether the covering of a woman's nipples is fully opaque, as the statute requires? (These statutes are full of absurd locutions, such as: "'Wholly or substantially exposed to public view,' as it pertains to breasts, shall

mean . . ."). . . . Most of us do not admire the Islamic clergy for their meticulous insistence on modesty in female dress. Many of us do not admire busybodies who want to bring the force of law down on the heads of adults whose harmless private pleasures the busybodies find revolting. The history of censorship is a history of folly and cruelty.

(It is worth reflecting, incidentally, on what might be made of this one paragraph alone in a Supreme Court confirmation hearing. If the confirmation process has evolved in a way that excludes a provocative and brilliant figure such as Posner, but gives us people who either have no opinions or are willing to deny the opinions they have, we are much the worse.)

Out of Posner's dissatisfaction with judicial opinions in cases such as *Bowers* (of which he is highly critical) came this extraordinary book. It is an ambitious and complex undertaking and really has three distinct goals. Its first and modest goal is to provide judges (and others) with information and arguments—historical, cross-cultural, scientific—on sexual matters likely to come before the courts. Its second goal, far more ambitious, is to provide a comprehensive explanatory theory of sexual behavior, drawing both on economics and on evolutionary biology. Its third goal is to advance a normative theory of sexual legislation that is "libertarian," defending the rights of individuals to regulate their sexual conduct by their own lights except in those cases where it can be shown to cause harm to or to infringe on the rights of others.

How are these goals connected? It seems important to ask this question at the start, since Posner pursues the first and the third with far greater success than the second. And readers of Posner's previous work will have another reason to press the question. For Posner is one of the leading defenders of the thesis that judicial reasoning, properly understood, is really like economic reasoning, that the procedure of judges in torts and contracts, and indeed in constitutional law as well, is actually reasoning that seeks to maximize society's wealth. He advances this thesis as a descriptive thesis (seeing things this way will help us to understand what judges actually do, though they use other language) *and* as a normative thesis (when judges do not proceed in this way, they are reasoning badly).

By appeal to the normative thesis, he has, in *The Economics of Justice* (1981), criticized the privacy jurisprudence of the Supreme Court as "topsy-turvy," suggesting that the economic meaning of privacy is "profitable secrecy"; a judge who proceeds rationally will build up protections for, say, industrial secrecy, while being far less concerned about the unprofitable privacy of the bedroom. And he has shocked his readers by trying out economic reasoning in the sensitive areas of surrogate motherhood (where he called for a "thriving market in babies") and even rape (where he speculated about whether the special pleasure derived by the rapist from the nonconsensual nature of his act is or is not outweighed by the woman's loss in property rights in her body). Posner defends this apparently crude way of looking at things by asserting, repeatedly, the extremely controversial thesis that whenever individuals (judges or anyone else) are thinking rationally, they are seeking to maximize their satisfactions: so, if we are to give individuals (including women) credit for rationality, we had better see how we can cast their reasoning in this "economic" form.

In his economic mode, Posner has struck many of his readers as dogmatic and quite insensitive to the history and the complexity of human phenomena. In his recent book, the ambitious *The Problems of Jurisprudence* (1990), he seemed to waver about whether the economic approach provides a sufficient account of judging, and even of rationality. In any event, in none of his judicial opinions in the area of sexual conduct is there the slightest mention of economic notions, or even of cost benefit analysis. These opinions display a sensitivity and a flexibility that were notably lacking in some of his earlier theoretical writing. All of this gives ample reason for Posner's readers to wonder about the role played by economic theorizing in his current account of judicial reasoning about sex.

All three of Posner's projects in this book are connected by an opposition to puritanism and to simple moralism, and by his closely related view that ethical norms in matters of sex are not "natural" at all, but are constructed by societies in different ways. This anti-puritanism and anti-naturalism supports Posner's determination to look to other times and other places for a more comprehensive understanding of human sexuality than a scrutiny of contemporary American intuitions might yield. And all this, in turn, supports his "hands-off" libertarian stance in areas such as homosexuality (where he holds that *Bowers* was wrongly decided), abortion (where he defends the general outcome in *Roe*, if not all the reasoning), and erotic art (where he wishes to give all expressive material full First Amendment protection, whether its content is political or not, propositional or not).

The informational and historical part of Posner's book is in many respects its most successful. Although the task of providing, in 100 pages of text, a short version of what judges ought to know about this topic is a daunting one, Posner, with his broad and accurate erudition, his curiosity and wit, does it remarkably well. He draws on the findings of anthropology, psychology, psychoanalysis, classical scholarship, and cultural history; and although the historical account is thin on material outside the Western tradition, it ranges very widely over times and places within that tradition.

Posner is especially interested in the ancient Greek world, and in analyses of ancient sexuality inspired by Foucault and the "social constructionists." The imaginary judges to whom this segment of the book is addressed would learn from even a cursory study of its contents that sexual categories and normative judgments about those categories are far more various than a modern American perspective might lead one to suppose. He or she would learn, for example, that in ancient Greece the fundamental distinction of sexual roles was between the active partner and the passive partner in the sexual act. For the active partner, the gender of the passive object was a matter of relative indifference. Thus the category of the "homosexual" as we know it—an individual who has an abiding preference for partners of a certain gender, regardless of the distinction between activity and passivity—did not really exist in that society. And in other ways, too, Posner is very good at showing the great diversity of attitudes that respectable societies have taken about many highly charged sexual topics, at setting contemporary America in perspective, among the cultures of the world, as a society marked by a singular combination of heterogeneity, puritanism, and "machismo."

The dominant position of the book's historical section is "social-constructionist," that is, it adopts the view that sexual norms do not derive from permanent and immutable laws of nature, but are devised by society and tradition. But Posner then goes on to defend as the best explanatory theory of human sexual behavior a theory that combines evolutionary biology with economics. The combined thesis is somewhat elusive, but one might attempt to capture it as follows. Large-scale patterns in sexual behavior—persistent behavioral tendencies and repeated social patterns—are best explained biologically, as ways that the species has found of maximizing its evolutionary fitness. Within the large constraints of biology, on the other hand, individuals, being rational agents (a characteristic that itself is held to derive from evolution), seek to maximize their own satisfactions, computing costs and benefits.

There is no reason in principle why someone who recognizes and stresses the great variety with which societies have constructed sexual categories and norms might not also believe that beneath this variety lay certain "natural" regularities. These regularities might even be invoked to explain why, in each concrete set of circumstances, the specific cultural manifestations take the form they do. Sometimes Posner attempts to integrate his bioeconomic with his historical argument in some such way, as in his attempt to explain ancient Greek homosexuals as of two different sorts: some (the "pathics") being males biologically determined to a preference for the passive role (which, quite confusingly, he simply equates with today's people who prefer a same-sex partner, regardless of what sexual role they take), others (the vast majority) being "opportunistic" homosexuals who prefer (young) male partners simply because access to women is difficult.

Still, even such an attempted reconciliation of the two theses runs into difficulty. For in fact the evidence shows that women, in the role of prostitutes, were widely available in ancient Athens; nor can Posner's argument explain the thriving business done by male prostitutes in that same city. Posner's account of the ways in which the changing social position of women influences social mores regarding marriage and related sexual matters is stronger and more interesting—though its interest derives far more from its historical than from its bioeconomic component.

In many other cases, Posner does not even try to reconcile his two lines of argument. For example, he asserts that the fact that women frequent prostitutes less often than men shows that women have, by nature, a lower "sex drive" than do men, failing to consider the manifold cultural and emotional factors that play a role in women's distaste for such choices. Again, he asserts that biology determines males to have a preference for women with large breasts and hips, although elsewhere in the book he stresses evidence that the sexual attractiveness of bodily shape is a matter of "social construction," the desirable shape varying a great deal from culture to culture. Some of Posner's bioeconomic assertions seem just as false and unsupported by evidence as those in the judicial opinions that he deplores: for example, the assertion that males are more sexually jealous than females—a fact that experience does not appear to bear out—and the assertion that a woman's ideal of an appealing sexual partner is a male who will be likely to protect and care for her offspring. (The plots of many works, from *Medea* to *Casablanca*, might be considered with these two theses in mind.)

And there is a more general problem about the fit between the two projects. The historical project speaks of sexual desire as a phenomenon characterized by a rich and complex intentionality: that is, as fundamentally directed to an object and concerned with the object seen in a certain way. Desire, in that picture, might contain instinctual components, but it is essentially a pull rather than a push, a response to the perception of some value. The biological argument, by contrast, and its economic companion even more clearly, views desire as simply a push, as a force that demands discharge and satisfaction and remains rather constant, whether a suitably evocative object is on the scene or not. It is by making this assumption that Posner can argue, for example, that a male deprived of access to females will choose an available male partner; that a female who, in the absence of a male partner, does not, like a similarly situated male, frequent a prostitute gives evidence thereby of a lower "sex drive." To have sorted out the "drive" component and the intentional component in sexual desire, and to have described some of the complexities of the interactions between the two, would have been a first step toward an adequate theory of human sexuality. In this sense, Posner's book doesn't even take the first step.

Nor is it clear that Posner's explanatory theory, such as it is, is really the alternative to moral and religious theories of sexuality that he believes it to be. His strategy is to demonstrate that if one understands that sexual matters have a non-metaphysical origin, an origin in our animal history, and if one can push this secular explanation far enough, so that it seems to explain what we want to explain at least as well as explanations of sex that invoke divine entities and laws, then we will have put those vestiges of religious moralism at a considerable disadvantage in the American legal process.

But this does not make biology a replacement for morality. As Posner himself is well aware, one may hold that biology has constrained human behavior in certain ways without believing that this goes very far in telling us how we ought to behave toward one another in sexual matters. The fact (if it is a fact) that certain forms of behavior promoted the evolutionary fitness of the species at a certain time in its history says nothing at all about whether intelligent reflective creatures should choose to perpetuate these patterns of action. Posner, as I say, knows this; and he insists, for example, on the fact that polygamy, while functional in certain contexts, is unlikely to promote the equality of women, a goal that many modern societies with good reason (in his view) pursue.

But then it is not clear why his theory is a replacement for moral theorizing—except in the sense that any Darwinian explanation tends to undercut modes of explanation and normative discourse that stress the discontinuity between humans and other animals, and that posit otherworldly origins for all that is valuable in human life. To stress the this-worldly and animal nature of sexuality, however, does not go far toward justifying the reductive modes of analysis ("search costs," "transaction costs," and so on) in which Posner takes such pride. For there are many ways of being a this-worldly animal; and one of those ways is to be an animal that is ethical. Such an animal will be likely to need a more complex language than Posner offers.

The largest problem in the book—and, I think, in much of Posner's other writing about secular morality—is that he supposes, in effect, that if God is dead, then everything is indeed permitted; that when religion goes out the door, morality goes out the door, too; that all we have left, if we deny ourselves the appeal to transcendent sources of authority in moral matters, is a situation in which the world is a great market and individuals are simply competing to maximize the satisfaction of their subjective preferences, any one of which is as good as any other. If not heavenly judgment, then hands off on all moral judgment. It is for this reason that Posner can oddly classify Ronald Dworkin's rights-based approach to sexual/legal matters as a species of religious view. He makes the mistake of thinking that humans cannot invent and commit themselves to moral categories on their very own hook, without the other world to tell them so.

This is the sort of error that will be made by someone all too fascinated by religion, and by human dependence on it; by someone who doesn't altogether trust human beings to use their very own wits to say what has value and how much. Posner, secular humanist that he is, should not make such an error. And, to be sure, he doesn't always. His book, far more quirky and fascinating than this summary of its argument makes it seem, contains constantly surprising reminders of its author's complexity and perceptiveness—as when, in a brief paragraph, he distinguishes between two types of erotic love, giving an account of love that cannot be integrated into the central argument, and is the richer for that. And at one point he seems to acknowledge that his own theory is simply a crude and somewhat shocking theory that will, like an "acid bath," peel away "layers of ignorance, ideology, superstition, and prejudice," and "clear the ground for a normative analysis" of a more complete and adequate sort.

How important is the bioeconomic theory for the concrete legal reasoning in the book's third section, where Posner unfolds his normative "libertarian" approach? Fortunately, at least as I see it, not very important. Posner frequently refers back to the bioeconomic theory for a general atmosphere of this-worldliness, hardheadedness, and sanity, but he might as well have invoked any secular moral theory. Indeed, there are some theories—say, Dworkin's rights-based theory—that would have provided a far more adequate philosophical foundation for Posner's libertarian judgments than his own theory does.

Revealingly, in his first reference to the "libertarian" normative theory, he borrows the language of Mill: conduct should not be regulated that does not damage another's "*liberty* or property" (my emphasis). Later, he says in his own voice that conduct will be regulable only on the basis of "economic or other utilitarian considerations." But protection of fundamental rights and liberties has not generally been a strong point of utilitarianism, which usually holds that such moral considerations are merely instrumental to satisfactions, and are to be overridden when the balance of satisfactions goes against them. Still, one might, with Mill (and with contemporary thinkers such as Amartya Sen), defend a general consequentialist conception—a conception in which the right question to ask about an action is whether it promotes the best consequences overall—and yet include the protection of fundamental human rights among the consequences that get promoted. I think that this is what Posner actually does, in many cases; and insofar as he follows Mill (and Sen) in this way, he is a lot closer to Dworkin's view of legal reasoning than his own statements suggest.

Posner's general strategy in this section of the book is to demand that we ask about social costs and benefits calmly and comprehensively, prejudice and disgust aside, using all the information available to us about the practices concerning which we are judging. Proceeding in this way, he arrives at results that will surprise those who are accustomed to making simple distinctions between "left" and "right," and who have long since decided that Posner, in virtue of his pro-market stances, must be a "right-wing" thinker. Describing his conclusions will not do justice to his arguments, but the conclusions are remarkable in their own right.

*Marriage.* On the whole Posner favors the gradual substitution of a secular form of contractual cohabitation (currently available in Scandinavia) for the institution of marriage as it is presently understood. Short of this, he would wish (*a*) to recognize non-marital cohabitation by some form of legal contract guaranteeing certain rights and benefits, and (*b*) to overhaul the system of alimony in order to provide compensatory benefits, in the case of divorce, for women who have sacrificed career opportunities to assist a spouse. He tends to favor allowing homosexuals to marry, although he would really like to solve this problem by "chucking the whole institution of marriage in favor of an explicitly contractual approach that would make the current realities of marriage transparent." Polygamy, he tentatively holds, should continue to be illegal, since it remains connected with hierarchy and the unequal social position of women. But women who have children outside of a recognized marriage should be protected somehow.

*Homosexuality.* The disgust that many Americans feel toward homosexuals is based on a combination of ignorance and machismo. (The only popular stereotype on this question that Posner finds reliable, on the basis of his cross-cultural study, is that homosexuals have a higher than average probability of having an artistic career, and "it is not the worst fate in the world to be condemned to a career in the arts.") Sodomy laws should be repealed, even if they are not enforced, since they tend to provide a basis for other exclusions—for example, from professions such as that of the judiciary, in which we would be reluctant to see an admitted lawbreaker. He is highly critical of the opinions in *Bowers* for "ignoring the ideological roots" of the Georgia sodomy law, for "lack of knowledge about this history and character of the regulation of sexuality," and, above all, for "profound lack of empathy for the situation of the male homosexual in America." And he supports the idea of a general constitutional right of sexual autonomy, which would cover this case along with many others. He also suggests that homosexuals should count as a suspect class for the purposes of the equal protection clause, and that, even given the *Bowers* result, this avenue of argument might possibly still be used by courts to rule in their favor.

As for the issue of homosexuals in the military, Posner provides a devastating criticism of the arguments most often used to support their exclusion: the security risk argument, the argument that gays are unstable, the sexual harassment argument. The one argument that he takes seriously is the view that the presence of gay men (he doesn't find this problem in the case of women) may well create serious morale problems, given the prevalence and the violence of male homophobia in America (by contrast to other countries, such as the Netherlands, which have unproblematically integrated gays into the services). Posner fears that homophobia is so deep in the self-definition of many American males that the danger of violence against gays is really rather great, and greater than in the parallel case of racial integration. Yet he thinks that the risk should be run, "for it is terrible to tell people they are unfit to serve their country, unless they really are unfit, which is not the case here." He favors a gradual policy of integration, beginning by keeping in the services gays who are already there and "come out," gradually accepting new recruits.

*Privacy and the Constitution.* Posner holds that the privacy cases involving contraception and abortion were, in general, correctly decided, although he does not approve of all the reasoning in the opinions. He thinks that in the end no compelling basis in the Constitution exists for the recognition of a general right to sexual autonomy, but that the courts should plug this gap and recognize one anyhow:

A constitution that did not invalidate so offensive, oppressive, probably undemocratic, and sectarian a law [viz., the anti-contraception law at issue in *Griswold v. Connecticut*] would stand revealed as containing major gaps. Maybe that is the nature of our, as perhaps of any, written

Constitution; but yet, perhaps the courts are authorized to plug at least the more glaring gaps. Does anyone really believe, in his heart of hearts, that the Constitution should be interpreted so literally as to authorize every conceivable law that would not violate a specific constitutional clause? This would mean that a state could require everyone to marry, or to have sexual intercourse at least once a month. . . . Yet we do find it reassuring to think that the courts stand between us and legislative tyranny even if a particular form of tyranny was not foreseen and expressly forbidden by the framers of the Constitution.

*Pornography.* In a discussion closely linked to Posner's opinion in the Kitty Kat Lounge case but ranging more widely, since here he is not constrained by previous Supreme Court pronouncements on obscenity, Posner holds that the only pornography that should be legally restricted is pornography that uses child models or inflicts damage on adult models. (His ruling in the case of *Robyn Douglass v. Hustler Magazine*, however, also shows that he is willing to support civil damage actions against such publications when photographs are used without consent.) His conclusion here is tentative; and yet, having argued that expressive artistic representations (for example, Robert Mapplethorpe's photographs) must be protected, he confesses that he can find no evident differences—with respect to the issues of violence and misogyny that are of most concern to feminists—between these "arty" works and the more popular pornographic forms.

Citing the arguments of the feminist historian of religion Margaret Miles concerning the patriarchal and misogynistic dimensions of much of classical art, Posner concludes that "if a *Playboy* pinup belongs to the same genre as a Renaissance nude, then since the latter is plainly protected by the First Amendment, so must the former be." In the *Kitty Kat* opinion, he notes that the category of "established art," sometimes invoked to try to make this distinction, would have excluded from protection Manet's *Déjeuner sur l'herbe*, and much else besides. And that is not his only worry. He plainly wants the dancers of the Kitty Kat Lounge to be free to express themselves in their own low-art way, and doesn't see why the protection of the First Amendment should be extended only to those who meet with the approval of highbrow tastes. Here Posner is openly at odds with many feminists. Though some of their arguments are powerful, and perhaps deserving of more scrutiny than Posner gives them, I am in sympathy with his conclusions.

Posner, plainly, is a complex character, difficult to pin down. One might do worse than to think of him as the George Bernard Shaw of American law. Like Shaw, he combines a passion for exposing humbug and pseudo-profundity with an odd but genuine sort of social compassion, a delight in shocking the self-righteous with a love of human diversity and freedom— and all of this, one must add, with a good deal of Shaw's inability to get inside the messier human emotions, with his tendency to think of emotion itself as a peculiar sort of religious dogma. Posner's bioeconomic theory is no better than Don Juan's theory of "the Life Force" (which it strongly resembles) as an explanation of the complexities of human sexuality. But as with Shaw, I think, so with Posner: long after the deeply flawed theories have been forgotten, we will remember, and profit by, the wit and the courage of his attacks on bigotry, folly, and cruelty.

# CHAPTER NINE

# Justice for Women!

SUSAN MOLLER OKIN (1989), *Justice, Gender, and the Family*

As Bangladesh was struggling to recover from the disastrous famine of 1974, Saleha Begum's husband fell ill, and they were forced to sell their land.[1] Like most women in rural Bangladesh, Saleha had never been trained to work outside her home. Although she raised her children almost single-handedly and did the hard physical work that daily household life required, she was illiterate, unprepared for any sort of wage-paying job, and without any claims to respect as a worker. To avoid starvation for herself, her husband, and her children, Saleha fought for and won the right to work at an agricultural project previously closed to women, in which food was given in exchange for labor. As the prize for her victory she was able to spend her days breaking up turf with a hoe and carrying heavy baskets of earth—all the while caring for her young children, who accompanied her to the field, and continuing to do all the housework when she returned home. (Women, studies show, can move forty cubic feet of earth per day.) She told an interviewer that she regrets her lack of professional training: "I could have had a profession to see me through these difficult days—without always dreading whether I will have work tomorrow or whether my children will be crying in hunger." When I saw her husband on film (too weak for field work, but otherwise apparently well), he was sitting on the ground and smoking a pipe while Saleha cared for their children.

Angela K. lives in the white middle-class American suburbs, but her story has much in common with that of Saleha Begum. Angela went to high school, but married shortly after she began college. She left school to go to work, supporting her young husband while he got both a bachelor's degree and a professional degree, and then quit work to have children. Ten years later she was divorced and awarded custody of the three young children; but the court ordered the family house to be sold and the proceeds divided. The child support payments and temporary "transitional" alimony ordered by the court were inadequate to keep the family from hardship. Forced to rely on her earnings, she is caught in an exhausting dead-end routine. She has to take jobs paying close to the minimum wage while also caring for her children and doing the housework, and she has no hope of pursuing any sort of professional training. Her frustration is increased by awareness that her ex-husband is flourishing. It takes the average divorced man only about ten months to earn as much as the couple's entire net worth. And divorced men are now more likely to meet their car payments than their child support obligations.[2]

Women suffer injustice not only through discrimination in the public world, but also through the ways labor is organized and income is distributed within the family itself. It is in families, indeed, that the cruelest discrimination against women takes place. The economist Amartya Sen, for example, has shown that patterns of female mortality in many parts of the world suggest that pervasive discrimination against women (and especially girls) deprives them both of adequate food and basic health care.[3] It is hard to prove who puts how much food on whose plate each night at dinner; but one can observe which members of a family die of malnutrition and draw the appropriate inferences about the inner life of that family.

And even when women are not actually dying as the result of discrimination, the patterns of family life limit their opportunities in many ways: by assigning them to unpaid work with low prestige; by denying them equal opportunities to outside jobs and education; by insisting they do most or all of the housework and child care even when they are also earning wages. Especially troubling are ways that women may suffer from the altruism of marriage itself. As the two stories show, a woman who accepts the traditional tasks of housekeeping and provides support for her husband's work is not likely to be well prepared to look after herself and her family in the event (which is increasingly likely) of a divorce or an accident that leaves her alone.

Such facts are all too familiar. Few who have lived through some variant of this story, or have seen their friends do so, would confidently maintain that the contemporary family is a just institution. And yet philosophical theories of justice have rarely considered the workings of the family; they have rarely treated it as an institution to which basic insights about justice and injustice must apply. The aim of Okin's important book is to bring this situation to light and to try to correct it.

Two reasons for this omission are frequently offered, Okin points out, either separately or in combination. Some theorists claim that the family is not an appropriate topic for a theory of justice because it is in some sense "beyond" justice, a sphere of life that embodies virtues of love and generosity that are "higher" than justice. (This claim has recently been advanced by thinkers as different as the communitarian political theorist Michael Sandel and the radical legal scholar Roberto Unger.)[4]

Even if such a claim is true of the family at its best, it is far from clear why generosity and love should be thought incompatible with a basic concern for justice—as if it were small-minded to inquire about equal opportunity when partners are bound by deep emotion. We should, as Okin says, be suspicious of that criticism, especially when we notice whose interests that idea of a love beyond justice has frequently served.[5] Real generosity and real love, we would insist, should at least be just; and it seems right to demand of the family that it meet the basic requirements of fairness, no matter what higher ends it pursues.

This point is all the more important since the dominant model of the family used in current economic theory—that of the economist Gary Becker—assumes a harmony of interests among family members, in which a beneficent head of the family acts "rationally" on behalf of the interests of all its members.[6] This approach, as Okin perceptively notices, is not very different from that of theorists who idealize the family. Like such theories, it fails to confront inequalities of power and problems of justice that can exist within the family itself.

It is also said that the family cannot be expected to meet standards of justice because, unlike the state, it exists "by nature," or "according to nature"—an argument recently made, for example, by Allan Bloom in his attack on women's demands for equality of opportunity.[7] But the word "nature," as J. S. Mill long ago observed,[8] is among the most slippery of many slippery terms in the philosopher's lexicon. If "according to nature" means "the way things are without human design or intervention," it is far from clear why we should be bound by nature when it comes to ethical choices. Many bad things happen according to nature in that sense—diseases, earthquakes, bodily weakness, and hunger. This hardly means that we should do nothing about them. Many good things, too, are in that sense against nature—including most of the ethical ideas we have.

Nor can the traditional patterns of family life be separated from other social norms and political institutions. As Okin shows in detail, the "private" realm of the family, so frequently contrasted with the "public" world of laws and institutions, is actually shaped by laws and institutions in countless ways: directly, by the impact of divorce law, tax law, and other family-related laws on the opportunities and living standard of family members; indirectly by the fact that the family members are deeply influenced by the societies in which they live. Their actions in "public" life also shape, and are shaped by, their ways of participating in family life. An unequal division of labor within the family presents obstacles to women in their lives outside the family; and these inequalities are often supported by social traditions and expectations.

And yet most major theories of justice have had little to say about women or the family. This, Okin argues, simply will not do: since women evidently suffer injustice, a theory of social justice forfeits its claim to our attention if it omits so much of its topic. The family, moreover, is the school of justice for the larger society, the place where children are first exposed to the models of fairness and unfairness that will affect their later behavior in the larger world. If young citizens' earliest experiences of family life include the experience of injustice, even of injustice masquerading as nobility or as nature, must this not work against the eventual possibility of a more just society?

Okin examines what some influential philosophical accounts of justice have to say about the justice of the family. If, as often is the case, little has been said explicitly, she asks whether the theory itself has the potential for an adequate treatment of injustice to women. Communitarian theories of justice, which hold that standards must be found in the deeply rooted traditions of particular societies, seem to her particularly inadequate.

Here Alasdair MacIntyre's account of justice within traditions[9] is of particular interest, since MacIntyre shows much sensitivity to issues of justice for women and goes to some pains to show that his Aristotelian-Thomistic account can avoid some of the discriminatory conclusions of Aristotle's actual treatment of women. Okin argues, convincingly in my view, that MacIntyre's appeal to the excellence of traditional arrangements is persuasive only to the extent that he makes his reader forget to ask what position he or she would occupy within the traditional society. It is one thing to be a Homeric warrior, quite another to be a Homeric slave, and MacIntyre always concentrates on the dominant class, failing to imagine the horrendous inequalities that are directly entailed by the standards of justice in these traditional societies. When much of the world seems to be seeking meaning in ethnic, national, and other traditions, and casting aspersions on the Enlightenment demand for impartiality, Okin reminds her readers of the dangers of romanticizing tradition.[10]

Equally vigorous is her attack on libertarian theories of justice, for example, Robert Nozick's rights-based account of a minimally interfering state.[11] Her criticism here is, I think, unfortunately narrow; it is aimed at finding an inconsistency within Nozick's account of ownership, and argues that he cannot avoid the conclusion that women own their children, since they produce them by their own labor. If this is so, she argues, nobody can ever own anything since they do not own themselves in the first place. In consequence, Nozick's theory of ownership and entitlement is flawed from the start. This seems to be a relatively superficial objection, of little help in investigating the general structure of theories of justice based on rights and what they have to offer women.

By contrast, Okin's criticism of John Rawls's theory of justice is one of her most valuable contributions.[12] Having great sympathy with Rawls's account of justice, she wishes to use it as the frame for her own account of justice between men and women in the family. She finds particularly attractive the well-known device of the Original Position, in which hypothetical people in selecting principles of justice are deprived of knowledge of their own particular place in society, their class, occupation, and so forth, and therefore have to consider the well-being of everyone, from the best-off to the worst-off, on the hypothesis that they could be any one of them.

This exercise of impartial moral imagination she finds enormously valuable for understanding the lives of women. She argues convincingly that principles chosen in such a way would not accept the huge inequalities between males and females, with respect to basic goods such as nutrition, health, the right to work, and political liberty, which now prevail in one or another form in most parts of the world. (Since Okin mainly discusses the problems of women in the United States and similar countries, she says little about hunger. But in an impressive recent paper she extends her analysis to women of developing countries, arguing that the problems they face are not different in kind from those she has described, but are simply, in many cases, worse and more urgent.)[13]

Okin is in fact rewriting Rawls. He did not stipulate that the persons in the Original Position are ignorant of whether they will be male or female in the resulting society. In fact, he said nothing one way or another about this question in *A Theory of Justice*—though in a later article he states that one's sex is, in fact, one of the morally irrelevant features that the veil of ignorance will hide; he now believes, it seems, that like wealth or social class, gender is not a feature that ought to affect people's entitlements in a fair and moral distribution of resources.[14] A further problem lies in his stipulation that the parties are "heads of households" who act on behalf of the interests of their households as a whole, not just on behalf of their own; for this seems to make the family and life within it, as Okin puts it, "opaque to claims of justice."[15]

Rawls doesn't seem to have thought much about the family. At one point he mentions that the family is part of the "basic structure" of society, for which principles are being chosen; and yet he says nothing about how the parties will choose to give structure to this particular institution, and, indeed, at one point he states that the family will simply be "assumed"—although "in a broader inquiry the institution of the family might be questioned . . . ."[16] As Okin says, "Why should it require a broader inquiry than the colossal task in which *A Theory of Justice* is engaged, to raise questions about the institution and the form of the family?" What is clear, however, is that the issue was not important to Rawls's view of what a theory of justice should accomplish. And this, as Okin notes, is all the more surprising since he devotes considerable attention, in a very valuable and little-read section of his book, to the way in which children learn moral sentiments, and eventually a sense of justice itself, from their early experience in the family. How can this happen, Okin quite rightly asks, if the family is itself unjust?

Okin's detailed criticisms of Rawls are telling and of wide interest. Her own positive proposal, Rawlsian in spirit, is elegantly simple. It is that we retain the device of the Original Position in selecting principles of justice, but (a) deprive the parties of the knowledge of whether they will be males or females in the resulting society; and (b) insist that since the structure of the family is in fact part of the basic structure of society, the parties would have to consider the basic principles of justice that affect it. From this, she argues, a truly "humanist justice" would emerge, one that would recognize the inequalities and deprivations deriving from the structure of family life, and that would correct these, both by legal institutions and by transformed patterns of daily life and activity within the home.

The society Okin imagines will insist, above all, on correcting the uneven division of boring and burden-some household tasks, which are very seldom equally distributed within the modern family, even when both parties pursue highly demanding jobs. (A recent survey in Finland, a country that has supported women's equal right to work more effectively, perhaps, than any other, providing well-designed and comprehensive schemes of subsidized child care and parental leave, found that working women do three times the housework done by working men.)[17] Caring for children, in Okin's view, should be in a different category, for it is both highly demanding and rewarding, so that what is being distributed is not just a task but also an opportunity to enjoy a basic human good.

Okin would like to see both work and education planned to achieve equality between men and women in careers, housework, and child care (by emphasis on flexible work time, child care at work, parental leave for both parents, and so forth). Such a plan, of course, would promote justice only if it were carried out in good faith by the men and women concerned. Education therefore becomes crucial. Public schools would prepare children of both sexes to take part in homemaking and rearing children, as well as in work outside the home, and would try to eradicate sex stereotypes. The laws of marriage and divorce would protect women like Angela K. far more than most such laws do now; they would recognize that the largest asset in most marriages is the earning power of its wage-working partner or partners; thus women like Angela K., who support their husband's work by keeping house, will, in case of divorce, be entitled to a portion of the husband's future earnings.[18] The primary aim of laws relating to alimony and child support should, she argues, be to ensure that the standards of living of the two post-divorce households are the same. This will be easier in any case in a society in which both parties to a marriage have been encouraged from the start to contribute to the family as both workers and homemakers. But where this is not the case, the law should intervene. And alimony of this sort, where necessary, should not end after a few years, as so frequently happens now. It should continue,

> for at least as long as the traditional division of labor in the marriage did and, in the case of short-term marriages that produced children, until the youngest child enters first grade and the custodial parent has a real chance of making his or her own living. After that point, child support should continue at a level that enables the children to enjoy a standard of living

equal to that of the noncustodial parent. There can be no reason consistent with principles of justice that some should suffer economically vastly more than others from the breakup of a relationship whose asymmetric division of labor was mutually agreed on.

These, practical proposals are not especially surprising. Many of them have long been endorsed by feminists, and some of them have actually been carried out in several of the Scandinavian countries. What makes Okin's argument for them novel and extremely important is the way in which she links them with underlying principles of justice. She argues, rigorously and convincingly, that principles that are widely endorsed as central to the moral point of view—for the device of the Original Position aims to provide a deeply shared picture of the moral point of view—when followed consistently, lead directly to the policies she advocates. But those principles will be seen to lead to these policies only when those who articulate them give to the lives of women and children in families the kind of attention that they have not so far gotten from most male theorists of justice.

Okin presents the problem of justice for women vividly and makes her philosophical case with exemplary clarity. Anyone concerned with social justice should study her book. Still, despite Okin's emphasis on the need for a theory of family justice, she does not address some of the deeper questions that such a theory would ultimately have to confront. First, one must wonder about her idea of "eliminating" gender distinctions, and what the proposed elimination would do to human love and desire. Okin believes that in a just society the difference between being male and being female would be no more significant than "one's eye color or the length of one's toes." And she plainly intends this elimination of difference to be a feature not just of public and legal institutions but also of daily life itself, as children grow up in families.

Her argument makes it evident that many, indeed most, of the ways in which differences between maleness and femaleness have been understood as significant by most societies have indeed been bound up with hierarchy and injustice; and her idea that we might regard gender as a category like eye color is certainly attractive by contrast to some of the hierarchical conceptions of gender that still influence the behavior of many of us. But how can the experience of being either male or female—and the experience of being sexually drawn to males or females, or both—be accurately compared to the feelings about oneself and others that are associated with the color of one's eyes? These experiences seem much deeper, and more intimately connected with one's life and identity.

Okin might feel this is neither a necessary nor a good state of affairs; but the sense of being male or female is so strong in most of us that a richer psychological and historical inquiry into the nature of human desire would be needed in order to make the case for the kind of society Okin seems to want. Even in societies like ancient Greece where the gender of sexual partners seems to have been far less important than it is for us, the experience of oneself as either male or female was a fundamental part of personal and social identity. Might we discover ways of retaining differences between the sexes while reconceiving them so that they would not entail hierarchy? Couldn't gender identity, for example, be like ethnic or national identity— fundamental ways that many people have of defining themselves, but not necessarily linked to the depreciation or oppression of any other group? I sympathize intellectually with Okin's views, but I can't see myself in the world she projects; and I find myself wishing that she were not so fond of making simple and unambiguous statements about matters that are deeply ambiguous and mysterious.

Then, too, we should know more about Okin's view of the family. She plainly has a strong preference for the nuclear family in something like its modern Western form, in which couples raise their own children in considerable privacy and with considerable freedom from outside interference. She rejects out of hand Plato's proposal for the communal rearing of children, simply asserting that the woman she is imagining "loves and cherishes her family life." She has little to say about unconventional family patterns, although she mentions the existence of homosexual couples—without expressing any view of their suitability as parents—and she approves of a limited amount of day care to assist working parents. But she never tells us what benefits she believes the modern Western family provides, or why, in view of the many alternatives that have been conceived, she still prefers the pattern that has proven, as she herself demonstrates, so resistant to reform in the name of justice.

Such arguments are all the more important now that Okin has extended her account to the women of societies very different from her own. Saleha Begum would be very unlikely to share Angela K.'s interest in the intimacy and privacy of the small nuclear family; and we know of many other societies in which the extended family, or village, is more important for child rearing than the couple. Furthermore, new technologies are now making it possible for a single woman, or a lesbian couple, or some larger group, to decide to have a child through artificial insemination. It will soon even be possible to arrange for children to be conceived and born entirely within laboratories and then raised in a variety of different ways.

We need to ask ourselves which ways are desirable, and this would require a historical and philosophical inquiry that is not even attempted in Okin's rather cautious analysis. Would the parties in Rawls's original position design a society with families in it at all? If so, what would be their arguments for doing so? Would they, for example, follow Aristotle, arguing that the intimate love and knowledge that are found within the nuclear family are better for the moral and psychological development of children than any more communal scheme could be? Okin, like Rawls, never addresses such questions.

All this points to the need for much more explicit consideration of what it is for human beings to flourish; for without some such account it seems difficult to say whether human beings might do better in families or in some sort of Platonic communal arrangement, or whether there is a clear case in fact for one or the other. Okin seems to make use of such an account implicitly when she imagines that both women and men will lead better lives if they share more activities than is now generally the case: for she implies that both caring for children and working outside the home are important human functions. Without either one of them, life might be said to be incomplete, however much money and security one may have. And yet, to develop this sort of claim would, it seems clear, take Okin beyond the boundaries of the sort of liberalism she has adopted, in which public policy is guided by basic principles of justice, but individuals are left to choose their own conception of the good.

Okin, following Rawls, is not, however, altogether neutral about the good;[19] for she seems to share Rawls's commitment to the importance of choice and autonomy, holding, with him, that satisfactions without choice are lacking in moral worth. And she insists, too, that in a just society religious views that teach the inferiority of women will simply not be admitted for consideration in the construction of basic institutions, any more than will views that teach the naturalness of slavery. But she never squarely confronts the issue of the good and the possible limitations of Rawls's views.

Rawls insisted that before they selected the principles of justice that should apply generally, the hypothetical persons behind the veil of ignorance would not know their own conceptions of the good: that is, what are the activities and goals in life that they take to have most importance. This, he held, was necessary if the resulting society was to be fair to people who came from different religious and metaphysical traditions. On the other hand, it was clear that in order to conceive principles for the distribution of things within society these individuals had to have some idea of what things were worth distributing. To this end Rawls provided his deliberating parties with what he called the "thin theory of the good"—that is, with a list of "primary goods" such as, for example, liberty, wealth, and income, of which, for all citizens, regardless of their personal conceptions, more was (allegedly) always better than less.

In his initial presentation of the list, Rawls spoke as if the primary goods were means to realizing any conception of the good one might have. In more recent work, he has denied this, connecting the list instead with the particular Kantian account of autonomy and rationality that he now uses explicitly to describe the parties in the Original Position.[20] But the claim still seems to be that these items are good, whatever one's conception of human goodness might be, and that more of them is always better than less; and he still claims that the "thin" list he gives is sufficient to give distributive justice a direction, without any further account of good human functioning.

Both of these claims have been questioned. Rawls's list of "primary goods" was always heterogeneous, including liberty, opportunities to act, and the social conditions of self-respect—all of which seem to be, or to be closely connected to, powers or abilities people may have—along with more traditional material resources, such as wealth and income. But certainly one might question, in at least some of the cases, the claim that more is always better than less. To say this about wealth and income, for example, is certainly to adopt a particular and highly questionable theory of the good, one very common in Western capitalism, but not for that reason the less controversial.

A feminist theory of justice should certainly question whether the unlimited acquisitiveness of modern capitalist societies has always been good for the family, for the bonds of community, or, indeed, for sex equality itself. Two people who believe that more income and wealth is always better than less are likely to have difficulties about the division of labor at home that people less attached to acquisition may not have; and professions that are based on this principle impose well-known burdens on their aspiring young members, making it very difficult for them to be just to their partners.

Nor should a feminist theory of justice simply assume that the "thin theory of the good" is sufficient to give direction to public policy in a just society. For one might argue—as Amartya Sen and others have recently argued against Rawls[21]—that such a list fails to demonstrate the very point and importance of those goods, which is to serve as instruments for human functioning. Unless we show how the goods on Rawls's list enable people to choose to live in ways that have value, we have not shown why they have any value at all; apart from its role in enabling people to act in various ways, money is only a heap of paper. But if we say, instead, that the parties in the original position need to identify the "capabilities"[22] for doing the things that people should be able to do, and to aim at equality of "capability," rather than at equality of resources such as income and wealth, we have already departed in some ways from the liberalism that lies behind Rawls's list.

The departure is not total, for in aiming to make people capable of choosing to function in various desirable ways we are preserving the emphasis on choice and autonomy that was basic to the spirit of Rawls's original proposal. The just society will make sure that people can be well nourished, but will not force-feed them if they choose to fast. And yet, even to say that the abilities to obtain food and to get an education are "primary goods" is to say more about the good human life than Rawls is willing to say.

Another departure seems of special significance for the good of women. In Rawls's approach, the well-off and the less well-off are defined according to the amount of primary goods each possesses. In Sen's approach, where abilities to take action, and not resources, are the primary goods, we can take account of the fact that individuals have varying needs for resources, in accordance with their social and physical circumstances, the special obstacles they face, and so forth. Two people may be given the very same amount of basic resources, and yet end up being extremely unequal in their ability to perform valuable human functions. A woman who, like Saleha Begum, performs hard physical labor eight or ten hours a day needs more food than a sedentary academic. Groups that have suffered from discrimination or oppression will often need special attention if they are to become equally capable of formal learning and of taking part in political and social life. Rawls treats such cases as rare exceptions that can be left to one side. But they are not exceptions, as the lives of women show clearly.

In order to deal with such individual variability, we have to say which functions we care about, and examine the varying needs of individuals in connection with these functions. Rawls's theory, which screens all this out, screens out too much. And its problems are more than usually evident when we consider the special problems of women, both in our own society and, even more urgently, in societies in which their basic nutritional and health needs are not being met.

When we begin to ask what functions are really important, we notice that institutions such as the nuclear family, which neither Rawls nor Okin is willing to question, suddenly need to be examined and justified. For we will have to ask, for example, what might be the consequences for people's capacities and abilities of being raised, or not raised, in a nuclear family. Okin, by ignoring such questions, does not provide a deep enough account of justice and the family.

Putting emphasis on the people's capabilities and what they can actually do, rather than on the resources available to them, raises the specter of paternalism—for if a theory of justice takes a stand about what capabilities are important, it seems to be telling people who may have diverse views of what is valuable in human life what they should be able to do and who they ought to be. How to deal with such objections is an urgent question currently being addressed by philosophers, economists, and others,[23] especially in connection with the attempt to develop a satisfactory approach to improving welfare and the quality of life in developing countries.[24]

If a theory of justice is to be persuasive it must to some extent take a stand on the question of what conditions and ways of acting are good ones, as Rawls does in favor of his short list of primary goods and in favor of autonomy and against mere satisfaction without choice. The question is how comprehensive the conception of good must be, and how neutral among competing religious and metaphysical views.

Even the limited accounts of the human good favored by Rawls and Okin are not neutral when it comes to religious conceptions; indeed, Okin's attempt to extend Rawls's scheme to women would reject as inappropriate to the structuring of public institutions the views about female inferiority that are expressed by most of the world's religions; and Rawls makes a similar commitment, though less explicitly. This kind of non-neutrality is firmly within the traditions of our own liberal democracy, which does not allow religions to justify the practice of slavery or polygamy, and holds the conduct of religious people and groups to standards of public justice in countless other ways. The arguments I have already given would justify an even more comprehensive account of the important human functions, one that would be more accurate in directing resources where they are really needed. What should be clear is that a theory of justice based only on the resources people should have is inadequate when it is not guided by a conception of what people do with these resources.

Such an approach to the problem of justice, in my view, could provide plenty of room for individuals to exercise choice.[25] If public policy takes a stand on the importance of being basically healthy, this still leaves individuals free to live in a very unhealthy way if they so choose; more important, it leaves them free to choose many different ways of life that may all be compatible with basic fitness and health. If public policy determines that the nuclear family in some form is an institution worthy of public support, this still leaves individuals with countless choices to make concerning whether or not to form families, and of what sort. And I suspect that a general theory of good human functioning might leave things more open-ended still, holding that there are a variety of different arrangements by which children may be raised with love and taught standards of justice, and that the capacities of children, rather than the institution of the family itself, are what society is committed to supporting. In giving such support, society should respect the desire of many people to realize these goals in accordance with their traditions and history. In any case, the relative merits of the Rawlsian liberal approach favored by Okin and the different approach emphasizing human "capabilities" that I have described here need much careful consideration before anyone can claim to have an adequate solution to the problems of justice in general, and women's justice in particular.

The story of Saleha Begum had a somewhat happy ending. She not only won the right she fought for, to work for food in the fields alongside men, but she organized the other women workers into cooperative groups that gradually became able to perform a variety of semiskilled tasks, including raising poultry and fish, growing silkworms, and even, in some cases, doing medical, veterinary, and legal work. She learned how to read and write, and eventually organized literacy classes for other rural women; she is now a respected local political leader. Her husband is under contract as "technical expert" to the women's cooperative. But all this has happened in spite of her domestic situation, with no basic change in family institutions that oppress and endanger women like her in every part of the world. Can these institutions, which at their best may be wonderful sources of love and intimacy for both children and adults, be made compatible with justice? Or was Plato right in thinking that real justice among human beings demands more radical measures? Liberalism will not confront these questions if it continues to lack, as it does, a satisfactory account of the human good.

NOTES

1. I take this real-life example from Marty Chen, "A Matter of Survival: Women's Right to Work in India and Bangladesh," in *Women, Culture, and Development*, a volume in the

World Institute for Development Economics Research series, ed. M. Nussbaum and J. Glover (Oxford, UK: Clarendon Press, 1995). The example of Angela K. below is a fictional composite, drawn from the data presented in Okin, chapter 7.

2. Okin draws this point and other related data from Lenore J. Weitzman, *The Divorce Revolution: The Unexpected Social and Economic Consequences for Women and Children in America* (New York: Free Press, 1985). Some of Weitzman's data have recently been challenged—see Susan Faludi, *Backlash* (New York: Crown, 1991), pp. 19ff. But Faludi still finds that pay inequalities in the work force, and the selfish behavior of divorced men, lead to serious economic hardship for divorced women. Criticisms of Weitzman are answered by Okin in "Economic Equality After Divorce," *Dissent*, Summer 1991, pp. 383–87.

3. Amartya Sen, "More than 100 Million Women Are Missing," *The New York Review of Books*, December 29, 1990; see also Sen, "Gender and Cooperative Conflicts," in *Persistent Inequalities*, ed. Irene Tinker (New York: Oxford University Press, 1990); Jean Drèze and Amartya Sen, *Hunger and Public Action* (Oxford, UK: Clarendon Press, 1989), pp. 46–64; and Sen, "Gender Inequalities and Theories of Justice," in Nussbaum and Glover, *Women, Culture, and Development*. Okin discusses the particular problems of women in developing countries in "Justice, Gender, and Differences," in *Women, Culture, and Development*.

4. Michael Sandel, *Liberalism and the Limits of Justice* (Cambridge, UK: Cambridge University Press, 1982), discussed in Okin, chapter 2; Roberto Unger, "The Critical Legal Studies Movement," *Harvard Law Review* 96 (1983), and also published as a monograph by Harvard University Press; also Roberto Unger, *Politics: A Work in Constructive Social Theory* (Cambridge, UK: Cambridge University Press, 1987), part I, both discussed by Okin in chapter 6.

5. See especially Sen, "Gender Inequalities and Theories of Justice," in Nussbaum and Glover, *Women, Culture, and Development*.

6. Gary S. Becker, *A Treatise on the Family* (Cambridge, Mass.: Harvard University Press, 1981), discussed by Okin in chapter 7; and in more detail by Sen in "Gender and Cooperative Conflicts," in *Persistent Inequalities*, and "Gender Inequalities and Theories of Justice," in Nussbaum and Glover, *Human Capabilities*.

7. Allan Bloom, *The Closing of the American Mind: How Higher Education Has Failed Democracy and Impoverished the Souls of Today's Students* (New York: Simon and Schuster, 1987), discussed in Okin, chapter 2. I discuss Bloom's treatment of issues concerning women in "Undemocratic Vistas," *The New York Review of Books*, November 5, 1987.

8. J. S. Mill, "Nature," from *Three Essays on Religion in The Philosophy of John Stuart Mill*, edited by M. Cohen (New York: Random House, 1961); see also the excellent treatment of this topic in Peter Singer and Deane Wells, *Making Babies: The New Science and Ethics of Conception* (New York: Scribner's, 1985).

9. Alasdair MacIntyre, *After Virtue* (Notre Dame, Ind.: University of Notre Dame Press, 1981), and especially *Whose Justice? Which Rationality?* (Notre Dame, Ind.: University

of Notre Dame Press, 1988). See my review of the latter in *The New York Review of Books*, December 7, 1989.

10. Okin draws the phrase "shared meanings" from Michael Walzer, *Spheres of Justice: A Defense of Pluralism and Equality* (New York: Basic Books, 1983); she is highly critical of the traditionalist strand in Walzer's theory, but finds considerable promise in other parts of his view, especially the criticism of dominance and hierarchy.

11. Robert Nozick, *Anarchy, State, and Utopia* (New York: Basic Books, 1974), discussed in Okin, chapter 4.

12. John Rawls, *A Theory of Justice* (Cambridge, Mass.: Harvard University Press, 1971); see also Rawls, "Kantian Constructivism in Moral Theory," *Journal of Philosophy* 77, no. 9 (1980); "Justice as Fairness: Political Not Metaphysical," *Philosophy and Public Affairs* 14 (1985); "The Priority of Right and Ideas of the Good," *Philosophy and Public Affairs* 17 (1988).

13. Okin, "Justice, Gender, and Differences," in Nussbaum and Glover, *Human Capabilities*.

14. Rawls, "Fairness to Goodness," *Philosophical Review* 84 (1975), p. 537, discussed by Okin on pages 91 and 196, note 9.

15. Here, Okin is citing Jane English, "Justice Between Generations," *Philosophical Studies* 31 (1977), p. 95.

16. Rawls, *A Theory of Justice*, pp. 462–63, discussed by Okin on p. 96.

17. This was reported to me in conversation by Päivi Settälä, Professor of Women's Studies, The University of Helsinki.

18. A similar proposal is now endorsed by Richard Posner in *Sex and Reason* (Cambridge, Mass.: Harvard University Press, 1992).

19. See especially Rawls, "The Priority of Right and Ideas of the Good."

20. See Rawls, "Kantian Constructivism in Moral Theory."

21. Sen, "Equality of What?" in *Choice, Welfare and Measurement* (Oxford, UK: Blackwell, 1982); I have made related arguments (with further references to other work of Sen's) in "Aristotelian Social Democracy," in *Liberalism and the Good*, ed. R. B. Douglass, G. Mara, and H. Richardson (New York: Routledge, 1990). The entire issue is very well summarized in David A. Crocker, "Functioning and Capability: The Foundations of Sen's and Nussbaum's Development Ethic," *Political Theory* 20, no. 4 (November 1992), pp. 584–612.

22. "Capability"—by now a standard term in the literature of economics and development—is intended to be the modern equivalent of the Aristotelian term *dunamis*, meaning, very generally, that condition in virtue of which one is *able* to do something. Some capabilities are internal "capacities" but many include states of the world external to the person's own condition. For example, the capability of voting

includes but is not identical to the internal capacity for making political choices: for it also includes being given the rights and privileges of a citizen.

23. It is being pursued by the International Development Ethics Association (IDEA), and also by the project on women and the quality of life at the World Institute for Development Economics Research (WIDER) of the United Nations University.

24. An example of the work of IDEA is Crocker's paper "Functioning and Capability"; the WIDER material will appear in *The Quality of Life*, ed. M. Nussbaum and A. Sen (Oxford, UK: Clarendon Press, 1992); and in *Women, Culture, and Development*, ed. M. Nussbaum and J. Glover (Oxford, UK: Clarendon Press, 1993).

25. Here I am summarizing the longer arguments I made in "Aristotelian Social Democracy," *Liberalism and the Good*, and also in "Human Capabilities, Female Human Beings," in Nussbaum and Glover, *Women, Culture, and Development*.

# CHAPTER TEN

# Divided We Stand

WILLIAM J. BENNETT (1995), The Book of Virtues: A Treasury of Great Moral Stories

How do we learn good character? Aristotle argued that we must begin with good "habits," meaning not mindless behavioral conditioning, but patterns of increasingly intelligent choice guided by attachment and love. A child is initiated into good choices, in the first place, through the love and the gratitude of family attachments. But as age brings greater independence and the need for greater critical discernment, a central role will be played by paradigmatic examples of virtue, and those examples will be given in poems, stories, and dramas. Reflecting on these examples, often in the company of the parent, the child becomes increasingly adept at identifying real life situations that call for courage or friendliness or justice or generosity. And the fact that the child learns to associate these examples with intense love for the parent lends them a radiance that exercises, in later life, a special power.

William Bennett thinks that Aristotle is correct. He also believes that the project of forming good character can and should be undertaken in a democracy independently of political debate about the issues that divide us. Despite the many vexing issues that separate us, he argues, we can agree in a general way about the traits of character that distinguish a good person and a good citizen; and it should not be greatly controversial to say that these traits ought to include compassion, self-discipline, courage, honesty, perseverance, responsibility, the capacity for friendship, some sort of faith in goodness. And if we focus on the cultivation of these common traits, we will do better at the deliberative resolution of the divisive questions—better, for example, than if moral instruction is left entirely to religious or ethnic traditions that seem to differ about the fundamentals of morality.

In order to form character in this democratically shared way, Bennett continues, we must recover paradigms that we once shared as a nation, before the triviality of television absorbed most of our children's attention, and before a prevailing cynicism made virtue seem laughable. And for this we need to think Aristotelian thoughts about stories and poems, building a conception of "moral literacy" for citizenship by gathering for parents the inspiring and character-building exempla on which earlier generations of Americans cut their moral teeth. This anthology of poetry, fiction, and philosophy is intended for parents to read with their children, selecting materials suited to the child's age and understanding.

Bennett's book comes wrapped up in a package that suggests a narrow ideological focus: a sentimental Norman Rockwellish cover, blurbs on the back from Margaret Thatcher (intelligent), Rush Limbaugh (abysmal), Roger Staubach. And of course Bennett's name will at once call to mind his bullying public manner and his unsubtle touch with many subtle issues. The reader may expect, therefore, crude moralism, and open the text eager to have a few laughs at Bennett's expense. This, it turns out, would be a big mistake. There is some awful stuff here, and there is some simplistic flag-waving stuff. But the project as a whole compels respect; and Bennett is revealed to be more complicated, and more passionately justice-driven, than many people will have understood him to be.

Let me put my cards on the table. I had an upbringing like the one that Bennett envisages. My father had many of Bennett's tastes in moral stories. He did not share, I hasten to add, the treacly Hallmark Card side of Bennett's pedagogy, but he certainly did share Bennett's emphasis on fortitude and sacrifice. To this day the smell of the sea is inexorably linked, for me, with an image of my father carrying me out to swim beyond the breakers, and both of these memories are bound up with William Ernest Henley's "Invictus" (a poem inexplicably omitted here). "Out of the night that covers me / Black as the pit from pole to pole": that severe pounding call to virtue, that joyful praise of the "unconquerable soul," is now forever mingled in my mind with the intense joy of those moments of love and adventure. So I agree with Bennett that these are the things that make one's responses to adversity. And if we let such lines be replaced by "Beavis and Butt-head"— or, at a more elite level, by an aesthetic preference for ironic distancing—we will quickly become a nation impoverished in citizenship.

Anyone who remembers Bennett as an arch-foe of "multiculturalism" will be surprised to discover that this is a fairly multicultural book. To be sure, its heart is firmly in the Western tradition, and in the American tradition above all; but there are also African and Native American folktales, Hindu, Buddhist, and Chinese texts, and very many works by, and about, women. The history of slavery and the history of race relations in the United States play a central role in the entire project. This material is scattered, and doesn't really succeed in conveying to children a sense of the world as a complex whole consisting of societies with richly different traditions. And yet there is the basic acknowledgment that "moral literacy" involves an acquaintance with the present and the past of other nations, and with the minorities within one's own nation. The reader experiences some astonishment, since the capacity to learn from his opponents never seemed to be one of Bennett's most salient traits. But there are even greater surprises in store as we proceed.

To illustrate the book's organization, which proceeds from the simple to the complex within each virtue, let me describe the section on compassion; it is among the best in the book, and a model of how such a project should be done. Bennett's introduction, in clear and simple language, presents the basic idea that compassion "is a virtue that takes seriously the reality of other persons, their inner lives, their emotions, as well as their external circumstances." Drawing deftly on Rousseau, Hume, and Josiah Royce, Bennett argues that the power of compassion to put oneself in the place of another lies at "the very heart of moral awareness," and inspires the desire to relieve want and suffering. He concludes by pointing out that the major obstacles to compassion are the forces of "animosity and prejudice," including "the divisive isms'. . . : racism, sexism, chauvinism and the rest." Is this really the Bennett that liberals love to hate?

Bennett now takes his cue from Rousseau, and begins with tales of kindness to animals—continuing on through several folktales and fairy tales to James Baldwin's retelling of "Androcles and the Lion," Andersen's "Thumbelina" and "The Little Match Girl," a fine version of "Beauty and the Beast," the rescue of Moses, the Good Samaritan, and, after other like things, on to the material for older children—Portia's speech on mercy, an extract from Dickens's *A Christmas Carol*, a story by Tolstoy, O. Henry's "The Gift of the Magi," a poem by George Eliot—and, moving on to greater reflectiveness, Aristotle's analysis of pity from the *Rhetoric*. Next, introducing Whitman's powerful "Vigil Strange I Kept on the Field One Night," Bennett observes that "true compassion runs deeper than the kind of grief in which we know only our own pain from another's death. True compassion seeks to understand . . . the tragedy dealt to a life suddenly lost." In the spirit of that thought, we turn to Lincoln's wonderful letter of consolation to Mrs. Bixby, who lost five sons to the Union cause; then to Whitman's "O Captain! My Captain!" and, expanding the scope of reflection to the general idea of poverty and need, Emma Lazarus's "The New Colossus." The material is enticing for the young reader, exhilarating for the more mature one.

The section ends with a remarkable extract from Tocqueville, which argues that compassion will not flourish where institutions do not work against hierarchy. For if people are not made equal by laws and institutions, how will they come to see themselves in one another, or view themselves and their fellow citizens as vulnerable to misfortune in similar ways? Thus American democracy, with its leveling of distinctions, offers the fairest hope for the virtue of compassion, for "the more equal social conditions become, the more do men display this reciprocal disposition to oblige each other."

Bennett's preface to the passage concludes: "we are forced to ask ourselves: How does modern America measure up to the portrait he painted more than a century and a half ago?" The child who gets to this thought—by a path that has led her through the Civil War and the anti-slavery cause and the ethnic migrations of the early twentieth century—will have a lot of questions here. (And not only the questions about race and ethnicity that Bennett repeatedly raises, but also questions about gender that he raises less frequently, questions about poverty and class that he raises only indirectly, and questions about sexual orientation about which he is completely silent.) How indeed have our institutions promoted, or failed to promote, the kind of equality that makes compassionate citizenship possible?

This sort of questioning is evidently what Bennett, in his Aristotelian mode, means by virtue. This is a conception of civic virtue that may seem to some readers difficult to square with the politics of Rush Limbaugh and Margaret Thatcher. But his book is not always this interesting. There is the problem, for a start, of Bennett's uneven judgment about poetry. There are many fine things, from Donne and Shakespeare to Blake and Emily Brontë and Emily Dickinson and Tennyson and Walt Whitman to Yeats and Frost. And Bennett is right to feel that some lesser classics, such as Emerson's "Concord Hymn" and Emma Lazarus's "The New Colossus," are still morally powerful. Let us grant him, too, his decision to stick to the past. (He cites the staggeringly high fees charged to reprint recent verse. Could this be the vice of stinginess?) But, even granting Bennett his premises, there is entirely too much poetry of the sentimental school—sometimes by reputable figures (Longfellow's "The Children's Hour") and sometimes by writers of doggerel, such as Ella Wheeler Wilcox ("Laugh, and the world laughs with you"), the deservedly obscure Laura E. Richards ("To the Little Girl Who Wriggles") and above all the rebarbative Edgar Guest ("Only a dad with a tired face, / Coming home from the daily race").

To paraphrase Wilde, one would have to have a stomach of stone to read these lines without nausea. If we took out all dross of this sort, we would have room for Whitman's "When Lilacs Last in the Dooryard Bloom'd," Blake's "Jerusalem," Stephen Spender's "I think continually of those who were truly great," Dylan Thomas's "Do not Go Gently," Wilfred Owen's "Strange Meeting"—and even for poems in which the child who wishes to think more about religion can get a sense of what religious joy may be in a life, at a level deeper than banality. There are peculiar prose omissions, too (no Thoreau, no Mill, no Gandhi), that could be remedied by a corresponding excision of banalities.

But the large amount of *Reader's Digest* material is not just an accident. I have so far described Bennett's project as Aristotelian. This is true, but not the whole story. Bennett has another side. It would be too imprecise, and too flattering, to call this other side Tolstoyan, but Tolstoy's argument in "What Is Art?" comes to mind. This other side of Bennett is exercised less by the ideal of an education aimed at reflective habits of choice and passion, and more by a conviction of moral simplicity, by a view of art as a force that unites people across divisions of race, gender, religion, and class through the simple power of basic moral sentiments. This side of Bennett is closer to the populist, demagogic, eternal-verities sort of conservatism by which he made his name.

And so Bennett is divided against himself. The complicating Aristotelian ideal and the simplifying populist ideal are deadly rivals, and Bennett, complicated character that he turns out to be, is pulled this way and that between them. In *The Book of Virtues*, one comes upon a kind of vulgar Tolstoyanism for Americans, according to which virtue entails a rejection of the complex and formally exacting in art and in ethics, a rejection of all that cannot be readily grasped by a child's simple faith. According to this conception, the moral poetry of Hopkins and Eliot and Owen and Spender—and even Donne, Blake, and Whitman, who are currently included—will have to go, to be replaced by Edgar Guest and Kipling and Service and (a superficial reading of) Frost.

Thus, the rhetorical complexities of Whitman's "Lo, the most excellent sun so calm and haughty . . . / the gentle soft-born measureless light" must yield before "Only a dad, but he gives his all / To smooth the way for his children small." For Whitman's stanza works on many levels, weaving its metaphysical and political and sensuous tapestry in language that challenges and divides, divides not only the educated reader, from the naive reader but also the reader who fought for the end of slavery from the reader who did not, the reader who thinks Whitman's radical democratic thoughts through to their conclusion from the reader who does not. Guest's homily, by contrast, does not divide, because it does not reach very deep into the recesses of personality, because its language is too bland to promote real thought. Poetry of this sort is a safe accomplice of conventional and unexamined moral assumptions. It prefers an easy unity of feeling to the hard puzzles of moral reflection.

Similarly, the philosophical complexities of Tocqueville and Aristotle and Aquinas and Plato and Rousseau give way in many parts of Bennett's book, and not only the parts intended for younger children, before folktales whose moral lessons are easily available to the untrained intellect. For philosophical argument, like really good poetry, also divides, in the sense that it requires an exacting effort of mind and promises no single, shared destination, no end to perplexity. It asks instead that the shared sentiments be subjected to the rigorous scrutiny of reason. And this is precisely the scrutiny that the simplifying populist must mistrust.

Aristotelian moral art, by contrast, begins from the idea that the moral life is an enormously difficult affair that requires us to cultivate great powers of discrimination, and surprising precision in passion. It originates not in faith but in wonder, at the complexity and the variety of life and of oneself. And this wonder is linked with joy, for the Aristotelian finds complexity and variety to be sources of delight, not sources of disgust. The real-life heterogeneity of human moral action is welcomed as a challenge to understanding and empathy, not banished as a barrier to a comforting sensation of certainty and unity. And wonder is also linked with a love of logic and clarity, with the conviction that rigorous thinking is the right way for a human being to respond to the mysteries of life. What an Aristotelian, not least an Aristotelian in America, wants from art is not, then, anything simple. Her interest in wonder will make her seek out and embrace poetry that sends a chill down the spine or makes tears stand in the eyes. And she will insist on combining poetic education with philosophical argument, knowing that even very young children make distinctions, and that it is never too soon to warn the young not to take moral truths on trust.

Bennett's book, as I say, is essentially torn between these poles. Thus the reader may be going along reading the Tolstoy-approved folktales and hymn lyrics, and suddenly find herself in the middle of Whitman or Shakespeare or Donne. Here are texts that testify to a simple, uniting type of faith, and there is Jefferson's instruction to his nephew that he examine the stories of miracles in the Bible exactly as he would scrutinize similar tales in the histories of Livy or Tacitus. And this tension in Bennett is closely linked to another one, between political quietism and a prophetic demand for justice.

The Tolstoyan conception supports, on the whole, a moral conservatism and a simple optimism about possibilities. Perseverance and loyalty and compassion and brotherhood are all at its core; but not the impassioned struggle for earthly justice. For if, indeed, the core of the moral life is a simple faith that can be conveyed to all without the rigors of education, then the struggle to extend educational opportunities bulks less large in one's idea of society; and if rich and poor, free and slave, peasant and landowner can alike attain to the summit of the moral life, and if the moral life is the core of our earthly life, then, once again, these differences seem to make little difference. The Aristotelian conception, by contrast, with its emphasis on the complexity of living well, the need for exacting education and the importance of material conditions for education and hence for virtue, supports a vigilant activism toward the equal extension of these possibilities for personal cultivation and for citizenship. (Aristotle himself, of course, did not extend these possibilities to women and slaves; but his approach to human capability has radical social implications.)

Thus it should come as no surprise to discover that this book, which announces from the start its determination to convey optimism and hope, wavers between a *Reader's Digest* optimism about the moral life and a more strenuous hopefulness. Simple patriotism and crude flag-worship are certainly in evidence, but there are also signs of a more exacting ideal. Bennett is repeatedly drawn to—almost obsessed by—stories of people who risk their lives or safety for a cause they believe to be right: Nathan Hale facing death at the hands of the British, Father Maximilian Kolbe volunteering to die in Auschwitz to save a stranger's life, Martin Luther proclaiming his defiance of his adversaries and his faith in his "mighty fortress," Mary Wollstonecraft asserting the dignity of Reason against the forces of prejudice, Susan B. Anthony fighting for the right to vote.

There is social radicalism in this brand of courage. Bennett knows it, and it grips him. Even his flag-waving has its radical side. His central exhibit here is Barbara Fritchie, who defied Stonewall Jackson out of her dedication to the Union: this was not knee-jerk patriotic sentiment, it was reasoned heroic defiance, connected to a moral imperative against slavery. Beneath his book's stale veneer of conservatism (and even inside it, as we see in the story of Vice Admiral Stockdale reading Epictetus in the POW camp so that he won't betray his men), it is this sort of heroic defiance for the sake of the just that Bennett most passionately wants to impart to his young reader. Bennett's public persona has often suggested an indifference to the claims of the weak, but here he is revealed, decisively if unevenly, to be profoundly concerned with justice and equality.

He is preoccupied, in particular, with the history of slavery, and he takes the struggle for racial equality in this nation with a seriousness that undercuts many of the book's more complacent utterances. The story of Harriet Tubman, writings of Frederick Douglass and Booker T. Washington and Lincoln, the story of Rosa Parks, writings of Martin Luther King: these are all to be found in Bennett's pages, and they promote a prophetic indignation about complacency, and encourage the young to reflect that conventional pieties may not be the stuff of true virtue. Introducing Douglass's scorching indictment of American conduct—"There is not a nation of savages, there is not a nation on the earth guilty of practices more shocking and bloody than are the people of the United States at this very hour"—Bennett writes, "Here is a brave soul holding America accountable for its sins." Will Bennett's conservative following be pleased by this judgment?

Sometimes Bennett tries to reconcile this prophetic tradition with the conservative tradition by suggesting that these American trespasses are all in the past, that we can now all feel good for having gone beyond them. But he cannot really accept this, for he has a sound instinct for the presence of injustice, and a love of the liberty of mind that confronts it. This tension emerges in an especially fascinating way in his treatment of Martin Luther King. The "Letter from the Birmingham Jail" and the "I Have a Dream" speech are quoted in full, and Bennett's prefaces confer upon their author a central stature in our national history. On the other hand, Bennett concludes his introduction to the "Dream" speech this way: "His soaring refrain of 'I have a dream' still inspires the American conscience. His perseverance and eloquence were rewarded." Where, pray tell? In this world, or in the next?

But then the reader reads the speech, and is encouraged by the paradoxical nature of Bennett's own preface to linger over the following lines: "We cannot be satisfied as long as the Negro's basic mobility is from a smaller ghetto to a larger one. . . . No, no, we are not satisfied, and we will not be satisfied until justice rolls down like waters and righteousness like a mighty stream." So the message once again is: question, be brave, take risks for justice, do not be satisfied.

Bennett's book contains a more Aristotelian vision of virtue and a more prophetic vision of America than its packaging lets on; and his ambivalence about this vision is itself an American ambivalence. For this country is historically and essentially divided between a desire to live by simple sentiments and a strict love of liberty. I hope that the parents who use this collection will remind their children, in Martin Luther King's words, that they "stand on the warm threshold which leads into the palace of justice," and that the threshold is still warm. Then they might skip "Only a Dad" and substitute a reading of "Invictus," or Blake's "Jerusalem."

# CHAPTER ELEVEN

# Looking Good, Being Good

ANNE HOLLANDER (1994), Sex and Suits: The Evolution of
Modern Dress; PHILIPPE PERROT (1994), Fashioning the
Bourgeoisie: A History of Clothing in the Nineteenth Century;
GILLES LIPOVETSKY (1994), The Empire of Fashion: Dressing
Modern Democracy

For many fashion-conscious Frenchmen, the triumph of the dark suit,
imported from England, was a source of national shame and aesthetic
distress. "The sun's rays have disappeared," wrote a Parisian journalist
in 1869, "giving way to the lugubrious shadows in which our tailors
envelop us." Another more vitriolic writer was quick to envisage the demise
of the hated costume:

> O . . . black suit . . . borrowed from perfidious Albion who inflicts it on
> every rank from a Peer of the Three Kingdoms to a Street Sweeper. . . .
> I won't miss you, dull, banal black suit that everyone wears on every
> occasion. May you disappear forever. May you emigrate with an export
> subsidy, go away threadbare, and, giving up the ghost through your broken
> buttons, may you metamorphose into a tabard on the back of a London
> cabby or on the rump of a Congolese or Zanzibarian as black as you. . . .
> The black suit is dying: . . . the black suit is dead!

In one way, this prediction has been a staggering failure. The suit is
alive and well. It is the costume of respectable dress for heads of state,
businessmen, lawyers, criminal defendants, and in a form remarkably little
changed from that of its Anglo-Parisian ancestor. In another way, it has
come true: for suits, without ever having left Paris, have taken up their
"export subsidy" and have moved to every nation of the world, replacing
traditional national dress for many functions connected with the serious
business of life.

What explains this remarkable stability, or, as Anne Hollander calls it, "the staying power of male tailoring"? No deliberate preservationist or antiquarian effort can be found, Hollander argues. It appears that we must look to human desire for the answer. The Parisian suit-hater left out one profound fact, which Hollander's scholarship produces: in their confident, forceful elegance, in their modern simplicity of line, in their remarkable ability to combine a look of virtuous personhood with a look of sleek and easy animality, suits are very sexy.

Hollander's brilliant, funny, exuberant essay is neither a straightforward history of dress nor a philosophical analysis of fashion. In its nonlinear manner, however, it suggests a thesis of serious political interest. It is commonly claimed that the ideals of personhood and equality that we owe to the Enlightenment lack motivational power. This is so, it is alleged, because these ideals are too abstract, too remote from our memories and dreams and wishes, to grip us and to inspire real passion. (This alleged lack during the Enlightenment is frequently mentioned to explain, or even to justify, the resurgence of interest in forms of local and ethnic identity.) Hollander's witty praise of the suit is, I think, a playful and yet serious defense of the Enlightenment against these charges.

Many men and women, Hollander suggests, have managed to remain passionate about equality and personhood in a way that transcends boundaries of class and gender and nation. This is partly because they have managed to embody these ideals in shapes that appeal to the erotic imagination, playfully combining aspiration with sex and humor, virtue with the delight of line and shape. In the enduring sexiness of the suit, we may read the triumph of Kantian ethics.

Before we examine Hollander's case for this unexpected thesis, we had better begin with the story told in Philippe Perrot's more pedestrian volume, a history of clothing in Paris during the nineteenth century, since Perrot tells a simple story of the rise of the suit, which Hollander will partly accept and partly undermine. *Fashioning the Bourgeoisie*, which was published in Paris in 1981 and now appears in Richard Bienvenu's fine translation, is filled with fascinating detail, but its argument is not complicated. By the middle of the nineteenth century, the French bourgeoisie had attained sufficient social and economic influence to dictate the course of fashion (which had been around as an institution for several centuries). The bourgeoisie prided itself on the virtues of thrift, responsibility, and self-control. The suit, dark, stiff, and austere, expressed the new self-image of the bourgeois male: men abandoned the "fashion game" of the old aristocracy to join "the inexorable tendency toward somberness and severity." Meanwhile, women, more frivolous beings, continued to be adorned, thus serving to demonstrate, as ornamental objects, the prosperity of the men who kept them. In this way men could manifest both thrift and opulence. The dress of both sexes became a form of male self-display.

Bourgeois dress manifested bourgeois virtues. At the same time, to a remarkable degree, it effaced distinctions of class and rank. The rise of ready-to-wear clothing made it possible for an astute male to look elegant, and males began to look all the same when dressed for serious business. With the democratization of attire went the democratization of shopping, as both sexes flocked to the newly created department stores, where one could wander and look and desire without pressure or demand. This gave equality another boost. The cultivation of consumer fantasy, Perrot argues, encouraged respect for the dignity and the freedom of each person's imagining. Those too poor to buy no longer had to stand outside, nose pressed to the window; they could consume in thought and they could touch, even when they could not purchase.

Perrot tells this story with a wealth of documentation that is frequently more interesting than the commentary it receives. He gives us rich details about the personal hygiene of this apparently fastidious middle class. (The medical rule was *saepe manus, raro pedes, nunquam caput*, "the hands often, the feet seldom, the head never"; and the habit of bathing more than once a month indicated "a certain indolence and softness that ill suits a woman.") We learn a great deal about the history of gloves, of footwear, of female and male underwear, including their laundering. (Perrot finds no evidence of laundry receipts for male undergarments, even in the most extensive of lists. One source comments that "information on underpants which have been worn for a long time is too vague to be used.") We learn that it was controversial whether male flannel underwear dulls sexual sensitivity by constant friction, or arouses it by an "electrogalvanic effect," as was maintained in a treatise of 1855 called "Study of the Action of Flannel in Direct Contact with the Skin."

As such a title shows, the issue of sex is never far away when clothing is the subject. In a particularly fascinating section of his book, Perrot shows us that nineteenth-century Paris had a way of discovering sexual pathology in the most apparently pleasurable and normal clothing-related activities. While bourgeois dress expressed (as Perrot sees it) an ascetic indifference to sexuality, the sexual vagaries of shopping and shoppers became the object of a medical discourse of obsessive complexity. The crowded department store was seen as a "compulsive, feverish, sensual" environment, in which the observer could discern manifold varieties of surreptitious male caressing of women. ("First come the 'gropers,' casual and haphazard, not yet fully corrupted. . . . Somewhat worse are the 'frotteurs,' easily recognized by their glances from top to bottom directed primarily toward women's necklines and bosoms. . . .")

Women, meanwhile, manifested the characteristically female pathology of hysteria. Given the sensuous appeal of clothing on display, this frequently expressed itself in compulsive shoplifting. (One wealthy woman stole 300 ties from a display stand; her house yielded 248 pairs of pink gloves.)

Interviewing 104 women accused of such thefts between 1868 and 1881, Dr. Legrand du Saulle made the following diagnostic analysis:

"Pathological" Thefts

| | |
|---|---|
| Very feebleminded: | 4 |
| Hysterical lunatics: | 9 |
| Hemiplegic lunatics: | 2 |
| Totally paralyzed lunatics: | 5 |
| Senile lunatics: | 5 |
| Total: | 25 |

"Semipathological" Thefts

| | |
|---|---|
| Hysterics, 15–42 years old, apprehended at the time of their menstrual periods: | 35 |
| Hysterics of the same age but not in their menstrual periods: | 6 |
| Girls or women hereditarily predisposed to mental illness (with a greater or lesser number of hysterical symptoms): | 24 |
| Women at menopause or seriously weakened by uterine hemorrhages: | 10 |
| Pregnant women: | 5 |
| Total: | 80 |

Foucault would have reveled in these classifications. Perrot has nothing much to say about them. He does not ask about those remarkable "totally paralyzed female lunatics" who somehow manage to pilfer alluring objects from Bon Marché. (Suits perhaps, their alleged stiffness and immobility matching the lunatics' condition?) He does not ask why, in the long career of female vice, there should be a crime-free interval between the age of 42 and menopause—a question of urgent philosophical interest to some readers. (Do women of this age look especially closely at men's suits, internalizing the lessons of virtue they afford?) And why are all these women who prowl department stores so bursting with pent-up sexual feeling (even when they are seriously weakened by uterine hemorrhages) if men, indistinguishable in their funereal suits, have never looked more boring?

For the answer to that question, we must turn from Perrot to Hollander. Hollander agrees with Perrot about a part of the story of nineteenth-century fashion: about the role of fashion in undercutting distinctions of class and rank, about the rise of ready-to-wear clothing as an opportunity for people of all ranks to look elegant. She takes a similar interest in the rise of consumer culture as an ally of democratization: each shopper, encouraged to devise forms of individual expression, becomes, far more than the original designer, the primary creative agent. But the story that Hollander tells about women and men is far more complicated than Perrot's, and more convincing. It is, above all, the story of the dark suit, which Hollander sees as a triumph of modern design, not as a dull anti-fashion dropout.

She urges that we begin with an undeniable fact: the suit looks wonderful. Flattering to almost any height and shape, moving easily and draping itself with grace as the wearer sits or rises, the "abstract tripartite envelope" is "relentlessly modern in the best classic sense." It is, moreover, "thoroughly erotic." (And she notes that this is so from points of view different in place and time.) Whereas earlier fashions in male dress had drawn attention to the clothing itself, displaying the beauty of the costume rather than the man, the suit's "careful fit without adornments, on the other hand, emphasizes the unique grace of the individual body—indeed creates it, in the highest tailoring tradition."

Hollander does not deny the connection of the suit with bourgeois ideals of virtue and sobriety. But she gives even this part of the story a complicated pedigree. Suits do, in a way, allude to austere ideals—say, the simplicity and the muted color of clerical dress. But they also contain allusions to military dress, and this, she insists, is a part of their lasting appeal: "Such a creative combination of opposites—the easy roughness of practical war gear blended with the reticence of clerical clothing—has had a lasting power over the masculine sartorial imagination."

And the suit's allusions to ideals of virtue are not exhausted by its references to clerical garb. Hollander's cover displays a nude Greek statue of a young man, with the powerful physique and the small genitalia by which classical sculpture traditionally suggests the virtue of moderation. It is one of Hollander's most original claims that the suit is, in effect, the nineteenth century's way of recreating this neoclassical ideal. Using wool, known as the common fabric of antiquity, and itself a "sculptural medium" able to "follow and complement the shapes and movements of the wearer's body without buckling and rippling," tailors constructed a costume of truly classical simplicity, referring to classical ideals of balance, naturalness, artlessness, moderation, and even rationality.

Just as nudity, for the Greeks, was the dress of personhood—the face and its expressions, undiminished by distracting decoration, showing, as Plato put it, the "traces of the soul"—so the suited man, with his muted colors and matte finish, became, paradoxically, more of a distinct moral character by virtue of his suited sameness to other males, his individual excellence becoming not less but more important against the simple background. At a formal evening occasion, when men wore suits and women each wore a different decorative gown, the women were individuated by their costumes, and their souls were lost, "as if the same doll were dressed in many different ways," whereas men were all soul, so to speak, in their apparently monotonous black and white.

The suit is the costume of virtue. It is also, Hollander has said, thoroughly erotic. This combination seems to be what explains, in her account, the staying power of the suit, and thus its contribution to serious social issues. But how should we understand the combination? Hollander expresses the relationship between the suit-as-virtue thesis and the suit-as-sex thesis in more than one way, and we must try to get clear about the connection. Does the suit make only superficial reference to ideals of virtue, its primary message being erotic? Does it refer only or primarily to ideals of virtue, though one may still see through to the body beneath? And if the suit refers to virtue and to sex, are these separable elements in the overall package, or does the suit eroticize virtue itself?

We can easily see that Hollander does not intend to claim that the suit's reference to virtue is merely superficial: she insists, consistently and vigorously, on the centrality of neoclassical ideals of excellence for the suit's design and success. We can also quickly conclude, I think, that the suit, in her view, does not refer only to virtue, while merely permitting the viewer to imagine the body. Hollander does suggest this idea at times, writing exuberantly of the way in which suits in motion reveal traces of the limbs beneath. But look closely at this fine sentence: "Knees and elbows pushed casually through the cloth, creating a few spare folds that echoed, with an austere and flattering rhythm, the easy dignity of the wearer's natural demeanor." This suggests that the eroticism of the suited body is no mere coincidence: it is created by tailoring itself. The sentence suggests, further, that in Hollander's view the suit eroticizes virtue. The same rhythm that is "austere" is at the same time "flattering," and the "easy dignity" characteristic of neoclassical virtue is also extremely sexy—as Hollander elsewhere puts it, the ease of an animal at home in its own skin.

I think that Hollander means to claim both that the suit eroticizes virtue and that it contains also some separate animal references. Like the nude statues that are, oddly, its archetype, suits make virtue seem sexy, by revealing it as housed appropriately in a forceful and well-balanced body. The young nude male of classical sculpture was an object of desire precisely because he looked so virtuous. (The old-fashioned speaker in Aristophanes' *Clouds* bemoans the fact that the youth of today, having lost old-time habits of virtuous self-discipline, look soft and sexually unattractive.) In a similar way, the suit, precisely by displaying its wearer as not a sensualist but as a moral agent of dignity and integrity, barely conscious of his body though it does indeed from time to time push through the cloth, makes him extremely alluring.

This effect is heightened by the way that the suit makes references to animality as well as to personhood. Because of its naturalness and its easy looseness by contrast to earlier male costumes, the suit creates—along with the image of the classical nude—the image of the sleek lounging animal, whose skin drapes easily around its powerful muscles and bones. The two images coexist in "a nonchalant counterpoint," creating a being who is remarkably complete, not only as a subject but also as an erotic object. (What more could one want than stable virtue allied to sexual power, rational integrity with knees and elbows?)

Hollander does not say so, but we can see here a powerful representation of a long-enduring ideal of marriage. Surely, the puzzle of the suit's longevity is bound up with the enduring appeal of that institution. The suit announces that one can harmoniously combine sexual fascination with stability, and that the combination brings not stress but relaxed delight. One might conjecture—though this takes us beyond Hollander's argument—that the lasting attraction of the suit is the lasting attraction of this profound human wish.

This brings us to the subject of women. Hollander's story of the rise of the suit is told as part of a larger story about the changing relationships between male and female costume. If (as I have extended her account) the nineteenth century's suited male embodies the contradictions of bourgeois marriage, only the twentieth century creates the possibility of a marriage between equals. As Hollander's discussion of the ball shows, the decorated female on the arm of the suited male is, in a sense, a more primitive creature than he: a dressed up doll on the arm of a person. Perrot saw the decorated woman only as an occasion for the display of male wealth. Hollander, as usual, sees more deeply.

She discerns in the wish to enclose women in yards of distracting drapery a deliberate if not fully conscious design to deny women full membership in the moral community. While the suit is adult and modern, women's dress infantilized and at the same time generalized them, deflecting attention from the signs of the soul to ribbons, bows, flounces—all feeding "the pernicious feeling . . . that women aren't ordinary persons, each naturally a human mixture." The concealment of female legs in particular reinforced mythic stereotypes of the woman as mermaid—human in voice, face, bosom, hair, neck, and arms, but beneath the yards of cloth a mysterious unseen region of oceanic unclean animality.

Hollander vividly tells the tale of the rise of truly modern female clothing, the liberation of legs by pants and short skirts, the creation of the classic female suit, "its brand of sexuality . . . similarly adult and essentially self-respecting, rather than exuberant, boastful, infantine or perverse." Although she recognizes that men can help themselves to decorative accoutrements that were for a long time taboo, she insists, plausibly, that the shape and the cut of acceptable male dress has changed remarkably little (even jeans and overalls are not a radical break from trousers as the suit created them). The big change is that females can now be equal partners in mobility and good tailoring.

Hollander doesn't say enough, I think, about the tensions and the conflicts that go along with this claim to equality, about men's continued demand for women as decorated children even after women have asserted their sartorial adulthood. After all, the "adult and self-respecting" sexuality of Rosalind Russell, Barbara Stanwyck, and Katharine Hepburn in their elegant tailored suits was followed directly by the "boastful, infantine" image of Marilyn Monroe's skirt swirling up to reveal her clenched legs, like the sea-foam billowing round the mermaid's tail.

Nor does women's claim to the attire of male respectability always win recognition in the workplace. To cite a representative example, in a recent court case in Indiana, Mary Carr, the first woman to be employed in the General Motors tinsmith shop, won a large judgment for sexual harassment. A central form of the harassment that she suffered was malicious cutting of the seat of her workman's overalls, as if her claim to that form of equal dress—the suit, so to speak, of that profession (Hollander treats overalls as a close relative of the suit)—constituted an especially keen threat to the self-esteem of her male coworkers.

Hollander's essentially exuberant and upbeat story of the expression of sexual fantasy in dress leaves too little room for the darker aspects of fantasy, its connections with oppression and inequality, its interconnections with struggles having real political and personal stakes. And there are other serious questions that she avoids raising. The worldwide triumph of the suit is treated as essentially a triumph of comfort and sexiness, rather than as a legacy of colonialism, or an outgrowth, more recently, of the dominance of Western-style markets and the related decline of traditional cultures. One need not think those latter economic developments wholly bad in order to feel that they call for moral evaluation. (Hollander is wrong, too, on some points of fact: it seems false that an American-style suit and tie is more comfortable than traditional male dress everywhere. Summer in Calcutta would prove the contrary.)

Hollander says that anyone with good taste can create a good look. But suits themselves are remarkably different from one another. And she does not mention what a really good suit costs—more, clearly, than the vast majority of people in this society can afford. Within the contemporary American context, Hollander does not take much interest in the issues of class that she rightly stresses in her account of the nineteenth century. Certainly it is correct that the suit, when it was introduced, was an equalizer, making the self-made bourgeois indistinguishable from the aristocrat. This is to some extent true today as well. Hollander rightly stresses that people from all origins can express their claims to respectability and status by dressing this way. But there are many walks of life in America in which we do not see suits; and even if she is again right to say that jeans and overalls are relatives of the suit, there are many subtle class distinctions evident in these differences.

Finally, the American culture of consumer fantasy that Hollander celebrates as democratic and delightful has its more questionable aspects. It has a problematic relationship to other aspects of culture, which it may be increasingly subverting. It seems dedicated to the creation of short-lived and ever-changing desires that are not clearly related to deep needs: these desires, in turn, engender a way of life that may well be in tension with the urgent needs of people elsewhere in the world.

*Sex and Suits* is such a captivating book that one's larger moral and political sense is a little narcotized as one reads. But finally the question of the fairness and the goodness of the way of life praised by Hollander cannot be avoided as one reflects, with whatever delight, on what one has read. Still, if Hollander largely ignores moral struggle, she gives even her most ambivalent, moralistic reader a powerful reminder of the fun that people actually have living—and that is not a small part of moral and political life. As Aristotle put it, we make war so that we may enjoy peace: we engage in these urgent moral and political struggles in order to fight for a life that has delight in it, and playfulness, and freedom.

Gilles Lipovetsky's *The Empire of Fashion*, which was published in French in 1987, does tackle these serious questions, but in a peculiar way. In contrast to Hollander's book, his is a terrible bore. It is ponderous, abstract, and gassy in the worst French manner. Lipovetsky notes, like Hollander and Perrot, that the fashion industry has created consumers with continually restless and shifting desires, always searching for the new; and, like Hollander and Perrot, he connects this idea with democracy, stressing the freedom that consumer culture gives to individuals to dream up an identity for themselves. But then he takes a further step. Acknowledging that many of the worst charges against this new culture are true—it has indeed bred nation upon nation of hedonistic narcissists wrapped up in trivial and superficial forms of pleasure—he now boldly asserts that it is this very fact that has enabled liberal democracy to survive in our century, and to extend itself.

How on earth might this be? Lipovetsky's idea is that the greatest danger to liberal democracy is fanaticism, and its expression in acts of individual and group hatred. But consumer narcissists are too busy staring at themselves in the mirror to give themselves over to the politics of hate. They do not wish to interfere with their neighbors, they tolerate their differences with equanimity, because they hardly know that their neighbors are there. The consumer society is an amiable, tranquilized society. (Lipovetsky's portrait recalls the "city of pigs" in Plato's *Republic*.) The paradoxical result is that "behind the scenes of seduction, the Enlightenment is at work; underneath the escalation of the ephemeral, the centuries-old struggle to conquer individual autonomy is under way."

How plausible is this? Like everything else in the book, this thesis is asserted abstractly and without empirical backing. There is no suggestion that the author has considered how such a thesis might be tested. But, like the view that men who masturbate to pornography do not rape, the view that the narcissistic consumer does no harm to others is testable, and ought to be tested. If it were true, for example, we might expect the political culture of California to be unusually free of ethnic and religious strife; but this does not appear to be the case. And we might expect that the advent of consumerism in Eastern Europe would have led to a decline in ethnic and religious violence; but this, too, does not appear to be true. Lipovetsky's proud assertion, made in 1987, that the European democracies are tranquil places of ethnic and religious harmony now strikes even him as a bit off. In a fascinating epilogue to the English-language edition, he grudgingly admits that the past few years have seen a considerable rise in ethnic violence, without any noticeable diminution in consumeristic narcissism. But he brushes this to one side, simply saying that all this violence is trivial, since it doesn't threaten the basic health of democratic institutions.

Still, there is an idea here, and it seems worth pursuing. It does seem possible, at least in principle, that the proliferation of sources of hedonistic self-fulfillment might divert erotic energy away from its noxious forms of expression. The real problem for Lipovetsky is that the culture he imagines and praises is not an Enlightenment culture any more. It is not inhabited by autonomous persons but by slaves of fashion, incapable of deep commitment and deep love. This Lipovetsky finally acknowledges at the end of the book, saying that the social system dominated by fashion will be characterized (or perhaps is so already) by a "tragic lightness . . . a tragic dimension that cannot be eliminated." Fashion may make us gentle to our fellow citizens (if it does); but it seems to prevent us from having lasting fulfillment in personal projects or intimate relationships. "The euphoria of fashion has its counterparts in dereliction, depression, and existential anguish."

This depressing conclusion to a lengthy praise of the fashion world sends us back to Hollander. It makes us wonder how she would respond to Lipovetsky's portrait of fashion and to his confession of doubt. (Or how she has responded, for Lipovetsky's work appears, like Perrot's, in her bibliography.) Hollander would certainly draw our attention once again to the suit as an aesthetic achievement that manifests both modernity and constancy, that partakes of fashion but at the same time rises above it. In Hollander's argument, the suit expresses the yearning of cultures for a marriage of stability with delight, virtue with pleasure. It promises a satisfaction that is more enduring than the fad of the moment. It also allows both men and women to represent themselves as virtuous citizens who demand (and greatly enjoy) such stable adult satisfactions. Finally, it represents virtuous personhood as equal across classes and races and religious groups and national origins and even, now, the sexes.

If Hollander is correct (and I am extrapolating from what she says), we do not entirely need to rely on narcissism to bolster citizenship, for we still have an erotic attraction to civic virtue. Isn't it strange to derive such a serious proposition from analysis of suits? And wouldn't Kant have been somewhat revolted by a defense of his normative notions in these playful, erotic terms? Certainly it is odd, and certainly Kant would have been dismayed; but it seems that he would have been wrong. For people are, after all, complex combinations of personhood and animality, and if it turns out that a basically Kantian ethics can animate that complicated combination, so much the better. (Kant could use some help here from Aristotle, who was more friendly to the body.)

In Hollander's argument, which is both playful and serious, the Enlightenment wins not because we are too auto-erotic to care, but because we have succeeded in eroticizing personhood and equality—not least in the suits we wear, which give rationalist cosmopolitanism a sexiness it might otherwise lack. This is a little too good to be true, and we should not be completely earnest about it, and it neglects many things. But it is not wholly false. Instead of "dereliction, depression, and existential anguish," we can see in our clothes the hope of equal personhood and dignity for all men and women of all nations—with "effortlessly integrated formal design," good tailoring, and knees and elbows pushing through the cloth.

# CHAPTER TWELVE

# Feminists and Philosophy

Louise B. Antony and Charlotte Witt (1993), A Mind
of One's Own: Feminist Essays on Reason and Objectivity

> — *And mustn't there be a type of woman that loves philosophy,*[1] *and another
> type that hates it?*
> — *Yes, both of these.*
>
> Plato, *Republic*, 456A

We'll encounter opposition, won't we, if we give women the same education
that we give to men, Socrates says to Glaucon. For then we'd have to let
women strip and exercise in the company of men. And we know how ridiculous that would seem.

Absolutely, says Glaucon—at least in the light of present practice.

Note, however, that it was not such a long time ago, Socrates says, when
the public calisthenics for men that now seem so natural and admirable
seemed themselves absurdly foreign—for we weren't used to the idea
of men stripping in public. But when we reflected about the reasons for
the change, and decided they were good, then "the appearance of
absurdity ebbed away under the influence of reason's judgment about
the best."[2]

Convention and habit are women's enemies here, and reason their ally.
Habit decrees that what seems strange is impossible and "unnatural"; reason
looks head on at the strange, refusing to assume that the current status quo
is either immutable or in any normative sense "natural." The appeal to
reason and objectivity amounts to a request that the observer refuse to be
intimidated by habit, and look for cogent arguments based on evidence that
has been carefully sifted for bias.

In our own society the arguments of feminists make such appeals to
reason and objectivity all the time, and in a manner that closely resembles
Platonic arguments. We now demand, with Plato, that reproductive
differences between men and women not be taken to be relevant to hiring

unless it can be shown that these differences affect job performance, as it rarely can.[3] We point out that these differences are not disabilities until law and custom treat them in certain ways; and we expect to be heard. Hiring in my own university between 1977 and 1992 was administered under a consent decree resulting from the settlement of a class-action lawsuit that vividly recalls Platonic arguments: for the males who denied tenure to a prominent female anthropologist held that her new type of scholarship, which concentrated on women, was theoretically weak.[4] The women prosecuting the class-action lawsuit did not hesitate to argue that by objective criteria (above all, the judgment of outside experts) this was not the case. The *claim* of objectivity had been used as a screen to mask mere prejudice against the new and strange. Critical to the case was this distinction between a pretense of objectivity and real objectivity. And so, at Brown as in Athens: "the appearance of absurdity ebbed away under the influence of reason's judgment about the best."

And yet today reason and objectivity are on the defensive in some feminist circles. We are frequently told that reason and objectivity are norms created by "patriarchy," and that to appeal to them is to succumb to the blandishments of the oppressor. We are told that systems of reasoning are systems of domination, and that to adopt the traditional one is thus to be co-opted. Our liberation as women, it is said, requires throwing over the old demand for objectivity and cultivating new modes of reasoning, which are not always clearly specified, but which are frequently taken to involve immersion in a particular historical and social context, and to be closely allied with some form of cultural relativism. Several distinct ideas have been involved in the attack—for example, the idea that traditional norms of objectivity insulate from criticism judgments about women that are false and politically motivated; and the idea that detachment from context is bound up with a traditionally male denigration of intimacy, emotion, and the body. I shall later return to these ideas, some of which have considerable merit.

The assault on reason has now reached the citadel of the alleged enemy: for feminists within philosophy itself have recently been very vocal in calling for the demotion of reason and its replacement by some different, politically more advantageous norm. Things have gone so far that the American Philosophical Association's *Newsletter on Feminism*, in a special issue on feminism and rationality, published (along with some admirable articles) a piece by Ruth Ginzberg, who teaches philosophy at Wesleyan University, alleging that *modus ponens*, one of the basic laws of logic,[5] was a male patriarchal creation oppressive of women.[6] The argument seemed to be that *modus ponens* is a male-invented way of defining who counts as a rational being, and that women very often (more often, it is suggested, than men) fail to recognize *modus ponens* as a valid form of inference. Indeed, Ginzberg generalizes, women tend to find "formal symbolic systems" "alien" and "foreign."

A related article in the same issue argues that the logic of the Aristotelian syllogism is "wonderfully fitted to hierarchical modes of thinking," because it separates the *form* of an argument from its material content. Since females have traditionally been linked to matter, males to form, this emphasis on form contributes to the marginalization and subordination of women.[7] One might have thought that such arguments would seem to any feminist retrograde maneuvers, capitulations to the worst denigrations of women as empty-headed and illogical. To some feminists, at least, they did not.

The feminist assault on reason is troubling because the arguments in its favor are for the most part weak, as I shall shortly argue, and because these arguments uphold a picture of women that feminists have worked for centuries to overturn. Nor do these weak arguments advance the political goals for which some feminists may favor them. For a mirror image of the assault on traditional conceptions of objectivity has recently been mounted by some conservative thinkers against the very norms of academic freedom and academic objectivity to which women in today's academy must look for the defense of their employment. For example, the eminent legal scholar Michael McConnell (a professor of law at the University of Chicago) has recently argued that professional organizations should not insist on the usual standards of objective judgment in academic hiring, and the usual norms of academic freedom, in their dealings with religious institutions.

These standards of objectivity, he claims, at least as currently realized, are sectarian and parochial, creations of a narrow liberal tradition. In some religious institutions, McConnell writes, standards of truth and reason require reference to "authority, community, and faith, and not just to individualized and rationalistic processes of thought."[8] Religious institutions are entitled to use these standards to deny jobs to those who do not conform. Liberals, he concludes, cannot claim that their standards of truth and objective judgment must take precedence in making academic judgments. In another article, McConnell explicitly invokes the aid of deconstruction to make these points, arguing that "the central insight of post-modernism is the exposure of liberalism as just another ideology"; relying on this insight, religion can confidently put forward its own criteria of truth.[9]

It seems unwise for a feminist to ally herself with McConnell's position on reason and truth, since this position could all too easily be used to defend the firing of women who criticize the position of their church on feminist issues. Yet by espousing deconstructionist ideas, many feminist academics have zealously denied that objective standards can be defended. If those ideas were convincing on other grounds, one might have to put up with these difficult practical consequences. But one certainly should not favor them for the sake of their practical consequences—as frequently happens, I believe, in feminist debate. And, as I shall shortly argue, the ideas are in fact far from convincing.

The issue raised by McConnell is of immediate concern to women in philosophy. In 1990, the national board of the American Philosophical

Association proved unable, after lengthy debate, to pass a simple resolution opposing discrimination in hiring, promotion, and publication. Some religious institutions protested that they wished to support a different resolution exempting them from the anti-discrimination provisions, which mentioned race, gender, religious affiliation, and sexual orientation among the impermissible grounds of discrimination. (The version that was finally passed was a compromise, allowing these institutions to discriminate only on the grounds of religious affiliation, and not where such membership was defined in a way that entailed any other form of forbidden discrimination.) My point here is not about the relationship between religion and feminism. The opposition to women's equality has many sources in our society, and in many cases religious traditions have been major sources of support for women's progress. What I am claiming is that the opposition to women's equality, whether in secular or in religious dress, derives support from the claim that traditional norms of objectivity are merely a parochial liberal ideology. Women in philosophy have, it seems, good reasons, both theoretical and urgently practical, to hold fast to standards of reason and objectivity.

Why, then, have they not done so? Why is the assault on reason so attractive to some feminist thinkers? Four reasons, I believe, can be offered for the trend. First, these feminists, like many other critical social thinkers, have been influenced by French theorists such as Jacques Derrida and Michel Foucault, and by their criticisms of reason. To my mind perversely, they believe that these positions, which try to reduce reasons for a conviction to causes of that conviction and claim that arguments merely reflect the play of social and political forces, have in them something liberating and politically progressive. But one might reflect that if argument is to depend on the play of forces, the weaker will always lose. What the weak seem to require is a situation in which reason prevails over force, and is given special respect. The deconstructionist might now reply that, as a matter of fact, this never happens, and it is liberating at least to recognize this fact. To this one should say that the descriptive claim seems false—and that to make such dire claims as if they reflected inevitable truth is likely to make them come true, by leading people to relax their vigilance about standards of argument.

Second, feminists working in philosophy note that the philosophical tradition has existed alongside patriarchal and oppressive institutions. Then, in a fallacious form of argument that one might designate *cum hoc, ergo propter hoc*, they blame the philosophical tradition for these abuses—even though some of the philosophers in the tradition were social radicals who argued vehemently against them, and still others provided in their thought the bases for a critical assault on unjust practices. Nor do they consider the historical analysis forcefully put forward by J. S. Mill in *The Subjection of Women*, according to which women's situation becomes far worse in eras mistrustful of reason and argument. It is hard enough at any time, Mill writes, to convince people of something that goes against their deeply entrenched interests and threatens their power. It is impossible to do so when they spurn the very mechanisms of reasoned persuasion.

Third, feminists note that males who wish to justify the oppression of women have frequently made a pretense of objectivity and of freedom from bias in sifting evidence, and have used the claim of objectivity to protect their biased judgments from rational scrutiny. More than a little perversely, some feminists have blamed this behavior on the norm of objectivity itself, rather than on its abusers.

Finally, a number of interesting philosophical criticisms of traditional norms of reason have recently been made within philosophy—concerning, among other issues, the role of human interest and desire in inquiry, and its cooperative or communal character; concerning, as well, the contribution of the emotions to good reasoning about personal and political choice. These issues are thought to have some relevance to feminism. Only this last point seems of any intellectual interest, and I shall return to it.

All this time, there have been many women in philosophy doing good work, along more or less traditional lines, in metaphysics, epistemology, moral and political philosophy, and the history of all of these. Many of these women are, politically, strong feminists. Thus they have been increasingly troubled by the strident claims of other feminists (both in and outside of the profession of philosophy), wondering whether there really is, as is claimed, something politically retrograde in their own activity. But at the same time they remained convinced that these charges were misguided, that traditional philosophical work, its traditional methods and also its traditional texts, still had a valuable role to play in feminism.

*A Mind of One's Own* is a collection of essays by women who are prominent in philosophy today and who wish to confront recent feminist criticisms of philosophy. Most of the contributors are under fifty and widely respected; most grew up with strong political ties to feminism. Few have written much about feminist issues in their work, and it is a question whether they would have achieved success had they done so. (Reason may not be male-biased, but many philosophers who use it certainly have been, and the profession has remained one of the most male-dominated in all of the humanities.) These women now ask: Are we right to feel, as we do, that reason and objectivity, the traditional "tools of our trade" (as the editors write) have important contributions to make to the lives of women who seek full equality?

The collection is important because women in philosophy have too long been silent about the question it poses, embarrassed by the shortcomings of some feminist philosophical work but reluctant to criticize people with whose politics they have much sympathy. The book is also distinguished by the quality of its contributors. On no previous occasion have so many of the most interesting female thinkers in philosophy contributed to a single book dealing with feminist issues. Most of the contributors tend to pull their punches, spending pages to say politely that a certain piece of anti-reason feminist writing fails to make some elementary distinction, or makes a basic logical error. For example, Margaret Atherton is too patient with writers who collapse the distinction between rationalism and empiricism; and Sally Haslanger spends ten pages showing that Catharine MacKinnon confuses being objective with pretending to be objective when one is not. Several other articles fail to reach the generally high standard of the collection. One should, I think, admire the motives of the editors, who describe their goal as promoting tolerance and respectful dialogue, while criticizing them for being on occasion excessively tolerant.[10]

The book begins with essays examining traditional writers in the "canon" of Western philosophy, and arguing, as the editors put it, "that the thought of traditional philosophers is rich with possibilities for feminist interpretations." Oddly enough, there is no essay on Plato or Mill—it is both a strength and a weakness in the collection that contributors write on whatever interests them most, without much regard for an overall plan. Marcia Homiak contributed a richly suggestive essay on Aristotle, a thinker of remarkable misogyny who has nonetheless recently come to be of great interest to feminists in both philosophy and the law.[11] Homiak eloquently shows the reasons for this interest, investigating Aristotle's norm of a life lived in accordance with reason. Unlike some modern pictures of reason prevalent in economics and elsewhere, the Aristotelian view, Homiak argues, does not neglect the role of emotions in practical reasoning, nor does it neglect the importance of attachment and affiliation in a complete rational life. On the other hand, it insists that this life of affiliation—marriage, friendship, citizenship—be lived in accordance with a plan endorsed through reflection; in this way it provides a model for feminists eager to endorse the emotions while also affirming the values of self-respect and self-determination.

Although this is not central to her argument, I wish that Homiak had taken the opportunity to be more critical of the traditional opposition between emotion and reason on which the denigration of emotion she mentions is based. Aristotle certainly gives good arguments for seeing this opposition as oversimple. And one reason he believes that anger, pity, and other emotions are so important to good reasoning is that he thinks these emotions themselves contain reasoning. (A part of being angry, for example, is to have the belief that one has been wronged.) But in general Homiak's essay goes to the heart of some of the more interesting feminist criticisms of traditional norms of reason; for she shows that the tradition itself has rich resources for the criticism of some accounts of reason that feminists have found impoverished.

A similar demonstration of the richness of the "canon" is to be found in Annette Baier's article on Hume, which argues that Hume's idea of reason as a natural embodied faculty can help us investigate some of the interesting questions feminists have asked about traditional ideas of intellectual detachment. According to Baier, Hume argues that reason is not a quasi-divine faculty, but a natural embodied capacity that human beings share with other creatures who learn from experience. He anticipates the modern feminist argument that human "norms, including norms for acquiring language, are social in their genesis as well as in their intended scope." Later in the book, Helen Longino, a philosopher of science, develops this very line of argument (though without reference to Hume), emphasizing the importance of social context and shared standards in acquiring scientific knowledge. Baier's claim for Hume's relevance to current feminist projects thus receives strong support.

Hume and Aristotle have often been invoked in feminist argument. It might seem to be a more difficult matter to reclaim more austere philosophers such as Descartes and Kant, whose views have frequently been denounced by feminists as based on culturally male standards of detachment and cold rationality. And yet Margaret Atherton convincingly argues that Descartes's arguments for a genderless reason separated from and not determined by the nature of the body were in fact sources of strength for women aspiring to equality. On the whole, the rationalist idea of a fixed human essence, far from promoting women's oppression, helped to advance their equality. For if we are not more than what we are made to be by society, and women appear to be different, then they are different; but if we all have an inalienable rational core, then that core may be seen to exert moral claims even on those who would deny its presence. This is the very argument in favor of Cartesian rationalism that was long ago made by Noam Chomsky, who might have been mentioned in this connection. Atherton gives the argument a firmer historical basis, and shows its continued appeal.

Finally, in an especially fascinating article, Barbara Herman, a leading moral philosopher, devotes her attention to Kant. Herman has elsewhere effectively defended many of Kant's basic moral ideas about respect, virtue, and what it means to be a person.[12] Here, therefore, she attempts the much less promising task of defending his ideas on sex and marriage. Kant's evident misogyny and disdain for the body have caused feminists to dismiss his arguments without seriously considering them. But, Herman argues, Kant's thinking about the possibilities of exploitation inherent in sexuality should be taken seriously: in his *Lectures on Ethics* and his *Metaphysics of Morals* he correctly points out that sexual interest in another's body frequently blocks respect for the other as a person, leading the person to be treated as a thing. The prospect of sexual pleasure, furthermore, also leads people to volunteer to be treated as things. Sexual activity involves mutual surrender and thus, for Kant, the conversion of persons into things. Legal institutions, in his view, should intervene to protect the status of the parties as persons. Marriage, for him, is the way in which law intervenes to define the parties to a sexual relationship as equal persons, thereby blocking the natural tendency to treat people as objects, and so to exploit them. The rules of care and support in marriage produce an artificial structure of moral regard by making sexual relations possible only where there are secure guarantees of concern for the other person's life and the acceptance of obligations with respect to that person's welfare.

Whatever we may think of these ideas, Herman argues, we must admit that they deserve the most serious scrutiny of feminists. Indeed, they anticipate the conclusions of some contemporary feminists,[13] while connecting those conclusions to a deeper analysis of personhood and equality. Feminists, Herman suggests, should be skeptical of Kant's solution to the problem— for they may judge, with good reason, that marriage has all too frequently promoted and protected the exploitation and the thing-like treatment of women.[14] Nonetheless, a modern critical analysis of sexual relations, marital and non-marital, can learn much from his diagnosis.

The most interesting essays in the rest of the collection offer eloquent defenses of aspects of traditional philosophy that have been severely criticized by feminists. Elizabeth Rapaport addresses the arguments of feminists who hold that out of respect for the differences among groups of women we should reject the concept of "woman" as a universal notion, and avoid claiming that women are members of a class whose oppression has certain common features the world over.[15] Concentrating on the work of Catharine MacKinnon, who has frequently been criticized for her "essentialism," she defends MacKinnon's appeal to such universal claims in moral and also legal argument, holding that a legitimate concern to emphasize differences should not cause us to deny common features—such features, for example, as sexual subordination and vulnerability to sexual violence—in the oppression of all women. Recognition of such common elements is frequently important to both moral and legal argument. But Rapaport should, with MacKinnon, go further: we need not only a concept of woman, but also a universal concept of the human being in order to say clearly what women need and what has been denied them. MacKinnon's well-known statement that "being a woman is not yet a way of being a human being"[16]—that is, that women are not granted the status of human beings—derives its argumentative force from a rather Kantian (or Platonic) notion of a common humanity that underlies gender and gives rise to claims of equal rights: "Being a tree is not yet a way of being a human being" has no moral force; it is only against a background assumption that women are indeed human (have needs, capacities, and rights similar to those of men) that the claim that their way of life is not fully human has moral force.

To invoke a notion of "the human being" is to engage in metaphysics— though not necessarily a type of metaphysics that seeks standards outside human experience. And feminists who regard all universal notions with suspicion have also put under suspicion the entire activity of doing metaphysics, which we might loosely describe as the activity of analyzing, the most general concepts that we use in talking and thinking about anything whatever, concepts such as cause and effect, substance and property, and so forth. Feminists have been particularly suspicious of concepts that appear central to feminist analysis: the concept of the human, the concept of the individual, and the notion of binary opposition or contrast. It has been claimed that the universal concept of the human being ignores morally salient differences among groups, and frequently imposes a male norm on women; that emphasis on the individual neglects values of mutual help and care that women rightly prize; and that binary contrasts are generally used to cordon off or marginalize groups that lack power.

Charlotte Witt—the author of one of the best books recently written on Aristotle's *Metaphysics*[17]—argues strongly that recent feminist criticisms of metaphysical analysis have been badly misguided. To the extent that they make interesting criticisms of the metaphysical tradition and some of its central notions, they have done so by using metaphysical analysis themselves. MacKinnon, she notes, employs her own concept of the human being and human self-realization: but because it is tacitly employed, it is never subjected to full critical analysis.

Carol Gilligan, in her famous criticisms of male norms of reasoning, also offers a contribution to our understanding of what it is to be human—namely, to value care for others and relatedness with them as well as justice and autonomy. This is a view, Witt writes, that would be much easier to assess rationally, and either accept or reject, if it were straight-forwardly presented through an ethical argument, with appropriately rigorous metaphysical analysis—rather than suggested obliquely through summaries of Gilligan's empirical research.

Empirical studies of gender differences are not sufficient to tell us what is good for either males or females, since we have no reason to think that the people being studied were brought up in circumstances designed to realize their best traits. Witt concludes that postmodernist thinkers such as Richard Rorty and Jean-François Lyotard, who have suggested that it is liberating to stop doing metaphysics, are simply wrong: rigorous argument promotes liberation by showing us clearly what in our practices is merely a matter of habit and what has a more powerful justification. And no postmodernist thinker has succeeded in showing that the distinction between good metaphysical analysis and bad, between rigorous and sloppy analysis, can no longer be used in the age in which we live. In short, the blanket rejection of metaphysical analysis, and even of essentialism, is a perilous theoretical position for feminists, and leaves them without the resources to make a convincing radical critique of unjust societies.

In "Quine as Feminist: The Radical Import of Naturalized Epistemology," Louise Antony confronts the central charge of the anti-analytic feminists: that traditional epistemology has been inherently male-biased in conceiving of reason as a faculty that enables us to grasp a reality which exists independently of human history and human concepts. As Atherton's article on Descartes already indicated, it is not at all clear that this traditional picture should be viewed as hostile to feminism; detachment from history can sometimes bring liberation. But Antony believes that there is more to be said about the charges against traditional epistemology. First, she makes the obvious point that the feminists who make the charge are way behind the times: for many years there have been few defenders of a strong form of metaphysical realism, according to which truth consists of correspondence to pre-articulated, "given" reality. Most prominent analytic philosophers have criticized that picture in one way or another, giving human faculties some role in constructing not just the conditions of knowledge but also the categories under which objects are objects of knowledge.

She then makes the equally obvious point (which still bears repeating) that the old norm of objectivity was in a sense more attractive for feminists than the norms that feminists now defend. For if we could get to the real truth by purifying ourselves of all social and historical influences, and if this were a project that had any real hope of being achieved, then arguments in favor of women's equality and dignity would be, at least in principle, easy to assess. If, on the other hand, we grant (persuaded by the arguments of W. V. O. Quine, Nelson Goodman, and others as well) that history, culture, and human interests always color inquiry in one way or another, we saddle ourselves with the much more subtle and tricky task of demarcating, in any inquiry, between the legitimate and valuable historical and cultural influences and those that are not so valuable. We run the risk that many will despair of accomplishing the task; they may suppose that the search for knowledge really is nothing else but a kind of power-seeking, in which ideology in effect displaces epistemology. This extreme conclusion is not warranted by any of the more convincing antirealist arguments. That is why post-modernist accounts, for example, that of Stanley Fish, are especially defective.[18] But those accounts raise a serious issue concerning the role of interests in knowledge. Therefore, to answer such people, we require an epistemology that separates legitimate from illegitimate human interests.

Having defined this task, Antony's essay does not attempt to carry it out. And I doubt whether Quine's thought has the resources to carry it further. Strongly influenced both by a form of behaviorism that would now not find much support even within cognitive psychology, and by an equally uncritical form of sociobiology, Quine does not offer subtle or fruitful insights into these social questions. Here one might have expected Antony to discuss the contributions of the American pragmatists, of the pragmatist-influenced work of Hilary Putnam, and of the work of Jürgen Habermas on the Continent. For these thinkers provide what Quine does not: an account of how human interests might be sifted and critically examined, in order to produce a process of knowledge-seeking that, while not free from interest, is free from illegitimate bias.

These themes are taken up—though with references to the Anglo-American social contract tradition of Locke and Hobbes, rather than to Habermas or Dewey—in Jean Hampton's fine essay, "Feminist Contractarianism." While developing her own version of social contract theory, drawing on both Hobbes and Locke, Hampton, an especially original and resourceful moral philosopher, argues that this tradition as a whole has rich resources for addressing feminist concerns about exploitation and manipulation. She concurs with Herman that their sort of concern for the underlying social contract need not signal a neglect of love and human relations. While one would be wrong to use a contract idea to evaluate bonds of love directly, such a concept can enhance these bonds instrumentally by making the parties aware of social imbalances and injustices that might ultimately subvert their relationship. It is only when the demands of distributive justice have been met, Hampton argues, that love can truly flourish.

The essays in this book testify to the richness and diversity of philosophical feminism and of female philosophizing. And they testify to something else, which Witt explicitly states, and several other contributors show without stating: that doing feminist philosophy is not really something different from doing philosophy. (Hence, I think, the sometimes tantalizing quality of the collection, which opens up more issues than it can resolve, leading the reader to want to read each of the contributors' more systematic work.) To do feminist philosophy is simply to get on with the tough work of theorizing in a rigorous and thoroughgoing way, but without the blind spots, the ignorance of fact, and the moral obtuseness that have characterized much philosophical thought about women and sex and the family and ethics in the male-dominated academy. It is in this way and no other, I think, that women in philosophy can go beyond the past achievements of males.

Answering a hypothetical opponent who charged that women have contributed nothing much to philosophy, J. S. Mill replied that philosophical creativity is not a spontaneous outpouring of untutored genius. It is an achievement that requires mastery of both the tradition and one's own disciplined rigorous practice within it. Women will achieve much in the field, he says, when that sort of mastery of traditions and practices is opened to them.[19] This is now happening, and it deserves recognition.[20]

But there is general agreement on campus that the existence of the guidelines very much improved the quality of both male and female faculty members, largely because of the requirement of public advertisement and search, which prevented weak departments from perpetuating themselves through informal hiring methods. For a description of the Lamphere case, see Louise Lamphere, "'Not So Much Worse Than Others': Forging a Career in the Context of Title VII Suit," manuscript on file with the author, Department of Anthropology, The University of New Mexico.

NOTES

1. Strictly speaking, my translation contains a redundancy: literally, the Greek says, "that loves wisdom," and "love of wisdom" is what philosophy is.

2. Plato, *Republic*, 442A-D. The best recent account of this section of the *Republic* is in *Plato: Republic* 5, translation and commentary by S. Halliwell (Warminster: Aris and Phillips, 1993).

3. Compare *Republic* 451D-E, where Socrates gets Glaucon to admit that female dogs are not considered to be incapacitated for all other tasks by the fact that they sometimes bear and suckle young.

4. The Title VII class action suit, initiated in connection with the tenure case of Louise Lamphere, resulted in a settlement that granted tenure to Lamphere and two other female faculty members who had been denied tenure, and a cash settlement to another who had been terminated earlier. A monitoring committee was set up to supervise hiring, tenure, and promotion at Brown, requiring that all jobs be duly and publicly advertised and that departments carefully document their search procedures, giving reasons for not hiring the best of the available female and minority candidates. It has been my experience that no statement in good faith of reasons for not hiring a candidate is denied out of a mechanical concern for minority and female hiring. (My own department, which has since 1984 had two tenured women, has recently hired six males in a row, with perfect justice so far as I am able to see, and with no impediment from the university.)

5. *Modus ponens* is the inferential form: if P, then Q; P; therefore Q.

6. Ruth Ginzberg, "Feminism, Rationality, and Logic," in *American Philosophical Association Newsletter on Feminism and Philosophy* 88, no. 2 (March 1989), pp. 34–39; see also Ginzberg, "Teaching Feminist Logic," same issue, pp. 58–62.

7. Vance Cope-Kasten, "A Portrait of Dominating Rationality," in *American Philosophical Association Newsletter on Feminism and Philosophy* 88, no. 2 (March 1989), pp. 29–34.

8. Michael McConnell, "Academic Freedom in Religious Institutions," in *Freedom and Tenure in the Academy*, ed. William van Alstyne (Durham, N.C.: Duke University Press, 1993), pp. 303–24; see the eloquent reply by Judith Jarvis Thomson and Matthew W. Finkin, in the same volume, pp. 419–29, which makes use throughout of appeals to reason, logical distinctions, and traditional philosophical analysis. McConnell replies to Thomson and Finkin in an unpublished response on file with the author. I note that one might agree with McConnell's conclusion without agreeing with this aspect of his reasoning: for, without granting that standards of objectivity are parochial and mere "ideology," one might grant on grounds of religious liberty that religious institutions should be in some cases exempt from those standards. This was in fact a central line of argument in McConnell's article.

9. Michael McConnell, "'God Is Dead and We Have Killed Him!': Freedom of Religion in the Post-Modern Age," *Brigham Young University Law Review*, Part 1 (Winter 1993), pp. 163–88. On a close reading of his argument McConnell does not finally embrace deconstruction; he argues only that its insights might be used to support religious freedom. McConnell's argument about tradition and religious freedom is subtle and complex; the reader should be aware that I have presented only a small and not altogether representative part of it.

10. This judgment should not be interpreted to apply to all the articles I do not explicitly discuss.

11. See, for example, Nancy Sherman, *The Fabric of Character* (New York: Oxford University Press, 1989); Linda Hirshman, "The Book of 'A,'" *Texas Law Review* 70 (1992), pp. 971–1012, with response by Richard Posner, 'Ms. Aristotle,' pp. 1013–17.

12. Barbara Herman, *The Practice of Moral Judgment* (Cambridge, Mass.: Harvard University Press, 1993).

13. Herman shows close links between Kant and the arguments of Andrea Dworkin in *Intercourse* (New York: Free Press, 1988).

14. Mill, I note, was on target here, arguing that the absence of laws against marital rape rendered a woman's status in marriage worse than that of the lowest slave.

15. For one influential example of the position Rapaport criticizes, see Elizabeth Spelman, *Inessential Woman* (Boston: Beacon Press, 1988).

16. Statement quoted by Richard Rorty, "Feminism and Pragmatism," *Michigan Quarterly Review* 30, no. 2 (Spring 1991). MacKinnon has since acknowledged the remark.

17. *Substance and Essence in Aristotle* (Ithaca, N.Y.: Cornell University Press, 1989).

18. I criticize Fish's arguments and those of Jacques Derrida in "Skepticism about Practical Reason in Literature and the Law," *Harvard Law Review* 107, no. 3 (January 1994).

19. J. S. Mill, *The Subjection of Women*, chapter III.

20. I wish to thank the following people for comments that contributed to the revision of this piece: Elena Kagan, Ruth Barcan Marcus, Michael McConnell, Richard Posner, David Strauss, Cass Sunstein, Judith Jarvis Thomson.

# In response to:

*Feminists and Philosophy,* from the October 20, 1994, issue

*To the Editors*:

Martha Nussbaum's review [*NYR*, October 20, 1994] of *A Mind of One's Own* deeply misrepresents the stated intentions of the editors of the volume, Louise Antony and Charlotte Witt. Although they share Nussbaum's skepticism about arguments connecting gender to notions of reason and rationality, they were concerned, as she clearly is not, to represent those arguments in the words of their proponents. The volume was conceived as a conversation between these two positions, something one would not guess from Nussbaum's review.

Rather than refer to any of the papers that most clearly present the revisionist side of the argument (aside from mine, there are those of Genevieve Lloyd and Robin Schott; they are the only papers Nussbaum does not discuss), Nussbaum offers her own speculations about what might motivate such arguments, and refers to two contributors to a newsletter. In one of those cases, she seriously misrepresents the views of the author, Ruth Ginzberg. Ginzberg, a philosopher who regularly teaches logic, is concerned to think through the resistance many of her students show to logic, with the aim, as she clearly states in the piece to which Nussbaum refers, of helping them to claim the tools of formal reasoning as their own and to be empowered in their use—for precisely the reasons Nussbaum gives. Such caricaturing of views is problematic enough on its own terms; in this case it takes the place of any critical discussion of the more contentious papers in the book under review.

Contributing to this volume, including participating in the conference that the editors organized as we were preparing our essays, was enormously rewarding. It was especially useful for me to be engaged seriously by other feminists and philosophers whose views are so deeply different from my own. No matter how negatively Nussbaum may have judged my paper or the others she didn't discuss, it would have far better served feminism and philosophy to have acknowledged that such a conversation, and not the promotion of one side of it, was the point of the book she was reviewing.

NAOMI SCHEMAN
Professor of Philosophy
University of Minnesota
Minneapolis, Minnesota

*To the Editors*:
It is surely boring to readers of these pages to read the lament that one has been misinterpreted, but it is also a little bitter to experience such distortion, especially at the hands of someone whose work I so much admire. Martha Nussbaum rightly observes that I think much of the theory of logic has some complicity in the subordination and marginalization of women, and then she somehow attributes to me the view to which I myself am objecting by explaining part of how it came to be sustained, the view that women are "empty-headed and illogical" (p. 59).

How she arrived at this attribution is very unclear, for she offers not a word of explanation. Omitting some prosaic possibilities as uncharitable as the language she employs, it may be that the key is that neither she nor I would be writing about these matters if there weren't something to worry about. I would surmise, furthermore, that we would agree on the generalization that women (and men, for all that goes) have at least as much ability to reason as is required by "logic," by theories about what is rational thinking.

What there is to worry about then is that "the subordination and marginalization of women" has involved both the refusal to recognize women's rationality and the unwillingness to provide even reasonable opportunities for its training, development, and employment. Whether or not "logic" is an accomplice to these disrespectful and wasteful practices, as I argued it was, the upshot is that at least some women sometimes accept the cultural stereotype of themselves as illogical, that they sometimes shun encounters where "logical argumentation" is the coin of the realm, that they sometimes develop an attitude toward logic that resembles the so-called "math phobia," and so on. If women come to think of themselves as "illogical" in these contexts—let alone what some men might be encouraged to think—these are real, if not unmixed, losses, and their consequences are indeed often something to worry about. And I would not have written for an essentially feminist publication if I did not think women are powerfully capable of worrying about these things in deeply and genuinely rational ways—including the development of more adequate theories of logic.

VANCE COPE-KASTEN
Department of Philosophy
Ripon College
Ripon, Wisconsin

*Martha Nussbaum replies:*

First I wish to express my personal respect for Naomi Scheman. Her perceptiveness and analytic sharpness are well known; I can think of few people whose comments, questions, and observations are as stimulating. It was largely because I believed that the article by Scheman in the Antony/ Witt collection did not give a fair representation of Scheman's philosophical ability that I omitted discussion of it.

I did not misrepresent the intentions of Louise Antony and Charlotte Witt. Indeed, I showed the manuscript of the review to them, and to all authors in the volume whose articles I discussed at any length, and revised it after taking account of their comments. I then read a second draft of the review at a session of the Society for Analytical Feminism with both editors and a number of the authors in attendance; again I was alert for criticisms, and revised the piece in response to some of them. I remained critical of Antony and Witt's decision to include some pieces of what I consider to be inferior work for reasons of balance, and I made that difference plain.

The Antony/Witt volume had a peculiar feature: the anti-reason positions that most of the articles were criticizing were not the positions of the "dissident" philosophers represented in the collection (with the exception of Lloyd, who was criticized in Atherton's paper). I chose to focus on the debate between the pro-reason essays and their target, rather than on the (sometimes idiosyncratic) positions represented in what I thought the weaker essays. The feminist debate over reason and objectivity is fruitful, and I hope it will continue. I do have a position in that debate, whose expression in the review should not have come as any surprise. I have criticized postmodernist attacks on reason and objectivity in print for about ten years. In recent years, furthermore, in the course of work on issues concerning the status of women in developing countries, I have observed the frequency with which such attacks on reason (and also on Enlightenment universalism) have been used to discredit feminist attacks on local traditions that subordinate them. These experiences have confirmed me in my conviction that feminism needs to be able to avail itself of robust notions of reason and objectivity. (See especially "Human Functioning and Social Justice: In Defense of Aristotelian Essentialism," *Political Theory*, 1992.) I repeated those points in the review.

Ruth Ginzberg's short essays on feminism and logic, which I discussed, are all I know of her work. Since Ginzberg is currently looking for a job (a fact of which I was unaware when I wrote the review), it is important to state that I have no intention of impugning her work generally; indeed, I have heard much good of her, as teacher and as writer. I trust that prospective employers will pass an unbiased judgment on the totality of her work. I think that the 1988 articles are unsuccessful. Although her writing is not always terribly clear, I am convinced that I characterized their argument correctly. Ginzberg writes that she herself is personally convinced that the inferential pattern called *modus ponens* (if *p*, then *q*; *p*; therefore *q*) is valid. On the other hand, she reports that female students in her classes have trouble seeing its validity more often than do male students. Her conclusion is that we should consider broadening our notion of logic to include the thinking of these women, who usually get branded irrational because *modus ponens* is taken to be definitive of the rational. She writes: "*As well-trained philosophers, though, we should realize that the mere fact that a young undergraduate can't describe the phenomenon of human reasoning upon first being asked the question is not* evidence in favor of the claim that *her* perception of the phenomenon is wrong" (emphasis in the original). She then refers to some other feminist critiques of reason and logic, and says that she can't help thinking that these criticisms are right.

In a recent interview in the *Chronicle of Higher Education*, furthermore, asked about her position in the *modus ponens* articles, Ginzberg is quoted as saying that "philosophy might do better to expand its definition of what counts as rationality"—presumably, once again, by admitting as rational what is usually taken to be illogical and therefore irrational. So I think that I have characterized the project correctly: only what Ginzberg calls a broader notion of the rational is what I would call the irrational, if it involves entertaining the possibility of doing without *modus ponens*. Indeed, notice, Ginzberg's own argument has the form of *modus ponens*. (If female students tend to have trouble with *modus ponens*, logic should be broadened to include the ways they think; female students do have trouble with *modus ponens*; therefore. . . .) Without that inferential form, which has not been challenged even by nonstandard logics, I don't see how Ginzberg or her students or anyone else can think or speak. Furthermore, I am skeptical of her alleged facts. Neither I nor any other teacher of philosophy I know has had Ginzberg's experience of a gender disparity with respect to grasping *modus ponens*. If there is something about Ginzberg's position that I have missed, all I can say is that I did my best to interpret the materials before me.

Cope-Kasten, like Ginzberg, offers a reconceptualization of the logical, with the intention of making logic more hospitable to women and their interests. His way, though well-intentioned, is even more perverse than Ginzberg's: he writes that the Aristotelian syllogism is oppressive of women because it separates the form of reasoning from its matter. (Traditionally, he says, women are associated with matter, men with form.) But if one cannot separate consideration of the logical form of an argument from the consideration of the truth or falsity of its premises, one is unable to think or argue. That distinction is fundamental to all reasoned discourse, both male and female. If I say: "All women are illogical; *W* is a woman; therefore *W* is illogical," I make a formally valid argument, but it is unsound because its first premise is false. If, on the other hand, I argue, "All mothers are women, $W$ is a woman, therefore $W$ is a mother," I make an invalid inference from true premises. Without this distinction there is no room for any reasoned criticism of anything, much less of bias and injustice. Therefore the *consequence* of Cope-Kasten's argument, I said (not, of course, his *intention*) would be to reinforce the view that women are illogical.

# CHAPTER THIRTEEN

# Unlocal Hero

KRISTEN RENWICK MONROE (1996), The Heart of Altruism: Perceptions of a Common Humanity; TZVETAN TODOROV (1997), Facing the Extreme: Moral Life in the Concentration Camps

Otto Springer was an ethnic German who lived in Prague during World War II. As the Aryan head of a Jewish firm, he protected his employees while also bribing Gestapo officials and concentration camp guards, forging false documents for Jews and working in the Austrian underground. He rejected an opportunity to be transferred by his company to India, where he might have spent the war in safety. Eventually he was sent to a camp himself, but he continued to work on behalf of others. All in all, Springer saved more than one hundred Jews from imprisonment and death.

Interviewed years later in San Anselmo, California, he denied that there was anything especially virtuous about his character. His morals, he joked to Kristen Monroe, were only slightly better than those of "an average American congressman." If you want examples of altruism, he told her, you should hear about this friend of mine—and he launched into a story of a non-Jewish man who went to the camp along with his Jewish wife, although it had been a marriage arranged to protect her. So why did Springer risk his life to save others? "One thing is important," he told Monroe. "I had no choice. I never made a moral decision to rescue Jews. I just got mad. I felt I had to do it. I came across many things that demanded my compassion."

A frail grandmother with a serious heart condition and braces on her legs and back, Lucille was the poetry editor for her local newspaper. One day in July, while working on a manuscript, she saw a woman, a stranger, being raped outside her window. Nobody else was around at that hour of the day. The ailing woman ran downstairs, screamed, and hit the rapist with her cane while he attempted to choke the victim. Lucille kept on hitting until he loosened his grip. After the victim ran away, she chased the rapist, unwilling to let him escape, and managed to close his car door on his foot. By this time help was on the scene and the rapist was arrested. In an interview with Lucille, Kristen Monroe discovered that she had a long history of such actions in the civil rights movement and in the army. Where did she get this courage? "It's really not a matter of courage," Lucille replied. "It's that you care enough about someone, about the human person, that you feel that you have to help no matter what." Does she have a personal ethical creed that guides her life? "As trite as it is, everything I do every day must always be aware of what's around me . . . always be aware of the humanity around me and what is their cause and what is their need."

Among the most influential accounts of altruistic behavior in our society are those that derive from economics. In a variety of ways, those accounts attempt to explain altruism as consistent with the model of the person as a rationally self-interested actor, maximizing his or her expected utility. Altruism is thus understood as a type of quid pro quo: the altruist acts in the expectation of a return. The return is an actual benefit from the recipient, or an enhancement of reputation or prestige, or the "psychic good" of self-approval and a quiet conscience. This personal utility is taken to be the real goal of the altruistic act, and the act itself only an instrumental means to that goal.

Such accounts have not gone undisputed within economics itself. In an essay called "Rational Fools," Amartya Sen argued in 1976 that such accounts could not explain the behavior of many people who, out of sympathy or commitment, sacrifice their own well-being. Introducing a more complicated account of human motivation into economics, Sen maintained, would have far-reaching consequences for the nature of many economic models.

Kristen Monroe is a psychologist, and she seems unaware of Sen's work, but she has set out on her own to test the economic accounts of altruism and to challenge them. Monroe has interviewed a large number of subjects whose actions fall into distinct categories with respect to altruism. At one end are the "entrepreneurs," creative self-made people, usually in business, who "take an idea and turn it to personal profit." The entrepreneurs conform well to the economic model of choice: when they do good for others, they always mention some motive connected with their own personal interest. A more varied group are the "philanthropists," chosen by Monroe as large donors to charities of various types. (Her inevitable failure to interview anonymous donors probably skews this analysis of philanthropy in favor of rational self-interest.) The philanthropists are less calculating than the entrepreneurs, and many obviously sacrifice a great deal of their personal energy and wealth for their causes; and yet Monroe finds that explanations in terms of reputation and "psychic good" are often (though not always) adequate accounts of their behavior.

Not so with her last two groups: rescuers of the Jews selected from the list of winners of the Yad Vashem medal, the award given by the Holocaust Memorial and Research Institute in Jerusalem, and "heroes" and "heroines" selected from the list of winners of the Carnegie Hero Awards, whose winners must have risked their lives to save someone in need. Lucille is among the latter; and like most "heroes" and "heroines" who won the award, she had never heard of it before she got it. Rescuers of Jews and heroes have in common that they saved strangers, apparently just because of the strangers' need. Since the class of heroes turns out to be heterogeneous— it includes highly disinterested people and people who were conscious of their own reputations—I will focus on the rescuers.

Monroe conducted exhaustive interviews with quite a few rescuers, a sampling of which she presents to us, along with summaries of her general findings. These interviews reveal different histories, personalities, and social backgrounds. The rescuers included peasants, urban workers, wealthy middleclass people, even a Silesian countess who worked as the veterinarian to a traveling circus. But there is remarkable commonality in certain significant traits. Without exception, the rescuers insist that what they did was normal and not extraordinary, that they behaved only as people ought to behave when someone in need is at hand. Without exception, they deny having agonized and calculated about the matter. Like Otto Springer, they felt that they had to do what they did. It was what there was to be done. Insofar as these people calculated the costs and the benefits of their altruism, the calculation concerned the "how" of the rescue operation, not the "why" or the "whether."

As for the goals of these rescuers, without exception they deny having received any material reward. (This is in any case ruled out by the arduous Yad Vashem investigation process.) They also deny being motivated by any expectation of recognition or gratitude or prestige. These denials are credible, since the rescuers operated in a society hostile to their aims, in which they knew they risked death. These people, finally, do not report feeling especially good about their actions: "Nothing special, no big deal" is a typical response.

What, then, separates these people from others? Monroe finds a recurrent distinguishing characteristic: a vivid awareness of a common humanity. Again and again, rescuers say things like "You should always be aware that every other person is basically you." And, "We live on one world. We are one people." They speak of people being "welded together," of how "everything is dependent on everything else." A Dutch rescuer named Tony says that the human race is like the cells of a single body: if one is damaged, all are damaged. Rescuers deny that this perception requires any special effort of role-playing or conscious empathy (though frequently they stress the fact that they have active imaginations, that they know how to picture life through someone else's eyes). The sense of a common humanity has become natural to them; it's just the way things are. (Several of them remarked that the Nazis succeeded in disrupting the normal order of things when they defined the Jews as outside the boundaries of common humanity, and thereby made cruelty toward the Jews seem legitimate.)

Some rescuers derived this sense of a common humanity from a religious upbringing, but Monroe finds that religion is not an independent predictor of altruism. Some owed it to a beloved parent or role model, but this factor, too, played no constantly predictive role. Some have an interest in philosophy: Otto Springer likes Kant, and Tony reports being helped by thinking that "Christ, Buddha, Gandhi, they're all the same person." But the one similar attitude in the lives of these altruists is their way of looking at people, no matter where it came from. It is this powerful consciousness of connectedness that makes them view their extraordinary actions as perfectly ordinary, "just common sense and common caring for people."

Monroe's general criticism of rational actor theory, and her defense of a wholly different theory that begins from the "perception of self," has not yet been completely worked out. Her positive theory is highly sketchy, and her concluding chapter sometimes seems imprecise and dismissive in its account of economic theories. Not so her analysis of her interview data, which gives powerful empirical support to Sen's common-sense observation. Monroe elegantly shows that altruism is not one simple thing, but many distinct things, and that the brand exemplified by the rescuers—and to some extent by the philanthropists and heroes—is not adequately captured by models based on rational self-interest.

The rescuers are a small and unusual group, but they themselves plausibly suggest that such altruism, on a smaller scale, is extremely common in the small actions of daily life. This implies that economic models are likely to have serious predictive failings. Monroe usually stresses the extraordinary character of the rescuers' achievements, but she may come closer to the truth when she says that Otto Springer's life gives just one example of "how a sensitive man lives his own life with integrity and dignity." Her data show that *Homo economicus* is not "a sensitive man." We should demand accounts that do more justice to the "integrity and dignity" of which we are actually capable.

Seeing the core of ordinary morality in the extraordinary time of the Holocaust is also Tzvetan Todorov's project. Todorov is a literary and cultural thinker, and so, unlike Monroe, he does not engage in strictly empirical research; his account is based on memoirs and letters. And although he briefly mentions the rescuers, he focuses on an altogether different population: the inmates of concentration camps, Nazi and Stalinist. His idea is to use the behavior of human beings under the weight of extreme circumstances as a kind of "magnifying glass" through which to glimpse key features of human morality generally.

Unlike many accounts that stress the dehumanization of the victims and their loss of moral dignity, Todorov points out that, short of circumstances of extreme physical pain or depletion, people in the reduced circumstances of the concentration camp often behaved quite well. They retained, in large measure, three components of ordinary morality: dignity, defined as the capacity to act as a subject with a will; caring, defined as the intention to help another individual person with whom one is personally acquainted; and the life of the mind, which, as a virtue, is defined as intellectual or artistic production intended to benefit particular individuals. Todorov argues that these virtues together are exhaustive of morality and that caring—which he associates with traditionally gendered images of maternal behavior—is the primary moral virtue.

To these three genuine and ordinary virtues, Todorov opposes "heroic virtue," by which he means, apparently, doing something for an abstract cause, whether or not it helps real people. This contrast is nowhere clearly laid out. Sometimes all "courage" and "loyalty" are classified by Todorov as heroic rather than ordinary, but sometimes the "heroic" is an especially cause-oriented and abstract form of these traditional virtues. It is not at all clear whether the pursuit of justice fits into either category. Nor is it very clear what precisely is wrong with the "heroic." Todorov's central example of how it goes wrong, the Warsaw Rising of 1944, seems to have been a failure, as he himself notes, largely owing to tactical stupidity. Its leaders appear to lack moral stature not because they were fighting for a noble ideal but because they didn't think very wisely about what they were doing and how it would affect the people involved.

Obviously this needn't be true of all noble ideals or of all the people who fight for them. We never understand just how far Todorov is ready to go in his critique of the abstract. Quite far, I suspect; but we don't really know on what grounds. We derive instead the sense of a powerful skepticism about any general pursuit of justice or goodness. It is a skepticism securely grounded in Todorov's own life, as we learn from the intermittent narratives of his childhood in Bulgaria. The experience of a state that crushed individuals while proclaiming high ideals shapes Todorov's book at every turn. Todorov's description of this experience commands the reader's respect and sympathy, but it culminates in conclusions that are nowhere justified by argument.

Todorov's experience of communist totalitarianism has left him with an abiding distrust of public and large-scale action, and with an unwillingness to see genuine virtue in any spheres but those of the home and the community. Let people encounter one another one by one, he suggests, in relationships of personal friendship and intimacy, and they will act pretty well. But let them start trying to benefit strangers, let them start pursuing universal justice, and they are bound to mess things up. Unfortunately, this larger argument remains submerged beneath data that do not exactly support it. For the evils of Nazism and Stalinism hardly provide an indictment of all movements dedicated to social justice and goodness. Nor do the moral successes of families and bands of friends and neighborhoods show that this sort of caring is always morally pure and reliable.

Todorov skews things by situating his "ordinary" actors in the camps—in circumstances, that is, in which they cannot act politically and in which "ordinary" actions focused on particulars are the only moral course open to them. In such situations of extremity, moreover, we are powerfully disposed to sympathize with them should they act like anything other than complete monsters. We might have arrived at a different evaluation of "caring" had

Todorov focused on the good behavior of Nazis to their spouses and children (which was probably about average), or even on the moral inconstancy of most of us in our everyday lives, where we certainly "care" for some people close to us but rarely exercise the constant moral attentiveness of which Lucille spoke. Had he investigated such unextreme cases, he would have had to ask different and deeper questions. Isn't it the case that we find the Nazis evil despite their many acts of ordinary "caring," precisely because they had a warped sense of justice in their larger dealings? Don't we rightly think badly of people who behave well at home and obtusely abroad? In this sense, the experience of extremity is not at all the best lens through which to view morality generally.

The contrast between Todorov and Monroe is a provocative one. Todorov prefers actions that express care for people whom one already knows. Monroe finds the essence of altruism in the choice to help a human being as a consequence of his or her humanity, without any special tie. Together, these books raise a question that lies at the heart of a long philosophical tradition: the question of the relative moral weight of duties to humanity and duties to our own. (Our own can be a family, an ethnic group, a nation.)

Addressing Greek and Roman cultures that were very attached to local group affiliations and to a sense of honor and pride based on such attachments, Stoic philosophers insisted, much in the manner of Monroe's rescuers, that people are all part of a single world in which the well-being of all humans is interdependent. Thus, wherever they are political citizens, people also bear duties as kosmopolitai, or "citizens of the world." What are these duties? Above all, they involve equal respect for the worth of humanity in each and every person—a Stoic idea that exercised great power over Kant, who captured the idea of world citizenship in his doctrine of the "kingdom of ends." We are all members of a moral community that constrains our political actions by instructing us to consider humanity as an end and never as a mere means. Historically, this idea influenced (and may have itself been further influenced by) Christian ideas of our fundamental equality as children of God and Jewish ideas about duties to the stranger and the alien, as these groups interacted in the Roman world.

In practical terms, Stoics held, like Kant, that world citizenship involves duties of hospitality to aliens who reside on our soil; stringent limits on the acceptability of war and on conduct during war; duties of benevolence to relieve the sick and impoverished; duties not to despise or disadvantage any human being on account of a fortuitous characteristic such as race, ethnic or national origin, even gender; duties to promote the equal education of all human beings. Stoics were among the first thinkers in the Western tradition to urge the equal education and citizenship of women. They did not focus as intently on material need as on respect, given their complex beliefs about the ultimate insignificance of "external goods" by comparison to one's inner virtue; but a modern cosmopolitan can easily hold, again with Kant, that we have stringent duties to promote the material welfare of others as well as to respect their humanity.

The question then becomes: Are we entitled to dwell on those who are near and dear to us, rather than seeking to benefit humanity as a whole? As the cosmopolitan tradition instructs us, actions benefiting humanity may take many different forms, from political support for international human rights efforts to financial sacrifice to local actions that express solicitude for a particular person considered as human rather than merely related. As Cicero vividly showed, all these aims give rise to conflicts. When may we devote ourselves to our own family if there are many people more urgently in need of our assistance? The cosmopolitan tradition holds that frequently we are so entitled, because our family is where we are situated. It makes most sense for each of us to care for our own neighbors and children, rather than to try to benefit all the world's children equally. But all our actions should be constrained by an awareness of common humanity, which may at times impose duties that limit our pursuit of local well-being. (Thus Kant held that these duties render any project of colonial domination absolutely unacceptable.) At this point, members of this tradition diverge in their accounts of these levels of obligation and the conflicts they generate. Some thinkers, such as Cicero and Kant, regarded duties of benevolence as relatively elastic, permitting preference for the local; others had a more stringent sense of what distant human beings rightly claim from us.

How would our two authors respond? Todorov would answer, I think, that we must always focus on the near when we act morally. The core of morality, he insists, is contained in daily acts of caring toward people "personally known" to us; and to seek to benefit people at a distance is to risk serving a bloodless abstraction. His test for the moral content of an act is about as far from Kant's as one can be: an act is moral if one's own connection to the recipient is an essential part of its motivation. He rejects the Stoic/Kantian tradition as dangerously unrooted in the daily stuff of caring. "Humanity" is one of the abstract purposes that he lists as robbing an action of its moral content, along with "the homeland or liberty or Communism."

In a book about the French Resistance, *A French Tragedy: Scenes of Civil War,* 1944 (University Press of New England), which appeared since the publication of *Facing the Extreme,* Todorov appears to embrace a more complex account of ordinary virtue. The resisters in his story of the French town Saint-Amand-Morntrond are rather like Monroe's rescuers. They see themselves as "advocates for those in need of help," without regard to personal ties. Although Todorov does not withdraw the account of virtue presented in the earlier book, or explore tensions between personal care and actions benefiting strangers, he obviously respects this attitude to strangers as an important kind of virtue, and thus moves closer to Monroe's account.

For Monroe's rescuers see things differently. They hold that morality originates in the recognition that we are all affiliated and attached, and that any human being as such demands our concern and our care. In this sense, they side with the cosmopolitan tradition. This does not mean that they prefer the distant to the local or insist on spreading their benefits evenly over all human beings: indeed, most often they responded to a claim of need that was at hand, saving these particular employees or this rape victim outside the window. But they did so because of the humanity of the person, and for no reason of personal relatedness. Moreover, they see this conduct as perfectly obvious and normal, "what everybody normally should be doing." It is simply "common sense and common caring for people," once one understands that all people are morally alike. Of course, they devote an unusual measure of concern and care to their own families and friends; but they understand this concern as a local way of expressing a larger and deeper concern. When the occasion presents itself, they are ready to extend that everyday concern to the stranger. Monroe's interviews show that there is nothing bloodless or inhuman about such people. In fact, their freshness of vision makes them remarkably attractive; one could hardly ask for better companions.

Todorov, writing out of a history in which abstract purposes were used as a screen for dehumanizing brutality, has such intense skepticism about any universalistic morality that in the end he robs care of some of its moral content. For him, all universalizing is a danger, and in this respect he differs from Monroe's altruists, who locate the danger in a particular type of universalizing that ignores human need or divides human beings into hierarchically ordered groups. "Caring cannot be universal," Todorov writes, "for it implies feeling personal sympathy with the object of one's concern." Surely this begs the question. For what the rescuers display is precisely a personal sympathy that responds to human need as such, to the stranger getting raped in the street, to the unknown workers who risk deportation and death. Todorov's perspective makes sense of some of what he describes: husbands following wives to their death, mothers valiantly protecting their children. But many of the "ordinary" acts of caring that Todorov finds in the camps do not concern long-term family relationships, and they are unintelligible without a sense of common human connectedness: the starving woman who shares the cranberries she has found in the wood with her fellow inmates; the woman who lies on top of a smaller woman whose name has just been called for the next selection and conceals her from her killers. These people knew each other in the sense that they were all imprisoned together; but they didn't choose each other for a moral relationship because they liked their looks or their personalities, or even because they were relatives. They responded to human need.

Nor does Todorov appear to admit as moral a pursuit of justice that involves a break with one's family or local group. Some of the rescuers came from anti-Semitic and even Nazi families. They chose to work against their own families, contributing ultimately, if indirectly, to the deaths of family members. Although Todorov does not discuss such conflicts, and although he values rebellion against tyranny, his account of morality seems unable to accommodate the decision to pursue justice against the interests of the near and dear. What the cosmopolitan tradition grasps is that morality must be grounded in something larger than the local, in a recognition of common needs and abilities. Todorov is wise to insist that universalism runs the risk of totalitarianism, but his own prescription for purely local foundations runs the risk of chauvinism and hierarchy, especially when we recall that our immediate surroundings always confront us with differences of race, religion, ethnicity, and gender. My country right or wrong, my club, my family, my religion, my sex: these are ways of fleeing from the fact that we are all naked, hungry, mortal, and dignified. And this equality exerts a moral claim, however we act on that claim concretely.

I do not wish to suggest that there is no place for the kind of long-term love and care that Todorov eloquently describes. Human beings care for one another best when they get to know one another personally. Such local loves, moreover, will raise vexing moral questions when their demands appear to conflict with those of larger loves. There will be conflict; but Todorov's perspective does not prepare us for such conflict, or help us to understand it.

Since these books focus on extraordinary circumstances, they may obscure a fact that most of Monroe's altruists stress: these extraordinary circumstances are really quite ordinary. There are always human beings who need our help, even in the absence of state-sponsored genocide. Having declared that he will use the extreme situation to understand the core of ordinary morality, Todorov concludes, oddly, that the extreme and the ordinary actually have very different requirements. It is only in extremities that the stranger demands our help: our goal "in peacetime should be to care about those close to us, but in times of trouble our goal should be to find within ourselves the strength to expand this intimate circle beyond its usual limits and recognize as our own even those whose faces we do not know."

Monroe's altruists, and Monroe herself, would respond sharply, and rightly. For a start, "peacetime" is hardly free of genocide. The fact that our nation is not at war does not make events in Bosnia and Rwanda less morally compelling. Moreover, there is a ubiquitous type of killing that does not involve death camps, but only the withholding of necessary nutrition and health care, and sometimes people are killed this way because they belong to a particular group.

Economists estimate that tens of millions and perhaps hundreds of millions of women, and especially girls, have died of such endemic and quiet deprivations, from having received nutrition and health care unequal to that given males. Some nations contain (or rather, fail to contain) tens of millions of such "missing women": 44 million in China, 36 million in India. We may use the term "genocide" or we may not. Call it what you will, this is injustice of mammoth proportions, and the silence about it is furthering it.

There is misery all around us that is morally compelling even when it does not add up to millions of deaths. Tony, Monroe's Dutch rescuer, says that most people he knows avoid the need of the homeless by saying that they are all a bunch of drunks who don't want to work. But "if they spent one afternoon in downtown L.A. or even in the park in Santa Monica and looked and learned to see through their eyes, they could not give that same answer. But most people look away." Just as they did in Germany, he says, where people clung to stories that make them feel safe, to local identities and affiliations that separated them from what they saw. Without such separate identities, however, "I suddenly would have to face my own humanity."

Could people learn not to look away? Monroe concludes her interview with Tony by asking what we should do "if we would like to have more people like you in the world." Embarrassed by her question, Tony deflects it: "Oh, I don't know if I'm really the world's most desirable citizen. Let's not get too focused on me. We live in one world. We are one people. Working together, basically we are all the same. We can behave or we can not behave." The important thing, Tony insists, is that "we're not doomed, you know. We can at any moment in our lives decide to change things, and that requires courage, too."

# CHAPTER FOURTEEN

# Foul Play

WILLIAM IAN MILLER (1997), The Anatomy of Disgust

Aristotle's students did not want to study the parts of animals. Recoiling in disgust from the study of blood and flesh, they found the distant stars cleaner and more appealing. But Aristotle advised them not to "make a sour face" at biology. Once, he told them, some visitors wanted to meet the famous philosopher Heraclitus, and when they arrived they "found him in the kitchen, warming himself in front of the stove." (Scholars suspect that this sentence really refers to toilet activities.) They halted outside, but Heraclitus said: "Come in, don't be afraid. There are gods here too."

William Miller is one of Aristotle's unregenerate students. He finds nothing but disgust in the contemplation of what he calls "thick, greasy life." No gods here: just ooze and stench and corruption, "the grotesque body, unrelenting physical ugliness, nauseating sights and odors . . . suppuration, defecation, rot." Miller maintains that our disgust with our own feces and sweat and hairiness and semen is a major element in our humanity—not only in the personal life, where it explains why sex is "so difficult," but also in public life, in political life. We are creatures who aspire to the cleanness of the stars, to "purity and perfection." And fueling a great part of that striving, in Miller's view, is disgust "with what we are . . . that we live and die and that the process is a messy one emitting substances and odors that make us doubt ourselves and fear our neighbors." Believing that any adequate investigation of these connections requires a multidisciplinary humanistic inquiry, Miller, who is a law professor at the University of Michigan, has written a wide-ranging and rich account of the emotion of disgust, drawing on psychology, literature, and history—all filtered through his own vivid narrative of the phenomena of bodily existence.

Miller recognizes that he is investigating (and expressing) a sensibility that has been shaped by an age-old Christian tradition linking disgust with sex, and linking both with the female body. Miller officially distances himself from this tradition's "gloomy and foul-spirited misogyny," but he doubts whether it is possible to distance himself from the "more generalized misanthropy" that lies behind it. Where misanthropy is concerned, he never tries: like Swift, he finds bleak pleasure in contemplating his own alienation from life. He sometimes tries to criticize misogyny, but this soon yields to a fascinated expression of its core ideas, as Miller repeatedly portrays the vagina as foul, smelly, and contaminated, and sex as a source of disgust to men as soon as its passion to defile its object is exhausted. Oddly, this doesn't make one dislike him. Miller is too astute about himself, too sad (and also very funny) about where all this has left him. Far from using these notions to dominate anyone, Miller seems, like Gulliver at the end, to be having enough difficulty just getting through a day with his fellow Yahoos. "Life," he reflects, "must be packaged just right not to make us cringe when it touches us." Perhaps the only way one can write well on this topic is to be unhappily in its grip.

Miller's book has three goals: to analyze the emotion of disgust; to give an account of when and where people experience disgust in daily life and in the sexual realm; and to investigate the role of disgust in morals and politics. Many writers about disgust have treated it as a bare feeling, with little or no cognitive content. Miller argues powerfully that this approach is inadequate. Disgust actually has a very complex and sophisticated cognitive content. Disgust is "about something and in response to something." It is not like a stomach flu: it "necessarily involves particular thoughts, characteristically very intrusive and unriddable thoughts, about the repugnance of that which is its object." These thoughts revolve around the notion of a particular type of danger for the self, "the danger inherent in pollution and contamination, the danger of defilement." Disgust evaluates its object both as base and as a threat. Thus it is closely linked both to fear (for the self) and to contempt (for the object).

Miller does not deny that, among the emotions, disgust has an especially intimate connection to the senses, but he does deny that this entails that disgust is just a bodily feeling. The connection to the senses comes through ideas: the defilement is seen in a uniquely sensory way, and described in a characteristically vivid sensory idiom. Disgust is "more visceral" than other emotions, not because it is less concerned with evaluation, but because "no other emotion forces such concrete sensual descriptions of its object."

Miller draws here on recent work in cognitive psychology, especially on the work of Paul Rozin, who stresses disgust's sophisticated cognitive character. But he argues against Rozin's claim that disgust originates in the areas of food rejection and anxiety about our animal origins. Plausibly enough, Miller holds that disgust has many different scenarios. While in some sense a cultural universal, it can take on a variety of forms, as societies shape both its relationship to other emotions and its sense of its proper objects.

This does not mean that disgust lacks an evolutionary role, an adaptive significance; Miller plainly thinks that it does, though he is not very interested in the issue. Those origins might give some disgust-experiences a certain rigidity or prominence; but they would not prevent the kind of social shaping that Miller describes.

It is important to note that one can accept this general analysis of the emotion—which is very well argued—without being utterly convinced by the chapters that follow, where Miller presents as universal data of human experience his own account of the typical objects of disgust. Indeed, his theoretical account calls his subsequent chapters into question, suggesting that any single cultural scenario is likely to be incomplete. But in one way the analysis is skewed by the phenomenology to come: Miller is so convinced from the start that disgust is "a necessary consequence of our consciousness of life itself—fat, greasy, teeming, rank, festering, viscous life"—that he pays little attention to connections between disgust and ideas of surprise or invasion. He mentions Mary Douglas's theory of boundary violation and pollution, suggesting that it might explain some aspects of the disgusting; but the suggestion never gets developed, so convinced is he that everyday life, without violations, is all the emotion needs.

Those who do not share Miller's extreme aversion to the quotidian may find an account modeled on Douglas's a valuable supplement to his theory. Here, for example, are two of my own core experiences of disgust. I go to the kitchen sink to do the dishes, and a baby bat, which has somehow gotten into the pipes, sticks its head up out of the drain. And at the Chicago Lyric Opera, near the end of the first act of *Norma*, a male stranger seated next to me vomits on my coat and then slumps into unconsciousness, leaving me stuck in my (non-aisle) seat with the stuff for the next fifteen minutes while June Anderson sings, undisturbed, about the gods' revenge. The peculiarly awful nature of these experiences is not explained by Miller, and could be explained by Douglas, who would connect my feeling of contamination with the sudden breaching of the boundaries by which we protect our safety. Bats should not intrude next to dishes and food; vomit is threatening when it invades the decorous precincts of the opera house. (You might say that Miller's core disgust experiences are ordinary sex and defecation, whereas mine are more like rape.)

Miller's reader now launches into the center of his book, a set of chapters describing disgust's occasions and objects, and the thoughts that lie behind the experience. He meticulously charts the connections of disgust to each of the bodily senses, describing with a wonderful richness of literary and historical detail the likely objects of the emotion (mostly bodily emissions) and the likely metaphors that characterize the disgusting qualities of these objects (slimy, mucky, viscous, oozy, scabby, and so on). The account is so erudite, so witty, and in a way so true (in that it seems on target about many people and many cultural norms of purity) that one can easily forget that the question of its social origins has already been put on the table, and can thus forget to ask to what extent Miller thinks he is uncovering relatively inflexible human universals.

It would seem that Miller does claim universality for the phenomena described; and yet what he gives us is a vividly rendered first-person account, bolstered by highly selective reference to his own culture. Sometimes he uses his own children as exemplars, as if their behavior (as they shrink from various types of contamination and dirt) proves the universality of a deep pre-cultural human repugnance toward bodily functions. In fact, the reader is likely to judge (as he guesses in one footnote) that children brought up by such a father are not a neutral sample of humanity. Too often, then, the parochial gets treated as the inevitable, and the question about cultural construction doesn't get squarely faced.

Consider Miller's account of sex. He says that, of all the bodily emissions, semen is the "most powerfully contaminating," with "the capacity to feminize and humiliate that which it touches." He argues that countless stories in a variety of cultures embody the idea that "male sexuality, embodied in an organ reminiscent of a slug that emits viscous ooze," pollutes the female, by the emission itself and by fertilization, making the vagina a "teeming, moist, swampy" place of "rank fecundity and generation." Joined to these thoughts is the thought that semen is emitted "under conditions that are dignity-destroying, a prelude to the mini-shames attendant on post-ejaculatory tristesse." The vagina is viewed as disgusting not so much in itself as because of what it tolerates, and it is more contaminated by semen than the penis is by having been inside it. "Since penises penetrate, they, like knives, do much less damage to themselves than they do to the other."

All of this, Miller notes, is a male view of semen, connected to self-loathing and to a fear of decay and death. He is well aware that these are the attitudes that lie at the origin of a great deal of misogyny, as males somehow come to blame the female for their own feelings of disgust and fear. And yet he acquiesces in the view at the same time as he criticizes it. He represents himself as sharing the attitudes described, and clearly views them as more or less inevitable. He never looks for alternative views, male or female.

It is no surprise, then, to find him endorsing, apparently as universally correct, the Freudian view that sex is made exciting and desirable only by the allure of hidden disgusting things. Disgust keeps desire in check, holding men back from excessive indulgence, and also creates the conditions under which desire can be sufficiently aroused to make intercourse possible. This means that men will desire sexual objects whom they believe they can defile—that a crucial part of what they desire is the pleasure of defilement. Once they have achieved this disgust-mingled pleasure, moreover, another type of disgust, the disgust of surfeit, arises to take its place. "Once our bodily appetites have been sated we do not want to be reminded of our prior uncontrolled urges." Referring here to Adam Smith (hardly an authority on the female body), Miller approvingly cites as "compelling" his account of surfeit, which begins "When we have dined, we order the covers to be removed," and he goes on to characterize the female body as similar to the plate from which one has just finished eating.

The reader cannot help recognizing here a familiar and highly influential male view. But what follows from this recognition? One is inclined to say, yes, plenty of men do see women that way, but one can quickly learn to detect the signs of that attitude and to keep out of the way of those who hold it. One is next inclined to say, how sad to go through life so constituted. But few readers, whatever they say, will agree with Miller that this is a complete account of what has aroused desire, even male desire, even in post-Christian Western culture. It leaves out too many things: the sense of wonder; the delight in beauty; the feeling of being taken over by something that one does not control; the sensation of losing one's boundaries; curiosity; the pleasure of being seen and known; the pleasure of seeing and knowing. Even the many pleasing ways that bodies smell and taste. These are things that are pleasant not simply because they are gross.

Think of the moment in the film *Elmer Gantry* when Jean Simmons, an evangelist tired of her sanctimonious entourage, makes a date with Burt Lancaster because "you smell like a real man." That is not a sign of the allure of the low; she just means that she is pleased and aroused by the way he smells. She associates the smell with fun and outrageousness and playfulness, with the relief of being able to be both an animal and a person, as opposed to a religious figurehead. Miller gives no time to these other sources of arousal; and he plainly agrees with Freud that none of them would suffice to "swell the tide of the libido to its height" (Freud's words) without the prospect of a loathsome roll in the sticky smelly ooze. Well, one can only say, not everybody is like that.

Love, says Miller, changes everything. When love is on the scene, various rules of disgust are relaxed or even suspended. Loving spouses endure one another's flatulence, bad breath, nose hairs, and so on, just as loving parents endure their children's diapers (something that Miller, predictably, says he had a hard time doing). And apparently love makes sex possible without disgust. On Miller's own account, however, it is hard to see why people who love each other would want sex at all. Freud, indeed, thought that they would not want it, or not very much: men need a degraded object to find sexual pleasure, and the wives for whom they have tender feelings do not arouse strong desire.

Miller hedges here, suggesting that people who love each other might still experience the "violative thrill" of "the mutual transgression of disgust-defended boundaries." But if the boundaries are no longer stoutly defended (as in love they are not, by his own account), and if the loved one is not thought of as disgusting (as she is not, by his own account), then it seems that there is little to thrill the Millerian lover. This comes about because his account of sex omits so much, and imputes so much to disgust, that when that prop is removed there is nothing left to get desire going. And so it is no surprise that the love of spouses merges into the love of parents for children, as if there really is no distinction between the two. Again, one can only say that Miller has given a wonderfully perceptive account of certain chunks of Western civilization. But he presents as the whole what is surely a (most unfortunate) part.

Miller follows his Freudian tack still further, producing an account of the progress of civilization (much indebted to Norbert Elias) that holds that civilization can be measured by the raising of the threshold of the disgusting, and by the repression or the concealment of the bodily. The more we find disgusting, and the less ooze and stench we tolerate, the more civilized we are. Miller's use of history here is highly eclectic and selective, as he leaps from the Icelandic sagas to the Middle Ages, and from there to the eighteenth century. He certainly does not persuade the reader that there is a unilinear progress of the sort that he depicts.

It is to some extent a mystery why people in different times and different places have had different levels of tolerance for dirt and smells. The average Roman soldier serving in Britain had better toilet facilities than most British people until well into the twentieth century. In much of India it is thought disgusting not to wash after a bowel movement, whereas in America we are content with paper. What is not clear is that these things are by themselves an index of the society's level of goodness or human quality, as Miller seems to think. The Romans had great plumbing, but they also had gladiatorial games, and slavery, and barbarous punishments; and India's fastidiousness shored up the caste system and the seclusion of women. Nor does Miller ever entertain the possibility that bodily fastidiousness might be carried to excess—a thought that is bound to occur to his reader. It might be more civilized to undo the props of misogyny than to foster them, more civilized of Gandhi to clean latrines than of his fellow Brahmins to relegate that task to "untouchables."

Miller's final chapters are devoted to the moral and political aspects of disgust. Here his good sense and his Swiftean immersion in the physically repulsive point in opposite directions. In one brief section, Miller draws an interesting contrast between disgust and indignation, suggesting that the latter is morally and politically more reliable than the former. Indignation embodies reasoning about harm and agency that is, if true, morally relevant; whereas disgust's sense of the personally contaminating sweeps far too broadly to be a reliable indicator of moral defect. He points out here that disgust is linked not only with misogyny, but also, throughout the ages, with the loathing of Jews, who have been seen as hyper-physical sensuous quasi-feminine beings, and therefore as threats to the clean masculine style of advancing civilization.

Having gotten this far, Miller might have been expected to expand on the theme of disgust's political and legal irrationality, and to criticize his own account of civilization in the light of these reflections. There is certainly a lot to be said about the role played by appeals to disgust in the oppression of homosexuality, and about the links between anti-Semitism, misogyny, and homophobia. But Miller is too caught up in what he criticizes to remain critical for long. And, though a law professor, he seems to have no interest in the role of disgust in the law. His book soon veers abruptly round to the positive role that disgust allegedly plays in maintaining political boundaries. Asking whether democracy has managed to eradicate hierarchies of class and rank that were sustained by physical loathing for the lower classes, Miller answers, with Orwell, that it has not and could not. The contempt for the dirty, smelly body of the working-class person is just too deep in any middle-class person's education to be surmountable.

Miller, like Orwell, doesn't think that this is a tragedy, or a scandal. He accepts it as a fact of life, a limitation that our bodies and our sense of the civilized impose on our efforts to achieve equality. By the same argument, he could also show that equality between the sexes can never be fully achieved, since it will always have to contend with the inevitable disgust that men feel for the contaminating vaginas into which they have just ejaculated. And so the first question must be, what truth is there to any of these claims of naturalness or inevitability?

The disgust described by Orwell, in the horrifying account of his working-class landlords, the Brookers, in *The Road to Wigan Pier*, is clearly a disgust that he wanted to feel for the working-class body. He moved from house to house (as Miller notes) until he found one that was dirty enough to inspire it, and then he came to the reassuring conclusion that class hierarchy had an inevitable bodily basis. But it just isn't true that working-class people are especially dirty. The Brookers were appallingly dirty, but so too are many English upper-class people. (I bet Orwell ate off of dishes that had been soaking in dirty soapy dishwater and set to dry without any rinse—a truly disgusting English habit that transcends class and rank. Yet even extremely poor manual laborers in the slums in southern India generally bathe and use talcum powder every day.) Miller seems sometimes aware that Orwell's disgust is a way of insulating himself from social change; but at other times he endorses it as ineluctable and necessary.

The problem is the same as in his treatment of sex: Miller first sees, but then loses sight of, the fact that the disgust that grips him is a particular and highly questionable historical formation, one that has the social function of maintaining injurious hierarchies. The really democratic act would be to criticize and to undo that social formation. Walt Whitman saw that this meant recreating our entire relationship to the body, and that the underlying project of democracy was precisely to "sing the body electric," to establish that the locus of common human need and aspiration was fundamentally acceptable and pleasing—still more, that it was the soul, the locus of personal uniqueness and personal dignity. Slave's body, woman's body, man's body; all are equal in dignity and beauty:

The male is not less the soul nor more, he too is in his place ...
The man's body is sacred and the woman's body is sacred,
No matter who it is, it is sacred—is it the meanest one in the laborers' gang? ...
Each belongs here or anywhere just as much as the well-off, just as much as you,
Each has his or her place in the procession.

It might be Miller himself whom these lines address. Miller may want to maintain, with Orwell, that the transformation that Whitman envisages is impossible. But then he needs first to come to grips with the physical-democratic ideal, with its realization in countless works of popular culture, and with its considerable reality in an America that sometimes does find bodies acceptable and appealing regardless of their class origins.

Indeed, as Whitman would have wished, the ideal goes further than simple acceptability, in the direction of a positive eroticization of the "real" body of the working-class person as far more interesting than the washed-up (not to say washed-out) bodies of his class superiors. When Jean Simmons is aroused by Burt Lancaster's smell (and note that this is a tony British actress playing opposite a notoriously lower-class uneducated actor who began life as a circus performer), she doesn't mean what Miller would mean, that the very disgusting nature of his lower-class body both lures and repels her. No, she means that it is refreshing and arousing to smell real sweat after being around the sanitized and the sanctimonious: it gives her permission to be an individual, rather than a representative of various idealized and loathed characteristics. And, of course, Burt Lancaster is the only one around who doesn't feel disgust at Jean Simmons's body (even the concealed disgust of worship): that is precisely why he is the only man that this businesswoman in evangelist's clothes will allow near her.

These blind spots in Miller's view of democracy surface with particular clarity in a lengthy story, told with his customary combination of literary eloquence and curmudgeonly self-scrutiny, about a mason whom Miller and his wife hired to do some work on their home in Ann Arbor. A "large, beefy man," this mason inspires Miller with disgust and contempt. For one thing, he has several tattoos, which Miller reads as "signs of his will to vulgarity." For another, he wears his jeans so low that when he bends over "his rear fissure (oh, the trials of decorum!) was exposed"—a posture that Miller cannot imagine himself ever willingly assuming. And the mason didn't like him either:

He had already been on the job for a few days when I rode up on my bicycle, back pack on my back, said hello and continued pedaling back to the garage. The mason said to my wife, "He a teacher?" The failure of the "is" to introduce that question captures only some of the contemptuousness of his tone.

This wasn't the end of the exchange. One day, when Miller's wife was wearing a t-shirt that read "Save Endangered Mammals," the mason (probably familiar with such righteous attitudes) came to work wearing one that said "Crack Kills," but "inscribed beneath a cartoon of a human being crushed between the cheeks of a naked backside." Miller feels contempt yet again, but he also sees that the mason is expressing his own contempt for the solemn style of the haute bourgeoisie. Miller uses the story to argue that while democracy has not removed disgust and contempt based upon class, it has created more space in which the lower can dish out the same attitudes toward the higher.

But consider what Miller does not tell us. Does the mason have a good body? (Some stray remarks suggest that the answer is yes.) When the guy bends over, Miller sees only the disgusting; but that's not the only way one might tell the story. A likely element of sexual display escapes Miller's notice completely, because he is so busy reacting in horror to the mason's lack of decorum. And isn't the t-shirt more of the same, a flaunting of an earthy masculine aggressiveness toward Miller's wife with her sanctimonious Millerian mottos, and toward the husband for whose style of masculinity he has unreserved contempt? Miller notes that the juxtaposition with the mason's t-shirt turns his wife's t-shirt into some sort of joke, but he doesn't seem to see that the joke could be against his whole outlook on life. Put the wife's t-shirt on Jean Simmons, and it can be read as mammalian humanity's plea for rescue from the etiolated purities of a civilization that is unable to put up with itself.

The serious Whitmanian point is this: if we think about the "body electric" with love and erotic excitement rather than with disgust, we will also see that in a crucial sense class doesn't matter, because sweat and muscle and hunger and thirst really do not differ. "Do you not see that these are exactly the same to all in all nations and times all over the earth?" Democracy creates a space in which one can be that kind of equal physical being, with needs and interests similar to those of every other one. Or, again in Whitman's words, "This is the meal equally set, this the meat for natural hunger . . . I will not have a single person slighted or left away."

Whitman grasped something profound when he suggested that democracy could not succeed without overcoming a good deal of our bodily disgust and shame, and perhaps not without eroticizing (in a positive non-Millerian sense) some of the very things that used to arouse it. Without some such strategy of decontamination, women (and homosexual men, for whom women, in Whitman, are also proxies) could not become fully equal citizens. But Miller, who is in the American democracy, is crucially not of it. He cannot understand its animating principle. The misanthropic and misogynistic sadness that animates his brilliant book is also, from the standpoint of democracy, a barrier to the acknowledgment of human equality, a moral and political weakness.

But doesn't this suggest that justice and joy might go well together? It's a pleasing thought. Maybe it's true.

# CHAPTER FIFTEEN

# If Oxfam Ran the World

Peter Unger (1996), Living High and Letting Die:
Our Illusion of Innocence

The basic life chances of human beings vary dramatically around the world. According to the 1996 *Report* of the United Nations Development Programme, the life expectancy of a child born today in Sierra Leone is 39.2 years, the life expectancy of a child born in Japan 79.6 years (U.S. 76.1, UK 76.3). In the developing world, daily calorie supply per capita ranges from 3223 in Barbados to 1505 in Somalia. The availability of these calories is not equally distributed in any nation, which means that there are many who suffer acute hunger. In Hong Kong in 1996, 100 per cent of the population had access to safe water, in China 67 per cent, in Haiti 28 per cent, in the Central African Republic 18 per cent, in Afghanistan 12 per cent. These facts suggest that there are big problems of human misery in the world, problems that should be addressed by theories both of personal morality and of global justice.

Peter Unger argues that we are culpably indifferent to this misery, and that our daily thinking about our duty to others is marked by self-serving irrationality. We typically believe that we do have a moral duty to rescue others who are at risk, especially where this can be done without great cost to ourselves. For example, most people would agree that a bystander has a duty to rescue a child who is drowning in a shallow pond (an example originally introduced by Peter Singer). On the other hand, we typically deny that we have a moral duty to send money to save children's lives at a distance, even though most people could do this with less effort than they would expend in saving the drowning child. This arbitrary distinction between the near and the far, Unger argues, can't ultimately be supported by any good ethical argument.

So, too, with another distinction we are fond of making to let ourselves off the moral hook: between doing harm and allowing harm to occur. If a trolley-car is about to run over six people and, by flipping a switch, we could divert it onto a track where it would kill only one person, we would no longer feel that inaction was a secure moral refuge (an example introduced by Judith Jarvis Thomson). But this suggests that the "out" we allow ourselves when we fail to do all we can to save people who are dying in poor countries is also irrational and self-serving; for we tell ourselves that we are not doing any harm, we are simply failing to intervene to prevent a harm that is occurring anyhow. Unger's vigorous investigation of irrationalities in our daily thinking, through these and related examples, suggests convincingly that we owe others far more than we typically think we do.

This, then, is a book on a topic of great importance, written with much moral passion by a skilful and ingenious philosopher. And yet its conclusion suggests that something is amiss. For Unger argues that a relatively affluent person, "like you and me, must contribute to vitally effective groups, like Oxfam and Unicef, most of the money and property she now has, and most of what comes her way for the foreseeable future." Unger's entire argument about our duty to give aid culminates in this recommendation; so we must take it seriously. Suppose all the people to whom it is addressed followed Unger's advice: what would the world then be like?

Oxfam and Unicef would suddenly become very rich, receiving both an annual fraction of people's incomes and significant amounts of their land and other property. Since Unger instructs us to choose these two above other charities such as religious groups and universities, for reasons I shall discuss, those other organisations would become impoverished. Religious groups would no longer maintain the charitable efforts they now support. Many universities and research centres would close their doors, no longer offering future world leaders training in economics, law, or the foundations of democracy, and no longer conducting basic scientific research on issues from AIDS to agricultural development. Nor would national and local governments be able to maintain such welfare efforts as they now fund, since so much property would have been given away. Within a few years, governments from India to Britain would be in disarray, as Oxfam became the owner of increasing amounts of everything. Although they would retain de jure authority, it is likely that governments would need to turn an increasingly large proportion of their operations over to these organisations (as, even now, NGOs operate the public education systems in some parts of the developing world).

The officers who run Oxfam and Unicef today are, it seems, excellent and competent people. But they are certainly not trained to manage a large fraction of the world's wealth, or to conduct basic scientific, medical, and economic research. This means that poverty and misery would almost certainly get much worse, as global health efforts fell into disarray, as the "green revolution" stalled for lack of intellectual input, and as debates about different types of economic organisation languished for lack of financial support.

Nor are the officers of these charities democratically elected or account-able in any public forum. They have views about matters ranging from man-datory population control to the religious dimensions of sex inequality, with which reasonable people can disagree. But they lack any mechanism for public deliberation. Who can tell how they would respond, when offered Unger's chance to become, in effect, the government of the world? The government of India is inefficient, ill-funded, and prone to corruption. But India is a democracy, and its government officials are accountable to its people. It is, to say the least, not clear that India would be better run by the largely foreign officials of Oxfam. Unger's solution would surely so dilute the rights and prerogatives of citizenship that most of us would be living in a world without effective liberty.

Moreover, it is by now clear that hunger is negatively correlated with political liberty: Amartya Sen has shown that freedoms of speech and of the press have a big role in averting the inequalities in entitlement that are at the root of disastrous famines. So Unger's proposal, insofar as it would under-mine democracy and create a world bureaucracy of agencies, threatens to self-destruct, creating conditions in which disastrous famine could exist without effective political remedies.

Finally, we simply have no idea at all what would become of economic incentives under such a regime, but we can have a suspicion that the lot of the poorest might well become worse than in a world that tolerated some inequalities. This, at least, is the likelihood, barring a radical change in basic human psychology, although perhaps it is just such a change that Unger is imagining.

In short, the world that would result if we took Unger's advice would be one in which the very problems he cares about would get worse and in which other items that are not at the centre of his agenda, such as political liberty, would end up in a disastrous condition. Unger doesn't even try to imagine this world, and he seems not to have asked himself any questions about what would actually happen if people took his advice. This would appear to be because he has assumed that people will not take his advice and that he will remain one of a small band of moral heroes, in a world of moral sloth and corruption.

How, then, did Unger arrive at his defective and undeveloped recom-mendation, from the starting-point of a sharply focused ethical argument? To begin with, there are grave problems in the way the argument itself is advanced, which go some way toward explaining why Unger never bothers to imagine the world that his recommendations would create. His implied reader is a moral imbecile, an affluent person who repeatedly tosses appeals from charitable organisations into the wastepaper basket and heedlessly goes on living the high life. This imbecile is not already thinking about how to do good, and can be reached only by being bullied and hectored. Unger keeps giving us phone numbers and addresses of charities, on the apparent assumption that we don't know how to find them for ourselves. His sentences are full of slogans and capital letters (the View that Ethics is Highly Demanding, or Pretty Cheaply Lessening Early Death). He writes as if trying to speak to someone who is not only obtuse but deaf. Even his examples presuppose moral heedlessness.

Consider his central example. Called the Envelope, and introduced at repeated intervals with the terminal self-righteousness characteristic of his style, it concerns the response we make when we receive a solicitation from Unicef. Unger can imagine no reason for our binning this other than moral blindness. Never, for example, does he consider that thoughtful people prefer to plan their giving ahead of time and to map out how much they will give to various groups, rejecting mail solicitations because they have already made a different plan. Perhaps recognition of this fact would introduce a dangerous asymmetry between duties to rescue and duties of charitable giving. But: "it's as easy as pie" to call in and make a Visa card donation, Unger gleefully announces, having pinned us into a moral corner. And: "Now, you can write that address on an envelope well prepared for mailing." Such instructions, as to a corrupt child, fill Unger's pages. It may be doubted whether this mode of address would be persuasive with the implied reader, even if a person so stupid and venal ever turned to a book on this topic.

Although this is a work of philosophy, the implied reader is also a philosophical imbecile. Near the end of the book, Unger astonishingly announces that "most of this book's mature readers" are "academic philosophers"; a little later he suggests that philosophers should be silent in public about some of the more unpopular conclusions of utilitarian argument, such as the conclusion that we sometimes have an obligation to steal in order to relieve misery. So whatever one might have thought, it turns out that he's been addressing professional philosophers all along. But it's a rare member of that profession who would get to the final page, given the work's lack of nuance and of engagement with the work of others.

Unger offers a crude choice, for example, between two philosophical methodologies: that of the "Preservationist," who likes to conserve as many of our current moral intuitions as possible, and that of the "Liberationist," who accepts Unger's brand of revisionary utilitarianism, rejecting some of our moral intuitions as ill-founded. It may be doubted whether any good philosopher has ever been a Preservationist, and Unger offers no discussion of the way intuition and ordinary belief are treated by serious non-utilitarian philosophers such as Kant and Rawls. Nor does he show us any reason why, having thrown over the traces of convention, we should choose to be utilitarians, rather than Kantians: none of the questions separating those two traditions is so much as mentioned. Only a philosophically illiterate reader (who is also pretty unimaginative as a human being) would believe that these two positions exhaust the space of morality. Unger's previous work has not prepared us for such oversimplifications, and one can only suppose that they are dictated by the intensity of his moral passion.

Nor is there any sophisticated discussion here of the writings of the many other people who have laboured on the question of beneficence and global obligation. Writers such as Derek Parfit, Liam Murphy and Shelly Kagan from the utilitarian tradition, Thomas Nagel, Thomas Scanlon, and Thomas Pogge from the Kantian, Gerald Cohen, Brian Barry, the economists Amartya Sen, John Roemer, and Partha Dasgupta, all get a nod in a footnote at most, and we hear nothing informative about how their arguments would be addressed. Major historical contributors such as Kant, Bentham, and Adam Smith don't even get a nod. So the implied reader is not a reader of philosophy (despite Unger's claim to the contrary), and can therefore be led to believe that evangelist Unger is a voice crying in the wilderness, rather than one of many thoughtful people who have been addressing the question for ages.

These problems in Unger's philosophical approach help explain why he doesn't give his own conclusion much realistic scrutiny. But there are other problems, connected with the excessively narrow approach he chooses. A helpful philosophical account of human misery and our responsibilities to alleviate it should address at least the following questions.

1. What would a good theory of global political justice look like, and how would it describe the basic entitlements of individuals and nations? Unger offers no help on this question, since he is basically not interested in institutional and political issues.

2. In the absence of globally just institutions, how stringent are the moral obligations of individuals to relieve human misery? Kant long ago argued that we have duties of beneficence only because "the injustice of governments" has created inequalities of wealth; he also argued that our duties of beneficence are "imperfect duties," allowing latitude for special obligations to the near and dear. Thomas Nagel has recently developed this position further. Unger confronts this question, offering his extremely stringent answer. But because he doesn't link it sufficiently to a question about the obligations of political institutions, he never adequately responds to the arguments put forward by Nagel and others who would distinguish the two spheres of obligation.

3. Are we morally required to devote only money and resources, or also time and effort? Unger spends one page on his question, apparently saying that we should devote both, but he doesn't offer any guidelines about how we should weigh these different contributions. (Indeed, he suggests that academics should become corporate lawyers if they can, so that they will have more money to give

away—once again slighting the contribution thought makes to practice.)

4. What should be the goal of our efforts: to maximise the sum of satisfactions? To maximise human functioning and capability? To maximise the access of individuals to certain basic resources? To ensure to as many people as possible a certain basic level of satisfaction, or of capability, or of resources? To maximise the situation (on any of these dimensions) of the least well-off? These questions have been at the heart of much of the modern debate about equality and global redistribution, but Unger neglects them completely, although at times he would appear to assume a classical utilitarian answer.

5. Should we think of human life as consisting of a single dimension, along which we can move individuals higher or lower, or should we think of it as consisting of a number of distinct dimensions, all of which should be promoted in any meaningful social policy? Again, this is a much discussed question on which Unger says nothing. It is highly pertinent to his eventual recommendation, since Oxfam and Unicef deal with some aspects of human existence (food, water, basic medical care, in some cases primary education), but leave others unattended (political liberty, religious freedom, higher education, artistic expression).

6. Should we, as givers, operate with a conception of the good that is our own, or should we attempt to promote a situation in which the recipients of our donations have choices to avail themselves of what we give in accordance with their own conceptions of the good? Can we usefully distinguish between a core of political values, which we may promote without offence to the liberty of others, and a more comprehensive set of values, which we may not impose on others through coercive political action? Again, nothing is said about this, and yet it seems crucial in determining the direction and admissible scope of our efforts.

7. What are the most effective strategies, if we want to use our resources to achieve one of the goals set forth under Number Four? This is a very tough question, involving many empirical issues (for example, issues about economic incentives), most of them under dispute. But there is one thing we can say: that there are many good-faith strategies people can take, without being moral imbeciles. Giving money to "élite institutions" may not be such a bad way of promoting progress in solving terrible social and economic problems. Giving to religious institutions is another way, both because those institutions support a great deal of direct relief and because they organise and assist the lives of poor people in many non-material ways. (Unger's brusque rejection of these groups is apparently based on the false belief that they do not relieve misery.) Writing a book or

going into politics or becoming a development economist is yet another way. Any defensible conception of human well-being ought to include a role for such contributions.

At the same time, any meaningful solution to the problems of developing countries must involve economic and structural planning and the appropriate use of markets. Direct giving, if it undermines these structures, will probably make things worse. That is not to say that public action and private philanthropy should not be combined with the market. Sen, for example, has written well about how these different approaches might be combined. But we certainly don't want to produce the situation Unger shoots for, where Oxfam runs the world.

Even in addressing the strictly economic aspects of human well-being, we are forced almost immediately to turn to other aspects. If we take the relief of acute hunger to be our only goal, we still must ask whether this is best promoted by addressing hunger directly, or by promoting political liberties, female literacy, and other constituents of a human being's quality of life. Unger is not unaware of these interrelationships, as one brief discussion shows; but he gives us no framework for thinking about them.

What, then, does Unger's book contribute? His discussions of the distinction between duties to rescue and duties to aid, and his general diagnosis of irrationalities in our thinking about people at a distance, are both ingenious and cogent. Much of this is not entirely original, however: many of the distortions that Unger describes have been recognised since Plato's *Protagoras*, and Unger's reliance on Peter Singer and Judith Jarvis Thomson for core examples is obvious. Nonetheless, he is a resourceful thinker who complicates the examples in interesting ways and adds others of his own. If one can abstract long enough from all the questions that crowd in unanswered, one may well find that he has made some progress towards establishing the stringency of our obligations to aid. A modest, tight, and interesting book could have been written along these lines. It would call into question many of the ways in which we live, and provoke the thoughtful reader to reflect on the seven questions and the practical challenge they contain. It would thus be an appropriate prolegomenon to a richer and fuller work in which the seven questions (or at least some of them) would be thoroughly tackled, and the competing answers of a variety of philosophers and economists debated.

Unger's sense of moral urgency betrays him, however. Because he is so eager to get readers to do *something* (even if it is strategically quite the wrong thing, at least those selfish folks won't be living so high and at least some good will in the short term be achieved), he short-circuits the work of reflection, and ends up offering little of philosophical interest. Philosophy is not political speechmaking or evangelistic arm-twisting. It offers nothing if not nuance and sustained reflection, and delicate theory-building. In the process of getting philosophy to be more practical, Unger has ultimately sold it out.

IN RESPONSE TO:

IF OXFAM RAN THE WORLD, FROM THE SEPTEMBER 4, 1997, ISSUE

*From Peter Unger:*

In her review of my *Living High and Letting Die: Our Illusion of Innocence*, Martha Nussbaum notes that I address the reader with the claim that an affluent person, "like you and me, must contribute to vitally effective groups, like Oxfam and Unicef, most of the money and property she now has, and most of what comes her way for the foreseeable future." She refers to this as "Unger's solution" to the heartbreakingly serious problems plaguing impoverished people in the poorest countries in the world. She tries to reduce this "solution" to absurdity by developing a vision of how the world would be if *everyone* were to comply with my injunction. Obviously the result would be chaos, as she observes at great length. But this is a bewildering misreading of my work. The injunction she cites was addressed to the conscience of the individual reader in the world as it is—a world in which governments do very little to save dying children in impoverished regions and in which organisations such as Oxfam America, US for Unicef, and Care together receive less money from private donations than Harvard University does. The injunction was, of course, conditional on the wholly realistic assumption that even after my book had its full foreseeable effect, this state of affairs would continue: that for the foreseeable future there would be no radical institutional changes, that most affluent individuals would continue to donate next to nothing, or even nothing at all.

My question was: in this actual situation, what should you, a person interested enough to be reading my book, do? My answer: give most of what you have in order to help save children who will otherwise die of preventable disease and malnutrition. The book offers several salient arguments in support of this but not one is so much as mentioned, much less addressed or discussed, in the review.

I never pretended to have articulated a programme for saving dying children by means of co-ordinated collective action at the institutional level. Doubtless it would be vastly more efficient to proceed at that level; and perhaps some day the world will be receptive to rational reforms of the global economic system. But until this Utopian condition prevails, there is much that a single individual can and should do.

Nussbaum also criticises the book for being insufficiently engaged with issues of theory. It doesn't offer "delicate theory-building," doesn't explain why we might or might not "choose to be utilitarians rather than

Kantians," and fails to say whether our goal should be "to maximise the sum of satisfactions . . . to maximise human functioning and capabilities" or whatever. But my concern in the book was explicitly not with theory-building, delicate or otherwise. Indeed, the strategy of my work was to avoid drawing my conclusions from all such evidently controversial theories, and instead to show that our own deepest moral beliefs themselves commit us to the costly conclusions for which I argued. It would of course be wonderful to solve all the problems of international distributive justice in a way that is economically rational, culturally sensitive, and based on a defensible account of the human good. But my ambitions didn't extend nearly that far, and it is fantastic that Nussbaum takes me to task for having failed to solve all the relevant problems which, as she notes, many excellent thinkers are working on.

As is indicated in Oxfam America's latest annual report, Nussbaum and I may well be the two American philosophers who most strongly support that organisation. It's with considerable sadness, then, that I read her distorted account of my book. Her focus on a fantasy world run by Oxfam is an irrelevant distraction from the serious problems with which Oxfam is concerned.

Peter Unger
New York University

*From Peter Singer:*
Martha Nussbaum writes that Peter Unger's "reliance" on Judith Jarvis Thomson and me for "core examples" diminishes the originality of his book. Her review shows, however, that she has failed to see where that originality lies. While Unger does start from an old example of mine, as he himself says at the outset, this example and the argument I built on it has—twenty-five years later—left many people unconvinced. Unger extends the example in ways that I never imagined, making the argument infinitely more difficult to escape.

The suggestion that Unger's originality is diminished by his reliance on examples from Judith Jarvis Thomson is even more startling. A significant body of philosophical literature has arisen around the "trolley problem" devised by Thomson (who, incidentally, got the core example from an article by Philippa Foot). Unger has effectively destroyed this body of literature. Thomson and others who have discussed the trolley problem rely on our common intuitions about a series of cases, and then draw moral conclusions from them. Unger has shown that these intuitions are affected by ethically insignificant factors in the way the examples are framed, the order in which they are presented and so on. No one will ever again be able to defend the use of trolley problem examples—or arguments based on intuitions in specific cases of these kinds—without dealing with Unger's critique.

Nussbaum does not like Unger's style. I find it original, amusing, and engaging, but I can easily see that some would find it extremely irritating. Less understandable, however, is Nussbaum's failure to discuss the central arguments of the book she is reviewing. Instead she goes off into a long account of "what if everyone did what Unger is suggesting?" This is transparently irrelevant to his arguments, which are based on the assumption—obviously true for the present and the foreseeable future—that a modest donation to an overseas aid organisation, of the kind that a middle-class person living in a developed country can easily afford, can do a lot towards saving lives. Nussbaum's argument is on a par with the argument that it is wrong to work late in order to avoid driving home in rush-hour traffic, because if everyone did that, the rush-hour would simply come later. I thought philosophers had long ago understood that the argument cannot be applied in so simplistic a fashion. Nussbaum has missed an opportunity to engage with the argument of one of the most significant works of ethics published this decade.

Peter Singer
Monash University

*From Martha Nussbaum:*
Peter Singer's response to my review of Peter Unger's book is strange, for he defends the aspects of the book that I praised and says nothing in defence of those that I criticised. I did not hold the non-originality of Unger's examples against him; I simply pointed it out. I said that Unger's "discussions of the distinction between duties to rescue and duties to aid, and his general diagnosis of irrationalities in our thinking about people at a distance, are both ingenious and cogent," and added that "Unger is a resourceful thinker who complicates the examples in interesting ways and adds others of his own."

My complaints against the book lay elsewhere. I objected to Unger's crude discussion of philosophical method, to his failure to grapple seriously with the arguments of others, to his failure to engage with non-utilitarians or to defend his own narrow utilitarian framework, and, especially, to his total failure to confront institutional and political issues that must be taken account of in any good analysis of duties to aid. I mentioned seven questions, all commonplace in recent political philosophy, that need to be addressed in any such work, and noted that Unger is silent about six of them. The non-addressed questions include such basic ones as: what would a good theory of global justice look like, and how would it describe the basic entitlements of individuals and nations? What should be the goal of our efforts: to maximise the sum of satisfaction? To maximise human functioning and capability? To maximise the access of individuals to certain basic resources? To ensure to as many people as possible a certain basic level of satisfaction, or of capability, or of resources? To maximise the situation (on any of these dimensions) of the least well-off? (Those are two of the six.) Unger makes claims that he cannot make plausibly without consideration of such familiar questions.

Unger makes, very seriously, a practical recommendation—we should all give most of what we have to Oxfam—that, if followed, would be disastrous. This fact is hardly irrelevant to the assessment of what he has accomplished. Philosophy of this sort cannot afford to be naive armchair rumination. Irresponsible speculation brings philosophy into discredit in just those circles where good philosophy may possibly do some good (a fact that Singer, a practical philosopher very concerned with fact, must know well). Even when ideal theory is in question, philosophy must confront economic and political realities. Many fine modern writers on international justice and the relief of hunger are aware of this. Unger is not.

# CHAPTER SIXTEEN

# The Professor of Parody

Four books by JUDITH BUTLER: Excitable Speech: A Politics of the Performative (1997); The Psychic Life of Power: Theories in Subjection (1997); Bodies that Matter: On the Discursive Limits of "Sex" (1993); Gender Trouble: Feminism and the Subversion of Identity (1990)

I

For a long time, academic feminism in America has been closely allied to the practical struggle to achieve justice and equality for women. Feminist theory has been understood by theorists as not just fancy words on paper; theory is connected to proposals for social change. Thus feminist scholars have engaged in many concrete projects: the reform of rape law; winning attention and legal redress for the problems of domestic violence and sexual harassment; improving women's economic opportunities, working conditions, and education; winning pregnancy benefits for female workers; campaigning against the trafficking of women and girls in prostitution; working for the social and political equality of lesbians and gay men.

Indeed, some theorists have left the academy altogether, feeling more comfortable in the world of practical politics, where they can address these urgent problems directly. Those who remain in the academy have frequently made it a point of honor to be academics of a committed practical sort, eyes always on the material conditions of real women, writing always in a way that acknowledges those real bodies and those real struggles. One cannot read a page of Catharine MacKinnon, for example, without being engaged with a real issue of legal and institutional change. If one disagrees with her proposals—and many feminists disagree with them—the challenge posed by her writing is to find some other way of solving the problem that has been vividly delineated.

Feminists have differed in some cases about what is bad, and about what is needed to make things better; but all have agreed that the circumstances of women are often unjust and that law and political action can make them more nearly just. MacKinnon, who portrays hierarchy and subordination as endemic to our entire culture, is also committed to, and cautiously optimistic about, change through law—the domestic law of rape and sexual harassment and international human rights law. Even Nancy Chodorow, who, in *The Reproduction of Mothering*, offered a depressing account of the replication of oppressive gender categories in child-rearing, argued that this situation could change. Men and women could decide, understanding the unhappy consequences of these habits, that they will henceforth do things differently; and changes in laws and institutions can assist in such decisions.

Feminist theory still looks like this in many parts of the world. In India, for example, academic feminists have thrown themselves into practical struggles, and feminist theorizing is closely tethered to practical commitments such as female literacy, the reform of unequal land laws, changes in rape law (which, in India today, has most of the flaws that the first generation of American feminists targeted), the effort to get social recognition for problems of sexual harassment and domestic violence. These feminists know that they live in the middle of a fiercely unjust reality; they cannot live with themselves without addressing it more or less daily, in their theoretical writing and in their activities outside the seminar room.

In the United States, however, things have been changing. One observes a new, disquieting trend. It is not only that feminist theory pays relatively little attention to the struggles of women outside the United States. (This was always a dispiriting feature even of much of the best work of the earlier period.) Something more insidious than provincialism has come to prominence in the American academy. It is the virtually complete turning from the material side of life, toward a type of verbal and symbolic politics that makes only the flimsiest of connections with the real situation of real women.

Feminist thinkers of the new symbolic type would appear to believe that the way to do feminist politics is to use words in a subversive way, in academic publications of lofty obscurity and disdainful abstractness. These symbolic gestures, it is believed, are themselves a form of political resistance; and so one need not engage with messy things such as legislatures and movements in order to act daringly. The new feminism, moreover, instructs its members that there is little room for large-scale social change, and maybe no room at all. We are all, more or less, prisoners of the structures of power that have defined our identity as women; we can never change those structures in a large-scale way, and we can never escape from them. All that we can hope to do is to find spaces within the structures of power in which to parody them, to poke fun at them, to transgress them in speech. And so symbolic verbal politics, in addition to being offered as a type of real politics, is held to be the only politics that is really possible.

These developments owe much to the recent prominence of French postmodernist thought. Many young feminists, whatever their concrete affiliations with this or that French thinker, have been influenced by the extremely French idea that the intellectual does politics by speaking seditiously, and that this is a significant type of political action. Many have also derived from the writings of Michel Foucault (rightly or wrongly) the fatalistic idea that we are prisoners of an all-enveloping structure of power, and that real-life reform movements usually end up serving power in new and insidious ways. Such feminists therefore find comfort in the idea that the subversive use of words is still available to feminist intellectuals. Deprived of the hope of larger or more lasting changes, we can still perform our resistance by the reworking of verbal categories, and thus, at the margins, of the selves who are constituted by them.

One American feminist has shaped these developments more than any other. Judith Butler seems to many young scholars to define what feminism is now. Trained as a philosopher, she is frequently seen (more by people in literature than by philosophers) as a major thinker about gender, power, and the body. As we wonder what has become of old-style feminist politics and the material realities to which it was committed, it seems necessary to reckon with Butler's work and influence, and to scrutinize the arguments that have led so many to adopt a stance that looks very much like quietism and retreat.

II

It is difficult to come to grips with Butler's ideas, because it is difficult to figure out what they are. Butler is a very smart person. In public discussions, she proves that she can speak clearly and has a quick grasp of what is said to her. Her written style, however, is ponderous and obscure. It is dense with allusions to other theorists, drawn from a wide range of different theoretical traditions. In addition to Foucault, and to a more recent focus on Freud, Butler's work relies heavily on the thought of Louis Althusser, the French lesbian theorist Monique Wittig, the American anthropologist Gayle Rubin, Jacques Lacan, J. L. Austin, and the American philosopher of language Saul Kripke. These figures do not all agree with one another, to say the least; so an initial problem in reading Butler is that one is bewildered to find her arguments buttressed by appeal to so many contradictory concepts and doctrines, usually without any account of how the apparent contradictions will be resolved.

A further problem lies in Butler's casual mode of allusion. The ideas of these thinkers are never described in enough detail to include the uninitiated (if you are not familiar with the Althusserian concept of "interpellation," you are lost for chapters) or to explain to the initiated how, precisely, the difficult ideas are being understood. Of course, much academic writing is allusive in some way: it presupposes prior knowledge of certain doctrines and positions. But in both the continental and the Anglo-American philosophical traditions, academic writers for a specialist audience standardly acknowledge that the figures they mention are complicated, and the object of many different interpretations. They therefore typically assume the responsibility of advancing a definite interpretation among the contested ones, and of showing by argument why they have interpreted the figure as they have, and why their own interpretation is better than others.

We find none of this in Butler. Divergent interpretations are simply not considered—even where, as in the cases of Foucault and Freud, she is advancing highly contestable interpretations that would not be accepted by many scholars. Thus one is led to the conclusion that the allusiveness of the writing cannot be explained in the usual way, by positing an audience of specialists eager to debate the details of an esoteric academic position. The writing is simply too thin to satisfy any such audience. It is also obvious that Butler's work is not directed at a non-academic audience eager to grapple with actual injustices. Such an audience would simply be baffled by the thick soup of Butler's prose, by its air of in-group knowingness, by its extremely high ratio of names to explanations.

To whom, then, is Butler speaking? It would seem that she is addressing a group of young feminist theorists in the academy who are neither students of philosophy, caring about what Althusser and Freud and Kripke really said, nor outsiders, needing to be informed about the nature of their projects and persuaded of their worth. This implied audience is imagined as remarkably docile. Subservient to the oracular voice of Butler's text, and dazzled by its patina of high-concept abstractness, the imagined reader poses few questions, requests no arguments and no clear definitions of terms.

Still more strangely, the implied reader is expected not to care greatly about Butler's own final view on many matters. For a large proportion of the sentences in any book by Butler—especially sentences near the end of chapters—are questions. Sometimes the answer that the question expects is evident. But often things are much more indeterminate. Among the non-interrogative sentences, many begin with "Consider . . ." or "One could suggest . . ."—in such a way that Butler never quite tells the reader whether she approves of the view described. Mystification as well as hierarchy are the tools of her practice, a mystification that eludes criticism because it makes few definite claims.

Take two representative examples:

What does it mean for the agency of a subject to presuppose its own subordination? Is the act of presupposing the same as the act of reinstating, or is there a discontinuity between the power presupposed and the power reinstated? Consider that in the very act by which the subject reproduces the conditions of its own subordination, the subject exemplifies a temporally based vulnerability that belongs to those conditions, specifically, to the exigencies of their renewal.

And:

Such questions cannot be answered here, but they indicate a direction for thinking that is perhaps prior to the question of conscience, namely, the question that preoccupied Spinoza, Nietzsche, and most recently, Giorgio Agamben: How are we to understand the desire to be as a constitutive desire? Resituating conscience and interpellation within such an account, we might then add to this question another: How is such a desire exploited not only by a law in the singular, but by laws of various kinds such that we yield to subordination in order to maintain some sense of social "being"?

Why does Butler prefer to write in this teasing, exasperating way? The style is certainly not unprecedented. Some precincts of the continental philosophical tradition, though surely not all of them, have an unfortunate tendency to regard the philosopher as a star who fascinates, and frequently by obscurity, rather than as an arguer among equals. When ideas are stated clearly, after all, they may be detached from their author: one can take them away and pursue them on one's own. When they remain mysterious (indeed, when they are not quite asserted), one remains dependent on the originating authority. The thinker is heeded only for his or her turgid charisma. One hangs in suspense, eager for the next move. When Butler does follow that "direction for thinking," what will she say? What does it mean, tell us please, for the agency of a subject to presuppose its own subordination? (No clear answer to this question, so far as I can see, is forthcoming.) One is given the impression of a mind so profoundly cogitative that it will not pronounce on anything lightly: so one waits, in awe of its depth, for it finally to do so.

In this way obscurity creates an aura of importance. It also serves another related purpose. It bullies the reader into granting that, since one cannot figure out what is going on, there must be something significant going on, some complexity of thought, where in reality there are often familiar or even shopworn notions, addressed too simply and too casually to add any new dimension of understanding. When the bullied readers of Butler's books muster the daring to think thus, they will see that the ideas in these books are thin. When Butler's notions are stated clearly and succinctly, one sees that, without a lot more distinctions and arguments, they don't go far, and they are not especially new. Thus obscurity fills the void left by an absence of a real complexity of thought and argument.

Last year Butler won the first prize in the annual Bad Writing Contest sponsored by the journal *Philosophy and Literature*, for the following sentence:

The move from a structuralist account in which capital is understood to structure social relations in relatively homologous ways to a view of hegemony in which power relations are subject to repetition, convergence, and rearticulation brought the question of temporality into the thinking of structure, and marked a shift from a form of Althusserian theory that takes structural totalities as theoretical objects to one in which the insights into the contingent possibility of structure inaugurate a renewed conception of hegemony as bound up with the contingent sites and strategies of the rearticulation of power.

Now, Butler might have written: "Marxist accounts, focusing on capital as the central force structuring social relations, depicted the operations of that force as everywhere uniform. By contrast, Althusserian accounts, focusing on power, see the operations of that force as variegated and as shifting over time." Instead, she prefers a verbosity that causes the reader to expend so much effort in deciphering her prose that little energy is left for assessing the truth of the claims. Announcing the award, the journal's editor remarked that "it's possibly the anxiety-inducing obscurity of such writing that has led Professor Warren Hedges of Southern Oregon University to praise Judith Butler as 'probably one of the ten smartest people on the planet.'" (Such bad writing, incidentally, is by no means ubiquitous in the "queer theory" group of theorists with which Butler is associated. David Halperin, for example, writes about the relationship between Foucault and Kant, and about Greek homosexuality, with philosophical clarity and historical precision.)

Butler gains prestige in the literary world by being a philosopher; many admirers associate her manner of writing with philosophical profundity. But one should ask whether it belongs to the philosophical tradition at all, rather than to the closely related but adversarial traditions of sophistry and rhetoric. Ever since Socrates distinguished philosophy from what the sophists and the rhetoricians were doing, it has been a discourse of equals who trade arguments and counter-arguments without any obscurantist sleight-of-hand. In that way, he claimed, philosophy showed respect for the soul, while the others' manipulative methods showed only disrespect. One afternoon, fatigued by Butler on a long plane trip, I turned to a draft of a student's dissertation on Hume's views of personal identity. I quickly felt my spirits reviving. Doesn't she write clearly, I thought with pleasure, and a tiny bit of pride. And Hume, what a fine, what a gracious spirit: how kindly he respects the reader's intelligence, even at the cost of exposing his own uncertainty.

III

Butler's main idea, first introduced in *Gender Trouble* in 1990 and repeated throughout her books, is that gender is a social artifice. Our ideas of what women and men are reflect nothing that exists eternally in nature. Instead they derive from customs that embed social relations of power.

This notion, of course, is nothing new. The denaturalizing of gender was present already in Plato, and it received a great boost from John Stuart Mill, who claimed in "The Subjection of Women" that "what is now called the nature of women is an eminently artificial thing." Mill saw that claims about "women's nature" derive from, and shore up, hierarchies of power: woman-liness is made to be whatever would serve the cause of keeping women in subjection, or, as he put it, "enslaving their minds." With the family as with feudalism, the rhetoric of nature itself serves the cause of slavery. "The subjection of women to men being a universal custom, any departure from it quite naturally appears unnatural. . . . But was there ever any domination which did not appear natural to those who possessed it?"

Mill was hardly the first social constructionist. Similar ideas about anger, greed, envy, and other prominent features of our lives had been common-place in the history of philosophy since ancient Greece. And Mill's applica-tion of familiar notions of social construction to gender needed, and still needs, much fuller development; his suggestive remarks did not yet amount to a theory of gender. Long before Butler came on the scene, many feminists contributed to the articulation of such an account.

In work published in the 1970s and 1980s, Catharine MacKinnon and Andrea Dworkin argued that the conventional understanding of gender roles is a way of ensuring continued male domination in sexual relations, as well as in the public sphere. They took the core of Mill's insight into a sphere of life concerning which the Victorian philosopher had said little. (Not nothing, though: in 1869, Mill already understood that the failure to criminalize rape within marriage defined woman as a tool for male use and negated her human dignity.) Before Butler, MacKinnon and Dworkin addressed the feminist fantasy of an idyllic natural sexuality of women that only needed to be "liberated"; and argued that social forces go so deep that we should not suppose we have access to such a notion of "nature." Before Butler, they stressed the ways in which male-dominated power structures marginalize and subordinate not only women, but also people who would like to choose a same-sex relationship. They understood that discrimination against gays and lesbians is a way of enforcing the familiar hierarchically ordered gender roles; and so they saw discrimination against gays and lesbians as a form of sex discrimination.

Before Butler, the psychologist Nancy Chodorow gave a detailed and compelling account of how gender differences replicate themselves across the generations: she argued that the ubiquity of these mechanisms of repli-cation enables us to understand how what is artificial can nonetheless be nearly ubiquitous. Before Butler, the biologist Anne Fausto Sterling, through her painstaking criticism of experimental work allegedly supporting the naturalness of conventional gender distinctions, showed how deeply social power-relations had compromised the objectivity of scientists: *Myths of Gender* (1985) was an apt title for what she found in the biology of the time. (Other biologists and primatologists also contributed to this enterprise.) Before Butler, the political theorist Susan Moller Okin explored the role of law and political thought in constructing a gendered destiny for women in the family; and this project, too, was pursued further by a number of feminists in law and political philosophy. Before Butler, Gayle Rubin's important anthropological account of subordination, *The Traffic in Women* (1975), provided a valuable analysis of the relationship between the social organization of gender and the asymmetries of power.

So what does Butler's work add to this copious body of writing? *Gender Trouble* and *Bodies that Matter* contain no detailed argument against biological claims of "natural" difference, no account of mechanisms of gender replication, and no account of the legal shaping of the family; nor do they contain any detailed focus on possibilities for legal change. What, then, does Butler offer that we might not find more fully done in earlier feminist writings? One relatively original claim is that when we recognize the artificiality of gender distinctions, and refrain from thinking of them as expressing an independent natural reality, we will also understand that there is no compelling reason why the gender types should have been two (correlated with the two biological sexes), rather than three or five or indefinitely many. "When the constructed status of gender is theorized as radically independent of sex, gender itself becomes a free-floating artifice," she writes.

From this claim it does not follow, for Butler, that we can freely reinvent the genders as we like: she holds, indeed, that there are severe limits to our freedom. She insists that we should not naively imagine that there is a pristine self that stands behind society, ready to emerge all pure and liberated: "There is no self that is prior to the convergence or who maintains 'integrity' prior to its entrance into this conflicted cultural field. There is only a taking up of the tools where they lie, where the very 'taking up' is enabled by the tool lying there." Butler does claim, though, that we can create categories that are in some sense new ones, by means of the artful parody of the old ones. Thus her best known idea, her conception of politics as a parodic performance, is born out of the sense of a (strictly limited) freedom that comes from the recognition that one's ideas of gender have been shaped by forces that are social rather than biological. We are doomed to repetition of the power structures into which we are born, but we can at least make fun of them; and some ways of making fun are subversive assaults on the original norms.

The idea of gender as performance is Butler's most famous idea, and so it is worth pausing to scrutinize it more closely. She introduced the notion intuitively, in *Gender Trouble*, without invoking theoretical precedent. Later she denied that she was referring to quasi-theatrical performance, and associated her notion instead with Austin's account of speech acts in *How to Do Things with Words*. Austin's linguistic category of "performatives" is a category of linguistic utterances that function, in and of themselves, as actions rather than as assertions. When (in appropriate social circumstances) I say "I bet ten dollars," or "I'm sorry," or "I do" (in a marriage ceremony), or "I name this ship. . ." I am not reporting on a bet or an apology or a marriage or a naming ceremony, I am conducting one.

Butler's analogous claim about gender is not obvious, since the "performances" in question involve gesture, dress, movement, and action, as well as language. Austin's thesis, which is restricted to a rather technical analysis of a certain class of sentences, is in fact not especially helpful to Butler in developing her ideas. Indeed, though she vehemently repudiates readings of her work that associate her view with theater, thinking about the Living Theater's subversive work with gender seems to illuminate her ideas far more than thinking about Austin.

Nor is Butler's treatment of Austin very plausible. She makes the bizarre claim that the fact that the marriage ceremony is one of dozens of examples of performatives in Austin's text suggests "that the heterosexualization of the social bond is the paradigmatic form for those speech acts which bring about what they name." Hardly. Marriage is no more paradigmatic for Austin than betting or ship naming or promising or apologizing. He is interested in a formal feature of certain utterances, and we are given no reason to suppose that their content has any significance for his argument. It is usually a mistake to read earthshaking significance into a philosopher's pedestrian choice of examples. Should we say that Aristotle's use of a low-fat diet to illustrate the practical syllogism suggests that chicken is at the heart of Aristotelian virtue? Or that Rawls's use of travel plans to illustrate practical reasoning shows that *A Theory of Justice* aims at giving us all a vacation?

Leaving these oddities to one side, Butler's point is presumably this: when we act and speak in a gendered way, we are not simply reporting on something that is already fixed in the world, we are actively constituting it, replicating it, and reinforcing it. By behaving as if there were male and female "natures," we co-create the social fiction that these natures exist. They are never there apart from our deeds; we are always making them be there. At the same time, by carrying out these performances in a slightly different manner, a parodic manner, we can perhaps unmake them just a little.

Thus the one place for agency in a world constrained by hierarchy is in the small opportunities we have to oppose gender roles every time they take shape. When I find myself doing femaleness, I can turn it around, poke fun at it, do it a little bit differently. Such reactive and parodic performances, in Butler's view, never destabilize the larger system. She doesn't envisage mass movements of resistance or campaigns for political reform; only personal acts carried out by a small number of knowing actors. Just as actors with a bad script can subvert it by delivering the bad lines oddly, so too with gender: the script remains bad, but the actors have a tiny bit of freedom. Thus we have the basis for what, in *Excitable Speech*, Butler calls "an ironic hopefulness."

Up to this point, Butler's contentions, though relatively familiar, are plausible and even interesting, though one is already unsettled by her narrow vision of the possibilities for change. Yet Butler adds to these plausible claims about gender two other claims that are stronger and more contentious. The first is that there is no agent behind or prior to the social forces that produce the self. If this means only that babies are born into a gendered world that begins to replicate males and females almost immediately, the claim is plausible, but not surprising: experiments have for some time demonstrated that the way babies are held and talked to, the way their emotions are described, are profoundly shaped by the sex the adults in question believe the child to have. (The same baby will be bounced if the adults think it is a boy, cuddled if they think it is a girl; its crying will be labeled as fear if the adults think it is a girl, as anger if they think it is a boy.) Butler shows no interest in these empirical facts, but they do support her contention.

If she means, however, that babies enter the world completely inert, with no tendencies and no abilities that are in some sense prior to their experience in a gendered society, this is far less plausible, and difficult to support empirically. Butler offers no such support, preferring to remain on the high plane of metaphysical abstraction. (Indeed, her recent Freudian work may even repudiate this idea: it suggests, with Freud, that there are at least some presocial impulses and tendencies, although, typically, this line is not clearly developed.) Moreover, such an exaggerated denial of pre-cultural agency takes away some of the resources that Chodorow and others use when they try to account for cultural change in the direction of the better.

Butler does in the end want to say that we have a kind of agency, an ability to undertake change and resistance. But where does this ability come from, if there is no structure in the personality that is not thoroughly power's creation? It is not impossible for Butler to answer this question, but she certainly has not answered it yet, in a way that would convince those who believe that human beings have at least some pre-cultural desires—for food, for comfort, for cognitive mastery, for survival—and that this structure in the personality is crucial in the explanation of our development as moral and political agents. One would like to see her engage with the strongest forms of such a view, and to say, clearly and without jargon, exactly why and where she rejects them. One would also like to hear her speak about real infants, who do appear to manifest a structure of striving that influences from the start their reception of cultural forms. Butler's second strong claim is that the body itself, and especially the distinction between the two sexes, is also a social construction. She means not only that the body is shaped in many ways by social norms of how men and women should be; she means also that the fact that a binary division of sexes is taken as fundamental, as a key to arranging society, is itself a social idea that is not given in bodily reality. What exactly does this claim mean, and how plausible is it?

Butler's brief exploration of Foucault on hermaphrodites does show us society's anxious insistence to classify every human being in one box or another, whether or not the individual fits a box; but of course it does not show that there are many such indeterminate cases. She is right to insist that we might have made many different classifications of body types, not necessarily focusing on the binary division as the most salient; and she is also right to insist that, to a large extent, claims of bodily sex difference allegedly based upon scientific research have been projections of cultural prejudice—though Butler offers nothing here that is nearly as compelling as Fausto Sterling's painstaking biological analysis.

And yet it is much too simple to say that power is all that the body is. We might have had the bodies of birds or dinosaurs or lions, but we do not; and this reality shapes our choices. Culture can shape and reshape some aspects of our bodily existence, but it does not shape all the aspects of it. "In the man burdened by hunger and thirst," as Sextus Empiricus observed long ago, "it is impossible to produce by argument the conviction that he is not so burdened." This is an important fact also for feminism, since women's nutritional needs (and their special needs when pregnant or lactating) are an important feminist topic. Even where sex difference is concerned, it is surely too simple to write it all off as culture; nor should feminists be eager to make such a sweeping gesture. Women who run or play basketball, for example, were right to welcome the demolition of myths about women's athletic performance that were the product of male-dominated assumptions; but they were also right to demand the specialized research on women's bodies that has fostered a better understanding of women's training needs and women's injuries. In short: what feminism needs, and sometimes gets, is a subtle study of the interplay of bodily difference and cultural construction. And Butler's abstract pronouncements, floating high above all matter, give us none of what we need.

IV

Suppose we grant Butler her most interesting claims up to this point: that the social structure of gender is ubiquitous, but we can resist it by subversive and parodic acts. Two significant questions remain. What should be resisted, and on what basis? What would the acts of resistance be like, and what would we expect them to accomplish?

Butler uses several words for what she takes to be bad and therefore worthy of resistance: the "repressive," the "subordinating," the "oppressive." But she provides no empirical discussion of resistance of the sort that we find, say, in Barry Adam's fascinating sociological study *The Survival of Domination* (1978), which studies the subordination of blacks, Jews, women, and gays and lesbians, and their ways of wrestling with the forms of social power that have oppressed them. Nor does Butler provide any account of the concepts of resistance and oppression that would help us, were we really in doubt about what we ought to be resisting.

Butler departs in this regard from earlier social-constructionist feminists, all of whom used ideas such as non-hierarchy, equality, dignity, autonomy, and treating as an end rather than a means, to indicate a direction for actual politics. Still less is she willing to elaborate any positive normative notion. Indeed, it is clear that Butler, like Foucault, is adamantly opposed to normative notions such as human dignity, or treating humanity as an end, on the grounds that they are inherently dictatorial. In her view, we ought to wait to see what the political struggle itself throws up, rather than prescribe in advance to its participants. Universal normative notions, she says, "colonize under the sign of the same."

This idea of waiting to see what we get—in a word, this moral passivity—seems plausible in Butler because she tacitly assumes an audience of like-minded readers who agree (sort of) about what the bad things are—discrimination against gays and lesbians, the unequal and hierarchical treatment of women—and who even agree (sort of) about why they are bad (they subordinate some people to others, they deny people freedoms that they ought to have). But take that assumption away, and the absence of a normative dimension becomes a severe problem.

Try teaching Foucault at a contemporary law school, as I have, and you will quickly find that subversion takes many forms, not all of them congenial to Butler and her allies. As a perceptive libertarian student said to me, Why can't I use these ideas to resist the tax structure, or the antidiscrimination laws, or perhaps even to join the militias? Others, less fond of liberty, might engage in the subversive performances of making fun of feminist remarks in class, or ripping down the posters of the lesbian and gay law students' association. These things happen. They are parodic and subversive. Why, then, aren't they daring and good?

Well, there are good answers to those questions, but you won't find them in Foucault, or in Butler. Answering them requires discussing which liberties and opportunities human beings ought to have, and what it is for social institutions to treat human beings as ends rather than as means—in short, a normative theory of social justice and human dignity. It is one thing to say that we should be humble about our universal norms, and willing to learn from the experience of oppressed people. It is quite another thing to say that we don't need any norms at all. Foucault, unlike Butler, at least showed signs in his late work of grappling with this problem; and all his writing is animated by a fierce sense of the texture of social oppression and the harm that it does.

Come to think of it, justice, understood as a personal virtue, has exactly the structure of gender in the Butlerian analysis: it is not innate or "natural," it is produced by repeated performances (or as Aristotle said, we learn it by doing it), it shapes our inclinations and forces the repression of some of them. These ritual performances, and their associated repressions, are enforced by arrangements of social power, as children who won't share on the playground quickly discover. Moreover, the parodic subversion of justice is ubiquitous in politics, as in personal life. But there is an important difference. Generally we dislike these subversive performances, and we think that young people should be strongly discouraged from seeing norms of justice in such a cynical light. Butler cannot explain in any purely structural or procedural way why the subversion of gender norms is a social good while the subversion of justice norms is a social bad. Foucault, we should remember, cheered for the Ayatollah, and why not? That, too, was resistance, and there was indeed nothing in the text to tell us that that struggle was less worthy than a struggle for civil rights and civil liberties.

There is a void, then, at the heart of Butler's notion of politics. This void can look liberating, because the reader fills it implicitly with a normative theory of human equality or dignity. But let there be no mistake: for Butler, as for Foucault, subversion is subversion, and it can in principle go in any direction. Indeed, Butler's naively empty politics is especially dangerous for the very causes she holds dear. For every friend of Butler, eager to engage in subversive performances that proclaim the repressiveness of heterosexual gender norms, there are dozens who would like to engage in subversive performances that flout the norms of tax compliance, of nondiscrimination, of decent treatment of one's fellow students. To such people we should say, you cannot simply resist as you please, for there are norms of fairness, decency, and dignity that entail that this is bad behavior. But then we have to articulate those norms—and this Butler refuses to do.

V

What precisely does Butler offer when she counsels subversion? She tells us to engage in parodic performances, but she warns us that the dream of escaping altogether from the oppressive structures is just a dream: it is within the oppressive structures that we must find little spaces for resistance, and this resistance cannot hope to change the overall situation. And here lies a dangerous quietism.

If Butler means only to warn us against the dangers of fantasizing an idyllic world in which sex raises no serious problems, she is wise to do so. Yet frequently she goes much further. She suggests that the institutional structures that ensure the marginalization of lesbians and gay men in our society, and the continued inequality of women, will never be changed in a deep way; and so our best hope is to thumb our noses at them, and to find pockets of personal freedom within them. "Called by an injurious name, I come into social being, and because I have a certain inevitable attachment to my existence, because a certain narcissism takes hold of any term that confers existence, I am led to embrace the terms that injure me because they constitute me socially." In other words: I cannot escape the humiliating structures without ceasing to be, so the best I can do is mock, and use the language of subordination stingingly. In Butler, resistance is always imagined as personal, more or less private, involving no unironic, organized public action for legal or institutional change.

Isn't this like saying to a slave that the institution of slavery will never change, but you can find ways of mocking it and subverting it, finding your personal freedom within those acts of carefully limited defiance? Yet it is a fact that the institution of slavery can be changed, and was changed— but not by people who took a Butler-like view of the possibilities. It was changed because people did not rest content with parodic performance: they demanded, and to some extent they got, social upheaval. It is also a fact that the institutional structures that shape women's lives have changed. The law of rape, still defective, has at least improved; the law of sexual harassment exists, where it did not exist before; marriage is no longer regarded as giving men monarchical control over women's bodies. These things were changed by feminists who would not take parodic performance as their answer, who thought that power, where bad, should, and would, yield before justice.

Butler not only eschews such a hope, she takes pleasure in its impossibility. She finds it exciting to contemplate the alleged immovability of power, and to envisage the ritual subversions of the slave who is convinced that she must remain such. She tells us—this is the central thesis of *The Psychic Life of Power*—that we all eroticize the power structures that oppress us, and can thus find sexual pleasure only within their confines. It seems to be for that reason that she prefers the sexy acts of parodic subversion to any lasting material or institutional change. Real change would so uproot our psyches that it would make sexual satisfaction impossible. Our libidos are the creation of the bad enslaving forces, and thus necessarily sadomasochistic in structure.

Well, parodic performance is not so bad when you are a powerful tenured academic in a liberal university. But here is where Butler's focus on the symbolic, her proud neglect of the material side of life, becomes a fatal blindness. For women who are hungry, illiterate, disenfranchised, beaten, raped, it is not sexy or liberating to reenact, however parodically, the conditions of hunger, illiteracy, disenfranchisement, beating, and rape. Such women prefer food, schools, votes, and the integrity of their bodies. I see no reason to believe that they long sadomasochistically for a return to the bad state. If some individuals cannot live without the sexiness of domination, that seems sad, but it is not really our business. But when a major theorist tells women in desperate conditions that life offers them only bondage, she purveys a cruel lie, and a lie that flatters evil by giving it much more power than it actually has.

*Excitable Speech*, Butler's most recent book, which provides her analysis of legal controversies involving pornography and hate speech, shows us exactly how far her quietism extends. For she is now willing to say that even where legal change is possible, even where it has already happened, we should wish it away, so as to preserve the space within which the oppressed may enact their sadomasochistic rituals of parody.

As a work on the law of free speech, *Excitable Speech* is an unconscionably bad book. Butler shows no awareness of the major theoretical accounts of the First Amendment, and no awareness of the wide range of cases such a theory will need to take into consideration. She makes absurd legal claims: for example, she says that the only type of speech that has been held to be unprotected is speech that has been previously defined as conduct rather than speech. (In fact, there are many types of speech, from false or misleading advertising to libelous statements to obscenity as currently defined, which have never been claimed to be action rather than speech, and which are nonetheless denied First Amendment protection.) Butler even claims, mistakenly, that obscenity has been judged to be the equivalent of "fighting words." It is not that Butler has an argument to back up her novel readings of the wide range of cases of unprotected speech that an account of the First Amendment would need to cover. She just has not noticed that there is this wide range of cases, or that her view is not a widely accepted legal view. Nobody interested in law can take her argument seriously.

But let us extract from Butler's thin discussion of hate speech and pornography the core of her position. It is this: legal prohibitions of hate speech and pornography are problematic (though in the end she does not clearly oppose them) because they close the space within which the parties injured by that speech can perform their resistance. By this Butler appears to mean that if the offense is dealt with through the legal system, there will be fewer occasions for informal protest; and also, perhaps, that if the offense becomes rarer because of its illegality, we will have fewer opportunities to protest its presence.

Well, yes. Law does close those spaces. Hate speech and pornography are extremely complicated subjects on which feminists may reasonably differ. (Still, one should state the contending views precisely: Butler's account of MacKinnon is less than careful, stating that MacKinnon supports "ordinances against pornography" and suggesting that, despite MacKinnon's explicit denial, they involve a form of censorship. Nowhere does Butler mention that what MacKinnon actually supports is a civil damage action in which particular women harmed through pornography can sue its makers and its distributors.)

But Butler's argument has implications well beyond the cases of hate speech and pornography. It would appear to support not just quietism in these areas, but a much more general legal quietism—or, indeed, a radical libertarianism. It goes like this: let us do away with everything from building codes to nondiscrimination laws to rape laws, because they close the space within which the injured tenants, the victims of discrimination, the raped women, can perform their resistance. Now, this is not the same argument radical libertarians use to oppose building codes and anti-discrimination laws; even they draw the line at rape. But the conclusions converge.

If Butler should reply that her argument pertains only to speech (and there is no reason given in the text for such a limitation, given the assimilation of harmful speech to conduct), then we can reply in the domain of speech. Let us get rid of laws against false advertising and unlicensed medical advice, for they close the space within which poisoned consumers and mutilated patients can perform their resistance! Again, if Butler does not approve of these extensions, she needs to make an argument that divides her cases from these cases, and it is not clear that her position permits her to make such a distinction.

For Butler, the act of subversion is so riveting, so sexy, that it is a bad dream to think that the world will actually get better. What a bore equality is! No bondage, no delight. In this way, her pessimistic erotic anthropology offers support to an amoral anarchist politics.

VI

When we consider the quietism inherent in Butler's writing, we have some keys to understanding Butler's influential fascination with drag and cross-dressing as paradigms of feminist resistance. Butler's followers understand her account of drag to imply that such performances are ways for women to be daring and subversive. I am unaware of any attempt by Butler to repudiate such readings.

But what is going on here? The woman dressed mannishly is hardly a new figure. Indeed, even when she was relatively new, in the nineteenth century, she was in another way quite old, for she simply replicated in the lesbian world the existing stereotypes and hierarchies of male-female society. What, we may well ask, is parodic subversion in this area, and what kind of prosperous middle-class acceptance? Isn't hierarchy in drag still hierarchy? And is it really true (as *The Psychic Life of Power* would seem to conclude) that domination and subordination are the roles that women must play in every sphere, and if not subordination, then mannish domination?

In short, cross-dressing for women is a tired old script—as Butler herself informs us. Yet she would have us see the script as subverted, made new, by the cross-dresser's knowing symbolic sartorial gestures; but again we must wonder about the newness, and even the subversiveness. Consider Andrea Dworkin's parody (in her novel *Mercy*) of a Butlerish parodic feminist, who announces from her posture of secure academic comfort:

> The notion that bad things happen is both propagandistic and inadequate. . . . To understand a woman's life requires that we affirm the hidden or obscure dimensions of pleasure, often in pain, and choice, often under duress. One must develop an eye for secret signs—the clothes that are more than clothes or decoration in the contemporary dialogue, for instance, or the rebellion hidden behind apparent conformity. There is no victim. There is perhaps an insufficiency of signs, an obdurate appearance of conformity that simply masks the deeper level on which choice occurs.

In prose quite unlike Butler's, this passage captures the ambivalence of the implied author of some of Butler's writings, who delights in her violative practice while turning her theoretical eye resolutely away from the material suffering of women who are hungry, illiterate, violated, beaten. There is no victim. There is only an insufficiency of signs.

Butler suggests to her readers that this sly send-up of the status quo is the only script for resistance that life offers. Well, no. Besides offering many other ways to be human in one's personal life, beyond traditional norms of domination and subservience, life also offers many scripts for resistance that do not focus narcissistically on personal self-presentation. Such scripts involve feminists (and others, of course) in building laws and institutions, without much concern for how a woman displays her own body and its gendered nature: in short, they involve working for others who are suffering.

The great tragedy in the new feminist theory in America is the loss of a sense of public commitment. In this sense, Butler's self-involved feminism is extremely American, and it is not surprising that it has caught on here, where successful middle-class people prefer to focus on cultivating the self rather than thinking in a way that helps the material condition of others. Even in America, however, it is possible for theorists to be dedicated to the public good and to achieve something through that effort.

Many feminists in America are still theorizing in a way that supports material change and responds to the situation of the most oppressed. Increasingly, however, the academic and cultural trend is toward the pessimistic flirtatiousness represented by the theorizing of Butler and her followers. Butlerian feminism is in many ways easier than the old feminism. It tells scores of talented young women that they need not work on changing the law, or feeding the hungry, or assailing power through theory harnessed to material politics. They can do politics in safety of their campuses, remaining on the symbolic level, making subversive gestures at power through speech and gesture. This, the theory says, is pretty much all that is available to us anyway, by way of political action, and isn't it exciting and sexy?

In its small way, of course, this is a hopeful politics. It instructs people that they can, right now, without compromising their security, do something bold. But the boldness is entirely gestural, and insofar as Butler's ideal suggests that these symbolic gestures really are political change, it offers only a false hope. Hungry women are not fed by this, battered women are not sheltered by it, raped women do not find justice in it, gays and lesbians do not achieve legal protections through it.

Finally there is despair at the heart of the cheerful Butlerian enterprise. The big hope, the hope for a world of real justice, where laws and institutions protect the equality and the dignity of all citizens, has been banished, even perhaps mocked as sexually tedious. Judith Butler's hip quietism is a comprehensible response to the difficulty of realizing justice in America. But it is a bad response. It collaborates with evil. Feminism demands more and women deserve better.

## Martha C. Nussbaum and Her Critics: An Exchange

*The Professor of Parody*, February 22, 1999

*To the Editors:*

In a recent issue, as an example of gullibility in the face of obscure prose, Martha C. Nussbaum trots out a secondhand quotation where I reputedly opine that Judith Butler is "probably one of the ten smartest people on the planet."

Had Nussbaum verified the quotation instead of citing a citation, she would have found a literary theory website introducing "The Grand PoohBahs: Often Named Jacques, but also Helene, Luce, Michel, and occasionally Fred" (which also features Michel Foucault's head pasted atop a Pez dispenser). The original quote: "Judith Butler's ideas are sophisticated enough that people usually simplify them in cartoonish ways. Engaging her in a profound way necessitates an understanding of an intimidating list of difficult thinkers. . . . Probably one of the ten smartest people on the planet, and damn her—he said admiringly—she's only 34." It's called irony. Discerning readers are welcome to join me.

Without doubt, theory-minded academics often dismiss objections with unwarranted impatience. But when self-appointed defenders of clarity are unwilling to do the basic research we would require of any first-year composition student, perhaps that impatience is warranted. For the original, campy discussion of Butler (and now, Nussbaum) visit: www.sou.edu/English/IDTC/Swirl/swirl.htm.

WARREN HEDGES
Assistant Professor of English
Southern Oregon University
Ashland, Oregon

*To the Editors:*
In her recent review of Judith Butler's work, Martha C. Nussbaum complains that feminists like Butler "find comfort in the idea that the subversive use of words is still available to feminist intellectuals." Her own essay is a better example of this confidence than anything written by Judith Butler.

Nussbaum believes that social-construction theories are the same as the analysis of gender as performative. And she will not allow Butler the freedom of expanding the Austinian performative into a more than verbal category. Since she so berates Butler for being impractical, she should have reckoned that social construction of gender theories being around since Plato is not quite the same thing as an intellectual pointing out that we all make gender come into being by doing it. Butler's performative theory is not the same as Austin's and not the same as social-construction theories. She is addressing conventions in use, social-contract effects, collective "institutions" of elusive materiality, the ground of the political. No legal or political reform stands a chance of survival without tangling with conventions.

As an Indian feminist theorist and activist resident in the United States and honored by the friendship of such subcontinental feminist activists as Flavia Agnes, Farida Akhter, Mahasweta Devi, Madhu Kishwar, Rajeswari Sunder Rajan, Romila Thapar, Susie Tharu, and many others, I refuse the implicit matronizing reference to "rape law in India today, which has most of the flaws that the first generation of American feminists targeted" with which Nussbaum opens her subplot of Indian feminists as an example of what Butler is not. (How are we to treat Anupama Rao's serious consideration of Butler in "Understanding Sirsgaon: Notes Toward Conceptualising the Role of Law, Caste and Gender in a Case of 'Atrocity,'" for example? Instances of the use of Butler by Indian feminist theorists can be multiplied.)

This flag-waving championship of needy women leads Nussbaum finally to assert that "women who are hungry, illiterate, disenfranchised, beaten, raped . . . prefer food, schools, votes, and the integrity of their bodies." Sounds good, from a powerful tenured academic in a liberal university. But how does she know? This may be her idea of what they should want. In that conviction she may want to train them to want this. That is called a "civilizing mission." But if she ever engages in unmediated grassroots activism in the global South, rather than championing activist theorists, she will find that the gender practice of the rural poor is quite often in the performative mode, carving out power within a more general scene of pleasure in subjection. If she wants to deny this generality of gender culture and make the women over in her own image, she will have to enter their protocol, and learn much greater patience and understanding than is shown by this vicious review.

"Butler's hip quietism . . . collaborates with evil," Nussbaum concludes. Any involvement with counter-globalization would show how her unexamined, and equally hip, U.S. benevolence toward "other women" collaborates with exploitation. The solution, if there is any, is not to engage in abusive reviews in the pages of national journals.

GAYATRI CHAKRAVORTY SPIVAK
Avalon Foundation Professor
in the Humanities
Columbia University
New York, New York

*To the Editors:*
We were disturbed by Martha C. Nussbaum's attack on Judith Butler in *The New Republic*.

One element we found particularly objectionable was Nussbaum's repeated attempts to dismiss Butler as a philosopher. At one point Nussbaum claims that Butler is seen as a major thinker "more by people in literature than by philosophers." She asks whether Butler's manner of writing "belongs to the philosophical tradition at all." As one who has contributed much to bringing literature and philosophy closer together, Nussbaum's questioning of Butler's attempts are disingenuous. Furthermore, Nussbaum's move is reminiscent of those who have tried to keep feminist concerns out of philosophy on grounds "that this is just not philosophy."

While Nussbaum raises some worthwhile questions, the element of vituperativeness in the essay is disturbing. Butler's contributions are not only described as "unconscionably bad" but the quietism Nussbaum claims to follow from them is said "to collaborate with evil." This rhetoric of overkill stands in striking contrast to the unquestioning adulation Nussbaum gives to Catharine MacKinnon and Andrea Dworkin. Given the authoritarian strains in the politics of MacKinnon and Dworkin, Butler's strong antiauthoritarianism is a useful antidote.

SEYLA BENHABIB
Professor of Government
Harvard University
Cambridge, Massachusetts

NANCY FRASER
Professor of Political Science and Philosophy
The New School for Social Research
New York, New York

LINDA NICHOLSON
The State University of New York, Albany
Albany, New York

*To the Editors:*
Martha C. Nussbaum's review of Judith Butler takes as its premise the belief that the test of a theory's goodness is its positive political outcome. Yet we are offered no empirical evidence for this claim. Instead, we are presented with a Manichean scheme which defines "good" theory as that which "is closely tethered to practical commitments," to "real" issues, to "the real situation of real women," to "real politics" and "real justice." It is irrelevant to Nussbaum's polemic that Judith Butler is on record in word and deed as a politically concerned person with "practical commitments" to "real politics," and that her writings have influenced what even Nussbaum would take to be "good" politics among Queer activists, feminist psychoanalysts, and lawyers working on women's rights. According to the logic of the argument, since Butler does not share Nussbaum's "normative theory of social justice and human dignity," Butler can only "collaborate with evil." In the guise of a serious book review, Nussbaum has constructed a self-serving morality tale in which she (along with Catharine MacKinnon and Andrea Dworkin) represents historically authentic and politically efficacious feminism, while Judith Butler (and the young, Francophile, sado-masochist minions who are said to follow her) indulge in "amoral anarchist politics" or "hip quietism" and so betray feminist goals.

Nussbaum conveniently omits all discussion of instances of "real" politics in her article, perhaps because the evidence is so damning to her argument. To deduce politics from theory, as Nussbaum does, is to misunderstand the operations of both. The job of theory is to open new avenues of understanding, to trouble conventional wisdom with difficult questions. The job of politics (in democratic societies, at least) is to secure some end in a contested, conflictual field. Politics and theory may inform one another at certain moments with successful or unsuccessful results—the outcomes are not predictable. Historically, though, one thing is sure: when the gap between theory and politics is closed in the name of virtue, when Robespierre or the Ayatollahs or Ken Starr seek to impose their vision of the "good" on the rest of society, reigns of terror follow and democratic politics are undermined. These are situations in which, to reverse Martha Nussbaum's reasoning, too much "good" ends up as "evil," and feminism, along with all other emancipatory movements, loses its public voice.

Sadly, Nussbaum's good versus evil scheme substitutes moralist fundamentalism for genuine philosophical and political debate among feminists— and there is much to be debated these days: Are all "women" the same? Who can speak for the needs and interests of "women"? How can political action address deeply rooted conventions about gender? Judith Butler has engaged these questions with great honesty and skill. Those of us looking for ways of reflecting on the situation of feminism today understandably prefer the provocative, open theories of Judith Butler to the closed moralizing of Martha Nussbaum.

JOAN W. SCOTT
Professor of Social Science
Institute for Advanced Study
Princeton, New Jersey

*To the Editors*:
Are feminist theorists now divisible into two distinct groups, the activists and the "hip defeatists"? While Martha C. Nussbaum raises some serious issues about the relation between feminist theory and the day-to-day struggles of women around the world to achieve recognition of their dignity, her dichotomy between those feminists who are "materialists" and those of a "new symbolic type" who "believe that the way to do feminist politics is to use words in a subversive way, in academic publications of lofty obscurity and disdainful abstraction" is not only simplistic but obscures the crucial focus of second-wave feminism on the role of representations in shaping our reality.

We don't think that any feminist, Judith Butler included, believes that feminist political goals can be achieved in the ways attributed by Nussbaum to this "new symbolic type." But feminists of all stripes—as well as many other groups in the second half of this century—have long seen that questions of how we represent ourselves and are represented by others are central to the quest for justice. In her article, Nussbaum contrasts Catharine MacKinnon as the exemplar "good" activist feminist to Judith Butler, her epitome of the "bad" language-oriented feminist. Yet for both MacKinnon and Butler, feminist work is grounded in an insistence upon the material force of representations, linguistic as well as visual. Catharine MacKinnon and other antiporn feminists have taught us that pornographic images and words brutalize us as women and that resisting repression means finding ways out of these representations.

Judith Butler's work, including her rightfully famous insight into the performative aspect of identity, likewise focuses on the ways in which representations have constitutive force, the way in which who we are is deeply connected with how we are represented. But whereas MacKinnon's focus on the materiality of representation has turned toward legal reform, including the creation of an innovative civil rights ordinance written with Andrea Dworkin, Butler has argued that the struggle over representations should be fought out in politics.

This is a real difference between them and needs to be addressed. Feminist theorists, including one of the authors, have sought for years now to address this question of the parameters of legal reform and the possibilities of change through politics. Part of this involves a problem that has historically plagued analytic jurisprudence: How do we reconcile freedom and equality in a concept of right?

Given the stakes and seriousness of the work of these two theorists as well as the complexity that their work and that of many, many others seeks to address, Nussbaum's facile division of theorists into two camps is not only inaccurate, it is less than productive. Reading her essay, actually not much more than an *ad feminam* attack on Butler, one is indeed reminded—if ironically, if paradoxically—of David Hume, whom Nussbaum accurately characterizes as "a fine . . . a gracious spirit: how kindly he respects the reader's intelligence, even at the cost of exposing his own uncertainty." Would that Martha Nussbaum had honored Hume's philosophical spirit in her own review of Judith Butler's work.

DRUCILLA CORNELL
Professor of Law, Political Science, and Women's Studies
Rutgers University
New Brunswick, New Jersey

SARA MURPHY
Lecturer
Gallatin School
New York University
New York, New York

*Martha C. Nussbaum Replies:*
Hedges's letter shows that I quoted him correctly. The larger context of his remark suggests that it may be hyperbolic; there is no sign that it is ironic. Perhaps Hedges confuses these two concepts.

Spivak is wrong to say that I equate social-construction theories with the thesis that gender is performative. I said that the latter, though built on the former, was Butler's one interesting new contribution. Butler can, of course, expand on Austin as she likes, but my claim was that Austin's views, which in any case she misrepresents, do not help her much with the project that she is pursuing.

I admire Spivak's work with tribal women: indeed I was thinking of it when I wrote that feminists in India, whatever their intellectual orientation, remain close to practical problems. But she should inquire about what I do before she makes assumptions. I have spent a lot of time during the past few years with activists and women's development projects in India. I have visited projects of many different types in different regions. I have never yet met a poor woman who told me she took pleasure in subjection, though there may be some who do. I have met countless women who struggle for access to credit, education, employment opportunities, political representation, and shelter from domestic violence.

My claims about rape law in India are correct: a victim's sexual history, for example, is still relevant evidence. I believe that there is nothing "matronizing" about making American readers aware of the fine work being done in this area by activists such as Indira Jaising, for whose advice and illumination I am grateful. In my forthcoming book, *Women and Human Development*, my claims about women in India are amply documented, as was not possible in a brief review.

Benhabib, Fraser, and Nicholson say that my claim that Butler is more sophist than philosopher is "disingenuous" because I have written that philosophy can derive insight from literature. This odd non sequitur might be valid if one supplied the tacit premise that sophistry is literature, or that Butler is a figure comparable to Proust and Henry James. But I see no reason to accept either of those assumptions. What I called "unconscionably bad" was not Butler's work in general, but her use of First Amendment legal materials in *Excitable Speech*. In that context, the phrase is appropriate. Finally, anyone who reads what I have written about MacKinnon and Dworkin will know that my attitude to them is not one of "unquestioning adulation," but rather of deeply respectful criticism.

Scott misses an important distinction. I was talking not about practical activities pursued by theorists, but about theorizing in a way that gives direction to practical political efforts. Butler may well have admirable practical commitments, but this does not change the fact that what she writes as a theorist offers no helpful direction for practice. I discussed many examples of theorizing that does provide such a direction, including writings about the reform of rape law, sexual harassment law, and the concept of sex equality more generally. Nor do I see how the scare-names of the Ayatollah and Robespierre undermine the value of the work of feminists who have helped make progress in legal reform.

Cornell and Murphy write an interesting letter that goes to the substance of what I actually argued. They are correct in noting that MacKinnon's thought has a significant symbolic dimension. The differences between

MacKinnon and Foucault deserve a subtle investigation. I hope they will write such a study. Far from dividing thinkers into two camps, I made it clear that I respect some work in the Foucauldian-Symbolic tradition, including the work of Foucault himself. Butler doesn't seem to me a thinker of the same caliber.

# CHAPTER SEVENTEEN

# Experiments in Living

MICHAEL WARNER (1999), The Trouble with Normal: Sex, Politics, and the Ethics of Queer Life

I

On the cover of Michael Warner's new book stands a row of male dolls. Half of them are hypermuscular and dressed in leather: gay men, it seems. They are dressed identically; they stand in identical stances. Alternating with them stands another set of male dolls, also identical to one another, also posed in identical stances. These dolls, dressed in white dinner jackets, hold out their arms as if to escort a partner: grooms in a wedding, it seems. And it appears that the leather dolls are all set to march down the aisle with the dinner-jacketed dolls, in a same-sex wedding that is also a wedding of outsider status with conformity, the "pathological" with the "normal."

In this way, Warner's book wittily announces its theme: the tyranny of public conformity and the irrational desire for sameness, even among people who, as social outsiders, ought to know the damage that this kind of tyranny can inflict on others. Thus Warner pointedly suggests from the outset that even the intense desire of many gays and lesbians for same-sex marriage may itself be an example of this tyranny. To the aspiration to conformity and the domination of the "normal," Warner opposes a moral argument based upon an ideal of autonomy and liberty, and upon the idea that a democratic culture needs to encourage, not to stifle, innovations and deviations in living, in order to discover the most fruitful ways to realize its ideal of human dignity.

Thus, although this book is the work of a leading queer activist and a defense of a radical subculture, it is also a descendant of Mill's *On Liberty*, which similarly inveighed against the tyranny of public opinion in the name of liberty and of "experiments in living." And it has another surprising, and more recent, antecedent: Richard Posner's *Sex and Reason*, which argued, appealing to Mill, that our public policy in the area of sex should reject the politics of moralism and should protect all consensual adult relations from state interference. But Warner acknowledges the complexity and the messiness of sex far more effectively than the economistic Posner or the somewhat squeamish Mill. His case for autonomy is stronger for being written as if the author knows something personally about the subject.

Warner is known to the nonacademic world as the founder of Sex Panic!, a group of gay activists united to protest various policies of New York Mayor Rudolph Giuliani in the areas of sex-related zoning and public sex. But he is also a professor of American literature at Rutgers University, and the author of a fine book about print culture and the public sphere in colonial America, and the editor of the Library of America's anthology of American sermons. Nor is his relation to religion merely scholarly. A remarkable article that he wrote in 1993 began with the sentence, "I was a teenage Pentacostalist," and went on to describe his upbringing in that community and his education at Oral Roberts University.

Although it seems natural to think of the two parts of Warner's life as radically discontinuous—natural even to him, as he admits—he cannot deny that there are deep links between them. Both communities in which he has lived are marginal "outsider" communities, alienated from the dominant culture and spurred in no small part by anger against it. (Warner tells us of a mother who, abandoned by her husband, spoke in tongues while she vacuumed the shag rugs.) So Warner knows well what it is like not to be normal, and to be pilloried by the normal; he also knows what it is to take a profound pleasure in marginality, and to regard it as the source of a deep seriousness. There are dangers in such a romanticization, and Warner's book does not altogether escape them; but on the whole Warner is a deft and thoughtful writer who turns his own experience of the margins into a source of genuine understanding about America and its sexual politics.

Warner's target is what he calls the "politics of sexual shame." By this he means a politics in which people's general unease about the fact of sex gets translated into a comforting set of hierarchies that brand some people as good and healthy, and other people as bad and deviant, and then uses the force of public opinion and law to curtail the consensual activities of those who have been stigmatized. Such a politics of shame, Warner contends, is behind sodomy laws and many other rules through which a majority seeks to define its own sexual activities as superior. We might also call this a politics of disgust, in the spirit of Lord Devlin's famous defense of sodomy laws as legitimate expressions of a society's disgust for some of its members' practices.

Warner argues—like Posner in *Sex and Reason*, and like critics of Devlin such as H. L. A. Hart and Ronald Dworkin—that public policy should never be based on a moralistic desire to tyrannize over the consensual sexual activities of others. Instead, the goal of public policy in this area should be to protect people's "sexual autonomy" from the tyranny of an interventionist moralism. In effect, he advocates making Mill's "harm principle" into a legal standard: if an activity does no harm to non-consenting others, it should not be legitimate to regulate it by law. Unlike Posner, however, Warner does not pretend that his proposal is value-free. He insists (correctly, in my view) that his argument against the politics of shame and his defense of sexual autonomy is itself a moral argument.

What is the shame all about? Warner says little here, but he makes it clear that he thinks we are all ashamed of our sexuality because sex represents a messiness, a lack of control, in human lives that anxiously strive for control and harmony. We could add, with Walt Whitman, that sex reminds us of the fact that we will decay and become part of the grass and the earth around us. Most of the time, of course, we would rather think that this will not happen, that we are pure spirits bound for eternity; and for this reason, too, the discomfort with a mortal and animal body elicits shame, a painful recognition that one has not reached a condition of invulnerability that one would very much like to attain.

Having a lot of shame about our own bodies—and disgust, too, a shrinking from contamination that derives from a deep ambivalence about our own animality and the animal secretions that are such a prominent part of sexual experience—we seek to render our bodies less disturbing; and this frequently involves projecting our own emotions outward, onto vulnerable people and groups who come to embody a shamefulness and a disgustingness that we then conveniently deny in our own person. This happens very young; children make "cootie catchers" and pretend to find disgusting bugs on the bodies of children who are a little bit different. But it is sex that most keenly provokes this troublesome dynamic.

Every society has its chosen "shameful" and "disgusting" sexual minorities who come to represent properties—stickiness, fluidity, sheer corporeality—that the dominant group would like to forget that it, too, possesses. Women play this role in more or less all cultures. But Warner is surely right in suggesting that this powerful emotional reaction to one's own perceived incompleteness is behind the virulence of much American homophobia, particularly when directed against gay men.

Warner does not expect that this shame and disgust will ever go away. (In this regard, the rhapsodic Whitman was too unrealistic: his paean to "the body electric" made the body so clean and unthreatening that it hardly seemed to be a body at all.) Warner asks only that we not make public policy in response to it, that we realize our own irrationality in these matters and decide to protect vulnerable others from its damages.

Warner makes two arguments, both of them Millean, one based on liberty and the other based on social advantage. Personal liberty (what Warner calls "sexual autonomy") is extremely valuable, and should not be curtailed where no harm to non-consenting others is at issue. This does not mean that we must refrain from making moral criticisms of them; it means simply that we not dragoon people into "normality" by legal restrictions. When we allow different groups more liberty to construct their own modes of sexual life, moreover, we are all likely to learn from these "experiments in living."

Warner's idea of sexual autonomy is underspecified. He makes it clear that sexual coercion should continue to be regulated by law; but he gives no hint of how he would resolve difficult cases. In his valuable book, *Unwanted Sex*, Stephen Schulhofer recently argued, for example, that the protection of sexual autonomy requires major changes in the law of rape. We need to protect people not only against physical force but also against intercourse accomplished by threat or intimidation, and by the abuse of positions of authority. Schulhofer notes that a high school principal who said to a student "Pay me $500 or you will not graduate" would surely be convicted of a crime; but a principal who said "Sleep with me or you will not graduate" was acquitted of rape because the woman did not say "no." Extortionate offers should be criminal, Schulhofer argues, in sex as in other realms of life, whether we call such cases rape or criminal assault. And Schulhofer extends his analysis to a defense of sexual harassment laws in the workplace, and of professional bans on intercourse between doctors and patients, lawyers and clients.

Warner never wrestles with these difficult cases. Had he spent more time confronting a wide range of feminist writings, he would have had to face the fact that law does not just compromise sexual autonomy, it also protects it. A simple "get the state off our backs" position may look attractive when we are thinking about the sex lives of middle-class men, but it is clearly inadequate to deal with the situation of women and other vulnerable groups. There is no consent where there is pervasive intimidation and hierarchy.

When radical feminists say that rape and "normal" intercourse cannot so easily be distinguished, they mean that a pervasive asymmetry of power makes it difficult for consent to be genuine. Just how this idea should be recognized by law is the difficult matter; but surely we should recognize that many instances in which there is no "no" are not instances of genuine consent; and we should recognize, too, that certain laws that interfere with some allegedly consensual sexual relationships (sexual harassment laws in the workplace, for example) have enhanced sexual autonomy, and not compromised it. I wish I knew what Warner would say about these questions; he will have a viable proposal for public action only when he has sorted them out.

Another issue that will need to be faced in the working-out of these notions of freedom is the issue of material inequality. Any attractive norm of sexual autonomy ought to contrast autonomous choice not only with choice coerced by a criminal act, but also with choice coerced by economic necessity. Warner tends to group "sex workers" with middle-class queer men, and to think of both as people whose sexual autonomy would be enhanced by getting the state out of their lives. Well, maybe for some sex workers. But many of them "choose" a risky and unappealing way of life because they have no good economic alternatives. We should question whether "choice" in those circumstances is really choice.

It is surely true that our society's unease about sex work is a result of the politics of shame; we do not extend the same anxious policing to boxing, or to risky types of factory work, or to any other dangerous and low-paid occupations to which working-class people with few skills tend to gravitate. But any politics of sexual autonomy will surely need to do more than to say "no shame here." It must ask also what material conditions are compatible with any meaningful type of human autonomy, and then seek to promote those conditions for everyone.

II

Warner is preoccupied with the tyranny exerted over people's liberty by public opinion and its insistent demand for conformity. In America, he argues, this demand takes a particular form. We tell ourselves, and others, that what is best is "normal." Ever since data about sex began to be gathered, we have been anxious to reassure ourselves that in sex, as elsewhere, we are right in the statistical middle, and in no way strange or eccentric. Of course, this hunger for the mean is not confined to sex: but in the realm of sex it exercises a particularly tyrannical power over minority ways of desiring and acting.

Why, asks Warner, would anyone want to be normal? If normal means the middle of a statistical range, there is nothing so good about that: it is normal to have back pain, or bad breath. Yet we persuade ourselves, somehow, that "normal" in that statistical sense is the same thing as "normative," or the way things ought to be: being normal seems already evaluative, as if it gives those in the majority a license to look down on the minority, who are definitionally abnormal. (Mill made the same point about the slippery use of the term "nature," which somehow slides from "the way things usually are" to "the way things rightly should be.")

Warner thinks that people have simply confused the idea of the normal with the idea of the normative. Yet intellectual confusion is not the whole story here. Warner's analysis of shame suggests a deeper story. People want to be like others, especially in sex, because then they can feel that they are less naked, less shamefully exposed. There is indeed safety in numbers. Somehow the numbers—like a fig leaf—hide the disorder of our bodies from us, and make us feel almost as if we had no bodies. It is this denial of the corporeal that finds expression, I think, in the convention that everyone wear a dark suit in the workplace. In suits, men are robbed of their physicality by their conformity. And so, when women came into a previously all-male workplace, with their alarming legs and flowing hair and brightly colored dresses, they represented sex. By standing out, they reminded everyone else that they, too, are sexual beings, and so an anxiety, or even a panic, was likely to ensue, and frequently did ensue.

Much the same, Warner suggests, is true of the American public response to gay men, especially when they will not oblige by hiding their sexuality. They remind everyone, but especially heterosexual males, of this common but scandalous aspect of human life, of the unreason that we are all in together. And so they have to be scorned and downgraded by an appeal to the normativity of the normal.

But of course gay men are not themselves immune to this logic. They are no more daring, no more reconciled to their mortality and their physicality, than anyone else. (Remember those identical male dolls.) So it is not surprising that they, too, should yearn for a kind of normality—and Warner is at his most incisive when he documents the recent trend in gay journalism toward the pretense that sex is not really the issue, that being gay has nothing to do with sex. In a way, there is nothing wrong with the gay dream of ordinariness. There is dignity also in the ordinary. But the gay movement was once about social criticism and social change, about the rights and the benefits of genuine and irreducible otherness. And it is worse than disappointing when those who have opted for the safety of the normal turn around and throw shame on others who have not. Sadly, "it does not seem to be possible to think of oneself as normal without thinking that some other kind of person is pathological."

In the remnants of defiant queer culture, by contrast, Warner finds a norm of dignity that makes a distinctive and worthy contribution to democracy. This is the Whitmanesque idea that human beings have dignity precisely in their mortality, in the disorder of their vitality. "If sex is a kind of indignity, then we're all in it together. And the paradoxical result is that only when this indignity of sex is spread around the room, leaving no one out, and in fact binding people together, that it begins to resemble the dignity of the human." Gay friendships, he argues, are based on a public acknowledgment that we have bodies that we do not altogether understand or control, and that this is a fundamental source of our equality and our characteristically human form of dignity. And these friendships need, for their flourishing, a public space within which to create their own public culture.

III

All this is appealing, as far as it goes. The queer community is indeed conducting a Millean experiment in living, and it is precisely such experiments that a democracy committed to liberty and dignity should protect, hoping that it will learn something from them. Here again, though, I wish that Warner had engaged more with the predicament of women, for it would complicate his romantic picture of the scorned aspects of queer life.

Think, for example, about pornography. In Warner's argument, the availability of sexually explicit materials is simply one of the freedoms that the experimenters want to have, and should have, as a part of their rebellion against the tyranny of the normal. Indeed, Warner pays pornography the compliment of portraying it as the opposite of the normal, as a kind of bad outsider other, in danger of being suppressed. But think about it from the viewpoint of many women, and things get terribly complicated. For the depiction of women in most pornography made for men is just an aspect—and a very powerful aspect—of the tyranny of the normal.

There is nothing rebellious or experimental about this sort of pornography. It is just the old message of male domination, made powerful by being packaged as a masturbatory aid. Men learn that women are objects for men's use and men's control; and many women, in the pornographic view of the world, even love abuse, and cry out ecstatically when they are beaten up. In short, pornography normalizes a very old way men have of viewing women: no subversive outsider, but the most inside of the inside, the sweat-stained leather armchair in the old boys' club.

If, then, you are a feminist interested in rebellion against the tyranny of the normal, it is by no means obvious that you will want to go along with Warner and seek the easy availability of sexually explicit materials, making no distinctions. You will first want to make, morally, a number of distinctions within the category of the sexually explicit; and you may even feel that here, again, legal interference with liberty might support sexual autonomy rather than undermining it. At any rate, the argument will have to be joined.

Even in the world of gay male pornography, Warner needs to argue that something like this is not the case. Male norms of objectification and domination are very powerful; it would be surprising if queer culture had simply thrown them off. After all, adult queer men are, almost all of them, brought up to be heterosexual men; it would be startling indeed if they had not internalized the norms of "straight" culture regarding women and the use of people as things. But then these norms might work their way into gay pornography in ways that would call for analysis and criticism, at least moral criticism.

It is wrong to congratulate oneself on the happenstance of statistical conformity, and still more wrong when that self-congratulation demeans and diminishes others. But the sheer rebelliousness of queer culture hardly guarantees that it does not contain pieces that tyrannically re-enact the normal. What makes Warner think that the queer community has been successful in liberating itself from the all-too-familiar patterns of domination and subordination that characterize the normal? So what we need is a more complicated argument. We need an argument for which autonomy is not just a matter of freedom from restriction—at least if it is to be connected, as Warner wishes, with equality and dignity.

IV

Warner draws from his general analysis a number of implications for public policy. One of his primary targets is the zoning policies of Mayor Giuliani. By restricting the places where sexually explicit materials may be sold, he argues, Giuliani has fractured a fertile and highly democratic gay public culture that focused on the street scene of the West Village. Now rich gays frequent expensive private clubs, while poorer gays go to the dangerous areas around the docks where these materials remain publicly available.

Thus, in Warner's account, the democracy of gay male culture has been undermined in the name of public disgust and shame. These are plausible examples of the divisive and cramping effects of a politics of shame, although, once again, Warner's arguments about pornographic materials lack complexity. But Warner's longest chapter, and the one that will surely bring him the most criticism from within the gay community, is his attack on the idea of same-sex marriage. Since there is likely to be a very heated debate about his position, it is important to be precise about what his argument is.

Warner's basic claim is that it is a mistake for the lesbian and gay movement to devote so much of its energy to seeking marriage rights for same-sex couples. Several distinct arguments support this conclusion. First, he argues, working for marriage rights is a deflection of valuable resources and energy away from causes that are both urgent and possible: AIDS prevention and education, and general non-discrimination in housing and employment. Indeed, there is no reason to think that the marriage struggle is winnable any time soon, so it may well be that a lot of money and time is being wasted.

But Warner also makes two deeper and more controversial arguments, closely connected. The first is that pushing for marriage rights unthinkingly validates the social status quo, when we should really be thinking hard about what living arrangements we want to support with what forms of state action. The second is that the status of marriage, as it exists in American society, is inherently discriminatory and hierarchical, defining some couples as worthy and thus defining other couples as less worthy. The two arguments are closely linked because Warner believes that a more reflective and experimental approach to the bundle of political privileges currently associated with marriage would be likely to disaggregate them, and that disaggregation would produce a less hierarchical state of affairs.

Marriage, as it currently exists in America, is not just a sentimental matter. It is also a large bundle of privileges and statuses, in areas including taxes, inheritance privileges, child custody, spousal support, courtroom testimony, hospital visitation, medical decision-making, immigration, and burial. To seek marriage as a right is not just to seek a public space within which to say "I love you." It is to seek that entire group of privileges, and thus to support the normative way of bundling them together.

Of course it seems wrong for opposite-sex couples to have the opportunity to get this bundle when same-sex couples do not. But Warner argues that what all of us should really seek is the regrouping of the entire set of privileges. There is no good reason why they should all be bundled together. Numerous European nations have been disaggregating them in various ways, with success. The Scandinavian countries have created registered domestic partnerships that have many of the privileges of traditional marriage. France has recently given legal recognition, in areas of property, inheritance, and care, to a wider range of living arrangements, not all of them based upon a sexual bond. (And India, I can add, gives government support to women's collectives, which promote women's employment opportunities, emotional solidarity, and shared child-rearing.)

Warner plausibly holds—here agreeing with Posner—that we should stop and think, learning what we can from these experiments, rather than jumping on the marriage bandwagon and cheering for an institution that does not, after all, have such a good record when we consider issues of sex equality (and, we might add, of child sexual abuse). Warner is aware of the argument that gay marriage itself is a radical experiment that may well revolutionize all marriage; but he is skeptical about such an outcome, holding that it is at least as likely that non-conforming styles of life will be dragooned by the institution of marriage into conformity with previous norms. Warner also plausibly holds that we should in any case prefer a disaggregated solution to the problem of marriage, because the traditional bundling of privileges tends to stigmatize people who, for whatever reason, do not want to enter, or cannot enter, the preferred kingdom. I think that these are excellent arguments, though I am not optimistic about our nation's willingness to deliberate seriously about the alternatives that other nations have embraced.

But isn't love an argument for marriage? Here Warner is tough with those who romanticize traditional marriage. Love, he points out, has been regarded, in large parts of the Western tradition, as a profoundly antinomian emotion, and not very comfortably at home with a settled arrangement such as marriage. What people who romanticize marriage are really after, Warner suspects, is something more like safety and insulation.

Insofar as a long romantic tradition does see marriage as a natural fulfillment of love, there is a peculiar paradox involved: marriage consecrates a love that represents itself as pure spontaneity, and offers a way for lovers to ally themselves with the dominant social order while still having the satisfaction of seeing themselves as daring protesters against all laws. There is nothing wrong with this very human tendency to want to have it both ways— but one's all-too-human insecurity is rarely a good source of law.

Warner is himself a peculiarly American kind of romantic. Just as he suggests that authentic love is radically antinomian, and that religions are at their most interesting when they set themselves against the dominant norms of society, so he sometimes suggests that all selves are authentic only if they are continually being remade. He ended his Pentacostalist article with this statement about minority religions: "They tell you to be somebody else. I say: believe them." In this spirit, earlier in the article, he admitted to a lack of sympathy with anyone who does not want to engage in ongoing experiments in living:

> I have never been able to understand people with consistent lives—people who, for example, grow up in a liberal Catholic household and stay that way; or who in junior high school are already laying down a record on which to run for president one day. Imagine having no discarded personalities, no vestigial selves, no visible ruptures with yourself, no gulf of self-forgetfulness, nothing that requires explanation, no alien version of yourself that requires humor and accommodation. What kind of life is that?

This same impatience with the absence of experimentation occasionally mars his book. There is sometimes a tone of disdain and superiority toward those who want to live routine lives, even when they do not try to impose their ways on others—as if those men who are at home "cooking for their boyfriends" are somehow less worthy of respect than those who make the rules up as they go along. Although Warner's most powerful position is an attack on all kinds of repressive "normalizing," at times he seems to "normalize" experimentation and to look down on conformity.

But most people need routines and even conformity, most of the time; and every person needs, at the least, a lot of parts of life that are not being called into question at every moment. In this sense, we all have to be married—to a job, a workout schedule, a daily routine of eating and washing, a breakfast cereal, a world of stable physical objects. Habit dulls perception and hobbles thought, but we need a lot of habit in order to live. Otherwise we would die from the pain of seeing.

If there are some people who find improvisational lives more tolerable than others, they should not look down on those others who cannot stand so much uncertainty. And really, isn't the queer life itself a kind of habit? Aren't people married to that life, as others are married to their domesticity? A little more gentleness toward humanity on Warner's part would not be amiss.

Still, to dismiss Warner's challenge on this account would be a mistake. For what Warner's book finally demands of us is not the chimera of romantic or existentialist self-invention. What it demands is genuine reflection. If we cannot dissociate ourselves from our patterns of desire and approval, including our desire to conform—and Warner knows that for the most part we cannot—we can at least think, and we can at least criticize, rather than just falling mindlessly back on the old ways and scorning those who are different.

This, in most good philosophical accounts of autonomy, is what autonomy means: taking an occasional step back from oneself, so that one can at least pose the question whether this is what one wishes to endorse, for oneself and for others. Warner, with Mill, is dead right when he says that the politics of sex has been ugly and mean-spirited in large part because we shrink from this kind of serious deliberation, and from being the kind of selves, and citizens, who engage in it. We call shame and disgust to our aid when we want to avoid looking seriously into our own sexual lives; and so the politics of shame is also the refusal of serious self-scrutiny. This invitation to thought, to the examined life, is the most attractive proposal, and the most challenging, indecent proposal, that queer culture makes to American democracy. They say to you, be someone else. I say: believe them.

# CHAPTER EIGHTEEN

# Review

ALLEN BUCHANAN, DAN W. BROCK, NORMAN DANIELS, and DANIEL WIKLER (2000), From Chance to Choice: Genetics and Justice

I

Katherine and Bill apply for the same management position in a large firm. Katherine's application contains a genetic enhancement certificate from Opti-Gene, stating that the bearer has purchased a package of genetic services that improve memory and boost the immune system. Bill, who could not afford genetic enhancement, protests that hiring on the basis of genetic enhancement is a violation of equal opportunity. He insists that the job should be assigned on the basis of merit. Katherine replies that merit means that the position goes to the best candidate, and she is the best candidate, so what is the problem?

Our growing knowledge of the human genome will pose complex ethical conundrums. Some of them are extensions of familiar perplexities. Looked at in one way, the dispute between Katherine and Bill is not unlike problems of equal opportunity that we have debated for a long time. Had Katherine been healthy and mentally sharp owing to a middle-class upbringing, and had Bill been less so owing to poverty and unkind circumstances, each would have had defenders, in the familiar debate over the meaning of equal opportunity in a context of social inequality. Had it been clear that Katherine inherited her good qualities from her parents' genes and Bill his defects from his parents' genes, most Americans would have said, well, that's who they are. But some determined egalitarians would have insisted that they do not deserve to reap any advantage from traits that they got by the luck of birth. They would have insisted that the job should probably still go to Katherine, but society's general scheme of rewards and opportunities must be adjusted to give Bill extra support. Katherine's talents are social resources that must be fairly used for the benefit of all.

But the moral terrain revealed by this case is not entirely familiar. The dispute between Katherine and Bill also poses some questions that are not covered by existing ethical theories. All existing theories make some sort of distinction between the realm of nature or chance and the realm of justice. Although it may be unclear where that line falls in any particular case, it looks as if our whole sense of life relies on there being such a distinction. Some things that go wrong for people are just tragedies, beyond human control; other bad outcomes might have been averted or controlled by better social arrangements, and so they belong in the general realm of social justice. Nature does not seem to be going away just yet, and a bad end still awaits us all. But the tale of Katherine and Bill does show us that we are living in a time characterized (to use the phrase of the fine philosophers who have produced *From Chance to Choice*) by "the colonization of the natural by the just." Many things that looked like unchanging accident now look like things that people can change, and may even have an obligation to change.

Thinking about justice, moreover, will now have to take a subtly new form. We are accustomed to thinking about justice in terms of distributing things to people, where the people remain who they are and are imagined as sharing a common set of human needs and abilities. When we are able to alter people in fundamental ways, however, we shall have to consider that justice may require some remaking of people: for Katherine's good health and quick memory are not just superficial properties, like a new haircut. And once we begin to travel this road, we will surely notice that it is quite unclear what we are promoting, because the idea of a constant human nature begins to slip through our fingers. And notions such as "human flourishing," or the "primary goods" that all human beings supposedly need in order to live, seem on the verge of slipping away with it.

In this eloquent and impressive book, Allen Buchanan, Dan W. Brock, Norman Daniels, and Daniel Wikler help us to sort our way through these perplexities. (Each takes primary responsibility for particular chapters, and there remain some subtle differences among them, which they debate; but the book as a whole is a joint production.) To put it crudely and briefly, they argue that we should use our new genetic knowledge to treat impairments against a baseline of some core human functions and abilities, but not necessarily (in most cases) to offer enhancements of human abilities above that baseline; that we should zealously protect reproductive freedom, and oppose most (though not all) attempts to persuade parents or to require parents to have a particular sort of child; that genetic counseling and certain types of genetic services should be offered in all health-insurance packages; that society must evolve toward greater respect for and inclusion of the disabled, but this concern should not make us shrink from treating serious genetic impairments to the extent that we can do so. But the authors of this book are not policy professionals, they are philosophers; and where philosophy is concerned, conclusions count for little without the arguments that lead to them. The most admirable contribution of *From Chance to Choice* lies in the density and the cogency of its arguments.

## II

Why should we care about what philosophical argument has to say to us in an era of scientific change? The authors' answer is that without it we are in danger of thinking badly. As we confront the bewildering new possibilities opened up by the Human Genome Project, three obstacles to good thought await us. First, we come immediately upon our fear of change. It is very easy to shrink back in horror from the whole idea of genetic treatment and enhancement, simply because we do not quite know what to say about it. The very prospect threatens notions that have been our moral bedrock for centuries. Instead of thinking coolly and analytically, therefore, we often warn darkly about the dangers of "playing God" or departing from "nature."

And yet, as the authors sternly tell us, that sort of phrase-making is no substitute for serious systematic reflection. We already "play God" in countless ways: we give inoculations, we treat diseases, we find new educational strategies to address learning disabilities. In so many areas of our lives, we are not passive before nature. And "nature" is hardly a moral norm for any sane person. (As Mill observed, "Killing, the most criminal act recognized by human laws, Nature does once to every being that lives.") So what is needed is not panic or piety, but a sober and thoroughgoing evaluation of the new possibilities for improvement opened up by our new genetic knowledge.

The second obstacle to proper deliberation in this era of genetic research is a kind of gene-fetishism that has always had its appeal, and that has become much more common of late. People like to say "it's all in the genes," meaning that the environment really has nothing to do with the outcome, and so we have no obligation to promote good environments. In such a view, the proper response to biology is resignation, and inequalities are all the result of fate. The authors spend a good deal of time tangling with misunderstandings of genetic causation, with the aid of an excellent scientific appendix by the philosopher of science Elliott Sober.

Sober gives a detailed account of the complex interrelationships between genes and environment, arguing that the right question to pose is always what the relative importances of genetic factors and environmental factors are in any outcome, since both factors are always causally involved. "A condition has a significant genetic or environmental component only relative to a range of genes and a range of environments." Moreover, genes often influence an outcome indirectly by changing the individual's environment: a physical difference may cause others to treat a person differently, for example, thus producing behavioral differences. Sober is particularly critical of the claim that a complex human and psychological phenomenon such as homosexual desire can be plausibly traced to a single gene.

And no less important is the authors' assault on the ideological function of genetic determinism. "If there were an all-powerful and all-knowing being," they write,

> who was resolutely committed to shielding the existing social and political order from critical scrutiny, it is unlikely that it could hit upon a better strategy than implanting genetic determinist thinking in peoples' heads. There is, of course, no such evil demon. There are, however, scientists who sometimes foster gene-mania by a combination of excessive enthusiasm for their own projects and breathless public relations rhetoric aimed at securing social and financial support. And there are biotechnology firms poised to unleash sophisticated marketing techniques that will no doubt encourage unrealistic hopes for genetic solutions to all sorts of problems.

Indeed, the authors show that the new genetic possibilities should make it harder for people to hide behind the gene as a rationale for quietism. If we can alter genes, after all, then they become a part of the social environment like anything else, and we have to think seriously about environmental change and its relationship to justice, whether we are so inclined or not.

The third obstacle to good thinking in this new era is by far the greatest. It is the half-heartedness, the sloppiness, and the lack of systematic effort that characterizes most human thinking about most topics in most times and places. The authors' methodology in this book is basically Socratic: they assume that most people have many sound ethical intuitions pertinent to the resolution of such dilemmas, but they believe that without sustained examination, the testing of alternative theories and principles, and the building of complex accounts that integrate particular judgments into a coherent whole, we will not face the future well. If that is so in areas where the facts and concepts are familiar, it is all the more so, they believe, in areas where new scientific possibilities require us to refashion some of our most basic principles.

Here, as they see it, is where philosophy comes in. The authors are among the most eminent philosophers in the United States who focus on medical ethics, but they are not simply "medical ethicists." They are also wide-ranging thinkers about social justice and individual happiness. They carefully distinguish their project from an approach that is too often found in the field of medical ethics, in which people simply parade out a small number of familiar principles, unlinked to any overall theory, and mechanically plug them into the cases. Such an approach hardly deserves to be called philosophy, as they scornfully suggest. (If you want to see an example of bad work prominently endorsed—this is my example, not that of the tactful authors—consult the section called "Philosophy" in the National Commission on

Bioethics report on Cloning, a disgraceful farrago of half-digested ideas thrown about as a screen for the fear of the new.)

Instead the authors believe, with Socrates, Aristotle, Sidgwick, and Rawls, that good philosophical work must be difficult, complex, and systematic. It must consider both people's judgments and the most prominent theories that organize those judgments. When considering genetic decisions, the serious thinker must integrate this discussion into an overall consideration of just social institutions and equal opportunity. Although inevitably such an inquiry must begin somewhere—and the authors begin with a familiar type of liberal theory of justice, close to that of Rawls—they show throughout the book a readiness to consider a range of alternative accounts and to test theories by the judgments they yield as well as testing judgments by their relation to the theories.

This holistic manner of argument, they insist, is even more important in this area than in other areas of political philosophy, because in this area it is especially likely that no current theory has fully adequate concepts. Thinking about how existing accounts of equal opportunity apply to the dilemma of Katherine and Bill is important; but equally important is understanding why our existing accounts are not adequate, and how they need to be improved. Thus this book, though clearly written and vividly illustrated with striking examples, is still very difficult, as serious thought about its subject ought to be. It should not be read by anyone hoping for quick solutions, because the work of analysis is far more significant, in these matters, than the "bottom line." But it should be read by anyone who wants to think well as a citizen about choices that we must increasingly make about our future and the future of our descendants. If we need a further argument to get us going, we should consider that if citizens do not establish what they want and articulate good reasons for their goals, the insurance companies will make most of these decisions for us.

The authors discuss genetic counseling and decisions about conception in one chapter; but this topic, because of its familiarity, occupies them less than do a number of topics on which little has as yet been written, most dealing with possibilities of genetic surgery or alteration. Thus: What genetic treatments should be offered, and should these be required parts of basic health care? Can we meaningfully distinguish between treatments and genetic enhancements, and, if so, should enhancements be subsidized as well, or left to individual choice? Should groups with a particular vision of the good human life be permitted to pursue genetic projects that aim at perpetuating the characteristics valued by the group, and cutting it off increasingly from the society that surrounds it? Should screening for widespread genetic defects be required as a public health measure? Should parents be held negligent if they fail to take advantage of possibilities for improving the lot of their children? How can we defend meaningful reproductive liberty in an era when we know so much about the child who will be born? And what are the implications of new genetic possibilities for the social standing of the disabled? Do they have a legitimate claim that ameliorative genetic programs be avoided, on the grounds that such shifts in the population will increasingly isolate and stigmatize them?

Our fear of genetic intervention is not motivated simply by irrational anxiety. It also has historical roots: for we recall the excesses and the indignities of the eugenics movement of the early twentieth century, with its forced sterilizations of the "unfit," the objectification and the vilification of disabled people, the disdainful class-based and race-based attitudes that masqueraded as science. The natural culmination of this movement, as most people see it, was the horror of Nazi eugenics. So the first step in the authors' argument is to perform what they call an "ethical autopsy" on the eugenics movement, asking what its moral failings were, and whether they must be endemic to any movement that pursues genetic treatment and enhancement.

After a complicated and revealing analysis that reminds us, among other things, that modern eugenics was popular in progressive social-democratic circles as well as on the reactionary right, the authors conclude that we can to some extent separate the idea of genetic improvement of people from the hideously flawed ideals of the old eugenics. First of all, those eugenicists had no respect for people's reproductive freedom; but any modern movement must start from a position of respect. At the same time, the old eugenics had no way of intervening in the reproductive process except by controlling who had children with whom. Modern eugenics will have a lot more space for improvement mediated by individual choice: for genetic surgeries and gene replacement therapies can be offered to parents in the way that other medical treatments are now offered, and governed by similar norms of informed consent. Such treatments will still raise questions in the area of liberty—for example, we will have to ask whether parents should be required to perform genetic surgery on a child in utero; but these issues will be similar to others that we have long faced in our debates about what medical treatments parents may be required to get for their children, on pain of being charged with abuse and neglect.

The question of prejudice against certain types of people is much more difficult, and the authors insist that any just society must be highly respectful of different views of what a good person is, and what a worthwhile life is. They are also very alert to the subtle interplay between person and environment: an impairment, they insist, becomes a disability only against the background of a particular social environment, and it is generally possible to design an environment in which any given impairment will be at least much less disabling. (Wheelchair ramps, wheelchair access on buses, and other such measures make impairments to mobility far less disabling for those in wheelchairs.) Thus the choice of a social environment always embodies choices in favor of some people and against others.

Still, these facts do not mean that all genetic treatment and enhancement are inherently in league with baneful forms of prejudice and contempt.

Even in a pluralistic liberal society, we still need to agree on a list of basic "primary goods" that are generally agreed to be valuable prerequisites for carrying out most plans of life. In the area under question, the authors are optimistic that we can come up with a list of basic human capabilities to which all citizens are entitled as prerequisite of meaningful choice and functioning. Not to care about such basic capabilities is itself illiberal, for it undermines people's real chance to choose the life they want. (I wish the authors had spent more time pondering the "capabilities approach" to questions of basic social justice, which insists that well-being should be measured not by looking at Rawlsian resources, but rather by asking what people are actually able to do and to be. The logic of their concerns leads them to use the language of capabilities, and yet they do not ponder the implications of this other theoretical approach.)

III

Using their account of central human capabilities as a "baseline," the authors approach the difficult question of how to protect equality of opportunity in a time when the rich may be able to purchase not just commodities, but also better selves. Equality of opportunity is a puzzling concept at the best of times, but it becomes more puzzling when we have the power to alter the person. The authors of *From Chance to Choice* consider two familiar conceptions of equality of opportunity.

One conception, associated with the Kantian ethical tradition, draws a line between person and world. It insists that equality of opportunity has been served when all the social and political aspects of the environment have been adjusted to be fair to the dignity of all persons. This conception might still require some redistribution of wealth and income from more talented to less talented people, as Rawls's view surely does; but the talents are permitted to remain part of the person, so to speak, and there is no push to redistribute those valuable abilities themselves, since all persons are taken to be fundamentally equal in dignity anyway, in virtue of their basic moral capacities.

But there is another, more radical conception of equality of opportunity. It asserts that talents themselves are simply resources: people have no right to them, any more than they do to the advantages of wealth or class. In our current world, all we can do about this is redistribute wealth and income, since we cannot really equalize talents. But suppose we become able to equalize talents: would equality of opportunity itself require massive genetic engineering to produce a nation of equally abled people?

The authors reflect in a fascinating way on this issue, and on its implications for the theories of equality themselves. They conclude that we are lucky. We do not really have to choose between these two theories, because another ethical concern intervenes at this point to make the two theories generate very similar conclusions. For we must confront the radical theory with the fact of value pluralism: people hold different views of the ultimate goals of human existence, and thus different accounts of what an ideally "able" person would be. And if we respect the different religious and other conceptions of the good that our fellow citizens hold, we cannot engineer people in ways that run roughshod over those differences. Thus we are back to the menu of basic human capabilities that figure in all plans of life: it is only those capabilities that the radical theory is justified in pursuing, and only up to a basic threshold level. But then it is quite similar to the Kantian theory after all, since the Kantian theory, too, focuses on a list of basic abilities as "primary goods" that enable all citizens to pursue their different plans of life.

What does this mean for what governments should give people? The authors consider, next, the problematic distinction between the treatment of genetic impairments and the enhancement of normal genetic equipment. They are not very happy with this distinction, because it is easy to think of cases that call it into question. Person A is short because of a genetically caused brain tumor that impedes pituitary functioning. Person B is short because his parents were short. It looks as if A has an impairment, and that the correction of it would be a treatment; but B has no impairment, and the treatment of his shortness would be an "enhancement." And yet both conditions are genetically caused, and both may be the source of misery and discrimination.

Problematic though the distinction is in some cases, the authors believe that we are justified in relying on it to map out an account of what a fair healthcare scheme would give all citizens: treatment for all genetic impairments that bring them significantly below the level of normal species functioning, as specified in the account of central capabilities. They believe that health insurance should offer such treatments, whether for genetic surgery in utero or for treatments after birth. It is far more problematic, they argue, to offer enhancements, and they believe that some enhancements, such as the purchase of extra intelligence or musical talent for one's own children, should actually be illegal, inasmuch as they will be ways through which the privileged create children who are better than other people's children, thus violating the spirit of equal opportunity.

The authors' approach to equal opportunity, like virtually all previous philosophical approaches, relies on a notion of common humanity. Yet they are acutely aware that the new genetics may eventually call that basis into question. What would the world be like, they ask, if ethnic or religious groups proved able to engineer their descendants and to develop traits prized by the group, until eventually separate kinds of humans were produced, and we ceased to have a notion of common abilities and needs as an ethical resource? They think, with good reason, that such an eventuality would threaten the very basis of morality. In this respect, we have good reason to fear the future, though it is not altogether clear what we should do to ward it off.

IV

Reproductive freedom is, throughout *From Chance to Choice*, at the heart of the authors' concern to distance their enterprise from the old and ugly eugenics. They spend a good deal of time working out what a suitably expansive conception of reproductive freedom would cover: the choice of whether to procreate, with whom, and by what means; the choice of when to procreate; the choice of how many children to have; the choice whether to have biologically related children, and of what sort. People should be offered extensive genetic counseling, they believe, as a part of any reasonable healthcare package; but in the end, in most cases, parents must be left free to decide what sorts of children they will bring into the world.

To be sure, parental neglect may be involved whenever parents fail to treat a serious genetic ailment, as it now is when parents fail to get medical treatment for an ailing child. But it is only in the very small number of cases in which we might argue that an individual's life is worse than no life at all that we should even consider prohibiting parents from having the child that they choose to have. In such cases—say, a child with Tay-Sachs or other extremely limiting and painful conditions has been born through either medical or parental neglect—the authors are sympathetic to the idea that a lawsuit for "wrongful life" might be brought against the negligent person. This does not mean that they defend mandatory abortion; on the contrary, they are deeply opposed to that idea, on the grounds that the freedom to have the biological child of one's choice is extremely important. But they point out that good genetic counseling about Tay-Sachs is already offered by at least one prominent Orthodox Jewish organization: parents and counselors can deliberate well before conceiving a child.

It is difficult to articulate the considerations underlying a "wrongful life" action using only our current notions of harm. Here is another area in which the authors discover a challenge to philosophy in the new genetic science. Usually we think that for something to harm person P we have to be able to compare P's unharmed state with P's harmed state: P has to be there both before and after the harm. But when a child is conceived with Tay-Sachs and is born, there is no other way that particular child could have lived. Had the parents used artificial insemination, or adopted, or had they simply had no children at all, the Tay-Sachs child would not have existed. So who is the person P who is worse off than he might have been? They suggest that we need a comparative notion of harm that could, for example, compare the state of the existing impaired child to the state of some other child who might have been conceived (or adopted) with wiser counseling.

Inevitably, discussions of parental choice with respect to genetically impaired children are very threatening to the impaired themselves. Even if these choices do not involve aborting already existing impaired children— even if, as in the authors' primary scenario, they mainly involve fixing disabilities in the womb, or after birth—there is still something alarming, at least for the near future, about the idea that Down syndrome, deafness, and blindness may gradually cease to exist. People with those conditions not only fear increasing stigmatization and lack of social support; they also maintain vigorously (especially in the case of the deaf) that they have a valuable culture that will be obliterated if a single norm of basic human capabilities is applied across the board.

The authors give a sensitive exposition of these arguments, but finally they reject them. They can find no reason to extenuate impairments that seriously affect the central human abilities in their baseline account. Discrimination and stigmatization must be combated, of course; and yet they doubt that this should be done by dooming future children to a life of deafness or blindness when we will have learned to cure those infirmities. We do not refuse to inoculate our children or to provide them with needed medical treatment on the grounds that our actions might stigmatize the ill or the disease ridden.

Neither should we hesitate if we can make a child see or hear who otherwise might not. There are many conditions about which we can argue, because they involve controversial values; but there is a core of basic human abilities, and not to have any one of them is to be at a disadvantage in any world remotely like our own. Society can make many changes that open up opportunities to the impaired, but it is not possible to make deafness and blindness no disability at all. Moreover, such changes as we might make would be terribly expensive, so we must ask why we should all be asked to foot the bill merely because some parents value the special culture that a particular disability would promote.

This is the most delicate and difficult set of issues raised by the book, and it is here, I think, that the authors' admirably hardheaded account leaves the reader with the greatest perplexity. For human life always has been a struggle against the limits of nature, and any real human being is the result of such a struggle. Moreover, we know that many of the most creative and valuable human lives are the result of particularly difficult struggles that forced people out of the mainstream and made them the targets of contempt and abuse. Anyone who has ever been bad in sports, or the wrong body type for some sexual stereotype, knows that genuine suffering is involved in these "impairments"—and so a caring parent might well demand genetic alterations to prevent them, thus producing a nation of large-busted women and muscle-bound men. But shouldn't culture be changed rather than nature? And where, in the culturally unreconstructed and genetically engineered world of gender stereotypes, will the artists and the intellectuals come from? If all children can be made into whatever the dominant norms of their society want them to be, won't human life be the poorer for it?

My daughter was born with a perceptual and motor impairment (not clearly genetic, but let us suppose that it was) that clearly puts her below the authors' base line for "normal species functioning." It is an impairment severe enough that any decent mother would have opted, ex ante, for a genetic "fix." (She learned to read when she was two, and to tie her shoe-laces when she was eight.) Although she is both gifted and beautiful, she has had to contend with abuse and teasing all her life. Her idiosyncratic, lively, humorous, and utterly independent personality is inseparable from those struggles. Not only do I not wish that I had had some other different child, I do not even wish that she herself had been "fixed." Maternal love aside (if ever it is), I simply like this unusual contrarian person so much more than I would have liked (or so I believe) the cheerleading captain whom I might have produced. And I certainly do not desire a world in which parents will all "fix" all their children so that nobody is an outlier, even though we all know that the lives of outliers are not easy.

But hang on, say the hardheaded authors of *From Chance to Choice*. You know, too, that many forms of injustice produce depth and insight in the personality. Forster was right, in *Maurice*, when he depicted his protagonist as a man who would have been a boring middle-class stockbroker but for his homosexuality and the prejudice against it. Adversity and difference led Maurice to introspection, understanding, and genuine individuality. And surely you do not want to keep homophobia around just so that boring stockbrokers may be improved by suffering.

No, I do not. And I think it is a very good thing that our society has decided (if it has so decided) that homosexuality is not a disease to be treated, but a condition against which irrational prejudice has been directed—that it has decided to fight prejudice rather than to eradicate homosexuality. In another time and another place, obviously, it might have been otherwise. (Indeed, some eugenicists had such a hope, and many gays and lesbians still fear that genetic knowledge might someday be used to eradicate them.) The problem is that I do not trust society to deal this way with prejudice against the short, the uncoordinated, the small-breasted, and the athletically impaired. It is likely that good parents will feel obliged not to work against the social prejudices that make the lives of such children difficult, but instead to "fix" those conditions before birth if they can.

Our world, already diminished by the tyranny of conformity, would be the poorer for such a change. What would Mill have said could he have contemplated a world in which middle-class conformism could affect not only the happiness of unusual people, but their very existence in future generations? What challenges to dominant social norms, what "experiments in living," would we have in such a world? "They wish I had never been born," said my daughter, when I told her the authors of this book favored genetic treatment of defects that depart from "normal human functioning." Well, yes: in a very real sense they do. But who, given the choice to spare one's future child suffering, could confidently disagree with them? It is just that the very fact of having such a choice seems threatening and in some ways tragic.

I have no good counterproposal to the authors' sensible recommendations. I believe that they are right to use as the baseline for genetic medicine a small core of common human abilities, and to protect pluralism in ways of life above that baseline. But we should remember that parents are likely to be poor judges of what lies within the core of the humanly normal; and also that they may also be far too zealous for the normal, at the cost of many good things in human life.

We are only just beginning to create a society in which children with Down's syndrome are respected as individuals, in which the deaf are seen to have a culture. We must support these developments, against the predictable tide of demand for normalizing genetic treatment. While not forbidding genetic surgeries of the sort that the authors recommend, we should also foster a public culture in which a wide range of putative disabilities are respected, understood, and seen with imagination, as valuable forms of human life—so that parents eager to have the "normal" will think again. The authors of this important book are right not to romanticize difference when it comes with huge suffering and gross impairment. But those people who were formed, and strengthened, and provoked to achievement, by their own difference—who became thinkers, say, because they could not be cheerleaders—should ponder their complicated but happy fate, and try to preserve a world where it may still befall others.

# CHAPTER NINETEEN

# Disabled Lives: Who Cares?

EVA FEDER KITTAY (1999), Love's Labor: Essays on Women, Equality, and Dependency; MICHAEL BÉRUBÉ (1998), Life As We Know It: A Father, a Family, and an Exceptional Child; JOAN WILLIAMS (2000), Unbending Gender: Why Family and Work Conflict and What to Do About It

I

Sesha, daughter of the philosopher Eva Kittay and her husband Jeffrey, is a young woman in her early thirties. Attractive and affectionate, she loves music and pretty clothes, and responds with joy to the affection and admiration of others. Sesha sways to music and hugs her parents. But she will never walk, talk, or read. Because of congenital cerebral palsy and severe mental retardation, she will always be profoundly dependent on others. She needs to be washed, fed, dressed, wheeled out into Central Park. Beyond such minimal custodial care, if she is to flourish in her own way she needs companionship and love, a visible response to the capacities for affection and delight that are her strongest ways of connecting with others. Her parents, busy professionals, both care for Sesha for long hours themselves and pay a full-time caregiver. Still other helpers are needed on the many occasions when Sesha is ill or has seizures, and cannot help by telling where she hurts. In *Love's Labor*, Kittay argues that Sesha's need for care suggests both major criticisms of our dominant theories of social justice and major changes that should be made in our political arrangements.

My nephew Arthur is a big, good-looking ten-year-old. He loves machines of all sorts, and by now he has impressive knowledge of their workings. I could talk with Arthur all day about the theory of relativity, if I understood it as well as he does. On the phone with Arthur, it's always "Hi, Aunt Martha," and then he goes right into the latest mechanical or scientific issue that fascinates him. But until recently Arthur has been unable to learn in a classroom with other children, and he cannot be left alone for a minute when he and his mother are out shopping. He has few social skills and he seems unable to learn them. Affectionate at home, he becomes terrified if a stranger touches him. Unusually large for his age, he is also very clumsy, unable to play games at which most younger children are adept. He also has distracting bodily tics and makes weird noises.

Arthur has both Asperger's syndrome, a type of autism, and Tourette's syndrome. His parents have full-time jobs, and they cannot afford much help. Fortunately his mother's job as a church organist allows her to practice at home, and church people don't mind if she brings Arthur to work. More important still, the state in which they live has agreed, after a struggle, to pay for Arthur's education at a private school equipped to handle his combination of gifts and disabilities. None of us knows whether Arthur will ever be able to live on his own.

Jamie Bérubé loves B.B. King, Bob Marley, and the Beatles. He can imitate a waiter bringing all his favorite foods, and he has a sly sense of verbal humor. Born with Down Syndrome, Jamie has been cared for, since his birth, by a wide range of doctors and therapists, not to mention the non-stop care of his parents, the literary critics Michael Bérubé and Janet Lyon. In the early days of his life, Jamie had to be fed through a tube inserted into his nose, and have his oxygen levels monitored by a blood gas machine. At the time his father describes him in *Life As We Know It*—using a detailed life story as the basis for a political argument on behalf of the rights of the mentally disabled—Jamie is three. A speech therapist works to develop the muscles of his tongue; another teaches him American Sign Language. A massage therapist elongates the shortened muscles of his neck so that his head can sit straighter. Movement therapists work on the low muscle tone that is the main obstacle to both movement and speech in Down children. Equally important, a good local preschool in Urbana, Illinois, includes him in a regular classroom, stimulating his curiosity and giving him precious confidence in relationships with other children, who react well to his sweet personality. Above all, his brother, parents, and friends make a world in which he is not seen as "a child with Down Syndrome," far less as "a mongoloid idiot." He is Jamie, a particular child. Jamie will probably be able to live on his own to some extent, and to hold a job. But his parents know that he will, more than most other children, need them all his life.

Extreme dependency comes in many forms. And it is not only the wide range of children and adults with disabilities who need extensive and even hourly care from others. The mental, physical, and social disabilities that I have just described all have rough parallels in the conditions of the elderly, who are generally even more difficult to care for than disabled children and young adults—more angry, defensive, and embittered, less physically pleasant to be with. Washing the body of a child with Down Syndrome seems vastly easier to contemplate than washing the incapacitated and incontinent body of a parent who hates being in such a condition, especially when both the washer and the washed remember the parent's prime. So the way we think about the needs of children and adults with disabilities is not a special department of life, easily cordoned off from the "average case." It also has implications for the way we think about our parents as they age—and about the needs we ourselves are likely to have if we live long enough.[1] As the life span increases, the relative independence many of us enjoy looks more and more like a temporary condition, a phase of life that we move into gradually, and which we all too quickly begin to leave. Even in our prime, many of us encounter shorter or longer periods of extreme dependency on others— after surgery or a severe injury, or during a period of depression or acute mental stress.

Who does all the work that extreme dependency requires? In most cases, as Eva Kittay and Joan Williams, a law professor and author of *Unbending Gender*, emphasize, this work is done by women.[2] Ordinary child care is still disproportionately done by women, since women are far more likely than men to accept part-time work and the career detours it requires. Fathers who agree to help care for a child who will soon go off to school, moreover, are much less likely to shoulder the taxing long-term burden of care for an extremely disabled child or parent. In the United States, furthermore, most women who do such work cannot count on much by way of support from an extended family or community network.

Much of the work of caring for a dependent is unpaid; nor is it recognized by the market as work. And yet it has a large effect on the rest of such a worker's life. My sister could not hold any job that did not allow her long hours at home. That the Bérubés and Kittays both share their child-care responsibilities more equally than most other ambitious professionals is made possible only by their flexible schedule of university teaching and writing. They also can afford a lot of help—most of it, as Kittay notes with unease, from women who are themselves, even though paid, neither paid very highly nor as generally respected by society as they should be for performing a vital social service.

Three urgent problems of social justice emerge in the books by Kittay, Bérubé, and Williams. First, there is the issue of the fair treatment of mentally and physically disabled people who need a lot of care throughout their lives. In another era, Sesha and Jamie probably would have died in infancy; if they had lived they would have been put in institutions and given minimal custodial care, never getting a chance to develop their capacities for love, joy, and in Jamie's case substantial cognitive achievement and, probably, active citizenship. Ten years ago, before Asperger's syndrome was recognized as a disease, Arthur would have been treated as a smart kid whose parents had messed him up emotionally. He would probably have been put into an institution, with no opportunity to learn, and they would have lived with crushing guilt.

Second, there is the related, but distinct, issue of providing adequate care for people who at times function relatively independently during phases of their lives in which they are profoundly dependent. The elderly always received some care, especially if they had children; but until recently they did not get, and many still do not get, the sort of care that shows respect for their dignity and encourages continued activity of body, mind, and heart. Providing such care looks like one of the things a just society would do.

A just society, we might think, would also look at the other side of the problem, the burdens on people who provide care for dependents. These people need many things: recognition that what they are doing is work; assistance, both human and financial; a chance at a rewarding career for themselves and at participation in social and political life. At one time, as Joan Williams shows, it used to be assumed that all this work would be done by women, who were not full citizens anyway and did not need to work outside the home. Women weren't asked whether they would do this work: it was just theirs to do.

We now think of women as equal citizens who are entitled to pursue the full range of occupations. We also generally think that they are entitled to a real choice about whether they will assume the burden of caring for a disabled elderly parent. Nor would most people say, if asked, that the accident of giving birth to a severely handicapped child should blight the prospects, for the parents or one parent, of living a productive personal and social life. But the realities of life in a society that still assumes that this work will be done for free, "out of love," still put enormous burdens on women across the entire economic spectrum, diminishing their productivity and their contribution to civic and political life.

II

What have theories of justice said about these problems? As Kittay insists, virtually nothing. Nor, she argues, can the omission be easily corrected, for it is built into the structure of our own strongest theories. Kittay believes that these theories have done real harm, shaping our practical political ideas through their subtle effect on the ways we speak and think. (For example, she plausibly suggests that attacks on providing welfare for non-working mothers are influenced by images of the citizen as an independent worker that come to us from centuries of social-contract thinking.) Thus she holds that more perceptive philosophical theorizing is important to addressing these issues in practical political life. Even if not immediately, theoretical conceptions shape public arguments, giving people the concepts they use and shaping the alternatives they consider. Her point has force: without explicit feminist arguments about rape and sexual harassment, for example, prejudiced conceptions of sexuality would very likely have continued to suffuse our political culture.[3] Persuasive theories are only one part of good political action, but they are a part.

Kittay plausibly suggests that our political discourse is pervasively shaped by the idea of society as based on a contract for mutual advantage, an idea that has dominated political theory in the Western tradition. All social-contract theories adopt a fictional hypothesis that appears innocent: the fiction of competent adulthood. The parties to the social contract are assumed, as John Locke wrote, to be "free, equal, and independent."[4] Contemporary advocates of social-contract theory explicitly adopt such a hypothesis. For the American philosopher David Gauthier, people of unusual need are "not party to the moral relationships grounded by a contractarian theory."[5] Similarly, the citizens in John Rawls's "Well-Ordered Society" are "fully cooperating members of society over a complete life."[6] And since the partnership envisaged is for the mutual advantage of the contracting parties, provisions for people who aren't part of the bargain will be an afterthought—not part of the basic institutional structure to which they agree.

Kittay is right to concentrate on Rawls—not only because his theory is among the strongest the Anglo-American philosophical tradition has produced, but also because it is committed to removing the unfair influence of various "morally irrelevant" accidents of life and to promoting equal respect among citizens. Just as race, class, wealth, and even sex do not give one person greater worth than another from the perspective of the principles of justice that should underlie society's basic institutions, so too, one would have thought, the facts that one person's body is more dependent than another's, or that one has a dependent aged parent, should not be sources of pervasive social disadvantage.

Kittay might have done well to observe that on this topic Rawls's Kantian starting point is likely to give bad guidance. For Kant, human dignity and our moral capacity, dignity's source, are radically separate from the natural world. Morality has the task of providing for human needs, but the idea that we are basically split beings, both rational persons and animal dwellers in the world of nature, never ceases to influence Kant's ideas.

What's wrong with Kant's distinction? Quite a lot. First, it ignores the fact that our dignity is that of a certain sort of animal; it is a dignity that could not be possessed by a being who was not mortal and vulnerable, just as the beauty of a cherry tree in bloom could not be possessed by a diamond. Second, the split wrongly denies that animality can itself have dignity; thus it slights aspects of our lives (our bodily desires, our sensory response to beauty) that have worth, and distorts our relation to the other animals. Third, it makes us think of the core of ourselves as self-sufficient, not in need of the gifts of fortune; in so thinking we misrepresent the nature of our own morality and rationality, which are thoroughly material and animal themselves. We learn to ignore the fact that disease, old age, and accident impede the moral and rational functions, just as they impede mobility and dexterity. Fourth, it makes us think of ourselves as not subject to the effects of time. We forget that the usual human life cycle brings with it periods of extreme dependency, in which our functioning is similar to that of the mentally or physically handicapped throughout their lives.

Rawls's contracting parties are aware of their need for material goods. But they are competent contracting adults, roughly similar in need. Such a hypothesis seems required by the very idea of a contract for mutual advantage.[7] In conceiving of persons in such a way, as Kittay shows, Rawls explicitly omits from the situation of basic political choice the more extreme forms of need and dependency that human beings may experience. Although caring for people who are not independent is "a pressing practical question," Rawls argues, it may reasonably be postponed to a later, legislative stage, after basic political institutions are designed.

Kittay is right to find this reply inadequate. Care for children, the elderly, and the mentally and physically handicapped is a major part of the work that needs to be done in any society, and in most societies it is a source of unfairness. Any theory of justice needs to think about the problem from the beginning, in the design of basic institutions.

Rawls's deferral of the question of extreme dependency makes a large difference to his political theory, as Kittay shows. For his account of the "primary goods," the things every society must arrange to distribute fairly to its citizens, is explicitly connected to his account of the capacities of "independent" citizens: it is said to be a list of what citizens need for their own lives, when they have the two "moral powers" (meaning, roughly, the capacity for instrumental reasoning and the capacity for ethical evaluation), as well as the capacity to be "fully cooperating." Although such a list might possibly be expanded to include care during intervals of dependency such people are likely to experience in their own lives (although Rawls does not so expand it), it has no place for the needs of people who are never going to be independent. Rawls's list of primary goods includes liberties and opportunities; income and wealth; and the social bases of self-respect—by which Rawls means institutional structures ensuring that all citizens are treated as having worth and dignity.[8] But care during lengthy periods (or a life) of extreme dependency is never mentioned.

Still more questionably (and something not emphasized in Kittay's argument), Rawls measures relative social position with reference to income and wealth alone, ignoring the possibility that a group that is denied dignity may not, as a class, be most deprived economically. Some handicapped people are economically disadvantaged and others are not; Sesha, Jeffrey, and Arthur are all relatively well-off. All encounter special problems in achieving self-respect that a just society ought to address.

Amartya Sen has made a related criticism of Rawls's theory of primary goods: that it ignores the fact that people have varying capacities to convert income and wealth into the ability to function effectively.[9] Take two people, one in a wheelchair and one not. If they are to have a similar level of mobility, a lot more will have to be spent on helping the person in the wheelchair. Moreover, a point that Sen does not emphasize, the expenditure will have to include ambitious social measures of a sort individual families, even well-off ones, cannot undertake on their own: building wheelchair ramps, ensuring that buses and trains have wheelchair access.

III

Can a liberal theory of justice adequately address these problems? Kittay doubts it. She holds that Western political theory must be radically reconfigured to put the fact of dependency at its heart. The facts, she says, that we are all "some mother's child," and that we exist in intertwined relations of dependency, should be the guiding image for political thought. Such a care-based theory, she thinks, will be likely to be very different from any liberal theory, since the liberal tradition is deeply committed to goals of independence and liberty. Kittay supplies few details to clarify the practical meaning of the difference. She seems to believe that a care-based theory would support a type of politics that provides comprehensive support for needs throughout all citizens' lives, as in some familiar ideals of the welfare state—but this would be a welfare state in which liberty is far less important than security and well-being.

Kittay is not altogether consistent on this point. At times she herself uses classic liberal arguments, saying that we need to remember that caregivers have their own lives to lead, and to support policies that give them more choices. While she rejects, in the abstract, solutions that emphasize freedom as a central political goal, the concrete measures she favors do not seem to have sweeping anti-liberal implications. She wants to restore and expand the Aid to Families with Dependent Children program, which was annulled in 1996, as well as expand the Family and Medical Leave Act of 1993. She advocates various educational measures aimed at promoting the dignity of the disabled, through a judicious combination of mainstream schooling and separate education (for those like Sesha). All these are familiar liberal policies, which can be combined with an emphasis on choice and liberty as important social goals. Kittay's most controversial proposal, that of a direct non-means-tested payment to those who care for family dependents at home, clearly has, or could have, a liberal rationale: that of ensuring that these people are seen as active, dignified workers rather than as passive noncontributors.

We could reformulate liberal theory without adopting Kittay's extreme theoretical alternative. Suppose we accept one of her suggestions, adding care during periods of dependency to a Rawlsian list of primary goods. Suppose we also make another change for which she expresses sympathy, conceiving of the entire list in Sen's way, as a list of "capabilities" for various types of functioning. In other words, a society is assessed not by the sheer amount of income and wealth it gives people, but by the extent to which it has made them capable of various important activities—mobility, for example, or access to political life.

Suppose we add a further change that she does not mention, but one that seems desirable: we reconceive the list of primary goods as a list of the basic needs of citizens of all types, and not only those who have, to a "normal" degree, the mental and moral powers Kant specified. In other words, we

substitute for the Kantian image of the citizen a more Aristotelian conception, thinking of people as animal beings with various needs to be able
to function—including, but not limited to, the needs for care by, and connection with, others. At this point, it is worth noting, we have moved rather
far from the social contract tradition and its basic idea of a bargain for mutual
advantage.[10]

Suppose, finally, we add to the list of primary goods some items suggested by Michael Bérubé's reflections on both what his son's life requires
and what it contributes. We say, that is, that all citizens need to develop
imagination and the ability to recognize the humanity in one another—
including those who have disabilities and unusual needs. Institutions
promoting the "social bases of the imagination"—humane schools,
public support for the arts—would have a place on the list, complementing
institutions that foster self-respect.

Still, the redesigned theory is basically liberal. For it emphasizes that we
want all people to have the chance to develop the full range of their human
powers, at whatever level their condition allows, and to enjoy the liberty and
independence their condition allows. Would we do better to reject this
theory in favor of Kittay's idea, jettisoning independence as a major social
goal and conceiving of the state as a universal mother? To be sure, nobody
is ever self-sufficient; the independence we enjoy is always both temporary
and partial, and it is good to be reminded of that fact by a theory that also
stresses the importance of care of dependent people. But is being "some
mother's child" a sufficient image for the citizen in a just society? I think
we need a lot more: liberty and opportunity, the chance to form a plan of
life, the chance to learn and imagine on one's own.

These goals are as important for the mentally handicapped as they are for
others, though they are much more difficult to achieve. Although Sesha will
never live on her own (and although Kittay is right to say that independence
should not be seen as a necessary condition of dignity for all mentally
handicapped people), I can hope that Arthur will, and hold a job, and vote,
and write his story. Bérubé, too, imagines his son writing a book about
himself, as two adults with Down syndrome recently have done.[11] One day
Jamie's kindergarten class went around the room, asking the children
what they wanted to be when they grew up. They said the usual things:
basketball star, ballet dancer, fireman. The teacher wasn't sure Jamie would
understand the question, so she asked it very clearly. Jamie just said, "Big."
And his literal answer, said the teacher, taught them all something about the
question. Bérubé, too, wants, simply, a society in which his son will be
able to be "big": healthy, educated, loving, active, seen as a particular
person with something distinctive to contribute, rather than as "a retarded
child."

For that to happen, his dependence must be understood and supported.
But so too must his need to be a distinct person and an individual; and
at this point Bérubé refers sympathetically to the ideas of John Rawls.

He argues that the concept at the heart of the Individuals With Disabilities Education Act (IDEA)—that every child has the right to an "appropriate education" in the "least restrictive environment" possible, based on an "Individualized Education Plan"—is a profoundly liberal idea, an idea about individuality and freedom. And thinking of the large differences between Jamie and Arthur helps us to see why this emphasis on individuality is central to respect. Jamie's educational needs and Arthur's are hugely different; any society that treated them as indistinguishable members of a "special education" class would be grossly unfair to both. One of the most important kinds of support that they both need is the support required to become adults who will make their own free choices, each in his own way. Insofar as Kittay suggests that we downplay or marginalize such liberal notions in favor of a conception of the state that makes it the parental supporter of the needs of its "children," I think she goes too far, misconceiving what justice would be for both the disabled and the elderly. Even for people like Sesha, who will never vote or be able to write, doesn't a full human life involve freedom and individuality—namely, a space in which to exchange love and enjoy light and sound, free from confinement and mockery?

IV

How, in practical terms, would a just society deal with such problems? Bérubé, like Kittay, discusses both the different images of dependent people and practical legal strategies to help them. An English professor accustomed to professional discussions of the "social construction" of various human categories, he writes that both the limitations and the value of that idea became much clearer to him as a result of his life with Jamie. Part of Jamie's condition is clearly not socially created, and Bérubé gives a detailed genetic and medical account of Down syndrome, with all its particular physical manifestations. But much of Jamie's condition is social: Will he be called a "mongoloid idiot"? A "retarded child"? Or will he get a chance to meet other children as simply "Jamie," a kid who is a little different, but then children are all different anyway—he's just a little more so? Such changes in labeling make a difference, Bérubé argues, and he is a staunch defender both of medical intervention and of a concern for language that might be seen pejoratively as "political correctness." Much of social justice, he argues, lies in the way we see and speak of one another.

Beyond good attitudes, though, we need good laws. And here both Bérubé and Kittay are worried. The progress that laws protecting the handicapped, such as IDEA, have made is fragile. It can easily be undone, particularly in a society determined to decrease the size of the public sector. Bérubé worries particularly about the current view that people who are not "productive," in a narrow economic sense, are a drag on the whole society. Children like Jamie may soon be seen as luxuries that society cannot afford.

Bérubé is also worried that in a competitive society such as ours, attending a regular classroom, which has been so important to Jamie, will be regarded as a waste of time, decreasing the more profitable learning time of other children. To this worry he responds that classrooms are not just for teaching skills: they are also for learning how to be a good citizen. And that means learning how to see the humanity of another citizen, whoever it may be. In that sense, Jamie has taught his classmates at least as much as they have taught him.

Bérubé sees complexity in the issue of "mainstream" versus special education. He and his wife have chosen for Jamie a combination of the two strategies. Special education can be indispensable to consolidate mastery and to give a child a sense of worth. And mainstream education, both he and Kittay agree, is crucial, since it shapes a society in which a wide range of human abilities are encountered every day as pretty normal, part of what being human includes. However, my sister, who used to be a staunch defender of mainstreaming, now opposes it, at least for children like Arthur, who look like other children and get teased because they behave oddly. After a month in a classroom with only other Asperger's children, Arthur is for the first time starting to make friends with other children his age.[12]

But what about the people who take care of children with disabilities and elderly parents? Williams, like Kittay, sees the work of caring for dependents at home as a crucial issue affecting the social equality of women. Holding that women are often subtly coerced by social norms into shouldering the burden of caring for a dependent, she argues that any solution to that problem has three parts, which must operate together. One part is the reallocation of domestic responsibilities between men and women in the home. A second (Kittay's primary concern) is the role of the state. The state may lighten the burden of people who care for dependents through a wide range of policies, including subsidized leave time, subsidies for special education and therapy through the school system, and the direct, non-means-tested payment that Kittay favors for the work of caring for a dependent.

But Williams emphasizes that the workplace should change as well. Through comparative data, Williams shows that in countries with a promising range of state policies (Sweden, for example), women still do most of the work of caring for dependents.[13] The reason, she plausibly argues, is that men do not want to jeopardize their careers, or to be perceived as marginal part-timers. They aren't against sharing domestic responsibilities, but they do not want their careers to pay the price that such a decision would now exact. For most jobs today, workers are expected either to work full time and have normal opportunities for promotion or to accept greatly diminished opportunities for promotion if they work part-time. In some occupations matters are even worse: there is a macho competition to work long hours on the job, and anyone who refuses to work overtime is seen as unproductive.

All of these problems need much more attention, about the possibilities both of state action and of reorganizing employment. None of these books offers more than sketches of approaches that might be considered, and the writers have little hope that any change will be tried, unless we first have better information about one another, and better images of decent relations among citizens.

Thus I think Bérubé is right to suggest that the key to social justice for both the disabled and those who care for them lies in enlarging the imagination. If we regard our fellow citizens above all as parties to a mutually advantageous bargain, we will never see much of value in the permanently handicapped. And we will see value in the disabled elderly only by thinking of them as formerly productive people who deserve some recompense for that earlier productivity; this is surely not all that their dignity requires. Finally, if we see little value or dignity in dependent people, we will be unlikely to see dignity in the work done dressing or washing them, and we will be unlikely to accord this work the social recognition it should have. We will confront these problems well only if we see human worth in Jamie's playful sweetness as well as in his brother's traditionally valued gifts, in Sesha's need to be dressed as well as in her parents' ability to dress themselves. Thus Bérubé's book, which can be read simply as a father's detailed and often quite humorous story about the life of his son, actually has an important theoretical purpose. All the detail and the humor are there to help readers understand the relationship with a "retarded child" not as a heart-wringing tragedy but as a valuable and enjoyable human relationship.

Although in both theory and practice American society has moved beyond earlier versions of the social contract tradition, by insisting on human dignity as a central social value, it is far from having shaken off a dark implication inherent in the very idea of a social bargain for mutual advantage— namely that those who remain dependent are not full participants.[14] "A more capacious and supple sense of what it is to be human"[15] is crucial if we are to think more clearly about problems of justice. One reason for optimism, as Bérubé says, is that we know that human beings are able to imagine and to communicate what they imagine even to someone who did not have that image before. If we were able to form the grim picture of the "mongoloid idiot," a generic being living out its hopeless future in an institution, it ought to be possible to learn to put in its place the image of Jamie, a particular child.

NOTES

1. According to the U.S. Department of Labor, Women's Bureau (May 1998), an estimated 22.4 million households—nearly one in four—are providing home care for family members or friends over the age of fifty. For these and other data I am grateful to Mona Harrington, *Care and Equality* (New York: Knopf, 1999).

2. See also *Human Development Report* 1999, published by the United Nations Development Programme (New York: Oxford University Press, 1999), pp. 77–83, which argues that in developing as in developed countries, such unpaid work is a major source of disadvantage to women, and increasingly so in the new global economy, which has often replaced home-based work by work outside the home.

3. Among these: the idea that if a woman does not resist with "utmost force" she has consented; that a woman with an active sexual life can be presumed to have consented to an alleged rape. For an excellent summary of the influence of feminist thought on criminal law, see Stephen Schulhofer, *Unwanted Sex* (Cambridge, Mass.: Harvard University Press, 1998); and see my own account in "American Women: Preferences, Feminism, Democracy," Chapter Five of *Sex and Social Justice* (New York: Oxford University Press, 1999).

4. John Locke, *Second Treatise on Government*, Chapter Eight.

5. David Gauthier, *Morals by Agreement* (New York: Oxford University Press, 1986), p. 18, speaking of all "persons who decrease [the] average" level of well-being in a society.

6. John Rawls, *Political Liberalism*, expanded paper edition (New York: Columbia University Press, 1996), p. 183 and elsewhere. Rawls's moral version of the contract doctrine is obviously very different from Gauthier's Hobbesian view, but in this respect there is a limited similarity.

7. Thus, for example, Rawls refuses to grant that we have any duties of justice to animals, on the grounds that they are not capable of reciprocity (*A Theory of Justice* [Cambridge, Mass.: Harvard University Press, 1971], pp. 17, 504–505); they are owed "compassion and humanity," but "they are outside the scope of the theory of justice, and it does not seem possible to extend the contract doctrine so as to include them in a natural way" (*Theory of Justice*, p. 512). His account of reciprocity seems very narrow, given the capacities of Jamie, Sesha, and Arthur for many types of interaction.

8. Presumably, though Rawls leaves all such matters abstract, constitutional guarantees of race and sex equality would be central examples of such structures.

9. Amartya Sen, "Equality of What?" in his *Choice, Welfare, and Measurement* (Cambridge, Mass.: MIT Press, 1982), pp. 353–72. Kittay refers with sympathy to Sen's views.

10. The idea of a mutually advantageous bargain also prevents the contracting parties from thinking about how they will support the needs of citizens who do not have the powers that they have. The premise that people are thinking of their own advantage is deeply built into the structure of the entire process of judgment in theories of social contract.

11. Mitchell Levitz and Jason Kingsley, *Count Us In: Growing Up with Down Syndrome* (New York: Harcourt Brace, 1994).

12. Another issue on which both books take nuanced positions is the issue of aborting fetuses known to have grave mental disabilities. Neither author would stigmatize parents who choose such a course; both are concerned primarily that parents not be coerced into such choices by lack of social support for the children they would otherwise bear.

13. As of 1986, 43 percent of working women in Sweden were employed part time, and women took fifty-two days of leave for every day taken by a man (Joan Williams, *Unbending Gender*, p. 51, with references).

14. Thus, Gauthier says that while the elderly have paid for the care they receive by earlier periods of productivity, the handicapped have not (Gauthier, *Morals by Agreement* [see note 5 above], p. 18, n. 30).

15. This phrase is Bérubé's, from a paper published after the book, entitled "Disability and the 'Difference' It Makes," delivered at the Smithsonian National Museum's conference Disability and the Practice of Public History, May 1999.

# CHAPTER TWENTY

# When She Was Good

Peter J. Conradi (2001), *Iris Murdoch: A Life*

I

How is moral philosophy related to narrative fiction? One would think that the relationship ought to be an intimate one. Both genres are concerned with character and choice, with motives and imaginings, with the vicissitudes of passion. And yet, from the time when Plato attacked the tragic artists, the relationship has often been characterized by mutual suspicion, philosophers viewing narrative literature as indulgent, emotional, and lacking in normative clarity, writers of fiction viewing philosophers as intolerant moralists who lack appreciation of what Proust calls the "intermittences of the heart." But some cultures and some periods have been marked by especially hostile relations between the camps. In the latter half of the twentieth century, fiction and philosophy drew close in France, with Sartre and Camus writing both kinds of books and blurring the distinction. In the English-speaking world, by contrast, things were very different. Very few noted philosophers attempted fiction, and Iris Murdoch was the only eminent novelist to publish serious works of moral philosophy.

To some extent, the reason for this estrangement was cultural. British academic society had a marked distaste for the public display of strong passions. For the typical Oxbridge don, novelists were a little like actors: amusing at a distance, embarrassing if they came too close. To some extent, too, the estrangement was stylistic. Anglo-American philosophy was written in a very austere and impersonal way, so that any incursion of narrative and emotion into the text would be regarded as an embarrassing anomaly. But how could a novelist not want to record the texture of concrete particulars—what Murdoch once memorably described in the hallowed precincts of the Aristotelian Society as "the smell of the Paris metro or what it is like to hold a mouse in one's hand"? Her remark was shocking in those quarters, because it insisted that such details of experience were the stuff of philosophy as well as the stuff of life. People were not yet ready to listen.

Above all, the estrangement between philosophy and literature was produced by issues of philosophical substance. Moral philosophy in the postwar period had become preoccupied—not surprisingly, given the tumultuous times—with the moment of ethical choice, and with the role of the will in choosing the appropriate action. R. M. Hare, who had spent time in a prisoner-of-war camp and on the Burmese railway, had no interest at all in the inner life, or in the effort to cultivate the thoughts and the feelings of a person of good character. He wanted a philosophy that would produce good in the world and help us understand the nature of good action. His analysis of moral language famously held that all moral statements were in essence commands to act, and this soldierly conception of morality became popular in a world intent on seeing the good defeat the bad. (On the Continent, a similar emphasis prevailed: Sartre depicted the moral agent as a free and isolated will, capable of choosing courageously for the sake of humanity only if it could first come to grips with the agony of being free.)

To this muscular conception of philosophy, the preoccupations of the novelist—the vagaries of emotion and desire, the variety of human character, the predatoriness of love—looked simply irrelevant, as if one had suggested that a grandiose salon painting of "The Choice of Hercules" could be improved by the addition of a floating indeterminate sky in the style of Turner. But the choice-of-Hercules conception of the ethical life left out a good deal, and these omissions were damaging to the postwar philosophers' own project of understanding how good can be done and evil can be avoided. For evil is very likely to begin in the inner world, with the struggle of love against infantile egoism and ambivalence, the laborious effort to form patterns of thought and action that defeat narcissism and acknowledge the reality of other people.

Oddly enough, these British philosophers were all teaching the Greeks, and they must have encountered there a richer view of the moral life. Teaching Aristotle, they would have reflected that a person's goodness does not consist in isolated moments of willing, but rather in a lifelong effort to cultivate patterns of motivation, attention, reaction, and, related to all these, choice. The effort was a virtuous one only if these patterns became genuinely rooted, suffusing the moral life. Aristotle certainly had too simple and too sunny a conception of the obstacles to goodness in the human personality, in part because he took no interest in children; but his conception is promising in its general shape, and it can be deepened by the addition of a more nuanced psychology. Still, teaching Aristotle did not affect the substance of what Oxford philosophers wrote—until much later, and under the influence of Iris Murdoch.

Murdoch was, for many years, an anomaly: a celebrated and also popular novelist, and at the same time a respected philosophy tutor at Oxford, who throughout her career (even after she quit teaching) continued to publish serious philosophical essays and books. For most of this time Murdoch opposed any effort to connect her two careers. In an interview with Bryan Magee in 1978, on the subject of "Philosophy and the Novel," she offered a caricature of Oxbridge philosophy at its driest as a definition of what philosophy was, and a similarly extreme definition of the novel as uncommitted play, as if to say to her baffled interlocutor: "See? You thought you'd do a program about how my two careers are connected. But there's no such connection, except in your well-intentioned head." As Peter J. Conradi's book makes clear, Murdoch had a constant desire to mystify and to prevent people from finding her where she was, and this interview was a splendid case in point.

Needless to say, there are profound connections between Murdoch's fiction and Murdoch's philosophy, and they become more apparent all the time. For Anglo-American moral philosophy has by now achieved a broader conception of its subject matter, which would today be agreed to include the virtues and the vices, the nature of imagination and attention, the vicissitudes of passion. And Murdoch's novels, which once looked like stylized social comedy portraying the foibles of the British upper middle classes, can now be seen more justly as complicated meditations about the nature of sin and the struggle of the personality with itself, in which artistic attention is not only the organizing force that drives the whole, but also, at the same time, an object of critical scrutiny.

The novels are a major part of Murdoch's philosophical contribution, because one cannot fully make the case for the moral significance of the strivings of the inner world without narratives that show at length and in detail what Henry James called "the effort really to see and really to represent," as it contends with "the constant force that makes for muddlement." Conradi misses this, and thus he misses Murdoch's large philosophical importance, assuming that like-minded souls in Oxford, such as Philippa Foot and John McDowell, are more important as philosophical writers about virtue because they were writing more of the conventional sort of philosophical work. What he fails to grasp (perhaps because he gets most of his information about philosophy from Foot) is that the ideas that Murdoch shares with these more conventional contemporaries require for their full exploration a different and riskier type of writing, which only she, with her complex erotic gifts, attempted to deliver.

II

In 1947, Iris Murdoch wrote in her journal: "For me philosophical problems are the problems of my own life." Conradi's biography makes it clear that Murdoch's life, like her work, was shaped by a moral struggle against the forces of destructiveness and sadism. Conradi is the editor of Murdoch's philosophical essays (a fine volume called *Existentialists and Mystics*) and the author of a good study of the novels. He was also a close friend of Murdoch's, particularly in the final decades of her life. *Elegy for Iris*, John Bayley's moving memoir of his wife's descent into Alzheimer's disease, is dedicated to Conradi and his partner Jim O'Neill, and the last chapter of Conradi's biography describes O'Neill bathing Murdoch at a time when she could only say, with bafflement, "I wrote."

Murdoch gave Conradi access to the journals that she kept for most of her adult life (with some pages excised), and her friends, many of whom are still living, have extensively confided in him. So this is a biography rich in information, written in a humble and tasteful way by an intimate whose aim is to put a lot of material at the reader's disposal, obtruding his own personality as little as possible. (Conradi, a Buddhist, introduced Murdoch to Buddhist conceptions of "unselfing.") As Conradi says, it is not the only sort of biography of her that will be written; but it is, I think, a fine example of its kind.

Murdoch was born in 1919, the only child of an Anglo-Irish couple who soon moved from Dublin to London, though they returned to Ireland frequently for holidays. (Murdoch's identification with the Irish was very deep.) Her childhood was a placid one, as she was evidently the delight of her gentle father and her able, enterprising mother. Success at school came easily, in studies and in sports. After Badminton School she went up to Somerville College, Oxford, in 1938, where she read Mods and Greats, the taxing undergraduate combination of Greek and Latin literature with ancient history and philosophy. Her interest in Greek conceptions of virtue thus got its start early, and she attended with great enthusiasm Eduard Fraenkel's famous seminar on Aeschylus's *Agamemnon*. (Fraenkel figures as a character in *The Unicorn*, one of her odder and less successful novels.) She was deeply influenced also by her philosophy tutor Donald MacKinnon, whose religious sensibility put him at odds with the times. She joined the Communist Party.

But this was wartime, and Oxford was greatly altered by the departure of so many young men for the front. Murdoch's first great love was Frank Thompson, the elder brother of the historian E. P. Thompson. They exchanged intimate letters while he served in Europe, and his death in Bulgaria in 1944 was a personal tragedy. After receiving a first-class degree, Murdoch went to London to work for the Treasury, sharing a flat with Philippa Bosanquet, later Foot. (Shortly before this, Murdoch left the Communist Party. Her past membership caused her no subsequent difficulty in Britain, though for years it made trouble every time she wanted to visit the United States.) In 1944, bored with the life of the bureaucrat ("I am inefficient and administration depresses me"), she joined UNRRA (the United Nations Relief and Rehabilitation Administration), and worked for two years with refugees and displaced persons, first in England and then on the Continent.

After a period studying philosophy in Cambridge—where she briefly encountered and was deeply impressed by Wittgenstein, though she was critical of his destructive use of his power, his capacity to destroy self-respect—she accepted a tutorial fellowship at St. Anne's College, Oxford. For the next six years or so, she taught philosophy by day, and by night she pursued the amazingly complex erotic life that she had already begun in London. The reader of Murdoch's novels tends to think that the constant changing of partners is fantastic high comedy; but life and art were closer than we thought. As Murdoch writes of herself, "Urge towards drama is fundamental. I am 'full of representations of myself.'"

Murdoch typically carried on simultaneous affairs with multiple men (and the occasional woman), affairs that were emotionally complex and often involved the betrayal of a friend. Sex, Bayley opines in *Elegy for Iris*, was of marginal interest to her where most of these men are concerned. Conradi's biography casts doubt on this, suggesting that she was a person of very strong physical passion. But sex was certainly, for her, about more than pleasure: it was about power, about mystification, about her own importance, about the desire, as she puts it in her journal, "to give moderately and yet have full attention."

She constantly caused pain to others, both the men who had to compete with other concealed rivals and the partners of these men. (Her friendship with Philippa Foot was broken for years on account of the suffering that she caused Michael Foot when she left him for the economist Tommy Balogh, a suffering for which Philippa consoled Michael. Murdoch wrote that Philippa "most successfully salvaged what was left after my behaviour," a characteristically self-dramatizing way of seeing the situation.) "Let me do no harm to [him or her]": this becomes a regular refrain in the journals. And yet she goes on doing harm.

Her lovers were almost all intellectually distinguished, and they fell into two types: the gentle and childlike (usually close to her own age) and the fascinating and cruel (usually much older). Murdoch indulged her fascination with the second sort while planning ultimately to settle down with the first sort. In the first category were the anthropologist and poet Franz Steiner, to whom she almost became engaged before he died young of a heart attack, and the literary critic John Bayley, whom she married—her "ideal co-child," in his words, with whom she had a relationship of immense gentleness and intimacy that seems to have kept at bay, at least for the most part, the more destructive aspects of her character. They created together a world of shared childhood, in which they called each other "Puss" and spoke a secret language, and at the same time shared a sense of life that only two sophisticated intellectuals could share. The marriage represented a remarkably successful incorporation of disparate elements.

But for some time before the marriage, and during the early days of her relationship with Bayley, the second sort held center stage. Murdoch formed alliances with a series of difficult and power-hungry older men, including

Balogh and, most prominently, Elias Canetti, a charismatic figure who was constantly surrounded by worshipful disciples. Why Murdoch would spend even one evening in his company is more than one can fathom from Conradi's and Bayley's accounts of this loathsome and sinister egotist. Here is Bayley, in *Elegy for Iris*, describing a conversation in which Canetti asks him what he thinks of *King Lear*, and Bayley, after doing his best to answer the question, asks Canetti the same:

> He continued to be silent for what seemed a long time. Finally, he spoke. "Friends tell me that my book is unbearable," he said. Fortunately, I knew this to be a reference to his long novel *Die Blendung*, and I nodded my head gravely. There was a further silence. "*King Lear* is also unbearable," he pronounced at last.
>
> I bowed my head. Shakespeare and his masterpiece would never be paid a greater compliment than this.

Is this story true? (Bayley, who has publicly admitted to making up love affairs in a more recent memoir, is certainly capable of fabrication in the cause of maligning a rival.) But true or not in its details, it seems to be largely right about Canetti, who was grotesquely self-preoccupied, patently sadistic, incapable of non-exploitative love. When she chose the gently devious Bayley over the "great man," Murdoch ultimately chose wisely. And perhaps Bayley's reaction to Canetti is the basis for that splendid moment in *A Fairly Honourable Defeat*, one of her finest novels, when Simon, the young, gentle, pleasure-loving gay man, simply tosses Julius, the destructive enchanter, into his hosts' swimming pool. Simon, like Bayley, looks like a lightweight, but his whimsical humor, his ability to wear his heart on his sleeve, his total lack of cruelty, are the novel's moral core.

The power of the enchanter, such a major theme in Murdoch's novels as well as in her life: where does it come from? And what was it in Murdoch that made it impossible for her to have the healthy "into the swimming pool you go" reaction to these loathsome tyrants? Murdoch puzzled over this, again and again, in journals and in novels. Why do people let enchanters walk into their homes and destroy their relationships? In part because of their distinction—but she casts doubt on this source of erotic power by stripping Julius, the Canetti figure in *A Fairly Honourable Defeat*, of any real achievement. In part, no doubt, because of their wit and charm. But Julius is charming in the way that Mephistopheles is charming: he mocks everything that people hold dear, he gives the appearance of depth and profundity because he claims that human life is at bottom a sordid affair in which the baser instincts are driving everything. (So, Canetti, casting doubt on Murdoch's political ideals, and insisting that the drives of the crowd produce all real historical events.)

So this just pushes the question back a step: why do people want this variety of enchantment? Murdoch's answer, in the end, is that it is the power of destructiveness and negativity itself that seduces, because many people have a sadomasochistic desire to be crushed, and to crush others in turn. She felt this at a personal sexual level. (Once she wrote in her journal that she felt herself to be a sadomasochistic homosexual man.) From the male enchanters, she endured—and evidently sought—an astonishing degree of exploitation and psychological abuse. With the gentle men, and also with women, she wanted to play, at times, the destroying man. (One journal entry reads: "Then I began to kiss her passionately and was desiring her very much. Understanding of what it would be to be a man, feeling very violent & positive, wanting to strike her body like an instrument.")

Murdoch connects sadomasochism with moral nihilism, and hence goodness with a gentleness that is free of sadism. For some, gentleness is a kind of grace with which they are fortunately endowed. (She once wrote that Bayley, like her father, was "a man entirely without the natural coarseness & selfishness of the male.") For Murdoch, who found in herself much "male" selfishness and coarseness, it became a lifelong project to achieve a non-destructive relation to people. This struggle is the source of much of her fiction.

It is natural for the reader of the biography to hope that it will trace the struggle to some early source. One close friend does tell Conradi that he thinks "something in Iris's past had introduced her to the idea of evil." But nothing reveals to us what this something is. Her father was a gentle man, her childhood was a happy one. At most one might say that she won the Oedipal struggle too easily, becoming her father's delight while her parents' very amicable marriage was apparently almost totally asexual. While Julius's destructiveness is explained—somewhat too easily—by making him a survivor of Belsen, young Iris was head girl in a prestigious school, a success at everything she tried, courted and loved by a large proportion of those who knew her. The darkness seems indigenous, lurking, inexplicable—and so it apparently seemed to her. While initially sympathetic to psychoanalysis, she came to feel that it told comforting, too-orderly stories about good and evil, which she preferred to see as real, absolute forces in human existence.

Murdoch thus came to see her own life, and life generally, as a moral struggle against what we might without melodrama call Mephistopheles: the nihilistic wiles of the self-insulating ego, which seeks power and comfort, exploiting and using other people. Its adversary is the moral imagination, which must strive constantly toward a clear vision of the reality of other people, one not marred by the ego's demands for control. One can see how difficult the struggle against her tendencies to control must have been from the extreme forms that it took, as she increasingly cultivated a shapeless and asexual physical persona and domestic surroundings whose squalor greatly exceeded even the British norm.

The novels, too, often associate neatness with egoism, vile filth with virtue. Thus Tallis Browne in *A Fairly Honourable Defeat*, who lives amid mold and vermin of all sorts, is a moral hero, in part because of this neglect of surroundings, and Julius's controlling sadism is revealed in his determination to clean the place up. Worse still, it is supposed to be good for Tallis to take a troubled teenage boy into his house—whereas this (no doubt all-too-controlling) American reader keeps feeling that charges of child abuse would be appropriate, both against Tallis and against the mother who promotes this life-threatening and (so it seems to me) quite sadistic arrangement. Bayley perceptively writes that Murdoch wanted to have objects around her and yet did not want to take care of them. Perhaps this neglect of the worldly was a part of her exacting idea of virtue, though it can easily look like a kind of aggression toward anyone who dares to come too close. Toward the end of her life Murdoch also re-wrote past journal entries, removing the names of sentiments, such as anger and contempt, that she felt she should not have had.

Conradi, who knew Murdoch in the last decades of her life, feels that her struggle was in the end successful. Her marriage to Bayley, though a source of great happiness, was not without tumult. A passionate lesbian affair in the early 1960s led her to resign from St. Anne's (this is the only instance in which Conradi conceals the name of a lover). One gets the impression that there were other lesser affairs. Still, as time went on Murdoch increasingly, if unevenly, distanced herself from her erotic self. The philosopher David Pears has remarked upon her "luminous goodness . . . when she came into a room, you felt better." And many have attested to her intense aliveness to others. Murdoch's moral serenity seems proportionate to her focus on her husband. As time went on, Bayley's elaborate jokes and small kindnesses struck her as goodness itself. "January 4, 1978. Puss singing in kitchen below. He is a good man." A year later, quoting a silly yet sophisticated impromptu Bayley poem about Strindberg and a skunk, she writes: "Of such is the kingdom of heaven."

III

For someone with such a tumultuous inner world, the muscular choice-is-all school of moral philosophy could not be satisfactory. Murdoch felt that we would get to the right choices only if we understood better the forces militating against goodness. And in her view the main force was our inability to see other people correctly. We are always representing people to ourselves in self-serving ways, she believed, ways that gratify our own egos and serve our own ends. To see truly is not the entirety of virtue, but it is a very crucial necessary part. And even where the overt choices go along well, if the inner vision is lacking, then an important part of virtue itself is lacking. (Here Murdoch agrees with Aristotle: there is a morally large difference between self-control and real virtue, even though the overt acts may look exactly the same, because the self-controlled person has not yet achieved the motives, the reactions, and the patterns of seeing that are characteristic of the good person.)

To make this point clear for philosophers, Murdoch invented an example that has become famous. In her lecture on "The Sovereignty of Good," she asks us to imagine a mother-in-law, M, who has contempt for D, her daughter-in-law. M sees D as common, cheap, low. Since M is a self-controlled Englishwoman, she behaves (so Murdoch stipulates) with perfect graciousness all the while, and no hint of her real view surfaces in her acts. But she realizes, too, that her feelings and thoughts are unworthy, and likely to be generated by jealousy and an excessively keen desire to hang on to her son. So she sets herself a moral task: she will change her view of D, making it more accurate, less marred by selfishness. She gives herself exercises in vision: where she is inclined to say "coarse," she will say, and see, "spontaneous." Where she is inclined to say "common," she will say, and see, "fresh and naive." As time goes on, the new images supplant the old. Eventually M does not have to make such an effort to control her actions: they flow naturally from the way she has come to see D.

Murdoch claims that this change is of moral significance. Getting the behavior right is one good thing; but getting the thoughts and the emotions right is another, and in some ways a more fundamental, good thing. She challenges moral philosophy to attend more to these long-term tasks in vision and self-cultivation, to focus on patterns of character that extend over a life rather than simply on isolated moments of choice. The challenge was first voiced in her splendid and highly critical book on Sartre, which appeared in 1953. Murdoch argued that because of his focus on the moment of choice, Sartre could not understand the sources of good or evil, which requires depicting "the mystery and contingent variousness of individuals." To Sartre's impoverished world she contrasts "the messy accidental world of the novel, so full of encounters and moral conflicts and love."

Murdoch's challenge to moral philosophy was given its most forceful articulation in 1970 in *The Sovereignty of Good*, which includes three of her most influential essays, and it was expressed strongly again six years later in *The Fire and the Sun: Why Plato Banished the Artists*. (The meandering *Metaphysics as a Guide to Morals*, Murdoch's expanded Gifford Lectures, which appeared in 1992, was a much less successful treatment of these themes.) It was Murdoch's early work that had a transformative impact on the discipline. Younger philosophers, themselves reacting against the neglect of the inner world, found illumination in the challenge of this example. Now few would deny that the then-unknown subject of "moral psychology" is one of the most important and fascinating branches of ethics; or that thinking about the nature of the emotions and the imagination, and what they contribute to moral choice, is one of the most significant tasks of the moral philosopher.

There are major gaps in Murdoch's philosophical vision. She seems almost entirely to lack interest in the political and social determinants of a moral vision, and in the larger social criticism that ought, one feels, to be a major element in the struggle against one's own defective tendencies. Her examples, and her characters, are almost always undone by something universal about the ego and its devious workings, almost never by prejudice or misogyny or other failings endemic to a particular society at a particular time. Indeed, although her journals fairly often complain about the hardship of being a woman at Oxford, she offers us little guidance in understanding how sexism thwarts perception. Race is almost totally unmentioned, except in the form of an erotic longing for, and anxiety about, Jews—a theme in her own life as well, but one that is never treated with the critical detachment that it deserves.

Only with regard to the lives of gay men does Murdoch retain a sense of the purely social and political obstacles to correct vision and action. She was a vigorous crusader for the abolition of sodomy laws, and in her fiction she depicted gay couples as fighting an uphill struggle for love and self-respect in a society that makes fun of them, or worse. In *A Fairly Honourable Defeat*, the older gay man Axel, working in Whitehall, has learned habits of secretiveness and denial that make it hard for him to express his love to Simon, or even to allow himself to be a person who fully loves. Simon, treated by straight society as a sex addict, has learned to doubt his own capacities for commitment and for goodness. But such suggestions of a complex relation between virtue and its social world should have played a more prominent role in the philosophical essays and the novels: all too rarely does Murdoch suggest that goodness requires reflection about social justice. Too often, indeed, the absence of a more textured social world impoverishes her characters, who seem to play out their erotic dance in a void.

Another problem, a deeper problem, is the tension between Murdoch's Platonism and her vision of particulars. Murdoch keeps on suggesting that "The Good" is a unitary abstraction of some kind, even while all her writerly instincts work in the direction of showing its irreducible many-sidedness and its kaleidoscopic variety; even while she also insists that what it is to be a good person is to see other particular people clearly. Her Platonism leads in the direction of the big abstract entity, but her moral instincts—I am tempted to call them Aristotelian—lead in the direction of the variegated world of surprising humanity. This tension is never fully resolved in the essays, where it simply sits there generating difficulty, or in the novels, where the vision of the particular predominates, but characters whom the writer appears to admire keep on talking what sounds like nonsense about "The Good." This fault in Murdoch's work may derive from her own experience of good and evil as original powers that stand somehow outside her, not generated by her particular biography. But they do mean that anyone who wishes to make philosophical use of her work must choose between the Aristotelian many-sidedness or the Platonic mysticism. (I know which I regard as the more fruitful, in philosophy and in life.)

Finally, there is an acute problem about action. Hare's vision of life is certainly incomplete; but it contains much that matters greatly. As the post-war generation knew, it does matter what one does. If one resists tyranny and saves the lives of the innocent, who cares if one was thinking "coarse" and "common" or, more virtuously, "spontaneous" and "fresh"? Murdoch is so preoccupied with the goings-on of the inner world that she seems almost to have forgotten about the difference that action can make; and the resulting obsession with one's own states looks strangely like egoism, in a world in which a forthright commitment to action can make the difference to people who are suffering, no matter whether the agents' intentions are pure.

Many years ago I had dinner with R. M. Hare in Oxford. With typical testiness, he complained about the new fashion for virtue ethics, which had eroded, he felt, philosophy's commitment to good works. Mentioning the cover of a book by one of his targets, which showed a naked man carrying a question mark over his shoulder, he said scornfully that this is what philo-sophy had become: meaning, I think, that it was all preoccupied with our naked insides and the interminable questions they pose, rather than armed for combat against real bad people and things. I have some sympathy with this way of seeing the movement that Murdoch inspired. Although there is no doubt that the big questions of social justice and human well-being need to be approached with an adequate moral psychology, Murdoch herself tended to veer sharply away from those questions, and even to suggest that in the end they did not matter, that the only important thing was each person's struggle for self-perfection.

That is a hopelessly egoistic vision of life, in a world in which sharp thinking about poverty and prejudice may actually make a difference to human lives. Whatever combination of Platonism, Christianity, and Buddhism shaped her sensibility, it was an oddly otherworldly sensibility in the end, as if we were already dead and in purgatory. But we are still on earth, so if we must try to see other people as well as we can, we must also try to create just institutions and just laws. This does not mean that it is the duty of every philosopher to talk only about justice; we all have our own projects. The mistake in Murdoch is her subtle suggestion that the search for justice is superficial.

IV

Murdoch's philosophical vision is fulfilled in her novels, which dramatize again and again the struggle to see clearly, in a world of self-delusion, the revelations and the blindings of erotic love. Although the more schematic essays were crucial in laying out the essential elements of her view, showing what is really at stake required the creation of extended patterns of vision and struggle. The best of her novels, such as *The Black Prince*, *The Bell*, and *The Sea, The Sea*, are plainly continuous with the themes of her philosophy, and make good on its promises in a rich, devious, and open-ended way.

Since the imagination played such a central role in Murdoch's moral thought, she arrived at a grave and highly critical view of the artist's moral role. In her view, artists are our guides to a vision of the world: they shape and nourish, or they fail to shape and nourish, the moral imagination. So art cannot evade morality. The artist is inevitably a moral figure: for art either assuages the ego, portraying an easy, flattering vision of the world and making us cozy within it, or it challenges us outward, toward the reality of others.

Where did Murdoch place her own fiction within the contrast between great art and egoistic art that she develops in *The Fire and the Sun*? In purgatory, no doubt: struggling to be pure, but full of silly self-regard. Conradi is probably correct to see her own parody of herself in the comic figure of Arnold Baffin in *The Black Prince*, a popular novelist who produces a novel a year, all full of high metaphysical matters and comforting the reader with the sensation of having experienced deep thoughts. And some of the later novels do seem pseudo-profound, in part because they give expression to a monistic metaphysical vision that she never made fully compelling in any genre. Still, the complex moral and literary richness of Murdoch's best novels grows more evident all the time, now that we no longer read them as realist social satire, and can appreciate their allegorical elements.

There is an odd paradox in the relationship between the novels and the morality that they (and the philosophical writings) contain. The paradox is that their very coming-into-being would appear, by the lights of Murdoch's morality, to be an immoral act, an act of manipulation and excessive control. No artist wants to give an unfinished work to the world as a token of her vision. "Here is my messy moldy verminous novel": no writer says this. That is why Tallis Browne is no artist; indeed, he cannot even finish the one lecture that he keeps trying to write. Murdoch's art, like all good art, is highly structured and controlled—a house neat and clean enough to satisfy the most morally obtuse of her upper-class British characters. Indeed, her novels draw attention more than most to the presence of centralized control, as the characters execute a complicated erotic dance whose choreographer is always just offstage.

For such an artist, as Proust's narrator says, real people are just material, the stones that the artist uses to build his monument. The artist's vision of reality is finally a vision that he makes completely, using and even exploiting others; and its relation to the real surprisingness of people can never be morally simple. Murdoch sought uncontrol and "unselfing" all her life, as a corrective to egoism and sadism. Yet she so plainly seeks control, too; and she knows it. Moreover, she herself makes Proust's connection: in one period of emotional suffering, she observes in her journal that "like Proust I want to escape from the eternal push and rattle of time into the coolness & poise of a work of art." Can the perfection of art possibly co-exist with the attempt to perfect one's life, as she sees that aim? In the form of such a question the struggle renews itself, as the morality of art and the artist's own rage for control become a topic of anxious rumination on the part of characters, such as Bradley Pearson in *The Black Prince*, who seem to be surrogates for Murdoch's own sense of herself as artist. Does the artistic enterprise record and extend the struggle against the ego, or is it the ego's most subtle victory?

I connect this problem, very tentatively, to my own acquaintance with Murdoch. We met in New York in 1985, and she invited me to lunch at the house in Charlbury Road, Oxford, where she and Bayley lived at the time. I went round to the house, very nervous and awkward, and sat for two hours in the chaotic kitchen, being scrutinized, as I felt it, by her sharp probing eyes. We talked about Proust and Henry James, about postmodernism and current developments in ethical thought, about Charles Taylor, whom she admired, and R. M. Hare, whom she did not. All the while I felt that her very intense gaze was going straight through me, to something that was not me at all, but to which I was somehow related. More than once I had the thought that Julian Baffin, in *The Black Prince*, has about Bradley Pearson: "You don't really see me." I cannot forget those predatory eyes, and the way they attended to something of immense importance that was, as I say, not exactly outside of me, and that was perhaps more real than me, but that was not precisely me, either. Nor can I ever forget the essential mysteriousness of her face, so much more alive than most people, so blazing with uncompromising passion, so intent upon things that were not exactly in the room. (I remember thinking a sad thought: that this was going to be the hoped-for friendship with a brilliant woman, but it is after all an encounter with just another predatory man. Erotic control and artistic control: where did one leave off and the other begin?)

If the gaze of art is fixed on the person and is at the same time intent on a creative work that appropriates and goes beyond the person, the question is whether this gaze can ever be, in the fullest sense, a humanly loving gaze, exemplary of the virtue that Murdoch's philosophy describes. Why not? It sees more truly than most loving people see. I had no doubt that Murdoch could have described me, after an hour, far more precisely than any lover of mine might have described me after some years. In this sense Proust seems right when he says that art is the fully lived life, life without patches of deadness and obtuseness.

And yet I believe that there is something more to loving vision than just seeing. There is also a willingness to permit oneself to be seen. And there is a willingness to stop seeing, to close one's eyes before the loved one's imperfections. And there is also a willingness to be, for a time, an animal or even a plant, relinquishing the sharpness of creative alertness before the presence of a beloved body. Does the artist's vision have about it these aspects of vulnerability, silence, and grace? Or does the artist's eye almost inevitably look down with something like disdain at the muddled animal interactions of human beings with one another, so obtuse and so lacking in nuance?

Still, if the novels were only tales of control, and their characters only the creatures of a sadistic enchanter, they would be, as Murdoch says, mediocre works. Some of them are indeed mediocre. *The Unicorn*, for example, is a rather sordid and pretentious melodrama about varieties of sexual sadism, in which Murdoch's own self-hatred becomes a hatred of humanity. And often the skepticism about human motivation is so thoroughgoing that one can hardly breathe. But the best of Murdoch's novels get beyond this. Perhaps this is because they are animated by a kind of humble opening toward reality in all its surprising diversity, by a quality of love for the world that even artistic polish cannot defeat.

And notice, really, that the moral problem I have outlined arises only for a writer who is both deeply moral (as Proust is not) and who has an extreme horror of her own destructiveness—who will not believe that anything she controls could possibly be all right for others. It is the same problem as the problem of the filthy house: only a certain sort of person would feel that her own efforts to clean up must inevitably be sinister, bringing death and destruction in their train. Someone less self-hating might think that there is glory, not sadism, in the beautiful thing.

In the end Murdoch transcended in her best books her own horror of control and cleanliness, allowing herself to express human love (and the artist's love for her characters) in a shapely and beautiful form. Consider this passage from A *Fairly Honourable Defeat*, in which good prose and tenderness unite, for once, to create a vision of happiness:

> Simon went on through the hallway and out into the garden. The sun was still warm and bright, though the evening star had strengthened. The vine was hung with grassy green translucent grapes and the leaves and tendrils glowed with a pale green radiance, outspread and welcoming and still in the quiet sunlight. Simon moved towards the vine, bowed his head under its shadowy arch, and touched the warm pendant beads of the grape bunches.
>
> Axel came out, removing his jacket and rolling up his white shirt sleeves. The sun made gold in his dark hair. "I've asked the patron to bring us a carafe of wine out here straight away. I'm just going up to look at the room. You stay here."
>
> Simon sat down at the table. The patron bustled over wearing purple braces, with a carafe and two glasses. "Merci." Simon poured out some wine and tasted it. It was excellent. The serrated green leaves extended above him, before him, their motionless pattern of angelic hands. The air quivered with warmth and a diffusion of light.
>
> Simon thought, it is an instinct, and not a disreputable one, to be consoled by love. Warily he probed the grief which had traveled with him

so far, and he felt it as a little vaguer, a little less dense. His thoughts of Rupert now reached back further into the past, to good times which had their own untouchable reality. He drank some more wine and raised his face to the dazzle of the sun among the leaves and felt his youth lift him and make him buoyant. He was young and healthy and he loved and was loved. It was impossible for him, as he sat there in the green southern light and waited for Axel, not to feel in his veins the warm anticipation of a new happiness.

What is surprising in this passage is not just the suggestion of happiness, but more particularly the suggestion of an erotic happiness and even an erotic goodness, the Dionysian images linked with the imagery of angels' hands. There is no false comfort in Murdoch, but sometimes there is a comfort that is true.

# CHAPTER TWENTY-ONE

# Dr. True Self

F. Robert Rodman (2003), Winnicott: Life and Work

I

Unlike Freud, Donald Winnicott is not a cultural icon, read in Great Books courses, revered and reviled. Unlike Jacques Lacan, he is not an intellectual cult figure, with a band of zealous disciples and an impenetrable jargon. There is no school of Winnicott; there are no courses in his methods. All this is as he wished it. Nobody was more skeptical of cults and the rigidities that they induced. All his life Winnicott was obsessed with the freedom of the individual self to exist defiantly, resisting parental and cultural demands, to be there without saying a word if silence was its choice. In his own writings he spoke with a voice that was determinedly his own, surprisingly personal, idiosyncratic, playful, and at the same time ordinary. One could not extract a jargon from it if one tried, and one cannot talk about his theoretical ideas without confronting live, complex human beings. That, perhaps, is why he has never had a secure home in the academy, which is so enamored of beautiful scientific or pseudo-scientific structures, and so often fearful of real people and the demands that their complexity imposes. And for these same reasons Winnicott has had an enormous influence on the practice of psychoanalysis, particularly in America.

When Winnicott burst onto the London psychoanalytic scene, an odd rumpled man exploding with ideas—he was like a Catherine wheel shooting off sparks, a colleague remarked—analysts still saw human emotions mainly in terms of Freud's account of primitive instinctual drives, with sexual gratification as their goal. Melanie Klein was already making her important contribution to Freudian theory by insisting on the crucial importance of the earliest stages of life; but she clung to Freud's hedonic theory, seeing the infant's search as aimed at pleasure, which she, apparently along with Freud, understood to be a single undifferentiated experience.

(Winnicott's great contemporary, the Scottish analyst W. R. D. Fairbairn, once wrote that Klein could have avoided this error by reading John Stuart Mill.) And she insisted that the infant's psychic drama was played out inside its own subjective space, with figures that were the demonic projections of its own inchoate sense of parts of reality. The actual environment and its people were of no interest to her.

Winnicott learned much from Klein, with whom he had a close if uneven friendship. He absorbed from her the importance of the young child's fantasy life, to which, as a practitioner, he had remarkable empathetic access. (The analysis of a little girl published under the title of *The Piggle* is one of the great examples in English literature of an adult entering the wild conflict-ridden world of a young child.) But he insisted that the infant seeks from the start complex forms of relationship and reciprocity, not simply its own pleasure. And also that the infant's development cannot be understood without looking at its real surroundings—at the objects, responsive or nonresponsive, that either create a "facilitating environment" for emotional growth or cause the self to hide, its place taken by a rigid mechanical surrogate. Thus, Winnicott famously said, "there is no such thing as a baby" on its own: we are always dealing with a "nursing couple." If psychoanalysis in America has largely become a theory of emotional nurture and exchange rather than one of hedonic satisfaction, it is thanks to Winnicott.

Winnicott also situated psychoanalysis far more accurately than had many of its other practitioners, seeing it as an imaginative humanistic endeavor, akin both to poetry and to love, rather than as an exact science with unvarying rules. To fellow analyst Harry Guntrip, who was his patient, he remarked that "we differ from Freud who was for curing symptoms. We're concerned with living persons, whole living and loving." (This somewhat unfair treatment of Freud shows the aggressive side of the gentle analyst's personality.) As for the goal of the process, it was not simply the removal of symptoms; it was also the ability to play, to be creative. "We are poor indeed," he said, "if we are only sane."

As F. Robert Rodman's fine biography makes plain, these insights grew out of a very troubled early life, followed by a successful and reasonably happy adulthood, though marred by cardiac illness, conflict with other members of the psychoanalytic community, and a series of questionable ethical judgments. Rodman, a practicing analyst, has edited Winnicott's correspondence, and this biography began as a quasi-official work co-authored with a member of the Winnicott Trust. He had the cooperation of Winnicott's widow, Clare Britton, who died in 1984, as well as numerous friends and associates. On his co-author's death in 1991, Rodman assumed the task on his own. This seems fortunate, for Rodman, though deeply sympathetic to both the man and his ideas, is free to express strong criticisms of Winnicott's ethical lapses, seeing him as "a person in conflict who expressed his genius, and also went awry, in manifold ways." With this combination of empathy and freedom, Rodman presents as balanced and insightful a portrait of the genesis of Winnicott's ideas as we are likely to have.

II

Donald Winnicott was born in 1896, in the west of England, to a prosperous middle-class Methodist family. According to a memoir written by his widow, his childhood was on the whole happy, but Rodman now makes it clear that matters were more complicated. Winnicott's father, a rigid man who never appears in photos without perfectly waxed moustaches, evidently imposed strict standards of behavior. The young Donald loved to play with a beautiful female wax doll, and his father so teased him about this non-male behavior that the little boy smashed his beloved toy. Shortly thereafter (Winnicott's widow reports in a fragmentary memoir) Donald decided, looking at himself in the mirror, that he was "too nice," and started to behave aggressively. One day his father heard him say "Drat!" and immediately sent him off to boarding school. If much of his life and thought was devoted to nonconformity and protection of the "true self" from invasion by the forces of conformity (including gender conformity, a topic that fascinated him), this is surely the outgrowth of his father's intrusiveness and the pain that it inflicted. In a late essay on the self, which he describes as "a protest from the core of me," Winnicott remarks that "rape, and being eaten by cannibals, these are mere bagatelles as compared with the violation of the self's core. . . . For me this would be the sin against the self."

In contrast with his father, Winnicott's mother is a shadowy figure. People who recall the family say little about her. But Rodman pieces the fragments together convincingly, arguing that Bessie was depressed and frightened of her sexuality. Winnicott once told a close friend that his mother weaned him early because she disliked the pleasurable feelings of nursing. Late in life, in a poem called "The Tree" (partly about Christ's suffering), he described the pain of having to keep his mother alive:

> Thus I knew her
> Once, stretched out on her lap
> as now on a dead tree
> I learned to make her smile
> to stem her tears
> to undo her guilt
> to cure her inward death
> To enliven her was my living

Here was another invasion of the self, which clearly involved forbidding himself both aggressive and sexual feelings. Not surprisingly, as far as we know, no member of Winnicott's family had a healthy sexual life. His two sisters, very attractive women, never married. Donald chose as his first wife a mentally disturbed woman, Alice Taylor, who rarely bathed and who used to commune with the spirit of T. E. Lawrence through her parrot. The marriage lasted for twenty-six years but was never consummated. Sexual impotence was a major theme in Winnicott's early life; he later connected the ability to enjoy sex fully with the idea of giving oneself permission to be aggressive. Several close associates link the strain of caring for his increasingly dotty wife with a series of heart attacks that made his health increasingly fragile.

After service on a destroyer during World War I (he spent much of his time reading Henry James), Winnicott took a medical degree at Cambridge and went into pediatrics. His interest in children had been strong for years. In a letter home from Cambridge he describes his delight in arranging theatrical games for the local Boy Scouts: it was "such a revelation of the powers of the imagination of the boys that I shall never forget that day. . . . Each one was absolutely different from the others, and half the charm lay there." Winnicott once estimated that during his career he had treated sixty thousand children. His rich experience gave psychoanalysis a new—and characteristically British—empirical dimension.

At the same time, no doubt owing to his own personal problems, his interest in psychoanalysis was already strong. While seeing pediatric patients, he went into training analysis with James Strachey (who wrote inappropriately gossipy letters speculating on whether "Mr. W" would "fuck his wife all of a sudden"). He graduated from the British Institute for Psychoanalysis in 1935 and began analysis with the Kleinian Joan Riviere. Here begins Winnicott's lifelong involvement with Klein's ideas, and with Klein herself. Chosen by Klein in 1935 to analyze her son Eric, Winnicott was drawn deeply into the Kleinian circle, where he never felt completely at home. Rodman depicts well the conflict between the Kleinians, so intent on theoretical purity and so insistent on orthodoxy, and Winnicott, who had a deep need to rebel and to go his own way.

Winnicott's friendship with Klein continued strong until her death, but increasingly, in letters to her, he urges her to watch out for her school, and to realize that theoretical closure and analytical perfection are inappropriate goals. Meanwhile, in a series of papers that won increasing attention, he was challenging the foundations of her theoretical approach, insisting on the importance of the real-life mother's actual behavior and of living human interaction. After Klein's death, and to some extent before it, her school treated Winnicott coldly. (Here Rodman may be too quick to impute blame to the Kleinians. They were a doctrinaire lot, but he needed to feel that he was in rebellion against conformity-demanding enemies. It seems unclear how much of the persecution that he felt was in fact genuine.)

Working with evacuated children during World War II, he met the social worker Clare Britton. In 1944 the two began an affair that led, in 1949, to the dissolution of his marriage to Alice (he waited until his father died before taking this step) and to a long and extremely happy marriage that lasted until his death in 1971. Plainly they did have a successful sexual relationship, and they shared a love of humor, music, and poetry. Clare was utterly different from Alice: "beefsteak," as one friend said, rather than "elderflower fritters." The couple indulged in elaborate jokes and wrote silly poems to each other during boring moments in conferences (including a lovely scatological putdown of the racist politician Enoch Powell). Another friend called them "two crazy people who delighted each other and delighted their friends." Asked whether they ever quarreled, the elderly Clare recalled that "in fact the question of hurting each other did not arise because we were operating in the play area where everything is permitted." Sometimes Winnicott would wake up in the night and say: "I'm potty about you, do you know that?"

Clare, a tough woman and a very successful worker with needy children (she eventually received the Order of the British Empire), seems also to have had a remarkable capacity for unanxiously "holding" Donald's mercurial temper, his vicissitudes, his health difficulties. After he had experienced an especially serious cardio-pulmonary illness, she found him up in a tree outside their home, sawing off a limb. Her first impulse was to get him down, to make him rest. But then: "I thought, 'No, it's his life and he's got to live it. If he dies after this, he dies.' But that was him. He wanted to live." At the opening of an autobiography that he was just beginning at the time of his death, he writes, "Prayer: Oh, God, may I be alive when I die." "And he was, really," Clare concludes.

As Winnicott's success increased, so did his confidence in his own judgment. The dark side of Rodman's story is that this confidence led to increasingly serious errors of judgment. We may already detect moral lapses in his collusion with Klein to conceal from her son the fact that his mother and his analyst were corresponding. Many such lapses follow. He analyzed Marion Milner, a close friend who was probably in love with him. He analyzed a patient who was at the time a tenant in the Winnicott house. He encouraged Clare to take up analysis with Klein while he was himself in close contact with her. He socialized with patients. In general he seems to have had little awareness of appropriate boundaries.

Most serious, however, was Winnicott's long analysis of and friendship with Masud Khan. A wealthy Pakistani emigre and self-styled prince, Khan has gradually been revealed as one of the most unprincipled and destructive analysts who ever practiced. He had affairs with some patients, and socialized with others in a show-offy way; he subjected patients to insult and humiliation; he used the therapeutic setting as a frame for his pathological self-aggrandizement, his obsessive tales of how he got the better of people. All this time he was in analysis with Winnicott, and Winnicott steadily supported him, first advancing his candidacy in the Institute, then supporting his continuation there. Rodman deals with this scandal tactfully and rather briefly, but he makes no secret of the serious issues that it raises about

Winnicott's ethical judgment. Khan was the son that Winnicott never had; clearly he was very devoted, although Clare managed to keep him at a distance and prevented him from becoming the editor of Winnicott's papers.

Although Winnicott did not want or need a "school," he did need someone to support his ideas and to share their genesis. But he made an egregiously bad choice, and he stuck with it in the presence of the mounting evidence of Khan's disgraceful conduct. Noting the evident high degree of "ongoing excitement and mutual self-indulgence" in the relationship, Rodman suggests that there was a sexual component, although it seems unlikely that this element was acknowledged. Khan's patient Wynne Godley, whose account of his analysis is a key document in the unmasking of Khan, reports that Khan took phone calls from Winnicott during his sessions; once they spent his time joking about fellatio.

On a trip to New York in 1969, Winnicott suffered a particularly serious cardiac crisis after a bout of the flu. Identifying himself with Cathy in *Wuthering Heights*, he wrote that he longed to come home before dying. He lived for another year, but in a weakened condition. During this period, amazingly, Winnicott continued to see patients; he wrote and delivered new papers, broaching significant new themes, such as the importance of recognizing the social rigidity of gender norms and the mixture of genders in all human beings.

Most impressively, he continued to correspond generously with strangers. Rodman himself, a young analyst just out of the army, received a four-page commentary on his first article. A troubled man from Oklahoma, writing to Winnicott out of the blue, got a helpful three-page letter about the roots of aggression. The analyst Alan Stone, who met him at this time (and found Winnicott unable to walk without stopping), reported that

> he held me in the center of his attention (or so it seemed to me) in a way that I have never experienced with any other human being. It was not that he made constant eye contact, or that he interjected the traditional psychoanalytic hum of empathy, or that he was selflessly accepting. As we walked he spoke of his own ideas, he reacted and responded with dignity and originality, yet all the time I felt recognized and encouraged—I was in a "facilitating environment."

Not all of Winnicott's correspondence was good-natured. To an analyst enamored of simplistic biological explanations of human phenomena, he wrote: "There seems to be no playing in what you write, and therefore a lack of creativity. Perhaps you reserve your creativity for some other area of your life, in friendships for instance, or in painting, I don't know."

He died in January 1971, after watching an old movie comedy on television.

Winnicott's main ideas emerged gradually over time, in a series of papers rich in clinical content. He never wrote a tidy summary of them, and it belies the nature of his thought to attempt such a summary. Still, one can at least sketch the narrative of infancy and childhood as he saw it, being careful to remember that, for Winnicott, particularity is everything and that, as Rodman emphasizes, he is the heir as much of Wordsworth and Emily Brontë as of Freud and Klein.

While Freud saw human beings as driven by powerful instincts that need to be tamed if morality and culture are to be possible, Winnicott had confidence in the unfolding of the developmental process, which would produce moral awareness as an outgrowth of early struggles if things went well enough. He believed (against his own experience, perhaps) that development usually goes well, and that mothers are usually "good enough." Mothers are preoccupied with their infants early on, and attend to their needs well, enabling the self to develop gradually and eventually to express itself.

At first the infant cannot grasp the mother as a definite object, and thus cannot have full-fledged emotions. Its world is symbiotic and basically narcissistic. Gradually, however, the infant develops the capacity to be alone—aided by its "transitional objects," a famous phrase invented by Winnicott for the blankets and stuffed animals that enable children to comfort themselves when the mother is absent. (He loved Charles Schulz and wondered whether Linus's blanket reflected the influence of his ideas.) Eventually the child usually develops the ability to "play alone in the presence of its mother," a key sign of growing confidence in the developing self. At this point, the child begins to be able to relate to the mother as a whole person rather than as an extension of its own needs. (Winnicott always spoke of mothers, and Rodman makes one of his strongest criticisms at this point: he seems to have had a blind spot for the role of the father until close to the end of his life. At the same time, he did increasingly stress that "mother" is a role rather than a biological category, that real mothers have aspects of both genders, and that analysts typically play a quasi-maternal role.)

Like Klein, Winnicott thought that this stage typically led to a painful emotional crisis. For the child now understands that the very same person whom it loves and embraces is the person against whom it has directed aggressive and angry wishes (when needs are not met automatically). But instead of Klein's somewhat forbidding concept of "the depressive position," Winnicott articulates this insight in terms of the concept of the developing "capacity for concern," showing how genuinely moral feeling bootstraps itself into existence out of the child's very love of its mother and the awareness that its aggression has projected harm. He thus was able to see morality as operating in tandem with love, rather than as a forbidding set of quasi-paternal demands. He stressed the crucial role of the imagination in coming to grips with this crisis: the child develops the capacity to imagine its mother's feelings, and thus becomes capable of generous and reparative acts.

Throughout this development, it is crucial that the mother should provide the child with a "facilitating environment" that allows it to express itself, even its destructiveness and hate, without getting the message that the mother will thereby be destroyed. Remarkably, mothers usually accept their children's hate and are not destroyed. (This ability was also an essential part of the good analyst's equipment, as he saw it. After Harry Guntrip talked at him aggressively for half an hour in a session, Winnicott said, "You see, you talked very hard at me, and I am not destroyed.") Most of the time this process goes reasonably well. It will go awry if the mother is too fearful or depressed (like Winnicott's mother), or if she too rigidly demands conformity and perfection in herself and in her child (like Winnicott's father).

One marvelous document concerning the latter sort of failure is Winnicott's analysis of a young male medical student, known as B, published in the volume *Holding and Interpretation*. (Rodman dislikes this case, but I have always found it especially rich.) Married to a man whom she saw as demanding perfection in everything, B's mother wanted to be a perfect mother and, hence, to have a perfect baby. This meant that she did not want her baby to be a real baby, needy, messy, crying. B got the message that his own needs were inappropriate and that the only way to achieve anything was to be quiet and "good." Nor could he, like most young children, gradually develop the capacity to release his mother from her need to be perfect by attending to her as an imperfect human being. This suppression of himself led to rigidity and emotional paralysis in later life. A competent intellectual "False Self" had developed capacities to cope with the world, but the needy childlike "True Self" had gone underground and remained at an infantile level, rather than gradually developing capacities to relate emotionally and to express itself in the world. B could have sex, but only with a woman whom he saw as an undifferentiated object, predictable as a masturbatory fantasy; he could not remember people's individuating features. "I feel that you are introducing a big problem," B says to Winnicott. "I never became human. I have missed it."

In the analysis itself, the patient repeatedly expects perfection from Winnicott, and is terrified by the space created by the analyst's own evident human imperfection. "The alarming thing about equality," he remarkably observes, "is that we are then both children and the question is, where is father? We know where we are if one of us is the father." Winnicott points out that in a good personal relationship there is an element of "subtle interplay" that presupposes an acceptance of human imperfection. Love means many things, "but it has to include this experience of subtle interplay, and we could say that you are experiencing love and loving in this situation." We might say (if oversimply) that for Freud, our cultural and personal problem is how to transcend the human. For Winnicott, it is how to bear the exposure of being imperfectly human. Play, art, and love come powerfully to our aid, but there remains "the inherent difficulty in regard to human contact with external reality."

Winnicott's theoretical writings emphasize empathy, imagination, and the highly particular transactions that constitute love between two imperfect people. One might have arrived at these ideas without being able to translate them into analytic practice. According to Harry Guntrip, who was analyzed by Fairbairn and then by Winnicott, Fairbairn had this problem. His theories spoke of the importance of a "personal relationship of genuine understanding" between therapist and patient, and when he discussed his ideas outside the office the two men communicated well. In the analytic setting, however, Fairbairn became rigid and formal, imposing theory-based interpretations rather than seeking out the core of the person. Winnicott was entirely different. He quickly attained a more satisfactory insight into Guntrip's idiosyncratic emotional history, because he did not insist on seeing everything in terms of a pre-established theoretical construct. And he was able to create for the sixty-year-old analyst, a man of personal courage and powerful intellect, a "holding environment," so that Guntrip's need for constant activity and talk ceased, and he could enjoy simply being himself. "I could let my tension go and develop and relax because you were present in my inner world," he wrote in his journal.

A pediatrician first and always, with adults or with children, Winnicott was always willing to play, to respond to the moment, to surprise, to adopt unconventional methods if they seemed right. (All too often, he wrote, the patient brings his False Self into analysis and the analyst addresses himself to that, because it is easy to talk to a False Self.) Sometimes he sat on the floor; sometimes he offered a cup of tea; sometimes he held a hand. Sometimes sessions were daily and sometimes months apart. In the case of "the Piggle," a little girl named Gabrielle who was two and a half when she began to see Winnicott and five when she finished, we have Winnicott's own detailed notes of every session. The sessions were held on demand by the child, often months apart, and sometimes included participation by the parents (sophisticated and analytically aware) as well as letters and phone calls from them.

This remarkable document shows us many things about Winnicott as therapist, but nothing more than his utter respect for the child's world of objects. Almost his first remark, in notes of the first session, is: "Already I had made friends with the teddy-bear who was sitting on the floor by the desk." And throughout the analysis, we sense that Winnicott's poetic capacity, his willingness not to be "only sane," enables a degree of entry rare for any adult into the unhappy child's world, with its "black mommy," its "Sush baby," and the terrifying "babacar." "To say that he understood children would to me sound false and vaguely patronizing," said one obituarist. "It was rather that children understood him." Such was his respect for his young patient that he refused to get ahead of her. "Importance of my not understanding what she had not yet been able to give me clues for," he writes.

But understanding was not the whole of it. As both the Guntrip analysis and the treatment of Gabrielle show, he also made both children and adults feel the presence of a good mother, before whom they were free to emerge. Rodman suggests that these great gifts were not unconnected to Winnicott's ethical failures. He sometimes felt, apparently, that he had moved beyond the need to consider normal ethical rules. Since he could on occasion defy convention with brilliant success, he trusted his own idiosyncratic judgment too far.

One can find much to criticize in Winnicott's ideas, as well as in his practical judgment. His account of the role of the father is grossly deficient, perhaps as a result of the fact that he never completely worked out his intuitive ideas about the malleability of gender and the relationship between rigid gender norms and the False Self. His ideas about the True Self sometimes verge on an excessive romanticism, as when he suggests that any communication with the outside world involves a deformation of a True Self, which is fundamentally incommunicado. At other times he more plausibly suggests that the True Self, if all goes well, will develop capacities for communication and reciprocity. But the mark of his childhood remained, and he repeatedly stressed (excessively, to my mind) the artificiality of the social, the radically asocial nature of all that is authentic. (Here he really is Brontë's heir.)

I am also unconvinced by Winnicott's constant connection between self-assertion and "hate," a word that he used too loosely. A person who has been repressed by demands for conformity might indeed hate those demands, and might feel the assertion of the self as a form of aggression; and such, clearly, was Winnicott's personal situation. But in the more benign case in which the capacity for concern and social interaction develops in partnership with love, self-assertion (and the sexuality that he linked to it) may take a wider range of forms. Winnicott implicitly acknowledges this, in his insightful remarks about art, culture, and play, but these notions remain inconsistently integrated into his writings.

These are trivial matters, though, in comparison with the rich re-orientation that Winnicott gave to the theory and the practice of analysis. He was a poet among theoreticians, as he was a compassionate doctor among analysts. If one can derive many related insights from the reading of his favorite authors, such as Shakespeare, Wordsworth, and Henry James, he was able to formulate these insights into guidelines for the therapeutic treatment of unhappy people, giving psychoanalysis a hopeful face, one that emphasized people's capacities for love and society's capacity for "holding" diversity, play, and freedom.

Indeed, one may learn many things about contemporary political life by posing systematically the question of what it would be like for society to become, in Winnicott's sense, a "facilitating environment" for its citizens. In thinking this idea through, one would come upon an enriched conception of the meaning of liberal "individualism": not selfishness, but the ability to grow and to express oneself; not solitary self-sufficiency, but "subtle interplay"; not the transcendence of human passions, but the secure "holding" of human need and imperfection.

In the end, the really important thing for Winnicott the theorist was the genuine flourishing of each person, and the same was true of Winnicott the doctor. At the end of his analysis of Gabrielle, as the five-year-old prepares to leave him, he remarks, "So the Winnicott you invented was all yours and he's now finished with, and no one else can ever have him." The two sit together, reading an animal book. Then he tells her, "I know when you are really shy, and that is when you want to tell me that you love me." And he records: "She was very positive in her gesture of assent."

# CHAPTER TWENTY-TWO

# For Once Clear to See

Mary Kinzie (2003), Drift

When Plato describes the journey of the soul out of life, he says that it is all but unrecognizable because of the "barnacles" encrusted all over it, slimy scaly deformities that time, society, and the violence of desire have caused it to wear. The human being looks like a monster. And yet, surprisingly, the soul itself, imagined above all as thought, is still there beneath. A primary job of society, if society is ever going to be just, would be, as Plato sees it, to bring up people who can imagine the soul beneath the barnacles, human freedom beneath the damages of life. If Plato had not had so much justified skepticism about poets (justified because poets are so often the servants of cultural deformity), he might have given them the role of nurturing this ability to imagine the soul's freedom. In spite of himself, Plato would have been drawn to Mary Kinzie's remarkable poems and to their vision of the human, assailed and deformed but still thinking, against time, against society.

The first source of damage to the human in Kinzie, as in Plato, is time, that force that creates this world's transient beauty ("The world is touched and stands forth," begins "Book of Tears"), but that also, gradually, inexorably, erodes particularity and removes hope. In "Looking In at Night," a mother sees her daughter's sleeping form and feels fear: "her shape makes me afraid. / . . . Every year the marble more decayed, / The lines less clear. Time starts its slide, / Curling the light along her shoulder blade." (Even here, in the formal perfection of the villanelle, there is resistance, thought's hard edge against the slide.) In "*Objet*" the same scene is revisited, and the mother considers "the body's / marble drift," both hard as stone and worn down every day by force.

The second source of damage to the human is society, a corrupt place of misogyny, racism, and blood, which makes young black men into killers, women into torn pieces of flesh or cunning self-concealers.

In "Flame Lounge: The Night Behind the Day," an extraordinary long poem set in a rough Chicago neighborhood, five young black men get out of a car to commit a crime:

> Then the car emptied the five men
>     their tall trunks moved
> their faces large
>     the rags of time
> whipping
>     along their torsos

And the speaker tries to imagine how and where they grew up, what deformities of class and race turned them into angry predators.

The primary focus of Kinzie's meditations on social violence, however, is the female body. These vulnerable sleeping daughters, what is going to happen to them? Even language contains hints of it. In "*Offoco*," Kinzie meditates on that Latin word, which means "to put toward the mouth / with the notion of force." Why would that word ever have existed, she asks, except to create a social space for a young man to "force against the teeth / of some strong person / a cup she could not refuse," making her "drink / until livid / jiggers of lead." In "Hornbeam," a meditation on the different versions of the Cinderella story, Kinzie ponders the shift in the story between a slipper of fur (*vair*) and a slipper of glass (*verre*), imagining how the "Hairy tenderness of the humble squirrel pelt" became, as the male story-tellers went about their business, a hard object that holds the foot prisoner and cuts it:

> *Was the young girl running*
>     *out of it because*
> *—recall the blood*
> *within the shoe?—*
> *it hurt her?*
> *or else—*
>     *or else—*

But what is this "or else"? Later in the poem, Cinderella is forced by the violence of "the world she looked upon" to

> dress in the worst rags and draw across her form the
> caul of cinders and deformity, her menial sluttishness a
> kind of cramp in the greater spirit she was born to be,
> the dirt stuck fast to her face and skin, an attitude of
> powerless dread in the bones — never to let others see
> her in the clear . . . a beauty at the edge of movement,
> alive, supple, still . . . ?

Poetry itself, Kinzie suggests in this book, is one way of stripping disguises away, as if to say: when language is clear, then, perhaps, we can see one another in the clear. The slipper, hard though it is, does not close that earlier sentence, does not exhaust the young girl's possibilities—one of which is freedom. As the poem ends, Cinderella speaks: "Don't forget, or *do*: I am a beast, / But oh, my thought is air." Women's sexual sluttishness is a disguise forced on them by social corruption, a cup held to the mouth with the notion of force, but there is thought beneath the deformity—or, in Plato's terms, some residual soul beneath the barnacles of time and violence.

True to their Platonism, though, these poems have the courage to see the space of the soul in the oppressor as well as the victim. Nowhere is this more clear than in the poem I mentioned earlier, "Flame Lounge: The Night Behind the Day." At first one reads this as the night of the predatory criminals behind the simple daytime activities of "Summer day in the cave of streets"—so night is evil and day is innocent. But then, in an extraordinary turning, Kinzie shows us that the night is also the dark untouched place where the soul still lives behind the daytime—the *ordinariness*—of evil:

> For once clear to see
> through the window
> in the door of the
> car for some time
> unopened
> from which no young
> black person
> had as yet
> unfolded himself
> into the air
> one of them
> might have seen
> breathing
> a complete
> ecocanopy
> of green
> within which
> turned a dome
> of darker green
> till from it rang
> birdsong
> reverberant
> with a sad
> absorbed sound
> as when wood
> or earth
> drinks down

to the clear
bottom of the
beaker
of silence
the bright
transferring clang
of iron
in a bell

Is the Platonism in these poems true? Is there always a space of clarity beneath evil, or an orientation to light, however absorbed, in whatever darkness? I find myself struggling with Kinzie, asking where her hope comes from, and whether we are entitled to hold out such hope. Perhaps, like Kant's idea of the "practical postulate," these poems are simply an assumption that human beings must make if we are to continue to try to love one another. But perhaps, and I think this is what Kinzie suggests, the poems themselves, their very possibility, are a demonstration of the soul, of the permanent possibility of thought, which is never exhausted by the world's assaults upon it. Their hope is clearer than cynicism, more difficult than despair.

# CHAPTER TWENTY-THREE

# The Founder

JUDITH M. BROWN (2003), Nehru: A Political Life;
SHASHI THAROOR (2003), Nehru: The Invention of India

I

Early in 2003, the website Samachar.com, which digests Indian newspapers for foreign Indiaphiles, conducted a poll that asked, "Which Prime Minister has contributed most to India's development?" When I checked the numbers in February, incumbent prime minister Atal Bihari Vajpayee was holding a huge lead with 596 votes, three times the number of his nearest rival. As for Jawaharlal Nehru, the chief architect of India's political system and its transition from colony to independent democracy, and the author of the speech about India's "tryst with destiny," which is as well known in India as Lincoln's Gettysburg Address is in the United States, a speech that similarly defines a nation in terms of the capacity for sacrifice and service—Nehru came in third, with a mere seventy-five votes. To judge from the expatriate community at least, Nehru's ideas had been roundly repudiated—though it was hard to say whether voters were applauding Vajpayee's record on foreign investment or his preference for a Hindu state. Coming less than a year after the mass killings of innocent Muslims in Gujarat, virtually condoned by Vajpayee and surely not protested, the vote did not express a robust commitment to minority civil rights.

Three months later, the voters of India expressed themselves very differently. They returned Nehru's Congress Party to power and roundly defeated Vajpayee's Bharatiya Janata Party, the party of Hindu nationalism. Sonia Gandhi, the widow of Nehru's grandson Rajiv Gandhi, declined the prime ministership in order to prevent the political process from being hijacked by the controversy over her foreign birth, but she still runs the party, and she has repeatedly stated that the electoral victory is a triumph for two central aspects of Nehru's vision of the state: the idea of equal respect for citizens of all religions, and the idea of a basic commitment to eradicating desperate conditions for the poor. It is clear that the votes for Nehru's legacy came in large numbers from poor rural areas, where voters, many of them illiterate (literacy rates are not much above 50 percent in the nation as a whole), vote with great commitment, overcoming many obstacles to get to the polls. Voter turnout in general elections in India is almost twice what it normally is in the United States; and this, too, is Nehru's legacy.

The biography of this extraordinary and controversial man is thus of more than historical interest. But what a difficult task it is to write his biography! Nehru lived for seventy-four years, from 1889 to 1964, and his life spanned the tumultuous period of resistance against British rule, the founding of the new nation, and the first fifteen years of its existence. In all these events he played a leading role, interacting with figures of his time who were as complex and historically significant as himself (notably Mahatma Gandhi, the Muslim leader Mohammed Ali Jinnah, and his own daughter Indira Gandhi, who succeeded him in power). The biography of Nehru must be at the same time a history of the nation and its leaders. And American readers know little about India's history, so a good biography of Nehru for the American public must be also a powerful narrative of largely unfamiliar historical events.

The difficulty of writing about Nehru is compounded by the fact that he himself was astoundingly prolific, which is not completely surprising, given that he spent more or less twenty years of his adult life in various British-run prisons, where reading and writing was virtually all there was to do. In particular, he is the author of a huge autobiography, first published in 1936, and thus including only the early portions of his political life, and of the monumental *The Discovery of India* (1945), with its sweeping coverage of Indian history, culture, and religion and its detailed commentary on British rule and the resistance to it. He also wrote thousands of letters, ranging from intimate love letters to paternal advice, political debate, and analysis of every kind. Even to read all that he wrote is a challenge to the biographer; but how to integrate it into a narrative unity?

And then there is the fact that Nehru is one of the supreme prose stylists of the English language in the twentieth century. What biographer's sentences would not look pedestrian by comparison to the serene yet deep emotion expressed in Nehru's will, as he asks that his ashes be thrown into the river Ganges:

> Smiling and dancing in the morning sunlight, and dark and gloomy and full of mystery as the evening shadows fall, a narrow, slow and graceful stream in winter and a vast, roaring thing during the monsoon, broad-bosomed almost as the sea, and with something of the sea's power to destroy, the Ganga has been to me a symbol and a memory of the past of India, running into the present, and flowing on to the great ocean of the future.

Or flat by comparison to the wit of the man who wrote of prison life, "This close association in a barrack has most of the disadvantages of married life with none of its advantages." Or humdrum by comparison to the political rhetoric of the end of the "tryst with destiny" speech:

> And so we have to labour and to work, and to work hard, to give reality to our dreams. Those dreams are for India, but they are also for the world, for all the nations and peoples are too closely knit together today for any one of them to imagine that it can live apart. Peace is said to be indivisible, so is freedom, so is prosperity now, and also is disaster in this one world that can no longer be split into isolated fragments.

Even the apparent awkwardness of "and also is disaster" works: the sentence, which begins like a trumpet call, modulates to a darker, more mysterious sound.

Nor was Nehru a simple man psychologically, as you can begin to see from these scattered fragments. He was painfully self-scrutinizing, yet with an ungovernable temper; a famously urbane and delightful guest, yet rightly described by Gandhi as one of the loneliest men in India; unreservedly given to the service of others, yet aware of a powerful egotism in himself; hungry for love and connection, but aware that "I had been, and was, a most unsatisfactory person to marry." The writer who would convey this personality to the public must be possessed both of human insight and a powerful narrative gift. And he or she would have to be able to add something to the already extensive self-analysis of Nehru himself, who criticized his own hunger for power in an anonymous article published in the *Modern Review* in 1937 that called Nehru a modern Caesar who has "all the makings of a dictator in him," and who wrote so pointedly of his own strange mixture of emotion and detachment: "I have loved life and it attracts me still and, in my own way, I seek to experience it, though many invisible barriers have grown up which surround me; but that very desire leads me to play with life, to peep over its edges, not to be a slave to it, so that we may value each other all the more." (And did he, noticing so much, see the egotism in that conclusion, which sets him on a par with life itself?)

Not surprisingly, even the most gifted writers of his own era hardly knew what to say of, or to, him. Consider this peculiar public tribute from the poet Sarojini Naidu, the first female president of the Congress, on the occasion of Nehru's fiftieth birthday: "I do not think that personal happiness, comfort, leisure, wealth . . . can have much place in your life. . . . Sorrow, suffering, anguish, strife, yes, these are the predestined gifts of life for you. . . . You are a man of destiny born to be alone in the midst of crowds—deeply loved, but little understood." Well, thank you very much. Naidu's statements are undoubtedly true in a way, but the biographer had better be able to do at least somewhat better than that.

It is clearly not impossible to write a biography of a complicated member of the Nehru family that meets all these challenges. Katherine Frank's biography of Indira Gandhi, which appeared in 2001, is an impressive success, weaving together acute psychological insight with a clear and compelling narrative of political events. Frank's emphasis is perhaps more on the personal and psychological than on the political, but there is a firm grasp of issues and policies, and political choices are illuminated from within, as Frank paints a telling portrait of a sickly child who took decades to realize her own strength, a woman who was treated as her father's son and called herself his "Indu-boy," and yet at the same time was treated by most of the dominant males around her as a weak woman and an outsider. Frank insightfully explains Indira's rigidity, her distrust of democratic deliberation and consultation, and her baneful tendency to rely on less than reliable members of her own family (especially her repellent younger son Sanjay) as growing out of her isolation in the male-dominated world of political conversation, and also out of her odd relationship to a father who wrote to her with enormous intimacy from jail but could rarely establish the same connection in person. Frank's book is hard to put down; it is highly accessible to people with little prior knowledge of India. And yet the more knowledgeable reader also comes away from it with a sense that new perspectives have been opened up. Indira is in one way an easier subject than Jawaharlal, because she did not write so much, or so well; but her father, too, emerges as a complex and compelling character in Frank's pages.

Unhappily, neither of these new biographies of Nehru offers nearly as much insight, psychological or political. Both have their virtues, and both are profoundly defective in different ways. Shashi Tharoor's book is a superficial popular life with no new research, not much analysis, and little psychological understanding. Tharoor addresses his book to the general reader who wants a rapid introduction. And so his biography is written with a glibness that belies the soul of its subject. Read it and you will get a vivid account of the main historical events and a general introduction to the life. You will also get an extremely superficial attack on Nehru's economic policies (Tharoor even gets facts wrong, attributing the start of economic reform to Narasimha Rao rather than Rajiv Gandhi), and a more substantial defense of Nehruvian religious pluralism, but simplistic still, in that it makes Jinnah the sole villain in the partitioning of India and Pakistan, not mentioning the rise of the Hindu right, and slighting the role of the British in fostering Muslim separatism. (Nehru never made that mistake: whenever he criticized Jinnah's religious communalism, he always mentioned the Hindu Mahasabha in the same sentence.) This is not a bad book for the American who knows little about India, but soon, if you are drawn in, you will need to turn to the man himself.

Judith Brown's scholarly tome is unsatisfactory for very different reasons. Unlike Tharoor's book, it contains lots of new material, including letters in the possession of Sonia Gandhi that were not available to other biographers.

It also contains at least some political and economic analysis. The later, thematically organized chapters are reasonably good, though nothing useful is said about links to contemporary events. Brown's treatment of Nehru's economic policies is nuanced and reasonable. She is good on Nehru's commitment to women's equality, and on the obstacles that he faced. (Tharoor is superficial here, getting crucial facts and even names wrong.) Her treatment of religious issues is far more complex than Tharoor's, though marred by an equal failure to discuss the rise of the Hindu right.

Brown's treatment of the Nehru-Gandhi relationship is particularly good, although she does not learn from this relationship that the question of what is "Western" and what is "Indian" in both men is a highly complex matter. Brown consistently treats reason and science as "Western" imports, and religion as a peculiarly "Eastern" preoccupation. Never mind that Gandhi tells us in his autobiography that two of the primary influences on his own religious thought were Ruskin and Tolstoy. Never mind that Nehru rightly emphasizes the richness and the prominence of the rationalist traditions in Indian religion and philosophy. Never mind that Nehru argues cogently that the British deliberately fostered the irrationalist strands in Hindu culture and religion and inhibited the rationalist, in order more securely to dominate a people who could not industrialize on their own without scientific development.

So Brown is not an entirely reliable guide on many matters, and one sometimes wonders what her relation to India actually is. Her simple concept of the "Western" would hardly survive an encounter with the Indian women's movement, for example, where women who cannot read and write, who have no televisions and no contact with "the West," are fighting hard for the very rights that the Nehru family is called "Western" for defending. Even on geography, Brown is hazy. She says, for example, that big cities in India look just like cities in "other modern countries": "Only in rural areas does it become apparent that the new and cosmopolitan is juxtaposed with far older economic and cultural patterns." This sentence makes me suspect that Brown has not ventured far outside the more prosperous parts of Delhi and Mumbai; she could not have written it had she spent much time in Patna or Ahmedabad or Trivandrum.

But the cardinal flaw in Brown's book is her complete lack of any narrative gift. The early sections of the book are virtually unreadable, a mass of details thrown in with little organization but the chronological. One feels that Brown is simply overwhelmed by the material. Sometimes she puts a piece of information in a wrong and misleading place—as when she mentions Rammohun Roy's reforms of Hinduism in Bengal in the middle of a paragraph discussing early twentieth-century reforms, even though Roy lived from 1772 to 1833. (This is important, because getting the chronology straight would establish that crucial reforms—higher education for women, for example—were introduced earlier in India than in Britain, and would thus put paid to the simplistic equation of modern reform with "Westernization.") Sometimes we get a mass of details on minor issues; and then, when a really large issue arises, we may hear virtually nothing about it. The brutal massacre of Indian civilians in 1919 at Amritsar, in which the British army under General Dyer opened fire without warning on a peaceful unarmed crowd, is well and accurately described in Tharoor's book. Brown gives a blurry compressed account, with crucial facts totally omitted, including Nehru's role in the investigation and the fact that the crowd was peaceful and unarmed, and that the British fired without warning. A similar contrast can be observed in the two accounts of Mahatma Gandhi's assassination: Tharoor gives us all the information we need and tells the story in a simple, moving manner, whereas Brown does not even tell us that the assassin was a Hindu right-wing fanatic who objected to Gandhi's sympathy for Muslims. (She calls him "a young Hindu man.")

Both books have curious omissions. Neither has any discussion of Nehru's law minister, B. R. Ambedkar, an extraordinary man from the group formerly called "untouchables" and now known as "dalits." Thus a chance is missed to confront issues of caste in the founding, on which neither book is of much use. And most unfortunately of all, neither says anything about the third giant of Indian thought and culture, alongside Gandhi and Nehru, namely Rabindranath Tagore. Tagore, who won the Nobel Prize for Literature in 1905, is best known in the West as a mystical poet, but he was also many other things: novelist, story-writer, composer, choreographer, and, most important, educational reformer with a developed vision of how India could come to grips with issues of religious division through an education emphasizing critical and independent thinking, world understanding, and the arts. To contrast Tagore's vision with Nehru's is crucial if we want to see what went right and what went wrong.

II

Jawaharlal Nehru was born in 1889, the only son of a prosperous liberal Kashmiri Brahmin family. His father Motilal, a lawyer, was a modernist and a reformer, comfortable with Muslims and mistrustful of all appeals to traditional religion. In Motilal's case it is not inaccurate to speak of Westernizing, since he required his children to study even Sanskrit texts in English translation, and dressed little Jawaharlal in a sailor suit, and encouraged the use of English nicknames for his two younger sisters. (Both became women of substantial achievement; one was the first woman president of the United Nations General Assembly.) At one point in the 1890s he decreed that no language other than English would be spoken in the home, despite the fact that his wife—a sickly woman, and traditionally religious—knew no English.

Jawaharlal was sent off to Harrow, where he was very happy. From Harrow he went on, in 1907, to Trinity College, Cambridge, where he studied chemistry, geology, and physics, graduating with a mediocre second-class degree. As important as any formal education that he received was his close relationship with his father, who in person and by letter deliberately cultivated Jawaharlal's capacity for argument, particularly on political topics. Resistance to British rule was growing, and Jawaharlal became increasingly radical in his views, ultimately influencing his moderate father to take a strong anti-British position. The Amritsar massacre radicalized many people who had previously been pro-British. (Tagore returned his knighthood.) Returning to India and taking up a career in law, Jawaharlal soon became close to Mahatma Gandhi and a staunch supporter of his non-cooperation movement. His influence within the Congress—the political movement that organized the struggle for independence—rapidly increased.

He also married, in 1916, seventeen-year-old Kamala Kaul, betrothed to him by family arrangement when she was only thirteen. Jawaharlal at first objected to an arranged marriage; when he yielded, he insisted that he and his betrothed should be allowed to get to know each other before marrying. Whether as a result or not, the marriage, though sorrowful on account of Kamala's ill health and premature death from tuberculosis in 1936, had great emotional depth. Kamala came to share her husband's passion for the cause of independence, and did valuable work for the cause when her health permitted. The sexual bond between them appears to have been deep, and perhaps increased over time. "Though we had sometimes quarreled and grown angry with each other," he later wrote, "we kept that vital spark alight, and for each one of us life was always unfolding new adventure and giving fresh insight into each other." Her death, in a sanatorium in Switzerland, brought him tremendous grief—all the more since his many years of imprisonment had deprived him so often of her company. Although he had affairs after her death—certainly with Sarojini Naidu's daughter Padmaja, perhaps later with his close friend Edwina, wife of Lord Mountbatten, the last viceroy of India—he never remarried. He once wrote to Kamala from prison, "I am a traveler, limping along in the dark night. Why should I drag others into this darkness, however near or beloved they may be; why should they suffer the travails of the journey?"

While still a young husband, in the 1920s, Jawaharlal became increasingly known as one of the leading pro-independence radicals of the Congress movement. He was frequently packed off to British jails, where he made a point of occupying himself with exercise, gardening, spinning (Gandhi's influence), and above all reading and writing. "I became obsessed with the thought of India," he records. Meanwhile, Gandhi was effectively mobilizing resistance through civil disobedience, most famously in the "salt march," in which he led a large group of followers on a long march to the sea, where he illegally made salt from seawater by allowing the water to evaporate in his hand, thus defying the British tax on salt. (This episode is described beautifully by Tharoor, badly by Brown.)

Nehru and Gandhi had a complex and troubled relationship. Nehru, ever the pragmatist, saw non-violence as only a tactic, and objected to a politics of unbending moral idealism. He also objected to Gandhi's romantic glorification of pre-industrial society, holding that India's future well-being required scientific, industrial, and technological development. During World War II, he and Gandhi had a very serious quarrel over India's stance toward the Axis powers. Nehru hated fascism from the first. He saw it up close on visits to Europe in the 1930s, where he made a point of purchasing Jewish products. "Amazed and disgusted" by Chamberlain's policy of appeasement, he called it "the difficult and intricate game of how to betray your friend and the cause you are supposed to stand for on the highest moral grounds . . . the utter collapse, in the moment of crisis, of all the so-called advanced people and groups." Summoned to a meeting with Mussolini in 1936, while in Italy, he refused, unwilling to let himself be used for fascist propaganda. Gandhi's much more equivocal stance included a willingness to support Japan if doing so would hurt the British; and Nehru found this horrifying. But the two remained deep friends and uneasy allies until Gandhi's assassination in 1948. Gandhi understood that Nehru was a practical politician of moral courage and superb practical perception; Nehru understood that Gandhi had an unparalleled capacity to inspire people for good ends, and he was deeply moved by the man always.

The piggish racism of the British during this period must be confronted to be believed, and Tharoor is ready to assist. He produces such gems as Churchill's remark "I hate Indians. They are a beastly people with a beastly religion," and his comment that Gandhi's visit to London involved the "nauseating" sight of "a seditious Middle Temple Lawyer . . . striding half-naked up the steps of the Viceregal palace . . . to parley on equal terms with the representative of the King-Emperor." Tharoor also reminds us that Gandhi, told that Lord Irwin (then viceroy) always prayed to God before making any major decision, remarked, "What a pity God gives him such bad advice." If the British couldn't have a dependent India, they were determined to have a fragmented one, and both these books tell with sadness the story of how the British fostered the cause of Muslim separatism, initially against the wishes of the vast majority of Muslims, until sentiment became polarized and the two-nation "solution," with its vast bloodshed, was the result.

After Independence on August 15, 1947, the story continues for seventeen more years, as Nehru worked tirelessly to build democratic institutions and to forge a policy whose key features were secularism (meaning not separation of church and state, since four major religions were given substantial roles in lawmaking, but equal respect accorded to the religions), a foreign policy of nonalignment and internationalism, and a socialist economic policy. Nehru was no admirer of communism, which he criticized for its failure to protect essential freedoms of association, speech, conscience, and religious practice; but in economic policy he did believe that socialism, meaning state ownership of the means of production and considerable top-down planning, was the best route to prosperity. These policies all had their difficulties, but they succeeded remarkably well, in part thanks to Nehru's endless capacity for hard work, his high moral tone, and his absolute freedom from corruption. His own personal qualities played no small part in holding India together in the early days, and also in winning respect from the other nations of the world.

In the 1960s, age began to sap his famous vitality. To Indira, increasingly his consort and companion, he wrote, "The sense of the work to do, so little done, and ever less and less time to do it, oppresses." In 1964 he had two strokes, but he quickly resumed his usual routine. On May 17, he died in his sleep of a massive aortic rupture. On his bedside table were found, copied in his own hand, these lines of Robert Frost:

The woods are lovely, dark and deep,
But I have promises to keep,
And miles to go before I sleep,
And miles to go before I sleep.

## III

How should we assess Nehru's "invention of India"? Let us begin where he began: "My legacy to India? Hopefully, it is 400 million people capable of governing themselves." India's population now tops one billion, but that legacy remains firm. The institutional structure that Nehru helped to design, with its separation of powers, its conception of the Supreme Court as defender of fundamental rights, and its role for federalism and local governance, has withstood the test of time, including the very strenuous test supplied by Indira Gandhi's suspension of civil liberties (approved by a cowardly Parliament) during the Emergency. An active electorate shortly turned her out, and the Supreme Court built up more robust safeguards for judicial review of parliamentary action.

Together with the institutional structure, we should credit the vigor of democracy in India to a strong and independent press, whose critical independence and commitment to free investigation was another part of Nehru's ideal. As Brown stresses, democracy and federalism made the realization of other cherished goals slow and uncertain: changes in the status of women in particular, central in Nehru's vision of India's future, have moved at a snail's pace because of the dominance of entrenched traditional ideas. Still, Nehru's patience with democracy was right and Indira's impatience was wrong. His one great weakness in this area, indeed, was a weakness of impatience, connected to his desire to get a lot done: namely, his reluctance to mold Congress into a genuine political party, one among others. Since Congress was always, under Nehru, both a movement and a party, multi-party democracy has not altogether flourished. The only other nationally influential parties organized along simply political lines have been the (two) communist parties and a short-lived market-libertarian party that never caught on. Apart from these (and communist influence is large in two states only), political opposition to Congress has typically come from parties organized along lines of religion, region, and caste. The resulting balkanization of politics has entrenched divisions that Nehru rightly wished to undermine.

As for the economy, both Tharoor and Brown easily make the hindsight judgment that Nehru relied too much on centralized planning—though Brown at least gives him credit for the progress that India made in heavy industry and for impressive economic growth in the early years. The failure of planning, more than any other single factor, explains the low esteem in which many businesspeople hold Nehru and Congress today. But it should be remembered that Nehru was always an empiricist, committed to following the evidence where it led. It is hard for me to imagine that he would not ultimately have supported the economic reforms of Manmohan Singh.

Yet one should not confuse a commitment to reform with indifference to the plight of the poor, and many voters in the Samachar poll may have made that confusion. The BJP's recent electoral campaign, which used as its central slogan "India Shining," offended and angered rural voters, for whom India is not at all shining. Reaction against a cynical politics of globalization without protections for the vulnerable played a large part in ensuring the party's defeat, in favor of a Congress committed to both economic reform and a decent social safety net.

In foreign policy, both Brown and Tharoor seem uneasy with Nehru's policy of non-alignment during the Cold War, and they are correct, to the extent that Nehru's sympathy with socialism blinded him to some of the evils of Soviet rule, with particularly bad effect in 1956, when he refused to protest the Soviet invasion of Hungary. He also took a rosier picture of India-China relations than was plausible. Yet one should admire his courage in standing up to demands from both sides that India become a pawn in their power games. And his internationalism, in a world that had not yet come to terms with the ideal of global cooperation, offers a moving model for an era in which that ideal is once again being increasingly called into question.

Where religion is concerned, both Tharoor and Brown are rightly impressed with Nehru's vision of India as a tolerant pluralist nation, showing all citizens and all religions equal respect before the laws. They are also rightly convinced that Nehru made mistakes in this area because he took religion too lightly. Nehru thought that science was the way of thinking for the future; he found religion embarrassing and primitive, a "terrible burden" that India had to get rid of if it was to "breathe freely or do anything useful." Brown puts this down to his Western education, but this underestimates the depth of religion in the West and the depth of rationalism in Indian religious traditions. Nehru knew a lot about all this, so his hostility to religion and his often facile contrast of religion with science is not easy to explain.

What is clear, however, is that his feeling that religion was an embarrassment led him to devote much too little attention to the public molding of religion, so that it could become a grassroots force for pluralism and respect rather than for fear and hatred. The result has been that the Hindu right went to work basically unopposed, creating a masterful popular program of indoctrination that has spread the gospel of anti-Muslim fear to every region. Given his emphatic recognition that Hinduism historically is the most pluralistic and tolerant of religions—its "essential spirit," he said, is "live and let live"—why didn't Nehru follow Gandhi's lead, putting forward a public version of religion that showed a way forward toward the removal of barriers of caste and faith? Or, better yet, since Gandhi himself stressed that the Hindu nature of India is more than compatible with a truly respectful pluralism, why did he not follow the example of Tagore, who forged in Bengal a public poetry of syncretism and inclusion, creating dance dramas, stories, poems, and songs (one of which is sung now as India's national anthem) that celebrate the strength that derives from diversity, the vigor that grows out of a willingness to criticize entrenched habits and to respect differences?

The major factor behind Nehru's failure to follow these examples, and create a public culture of equal respect that could hold people's emotions and hopes and fears, was, I believe, the influence of Marxism. Nehru greatly loved the people of India, but he writes about them oddly, using crude words such as "the mass" and "the masses." One minute he is writing about his own personal emotions with the greatest acuity; the next he treats "the mass" as a proletarian class that has no such personal emotions, but will somehow behave like a class, rising and flourishing as such. This was not elitism so much as a theoretical view of class that screened him from the reality of what people feel in their hearts. The Marxian idea that religion is an "opiate" impeding the proletariat from realizing its destiny is an idea that Nehru expresses repeatedly in his own words.

He failed to see, in short, what Tagore saw very clearly: that each human being of every caste, creed, and class is a separate person, with fear and longing and hope. If he had understood this, he would perhaps have understood, too, that the people of India, each and every one, need what he needed: poetry and music and mourning and love, in a religious or non-religious form—and also a group of like-minded Indians with whom to share poetry and music and mourning and love. The Hindu right understands this very well.

And these limitations in Nehru's imagination of humanity explain also his other great failure: namely, the failure to create a system of public education that would provide robust underpinnings for a democratic political culture. India does splendidly in scientific and technological education, because that is what Nehru cared about and fostered. If the teaching of basic science and computer technology were as primitive as is the teaching of history and literature and critical thinking, it would be a public scandal. But, with all the arguments that rage about what account of history should figure in textbooks for seventeen-year-olds, one more rarely hears the complaint that seventeen-year-olds are learning history by rote from textbooks—that, indeed, virtually all their schooling takes the form of rote learning. Over the years basic literacy has spread, but access to really high-quality education is virtually restricted to elites who can attend private schools.

The dismal quality of rote learning in public schools (when the teachers even show up, which is not always) surely augurs badly for the future of Indian democracy. In fact, one reason why the rural poor are such thoughtful and active citizens is possibly that they often don't go to public schools. I have observed education in India for the rural poor, as conducted by NGOs that work with working children and adults, and that education is almost always imaginative, vigorous, animated by a sense of education as a humane mission connected with empowerment and citizenship. In the average public school classroom, there is not much idealism or imagination on offer. In some crucial respects, then, the middle class gets a worse education for citizenship than the rural poor. (Here again it was Tagore who showed the way, creating an educational vision, in his Santiniketan school and the related university, that focused on the activation of critical and imaginative capacities.)

For all his blind spots and his failings, however, Nehru's achievement was staggering: the creation of the largest democracy in the world. So far, this democracy has grappled with enormous tensions and unparalleled diversity without losing its basic commitments to pluralism and the rule of law. Where Nehru's vision has gaps and defects, he himself was the first to acknowledge that his task was both shared and ongoing. At the head of the epilogue to his autobiography he placed an epigraph from the Talmud: "We are enjoined to labor; but it is not granted to us to complete our labors." If blind greed, technocratic elitism, and religious bigotry do not derail the "labor," it may possibly be—not completed, for it never can be, but continued, by all of us, in this "one world that can no longer be split into isolated fragments."

# CHAPTER TWENTY-FOUR

# Epistemology of the Closet

BART SCHULTZ (2004), Henry Sidgwick: Eye of the Universe:
An Intellectual Biography

When most people think of Utilitarianism today, they are likely to think of the idea, central to much modern economic thought, that people are by nature maximizers of the satisfaction of their own interests. In its economic form, with the accent on natural selfishness, Utilitarianism looks like a cynical creed that denies the possibility of genuine altruism. If social good for all or most people is to be achieved, it will be because somehow or other the selfish decisions of many people combine to produce it. Such Utilitarian ideas, however, are but an amputated limb of the radical philosophy that once went by that name. For the three great British Utilitarians—Jeremy Bentham (1748–1832), John Stuart Mill (1806–1873), and Henry Sidgwick (1838–1900)—the proper social goal was the greatest happiness of the greatest number, a calculus in which, in Bentham's famous slogan. "Each [is] to count for one, and none for more than one." Far from being a complacent egoistic philosophy, Utilitarianism was radical in both its methods (counting all people equally) and its results, which often urged sweeping change in existing social structures.

Nor were Utilitarians political conservatives, as their modern descendants in economics tend to be. On the contrary, in line with their philosophical convictions, they supported an end to religious establishments, the equality of women, a demanding globalism, and, in the case of Mill and Bentham, a dedication to animal rights (since "each" included all sentient beings). Arrested at the age of 18 for distributing contraceptive literature among the poor of London, Mill went on to introduce a motion for women's suffrage as a member of Parliament. Bentham issued the first Western philosophical defense of animal rights since Greco-Roman antiquity, and Mill left much of his estate to the SPCA. Both, as atheists, were unable to hold an academic appointment, which at that time required swearing belief in the Thirty-Nine Articles of the Church of England. Even more radically,

Bentham condemned laws against same-sex relations, commenting, "It is wonderful that nobody has ever yet fancied it to be sinful to scratch where it itches, and that it has never been determined that the only natural way of scratching is with such or such a finger and that it is unnatural to scratch with any other."

Henry Sidgwick is usually regarded as the tame Victorian among these radicals, the person who domesticated Utilitarianism and made it both academically and socially respectable, in the process smoothing its rough edges. This facile story runs up against some inconvenient facts, such as Sidgwick's resignation of his Cambridge fellowship when he decided that he could not support the Thirty-Nine Articles (he resumed it again only when the rules were changed), and his key role, with his wife, Eleanor, in founding Newnham College, the first women's college to be located right in the heart of Cambridge, not (like Girton) at a safe distance from the centers of power. Despite these signs of radical commitment, however, Sidgwick's reputation for tameness has persisted, an impression reinforced by the dry, dense, and academic style of his great work, *The Methods of Ethics*. Both of these factors combine to make Sidgwick of little interest to the general public, at a time when Mill, especially, is enjoying a renewed popularity, helped in no small measure by the eloquence and insight of his famous *Autobiography*.

Professional philosophers, by contrast, admire Sidgwick, even when they differ sharply with him. Both John Rawls and Bernard Williams, for example, have focused very respectfully on Sidgwick in their critiques of Utilitarian thought, and Rawls praised Sidgwick as one of the most impressive of historical figures for his rigor and complexity. But most philosophers, too, would have thought that Sidgwick, unlike Mill, could not possibly have written anything that showed deep emotion or human insight, much less anything that issued a radical challenge to Victorian sensibilities.

Bart Schultz's mammoth biography shows that we would have been entirely wrong. Schultz, a lecturer at the University of Chicago, argues that Sidgwick was not just a very distinguished academic thinker but also an authentic social radical, if a conflicted one. He tried hard to be a proper Victorian, but he failed in two big ways, losing faith in God and owning up (though not publicly) to forbidden desires for sex with men. The exploration of these themes and related ones (Sidgwick's feminism, his radical views about education and his somewhat more conventional attitudes about race and empire) make this book not only a superb biography but also an invaluable contribution to the history of Victorian England. And because, in addition to these virtues, it is written with a high degree of philosophical understanding and a good deal of sophisticated philosophical discussion, it is the best biography of a philosopher to appear in many years, and perhaps the best ever produced about a British thinker.

Schultz's book is very long, and even longer than it seems, because it is full of lengthy quotations from letters and diaries set in smaller type than the text. But it should not have been shorter, because he has uncovered so much previously unknown source material that is not likely to be assembled again. The reader who doesn't want to read every bit should still be happy it is all there, ready to be mined whenever one wants. And the volume is intelligently arranged. Straight biographical narration occupies its beginning and end, but the middle chapters are thematically organized: one long one on the central philosophical ideas, one on Sidgwick's investigations into the paranormal, one on sexuality, and one on race and ethnicity.

Unlike Bentham and Mill, Sidgwick wanted badly to believe in conventional religion, but it took him many years to figure out that he could not do so. Nor did he give up the ghost, so to speak, when he decided that ordinary Anglican piety was not and could not be rationally well grounded. Instead, he tried to prove the existence of a life after death scientifically, co-founding the Society for Psychical Research and devoting a great part of his later life to experiments that tested the claims of mediums, clairvoyants, and hypnotists. Bentham and Mill would have mocked these doings because they cared little about heaven in the first place. (Mill once said that our interest in it would be likely to drop away as civilization progressed— although he could not let go of the hope of being reunited with his beloved Harriet.) But the fact that Sidgwick still felt that conventional religious ideas were crucial to solving the conflict between egoism and altruism should not conceal from us, Schultz argues, the highly unconventional means he used to recast them. To the reader who finds all the ghost stuff ridiculous, Schultz points out that at the time many utterly serious people believed it, and that at least some of it (hypnotism) turned out not to be ridiculous. How would we know, without testing? Moreover, Sidgwick's attitude was invariably skeptical and scientific. For that reason he was never satisfied that his hope for communication from beyond the grave had been realized—although some members of the Society firmly believed that he had succeeded in communicating with them after his death.

While Sidgwick was testing the limits of religion, Schultz shows in the most surprising portion of his book, he was also profoundly unconventional in matters of gender and sexuality—much more so indeed than Bentham, a lifelong solitary bachelor, or Mill, whose most scandalous act was to go about with a beloved married woman for many years, probably without sleeping with her, and then to marry her after her husband's death. Sidgwick, by contrast, was not just a feminist, which we knew, but also a lifelong homosexual, which we have never clearly known. Much of the book is devoted to probing Sidgwick's role in a circle of men of homoerotic inclinations, prominently including John Addington Symonds, the independent scholar who (in a monograph titled *A Problem in Greek Ethics*) did more than anyone prior to Sir Kenneth Dover to put our knowledge of ancient Greek sexual practices on the right track. Although it is unclear whether Sidgwick ever expressed his inclinations in sexual intercourse, and although he did eventually marry the estimable Eleanor Mildred Balfour, whom he met in the Society for Psychical Research, Schultz does establish that he was entirely impotent sexually with women (Symonds and most of the other men in the circle were not, and fathered children), and that he struggled throughout his life with issues of hypocrisy and openness in connection with his own forbidden desires. His fear of scandal kept him from embracing his sexual identity, and he aggressively protected his friends from exposure and disgrace, at one point making Symonds lock up a box of his passionate homoerotic poems and dumping its key, himself, into the river Avon. "I feel often as unrelated and unadapted to my universe as man can feel," Sidgwick summarized himself to a male friend.

Stories like Sidgwick's have been told in histories of Victorian sexuality, but Schultz has mined the intimate correspondence of Symonds and Sidgwick for priceless insights into the way gay men experienced the world in the time of Oscar Wilde. What we see here more clearly than ever before is the cruel deformation of personality wrought by the Victorian closet, with its looming fear of disgrace and imprisonment. Consider the case history of himself contributed by Symonds to Havelock Ellis's *Studies in Sexual Inversion*:

At about the age of 30, unable to endure his position any longer, he at last yielded to his sexual inclinations. As he began to do this, he also began to regain calm and comparative health. . . . In the third period the gratification became more frankly sensual. It took every shape: mutual masturbation, intercrural coitus, *fellatio, irrumatio,* occasionally *paedicatio,* always according to the inclination or concession of the beloved male. . . . Coitus with males, as above described, always seems to him healthy and natural; it leaves a deep sense of well-being, and has cemented durable friendships. He has always sought to form permanent ties with the men whom he has adored so excessively.

He has suffered extremely throughout life owing to his sense of the difference between himself and normal human beings. No pleasure he has enjoyed, he declares, can equal a thousandth part of the pain caused by the internal consciousness of Pariahdom [Symonds describes the ruin of his health by anxiety in early years, and his gradual restoration, after sexual fulfillment was found]. . . . Although he always has before him the terror of discovery, he is convinced that his sexual dealings with men have been thoroughly wholesome to himself, largely increasing his physical, moral, and intellectual energy, and not injurious to others. As a man of letters he regrets that he has been shut out from that form of artistic expression which would express his own emotions. He has no sense whatever of moral wrong in his actions, and he regards the attitude of society towards those in his position as utterly unjust and founded on false principles.

Not for Sidgwick, however, even this hard-won journey to self-acceptance and spiritual repose. Guilt and fear keep on oscillating unsteadily with the sense that his desires are good and their objects beautiful and lovable. To read the following extract from Sidgwick's private jottings marked "(May 1867 to JAS)" is to take on an utterly new view of the arid academic we thought we knew:

1. These are my friends—beautiful, plain-featured, tender-hearted, hard-headed.
2. Pure, spiritual, sympathetic, debauched, worldly, violent in conflict.
3. Their virtue and vice are mine and not mine: they were made my friends before they were made virtuous and vicious.
4. Because I know them, the Universe knows them and you shall know them: they exist and will exist, because I love them.
5. This one is great and forgets me: I weep, but I care not, because I love him.
6. This one is afar off, and his life lies a ruin: I weep but I care not because I love him.
7. We meet, and their eyes sparkle and then are calm.
8. Their eyes are calm and they smile: their hands are quick and their fingers tremble.
9. The light of heaven enwraps them: their faces and their forms become harmonious to me with the harmony of the Universe.
10. The air of heaven is spread around them: their houses and books, their pictures and carpets make music to me as all things make music to God. . . .
13. Some are women to me, and to some I am a woman.
14. Each day anew we are born, we meet and love, we embrace and are united for ever: with passion that wakes no longing, with fruition that brings no satiety.

Reading such passionate and slightly mad utterances, we understand that the closet enclosed Sidgwick's poetry as well as his body. And we attach a new sense to his constant insistence that moral judgments are best made from the "point of view of the Universe." For Bernard Williams and other critics, this preference for the detached point of view shows Sidgwick's emotional obtuseness, his inability to see the value of the personal point of view. Schultz shows that things are much more complex: The Universe (unlike "my universe," in the other quotation) is a place beyond Victorian morality, a place that knows the good of love and sees the surpassing beauty of the men who are its objects. Perhaps the saddest aspect of this fantasy is its unmistakably Victorian character. (Sidgwick loved Pre-Raphaelite verse and called Christina Rossetti's "Remember" "perhaps the most perfect thing that any living poet has written.") Whereas Bentham and Mill derived happiness from their outsider status (Mill insisted on being buried in France because he was utterly fed up with England and the English), Sidgwick cannot stop being of his time even in the act of spurning it.

Were Schultz's book only a record of these aspects of Sidgwick's life and conduct, it would already be an estimable volume of history. But of course Sidgwick is worthy of our attention because he is a first-rate philosopher, and much of Schultz's volume is taken up with a close reading of his great book. *The Methods of Ethics* is an important work in part because of its systematic ambition and rigorous argumentation. Unlike Bentham, who was simply not a very good arguer, and unlike the much greater Mill, whose journalistic style often frustrates the philosophical reader by leaving essential matters to be filled in on one's own, Sidgwick lays out Utilitarianism with great philosophical detail, showing with close argumentation why it seems to be preferable to the two other prominent approaches to ethics in Sidgwick's time, ethical egoism and "intuitionism," the commonsense-based morality made famous by the anti-Utilitarian William Whewell. (The absence of the Kantian alternative is striking; it led Rawls to suggest that his own Kant-inspired political theory might be seen as the next chapter in Sidgwick's opus.) Tracing his method to Aristotle, Sidgwick purports to go through the view of "the many" and "the wise," and to show that Utilitarianism preserves the "appearances" of reputable ethical thought better than its alternatives.

Utilitarianism can be usefully characterized (following an analysis proposed by Bernard Williams and Amartya Sen) as involving three ideas. First, consequentialism: The right choice is the one that produces the best overall consequences. Second, sum-ranking: The way we aggregate the satisfactions of different persons into a social whole is simply by adding them all up (rather than, say, by focusing on getting the worst-off person as high up as possible, or by insisting on some constraints on how unequal people can be allowed to be). Third, some substantive view of what the good for a person is, such as pleasure, or the satisfaction of desire. Sidgwick, like Bentham, opts for pleasure, though he is much more sensitive than Bentham to the difficulties involved in comparing different pleasures of the same person and the even greater difficulty involved in comparing the pleasures of different people.

Utilitarians typically commend the choice of pleasure as the goal by pointing to the alleged ubiquity of the pursuit of pleasure (not the best and surely not the only way to justify a central ethical value, one might have thought). They then encounter a difficulty: If what each person pursues, and should pursue (according to them), is maximal personal pleasure, how are we going to defend the view that the right goal for society is the greatest happiness of the greatest number? And how, having defended the view, are we going to convince people that it is that goal, rather than the egoistic goal, that they should pursue, since for many people pursuing overall happiness will involve personal sacrifice? Mill had a lot of difficulty with the philosophical argument, and he needed ultimately to depart from strict Utilitarianism in order to solve it to the extent that he did; but he was optimistic about the social process, believing that civic education could produce people who really did think of the happiness of others as an integral part of their own happiness. Sidgwick was hung up on this problem all his life; he called it the "dualism of practical reason," and in the end he believed that he had failed to solve it—unless life after death should turn out to produce a coincidence between personal happiness and service to others. But he made much more headway than his predecessors on the philosophical side of the issue, with his probing work on ethical methodology and his defense of a perspective of impartiality ("the point of view of the Universe") as the right place from which to make ethical judgments. (Schultz rightly notes that Sidgwick owes a considerable debt to Kant, although it is scarcely acknowledged, and to the Kantian idea that one must not favor one's own case but rather must test one's own actions by thinking about how they would look as universal features of the world.)

Non-philosophers will want to read this material slowly over time. One part of it they should not miss, however, is Schultz's lucid account of Sidgwick's defense of "indirect Utilitarianism" and of the central role of an elite who will run society for its own overall good. Sidgwick was far less democratic than Mill. He retained from his youthful days in the Apostles (the secret Cambridge intellectual society that gave birth to the Bloomsbury Group, as well as, later, to notorious traitors and spies) a strong elitism about morality, holding that only a select few could be trusted to know the true principles of Utilitarian ethics, and that the rest of the people would be better off believing in ordinary morality, with its notions of virtue and vice. This two-level Utilitarianism has seemed to some to solve some of its thorniest philosophical problems; to others it is an index of its moral bankruptcy. Schultz's rich discussion lets the reader decide.

Sidgwick spent his life on one of philosophy's most difficult problems, which is also one of the most difficult problems of personal and political life: How can we be happy while at the same time pursuing fairness? If he himself did not solve it, he contributed more than all but a few to our understanding of its dimensions and our sense of where to look for its solution. How odd that his widow and friends became so obsessed with his putative communications from beyond the grave, when he had already achieved this far worthier, and genuine, immortality, in a life marked, as we now know, by painful struggle and a strange combination of radical openness and fearful self-concealment.

# CHAPTER TWENTY-FIVE

# The Prohibition Era

KENJI YOSHINO (2006), *Covering: The Hidden Assault on Our Civil Rights*

I

In 1998, a Missouri court granted custody to a lesbian mother, after finding that "the children were unaware of Mother's sexual preference, and Mother never engaged in any sexual or affectionate behavior in the presence of the children." Many courts have gone the other way, after determining that same-sex parents engaged, not in overt sexual conduct that would be inappropriate for any parent to display before any child, but in displays of affection, such as hugging or holding hands, which clearly revealed the parent's sexual orientation. Courts in these cases are not demanding that same-sex parents stop being gay, or even that they pretend not to be gay. Instead, they are making a demand that Kenji Yoshino (following Erving Goffman) calls a demand for "covering": a demand not to express their identity in public and visible ways.

The repression of a minority, Yoshino argues, does not end when it is permitted to exist in society, and is no longer forced to "convert" to some other way of being and acting. Nor does it end when members of the group are not expected to "pass," concealing their minority identity from all but chosen intimates. Even when minorities who reveal their group member-ship openly are tolerated, they are often required to assimilate in ways that "cover" that identity. Thus, it was all right for the lesbian mother to be known as a lesbian, but not all right for her to hold hands with her partner. It is often all right for African Americans to be prominent in the workplace, but they have to dress for success and play nice, conforming their behavior to a stereotype invented by the dominant culture.

An interesting example that came too late for inclusion in Yoshino's account of "covering" has been the media's treatment of the Olympic medal-winning speed skater Shani Davis. White society was all set to pat itself on the back when an African American finally medaled in the lily-white sport, and Davis would have been warmly welcomed into its bosom had he been cheerful, docile, and grateful. Stories of how Davis overcame his "gang-infested" neighborhood (he comes from my own neighborhood, Chicago's Hyde Park, a multiracial university community that can be criticized as boring but not as gang-infested) were trotted out to prepare the way for a warm reception. Instead of gratitude and proper "white" behavior, however, Davis was spiky, brusque, and clearly annoyed at the press's quite ridiculous treatment of his origins. He talked to Chicago newspapers, which treated him with respect and got his story right, but he turned a cold shoulder to the others. ("Are you angry, Shani?" a network reporter asked, as if that would be the unforgivable sin, when the white community was being so very nice.) A similar treatment often befalls African Americans who wear cornrows, or "talk black," or in other ways refuse to make the majority comfortable.

Similar stories can be told about other minorities. There was once a time when Jews were forced to convert to Christianity if they wanted to escape persecution. Overlapping with this time were times when many Jews persisted in their religion but kept it secret, "passing" as Christian, while revealing their Jewish identity to intimates. By far the most significant form of discrimination suffered by Jews in Europe and North America in the modern era, however, is the form that Yoshino calls "covering": they may be full and equal (sort of) members of Protestant society if they talk and dress like WASPs, and do not flaunt their religion before others; in short, if they are not "too Jewish." In the mid-twentieth century, upwardly mobile Jewish parents gave their children WASP names, urged them to avoid their too-Jewish peers, and made sure they went to WASP schools where they would get the "right" social connections. I know older Jews who flinch, even today, before "out" Jews of their own generation, because the expressions and mannerisms of those Jews are exactly what their parents drilled them not to display.

Women, too, encounter a demand for "covering," but in a more complicated, mixed-up form. At times, women are urged to adopt stereotypical male behavior. A female law student is urged to be aggressive and talkative, to wear a black suit, to mask her emotions, not to have children or to say nothing about them if she does. But at other times (and in other careers), women are penalized if their dress and manner are not "feminine" enough. How on earth any sane person could ever decode these social rules is beyond me. Our confusion is clearly revealed by Yoshino's lists of women's "masculine" and "feminine" characteristics, since many professional women possess most of the items on both lists: they avoid pastels and floral designs, and they are aggressive, ambitious, assertive, athletic, competitive, individualistic, and self-reliant; but they also wear earrings and makeup, are sympathetic and yielding, and perform "nurture" functions at work, "like counseling and mentoring." So who would be surprised that women get criticized and downgraded from both directions: sometimes for being "too masculine," sometimes for being not "masculine" enough?

The story of any minority's progress, argues Yoshino, can be charted by examining these three stages: first, the demand for conversion; second, the demand for "passing"; third, and last, the demand for "covering." Not all three categories apply to all groups. Women were never asked to "convert," for obvious reasons, or even to "pass," and African Americans had no realistic option of "conversion." Most minorities in America today, according to Yoshino, no longer face demands for conversion or passing—but all, to some extent, face the demand for covering, for assimilation to majority norms. And this demand, while less oppressive than the other two, is profoundly unfair, burdening minorities in ways that majorities are not burdened.

Moreover, the demand is fraught with psychological danger. How can a person really have equality when she has to push some of her most deeply rooted commitments under the rug, treating them as something shameful and socially inappropriate? Surely the lives of gays in America have improved markedly now that they are typically not subjected to enforced conversion procedures, and may even be "out" with impunity; but being "out," as Yoshino rightly shows, is a spectrum, and the law professor whose colleagues tolerate his known gayness but who urge him not to engage in gay politics, or not to teach sexual-orientation law, or not to "flaunt" his orientation through public displays of affection, encounters a demand that is constricting. So, Yoshino concludes, we should not pat ourselves on the back because we tolerate people who are different, when we are imposing demands that deform and humiliate. Instead we must think about how we can produce a society where people are free to be themselves.

This is a helpful and important idea, and Yoshino argues well that we need to make it central to our social debates. But what is original about his book is not so much its central argument, which was adumbrated by Goffman, as the way in which it puts flesh on Goffman's concept through an arresting personal narrative. Yoshino once wanted to be a poet, he tells us, and it was his struggle with his gay identity that turned him to law. But he is still a wonderful writer, and what makes his rather routine "coming-out story" interesting is its literary beauty, which may have a kind of Brokeback Mountain impact on the parts of "straight" society that encounter the book. Here is how Yoshino describes his first realization that he was in love with a man:

One glittering afternoon, we walked along the Charles River. It was a Sunday—the riverside drive was hedged with sawhorses, closed to cars. The cyclists sheared the air. Dazzled by the needles of light stitching the water, I turned to watch him watch them. I noticed his eyelashes were reflected in his eyes, like awnings in windowpanes. As I tried to make sense of that reflection, I found I could not look away. His irises were brown, clouding into orange, with brighter flecks around his pupils. . . .

It hardly mattered that I knew he was straight. I experienced my desire for him, which was a pent-up desire for many men, as having an absolute absolved necessity. Just as the brain seems larger than the skull that contains it, so did my desire seem grossly to exceed the contours of my body. I thought if I could only make him experience the strength of what I felt, he could not demur.

Yoshino's daring choice to alternate between narrative and analysis is vindicated by the skill with which he does both. What emerges from the long account of his depression, his search for love, his coming out to his parents (whose first thought is that now they can never go back to Japan), his turn to law and political activism, is a picture of a strong and decent man who has managed to protect his capacity for love and joy despite the social pressures that he so shrewdly exposes. Although he is an activist and feels solidarity with other gays and lesbians, he does not romanticize defiance or trash stable affection; indeed, one of the biggest costs he ascribes to the "covering" demand is a cost in the ability to express love in a way that is simply first-personal and not tinged with political shock.

The first part of the book is devoted primarily to this autobiographical narrative, with brief glimpses of the analysis to come. Yoshino then presents a detailed analysis of gay covering and somewhat shorter analyses of race-related and gender-related covering. He briefly alludes to similar issues in the areas of religion and disability. Finally, after some consideration of potential legal remedies for the covering problem, he concludes that law will not really be of much avail in this area, that the real struggle must be fought informally, in families and in civil society. As a first step, we can at least promote a lot of public conversation about the demands we make on people.

II

In its contention that covering is a central human problem in American society today, Yoshino's book is convincing, and also moving. But there is more that needs to be said. I wish the book had somewhat more of a comparative and historical dimension, because it is clear that, whatever problems afflict the United States today, this country is much more accepting of public differences of many sorts than societies in most other times and places. One has only to think of the Victorian Britain assailed in Mill's *On Liberty* to see that a good deal of progress has been made.

It would also have been very instructive to do a detailed comparison of the assimilation demands made of Jews in present-day Europe and in the United States. Yoshino is just wrong, I think, when he says that there is increasing pressure on Jews today to conform to the WASP paradigm. Indeed, you can chart the progress Jews have made against "covering" in many ways, not least by noticing the flowering of Hebrew, yarmulkes, and even prayer shawls in Reform Judaism, that once most middle-class and assimilationist of denominations. On a recent visit to Hebrew Union College, the cradle of Reform, I studied the photographs of graduating classes of rabbis from the 1860s until the present day. The biggest change—apart from the inclusion of women—was the gradual de-covering of rabbinical dress. At one time all wore black suits, all were clean-shaven and bare-headed. Today many have beards, all wear yarmulkes, and almost all (including the women, of course) wear a tallis. We really have moved beyond the melting pot.

So how did America come to permit the gradual self-expression of Jews as Jews, and why is that expressive freedom still largely denied them in Europe? Most Americans recoil at France's insensitivity to the marks of religious identity (yarmulkes are banned in school along with the more notorious Muslim head scarf), and at Italy's insistence (until now) that hanging a crucifix in front of every public school classroom is just fine as an expression of "our culture." My peeve of the week is that Finland just scheduled a major public discussion of the future of the Finnish democracy (including the entire parliament) on Yom Kippur—and despite the presence of Jews in the legislature. I (as an invited speaker) was the first to break this news to them. Either these Jews are very ignorant, or the demand for "covering" silenced them.

This is a general issue, and it goes way back to the founding. From the mid-seventeenth century on, one can find public sensitivity at least to religious difference: to Quakers who refused to take their hats off in court; to Jews who refused to testify on Saturday; even to refusals of military service, as George Washington reassures the pacifist Quakers that their "conscientious scruples" will be treated with "the utmost delicacy and tenderness." Europe was not like this until a long time later—if, indeed, it has ever become like this, since we see rather little "delicacy and tenderness" in European debates about Islam these days.

If, then, covering is the regime of the hour in America (or in some parts of America) with respect to same-sex relationships, it might be helpful to ask whether this is because we are in general a land where covering reigns, or because we are a land that has particular difficulty with sexual matters generally, and sexual orientation in particular. It is the latter, I think; and so the public conversation demanded by Yoshino needs to be not a conversation about the prejudice and conformism, the excessive and even coercive universalism, that allegedly frustrates the multicultural realities of American life, as a result of which we all agree to respect difference and authenticity but, rather, a more specific and deeply uncomfortable conversation about sex, gender, and family.

Since Yoshino's tone is romantic, and poetically discreet, his book never really talks about sex. But if sex between men is what the panic is all about, as I think on the whole it is, then romantic talk will not reach the problem. In this way, Yoshino's narrative is quite unlike *Brokeback Mountain*, because it lets readers have an easy time of it: they can, if they want, imagine Yoshino as a disembodied spirit, and they are not forced to think about sex acts that many Americans find revolting. A significant part of the problem of gay life in America goes unaddressed, since anti-gay feeling is not just about difference, it is centrally about sex.

Another problem with Yoshino's analysis is its concept of authenticity. Yoshino smartly refuses the easy idea that authenticity can be measured by the extent to which a minority group buys into a specifically minority stereotype. Though at times, early in the book, he appears to suggest that a woman who fixes her own car, or an Asian who listens to NPR (his example), or a gay man who does not care about political activism is by definition inauthentic, he ultimately rejects this notion—and a good thing, too, since it is just as tyrannical as the regime of covering that it opposes. Just as an adolescent needs to learn that individuality does not mean doing the opposite of what one's parents recommend—such oppositional behavior is no less determined by parental norms than is perfect conformity—so, too, minorities are cruel and deforming if they insist that only stereotypical behavior (of a sort that is quite likely to be a back-formation of some type from dominant norms) defines one as a "real" black and not an "oreo," a "real" gay and not a "normal."

While Yoshino refuses (somewhat inconstantly) the bankrupt route of defining authenticity as rebellion, he does not provide a positive analysis. Philosophical accounts of autonomy (which require reflection, critical scrutiny of traditions, and so on) have a lot to contribute to the further analysis that never emerges. Mill, Kant, and modern writers such as Gerald Dworkin and Marilyn Friedman would all have been quite helpful to Yoshino in crafting a normative account of autonomy that could separate mindless conformity from a genuinely thoughtful choice of a mainstream way of life. Yoshino appears not to be interested in philosophy. Instead, he turns to the psychoanalyst Winnicott and his conceptions of the "True Self" and the "False Self."

Now, I love Winnicott as much as Yoshino does (and have said why in these pages), but the True Self is a concept that Winnicott defined in several ways, some of them verging on an excessive romanticism. At times Winnicott suggests, helpfully and attractively, that the True Self is something like the autonomous self of the philosophers: it is the organized set of whatever commitments and values stand the test of reflection, so that we are willing to identify our life and our selfhood with them. That is the sort of concept Yoshino needs in order to ask which aspects of a minority identity are truly central, part of our autonomy, and which parts are more peripheral. This aspect of Winnicott fits well with Yoshino's call for more reflection and debate—but often Winnicott (who was so deeply bruised by the puritanical conformism of his Methodist family that he was sexually impotent until he was past forty) speaks in more romantic terms of a hidden inner core that is incommunicable in language, suggesting that any contact at all with other people and the world deforms the True Self. (Emily Brontë was one of his favorites, and he particularly identified with Cathy in *Wuthering Heights*.) So it really is not helpful for Yoshino to refer vaguely to Winnicott: he needs to tell us which Winnicott he means, and to give some analytical precision to what Winnicott left vague and amorphous.

We see clearly enough what Yoshino is against, but until we see more clearly what he is for, we have no confidence that we have really understood him. He writes as if there is only one thing that a person really is, and all other social presentations of self are somehow "false" (though, with Winnicott, he does admit that the False Self can be useful). But people are usually a tumultuous mixture of elements, and it may be very unclear what any person "really" is; it is very unlikely that there is one unitary thing that each of us "is." A "covered" self might be the real and sincere way one presents oneself as a worker (say, not alluding to one's own personal problems at work), or even as a friend or lover (say, trying to suppress one's selfishness, or anger, or anxiety). Sometimes covering is just discretion, and protective of others. Discretion, like self-expression, is often a social good. There may be wild or silly or childlike elements of the self that emerge in intimate contexts, and these would be utterly out of place elsewhere. They would lose their delight if the workplace suddenly opened itself to admit them. This does not make these other contexts repressive, or one's behavior in them somehow squeezed and defective.

Often, too, external demands help people develop richer and more variegated selves. Educators who believed that the best school was one that imposed no external demands, letting children express themselves as they pleased at all times, soon learned that the children grew up not free but unfree, lacking both crucial knowledge and trained expressive capacities. After all, what art worth anything is created spontaneously by children? As a once-aspiring poet, Yoshino should know that external discipline is usually a necessary condition of all expression worthy of the name. And what is true of art is also true of virtue: one does not learn to be sensitive to the needs of others without taxing discipline, which imposes covering demands that often last the entirety of a life. All this needs sorting out. Yoshino clearly does not accept the extreme romantic view according to which all social norms are bad; but he says much too little about what he is for. There is a large hole at the heart of the book, to be filled in by whatever the reader can come up with that works better than slavish adherence to conformity.

More troubling, since this is a book by a law professor, is that Yoshino seems to have relatively little interest in the law. He does not even state legal issues accurately. His treatment of the legal issues involved in the major gay-rights cases is cursory but not truly bad; the same cannot be said of his casual treatment of the legal issues surrounding disability and, above all, religion. Yoshino says that in these two areas America has adopted a "principle of accommodation," and he goes on to give some examples of how that principle works in practice (accommodations for persons with disabilities in the workplace, the Supreme Court's decision that the Amish need not send their children to the last two years of required public school). Analytically, however, he does not even get started, since he never makes a distinction that is absolutely basic: between accommodations resulting from legislation and accommodations resulting from judicial interpretation of constitutional requirements.

The Americans with Disabilities Act is legislation. The Supreme Court has a role in interpreting it, but it did not create it. Very different are some of the accommodations granted to religious minorities, such as exemptions from the draft, or the educational dispensation given to Amish children: these are judicially mandated accommodations that give people the right to be exempt from laws passed by a majority and applicable to all citizens. This distinction is crucial because virtually nobody thinks that legislative accommodations are a bad thing (though there may be some limits to how some of them can be made consistent with the establishment clause). A long judicial tradition, by contrast, thinks that judicially created accommodations are a very bad thing, an example of courts riding roughshod over democracy.

Yoshino not only fails to state this conflict, he rides roughshod over it. Quoting from Justice Sandra Day O'Connor to exemplify the "accommodation principle," he neglects to inform the reader that she is describing the regime of accommodation that once existed but that the majority opinion in *Employment Division v. Smith* (1990) has just uprooted, to her great displeasure. Nor can we capture the ongoing judicial debate well in Yoshino's terms, as a debate between people who like covering and people who do not like it. Justice Antonin Scalia is happy to go along with many legislative accommodations (even when they concern religious drug use, which was the issue in Smith); he just thinks that judges should not usually be in the business of imposing them.

And even under the less accommodation-friendly regime that Scalia initiated in Smith, there is room for minorities to complain. Santeria worshippers in Hialeah got the Court to toss out a regulation forbidding animal sacrifice that clearly targeted them in particular, and this with Scalia's approval, since he found clear evidence of discriminatory intent. More daringly, Justice Samuel Alito, while an appellate judge, ruled that the Newark police might not deny Muslim police officers the right to wear beards for religious reasons, given that they had allowed a secular exemption for people with a rare skin condition. This case went further than Scalia's "neutrality" theory suggested, since there was no finding of discriminatory intent. It was, and is, an admirable decision, within the confines of the present legal regime.

But Yoshino does not even give us the difference between the pre-*Smith* and the post-*Smith* regimes, or state the current judicial understanding at both state and federal levels. (Many states have adopted the pre-*Smith* accommodation-friendly principle as a feature of state law, and the Religious Land Use and Institutionalized Persons Act has protected important areas of accommodation at the federal level, including, recently, the right of minority-religion prisoners to opportunities for worship that many states had denied them.) It was a mistake to treat this fascinating area of law so casually, because it gives us rich insights as to how a regime that is concerned not just with conversion and passing, but also with expressive conduct, can be implemented through law.

If Yoshino had gone into the religion cases, he would have had to face an issue that he nowhere faces: what reasons for exemptions from laws of general applicability should a legal regime recognize? Or, to use Yoshino's language, what types of covering should it forbid? Ours has focused on the specialness of religion—after all, that is what the free exercise clause protects, not the "free exercise of culture," or the "free exercise of identity," or anything else. "Religion" was clearly understood at the time of the founding as a broad concept: early drafts often use the term "rights of conscience," and my guess is that the final wording came in only because of the decision to focus on "exercise" as well as belief, and because the phrase "free exercise of conscience" was an anomaly, just not a phrase that anyone had used in these debates.

Whatever the Framers meant to protect (and we should remember that around 80 percent of Americans in the early years of the republic were not members of any organized church, though most were Christians of some kind), the tradition of interpretation has understood the notion of "religion" relatively capaciously—at the very least to include non-theistic religions such as Buddhism, Confucianism, and Taoism. During the Vietnam War, the Court went still further, giving exemptions from the draft to two young men whose beliefs were *sui generis*. One, Seeger, called his view "religious" and provided a metaphysical account to go with it. The other, Welsh, crossed out "religious" on his conscientious objector form, and plainly had what we might call a comprehensive ethical doctrine entailing non-killing. The Court stretched "religion" to the limit here, obviously trying to show respect for conscience even when conscience did not take an organized or traditional shape.

Yet the Court has never dropped the general idea that religious reasons are special. A worker who refused to work on Saturday because the day-care centers are closed, citing reasons of family obligation, or one who pointed out that her ethnic minority held its regular group meetings only on Saturday, would get the brush-off. A Jew or a Seventh-Day Adventist would not, because our tradition believes that reasons of conscience are somehow special. What exactly reasons of conscience are, and why they are special, remains deeply obscure, and some legal thinkers find the special place for religion simply unconscionable. (They tend to defend Scalia's less protective *Smith* standard, for quite different reasons from the institutional reasons Scalia used.)

I would like to know what Yoshino thinks about all this. When an employee wants to wear cornrows at work, is this an issue of conscience?

(Of course, race is constitutionally special for different reasons, so what we need here is an example of ethno-cultural dress that is not racially coded.) What if I have large and conspicuous tattoos, which express my personal conception of an authentic life, and my employer tells me that I have to cover them in the workplace? Is there any reason why the law should listen to my complaint, and, if so, what account of the protected areas of expression could coherently be given?

Yoshino tells us—and this is all that he tells us about the law of accommodation—that certain reasons for making "covering" demands should be disallowed: prejudice, bias, animus. But most of the covering demands in today's world are motivated not by those things, but by a love of uniformity, or administrative simplicity, or even a love of country (as in the compulsory flag-salute cases). And even these otherwise admirable reasons have an uphill battle when issues of conscience are at stake, or at least they did before *Smith*, and do now, in a narrower set of cases. What O'Connor valued about the pre-*Smith* regime (rightly, in my view) was that it ensured that the state had to show a "compelling interest" if it was going to override a reason of conscience and impose a "substantial burden" on the free exercise of religion of any person. Just any old hand-waving about administrative efficiency would not do.

Should this asymmetry between reasons of conscience and other reasons exist? Can it be defended? If it cannot be defended philosophically, should we still wish to retain it in the light of history, which shows us how conscience has been trampled by the state again and again? And if we do not retain the idea of the specialness of conscience, don't we just have to get rid of the idea of accommodation as a workable legal idea? There is a lot about law in this topic, then, and Yoshino seems oddly uninterested in these decisive dimensions of his complaint. In this sense, the book's melodramatic subtitle is deceptive. Although Yoshino does speak of a new attitude to "civil rights" that thinks of universal human rights norms as being gradually applied in informal social interactions, the term "civil rights" usually refers to enforceable legal rights, which is what Yoshino, in the end, does not think most rights against covering demands are.

Perhaps Yoshino's lack of interest in real civil rights is not so surprising, given his central focus on gay issues. People usually are not disgusted by the religions of others. (There are exceptions: the Mormons come to mind, and perhaps the Jehovah's Witnesses.) So those inequalities are amenable to legal redress, and even in colonial America people could understand that liberty of conscience is something precious to all, as much to those one considers damned as to those one considers saved. When people are disgusted by the sex acts of others, by contrast, law is a pretty blunt instrument, as Yoshino in the end concludes. People who are disgusted really do not believe that liberty of sexual self-expression is valuable for all. Law can tell people that they cannot turn their disgust reactions into legal penalties, and that, at last, is something. Sodomy laws are no more, and in many areas of life gays and lesbians have also won protections against workplace discrimination. In some places they are winning at least the civil rights associated with marriage, if not marriage itself. To counter the persistent demand for covering, however, it seems likely that time and social change will be necessary, because law has done almost as much as it can do on its own.

Yoshino calls for public debate and reasoned conversation. Those are good things to call for. But the issue demands more. It demands also an effort of culture: works of art, high art and popular art that touch the public imagination and inspire it to feel empathy with relationships that are now viewed with loathing. To that humane public poetry, Yoshino's lyrical and thought-provoking book makes a significant contribution.

# CHAPTER TWENTY-SIX

# Man Overboard

HARVEY C. MANSFIELD (2006), *Manliness*

I

Suppose a philosophical scholar—let us call this scholar S—with high standards, trained in and fond of the works of Plato and Aristotle, wished to investigate, for a contemporary American audience, the concept of "manliness," a concept closely related to the one that Plato and Aristotle called *andreia*, for which the usual English rendering is "courage." (Harvey Mansfield himself tells us that *andreia* is his subject.) How would this scholar go about it? Well, following the lead of Aristotle, S would probably begin by laying out the various widespread beliefs about the topic, especially those held by reputable people. S would also consider the opinions of well-known philosophers. In setting down all these opinions, S would be careful to get people's views right and to read their writings carefully, looking not just for assertions but also for the arguments that support them.

Inevitably this welter of opinions would contain contradictions—not just between one thinker and another, but also within the utterances of a single thinker. People are amazingly able to live with contradictions, since most people do not stop to sort these matters out in the way that Socrates recommended. People also use terms imprecisely and ambiguously, so S's inquiry would uncover much fuzziness and equivocation. Nor do most people most of the time, when they make statements of the form "Manliness is X," pause to tell us whether they mean to say that X is a necessary condition of manliness, or a sufficient condition, or both, or neither. So S would have to sort all this out, too. ("Don't use your feminine logic on me," I can already hear my partner saying teasingly in the background, as he typically does when words such as "necessary condition" are wheeled onto the stage.)

Carefully, S would set out the puzzles, untangling opinions like tangled strands of yarn. (Women do so well at logic, says Aristophanes' Lysistrata, because they have all that experience detangling and delousing, whereas men, who are impatient creatures, just like to wave their shields around.) Finally S would try to produce an account that seemed to be the best one, preserving the deepest and most basic of the opinions and discarding those that contradict them. S would then hold this definition out publicly, inviting all comers to try things out with their own reasoning, and then accept the proposed definition or improve upon it.

Being a friend of the Greeks, S would naturally have curiosity about the cross-cultural aspects of this particular topic. It is evident that Athenians of the fifth and fourth centuries B.C.E. had rather different ideas about manliness from those of modern Americans. A lot of them thought that manliness naturally expressed itself in a preference for young men over women as sexual partners, and that the most manly of the gods, Zeus and Poseidon, enjoyed such lovers. Most Americans, even if they grudgingly grant that men in same-sex relationships are potentially manly, would shrink at the thought that Jesus or Jehovah had any such inclinations. Many Athenians, moreover, and even more Spartans thought that erotic attraction between males was a fine cement for a military combat unit—something that the American military is so far from thinking that it would rather not think anything at all about the topic. So S would investigate these differences, and these would naturally lead S to the copious cross-cultural literature on manliness that by now exists: to the work of, say, Daniel Boyarin, on how Jewish males refashioned Roman norms of manliness, making the astonishing claim that the true man sits still all day with a book, and has the bodily shape of someone who does just that; or to work on Indian conceptions of manliness, contrasting the sensuous Krishna, playing his flute, with the tougher norms of manliness recommended by the Raj. A scholar with S's curiosity and love of truth would find in this material rich food for reflection.

Harvey Mansfield's credentials suggest to the reader that he will behave like S. He is a prominent political philosopher, recently retired from a chair at Harvard University, who has written widely about philosophical texts. He regularly taught a well-known class in the classics of Greek political thought. By his own account, the works of Plato and Aristotle are particularly important to him. Moreover, Mansfield has become famous as a defender of high academic standards and an opponent of "grade inflation." He likes to excoriate his faculty colleagues for their alleged laxness and looseness.

It quickly becomes evident, however, that *Manliness* is not the book that our imagined S would have written. To begin with, it is slipshod about facts—even the facts that lie at the heart of his argument. He repeatedly tells us that "all previous societies have been ruled by males," producing Margaret Thatcher as a sole recent exception. Well, one has to forgive Mansfield for not adducing Angela Merkel or Han Myung-Sook or Michelle Bachelet, since these female leaders won their posts, presumably, after his book went to press. One might even forgive Mansfield for not knowing about female heads of state in Mongolia, Argentina, Iceland, Latvia, Rwanda, Finland, Burundi, Bermuda, Mozambique, Jamaica, Nicaragua, Dominica, Malta, Liberia, and Bangladesh. Those are relatively small countries, and one would have to be curious about what is going on in them. But one can hardly overlook Mansfield's neglect of the very newsworthy recent or current female leaders of New Zealand (Jenny Shipley, Helen Clark), Turkey (Tansu Ciller), Poland (Hanna Suchocka), Norway (Gro Harlem Brundtland), France (Edith Cresson), Canada (Kim Campbell), Sri Lanka (Sirimavo Bandaranaike, and now her daughter), the Philippines (Corazon Aquino, Gloria Arroyo), and Pakistan (Benazir Bhutto, a government major at Harvard who might have taken Mansfield's class). And what might one say about Mansfield's utter neglect of Indira Gandhi and Golda Meir, two of the most influential politicians of the twentieth century? Don't we have to think, in the face of these cases, that his assertions are some sort of elaborate charade, a pretense that the world is the way some audience would like it to be, whether it is that way or not?

So Mansfield is not overly concerned with fact. A few minutes on Google would have made these facts available to a minimally inquiring mind. Is he, then, at least concerned with logic? Only if his concern is to demonstrate, boldly, his disdain for it. After being confronted with a bewildering range of attributes of manliness—confidence, aggressiveness, protectiveness, independence, ability to command, eagerness to feel important, love of attention—we think that we are finally getting somewhere when Mansfield announces that his own definition of manliness is "confidence in the face of risk." We might have some issues with the proposal. Don't brave people often feel afraid? Aristotle thinks they do, and rightly, for the loss of life is especially painful when one has a good life. And what about risk? Doesn't manliness also come into play in facing the inevitable, such as each person's own death? And what sort of risk? Are we talking about the physical realm or the moral realm? Barry Bonds has a lot of physical confidence while being (apparently) a moral coward. Socrates probably wasn't up to much furniture-moving, and Seneca is always whining about his stomach problems; but both had the confidence that counts morally, when they stood up to unjust governments and went to their deaths. So the candidate definition—"confidence in the face of risk"—needs to answer a lot of questions. But at least it is something, a definite proposal from which we can move forward.

Imagine the shock to the feminine logic-loving mind, then, when within two pages the definition is, if not withdrawn, at least ignored, and quite different formulations, inconsistent with it, trot forward like eager children vying for attention. Manliness is aggressiveness, combined with promiscuousness in sex. It is the "brute spirit of aggression." It is not mere aggression, but only "aggression that develops a cause it espouses." It is "a claim on your attention." It is the "willingness to challenge nature combined with confidence . . . that one can succeed." "In the end aggression is all there is." It is "stubbornness added to rationality."

Mansfield does tell us that his definition will shift as he moves, in later chapters, "from aggression to philosophical courage." But these examples are all quite close together in the early portion of the text; and the later chapters do not supply a new, coherent, contradiction-free account. Things do not get better, then. Philosophers get mentioned more often, but are never emulated. We never find Mansfield even worrying about his mass of contradictions or trying to clean up the account. On the logical principle that from a contradiction everything and anything follows, I conclude that *Manliness* says it all. Try that out on the back jacket.

As for the careful reading of other thinkers' works that our friend S would recommend, such reading is nowhere to be found in these pages. Mansfield is horrendous when he reads feminist thinkers. He gives us a hasty, superficial summary of several bits of some early works (de Beauvoir, Millett, Greer, Firestone), but absolutely no sense of how any of these women argues, and no sense of what the women's movement has produced since the early 1970s. (Cursory references to Carol Gilligan and to an exchange between Judith Butler and Seyla Benhabib do not tell us anything about the framework of their ideas.) Susan Okin is mentioned once in the text, and Andrea Dworkin is ignored altogether. (Catharine MacKinnon turns up in the bibliography.) By such strategic omissions, Mansfield is able to hoodwink his implied reader into thinking that all feminists want to have a lot of sex without commitment, and that they ignore or denounce the family, and that they "do not worry about violence in sex, and they do not refer to the respect in which one should hold one's partner." This last is the most extraordinary claim of all. If any topics could be said to be absolute clichés of modern feminist thought, they would be the topics of sexual violence and sexual respect (treating a person as a person instead of as an object).

But never mind. It turns out that Mansfield is an equal opportunity misreader. Male philosophers get the same slipshod treatment. To mention a typical example, Mansfield evidently believes, and asserts with high-spirited glee, that for him to require the reading of Mill's *On Liberty* in his class at Harvard, a private university, is "contrary to [the work's] main thesis." He seems to think that Mill's "harm principle" supplies limits on all human conduct, not just on the legal regulation of conduct: nobody can require anything of anyone, including the young, unless that person is harming others. This "reading" flies so flatly in the face of Mill's elaborate views about education, not to mention the plain meaning of the text of the fourth chapter of *On Liberty*, that one thinks with distress of this jokey aside being retailed to pseudo-knowing undergraduates almost as another example of manliness: "See? I can teach Mill as a required text, thus showing that I have contempt for his main idea."

Indeed, when we compare Mansfield to our decent-if-not-very-flashy S, it seems appalling that Mansfield has spent decades teaching great philosophical texts to undergraduates who cannot easily tell a careful reading from a careless one, or low standards from high ones—especially when the teacher keeps portraying himself as the bold defender of standards. Undergraduates typically take a while to learn to analyze the arguments in Plato logically and to care about things like validity, ambiguity, and contradiction. Many of them, then, will not notice how riddled with logical error and verbal ambiguity their teacher's pronouncements are. That is the sort of thing that they are in class to learn. But surely other, older people know. How did someone whose every paragraph is a stake in Socrates' heart come to be an exemplar of philosophical seriousness?

If the author of *Manliness* is far from being the patient philosophical type for whom we have been searching, who might he be? Plato's dialogues knew the answer: he is a rhetorician or a sophist, one of those theatrical types so admired by the conventionally ambitious men amply on display as Socrates' interlocutors. Far from seeking truth, the sophist seeks to put on a good show. Far from wanting premises that are correct, the sophist seeks premises that his chosen audience will find believable. Far from seeking analytical rigor, he offers a show of rigor in arguments that are riddled with ambiguity and equivocation and logical error. Far from submitting bravely to Socrates' questioning, he slinks away when the going gets tough, or cranks up the volume in order to try to drown out the courageous voice of the truth-seeking philosopher. Audiences love him—because, says Socrates, he is like a clever cook: instead of promoting true health, he goes after what his audience will eagerly gobble up.

That is Mansfield to a T. In this book that repeatedly proclaims its own manly boldness, offering its author as a John Wayne of the intellect, he serves up a concoction that is contrived mainly to delight the conservative audience that already lionizes Mansfield as the hero of high standards, the enemy of grade inflation, and the foe of feminism. Mansfield's daring physical prowess, he told a *New York Times Magazine* reporter, is displayed in his ability to move furniture around his house. His daring moral prowess is displayed in his ability to make speeches on the floor of the Harvard faculty opposing the creation of a women's studies program, a risky feat indeed. Should average readers wonder whether this does indeed bring him into competition with John Wayne, or even with the questionable Barry Bonds, Mansfield does not care an iota, because he has his expected audience dead to rights. Readers of *The Weekly Standard* and *National Review*, they are already devouring the logic-free, ambiguity-riddled concoction he has served up and smacking their lips.

Mansfield's intended readers do not care what modern feminism really says, and they know so little about the subject that they are likely not even to see how little of it Mansfield has described. From their youth they remember the chilling names of Millett, Greer, and Firestone, and they are sure that feminism cannot have had a thought since then. They certainly relish the tasty claim that sexual promiscuity is a central goal of the new feminism.

And just to be sure that they are utterly delighted, Mansfield smears all over the top of his dish a thick layer of sneers and jibes, rather like anchovy paste, delicious to some but revolting to others—patronizing characterizations of women as harboring a "secret liking for housework," or enjoying "the pleasurable duty of henpecking." Or this: "One has only to think of Jane Austen to be assured that women have a sense of humor, distributed in lesser quantities to lesser brains." At this point, I think, even some of the implied readers of this book might turn away. In fact, I suspect that Mansfield underestimates the care and the acuity of his chosen audience (or some of it) throughout his book.

## II

Mansfield's assertions (I cannot quite call them arguments) seem to be as follows. Manliness, the quality of which John Wayne (says Mansfield) is the quintessential embodiment, is a characteristic that societies rightly value. But modern feminism wants a society that has effaced all distinctions of gender, a society in which men and women have the same traits. This is a dangerous mistake, because manly aggression, though not altogether reliable, supplies something without which we cannot have a good or stable society. (Mansfield connects manliness not only to military performance but also to the ability to govern a nation, and, as we have seen, he denies that women who are not Mrs. Thatcher have this trait.) Since women are only rarely capable of manliness, a society in which both sexes have the same traits will have to be lacking in manliness. We should reject this aim, and, with it, modern feminism.

The second half of the book contains, as Mansfield has warned his reader, a more complex set of assertions, though they all lead to the same bottom line. Taking Theodore Roosevelt as his more complex icon of manliness, Mansfield notes that traditional John Wayne-style manliness is not necessarily combined with virtue. Indeed, traditional manliness is often linked to a Nietzschean sort of "nihilism," which accepts no restraints and desires to soar "beyond good and evil." (This reading of Nietzsche, like so many readings in the book, is not defended by any close look at an actual text. Is this the Nietzsche who prizes the disciplined virtue of the dancer, who teaches that *laisser aller*, the absence of restraint, is incompatible with any great achievement of any sort?) Theodore Roosevelt, though, did combine traditional manliness with virtue, thus showing that it is both possible and valuable to do so.

On the whole, however, men will allow the constraints of virtue to drag down their manly flights only if women insist on virtue as a condition of sex. So women's non-manly inclinations hold men in check. This old saw, which one encounters over and over again in the writings of Leo Strauss's followers, seems to derive not from a realistic look at life but from an opportunistic reading of Rousseau's *Emile*, minus all Rousseau's complexity and nuance. Rousseau shows clearly that the difference between Emile and Sophie is produced by a coercive regime that curbs Sophie's intelligence and even her physical prowess—she would have beaten Emile in the race had she not had to run in those absurd clothes. He also demonstrated, in his unpublished conclusion to the Emile-Sophie story, that a marriage so contracted would be a dismal failure, since parties so utterly distinct in moral upbringing would be totally unable to understand one another.

But back to feminism. Feminism (exemplified in Mansfield's book by a few carefully selected bits of early 1970s authors) wants women to reject virtue and to seek sexual satisfaction promiscuously. In effect, it teaches women to be as "nihilistic" as men. But women are doomed to dismal failure at this task, because their manliness is puny. Meanwhile, they will lose the hold they once had on men through modesty and virtue. They will therefore be more endangered: Mansfield actually asserts that a woman can resist rape only with the aid of "a certain ladylike modesty enabling her to take offense at unwanted encroachment"! (How does he handle the well-known fact that a large proportion of rapes are committed by men with whom the victim has already had an intimate relationship, or with whom she currently has one?) Society, meanwhile, will come to grief. So, once again, the lesson is that we ought to rid ourselves of feminism.

Where to begin? Since in Mansfield all roads lead back to the bogey of feminism, let us begin there. Modern feminism is a hugely diverse set of positions and arguments, but almost nobody has seriously suggested that gender distinctions ought to be completely eradicated. Indeed, much of the effort of legal feminism has been to get the law to take them seriously enough. Thus feminists have urged that rape law take cognizance of women's unequal and asymmetrical physical vulnerability. Some courts had refused to convict men of rape if the woman did not fight her attacker. In one recent Illinois case, the conviction was tossed out because the woman, about five feet tall and less than one hundred pounds, did not resist a two-hundred-pound attacker in a solitary forest preserve. But in a situation of great physical asymmetry, feminists have urged, fighting is actually a stupid thing to do, and in the Illinois case even crying out "No!" would have been stupid, given the extreme solitude of the place and the likelihood that shouting would provoke the attacker to violence. (I take this example from the feminist legal scholar Stephen Schulhofer. Mansfield utterly ignores the existence of male feminists, though they are many. Feminism is a concern with justice, not an exercise in identity politics.)

Feminists have also taken exception when insurance companies refused to offer pregnancy benefits and then claimed that they were not discriminating, because their policies protected all "non-pregnant persons" and refused to protect "pregnant persons," male and female. Catharine MacKinnon made the valuable observation that sameness of treatment is not enough for the truly "equal protection of the laws," when there are underlying physical asymmetries that significantly affect women's social functioning. The "equal protection of the laws" requires, instead, that society dismantle regimes of hierarchy and subordination. MacKinnon's strategy was based upon existing law in the area of race. Laws against miscegenation had been defended on the ground that they treat everyone alike: blacks cannot marry whites and whites cannot marry blacks. Yet the Supreme Court held that these laws violate the equal protection clause of the Fourteenth Amendment, because they uphold and perpetuate "white supremacy." The denial of pregnancy benefits, MacKinnon argued, was like that, a regime of male supremacy. The refusal to offer pregnancy benefits is now seen as a form of sex discrimination, thanks to feminist argument.

Feminists, then, have not typically sought a society in which there are no gender distinctions. They have challenged imposed and unchosen gender norms that interfere with women's freedom and functioning—seeking clothing, for example, in which one can do what one wants to do and is capable of doing (not like Sophie's absurd doll clothes). Anne Hollander has written eloquently of the way in which women have claimed the suit, that attribute of the successful man the world over, as their own, replacing with it those billowing petticoats that made women seem vaguely like mermaids, human on top and some hidden uncleanness below. But women's suits never have been and never will be precisely like men's suits—perhaps because women have better fashion sense, perhaps because color-blindness is a male sex-linked gene.

What feminists have sought above all is a society in which there are no sex-based hierarchies, in which the sheer luck of being born a female does not slot one into an inferior category for the purposes of basic political and social functioning. Just as society now refuses to discriminate on grounds of religion and race, so too it should refuse to discriminate on grounds of sex.

If we now consider the example of religion, we can easily see that non-discrimination does not entail homogeneity. Indeed, the connection, if any, works in the opposite direction. Precisely because the United States does not have an established church, and refuses to discriminate politically on grounds of religious membership, people are extremely free to choose any religion they want, to make one up if they want to, or to have none if they want none. Wherever political privileges are attached to religious membership, this freedom, even if nominally protected, is not total: most people want to be in the dominant group, so it is not surprising that there are lots of Protestants in officially Protestant nations, and so forth. What makes the United States the most religiously diverse and colorful nation in the world (perhaps in company with India) is its firm commitment to non-discrimination (which it also shares with India). Go and convert to Buddhism if you want, or to the newest sect of Pentacostalism. Be a Jew and do not feel pressure to convert to Christianity, as Jews always did in Establishmentarian Europe. Your political privileges will not be affected by your religious choices.

What non-discrimination means for gender difference is not yet clear, because people have only begun to experience non-discrimination. Using the religion analogy, however, we might predict that once gender is no longer a source of hierarchy and subordination, people will express themselves more and more personally where gender is concerned. Even now, some women wear skirts and others feel more comfortable in pants. Some wear their hair very short and others very long. More and more, form follows function. Women's athletic clothes are not the same as men's athletic clothes; gone are the bad old days when female runners had to wear an ill-fitting garment designed for the male torso. But they are suited to running, which is what matters here; and the same garment is not suited to the office (whereas Sophie had to wear her modest housewifely clothes for running and studying and flirting alike).

In sum, when people are not forced, their choices make sense for them and the lives they want to lead. So, too, in relationships: some women will choose flirtiness, others a "manly" directness. Some men will like taking care of children (if government and employers give them decent support); others will try to avoid care, and women will be able, let us hope, to see that one coming in advance and make the choices they want to make in response. Some women will attach great importance to their identity as women (as some African Americans attach great importance to that identity), and others will care less. What really troubles Mansfield, I fear, is personal liberty itself, and the diversity that a culture of personal self-expression, fostered by non-discrimination, brings with it.

### III

But what about manliness? Do we want John Waynes around, or don't we? Manliness, all of Mansfield's singulars and abstractions notwithstanding, is clearly not a single trait. It is a family of traits: upper-body strength, aggressiveness (and there are many forms of that), physical endurance, mental endurance, physical courage, moral courage, and probably many more. Barry Bonds might be said by many to be "manly," but if we are thinking of the Gary Cooper of *High Noon* as our paradigm, we will find Bonds quite unmanly. When the Chicago Cubs catcher Michael Barrett slugged the Chicago White Sox catcher A. J. Pierzynski, unprovoked, callers on Chicago sports talk shows (overwhelmingly male) generally agreed that Barrett's gesture, "manly" by the Mansfield standard of "brute aggression," was a sign of weakness, not strength. They understood that he was cracking under the stress of a miserable season, and that a "real man" would (like Gary Cooper) avoid conflict unless it were inevitable.

Sure, we need upper-body strength, at least in some functions, though these are fewer today, even in the military. (Even Mansfield grants that women outdo men in endurance, another valued physical characteristic.)

And sure, we need some of that old punch-'em-out aggression, though boys need to learn that some types are better and other types are worse. (Significantly, all Chicago White Sox fans, including this one, applauded rookie Brian Anderson when he ran out of the dugout and joined in the ensuing brawl, punching Barrett's teammate John Mabry and thus standing up for his own teammate—the very teammate who had made the six-foot-two, 215-pound rookie walk around in a female cheerleader's outfit, as a comic form of hazing.)

Above all, we need to follow Aristotle's lead and distinguish the sort of courage that stands up for a valuable goal from both upper-body strength and punch-'em-out aggression. That sort of courage, which was the only sort that Aristotle thought a true virtue, always good no matter what the circumstance, requires the ability to reflect on what risks are worth running, on what goals are noble, and what goals are trivial or even base. It is because the Gary Cooper character exemplifies this sort of reflection, and not only because he is unafraid to face a villain, that he is deemed a hero; but one can have that sort of reflection and not have much in the way of physical strength. If we take Mansfield's candidate definition, "confidence in the face of risk," and ask which American presidents have exemplified this trait—when understood in Aristotle's way, meaning risks for ends that have been reasonably deemed to be important—who could be a better candidate than the other Roosevelt, who is mentioned only once in Mansfield's book?

Franklin Delano Roosevelt had that famous optimism that kept a nation together through the dark times of the Depression and then through global war. He stood up for people in situations that were risky in all sorts of ways (the danger of a socialist revolution, the dangers of countless deaths of innocent people, the dangers of Nazi Germany and imperial Japan). His ends can be plausibly seen as valuable and good. And yet he was hardly an icon of manliness in Mansfield's sense. He was reassuring more in the way that a good parent is reassuring than in the way that T.R. was (if he ever was) reassuring. Yes, he dissembled, making people think he could walk at least a little bit. So he did understand that the American public needed (and perhaps still needs) to see its president as manly in a more vulgar sense. But how many would have thought him a John Wayne, even then? There are some things to be said for T.R., but for Aristotelian manliness I'll take FDR any day.

Now let us come back to the gender question. If we ask whether the Aristotelian virtue of courage belongs more to men than to women, we will need to ask, first, what it is that makes people willing to take enormous risks for the sake of others. It is difficult to study that topic, but a beginning was made by Samuel P. Oliner and Pearl M. Oliner in their book *The Altruistic Personality*, a famous study of rescuers of Jews during the Holocaust. With careful social science techniques, they identified a number of variables that might be highly correlated with those courageous acts, and then they questioned rescuers to discover what traits they had. The two traits that they found most highly correlated with this sort of courage were what they call a "caring attitude" and a sense of "responsibility." The rescuers had all been brought up to think that people ought to care for one another, and that it was unacceptable to shirk responsibility for someone else's suffering if one could do something about it. That was why (the Oliners conclude) they stood up for strangers as they did, risking their lives in the process. Rescuers were, of course, both male and female. Their common bond was, however, a set of traits that, at least in terms of common gender stereotypes, are more "feminine" than "masculine." Kristin Monroe, working with the list of "righteous gentiles" from Yad Vashem, came to a similar conclusion in *The Heart of Altruism*.

If this is right, and if we want to produce young people who have the sort of courage that these rescuers embody, then we will want to be sure that boys and girls both grow up with the capacity for concern and care, and the ability to take responsibility for the situation of others—traits that seem to be sorely lacking in American society at present. It would have been nice to have a book on manliness that focused on this problem. Clearly ordinary people can become virtuous in the way that Aristotle recommends, and clearly neither gender has a monopoly on the virtue in question. The problem we have is that so many young people in our money- and fame-focused society do not get much experience taking care of anyone or anything, and are all too lacking in a sense of responsibility, as has been clearly shown in Dan Kindlon's *Too Much of a Good Thing* and other recent social scientific research on American adolescents.

What might one do about this, if one thought it a problem? A mandatory program of national service might be one way to begin bootstrapping courage—or true "manliness"—even if the materialistic and competitive culture of our high schools has left character in a pretty bad way, and even if families are all too uneven in the values they communicate to their children. We could also try to make primary and secondary education settings in which children learn the importance of care and social responsibility—a goal that has been greatly set back, of late, by the constant harping on scientific and technological proficiency, so important for competition in the global market, and the relative neglect of history, the humanities, and the arts.

Such reasonable and decent goals will be greatly impeded, however, if we do not even get to the point of distinguishing Franklin Delano Roosevelt from Michael Barrett, or, worse still, if we encourage young people to believe that the latter is better than the former. Even die-hard Cubs fans know better. Harvey Mansfield does not utterly reject such goals (I think), but his cavalier way with logic, his lack of definitional clarity, his ideological enthusiasm, and his tendency to romanticize characters similar to Bonds and Barrett make his book, well, uncourageous, just when we badly need to think well about how better to cultivate true courage.

# CHAPTER TWENTY-SEVEN

# Legal Weapon

CATHARINE A. MACKINNON (2006), Are Women Human?
And Other International Dialogues

Inequality on the basis of sex is a pervasive reality of women's lives all over
the world. So is sex-related violence. Rape by strangers and acquaintances,
rape within marriage, domestic violence, trafficking into sex work, the abuse
of women and girls in the pornography industry: In all these ways, argues
Catharine MacKinnon, women suffer aggression and exploitation, "because
we are women, systemically and systematically." Although violence against
women is certain to be underreported and undercounted, data still show a
tremendous amount of it everywhere. (Cross-cultural studies cited by
MacKinnon show that rates of violent domestic abuse are similar in the
United States, Japan, and India.) As a 1989 United Nations report summarizes, "The risk of violence and violation within the household is one thing
women, irrespective of their social position, creed, colour or culture, share in
common." So, too, is vulnerability to rape in wartime—the well-documented
mass rapes of Bosnian women being just one recent example of an appalling
reality that has characterized most armed conflicts.

Despite the prevalence of these crimes, they have not been well addressed
under international human rights law—if, indeed, they have been addressed
at all. Typically, there has been what MacKinnon calls a "double-edged
denial": The abuse is considered either too extraordinary to be believed or
too ordinary to constitute a major human rights violation. Or, as MacKinnon
says, "If it's happening, it's not so bad, and if it's really bad, it isn't happening." Until recently, abuses like rape and sexual torture lacked good human
rights standards because human rights norms were typically devised by men
thinking about men's lives. In other words, "If men don't need it, women
don't get it." What this lack of recognition has meant is that women have
not yet become fully human in the legal and political sense, bearers of equal,
enforceable human rights.

In recent years there has been progress. International agreements, above all the 1979 Convention on the Elimination of All forms of Discrimination Against Women (CEDAW), have given salience to sex-specific abuses such as domestic violence and sexual harassment. Creative use of existing laws has made it possible, in some instances, for women to win against their abusers in cases that cross national boundary lines. Meanwhile, women organizing through the informal social networks of nongovernmental organizations and the international women's movement have pressured states and the international community to act on issues like trafficking and rape in war. Indeed, as MacKinnon notes, "Women's resistance to their status and treatment" is now "the cutting edge of change in international human rights."

MacKinnon herself has played a moving role in these developments. Because she is so well known as a feminist thinker, it is easy to forget that MacKinnon is also a lawyer, and a very shrewd one. Representing a group of women who had been raped during the Bosnian conflict, in a case called *Kadic v. Karadzic*, she employed a little-known American law, the Alien Tort Claims Act, which allows plaintiffs to file civil suits against foreign citizens in U.S. courts, provided that the defendant can be served on U.S. soil. Previous users of the statute had been isolated individuals. While rejecting a class-action approach on the grounds that it would impose plaintiff status on women who might be unwilling to join in—the process, she argues, must be "accountable, personal, and responsive"—MacKinnon brought suit against Bosnian Serb leader Radovan Karadzic on behalf of a specific group of female clients, seeking damages for injuries consisting in "genocidal sexual atrocities perpetrated as a result of [his] policy of ethnic cleansing." Damages were sought for the named individuals, as was an injunction that Karadzic order the genocide to stop. On August 10, 2000, a jury in the State of New York awarded the plaintiffs a total of $745 million in compensatory and punitive damages and issued a permanent injunction. For her role in this landmark prosecution, MacKinnon was honored as one of the finalists in the 2001 "trial lawyer of the year" competition by the Trial Lawyers for Public Justice.

Now MacKinnon has gathered the speeches and articles that she has delivered over the past twenty years on sex equality and international law. The result is a sparkling book, perhaps her finest. Unsettling in the best sort of way, *Are Women Human?* shows her to be not only a prodigiously creative feminist thinker who can see the world from a fresh angle like nobody else (and I mean the angle of reality, as opposed to the usual one of half-reality) but also one of our most creative thinkers about international law. As elsewhere in MacKinnon's work, we find plenty of trenchant and eloquent writing; but we also find more systematic analysis and more extensive scholarship than we sometimes get, and the book is the richer for it.

MacKinnon's central theme, repeatedly and convincingly mined, is the hypocrisy of the international system when it faces up to some crimes against humanity but fails to confront similar harms when they happen to women, often on a daily basis. There is a category of torture, and we think we know how to define it. We think we know what it does: It uses violence to control and intimidate. And yet when violence is used to control and intimidate women "in homes in Nebraska . . . rather than prison cells in Chile," we don't call it torture, and we somehow think it is not the same thing. Torture in Chile is not explained away as the work of isolated sick individuals. We know it is political, and we can see how systemic it often is. When violence happens to women in Nebraska, we say, Oh well, that was only some sicko, and men really aren't like that. Well, given the numbers, shouldn't we ask more questions about that?

Again, we have a concept of war, and we think we know what war is: People get maimed and killed fighting over land and power. And yet when women get raped and beaten up by men who want to control them, we pay little heed. "It is hard to avoid the impression that what is called war is what men make against each other, and what they do to women is called everyday life."

As in her prior work, MacKinnon is caustic about the damage done by the traditional liberal distinction between a "public sphere" and a "private sphere," a distinction that insulates marital rape and domestic violence from public view and makes people think it isn't political. "Why isn't this political? . . . The fact that you may know your assailant does not mean that your membership in a group chosen for violation is irrelevant to your abuse. It is still systematic and group-based. It . . . is defined by the distribution of power in society."

In the two most deeply troubling articles in the collection, "Genocide's Sexuality" and "Women's September 11th," MacKinnon examines the internationally accepted definitions of genocide and terrorism, and argues that many acts of men against women meet one or both of these definitions. As defined under the UN convention on genocide, genocide is either killing or inflicting serious bodily or mental harm on members of a group, with intent to destroy that group either entirely or in part. The groups mentioned are "national, ethnical, racial, or religious" groups: So in that sense violence against women clearly doesn't qualify. On other grounds, however, one could argue that a great part of violence against women does involve a similar infliction of "serious harm" on women because they are women, and its aim can be said to be to destroy "in part"—for "destroy," if mental harm is sufficient for genocide, must mean not "kill" but "remove from the ranks of the fully human"—something that happens to women all the time.

Examining a wide range of cases in which rape occurs in the context of a recognized genocide (including both the Holocaust and the Bosnian conflict), MacKinnon argues that these rapes are not *sui generis*. Similar violations take place all the time. "In this light, what rape does in genocide is what it does the rest of the time: ruins identity, marks who you are as less, as damaged, hence devastates community, the glue of group." It's convenient not to notice a genocide this dispersed, this multinational, this perpetual. MacKinnon summons the international community to notice, and to grapple with the question of how to dignify violence against women as an atrocity worthy of the name. "If women were seen to be a group, capable of destruction as such, the term genocide would be apt for violence against women as well. But that is a big if."

Terrorism, she believes, is another concept that needs to be recast with women's lives in view. In confronting the reality of terrorism after 9/11, the international community had to find ways to conceptualize and condemn a new sort of organized violence that didn't fit previous definitions of war. It did so—but, again, it didn't notice the implications of the new concepts for the lives of women. Terrorism is unlike war in that the perpetrators are non-state actors who are not combatants in a formally declared conflict. "Common elements include premeditation rather than spontaneity, ideological and political rather than criminal motive, civilian targets (sometimes termed 'innocents'), and subnational group agents. What about violence against women fails to qualify?" A lot of this violence, including gang rapes and much stalking and sexual harassment, and most trafficking, is planned. Its victims are "innocents"—aren't they? And surely the status of women in relation to men is "political"—isn't it? And once again, the motives of men are not just those of the isolated criminal "sicko"; they are often quite fully ideological, expressing a view that women are there for men's use and control. What the precise consequences of the recognition of these similarities should be for law are not exhaustively developed. But one thing is very clear: States that make a big deal of saying that they will do this or that to states that "harbor terrorists" and yet fail to have the slightest interest in states that don't enforce laws forbidding violence against women are hypocritical. MacKinnon's aim is to expose this hypocrisy and get people involved in seeking creative legal remedies, acknowledging, as they do so, that women are full-fledged human beings deserving of the dignity of legal protections: "When will women be human? When?"

Throughout the book MacKinnon reasserts the conception of equality that has been, so far, her most influential contribution to legal thought. Similarity of treatment, she has argued throughout her work, is not sufficient for the true "equal protection" of the laws. Mere formal equality often masks, or even reinforces, underlying inequalities. We need to think, instead, of the idea of freedom from hierarchy, from domination and subordination. This insight had been influential in the law of race prior to MacKinnon's work. Thus, laws against miscegenation were defended on the ground that they treated blacks and whites similarly: Blacks can't marry whites, and whites can't marry blacks. The Supreme Court, however, invalidated those laws under the equal protection clause of the Fourteenth Amendment, saying that they upheld a regime of "White Supremacy." MacKinnon makes a parallel move in the area of sex: To deny women benefits that they need in order to function as equals (medical pregnancy benefits, for example) is to violate equal protection, even when the treatment of men and women is similar (no men get pregnancy benefits, and no women get them either). This insight has shaped legal thinking about sex equality, sexual harassment and the nature of the equal protection clause. It is widely agreed, for example, that MacKinnon's *Sexual Harassment of Working Women* is one of the most influential books by a legal academic, in terms of its actual influence on the law. The present book helpfully explains her equality theory again and shows how it operates in a range of international contexts.

While advancing ambitious theoretical arguments, *Are Women Human?* also shows MacKinnon's wide range as a comparative legal scholar, as she discusses tensions between Canada's Charter, which guarantees substantive sex equality, and the Meech Lake Accord, a failed set of amendments that offered protections for regional group rights; as she addresses an audience in India about related tensions between India's religious systems of "personal law" and its constitutional guarantee of sex equality; as she investigates the role played by rape and forced prostitution in the Holocaust; and as she reflects on the role that rape played in the genocide in Bosnia, drawing upon her clients' wrenching narratives of violation. The book also contains valuable insights at the meta level, particularly on feminist theory and its relationship to political reality. In "Theory Is Not a Luxury," MacKinnon addresses critics who doubt that "theory" provides anything useful for marginalized people. Some are uncomprehending men, for whom calling something "only a theory" is a way of devaluing it in contrast to (their view of) "reality." Some are women, who see theory as a male tool and would urge feminists to eschew it. Feminism needs theory, argues MacKinnon, because theory shows the world in a new way, using method to make it "accessible to understanding and change." Theory is not an enemy but a necessary ally of the "reality of women's lives," because that reality is frequently invisible until theory brings its salient features into prominence.

Unlike some types of theory, feminist theory, she argues, is bottom-up: It starts from the silenced reality of women's lives. Its "development as theory is impelled by the realities of women's situation." Its goal is to make that situation more visible, more comprehensible—not as a mere ideological construct but as what was, and is, happening. "As it turned out, once rescued from flagrant invisibility, women's realities could often be documented in other ways, and nearly anyone proved able to understand them with a little sympathetic application. . . . What we said was credible because it was real."

Because feminist theory, in her understanding, is committed to reality, MacKinnon is deeply troubled by some of the excesses of academic postmodernism. One of the gems in the collection is an essay called "Postmodernism and Human Rights," which ought to be required reading for all undergraduates and graduate students in the humanities. Here MacKinnon makes points that have also been made by other left-wing critics of postmodernism, notably Noam Chomsky and Tanika Sarkar, but she makes them with a devastating wit that is all her own. To say that gender is a social construct, she argues, is hardly to say that it is not there. "It means that it is there, in society, where we live." To say that feminists wrongly "essentialize" by ascribing common properties to women is to raise

> An empirical rather than a conceptual question. Do characteristics exist that can be . . . found in the reality of . . . the status of women across time and place. . . ? Women report the existence of such regularities: sex inequality, for one. It is either there or it is not. . . . Once it has been found to exist, to say it isn't there, show it isn't there—show, for example, that female genital mutilation is a collective delusion or harmless or a practice of equality. . . . What the postmodernists seem to be saying here is that they don't like the idea that women are unequal everywhere. Well, we don't like it either.

As for postmodernism's critique of universality and binary oppositions, she has this to say:

> The postmodern attack on universality also proves a bit too much. Inconveniently, the fact of death *is* a universal—approaching 100 percent. . . . Much to the embarrassment of the anti-essentialists, who prefer flights of fancy to gritty realities, life and death is even basically a binary distinction—and not a very nuanced one either, especially from the dead side of the line, at least when seen from the standpoint of the living, that is, as far as we know. And it is even biological at some point. So the idea that there is nothing essential, in the sense that there are no human universals, is dogma. Ask most anyone who is going to be shot at dawn.

MacKinnon's attack has no particular target or targets, although there are footnote references to several specific postmodern feminists. Instead, she issues a cheerful invitation: "Far from attempting to tar them all with this brush, I invite anyone to disidentify with what I describe and to stop doing it any time."

*Are Women Human?* is a major contribution both to feminism and to international law. About some of MacKinnon's specific claims, however, I have doubts. I wonder, for example, whether her expressed preference for civil over criminal law as a vehicle for pressing sex-equality claims is not unduly influenced by the particular success of her strategy in *Kadic v. Karadzic*. She is certainly right that criminal laws are frequently underenforced, and that when criminal prosecution is impossible, a civil suit may be a victim's only way of attaining justice. But that doesn't show that civil remedies ought in general to be "favored"; and surely women's lives will not improve much unless and until the criminal law in the place where they live has become both adequate in its content (defining rape appropriately, recognizing that it can take place in marriage, etc.) and adequately enforced.

I have a more serious worry about MacKinnon's expressed preference for the international realm, in contrast to the state realm, as a place where women should focus their energies. It is certainly true that the abuses suffered by women are depressingly similar from one nation to another, and that the international women's movement has therefore been able to identify similar problems in many nations and to jump-start the search for creative solutions. It is also true that when states are doing nothing, women can goad them into action by making a big noise internationally, and that this has happened, often helpfully. Finally, it is true that some specific problems require international solutions. Trafficking, for example, as MacKinnon points out, will not stop without international sanctions, because otherwise the traffickers will just keep moving on from states that have adopted strong laws to states that have weaker laws or that don't enforce the ones they have. Much the same is true of labor accords, as she mentions: Here, too, a solution has to be transnational because piecemeal solutions just make the problem move elsewhere.

None of this, however, adds up to saying that the state is not a crucially important place for sex equality to be enacted and realized. MacKinnon sometimes comes quite close to saying that the modern state is a sexist relic that has had its day. Surely, however, the state is the largest unit we know of so far that is decently accountable to people's voices, and thus it is bound to be of critical importance for women seeking to make their voices heard. I think there is also a moral argument for the state: It is a unit that expresses the human choice to live together under laws of one's own choosing. Once again, it is the largest unit we yet know that expresses this fundamental human aspiration. A world state, should it exist, would either be too dictatorial, imposing on Indians and South Africans and Canadians alike a Constitution that each group might like to determine and fine-tune separately, or else it would be little more than a charade, as some international agreements are today.

MacKinnon is a lawyer, and her imagination has always been galvanized by the experiences of women in specific legal situations, whether they are her formal clients or not: the plaintiffs in the landmark sexual harassment cases, the victims of abuse in the pornography industry whose testimony is gathered in her book *In Harm's Way*, the Bosnian women she recently represented. I think that this powerful empathy explains why she is impatient with the slow work of Constitution- making and Constitution-changing that is required for sex equality at the state level, and drawn to the more personal and informal encounters among women in the international women's movement. If the state has in many ways been deaf to women's voices, however, why should she believe that—without changing the nature of each liberal state, one by one—women can get good results at the international level? Surely the two levels need to work in tandem, informing each other. And both need to be informed by grassroots work at the most local level, as India's democracy has been powerfully influenced recently by the insights and achievements of women who now, by constitutional amendment, hold one-third of the seats in the *panchayats*, or local village councils.

MacKinnon is clearly correct, however, that change will not take place through state-based laws and institutions alone, and that all levels of civil society must be enlisted to play their part. "Opposing violence against women teaches," she concludes, "that peace-building is an active social process, not a mere lack of overt fighting, far less a document-signing ritual of contract or an arm-twisting exercise to get the parties in bed together in the silence of power having prevailed." By casting herself as a peace-builder, MacKinnon issues a pointed challenge to her adversaries, who boringly stereotype her as a fierce amazon on the warpath against male liberties. This book is indeed fierce, unrelenting in its naming of abuse and hypocrisy. In a world where women pervasively suffer violence, however, it takes the fierceness of good theory to move us a little closer to peace.

# CHAPTER TWENTY-EIGHT

# Review

MARTHA ALTER CHEN, Perpetual Mourning:
Widowhood in Rural India; Widows in India:
Social Neglect and Public Action;
DEEPA MEHTA, Water (Film); BAPSI SIDHWA, Water: A Novel;
DEVYANI SALTZMAN, Shooting Water: A Memoir of
Second Chances, Family, and Filmmaking

I

"I may die," says Metha Bai, "but still I cannot go out. If there is something in the house, we eat. Otherwise, we go to sleep." A poor but upper-caste widow from rural Rajasthan (a state in northwest India), Metha Bai was widowed at the age of twenty-eight, when her husband succumbed to internal injuries caused by electrocution, as he rescued one of his sons, who had fallen against a live wire. Left with the care of two young boys, one of whom is mentally disabled as a result of the electric shock, Metha Bai is unable to go out of the house to look for work, because her in-laws insist on upholding caste norms of proper widow behavior. She does not want to move back to her parents' home, because this would mean abandoning any claim to her husband's share of the family land, the only asset her sons have. But she cannot cultivate the land herself, since she lacks the skills and the strength, and the in-laws throw stones at her if she ventures outside. Her sons are too young to help. For now, her father travels a considerable distance to till the field. "When my father dies," she says, "I will die."

The death of a spouse is likely to be a stressful event whenever and wherever it occurs. Whether the surviving partner loved the deceased partner or not, such a death, early or late in life, is likely, at the very least, to cause a stressful jolt, as familiar life patterns are turned inside out. When the surviving partner is less well off than the dead partner—with fewer assets, fewer employment-related skills, and/or insecure inheritance rights—the event may also cause acute economic stringency for the survivor and any surviving children. Such hardships beset women more often than men in most nations of the world, since women's wealth and earning power are still on average very unequal to those of men, and since property law in many nations gives women unequal inheritance rights. Economic problems for widows are far from unknown even in wealthy nations, as is shown by the plight of many U.S. women widowed in the Iraq War, whose military pensions have been delayed.[1]

If, moreover, the female partner has been brought up to think that her main purpose in life is to support her husband, not to achieve and act in her own right, a husband's death may lead to a sense of low value and purposelessness, a sense all the more enveloping if the surrounding society tells the widow that she has little worth. Once again, this women's problem is all too frequent in many if not most countries. Widowers have other problems— learning to cope with daily life, for example, when the person who took care of all that is gone. But men are rarely brought up to believe that their main role in life is to prop up their wives, so the death of a wife is less often connected with an acute crisis of self-worth.

It is not surprising that these pervasive problems of widowhood have led to the formation of international groups and organizations dedicated to improving the living conditions of widows in many nations. One impressive example is the London-based Widows Rights International, which works across Asia and Africa to protect widows' property rights, inheritance rights, right to work, rights against social ostracism, and rights of choice in the matter of remarriage.

Metha Bai's case exhibits some pervasive problems of widowhood, but it also has some special features that are peculiar to specific Indian traditions. India has a very large number of living widows—around 34 million, in the last census, out of a population of slightly over 1 billion. Ten percent of all women and 55 percent of women over fifty are widows. This large number is connected to social norms discouraging widow remarriage, as well as to age discrepancies between women and men at the time of marriage and the virtual universality of marriage. Meanwhile, norms forbidding women of certain castes from working outside the home, and a history of unequal land rights, have caused the situation of Hindu widows to be even more precarious than it is in lots of nations where women struggle against social and economic inequality. The economic and social situation of widows is clearly a major problem, or set of problems, for India as a whole. Unfortunately, these problems have not received the attention they deserve, even after close to sixty years of economic planning—in part because economic data about poverty, as Chen notes, typically aggregate all members of a household into a single unit, rather than studying the well-being of individual family members. This practice means that it is difficult to get reliable information about widow poverty, since many impoverished widows, like Metha Bai, live in families of adequate means who simply refuse to support them. (Economic theories of the family that make the simplifying assumption that the head of the household is a beneficent altruist who distributes well-being adequately to all family members are particularly misleading when applied to Indian widows' situation.)[2]

To understand the many problems posed by widowhood in India, however, it is crucial not to think in terms of a fictive monolith called "Indian traditions," or even "Hindu traditions," but to confront the many different ways in which economic, social, and regional differences produce different outcomes. Understanding Metha Bai's case, for example, requires understanding how Rajasthan, in the northwest, is different from states in the south. Rajasthani wives marry by moving out of their parental communities, and they move to a considerable distance (making it hard for Metha Bai's father to till her field). In parts of the south, by contrast, the husband moves into the wife's home. Southern wives, therefore, are less dislocated by the spouse's death, more able to count on the support of a community they have known all their lives, independently of their relationship to the husband. They are also less hobbled by the proverbial, and frequently all-too-real, hostility of in-laws, after the man who brought the alien woman into his mother's home is gone. Some southern communities also transmit property through the female line, a custom that would have made it more likely that Metha Bai could expect inheritance from her natal family, not just from her husband.

We need, as well, to think about caste. Most of the restrictive norms about Hindu widow behavior originally bound only the upper castes, Brahmins and Rajputs (Metha Bai's caste), leaving lower-caste widows free to work outside the home and even to remarry, although recently upward mobility has led some lower castes to emulate the restrictive behavior of the upper. So it is just wrong to think that "Hindu widows" in India are forbidden to remarry, or even discouraged from remarrying. We cannot make any statement about the applicable social norms until we place the woman in her caste.

Metha Bai's case shows, further, the importance of analyzing widowhood from a number of distinct disciplinary perspectives. To see why her situation is so bad, and how it might be made better, we need to ask questions about religious texts, traditions, and norms, and also (often not the same thing) about social traditions and norms in each region and caste. In each case, we need to understand not just what official normative statements have been made, but also how they have been contested, what sort of dialogue exists around them. We need, further, to ask about laws relating to widowhood and about state action or inaction. We need to ask about the access of a widow like Metha Bai to the political process, and to potentially helpful nongovernmental organizations. Perhaps particularly important, we need to ask about economic issues. What laws and norms govern her land rights in both her father's and her husband's family? What education and employable skills has she learned, and what options are there for an unskilled but genteel worker like her? If she wants to start a home-based business, or even to pay back the money her husband owed, can she get a loan? A good account of her predicament will investigate all these dimensions.

Needless to say, scholars with the requisite breadth are not numerous. An important paper on Indian widows was published in 1990 by economist Jean Drèze (longtime collaborator of Amartya Sen),[3] but Chen's book is the most extensive and ambitious study yet. A professor of development studies at Harvard's J.F.K. School of Government, Chen has an auspiciously multi-disciplinary background. Trained as a Sanskritist and scholar of Indian religions, she later turned to social anthropology. She has also collaborated closely with development economists. Perhaps more important still, she grew up in India, speaks several Indian languages fluently, and has spent roughly half her life there, a lot of it in the field in rural areas. She is known for the ability to do excellent fieldwork on rural women in India and Bangladesh, and then to write about it in a human voice, clear and compelling, prominently including the voices of the women whom she studies. Her 1986 book *A Quiet Revolution: Women in Transition in Rural Bangladesh*,[4] which studies an integrated development program for rural women, prominently including adult literacy training, is a fine example of the value of a narrative approach for social science. Because she approached the women involved as individual human beings, with an interest in each person's story, Chen got these women to trust her and to give her information of a depth and complexity that rarely emerges in standard survey literature. She is also able to use her considerable literary skill to convey to readers who know nothing at all about rural Bangladesh the look and feel of the place where these women live, the texture of their daily lives.

The *Widows* book has all these virtues on a much larger canvas. For years Chen went around rural India, studying all ever-widowed women in a set of fourteen predominantly Hindu villages in seven states, a total of 562 widows in all. Chen is not the sort of social scientist who ventures out into the field from the sheltered confines of a four-star hotel. In each place she lived with the women she was studying, often enduring considerable hardship. Of one hut where she lodged in West Bengal, she writes, "When the rats ran through the rafters at night (which they seem to do all night every night) bits of plaster fell on me. I learned to cover myself like a cocoon in my thin cotton shawl (*dupatta*). I tried shining my flashlight on the rats, as their noses quivered through the holes in the ceiling." Before systematic analysis commences, Chen's reader is brought into the world of each village in turn, through vivid description and extensive quotations from the women involved.

This method is not just an engaging way to write social science, although it is that. It stems from a deeper set of theoretical commitments. One commitment is to the individual. Chen feels that widows are so often seen simply as members of a group, either as "ideal images" or as "hapless victims," their distinctiveness hidden beneath vague, homogenizing cultural categories. She aims, instead, to show each as a distinct individual, both because she believes that this method shows respect, and because she believes that social processes are best understood by looking up close at the many ways in which diverse individuals, situated in complex regional, social, and economic contexts, pit their agency and ingenuity against the constraints of their specific surroundings.

A second commitment, equally fundamental, is to the importance of the daily. Chen regrets the fact that foreign images of Indian widows often focus on sensational but rare events, such as *sati* (the immolation of a woman on her husband's funeral pyre), a practice that was always limited to wealthy families in one or two regions, and that has been known in recent years in only a handful of notorious cases. More common by far are the many quiet deprivations widows experience: hunger, unemployment, bad treatment by in-laws, bureaucratic inefficiency, the inequities and delays of the legal system. Her aim is to use vivid narratives of particular cases to put these daily predicaments before the reader and to show how they interact with one another—in a way that shows, as well, many instances of creative resistance against these ills. Focusing on the dramatic images stymies the political imagination, making one think that all will be well if one or two notorious abuses are ended. Focusing on the daily reveals that raising the living standard of widows requires a complex set of strategies, economic, legal, and social.

Finally, Chen insists on the importance of recognizing diversity and struggle in any region and tradition. By getting close to the stories of individuals, we see what ought to be obvious but is frequently missed: the fact that no tradition, religious or social, is ever completely monolithic or completely uncontested. Seeing where these fissures and points of contest lay helps us see where intervention may be most effective.

II

After Chen has introduced the widows who form the core of her story, she turns to religious history, arguing that there is no single "Hindu tradition" concerning widows. The oldest sacred texts, the Vedas (of disputed date, but at least as old as 1500 B.C.E.), say nothing forbidding widow remarriage, and examples of the practice occur, not always involving marriage to kin of the late husband. The same is true in the later epics, *Mahabharata* and *Ramayana*. A more restrictive set of norms creeps in between 400 B.C.E. and 200 C.E. The *Laws of Manu*, a central text of religious law produced over several centuries during this period, contains contradictory statements about widowhood: some sentences permit remarriage, others remarriage only of childless widows, and still others no remarriage at all. Lifelong asceticism is recommended as the most desirable practice. As time went on, commentators on this text increasingly construe an ascetic life as mandatory for widows and forbid all remarriage By 1000 C.E., the upper castes had accepted this ban, although lower castes never did. In short, "remarriage appears to be an ancient Indian practice which higher castes have given up, rather than a tribal or lower-caste custom."

Nor did the restrictive norms remain uncontested. Beginning in the early nineteenth century, indigenous religious reformers, particularly Ram Mohan Roy (1772–1833), founder of the reform movement within Hinduism known as the "Brahmo Samaj," and Ishvarchandra Vidyasagar (1820–91), a second giant of what is sometimes called the "Bengali enlightenment," spoke against *sati* and in favor of marriage permission for girls widowed in child-hood (a common problem, given that marriages were often contracted at a very young age, long before the bride would move into her husband's home). The British, as so often, made a mess of things, failing to understand that the restrictive norms had never applied to the lower castes. Their Remarriage Act of 1856 loosened the conditions of remarriage for upper-caste widows, but made things worse for lower-caste women who had never previously been under any restriction.

Meanwhile, Indian women themselves took a leading role in the struggle for widows' rights: Pandita Ramabai (1858–1922), a widely respected scholar of Sanskrit and the first woman to be given the honorific title Pandit, or "learned teacher," started a residential school for Hindu widows and orphans in Mumbai in 1889. (She also translated the Bible into Marathi: reformers of the time often sought common ground between Hinduism and Christianity.) One of her pupils, Baya, widowed at the age of nine, was remarried to a prominent Brahmin widower, Professor Karve, and that couple in turn set up an institute for widows in Pune. Baya's Brahmin father said that he was convinced to allow the remarriage by what he learned at a conference of Hindu *shastris* (commentators on religious texts) and *pandits* (learned religious teachers) in Pune that debated the issue of child-widow remarriage—so it appears that a large proportion of learned religious scholars must have argued in favor of the reform.

Reform movements were not confined to Bengal. Gandhi's well-known interventions on behalf of widows emerged from a Gujarati tradition of reform, and were neither novel nor radical. He favored remarriage for women widowed in childhood, and indeed opposed child marriage, but recommended a chaste and ascetic life for adult widows. Of course he preferred such a life for everyone who was capable of it, and even advised his widowed son Harilal not to remarry, saying that one ought to renounce sex. But there is a large difference between personal advice and the enormous social pressures that widowed women faced, and he seemed content to leave these pressures in place for adult widowed women.

In today's India, the remarriage of widows is widely accepted. Most Backward Caste communities and almost all Scheduled Castes (traditionally the lowest groups in the caste hierarchy) permit it, although exceptions are found when a group aspires to rise in the hierarchy by imposing upper-caste–like restrictions on their women, forbidding widows to remarry and all women to work outside the home. (One might compare the United States in the fifties: in the upper-middle-class community where I grew up, people understood that a working wife meant lower-class status, so aspiring transitional families often imitated the custom of the stay-at-home wife to show their gentility, even at the cost of some economic strain.) Remarriage, however, is much less frequent than its wide acceptance would suggest. Drèze estimated that only one in five or six widows remarries—and this includes those whose communities require a childless widow to remarry her husband's brother, or some other chosen representative of the family line. In Chen's sample of 562, only fifty-two widows remarried, and almost half of those were less than twenty when they remarried. Chen's sample, however, did not include any child widows, though it did include older women who had been widowed in childhood some time ago. The practice of denying remarriage to widowed children, then, seems to be gone, or at least on the way out.

The reasons widows do not remarry are diverse. Some are just not interested in remarriage, because the experience of marriage has not been a happy one. If they can get by on their own, they prefer to do so. Others encounter social resistance and social isolation that makes remarriage virtually impossible. Still others are seen as too old to be sought out for marriage. The lives of widows who do not remarry are often difficult. Many still confront the social stigma traditionally attached to widowhood. Widows have been thought to be both threatening (because an unattached woman is seen as sexually dangerous, a risk to good social order) and inauspicious (because it is widely believed that they were somehow responsible for their husbands' deaths). The age-old requirements that they wear only white, eat only nonspicy foods, shave their heads, and remove their ornaments are still imposed by custom in many regions, though less often than formerly. Many widows are still told that they cannot attend auspicious events: one widow in Chen's sample, who had sacrificed greatly to raise her daughter, was told that she could not attend the girl's wedding.

Even more difficult to bear, it would seem, is the economic hardship that many, if not most, widows routinely encounter. Even if a widow's caste, unlike Metha Bai's, permits work outside the home, she may have no employable skills, and she may not be accustomed to dealing with men out in the world. Women who live with their in-laws routinely encounter deprivations, being insufficiently fed and clothed, being made to sleep on the floor, and so forth. Although most widows live in the villages of their late husbands, and often in the same house with his relations, few share food fully, and the widow's kitchen is likely to be the poorer. By far the most secure among widows, Chen finds, are those who have adult sons. (Relying on daughters is thought shameful, and daughters are all too soon married into a family that very likely has no concern for the woman's mother.) Public support for widows, meanwhile, is a matter left to the state level of government in India, and states vary greatly in what they provide. Even in a state like Kerala, famous for the quality of its social services, widows may have a

difficult struggle to collect a pension. Jayamma, an elderly brick worker profiled by Leela and Mitu Gulati in the edited volume, was told that she could
claim nothing because she has adult sons, although in fact her sons live at a
distance and refuse to support her.[5]

What strategies are likely to prove most effective in helping widows
achieve a more secure livelihood? Paid employment outside the home is
obviously a good thing to promote, and projects that offer food for work
have helped many poor women, including widows.[6] Employment, however,
requires education and skills training, so this strategy will require, in turn,
long-term efforts at improving the educational status of girls. Particularly in
regions like Rajasthan, where child marriage is still widely practiced
(although it is illegal), families often have no interest in educating a girl
child, since once betrothed, often at the age of four or six, she already
belongs to someone else's family. Aggressive state action makes a large difference here. By campaigning tirelessly for school enrollment, with flexible
school hours and a nutritious midday meal, Kerala has achieved 99 percent
adolescent literacy in both boys and girls; the midday meal has now been
held by India's Supreme Court to be a mandatory measure for all states,
under the new constitutional amendment that makes primary and secondary education a fundamental right. Kerala begins with some unique advantages, given its matrilocal custom of residence after marriage and its
matrilineal tradition of property transmission. Even in a less advantaged
state such as West Bengal, however, a study by Amartya Sen's Pratichi
Trust has found some improvement in attitudes toward female education,
probably resulting in part from state action.[7]

Employment and education are important, then, but they are long-range
goals that will do little for many adult widows, and certainly will not improve
the lot of Metha Bai, whose in-laws are prepared to use violence to prevent
her from going to work. A more immediately productive strategy is to make
credit available to widows and other poor women, through the many micro-
credit schemes currently managed by nongovernmental organizations in
many parts of the nation. A loan can enable a woman to begin a home-based
business, such as tailoring or craft labor, or, if she has some land, raising
sheep or goats, or farming. (Already in fourth-century B.C.E., Kautilya, in his
great economic treatise *Arthashastra*, urged that widows earn money by
home-based work.) More than 90 percent of working women in India
work in the "informal sector" of the economy (including home-based labor,
hawking and vending, and agricultural labor), so enabling a home-based
business to get started can be very significant. For Metha Bai, credit through
a women's organization was crucial in enabling her to pay off a bank loan
taken by her husband that almost led to the loss of her land.

Chen stresses that government can do more for widows than is currently
the norm, by better guarantees for widows and by easing access to the
guarantees that are already available—also, by protecting widows
against the violence that so often threatens them. One hopeful aspect of

government's role that came too late to be included in her study is the pair of constitutional amendments in 1992 that guaranteed women one-third representation in the *panchayats*, or local village councils. By now it has become clear that this system has actually produced benefits for women. It has increased support for the education of girls, since females are seen by their families as people who may play an influential political role; it has also sharpened the focus, in *panchayat* discussions, on issues such as health and domestic violence.[8] Although I am not aware of any study that focuses particularly on the influence of the new system on the status of widows, there is surely work to be done here, and we may hope that giving women an enhanced presence in politics at the local level is leading to some important changes.

Probably the most important single determinant of a widow's future, Chen stresses, is land rights. Here the definitive work has been done by economist Bina Agarwal, whose *A Field of One's Own: Gender and Land Rights in South Asia*,[9] prominently discussed in Chen's book, studies gender-inequalities in India's various systems of land tenure. Agarwal is also prominently represented in the edited volume.[10] Having a piece of land in her own name, however small, gives a widow a potential source of income, offers her access to credit, and increases her bargaining position in her late husband's family. It also enhances her power over her own sons, who may, like Jayamma's, be indifferent to her welfare but who may be brought round by the threat of disinheritance. A more recent study by Agarwal shows that land ownership is a highly significant factor in protecting women against physical violence in the home.[11]

Unfortunately, the law governing Hindu land tenure has given women in general, widows in particular, very unequal rights, particularly in regard to agricultural land. In 2005, the Hindu Succession Act was amended to remove the major inequities, after tireless campaigning by several women's non-governmental organizations, in consultation with feminist academics, prominently including Agarwal. Inequities in widows' rights to inherit a deceased husband's property if they remarried were also removed. This national success grew out of a long-term set of grassroots lobbying efforts by women's groups in a number of states, which had already achieved changes at the state level. "Women did not receive these rights without struggle," remarks Agarwal, noting that women had been lobbying for better laws even before 1956, when the longlasting defective law—much better, however, than what preceded it—was adopted.[12]

Land rights are not everything: Agarwal stresses that women who know and demand their rights are often faced with violence from their in-laws and indifference by government bureaucracy. These rights are, however, a crucial first step, and Hindu widows have now made that step.

Above all, then, Chen's work and the related work of Agarwal show us that the agency of women has been crucial in improving widows' lot, both in the time of Pandita Ramabai and today. As elsewhere in the Indian women's movement, networking among widows crosses lines of caste, religion, even language and region. Sometimes this solidarity emerges spontaneously: three elderly widows from the northern state of Uttar Pradesh told Chen that their common problems brought them close to one another. Although from different castes, "We are friends. We have affection for one another. We have sympathy for one another." Given the isolation in which widows frequently live, however, solidarity sometimes needs to be helped along by groups that create opportunities for widows to get together. At a national workshop on widowhood organized by Chen and Drèze in 1994, widows from all over India strategized together, sometimes meeting other widows for the first time. They garlanded one another with flowers, pledged to wear traditionally taboo colors, danced, in some cases for the first time in decades, and shared economic and political proposals. This experience of solidarity was powerful, Chen stresses, because it offered these women a new social identity—as citizens with rights and active members of a mutually support-ive network, not as discarded members of someone else's household, as women bound by ties of mutual responsibility, as well as by shared predica-ments. At that workshop, as Metha Bai showed Chen the bangles and colored clothes that she had bought on a field visit to a local women's orga-nization, Chen, who was accustomed to seeing her sad, and even in tears, saw her smile.

By now, the connections forged at the Bangalore workshop have led to the formation of a network of organizations working with widows, including, in Rajasthan, an organization of single women (80 percent of whom are widows), with 19,000 paid-up members. Called The Association of Strong Women Alone (*Ekal Nari Shakti Sangathan*), the group fights for land rights, access to government resources, and other social and economic entitlements. After a large convention of widows in North India in 2004, other states began to set up similar networks. Ginny Srivastava, herself a widow and one of the organizers, writes, "No ashram or widow home for these women. . . . Widows are not weak women—they are strong, and in India, they are on the move."[13]

III

What sort of film might possibly do justice to the reality Chen records and the spirit in which she records it? No film could depict the enormous variety with which Chen's book confronts us, although some way might be found to allude to differences of region, caste, and class. But a film might yet embody the deeper spirit of Chen's encounters, if it could find a way to depict a single story, or, better, several interlocking stories, with her respectful concern for the individuality of each woman; the agency and creativity of women struggling to make something of their lives in difficult conditions;

the presence of friendship, love, active planning, and even humor in their seemingly grim lives. Such a film would need to take context seriously, depicting economic and social realities with precision and leading the viewer to find such daily details interesting. Above all, if it were not to betray utterly the spirit of Chen's work, the film would have to locate dramatic interest not in some splashy tragic or sensational tale, evoking, as Chen says, "pity and horror," but in the small movements of daily life and conversation.

Satyajit Ray could have made such a film, and indeed he did, twice—first in *Aparajito* (1957), the second part of the Apu trilogy, which depicts the loneliness, grief, and poverty of Apu's widowed and impoverished mother. Here, as throughout the trilogy, Ray illuminates daily life by the sheer respectfulness of his attention, as the rural poor become not masses, but individuals, objects of interest in their own right. This focus was what made Ray a radical in the Indian cinema, dominated then, as it still is today, by a Bollywood film industry enamored of spectacle and sensation, prone to drawing character with large generalizing strokes rather than revealing it slowly in the grit and sweat of daily struggles. Bollywood often transcends its thin character portrayal through the ability of gifted actors to endow a weak script with their own more nuanced inner life. (Consider, for example, Om Puri's harrowing performance as a corrupt chief of police who betrays his best friend in *Dev*, Govind Nihalani's mostly forgettable film about the Gujarat riots of 2002. Despite the fact that the lines written for him are of crashing banality, Puri's suicide scene is Shakespearean in its resonance.) In Ray, however, nuance and complexity arrive, not by lucky casting, but as the result of a deeply reflective and compassionate directorial intelligence.

In 1984, Ray approached the topic of widowhood again, in *The Home and the World*, based on Rabindranath Tagore's 1914 novel about the rise of Indian nationalism. Here the widow story, being a story told with attention to context and individual character, is utterly different from that of *Aparajito*. Nikhil's sister-in-law, known in the novel only as the Bara Rani, the Senior Woman, widowed without children while still a widely admired beauty, envies Nikhil's young wife Bimala the love and affection she receives from her husband—not to mention the colorful clothes, the education, and the social attention that she herself has had to forgo. In the highly specific story of this widow, a subplot in both novel and film, we see the tremendous waste of life and intelligence that the widow system can create, even in a wealthy and decent family in which everyone is well fed and clothed. Hair shorn and dressed in white, but otherwise doing very nicely, the Bara Rani has no complaint to make about her economic situation, since she has a secure life interest in her husband's property—nor indeed about violence, now that her drunkard husband has died. But she does suffer from not really having a life, and she envies the less articulate younger woman the sheer luck of having a kind and healthy husband, luck that the younger woman does not sufficiently appreciate. The Bara Rani's eye for transgression is unerring, her sympathy for weakness utterly withered. Not having any other outlet for her considerable talents, she lives on an emotional diet of sarcasm and petty revenge. And yet she is no mere passive victim: even her envious plotting is a way of making something real of her days. Through her story Ray suggests further criticisms of traditional widowhood, but in a way that respects the utter particularity of this widow's story, so unlike that of Apu's mother.

Deepa Mehta, the director of *Water*, has sometimes been compared to Ray, but the comparison is problematic. *Water* does contain moments of a Ray-like vividness and particularity, but these moments are largely supplied by two of Mehta's leading actors. As the middle-aged widow Shakuntala, whose compassion shelters both the gentle doomed Kalyani and the child widow Chuyia, Bengali actress Seema Biswas gives a performance worthy of a Ray film, her grief-toughened face yielding haunting glimpses of longing and tenderness. And as Chuyia, the Sri Lankan child actress Sarala—selected after Mehta had rejected dozens of Bollywood cuties who (as we learn in her daughter's narrative of the filming) all were trying to look like Britney Spears—has a fierce energy and a seething emotional life that galvanize the film whenever she is on camera. Whether she is biting the leg of the fat director of the widow ashram, wringing the neck of the duplicitous woman's beloved parrot, or pleading with a street vendor to sell her a sweet (forbidden for widows) so that she can give it to an elderly friend who longs to taste one before she dies, we see not only the unaffected directness that we'd expect in Ray but also a marvelous embodiment of some Chen's major themes: the undefeated agency of widows in difficult circumstances, the solidarity that links women utterly different in class, history, and, in this case, age.

The film as a whole, however, is something else again. An independent filmmaker who grew up in India, but who has lived in Canada since the age of twenty-three, Mehta has an eclectic cinematic style, for which Bollywood supplies major ingredients. The film's visual aesthetic, albeit pleasing in its color palette of soft blues and grays, is far too addicted to prettiness to capture the feel of a real Indian city. A series of Bollywood songs breaks up the dramatic tension, without even supplying the usual elements of spectacle and movement. The scripting of character is so Bollywood-thin that it borders on the cartoonish. Most Bollywoodish of all are the lead actors, Lisa Ray and John Abraham, who play the young widow Kalyani and the rich young social activist Narayan, who tries to marry her. Both Ray (half-Indian, half-Canadian, with a Polish mother, green-eyed) and Abraham are successful fashion models who are just beginning their film careers as Bollywood ingenues. Their fortunes so far have been made by their pretty looks and their light skin. Both exude a bland sort of niceness, and Saltzman's memoir of the shooting of the film convinces us that in real life they are both extremely amiable. (Ray, for example, befriended Saltzman, Mehta's daughter, while she was working out her difficult emotional relationship with her mother.) But neither has the slightest capacity to convey emotional complexity, or even erotic tension and chemistry. So the initially happy and ultimately tragic love story that is meant to be the film's heart never even reaches the aesthetic level of *Sex and the City* (since neither has a capacity for humor either), and the film as a whole remains a Bollywood romance with pretensions to political profundity, transfigured from time to time by the two wonderful supporting actors I have mentioned.

*Water* is the third film in Mehta's "elements" trilogy. Each of the trilogy's films addresses a major political topic, and two of the three have occasioned considerable political controversy. *Fire* (1996) concerned a lesbian relationship between two lonely married women. Tasteful and not particularly aggressive, though not particularly wonderful either, the film was greeted with violent protest in several cities by right-wing Hindu mobs. The ensuing controversy led to a productive public debate about freedom of speech, about same-sex relationships and their relationship to Indian traditions, and about the relationship between lesbianism and feminism. India's feminist community had not previously been very eager to speak publicly in support of same-sex relationships. Mehta's film, and talking about it, led many feminists to conclude that they could not defend women's equality well, especially during the ascendancy of the Hindu right, without defending the right of same-sex couples to respectful treatment. So the film, whatever its aesthetic merits, did some real good.

*Earth* (1998) was far and away the trilogy's most successful film, in part because it was based on a good novel, *Cracking India*,[14] an autobiographical tale of religious violence by Pakistani novelist Bapsi Sidhwa. (Sidhwa remains a collaborator of Mehta's, and has recently turned the screenplay of *Water* into a novelized version, which follows the screenplay more or less verbatim and supplies a few extra background details.) Set in 1947, during the struggles surrounding the creation of independent India and the partitioning of India and Pakistan, *Earth* showed escalating religious tensions through the eyes of an eight-year-old Parsi girl, Lenny, whose family, being Parsi, considers itself *hors de combat* as Hindus and Muslims square off, and as both resist British domination. This very aloofness, however, is seen by others as cowardice (In one marvelous scene, Lenny asks her mother about a phrase she has heard: Parsis, people say, are "bumlickers of the British." Her hyper-elite mother explains, undisturbed, that "we" are "like the Swiss, dear. We've always been neutral.") Because *Earth* followed the particular stories of characters whom the novel had already endowed with considerable psychological complexity, it was able to illuminate the phenomena of religious hatred, showing how it happens that people who have been friends the day before can suddenly begin butchering one another, under the suasions of a polarized leadership and a conforming peer community—and how all too easy it is for other well-intentioned people to sit on their hands.

So *Earth* could certainly be called a "political film," but its success, like that of Satyajit Ray's films, rested on its ability to reach toward large themes through a well-told particular story. In *Water*, by contrast, Mehta has obviously set out to make a political statement first and foremost, and to line up particular cases that illustrate that statement. Watching it, I recalled the experience, in the 1970s, of reading Marilyn French's popular novel *The Women's Room*, which follows a diverse group of women, as, one by one, with no apparent capacity for agency or resistance, they succumb to the whole panoply of injuries that men can inflict upon women. Despite French's undeniable cleverness as a story-teller, one felt used, almost soiled, by the sense of a set-up, a *parti pris*. And one felt, even more, that the characters had been used, denied their own freedom to be something, by the edifying set of fates that had already been meted out to them by the novelist's sermonizing hand. So, too, in *Water* we follow a sample group of widows as, one by one, they meet all the bad fates that are known to befall widows in Indian society. And one feels, similarly, that the characters are being used, as pawns of a larger theoretical intent, denied the freedom to intervene in their circumstances that Chen's book so powerfully conveys.

*Water* is set in a widows' ashram, or devotional religious retreat, in a fictional Indian city, Rawalpur, which Sidhwa's novelization tells us is on the Bengal-Bihar border. The year is 1938, an intense period of struggle between Indian fighters for independence and their British masters, and this struggle forms the film's backdrop. Chuyia, an eight-year-old girl, has been married to a much older man, who falls ill and dies. (The novel helpfully tells us that Chuyia's parents are poor Brahmins who married her to an older widower because he would take her without a dowry.) As was the norm, she does not actually cohabit with the husband yet, but she is firmly married. The widower falls ill and dies. Suddenly widowed, she is taken by her apparently loving father to a widows' ashram in the city on the Ganges where her husband has been taken to die and have his last rites (as many people have their last rites in Benares). The father and all concerned behave as if there is absolutely no alternative to Chuyia's going into the ashram. Her hair is shorn, her bangles broken. At this point, reasonably furious at being abandoned by her parents, she bites Madhumati, the head of the ashram. Shakuntala befriends her, as does Kalyani, a beautiful young widow whose hair, mysteriously, is unshorn.

We soon learn that the ashram is partly a brothel, and that Kalyani is regularly prostituted to wealthy men around the city by Madhumati as pimp and the eunuch go-between Gulabi. Both Madhumati and Gulabi are stock figures out of Bollywood comedy, although the former is effectively acted by the Tamil actress Manorama, and she provides the one example of female economic resourcefulness in the film, as she runs a side prostitution business to get a steady income and a reliable source of drugs.

One day, while Kalyani and Chuyia are out washing a little dog that they have hidden in the ashram, Kalyani's beauty is spotted by the wealthy young Narayan, a Bengali Brahmin from a conservative family who has recently become involved in the independence movement, as a follower of Gandhi. The two meet, talk romantic Bollywood talk, fall in love, move around to music, and eventually plan to marry. Angered at the potential loss of income, Madhumati cuts off Kalyani's hair. Narayan, however, loves her still, and Shakuntala defies Madhumati by unlocking the door to the ashram so that Kalyani can go to her lover. All seems well. But on the way across the river to Narayan's home, Kalyani recognizes with horror that the house to which they are being taken is the very place where a wealthy customer has repeatedly slept with her. After a question or two, she realizes that the patron is Narayan's father, Seth Dwarkanath. (Apparently she never knew Narayan's last name until this moment, despite being engaged to him.) Unable to tell him what is wrong, she asks him to turn the boat around and take her home. She then drowns herself in the river—just before Narayan, having had an angry confrontation with his father, comes to tell her that he knows all and wants to marry her anyway.

Desperate for a renewed income source, Madhumati sends Chuyia to one of Kalyani's other clients, the father of Narayan's best friend, Rabindra. (Thus the only middle aged men we meet both hire the same prostitute and both make assignations with her, implausibly, in their own homes, under the nose of their wives. This is necessary for the plot, since Kalyani recognizes her fate by seeing the appearance of the house.) The little girl, who thinks that she is being taken to her parents, is drugged and raped. Shakuntala picks up her almost lifeless body and carries her to the railway station, where Gandhi is due to appear. Gandhi appears. To the assembled crowd he briefly states that he used to think that God was Truth, but he now sees that Truth is God. Narayan turns up in the window of the crowded train, and Shakuntala hands the still-comatose Chuyia to him, imploring him to be sure that she gets Gandhi's attention and care. (Shakuntala's agency stops here: apparently she has no plan for herself, other than returning to the ashram.)

The filming of *Water* was delayed for four years. While Mehta was initially filming it in Benares, hooligans of the Hindu right destroyed the sets and made life impossible for the film crew by a range of other stunts, including a repeated "attempted suicide" of protest by a man who turned out to be a professional suicide stunt man. Saltzman's sensitive and well-written memoir focuses on her estrangement from Mehta and their gradual reconciliation during the two filmings. But it also gives a vivid account of these events, as Mehta tries to accommodate demands of Hindu-right politicians for minor script changes, but sees, ultimately, that the official approval of both the local Hindu-right government and the most powerful Hindu-right social groups was specious, masking an unbending intent to disrupt. Backing off, Mehta eventually returned to the project four years later in Sri Lanka, where, despite being in a country torn by widespread sectarian violence, she found the peace she needed to finish her film—mostly on an artificial set (hence the film's impossible prettiness).

The passage of time evidently left intact Mehta's determination to make a political statement, confronting Hindu traditions that oppress women. Indeed, Saltzman's memoir, despite its highly favorable portrayal of Mehta, lets slip some signs that this is an artist very self-conscious about her own importance as a political figure. In one particularly unpleasant anecdote, Mehta visits a Tamil Tiger cemetery guarded by the Sri Lankan government and spends time negotiating with government officials to get a Tamil Tiger flag to take home to Canada with her. It's easy to imagine, behind this, the thought: "Like them, I'm a courageous revolutionary, and this red-eyed tiger emerging from a ring of bullets is my symbol too; what a nice thing to hang up in my study." It's a pretty disgusting response to murderous terrorism. (Saltzman notices that their young government guide has a plastic leg.)

We know even before it gets going that *Water* is meant to be "The Story of Indian Widows," not just a story of some women who are widowed, since the sentences of the *Laws of Manu* that offer the most repressive account of widows' duties and possibilities appear on the screen right off, the first thing we see, as if these words constitute the Hindu tradition's sole text concerning widowhood. What Chen's book shows (and Mehta acknowledges her work in the novelization, despite flouting some of its best insights) is that the Hindu tradition contains tremendous variety and debate around this topic—debates in which women themselves are leading participants. In *Water*, by contrast, the only woman who does something enterprising with her life is the comic Madhumati. Apart from this buffoonish and negative example, *Water* is a film in which controversy and debate are virtually absent—until Gandhi appears, more or less as a *deus ex machina*, at the story's end. It's a sad romantic fable in which women, at least all women who are not hideously fat, are sad passive victims of a fate that has existed unchanged since time immemorial. Their only hope is to be rescued by a man on a white horse (in this case, a shiny American car)[15] or, in Chuyia's case, to be sheltered by the magical presence of Gandhi. Instead of the fascination of daily struggle, Mehta goes straight for Bollywood "pity and horror," the very thing Chen was trying to take us beyond. She has no interest in economic context, in property, in employment, in women's challenge to existing laws and traditions. The controversy about the film is in that sense quite absurd, since a more innocuous and apolitical take on widowhood would be difficult to imagine. Indeed, the film is positively anti-political, since its fatalism discourages any thought that widows could possibly improve their life conditions—unless some man, whether the glamorous Bollywood hero or the suddenly appearing Gandhi, carries them off. (Saltzman, a balanced and astute, if somewhat depressive, observer of the scene connects the film's plot to her own romantic mess with an older Indian man, concluding that she is "sick of women seeking salvation in the image of a perfect man.") The really political issues about widowhood—changing property rights, providing employment, teaching people to read—appear not to engage Mehta at all. (Indeed, Chuyia's impoverished mother, who in real life would almost certainly be illiterate in 1938, is improbably endowed, in the novelization, with the ability to read from classical Sanskrit texts, or perhaps some vernacular translation: she reads to Chuyia from a "tattered copy" of the *Mahabharata*—no mean feat of arm strength, holding this "copy," since this work is more than eight times the length of the *Iliad* and the *Odyssey* combined.)[16]

As in French's novel, Mehta's screenplay provides us with a representative collection of widows, so that we can see how, one by one, they suffer various disasters. This she does by setting the story in the widows' ashram, where about twenty widows live together. By bringing a large group of widows together in one place, Mehta does provide interesting glimpses of widowhood at different ages. The elderly toothless widow Bua, who dies happy after eating the sweet that Chuyia brings her, is a particularly telling cameo. Mehta gets this representativeness, however, through complete unrepresentativeness. Almost no widows, if any, have ever lived like this. To a *Chicago Tribune* reporter, Mehta made the astonishing statement that "they" think that 11 million of India's 34 million widows currently live in ashrams.[17] She doesn't say who "they" are, but Jean Drèze told me he would be astonished if the number was even 1 percent of that.[18] Chen's research, moreover, emphasized that even where such religious ashrams exist today, women don't actually live there. They go there for devotional exercises, but they live in lonely little huts outside, in the city. So Mehta's allegedly typical place is actually a fictional construct, rather like French's women's room, whose function is to make it possible to have lots of tragedies in the same story.

This fiction, at least, has a clear aesthetic function—although the sense of inevitability surrounding Chuyia's entry into it is utterly bogus. A loving father in 1938—and this father is depicted as intensely concerned with Chuyia's welfare—would have been able to take her back home and make other plans, perhaps another marriage to an older widower, numerous examples of which turn up in Chen's book. Far less understandable are the numerous other ways in which the film flouts history. It is 1938. Much is made of this date. It is flashed on screen at the beginning, and alluded to throughout. In 1919, British troops led by General Dyer opened fire without provocation on a peaceful crowd of Indian civilians gathered at Amritsar, in a place called Jallianwalla Bagh, killing 379 and wounding 1137. This event galvanized the nascent independence struggle. Previously moderate elites, such as the Nehrus, were radicalized by the event. Motilal Nehru, as British an Indian as there has ever been, stopped wearing Harris tweeds and began wearing homespun cotton. Appointed to take charge of the official investigation of the shootings, he sent his son Jawaharlal to make a report. The report was devastating: the crowd was unarmed, the place a closed area with no means of escape. Meanwhile, in Bengal, Rabindranath Tagore, who had won the Nobel Prize in 1914 and was knighted shortly thereafter, returned his knighthood in 1919, saying that he really could not hold any honor from people who could behave in this way. "I for my part want to stand, shorn of all special distinctions, by the side of those of my countrymen who for their so-called insignificance are liable to suffer a degradation not fit for human beings." This letter was very famous. The British, unapologetic, escalated their campaign against the independence movement: both Motilal and Jawaharlal were tossed into British prisons in 1921, and repeatedly thereafter.

And yet in Mehta's film the elites of 1938 are just beginning to hear talk of independence. The family of Seth Bhupindranath had the Bengali patriotism to name their son (Narayan's best friend) Rabindra, evidently after Tagore. (One could not name a Bengali boy Rabindranath without naming him after Tagore, so central is Tagore's presence in Bengali culture.) And yet they somehow never mentioned to their son the inconvenient fact of Tagore's critique of imperialism, and allowed him to grow up thinking that the British are A-OK, as he tries to tell Narayan, who has heard otherwise from Gandhi. No educated Bengali in 1938 would be a blank slate in this way, and it is also quite absurd to portray Gandhi as *the* person who has put the idea of independence into people's minds, although his leadership surely contributed greatly to the movement's success. Furthermore, by presenting Rabindra as a total clod, who misquotes Shakespeare and sings Shubert off-key—all in order to demonstrate his British learning—Mehta turns into a silly cartoon the tragic relationship between elite Indians and British culture, as they struggled to chart a new relationship to a culture that they had profoundly loved and internalized, and that had always supplied them with some of their best resources for artistic self-expression.

So much for political history; now to Gandhi. It is 1938. By this time, Gandhi was a world-famous figure. His foundational book about non-violent struggle and Indian independence, *Hind Swaraj*, was published in 1909, his even more famous *Autobiography* in 1925. Beginning in 1919, he was working with Motilal and Jawaharlal Nehru to organize the Congress, and from then on he played a leading role in the independence movement. The great Salt March, in which Gandhi, with a huge band of supporters, walked 241 miles from his home in Gujarat to the sea and made salt in defiance of British law, by letting the water evaporate in his hand, galvanized all India and the world, making Gandhi a household name. This march took place in 1930. All over the world, people were talking about Gandhi—whether with contempt (Winston Churchill) or with love and reverence. In Cole Porter's *Anything Goes* (1934), Ethel Merman sang, "You're the top, you're Mahatma Gandhi." So his fame had even reached Broadway. And yet in 1938 the film's characters seem only to be hearing about Gandhi for the first time, and they have no clear idea of who he is. Madhumati actually says, "Mohandas who?"—and asks whether he is a new client for the brothel.

Nor does Mehta have any interest in portraying Gandhi's ideas precisely. We are told, "Gandhi said that widows are strangers to love. And nobody should be a stranger to love." This suggests that Gandhi favored remarriage for all widows, and favored it on grounds that earthly, physical love is a good thing. Of course this was far from being his view. He did favor remarriage for child widows, mostly, it would seem, on grounds of procreation and perhaps also because it gave them economic sustenance. He opposed remarriage for adult widows and also for widowers, because he thought that it was best to resist the sexual impulse. So the norm of ascetic life that Mehta depicts as belonging to a repressive Hindu tradition from which Gandhi will rescue us was one that Gandhi deeply endorsed, albeit in his own sex-equal way. The one remark that is placed in Gandhi's mouth, the remark about Truth being God, is something that he famously said, but by taking it out of the context of his other voluminous statements and writings Mehta creates the impression that Gandhi was an anti-religious figure who spurned the Hindu tradition. This is far from true. He was a radical reformer, who (like reformers in many religious traditions) put conscience ahead of tradition and text. But he loved the Hindu tradition, and he always thought of India as a fundamentally Hindu nation, much though he favored equal citizenship for Muslims. He always saw himself as Hindu, and he argued that his own view expressed the true essence of Hinduism. His politics of non-violence and self-rule grew out of a deep set of religious commitments. By failing to portray that and indeed by arranging to withhold this information from her viewers, Mehta is able to situate goodness and compassion outside of religion and to portray religion as monolithically conservative and anti-woman.

This strategy is helped along by her silence about currents of reform and debate within Hinduism. The only religious text that is mentioned is the one sentence of *Manu*, which is not even the whole story about that very conservative text. The fact that the Vedas and the epics tell a different tale would have been interesting to note. As for nineteenth-century reform, where women themselves, as we have seen, took a leading part, it appears in the film in the most laughable manner. Narayan is trying to convince his mother that it is all right for him to marry Kalyani, despite her widowhood. He tells her, "Raja Ram Mohan Roy says widows should get remarried." The mother replies, "And Raja Whoever—what does he know about our traditions?" Mehta makes a twofold mistake here: "Raja," an honorific title like "Sir," is treated as the man's first name: no Bengali matron would make this error. And Roy, one of the great luminaries of Bengali culture, is treated as a character who is completely unknown to this wealthy and reasonably well-informed woman. She doesn't even appear aware of his date: for after all, having lived from 1772 to 1833, he *is* their tradition. It is as if a young American man, trying to convince his mother of some point, alluded to the ideas of Thomas Jefferson, and the mother replied, "Thomas who?" Sidhwa, a Pakistani Parsi, seems equally in the dark; in the Glossary to the novelization, approved by Mehta, Roy is identified simply as "a social activist," no dates given. By such slipshod ways with history, Mehta manages to portray critique and disputation as utterly new phenomena, identical with Gandhi's (allegedly) anti-religious presence.

There's irony here. While Mehta sees herself as a courageous opponent of the Hindu right—and in some ways is so, favoring far more equality between the sexes than this movement would endorse—she more or less buys into the version of Hinduism that the Hindu right has been purveying for years: namely, that Hinduism is a single thing, that its essential beliefs and categories are one and unchanging from time immemorial, and that these traditions are uniformly quite conservative in the roles they allot to women. Hinduism always has been a hugely diverse set of traditions, varying by region, caste, and time. In order to lay the foundations for a Hindu state, the intellectual forces of the Hindu right set about concealing evidences of complexity, debate, and dynamism. Who would commit acts of violence in order to build a Rama temple at Ayodhya if they were brought up to think that the importance of Rama, the divinity of Rama, and even the goodness of Rama, have varied greatly in different places and at different times? In the hugely successful TV versions of *Ramayana* and *Mahabharata*, the rising Hindu right captured the imagination of a public that, by and large, had not learned much comparative religious history in their schooling or in the general public culture, foisting on them a picture of a monolithic Hinduism that is precisely the one that Mehta foists upon her unwitting viewers. Even the attitude to Gandhi is uncomfortably similar. The Hindu right doesn't quite know what to do about Gandhi—after all, his assassin, Nathuram Godse, was one of them, and yet it is not politically expedient, today, to show open sympathy with Godse's ideas. Gandhi is widely beloved, and yet his version of Hinduism is not one that today's Hindu right can accept, any more than Godse could. One way round this dilemma is to represent Gandhi as anti-religious, as attempting to overturn Hinduism in the guise of internal reform. (This strategy was taken by in BJP politician Arun Shourie, in an odd book on Hinduism that ends up showing considerable sympathy with Gandhi.)[19] So, too, Mehta—although of course she detests the Hinduism she depicts, whereas her opponents presumably love it.

Mehta's mistake is not just the mistake of someone who has been away from India for too long, or who doesn't care enough about history. It is a more significant, and more pernicious, error. Progressive elites in today's India—intellectuals, artists, journalists—often take the attitude to religion that Nehru fostered: that it is backward, that it impedes human progress, and that enlightenment will come only from a type of scientific rationalism that displaces religion. When one talks to Indian university students about the progressive movements in U.S. history in which religion played a formative role (the abolition movement, the civil rights movement), they seem utterly astonished: to them, religion is merely a source of reactionary constraint. Nehru himself was not ignorant of the progressive elements in India's religious traditions: his *Discovery of India* contains moving material on the tolerant Buddhist emperor Ashoka, the tolerant Islamic reformer Akhbar, and all the more recent reformers whom I have mentioned within the Hindu tradition. And yet in Nehru's own mind religion was slightly contemptible stuff for the masses, something that kept them down.

Gandhi never made this error: he understood that religion can be a source of hatred and violence, but that it can also be an essential source of the struggle against hatred and violence. If real people are going to fight successfully every day against the urge to dominate others, many of them, at least, would need, he believed, to do so through religious devotion, which he himself found invaluable. (Here Gandhi agreed with Immanuel Kant: we want to purify religion of some of its historical crudities and prejudices, but we need to keep it around as a social and psychological force that helps people resist the pressures of "radical evil" within themselves.) So Gandhi would never have created a system of education and a public culture in which people learn little about the diversity of their own religion, as is so generally the case with Hinduism in India today. (Kant favored generous subsidies for critical religious scholarship.) Nor would Gandhi have thought that a healthy society was one in which scientific and technical approaches to life dominated spiritual and moral approaches. He was too much opposed to scientific progress, which can be invaluable for the rural poor; but he rightly saw that a life based on material achievement was not a complete life, and not a sufficient foundation for a decent political culture.

Gandhi, however, died too soon to have much influence on the direction of Indian education. The result has been that most centrist and liberal Hindus, and intellectuals above all, are disdainful of religion, taking Nehru's and Mehta's attitude that it is a monolithic backward oppressor. Mehta speaks for a large number in India when she suggests that progress requires the wholesale rejection of Hinduism, when, in the service of this idea, she utterly ignores the prominent strands of reform and critique and feminism inside India's varied religious traditions.

In the end, Mehta's two disturbing errors—her effacement of women's struggle and agency, and her effacement of religious debate and reform— stem, it would seem, from the same distorted picture of human beings, one that could be called Foucauldian, although Foucault himself had doubts about it later in life. According to this picture, ordinary people are not agents, but relatively passive constructs of a monolithic power structure that envelops and suffuses them. They have little space for challenge and negotiation, and they certainly can never change the structure itself, since it has created their very categories of thought, their emotions, their very selves. Real history, and a real look at history's women, the sort exemplified in Chen's book, shows us that in daily life, people who are oppressed by convention, by political power, and by economic inequality do not lapse into mere victimhood. They think and they act, often in creative and unscripted ways. Sometimes they are cruel, sometimes they are envious, but they are rarely simply "docile bodies," to use Foucault's famous phrase. Much though Mehta expresses admiration for Satyajit Ray in interviews about her film, Mehta and Foucault basically see the world one way, Chen and

Satyajit Ray another. As Ray emphasized, it is from this other vision, the vision of human beings as unsubdued, that the excitement of good social art is generated. Indeed, the artist himself, he stressed, is just such an unsubdued agent in frequently unpromising circumstances. In an essay entitled, "The Odds Against Us," Ray wrote: "[T]here is something about creating beauty in the circumstances of shoddiness and privation that is truly exciting." A viewer curious about India's poor should go to *Water* with skepticism. A more exciting, and illuminating, evening might be spent watching any of Ray's great films on DVD.

## NOTES

1. See "Military Fails Some Widows Over Benefits," *New York Times*, June 27, p. A1.

2. Gary Becker's influential theory of the family (*A Treatise on the Family* [Cambridge, Mass.: Harvard University Press, 1981]), which makes this assumption, has had widespread influence on the way data are gathered. Becker himself does not deserve criticism for this problem, however, since he has long noted the inadequacy of this particular assumption: see "The Economic Way of Looking at Behavior," Nobel Lecture, in *The Essence of Becker*, ed. Ramón Febrero and Pedro S. Schwartz (Stanford, Calif.: Hoover Institution Press), 633–58.

3. "Widows in Rural India," DEP paper no. 26, Development Economics Programme, STICERD, London School of Economics.

4. Cambridge, Mass.: Schenkman Books.

5. "Jayamma: Profile of a Widowed Brick Worker"; Jayamma was profiled, earlier, in Gulati's *Profiles in Female Poverty;* my own profile of her, in *Women and Human Development* (Cambridge, UK: Cambridge University Press, 2001), was based on an interview conducted jointly with Leela Gulati at the time when she was preparing the later article.

6. See Chen, "A Matter of Survival: Women's Right to Employment in India and Bangladesh," in *Women, Culture and Development*, ed. M. Nussbaum and J. Glover (Oxford: Clarendon Press, 1995), 37–57.

7. *The Pratichi Education Report*, no. 1, 2002 (New Delhi: TLM Books). Ninety-six percent of parents believed that boys should acquire elementary education, as opposed to 82 percent for girls. Reasons cited were not merely economic: parents saw the education of girls as "a part of necessary social change. We were struck by the reflective and mature nature of these radical aspirations," writes Amartya Sen in the preface (p. 4). (The attitudes are radical because at present, in the nation as a whole, female literacy is only slightly above 50 percent.)

8. See Niraya Jayal, *Gender and Decentralisation*, monograph, Jawaharlal Nehru University Center for Law and Government; Nirmala Buch.

9. Cambridge, UK: Cambridge University Press, 1994.

10. "Widows Versus Daughters or Widows as Daughters? Property, Land and Economic Security in Rural India," in Chen, *Widows*, pp. 124–69.

11. B. Agarwal and P. Panda, "Home and the World: Resisting Violence," *The Indian Express*, August 7, 2003, p. 9.

12. Bina Agarwal, interview, *The Indian Express*, September 13, 2005.

13. E-mail correspondence, June 30, 2006.

14. In Britain the novel is titled *The Ice-Candy Man*.

15. Sidhwa's novelization calls it a Model T Ford, but the Model T was manufactured between 1908 and 1927, and Rabindra's car looks quite new—perhaps another case of the film's indifference to specifics of place and time.

16. At another point, Sidhwa portrays the mother as chanting passages "from the Bhagavad Gita or the Mahabharata," apparently unaware that the former is one part of the latter.

17. "No Tears for Film by Mehta," by Michael Wilmington, *Chicago Tribune*, May 10, 2006.

18. Jean Drèze, e-mail correspondence, June 17, 2006, cited with permission.

19. Arun Shourie, *Hinduism: Essence and Consequence* (Delhi: ASA, 1980).

# CHAPTER TWENTY-NINE

# Texts for Torturers

Philip Zimbardo (2007), The Lucifer Effect:
How Good People Turn Evil

In August 1971, the Stanford University psychologist Philip Zimbardo and his team of investigators selected twenty-four young men to participate in their study of the psychology of imprisonment. The men, only a few of whom were students, had answered an ad placed in both the student newspaper and the local town daily that offered subjects fifteen dollars per day for two weeks to participate in a study of "prison life." The successful applicants were randomly assigned to the roles of prisoner and guard, fifty-fifty. Prisoners were to stay in the prison for the entire two weeks; guards served in eight-hour shifts, three groups per day. Thus began the now famous Stanford Prison Experiment (SPE).

The prison was built in university facilities, after local police refused to allow the use of the real town jail. They did, however, agree to "arrest" the future prisoners, coming unannounced to their homes in a way that enhanced the verisimilitude of the situation. Because Zimbardo, who had been teaching a course on Psychology of Imprisonment, initially conceived the study as an investigation of the isolation and loss of individuality that occur during imprisonment, he gave the prisoners no detailed instructions, although he initially told them that they, like the guards, were free to leave the experiment at any time (forfeiting all the cash). He also assured them that there would be no physical abuse. (This assurance proved false, since guards were permitted from the beginning to deprive prisoners of sleep, a very damaging form of physical abuse.) Guards, by contrast, initially seen as "ensemble players" whose role was to help Zimbardo study the prisoners, were given a detailed "orientation." Zimbardo told them that in order for the study of prisoner psychology to be successful, they had to play their roles with vigour. He urged them to create an experience that included frustration, fear, and loss of control. "In general, what all this should create in them is a sense of powerlessness. We have total power in the situation.

They have none. The research question is, "What will they do to try to gain power, to regain some degree of individuality, to gain some freedom, to gain some privacy." He told the guards that initially the prisoners would think of the situation as just a game, but "it was up to all of us as prison staff [Zimbardo doubled as head experimenter and prison superintendent] to produce the required psychological state in the prisoners for as long as the study lasted." From the beginning, the prisoners were rendered anonymous, made to wear baggy uniforms and stocking caps that concealed their hair; they had to be referred to by number rather than by name. Guards were required to wear reflecting sunglasses, which inhibited any human connection with the prisoners.

In very short order, the situation began to go bad. The prisoners (deprived of sleep) began to exhibit symptoms of depression and dislocation. Guards, meanwhile, engaged in acts of humiliation, which escalated as several aggressive guards took the lead and the more sympathetic guards failed to protest. As time went on, one prisoner, either cracking up or pretending to, succeeded in dropping out of the experiment; two others engaged in individual forms of resistance against the guards, but, much to Zimbardo's disappointment, nobody organized any group protest. On the fifth day of the expected two weeks, Zimbardo called a halt to the experiment. His future wife, the psychologist Christina Maslach, shocked by the abuse she witnessed, persuaded him that it was unethical to allow the experiment to continue.

In Zimbardo's new book, *The Lucifer Effect*, the shocking events of the SPE (later documented in the film *Quiet Rage*) provide the lead-in to a detailed examination of psychological research showing the power of situations to overcome people's better judgement. Zimbardo usefully describes a large body of research: Solomon Asch's research on perceptual judgement, which documents the power of peer pressure to lead people to make statements about lines and shapes that they can easily see are untrue; Stanley Milgram's experiments on authority, often replicated in many countries, which showed that about three-quarters of subjects would administer a shock labelled as seriously harmful to a person who was supposed to be a subject in an experiment on learning, if ordered to do so by the researcher; and a host of less famous but equally convincing experiments, all showing disturbing and even cruel behaviour by ordinary people. One particularly chilling example involves schoolchildren whose teacher informs them that children with blue eyes are superior to children with dark eyes. Hierarchical and vindictive behaviour ensues. The teacher then informs the children that a mistake has been made: it is actually the brown-eyed children who are superior, the blue-eyed inferior. The behaviour simply reverses itself: the brown-eyed children seem to have learned nothing from the pain of discrimination.

Zimbardo concludes that situational features, far more than underlying dispositional features of people's characters, explain why people behave cruelly and abusively to others. He then connects these insights to a detailed account of the abuses by United States soldiers at Abu Ghraib prison, where, he argues, the humiliations and torments suffered by the prisoners were produced not by evil character traits but by an evil system that, like the prison system established in the SPE, virtually ensures that people will behave badly. Situations are held in place by systems, he argues, and it is ultimately the system that we must challenge, not the frequently average actors. He then sets himself to analyse the features that make systems and situations bad, and to suggest ways in which they might be remedied.

*The Lucifer Effect* focuses on the SPE and its aftermath. The story Zimbardo tells, however, is not well served by his own experiment, which has not been replicated and which is profoundly flawed. Asch and Milgram (like most psychologists doing this sort of work) do not inform subjects about the real object of their study. Subjects think that they are engaged in a study of perception or of learning. In this way, they are prevented from playing into a preconceived role or gratifying the experimenter's wishes. Zimbardo's subjects, by contrast, not only knew what he was studying, but were even encouraged to act their roles to the hilt to make the study work. The "orientation" given the guards is particularly problematic, in the light of their subsequent behaviour.

Much though we may suspect that some of the behaviour that emerged in the SPE was behaviour that a non-fictional situation of similar type would also have elicited from those people, solid scientific results cannot be built on such self-conscious role-playing. (When the guards wanted to take off the reflecting glasses that dehumanized their relationship with the prisoners, they were reminded that they were required to wear them as a part of the experiment.) There are other problems. The drama of arrest and imprisonment, for most prisoners, is centrally a drama of guilt and innocence. If a prisoner is innocent, he is preoccupied with proving his innocence; if he is guilty, he is probably trying to assess the weight of the evidence against him and to decide whether a guilty plea is his best strategy.

Finally, there is the drama of Zimbardo's own dual role as investigator and prison superintendent. He is much too emotionally involved in the outcome, and too present on the scene, steering his actors around, for the resulting behaviour to be scientifically reliable. He himself criticizes this aspect of the SPE, but he doesn't fully see how thoroughly his own personal drama permeates the entire set of events—in particular the fact that the experiment was brought to an end because his own future wife (to whom he is still married, more than twenty-five years later, and whom he describes as "the serene heroine of my life") got very upset with him.

All in all, then, the reader should regard the SPE as a side issue, a curiosity. Its conclusions are very likely true, or at least somewhat true, but it did little to establish them. It is not surprising that Zimbardo—still, thirty-five years later, with much investment in the significance of the SPE—devotes about half of this book to it, but the real work of establishing his conclusions is done in other research that he describes. He is at his best, then, when analysing the current state of our knowledge about the role of situations in eliciting bad behaviour. Research has amply confirmed that people of many different kinds will behave badly under certain types of situational pressure. Through the influence of authority and peer pressure, they do things that they are later amazed at having done, things that most people think in advance they would never themselves do.

Zimbardo's first plea, appropriately, is for humility: we have no reason to say that atrocities are the work of a few "bad apples," nor have we reason to think that they are done only by people remote from us in time and place. We should understand that we are all vulnerable, and we should judge individuals, accordingly, in a merciful way, knowing that we don't really know what we would have done, had we faced similar pressures. His second appropriate plea is that we learn to "blame the system": namely, to look at how situations are designed, and to criticize people who design them in ways that confront vulnerable individuals with pressures that human beings cope with badly. Zimbardo served as an expert witness on behalf of one of the officers accused of presiding over torture at Abu Ghraib, and his point was that we must not think that this is the work of a few unusual "defectives." We must understand that good people can do bad things under pressure, and we must learn how to structure situations so that they do not put such pressures on individuals. In short, he calls for collective responsibility—not as a total replacement for personal responsibility, but as its necessary concomitant, if people are not to be faced, again and again, with demands to which they are very unlikely to respond well.

Zimbardo sometimes speaks as if situations are all that is important, and the insides of people explain nothing at all. That is clearly a wild over-extrapolation from his data, which support a much more qualified view. Even if people in these experiments had all behaved in precisely the same way, we could not conclude that their inner psychology supplies nothing at all: for they might be motivated by common human emotions and tendencies, one or many, and it would then be extremely important to know what these forces are. Fear and insecurity have often been linked with aggressive behaviour—at least as long ago as the days of Jean-Jacques Rousseau, who concluded that education should aim to give people strategies to cope with life's uncertainties, and, importantly, to make them understand how compassion and cooperation can support our intrinsic weakness. Recent psychological research on disgust, by Paul Rozin and others, suggests a connection between aggression and an inability to tolerate one's bodily nature, with the ominous forecasting of death and decay that its effluvia suggest. Again, thinking about that source of aggression has consequences for education, not far removed from those Rousseau emphasized: we would encourage people not to repudiate their animality, but to understand that we are all mortal together and must learn strategies of mutual aid. Yet other research suggests that deformed images of masculinity are to blame for at least some of the readiness for aggression that we see around us: people are brought up to think that a "real man" should not need others, should not ever be weak, should not be human, really. So they react with violence against a reminder of their weakness. This research, again, suggests a Rousseauesque conclusion: we should bring up young men (and women) to understand that mutual interdependence and caring are not shameful or "unmanly." These intersecting areas of psychological research are of vital importance to Zimbardo's overall project, but he ignores them, suggesting that situations are all there are. Situations, however, don't elicit bad behaviour from a stone, or even an elephant. So what is it about many humans that makes them vulnerable? Zimbardo should press this question.

People, moreover, are not all alike. The research described by Zimbardo shows a surprising level of bad behaviour in the experimental situations, but nothing like uniformly bad behaviour. First, there are active perpetrators and fearful but humane collaborators. Both of these are morally defective, but in different ways. Finally, there are whistle-blowers who do have the strength to challenge the system, and Zimbardo devotes his final chapter to the characteristics of such people. So he himself knows that the individual does matter, and he is actually very interested in asking not only how situations can be better designed but also how people can be brought up to be good actors in bad situations. (Unfortunately, the sort of self-report questionnaire used by psychologists before such experiments can tell us little about subtle differences in upbringing and education that contribute to these individual differences.) What would a good society focus on, according to Zimbardo, if it wanted people to be capable of behaving well under situations of moral stress?

First of all, he calls for a society-wide emphasis on critical thinking, beginning in childhood. From their earliest days, children should be encouraged to think about the traditions and norms that govern their lives, and to ask uncomfortable searching questions. We need a culture of timely whistle-blowers, and we will only get this, he rightly argues, if we encourage Socratic questioning of authority both in the family and in the classroom. Beyond this, Zimbardo emphasizes the importance of fostering a culture of personal accountability. As anyone who has ever violated the speed limit knows, when people are anonymous or think they will not be seen, they are more willing to do bad things: so, making people aware of themselves as individuals, with personal responsibility, makes them less likely to act on aggressive impulses that they might have. Training individual responsibility is both a developmental and a situational matter. Zimbardo emphasizes the latter (foster structures that promote individual accountability), but we, with John Stuart Mill, should also pursue the former, thinking of ways to bring up children so that they are ready and eager to see themselves, not as the anonymous heirs of a tradition, but as individuals. We should promote the perception of others as individuals: when people are led to see others as anonymous members of a group, they are more willing to do bad things to them than when they see them as individuals with names and distinctive histories.

Philip Zimbardo does not focus on emotional development, but it is surely a key part of the future of any society that is going to refuse to go down the road of the SPE and Abu Ghraib. What the guards in the experiment crucially lacked, when they lacked the ability to see the other as human, was empathy and its close relative, compassion. Compassion, as Daniel Batson's wonderful research has shown, is closely linked to the ability to follow the story of another's plight with vivid imagination. Situations can certainly encourage this ability, as Batson's experimental situation did. Nonetheless, the imagination is a muscle that gets weak from routinized thinking and strong from vigorous challenges, and this suggests a vital role for the arts and humanities in any curriculum for good citizenship.

Let us hope that *The Lucifer Effect*, which confronts us with the worst in ourselves, stimulates a critical conversation that will lead to more sensible and less arrogant strategies for coping with our shared human weaknesses.

# CHAPTER THIRTY

# Stages of Thought

A. D. NUTTALL (2007), Shakespeare the Thinker;
COLIN MCGINN (2006), Shakespeare's Philosophy: Discovering
the Meaning Behind the Plays; TZACHI ZAMIR (2007), Double
Vision: Moral Philosophy and Shakespearean Drama

I

Philosophers often try to write about Shakespeare. Most of the time they are
ill-equipped to do so. There is something irresistibly tempting in the depth
and the complexity of the plays, and it lures people who respond to that
complexity with abstract thought, even if for the most part they are utterly
unprepared, emotionally or stylistically, to write about literary experience.
Such philosophers see profound thought in Shakespeare, not wrongly. But
armed with their standard analytic equipment, they frequently produce
accounts that are laughably reductive, contributing little or nothing to
philosophy or to the understanding of Shakespeare.

To make any contribution worth caring about, a philosopher's study of
Shakespeare should do three things. First and most centrally, it should really
do philosophy, and not just allude to familiar philosophical ideas and
positions. It should pursue tough questions and come up with something
interesting and subtle—rather than just connecting Shakespeare to this or
that idea from Philosophy 101. A philosopher reading Shakespeare should
wonder, and ponder, in a genuinely philosophical way. Second, it should
illuminate the world of the plays, attending closely enough to language and
to texture that the interpretation changes the way we see the work, rather
than just uses the work as grist for some argumentative mill. And finally,
such a study should offer some account of why philosophical thinking
needs to turn to Shakespeare's plays, or to works like them. Why must the
philosopher care about these plays? Do they supply to thought something
that a straightforward piece of philosophical prose cannot supply, and if
so, what?

Two of these new books do very badly by these criteria. To be fair, A. D. Nuttall, who died not long ago, was not a philosopher, but a literary critic who did impressive work on the margins of philosophy. (*A Common Sky: Philosophy and the Literary Imagination* was a marvelous exploration of epistemological themes in the Romantic poets.) It is not terribly surprising that his book contributes nothing of original philosophical interest, though it is disappointing that the ideas on offer in this tired, diffuse book are so far beneath Nuttall at his best. Nuttall believes that it is doing philosophy to, say, poke fun at Stoicism in the context of Julius Caesar—but without the least philosophical puzzlement about why so many people lived and died by and for that philosophy, or about what might have motivated its more controversial positions. In general, Nuttall's book exudes a complacency that is most unphilosophical.

Nor does Nuttall satisfy on the second count. He has isolated illuminations to offer about this line or that scene, and he discusses current trends in literary theory well. But he spends such a short time on each play that no real insight is possible, no surprising new interpretation. Even the writing is flat and tired, the voice of someone who is no longer electrified by the dramas and who finds the task of interpretation rather boring. And Nuttall has nothing to say about why someone interested in philosophical problems should turn to Shakespeare.

Colin McGinn's book is much more intelligent, and it is the book of a real philosopher, with reasonably useful things to say about gender as performance, about the fluid nature of the self, about knowledge of other minds. Still, it is all at the level of Phil 101. McGinn does not offer anything subtle or new; he just identifies familiar philosophical themes that figure in the plays. The impression conveyed is that Shakespeare has gotten a good grade in Phil 101, with McGinn as his professor and his superior in understanding. This is a terrible way to approach Shakespeare's complexity.

McGinn's attention to language and dramatic structure is so hasty that he, too, has no new or convincing readings of the plays he tackles; he just gives the reader a breezy tour through them, never pausing to be puzzled. Nor does McGinn give any account of why we might need to turn to Shakespeare for philosophical illumination. McGinn obviously enjoys reading Shakespeare, but Shakespeare himself does not make a creative contribution to the thought distilled from the plays. McGinn already knows what to think about the philosophical issues, and, with a certain narcissism, he is pleased to find confirmation of himself in Shakespeare.

How might a philosopher do better? The most distinguished Anglo-American philosophical writing on Shakespeare in recent years, by a long distance, may be found in the work of Stanley Cavell. Cavell's essays, collected in the book *Disowning Knowledge in Seven Plays of Shakespeare*, amply fulfill my first and second standards for this enterprise. His sometimes mysterious and idiosyncratic readings of a group of plays offer philosophical insights that are surprising and subtle, while genuinely illuminating themes of love, avoidance, skepticism, and acknowledgment in the dramas.

Cavell's writing is difficult, at times opaque. But we should see this way of writing as expressing the agony of human emotions and the intense difficulty of philosophical thought.

Despite the great merits of Cavell's particular insights, however, he has little to say about why we would want to turn to poetic drama in general, and to Shakespeare in particular, in pursuit of philosophical themes. His readings of Shakespeare tend to confirm the philosophical notions for which he has already argued independently, in readings of Wittgenstein, Descartes, and other philosophers. Anyone who fails to read Cavell's justly famous essay on the avoidance of love in *King Lear* can discover the same theme amply explored by way of Wittgenstein in *The Claim of Reason: Wittgenstein, Skepticism, Morality, and Tragedy* (or by way of Hollywood film comedy in *Pursuits of Happiness: The Hollywood Comedy of Remarriage*). Little is said about why it might be important to engage with Shakespeare's plays, among all other texts, on those questions. Indeed, Cavell's remarkable reading of *Othello* was originally published as the tragic conclusion to his philosophical magnum opus, *The Claim of Reason*, where it follows four hundred pages of argument about Wittgenstein, Austin, and many others.

But now we have Tzachi Zamir's *Double Vision: Moral Philosophy and Shakespearean Drama*, head and shoulders above its rivals. A first book by a young Israeli philosopher, *Double Vision* stands comparison with Cavell for philosophical subtlety and insight (though not for a more systematic philosophical contribution), and Zamir is, happily, much more upfront about what the enterprise of doing philosophy by consulting works of literature is all about, and why it might be important. Helpful, too, is the fact that Zamir writes with an evocative grace that shows a deep emotional response to literature and a sense of its complexities and its mysteries. His style itself helps to convince us that Shakespeare is not simply being used as a primer for Philosophy 101, or reduced to an analytic paragraph. Unlike McGinn, Zamir writes as someone capable of being puzzled, capable of delving into the painful or exhilarating depths of certain problems with Shakespeare as his guide rather than his pupil. *Double Vision* is quite a brilliant book.

II

Zamir understands that it is crucial not just to show that there are themes in the plays that philosophers have also discussed, and not just to show, through interpretation, what the plays contribute to our understanding of those themes, but also to say why it is important to turn to plays in particular, and to literary works in general, for philosophical guidance. His argument is complicated, but we may summarize it as follows. Literary works offer their readers a range of experiences that philosophical prose cannot provide, reshaping their perceptions in a variety of ways. Some of these experiences are varieties of emotional response; some are experiences of dislocation and a loss of meaning; some are experiences of losing a sense of meaning and then finding it again; some are experiences of not being able to figure out who or what a certain person is, or even what a person or self might be. And sometimes the experience is that of following the shifting trajectory of a human relationship.

So there is not just one thing that literature offers. It portrays and dissects a wide range of human experiences, all of which we have in life, but which literature offers in a concentrated and heightened form. And when we are dealing with not just any writer, but with Shakespeare, we find again and again that the shaping of plot and the resources of language are used to construct and then to deepen a set of these experiences in ways that provide resources for knowledge. If what we are after is to understand the search for value against the threat of nihilism, we would do well to engage with *Macbeth*; or to understand how a certain theatricalization of the self can be employed to deflect attention away from the indeterminacy and ineffability of the self, with *Hamlet*; or to understand whether and how far successful parenting requires the willingness to engage with, and not repudiate, the childlike parts of the self, with *King Lear*. We would do well to engage with these works because they provide us with experiences that are epistemically relevant to our search.

That is a very general claim, as it should be, avoiding any narrowly reductive account of literary meaning. But the claim is so general that it risks vacuity. It must be immediately backed up by detailed readings that again and again make good on the promise of new understanding, returning in each case to the question, What have we learned from the specifically literary quality of the works? At the heart of Zamir's book are three chapters on erotic love in *Romeo and Juliet*, *Antony and Cleopatra*, and *Othello*. He prefaces his readings by pointing to the great difficulties that philosophy has had investigating love, especially erotic love; and he suggests that only works that convey to their reader the texture of complex human experiences, with all their internal tensions and contradictions, will put us in a position to make any philosophical claims at all.

*Romeo and Juliet* conveys the hyperbolic, extravagant, and rather abstract character of young love, with its focus on a generalized and aestheticized image of the body ("I ne'er saw true beauty till this night"), and its humorless mutual absorption, its search for a transcendence of mere earthly humanity. Juliet is the sun, her eyes "two of the fairest stars in all the heaven." She is a "bright angel," soaring above the heads of mere mortals. This sort of love, Zamir shows, works by distancing, and even bracketing, reality; it is actively hostile to fact and evidence. Since it is determined to rise above the earth, it is also lacking in particularity: Juliet is an abstract image, an angel, and neither Romeo nor the audience knows a great deal about the earthly attributes that distinguish her from others.

One sign of these qualities in their love is the play's constant fascination with images of sleep and dreaming. Like many critics before him, Zamir notices that the play itself draws readers into a lulled and dreamy state.

Such a state might be seen as mere forgetfulness; it might also be seen as infantile narcissism. Zamir rejects both these interpretations in favor of one that focuses on the transfiguring experience of the perception of beauty: "Love in the play is not only an abandonment of the world, a dim or foggy experience, but also a penetration of it through heightened perception." By allowing ourselves to be drawn into this complex state, we instantiate, and learn more fully to understand, our own relationship to aesthetic beauty, and to the blindness to daily life that its perception frequently involves.

By contrast—in what for me is Zamir's most fascinating chapter—*Antony and Cleopatra* depicts "mature love," love between people who enjoy being grown-ups together, and who have no project of transcending human life, because they are taking too much pleasure in life as it is. Romeo and Juliet do not eat; Antony and Cleopatra eat all the time. Romeo and Juliet have no occupation; Antony and Cleopatra are friends and supportive colleagues with a great deal of work to do running their respective and interlocking empires. Romeo and Juliet have no sense of humor; Antony and Cleopatra live by elaborate jokes and highly personal forms of teasing—what Zamir calls "idiosyncratic practices." ("That time,—Oh times!—I laugh'd him out of patience. . .") Romeo and Juliet, utterly absorbed, pay no attention to anybody around them; Antony and Cleopatra love to gossip about the odd people in their world, and spend evenings wandering through the streets watching the funny things people do. Romeo and Juliet speak to each other only in terms of worshipful hyperbole; Antony knows how to make contact with Cleopatra through insults, even about her age (he calls her his "serpent of old Nile"), and she knows how to turn a story about a fishhook into a running joke that renews laughter each time it is mentioned. All this suggests a romance that, unlike that of the younger couple, "does not work through transcending life, through perpetually setting its intensities at odds with what life is, but rather structures itself through life and the daily pleasures it affords."

It's not that they do not pay attention to each other's bodies, says Zamir—but in contrast to the teenage lovers, the body in *Antony and Cleopatra* is always seen as animated by a searching and idiosyncratic mind that makes contact with another particular mind through intimate conversation. Cleopatra is clearly supposed to be attractive, but, as Zamir notes, the play, by contrast to Shakespeare's sources, downplays this aspect of her attraction. It is her complicated personality, full of surprises, to which Shakespeare most draws our attention. ("Age cannot wither her, nor custom stale / Her infinite variety.") Her mode of seduction, in Zamir's persuasive reading, is above all mental. "Cunning past man's thought," as Antony describes her, she ingeniously elaborates a battery of stratagems to keep herself in the forefront of his attention: flirtation, capricious annoyance, the constant private teasing, frustrating allusions to significant undelivered information—but also shared ambition, trusting collaboration, sincere and deeply felt admiration for his achievements, and insistence on her own equality.

(When Charmian advises deference and flattery, Cleopatra is appropriately contemptuous: "Thou teachest like a fool; the way to lose him.") Zamir is particularly insightful, and adds something that I believe to be new in the literature on the play, when, examining the scene after the battle of Actium, he shows the love expressed in Cleopatra's delicate attunement to the phases of Antony's career, her subtle sense of when to approach him and of what should and should not be said. I do not know another critic who gives Cleopatra the credit for empathy that she plainly deserves.

But does she really love Antony? The question is Zamir's. In part because many critics do not like Cleopatra, feeling that any such complicated, capricious, and powerful woman must be incapable of love, Zamir feels compelled to press this question repeatedly. He seems to have a hard time trusting the reality of this middle-aged love, so lacking in outsize rapture, so immersed in the daily movement of work and conversation. Zamir eventually finds an affirmative answer to his question in the scene in which news of Antony's marriage to Octavia is delivered to Cleopatra by a messenger—whom she first upbraids and then, in a bizarre tantrum, drags physically around the room by his hair. (Stage direction: "She hales him up and down.") Her angry reaction, says Zamir, must convince "even the most suspicious of audiences that this woman's love . . . is genuine." And here, I think, Zamir missteps: he reads Cleopatra's reaction as a pure case of erotic jealousy. But of course it cannot be that, since Cleopatra knows that the marriage is politically motivated, and not at all based on overwhelming passion. And she intuits quickly that Octavia is no rival in brains or fascination.

Zamir himself makes much of the fact that Octavia is later described as "of a holy, cold, and still conversation." With her "modest eyes / And still conclusion," she "shows a body rather than a life." (In fairness to Octavia, we should observe that, though the first of these judgments comes from the relatively impartial Enobarbus, the second remarkable insult is uttered by Cleopatra herself, and the third by that same messenger, no doubt averse to a second "haling," and happy to echo exactly what Cleopatra wishes to think about Antony's marital relationship.) So jealousy, focused on the sexuality and spirit of the rival, is not what her emotion is about. She does eventually get around to asking what Octavia looks like, at the end of this scene and in a later one, but it is an afterthought, well after the unfortunate messenger has been dragged about, and after she has asked him, three times, "He is married?"

So it is clearly the fact of marriage, and not the particularity of the wife, that is the target of her fury. This formidable woman, powerful, unique, who has wit, achievement, success, and glamour, who rules a kingdom, who seems an utter stranger to banality—this woman suddenly sees that she is circumscribed by the world's most banal form of power. This fact seems to her so completely outrageous and absurd that she can react only by behaving in an absurd, even infantile, way. Zamir is correct, then, that she does love him—but it is not jealousy that is the proof, it is her regal intolerance of mere social impediments, and, far more, her utterly submissive tolerance of them, as she accepts and lives with the limitations entailed by the news, whatever they may ultimately turn out to be. (But does she really accept limitation, or is all that dragging by the hair, that funny threat to put the messenger in brine and turn him into a pickle, itself one more outsize joke, a theatrical display of determination and indomitability? Cleopatra is certainly capable of games more elaborate by far. An actress might play the scene in many ways.)

Romeo and Juliet's love transfigured the world by raising love into the heavens: Juliet is the sun, and, as with the sun, we have no idea what, if anything, makes her laugh. Antony and Cleopatra transfigure the world from within, making each daily experience more vivid, funny, and surprising. Without each other, the world is sadly boring. "Shall I abide / In this dull world," she asks him as he dies, "which in thy absence is / No better than a sty?" What is piggish, in her view, is not the body, it is the absence of interesting conversation. So the world needs to be transfigured here, too, but the transfiguration is human and particular, rather than celestial and abstract.

What does all this have to do with philosophy? Well, in the first place, no philosopher has ever given a decent account of the complexities of "mature love." (John Stuart Mill's letters and autobiography come close, but they are not philosophical works, and Mill, despite his many virtues, is not exactly the man to describe the role of jokes and erotic teasing in love.) Nor is this failure just an accident, or a social fact about cultural reticence. Zamir plausibly argues that philosophical prose all by itself could not convey the quirky and uneven nature, the incommensurable particularity, of this type of love, the way genuine feeling is embodied in a fish story. And so he contends that the experience of the spectator or reader, as she goes through the variegated moods of this relationship, is epistemically significant, putting her in a position to make claims about love, and to assess claims about love, as no abstract account could do.

### III

If Antony and Cleopatra's love faced fatal political and military obstacles and was for that reason tragic, wrecked on "the varying shore o' the world," still there is nothing fundamentally tragic in the texture of the love itself, which is at its heart more akin to comedy. In *Othello*, by contrast, Zamir finds a love that is tragic at its core, fated for violent death—because of one party's determination to see and to deeply love, and the other party's horror of being seen and being deeply loved.

Any successful interpretation of *Othello* must explain Othello's readiness to be deceived. Iago is certainly skillful, but he has an all-too-willing victim. At every point, Othello picks up Iago's suggestions and runs with them.

No other character, despite receiving the same information, shows the slightest inclination to believe that Desdemona is unfaithful. Here McGinn writes his best chapter, showing how the play takes the classical philosophical problem of the knowledge of other minds and displays its agonizing human reality—but, focusing on enumerating passages that highlight epistemological themes, he does not finally show us why Othello is driven mad by this problem in a way that other characters are not. Some interpreters impute the Moor's collaboration with his tormentor Iago to his racial insecurity in a society that stigmatizes him. Yet this suggestion by itself does not tell us why the insecurity should take the form of sexual jealousy and ultimately violence—especially violence directed against the one person who appears to have no awareness of his racial difference. ("I saw Othello's visage in his mind.")

Stanley Cavell's famous interpretation goes further. Othello, he believes, has become heavily invested in the idea of his own purity, a project no doubt supported by his awareness of being black, and a Moor, in a white Christian world. So, says Cavell, when Othello makes love to Desdemona and sees the passion he arouses in her, he cannot bear it, because this passionate response proves to him that he is a sexual being, not a pure heavenly will. Cavell's sentences express, in their haunted and hesitant structure, the torment of that discovery:

> In speaking of the point and meaning of Othello's impotence, I do not think of Othello as having been in an everyday sense impotent with Desdemona. I think of him, rather, as having been surprised by her, at what he has elicited from her; at, so to speak, a success, rather than a failure. . . . Rather than imagine himself to have elicited that, or solicited it, Othello would imagine it elicited by anyone and everyone else—surprised, let me say, to find that she is flesh and blood. It was the one thing he could not imagine for himself. For if she is flesh and blood then, since they are one, so is he.

Cavell then generalizes, in a memorable observation: "If such a man as Othello is rendered impotent and murderous by aroused, or by having aroused, female sexuality; or let us say: if this man is horrified by human sexuality, in himself and in others; then no human being is free of this possibility." Sexuality, Cavell continues, is the field in which the idea of human finitude, "of its acceptance and its repetitious overcoming," is worked out. In other words, we are all to some degree ashamed and horrified at our own sexuality, of which another person's sexual response to us is the proof. We are horrified because we wish not to accept our finitude. We wish to be pure souls without limit or imperfection.

Cavell's essay is one of the best things written about the play, and one of his own best essays, haunting and devastating to experience. I recall the sense of sudden revelation that swept over all of us when Cavell first presented it in a class I taught with him at Harvard in 1980. But now, with the distance of time, I must say that what Cavell is describing looks to me not like a universal human reality, but like a common style of misogyny, in which people—usually males—have a stake in being above the merely bodily, and find themselves reminded by women's sexuality that they are not in that way lofty. But this sort of shame and revulsion at sexuality is hardly inevitable. Why on earth should one think that "no human being is free of this possibility"? (Antony and Cleopatra are utterly free of this type of disgust-misogyny. What disgusts her, and turns the world into a "sty," is the absence of humor, not the presence of the body.) As a reading of the play, Cavell's assimilation of *Othello* to *The Kreutzer Sonata* is much too quick, neglecting the fact that Desdemona's primary mode of interaction with Othello is not sexual rapture but compassionate understanding, directed at the suffering that he has experienced during his exploits.

Here is where Zamir gets going, in another wonderful chapter. Othello, he argues, has become deeply invested in seeing himself as identical with his heroic role. He is that outsize hero, and the vulnerable shapeless person within has been concealed by that grandiose construction, to such an extent that Othello himself does not even remember that he really is that vulnerable inchoate self. Desdemona sees past the persona to the self within: she recognizes, and pities, his vulnerability. Othello is erotically drawn to her by her compassionate response: "Othello falls in love when he encounters pity directed at him, when, for a change, he is not being used but is understood." But committed as he is to invulnerability, to being nothing more nor less than the grand heroic construct, he simply cannot stand the loving knowing gaze that reaches past his achievements to "some deeper foundation of his being," "an unbearable penetrating love that sees through to his source." He has to extinguish the eyes that see him, and love him, too deeply. "In his growing abuse of her, Othello wants this kind of love to stop somehow."

In other words, the general human problem raised by the play is the problem of the "false self" (Winnicott's term) with which we so often mask our real, childlike selves. All human beings have this problem to some degree, wanting to hide from the gaze of those who see our vulnerability too clearly (although it is also seductive to be so seen). For some people, however, the problem is more agonizing than for others, because some people have become so invested in being competent and in control that they have not attended to their inner selves or cultivated the emotional and receptive parts of their personalities. The result is that the true self, the one within, remains in an infantile condition, and the controlling adult has little conscious access to it. When it is seen and addressed, it can be a terrifying experience.

Zamir does not make use of Winnicott's concepts, but that is how I would make sense of his shrewd suggestions. Still, his reading has a harder time than Cavell's in making sense of the sexual form that Othello's fantasies take. For Cavell, "rather than imagine himself to have elicited that, or solicited it, Othello would imagine it elicited by anyone and everyone else." Moreover, the very fact that Desdemona is aroused means, for him, that she is a whore, to be distanced from the self who is striving for purity. (Misogyny often works this way, by projecting the feared and loathed aspects of the self onto others: she, not I, is the body; she, not I, is an animal being.)

How would Zamir, by contrast, make sense of Othello's sexual focus? He would say, I suppose, that by portraying his wife to himself as a whore, attending to many men, Othello can deny that she is focused all too intently on loving him. "Iago," says Zamir, is Othello's "mode of resistance and something in him is using Iago so that it can bloom to full expression." What he cannot stand is the real love that she offers, and so he would prefer to believe anything else. I am not entirely satisfied with such an account of Othello's obsessively sexual fantasies, and I wish that Zamir had said more about this issue.

Yet Zamir's reading is very strong in explaining Othello's odd and disjointed language in the murder scene, in which a carefully constructed persona has unraveled and he no longer knows where or what his selfhood is. He speaks in strange third-person abstractions. He seems to have lost hold of his "I." ("It is the cause, my soul.") Above all, Zamir makes better sense than Cavell of Othello's obsession with extinguishing Desdemona's vision: "Put out the light, and then put out the light." And later, "This look of thine will hurl my soul from heaven." On Cavell's reading, he should be obsessed with her bodily movements, her sexual organs. Zamir convincingly shows us why he is so afraid of her eyes.

Zamir simply offers, side by side, his readings of *Antony and Cleopatra* and *Othello*. He draws no explicit conclusion from the juxtaposition, but these readings, juxtaposed, make us wonder why Antony and Cleopatra do not fall prey to the same romantic agony. It's not that they do not feel jealousy—but the jealousy that they know is of a limited and daily sort, not monstrous or murderous. The answer, it would appear, is given by Zamir's fine passages on their "idiosyncratic practices": they are willing to acknowledge what is uneven, silly, and odd about the self—to let it be seen, to let it be. In their way highly regal and heroic, they have no stake in being only that. The most intelligent and commanding woman in all of Shakespeare, Cleopatra is also one of the silliest and most childlike—and it is this capacity for allowing silliness to be seen that is their personal salvation and, by its absence, Othello's doom.

Zamir's book has its defects. Like many first books, it opens up more questions than it pursues. It lacks, to some extent, what Cavell always gives us: the sense of a coherent and distinctive philosophical sensibility with its own well-thought-out views on the significant questions. Yet those faults can also be seen as virtues: openness rather than dogmatism; a willingness to be puzzled rather than to assert; an acknowledgment that the world, and Shakespeare, does not fit into a single tidy philosophical picture. Nuttall and McGinn fail because they make Shakespeare look simple, reducing him to a primer. Cavell brilliantly succeeds at being Cavell, which is to say that his readings always illuminate issues of human significance; but one often has the sense that the plays are being used as occasions for the pursuit of Cavell's own preoccupations. In Zamir, however, the plays challenge the philosopher to new thought. Zamir's approach is respectful of mystery and complexity, and always suggests that the plays contain more than his interpretations have elicited.

To write philosophically about Shakespeare, or any other great author or artist, one needs not so much philosophical learning, or even philosophical argument, but a genuinely philosophical temperament, puzzled and even humble before life's complexities, and willing to put one's sense of life on the line in the process of reading a text. As Plato rightly said, it is no chance matter that we are discussing, but how one should live. The philosopher needs to turn to literature because literature gets at depths of human experience, tragic or comic, that philosophical prose does not reach; but then the philosopher will need to show the imprint of that complexity, to reveal something of the pain or the joy that the work evokes from his or her own character. *Double Vision* owes its success precisely to this capacity for philosophical puzzlement, for laying the plays newly open both to emotional experience and to serious reflection.

# CHAPTER THIRTY-ONE

# The Passion Fashion

CRISTINA NEHRING (2009), A Vindication of Love: Reclaiming Romance for the Twenty-First Century

Women today are too risk-averse in love, charges Cristina Nehring. We "settle," and seek comfort rather than passion. In flight from pain, we end up too often with mediocre and cramped relationships. Obsessed with control, we lack "the generous fault to put oneself entirely in another's hands and thus be at his mercy." We employ a whole battery of devices to lessen our exposure to experience, to distance ourselves from real vulnerability: we regard our passions with ironic distance; we convert sex into a commodity; we glorify momentary pleasure rather than lasting emotion.

In the process, Nehring continues, women are losing out on one of life's great goods. For love is not just wonderful in itself, it is also a source of energy for the rest of life's activities—particularly, perhaps, for artistic and intellectual creativity. And it is a source of insight, leading us to see ourselves and others with more generous and accurate eyes. (Here Nehring draws persuasively on Plato's *Phaedrus*.) In sum, love makes the entire person come alive—but only if it is pursued with sufficient openness and daring that it brings with it a constant danger of pain and loss.

So far, so good. Nehring certainly raises an important issue—although it is not only with respect to love, and not only yesterday and today, that people have preferred to live in an excess of caution. Most people in most times and places have been averse to risk, avoiding deep commitments of all sorts—to work, to justice, to a cause, to a country—because they can see that through such commitments they would risk failure on a large scale. Most people enjoy contemplating the sufferings of tragic heroes, but they do not wish to be called upon for heroism themselves. Not caring deeply; looking at everything with irony, as a mere spectacle; and pursuing superficial pleasures: these are clever ways of evading or thwarting tragedy—in love, but also in every department of life. The smallness of aspiration against which Nietzsche inveighed in his portrait of "the last man" is not, as he suggested, a recent creation of bourgeois European Christianity. It is a pervasive inclination of ordinary human life.

But it is certainly possible that in America in our own era we are seeing a rising tide of risk aversion. If I compare my students today with my student contemporaries of the 1960s and 1970s, they certainly do seem to be more cautious and more calculating about career choice, political engagement, and aspiration generally. They make prudent life plans, and they are unembarrassed by all their prudence. It would not surprise me if attitudes toward romantic love have become similarly cautious and calculating, and perhaps also similarly ironic and detached. How could they not, if people are determined not to take large risks in any precinct of life?

Nehring provides no systematic evidence for the claim that attitudes toward love have changed. She ignores a huge stretch of popular culture when she says that we badly need some books that make passionate romance sexy for women. Can it be that she has never encountered romance novels? Does she not go to the movies? Still, she is on solid ground when she contends that many people miss a lot in life, including a deeper under-standing of self and other, because they are determined not to fail and not to suffer—because they hold the conviction that it is not better to have loved and lost. If you are a person globally averse to risk, then you will circumspectly avoid profound personal love, because its riskiness is obvious.

Nehring seeks to "reinvent" romantic love for our time, and to accom-plish this by telling great love stories from literature and history, trying to get us to see how appealing they are in their proud openness to risk and in the magnitude of loss to which they make themselves vulnerable. Abelard and Heloise, Antony and Cleopatra, Mary Wollstonecraft and William Godwin, Margaret Fuller and Count Giovanni Ossoli, Jean-Paul Sartre and Simone de Beauvoir, Frida Kahlo and Diego Rivera—they are all fun to read about, and they do remind us of the joyousness and the wisdom that can come from life lived on a grand scale, without crippling self-protectiveness. (Although most of Nehring's key examples are heterosexual, she expresses sympathy with same-sex lovers too, and evidently thinks that the same analysis applies to their choices.) Nehring rarely mentions the fact that some of these examples are fictional and some real, but blurring that line does not cause confusion, because her strategy is to show the lasting appeal of these stories for women today, as models and possibilities.

Unfortunately—since there is a good idea here—Nehring does not have terribly good taste about what is sexy in literary love. She adores the large melodramatic gesture, but does not seem drawn to subtlety, playfulness, or finesse. There is "hardly a sexier moment in the history of opera," she pronounces, than the scene in *Carmen* in which Carmen convinces Don José to release her. Well, all right, the music is first-rate, but the view of love on offer is so adolescent that even Nietzsche—famous for his silly views about women and love—went for it. The simple man brought low by the wiles of a heartless seductress: this is a banal male fantasy, and it has very little to do with anything like love.

One suspects that Nehring would be utterly bored by the passages in opera—which is indeed a vast literature about love—that explore love and sexuality in a more subtle and, I think, more genuinely erotic manner: the playful, tender seduction duet "Il core vi dono" in *Così Fan Tutte*, which surely depicts risk in its own way, by showing how one can search for one's own heart and then discover that it is beating over there, in someone else's body; or the ecstatic final duet "Pur ti miro, pur ti godo" in *L'Incoronazione di Poppea*, which shows why one would want to take a risk in the first place— so as to attain a rapturous focus on the person one loves. Notice that in both lyrics the "you," not the "I," is paramount: these lovers are savoring one another, not their own interesting mental states.

For Nehring, only the crashingly obvious and way-over-the-top is sexy. This is a considerable defect in a book that aims to re-invigorate romantic love. Similarly, and astonishingly, she dismisses Shakespeare's comedies as sources for insight into romantic love, calling them "frivolous," "light-hearted," and "without gravity." (A part of the problem is that she appears to think that laughter is incompatible with passion.) And Nehring's aesthetic deficiencies are amply on display in her writing, which is breathless, full of cheap effects, and as narcissistic as a teenager's diary:

As I write these words, I bear the bodily scars of a loss or two in love. I have been derailed by love, hospitalized by love, flung around five continents, shaken, overjoyed, inspired, and unsettled by love.

There is a lot more writing as bad as this in Nehring's book. Her bad prose has an ethically unpleasant flavor, in its fascination with her own experience, her own pain, and her own ecstasy. This is surely not helpful if what one is pursuing is love, which is, after all, directed at another.

Her style is not Nehring's only problem. Her central thesis is really two distinct arguments, one sensible and wise, the other adolescent and silly. The wise thesis is that one should be willing to incur risk for the sake of a deep and valuable love. This advice may not be for everyone, but for those who have the strength to live that way, such a life does, as she says with Plato, promise great rewards—even when, as often happens, the love turns out to involve reversal or some other type of suffering. (There is always death at the end of even the happiest love.) We can add to the wise thesis a corollary that Nehring at times endorses: given that people tend to be self-insulating and risk-averse, valuable love involves "conquest and self-conquest," a struggle against one's own selfish and self-protective propensities. In this sense, struggle does seem intrinsic to the valuable type of love.

The second thesis, which Nehring regularly confuses with the first, is that the quality of a love can be measured by the amount of danger, distance, riskiness, suffering, and so on that it involves. In the pursuit of this melodramatic idea, Nehring writes chapters with subtitles such as "Love as Inequality," "Love as Transgression," "Love as Absence," "Love as Failure." The idea that love is improved by suffering and loss is an adolescent view (despite the fact that some great Romantic writers have had it—but then Romanticism had its elements of immaturity). This argument generates some of the book's silliest parts, in which Nehring recommends to today's women a life spent in unseemly narcissistic reveling in their own tribulations.

The second thesis is not the same as the first. All of Nehring's favored lovers were willing to endure suffering for love, if life brought suffering their way—but they did not seek it out. They were quite prepared to live happily, and they eagerly did so, until illness and death took their inevitable toll. Sartre and de Beauvoir, Wollstonecraft and Godwin, Antony and Cleopatra: none of these lovers courted suffering as a good in itself. By Nehring's own account, they enjoyed life and one another—and then, because of the way life is, they had to deal with adversity, loss, and death. But the roiled Romantic sensibility of Nehring's second thesis, and the characters who are its exemplars, is quite different: Werther was not prepared to live happily with anyone, and he clearly regards his love as deep in proportion to its painfulness. Nehring clearly loves the Werther model of love, but I would question whether this is a model of love at all, and not a type of acute self-preoccupation—narcissism masquerading as love. Unlike love (as Nehring in her Platonic mood describes love), it yields no insight into any other person, because the gaze is resolutely on the vicissitudes of the self. Nor does it yield any insight into nature, since nature is seen through a fog of the sufferer's own projected emotions. Nehring asks women to take generous risks, rejecting self-concern and self-protectiveness, but in her fascination with the pain of the self she moves awfully close to the invincible self-involvement that she rightly criticizes.

Each of Nehring's chapters generates its own version of the two theses, and of the tension between them. Real love may be able to surmount social inequality—but does it require or thrive on social inequality? Real love may require suffering or loss, and this suffering may move us when we contemplate it—but does the love itself really get better or more "purified" the more the lovers suffer? Nehring certainly does not show that lovers are more open to one another because of the suffering that they endure. Again, deep love may at times lead lovers to transgress restrictive social norms, but surely it does not follow that love is deeper and more real the more transgressive it is. And this confusion about transgression is nothing other than a staple of male mid-life crisis. Politicians seem particularly prone to this confusion, perhaps because that profession selects for a high degree of narcissism.

Nehring addresses her book to women. She thinks that it is women in particular who need to hear her message, because she has an unusual diagnosis of the reasons for today's risk-averse living. Bypassing such plausible causes as pervasive human anxiety, the desire to control the uncontrollable, the felt need to surmount mortality and the limits of the body, she pins the whole thing on—fanfare of operatic trumpets!—feminism. Feminism is to blame for women's rejection of romantic love because, says Nehring, feminism asks women to be always rational and always in control, rejecting the romantic emotions as sources of low status or even of servitude. Moreover, feminism urges us to see love in contractual terms, and that sort of calculation is incompatible with real passion.

Let us admit that some feminists have mistrusted love altogether, and have urged women not to allow themselves to fall under its sway. One can always find such passages from some of the early radical feminists (though Nehring is quite wrong to pin this view on Andrea Dworkin, who wanted to open a space for real passion by getting rid of the idea that the man is always entitled to use force to gain his ends). And let us also admit that some feminists have at least suggested that correct sexual relations should not involve anything like abandon, or play with power relations—a view that Nehring appears to target, albeit unclearly. Some feminists may have been so severe in their critique of inequality that they insisted on too vigilant a control over people's unruly fantasy lives. But the dominant view in feminism, I think, has been that the context of the relationship as a whole is all-important: in a context of mutual respect, intimacy, and trust, there is nothing problematic about experimenting with passivity, abandon, and temporary power and powerlessness.

Let us admit, too, that some feminists have wrongly criticized Mary Wollstonecraft for her passionate erotic life, in which she seems to them to be too susceptible, too lacking in pride. To the extent that some feminists have said this, Nehring is right to point out that the energy of some of the best feminist work comes from a willingness to seek passion without self-protection.

On the whole, though, the idea that women who are romantic and sexually passionate cannot be real thinkers has come more from males than from females, as Nehring herself notes. Men have had an irritating propensity to react to the presence of a sexually and romantically charged woman as if she were a source of trouble and confusion, and to feel that clear thinking can only take place if she is ushered out of the room. But that is their problem, not ours; and Nehring is right to say that women should never have listened to them. Male artists, as Nehring emphasizes, have always been allowed to have love lives, and women should have demanded the same right from the start. So I agree with Nehring that a productive feminism should not internalize the male critique of female sexuality, and that it should claim the right to equal erotic lives. How far this is the problem of feminism, and how far it is just an understandable reaction to a real problem that women were having in the workplace, still needs to be determined.

What certainly cannot be maintained, however, is that the search for equality itself is the death knell of passion. Nehring agrees that women did not get much opportunity to take risks for love until feminism came along: they were treated like property, and they could not really choose a mate for love. They were subject to force, and this was taken to be normal, the way things were, especially in marriage. Real sexual agency, for all but a lucky or privileged few, required feminism, with its insistence on the right to divorce, and its protection against marital rape, and increased attention to problems of sexual coercion in the workplace. Nehring seems to grant this—but then she should grant also that the entry of law into the domain of intimacy is not the end of romance, but its necessary condition. Unless and until women can earn money without depending on men; unless and until they can protect their bodies against assault, even in an intimate relationship; unless and until they can protect themselves from unwanted pregnancy; unless and until they feel free to go to the police when they have been assaulted—unless all these conditions of freedom and autonomy are in place, the pursuit of adult romance may be jeopardized for many women. Fear and silence will reign supreme. Why were the students of my generation so joyful and so willing to accept risk? In part, because feminism had cleared a space for risk of the valuable sort, by beginning to control the bad and non-necessary risks that women used to run every day in a male-dominated world.

But, says Nehring, love thrives on inequality. Here, of course, we have the two-theses problem. The first says, wisely, that real love should be prepared to overcome inequalities of power, class, and station. (That is the plot of more or less every Victorian novel.) The second says, foolishly, that real love requires inequality of power, class, and station. So confused is Nehring at this point that she interprets *Pride and Prejudice* as confirmation of her second thesis rather than her first: it shows, she says, that people always eroticize class difference and would never love people of similar station. What a trivialization of Elizabeth Bennett and Mr. Darcy! Their deep moral and intellectual affinity, and their strong romantic attraction, gradually manage to surmount the obstacles imposed by rigid social norms and the internal dispositions (prejudice and pride) that they engender. It is true that there would be no novel without the distance; after all, there has to be a plot. It seems obviously untrue, however, that there would be no love without the distance. Far from social distance being eroticized, it is, until late in the novel, a source of erotic blindness. At this point Nehring's argument loses all clarity, as, seeking confirmation for her anti-feminist thesis, she begins to treat any qualitative difference at all as "inequality": the very fact of heterosexuality, she now says, shows that sexual desire thrives on inequality.

But does passion even require qualitative difference? Here Nehring appears to endorse a view of sexual attraction that Roger Scruton popularized some time ago in his book *Sexual Desire*. Really valuable sexual passion, Scruton said, requires qualitative differences between the parties, because sexual love, when valuable, involves a kind of risky exploration of strange terrain, and we should think less well of those who stick to the familiar. Scruton could not advance this claim as a descriptive thesis about sexual choices, for nothing is more obvious than that people tend to choose people close to themselves in all sorts of ways—religion, class, education. But he did put it forward as a normative claim, and he used it to argue that hetero-sexuality is superior to homosexuality, because it involves greater adventure and risk. Something like this is probably what Nehring has in mind, although she has no disdain for same-sex passion.

What should we think of this? Do people who choose qualitatively simi-lar partners really lack courage? The most obvious problem with Scruton's thesis was that it was capriciously and inconstantly applied: to sexual orien-tation, but not to romances between adults and children, between Protestants and Catholics, between the virtuous and the immoral. A more subtle prob-lem with his argument is that it is not even clear how it could be assessed: for, as the philosopher Nelson Goodman showed in his great essay "Seven Strictures on Similarity," the concept of similarity is so slippery that it has basically no content. Any two things are similar and dissimilar to one another in manifold respects.

But the real problem with Scruton—and Nehring, who speaks, Scruton-like, of the "enigmatic Other"—is that they both mislocate erotic risk. What is risky is not getting in touch with some trait that is dissimilar to some trait of one's own. It is the whole idea of becoming vulnerable to an inner life that one cannot see and can never control. It is not qualitative difference, but the sheer separateness of the other person, the idea of an independent source of vision and will, that makes real love an adventure in generosity—or, if one is like Proust's narrator, a source of mad jealousy and destructive projects of domination and control. And this has nothing at all to do with class difference, or gender difference, or even temperamental difference. It has to do only with the fact of human individuation—that minds and bodies never merge, that intimacy is not a fusion but a conversation.

There is a grain of truth in Nehring's thesis about personal qualities: it is at least plausible to maintain that loving someone who is complicated, opaque, and in some respects concealed can be of particular interest or value. At any rate, we often think less well of people who are willing to love only people who are altogether obvious and lacking in complexity. Rightly or wrongly, we think that such lovers are refusing some challenge, or lacking in curiosity. And yet an erotic attraction to psychological complexity does not require pursuing class difference, career difference, power difference, or some other obvious kind of difference. Indeed, it is difficult to imagine how one could ever pursue a relationship with persons as complicated as some of the artists and writers adduced by Nehring without a context of shared activities, commitments, or aspirations that would generate the kind of friendship and openness that make insight into another person's complexi-ties possible. The way she tells the stories of those complicated artists and writers, they understood this well.

Nehring's complaint against feminism appears to be groundless (apart from offering a fair critique of some of its radical excesses). Pursuing equal respect is perfectly compatible with love. And what's more, Nehring herself seems to think so. I would say that she is a feminist in spite of herself. For among the many relationships that she depicts, she keeps being drawn to the ones that assuredly do involve equal respect and reciprocity: relationships between strong thinkers or artists who respect one another's work and sphere of action, and find a way to enact equality even in a world of inequality. In the case of Margaret Fuller, she makes it clear that she finds the Cambridge suitors who fail to appreciate Fuller's intellect pathetic and contemptible, and she is very glad that Fuller ended up with Ossoli, who did know how to respect her.

All these are feminist paradigms, in the sense that the male of the couple is prepared to defy convention by giving the woman a respect, and a sphere of action, that the surrounding world does not give her. They involve deep connection and a willingness to risk difficulty and adversity, but they combine these qualities with reciprocity. Indeed, it is clear that much of their depth is owed precisely to their reciprocity, because mutual respect generates trust, and trust in turn promotes greater openness and generosity. Nehring herself concludes that "romantic love is better between partners with equal rights. . . . We can have both knowledge and mystery, equality and abandon."

Nehring seems like a very sensible person with some provocative and useful observations, and some wonderful historical and literary material. If her book has an emboldening effect on some of its readers, if it makes them question their inclination to prudence and calculation, then it will almost certainly be for the better. How unfortunate, then, that—led on, perhaps, by the demand for hype and extremism that is a large part of the book-marketing industry these days—she should have rushed into print with an unrefined and not fully disciplined set of ideas, uttered in breathless and melodramatic prose. Her own thoughts deserve better.

# CHAPTER THIRTY-TWO

# Becky, Tess, and Moll

Nicola Lacey (2008), *Women, Crime, and Character:
From Moll Flanders to Tess of the D'Urbervilles*

Early in the 1870s, the London publishing house Leadham and Loiter published a new work on female criminality. Entitled *Criminal Queens*, it appealed to popular fascination with extreme female behaviour and crime-generating mental states. Its author, however—a middle-aged widow struggling to support two adult children on a literary income—refused to pander by depicting women as frail pathological creatures incapable of responsible moral agency. "After all," she writes to a prominent critic, justifying her decision to write the biographies of famous criminal royalty, "how few women there are who can raise themselves above the quagmire of what we call love, and make themselves anything but playthings for men." The author herself, not surprisingly, aspires to the same condition: a clever con artist, who "used her beauty . . . with a well-considered calculation that she could obtain material assistance in the procuring of bread and cheese, which was very necessary to her," Matilda Carbury seeks financial independence and control over her future, a difficult goal for a woman of slender means and equally slender talent.

Matilda Carbury and her book are of course fictitious, the invention of Anthony Trollope in *The Way We Live Now* (1875). The portrait derives additional interest from Trollope's suggestion, in his *Autobiography*, that it is partly based on the career of his mother. Fanny Trollope was a successful novelist who actually did support her struggling family on a literary income, producing her first volume at the age of fifty and completing 114 books in all. She, however, probably did not seduce her reviewers, and her topics were industrial life and the evils of slavery, not female criminality. But Lady Carbury's fictional career neatly draws together the central themes of Nicola Lacey's engrossing historical narrative: the British public's fascination with female crime and extreme mental states; the restrictions to women's freedom that the Victorian era brought; and the resilience of women in the face of these constraints, their refusal to be treated as mere "playthings of love."

Although Lacey bases her study largely on novels, she does not mention Trollope, and this is a pity, because he is a gold mine for all of her themes. Otherwise, her coverage of eighteenth- and nineteenth-century novels dealing with gender and power is impressive (ranging over Defoe, Fielding, Richardson, Austen, Dickens, Thackeray, Hardy, and Eliot), and her aim to show thinking about criminal law reform and changing perceptions of female criminality through the prism of the novel is original and illuminating. A professor of criminal law and legal theory whose book had its origins in her Clarendon Law Lectures, Lacey vigorously defends her focus on novels as sources for social and legal ideas. First, novels aspired to social realism, so they can be used as evidence for social norms and practices alongside other historical sources. Second, in the process of re-creating crimes, investigations, and trials, they draw heavily on juridical sources that are otherwise lost or obscure. Third, leading novelists were also prominent thinkers about criminal law reform: this is most obviously true of Fielding, but most of the others have a strong interest in this process. Finally, the genre has a didactic purpose: it attempts to engender those habits of vision and sympathy that are (in the novelists' view) essential to a productive social dialogue about criminal law and its reform. They are thus a creative force in the process that they also depict. All of this is powerful and persuasive, although Lacey pays less attention than she might to individual differences in novelists' views of human beings and society. Eliot, Hardy, and Trollope, for example, are rough contemporaries, but each has a distinctive moral and social vision. Differences of outlook are largely absent from the book, which treats shifts from one novelist to the next entirely in terms of diachronic change.

After justifying her focus on the novel, Lacey rehearses the familiar evidence that the period saw a gradual shift—not complete until the mid-twentieth century, in her view—from a character-based mode of assessing criminals (where "character" can mean anything from status to a habitual pattern of acts) to a concentration on evidence concerning the particular case, including the defendant's mental state. With this change go the rise of the professional defence lawyer, new methodological constraints on the investigative role of the police, and the development of rules of evidence— in short, the professionalization of criminal procedure. Lacey's intriguing question then is: how is this change related to an equally obvious shift in novelists' depictions of female criminals—the shift, mentioned in her subtitle, From Defoe's Moll Flanders to Hardy's Tess? Moll, a cheerfully amoral thief, independent of male control, can be the heroine of a novel in the eighteenth century. By the Victorian era, contends Lacey, no such criminal heroine is even thinkable. Tess's murder of her seducer can be described only in terms of victimhood, punishment, and retaliation.

The thread of Lacey's argument is not always easy to follow, in part because she spends too much time summarizing the views of literary scholars.

Especially in so short a book, she might have had more confidence in her own good judgement. But her basic contention is clear: one common story of the connection between the two shifts is false. The false story is that women came to be viewed as delicate, mentally unstable creatures whose crimes were typically the product of some pathological mental state for which they were not responsible. This shift, claim Lacey's opponents, explains both the new focus on mental state in criminal trials and the impossibility of a heroine like Moll. Of course, even if women were generally viewed as mentally incompetent, that would not explain why trials of all criminal defendants, male and female, shifted in the direction of crime-specific evidence (including evidence of *mens rea*). But Lacey makes a more fundamental objection: novels of the period show us that women simply were not regarded as flighty things without responsibility for their acts. To judge from literary evidence, Lacey argues, the Victorians did take a keen interest in extreme or pathological mental states. (Here again differences should be noted: Wilkie Collins is obsessed with them, Trollope not very interested.) They did not, however, represent these states, even when present, as removing women's agency. Instead, they portrayed women, on the whole, as morally responsible agents acting within a newly constrained social frame. Even Hardy's Tess and Eliot's Hetty Sorrel, extreme though their emotions are at times, emerge as agents who can be expected to take responsibility for what they have done. What makes these Victorian heroines different from Moll is the world in which they live, a world that is newly confining, newly intolerant of transgressive female behaviour. (Lacey points out that Thackeray's Becky Sharp is like Moll in deeds, but the judgement on her is utterly different.) Women who transgress "the bounds of conventional femininity" aren't necessarily crazy, but they do have to be punished.

By the time we get to *Middlemarch* (1874), we find that a strong woman has little room for agency of any sort. Eliot sees the walls that hedge in Dorothea Brooke as socially constructed, rather than inherent in female nature, and she sees them as pernicious. They are, however, there; and Eliot can imagine a happy ending for her heroine only by leaving its details utterly obscure. Here one feels especially acutely the absence of Trollope. Hardy, with his dark fatalism, does show life as meting out punishment to more or less everyone who aspires, though certainly not to women only: Bathsheba Everdean exercises agency far more successfully than Jude, or Michael Henchard. But in Lacey's account, Hardy's sex-equal bleakness goes unremarked, and Tess's problems are chalked up to women's (recent) lot. As for Eliot, sympathetic though she is in some ways to the constraints surrounding women, she nonetheless has an unsettling fondness for seeing ambitious women punished. Both Hetty and her illegitimate child have to die, and, as Lacey notes, Eliot's three most "luminously agentic female figures"— Dorothea Brooke, Gwendolyn Harleth and Maggie Tulliver—are, as she puts it, "buried"—in, respectively, "an unbelievable marriage, an unbearable marriage, and a premature death." Is this the Victorian era, or is it Eliot's own moral/aesthetic preference for the punishment of transgression? Here Lacey's flattened view of authors—they all have basically the same social vision to impart, differing only by chronology—is in a troubling tension with her more generous view of novelists as creative social agents, each with a distinctive moral vision.

This summer I happened to read Trollope's *Doctor Thorne* (1858) right after reading Eliot's *Adam Bede* (1859). Both concern the aftermath of a seduction and the birth of an illegitimate child. Hetty Sorrel is rescued from the death penalty and transported to Australia, but then the novelist decrees that she must die there. The law releases her, but Eliot will not. The illegitimate child has died long since, and everyone involved seems to feel that it would never have had a decent life. In Trollope, by contrast, the seduced mother accepts a marriage proposal from a nice man who carries her off to America, where she has several more children and, apparently, a happy life. Since the nice man can't quite see his way clear to taking the illegitimate baby to America with them, she gives it to her friend the village doctor, who brings "Mary Thorne" up with all love and favour, and she becomes a fine young woman. Eventually she marries for love. Only after her lover has embraced both her illegitimacy and her poverty does she turn out to have money after all (inherited from a working-class relative who broke all social norms through his talent at engineering and ended life as a peer of the realm). Moreover, even the snooty characters who object to Mary's illegitimacy treat it, significantly, not as a moral stain but as a class problem— repeatedly they compare it to the birth of the wealthy Miss Dunstable, who has come from tradesman-class (but not illegitimate) origins and inherited a fortune her father made by developing a patent pharmaceutical called the Oil of Lebanon. So illegitimacy is not damning, and Trollope clearly approves the kindly doctor's view that illegitimacy is an utterly ridiculous ground for the punishment of a child.

In short: there are spaces for subversion and evasion even in the Victorian world (as Eliot knew in her life, if not in her fiction). The merciful eye of Trollope finds them out, urging his readers to cultivate them, whereas the austere eye of Eliot closes them up. Trollope, we might say, is the emotional Harry Houdini of fiction: the one who shows how ingenuity, love, and honesty can extricate people from the most apparently inexorable death-dealing constraints, all of which are imposed not by fate, but by fashion, wealth, and their slavish adherents. He urges his reader to view people with generous and merciful eyes: one may then be able to imagine one's way out of many apparently fixed situations. The character who is punished in Trollope is Augusta Gresham, who refuses a man she really loves, a solicitor named Mortimer Gazebee, because a snobbish female friend tells her that the "blood" of a mere lawyer is not good enough for her. Augusta does not marry; a few years later, the snobbish friend walks down the aisle with Mr. Gazebee. That is punishment, certainly: but for lack of emotional integrity, not for ambition and agency.

Let us now return to Lady Carbury of *The Way We Live Now*. For, of course, she is my answer to Lacey's contention that a successful transgressor like Moll Flanders is impossible in the Victorian era. (Published in 1875, one year after *Middlemarch* was first issued in a single volume, the novel is the antitype to that tale of female doom, just as *Doctor Thorne* is the antitype to *Adam Bede*.) Trollope knew first-hand, as a child watching his remarkable mother, how at least some of the confines of a woman's lot could be transcended by ingenuity, hard work, and a capacity for joy. (He says that his mother had more of the last than any person he ever saw.) He invests his heroine with similar qualities. Married to a physically abusive husband, Lady Carbury defies convention by leaving him, apparently running off with a lover. She then defies it again by returning to the husband out of sympathy, to take care of him when he is in decline (from alcohol). After his death Lady C. therefore receives double opprobrium, both for the transgression and for the lack of firmness exhibited in her compassionate return. A penniless social outsider with two children to support (one a prodigal), Lady Carbury finds that the best way to survive is to write the type of book that the public wants to read. So her first offering is *Criminal Queens*, a series of sensationalized historical tales that includes Cleopatra, Semiramis, and Mary Queen of Scots—all women who are able to commit crime on a grand scale because they refuse to be simply "playthings of love."

Interestingly, Trollope is with Lacey here: he represents the public as eager for tales of agency, not details of pathology, and as eager to see what women can do in the realm of criminality when, being royalty, they are not circumscribed by the usual confines of middle-class morality. That is Lady C.'s view of her public, of course, not the novelist's directly. But the criticism she is represented as receiving focuses entirely on the historical inadequacy of her work, not its moral message. Matilda Carbury knows that *Criminal Queens* is a badly written book and that she has no talent—but she needs money. So she tirelessly promotes the book by flattery and flirtation, trying to get all of London's prominent reviewers on her side. "It is so very hard to get paid for what one does," she observes with understatement. Bitter towards men and marriage, she does not mind a little mild sexual bribery, a kiss or two in the service of a favourable review. In her way, Lady C. is a reprobate in the tradition of Moll and Becky Sharp. She is, however, also much more, and, as the novel goes on, her dauntless pluck and ingenuity, and her generous and determined, if at times unwise, love of her children, inspire the reader with increasing admiration. What Trollope writes of his mother (even while criticizing her indifference to factual accuracy) could as well be said of his fictional creation: "She was an unselfish, affectionate, and most industrious woman, with great capacity for enjoyment and high physical gifts. She was endowed too, with much creative power, with considerable humour, and a genuine feeling for romance."

Towards the novel's end, something very surprising takes place. Lady Carbury decides to permit herself to love. She suddenly realizes that while she has been flirting with Mr. Broune, the literary critic of the *Morning Breakfast Table*, she has actually formed a friendship, based on fun, shared conversation, honesty, and mutual respect. (Another great Trollope theme is how love develops in middle age, a phenomenon no other Victorian novelist acknowledges.) She finds that she cannot play around with him any more. In a wonderful sentence that depicts the transition from flirtation to love, Trollope reports that she "found herself almost compelled to tell him what she really felt and thought." So—she decides to be happy. Trollope tells us that younger readers would probably find their bodily posture awkward, as they embraced: but then, he adds, "Youth always fails to appreciate that Age can feel, and acknowledge, physical passion."

Lady C. does abandon her literary career, and she even takes her husband's name. Trollope depicts this change, however, not as a diminution of her, but as a new readiness to pursue integrity—she always knew the novels were a con game—rather than money. Lacey might see this as a conversion from profitable criminality to Victorian propriety, but I think we should say instead that she is giving herself permission to enjoy life, rather than trying to defeat it. Far from becoming a mere "plaything of love", she is empowered. Of the many escapes from constraint depicted in Trollope's novels, perhaps this one, in which a woman escapes from her own traumatized bitterness into emotional freedom, is the most moving and the most hopeful. (Another comparable case is that of the cynical Oil of Lebanon heiress Miss Dunstable in *Doctor Thorne* and *Framley Parsonage*—never sought out for herself, but always for her fortune—who learns, in late middle age, to escape from her own scepticism by permitting herself to love the middle-aged Doctor Thorne, whom she is right to trust.) Trollope's world has its limits, to be sure. Even in *The Way We Live Now*, Mrs. Hurtle, the American woman who might or might not have a living husband from whom she might or might not be divorced, and who might or might not have shot a man in Oregon, must ultimately surrender Paul Montague, the proper Englishman she loves, to a more socially acceptable and boring mate, Lady Carbury's daughter Hetty. Even here, however, the novelist lets us know where true emotional depth and integrity reside, and his sympathy for Mrs. Hurtle quite unbalances the novel. As she returns to an open future in America, much of its energy departs with her. (Trollope's mother, we can't help remembering, once ran a retail business in Cincinnati.) Victorian novels, in short, show us constraint, but they (or some of them) also show us the subversive energy that led to women's suffrage and to all the countless changes in women's lives that have been made since, and that still need to be made. Nicola Lacey's book is so much fun to argue with that these ripostes are a sign of its strength.

# CHAPTER THIRTY-THREE

# Examined Life (Inheriting Socrates)

Astra Taylor (2009), The Examined Life (Film)

Astra Taylor is a gifted young filmmaker. *The Examined Life* shows a keen visual imagination and a vivid sense of atmosphere and place. It also testifies to a personal passion for philosophy. What I shall say in criticism of the film should not be taken as denigration of Taylor's talent, her creativity, or her deep sincerity.

Still, I found *The Examined Life* upsetting, because it presents a portrait of philosophy that is, I think, a betrayal of the tradition of philosophizing that began, in Europe, with the life of Socrates, although similar movements have flourished in other cultures.

One might quarrel, first, with the choice of participants. Peter Singer, Anthony Appiah, and I are all solidly within philosophy, as that discipline is usually understood. Most of the others in the film are figures in culture studies or religious studies or some other related discipline (I'd call West a political theorist), but what they do is not exactly philosophy, as I understand it. They aren't, even in their books, all that concerned with rigorous argument, or with the respectful treatment of opposing positions.

But I have not yet said what philosophy, as I understand it, is. So, let's think about Socrates, as he is portrayed in the early Platonic dialogues, such as *Euthyphro, Laches, Lysis, Charmides,* and as he describes his own way of life in the Platonic *Apology.* Socrates has a passion for argument. He doesn't like long speeches, and he doesn't make them. He also doesn't like authority. He takes nothing on trust, not from the poets, not from the politicians, not from any other source of cultural prestige and power. He questions everything, and he accepts only what survives reason's demand for consistency, for clear definitions, and for cogent explanations. This also means that Socrates and his interlocutor are equals: the fact that he is a philosopher gives him no special claim, no authority. Indeed, he practices on himself the same techniques of examination and refutation he practices on others.

If he is one step ahead of his interlocutors at times, it is only because he knows what he does not know, and they sometimes fancy that they have answers—which soon fall to bits.

What this Socrates says to a democratic culture impatient with deliberation and prone to yield to demagoguery of all sorts is: "Slow down. Think clearly. Do not defer to authority or peer pressure. Follow reason wherever it takes you, and don't trust anything else. Indeed, don't trust even reason: keep probing your arguments for faults, never rest content."

Socrates also teaches this impatient culture a new way of dealing with political or cultural disagreement. Instead of thinking of an opponent as an enemy to be defeated by the sheer power of one's words—what I might call the "talk-radio" conception of disagreement—he teaches us to think of opponents as people who have reasons, and who can produce them. When reasons are produced, it may turn out that the disagreement narrows: the "other side" may accept some of the same premises that "my side" starts from, and then the exercise of finding out where and why we differ will become a subtle search, not a contest of strength.

American culture, like the ancient Athenian democracy, is highly prone to authority and peer pressure, and to seeing political argument as a matter of boasts and assertions, of scoring "points" for one's side. That is why Socrates has so much to offer us, why Socrates is so urgently needed. I once talked with a student in a business college who had had to take a required philosophy course in which he studied the life and career of Socrates, and learned to argue, himself, in a Socratic manner. The instructor included a segment in which students conducted classroom debates on political issues, often being assigned to defend a position that was not their own. He said that this experience taught him a wholly new attitude to people who disagree with him in politics. He had never understood that it was possible to argue on behalf of a position that you yourself do not hold. Learning this, in turn, taught him that people on the "other side" could have reasons and be respected for those reasons. It was even fun and exhilarating to figure out where the source of the disagreement lay.

It was this aspect of Socrates—this insistence on deferring to nothing but what one had figured out with one's own reason—that inspired Kant and the philosophers of the Enlightenment, and this deliberative and egalitarian conception of philosophy continues to animate philosophy teaching all over our country and in many other countries. In our present polarized and hysterical political culture, we need Socrates more than ever.

In Astra Taylor's film, philosophers are cultural authority figures who think deep thoughts and make deep pronouncements. Trouble begins with the basic conception: the philosopher is always alone. This was not evident in the process of filming, since Taylor engaged me in a very intelligent Socratic process of question and answer, and she also allowed me to be Socratic with myself, so that I expressed throughout the objections to my own views and the give and take between me and my opponents. In the final version of the film, however, all this was lost, and each of us appeared as a pronouncer, a talking head. There was no sense of equality: the philosopher was a kind of deep and venerable guru, and spectators are supposed to find that inspiring. There was also virtually no sense of the structure of an argument: we each came across as people who had positions, rather than arguments for conclusions. So, we ended up looking just like those poets and politicians that Socrates subjected to his stinging critique.

Portraying philosophers as authority figures is a baneful inversion of the entire Socratic process, which aimed to replace authority with reason. Taylor, instead, replaces reason (since I'm sure some of us were at least trying to offer arguments) with authority. But authority is all over the place in our culture; we certainly don't need more of it. What we need is deliberation, and careful listening to one another, careful dissection of one another's positions.

It's not as if Taylor's portrait of the philosopher as a solitary profound thinker has no historical antecedents. One post-Enlightenment continental tradition does indeed portray the philosopher as a lonely thinker of profound thoughts. I'd mention Nietzsche and Heidegger as two sources of the picture that seems to animate the film. (Both, not coincidentally, preferred the Pre-Socratic philosophers to Socrates.) Heidegger was particularly energetic in setting himself up as an authority figure and encouraging deference. This example had a lot of influence, but I'd call it a pernicious influence, and a betrayal of the whole enterprise of philosophizing.

If I were making a movie about philosophy, I would try to show what philosophizing in the Socratic mode can contribute to a democratic public culture. This means that I would want to film interactions. I might start with a good philosophy class, showing the kind of enlivening that takes place under the pressure of questioning, and then I'd have the film follow up with the students later to talk about how the experience influenced their view of political and cultural debate. I would be sure to have opposing viewpoints represented, and treated respectfully and attentively by all participants. There would be no stars in my movie: the professors would be there only as facilitators of dialogue.

But we do not need to imagine what I *would* do: for I helped to do something just like this. Approached last year by the Dutch public TV company VPRO, who wanted to make a TV documentary about the ethical implications of the financial crisis, and wanted to show its impact on thinking at the University of Chicago Law School, where Barack Obama taught, I agreed to help them make the film, and they shot it in January 2008. Now it exists on DVD: *The Chicago Sessions: Law and Ethics of the Credit Crisis*, available from backlight.vpro.nl. I made the initial decision to entrust most matters to two very capable students: one a law student named Alexandra Kolod (a former graduate of the College, where she majored in Philosophy), and the other a former NPR broadcaster named Gretchen Helfrich, who used to run an excellent program called "Odyssey," which was cut, and who then went to law school. Last year, like Alex, she was a third-year law student. Alex and Gretchen had knowledge of the student body, so, in consultation with the Dutch producers, I charged them with selecting a group of students diverse in political viewpoint, as well as gender, race, ethnicity, and intellectual background. There were eight law students and four philosophy graduate students. We then selected pairs or trios of contrasting faculty members who would serve as the facilitators for each of the three sessions (six hours were filmed to make a one-hour program), and we told them that their role was to stimulate focused discussion of key ethical issues surrounding the financial crisis. We deliberately chose faculty with opposed starting points, and of course all of them were as committed to the rigorous and open exchange of critical argument as we were. I was one of the faculty, in the segment concerning "first principles and foundations." I argued with Eric Posner, a Utilitarian, but of course it was the students who did all the real work. I appear only once or twice in the finished product—contrary to the initial expectation of the producers, who knew me from another Dutch film, and expected me to play a sort of star role. But then they, too, got into the Socratic spirit.

I recommend viewing this film. Like Taylor's, it, too, has its moments of haunting visual beauty—shots, for example, of one of our law students taking the producers on a walk through a South Side neighborhood with lots of boarded-up houses, in the silence (it was a week so cold that nobody went out), and the deep white snow. But the real action was in the classroom. Even though the film is so greatly cut from its original length, you will still see the atmosphere of argument and dialogue that we were trying to achieve. Despite the bleakness of the topic, I think there is reason for hope if a group of young people so gifted, headed for positions of leadership, can listen to each other this well, and exchange ideas about matters touching their lives in an atmosphere of respect for reason.

Our public culture needs philosophy, but it needs what is on display in *The Chicago Sessions*, not what is on display in *The Examined Life*.

# CHAPTER THIRTY-FOUR

# Representative Women

CHRISTINE STANSELL (2010), The Feminist Promise: 1792
to the Present

For much of its existence, the feminist movement in the United States has looked like a loosely knit coalition of upstarts and insurgents making common cause around an evolving list of issues: suffrage, access to divorce, property rights, contraception, antidiscrimination law, sexual harassment, domestic violence, rape law and abortion rights, to name a few. In turn, feminism has apparently struck many historians as being both too topical and too diffuse to have a history. At least such a view offers the most likely explanation for an enduring deficiency. Although American historians have written incisive histories of marriage with attention to women's concerns (Nancy Cott's *Public Vows: A History of Marriage and the Nation*, Hendrik Hartog's *Man and Wife in America: A History*) and landmark biographies of feminist pioneers (Ellen Chesler on Margaret Sanger, Elizabeth Griffith on Elizabeth Cady Stanton, Nell Irvin Painter on Sojourner Truth), they have not given us any comparably authoritative history of the feminist movement in the United States. But now we have one.

Christine Stansell's magisterial *The Feminist Promise* traces the movement from its eighteenth-century inception to the present day, sorting out its crosscurrents and offering a useful narrative framework within which to situate its varied struggles. Stansell is an acclaimed scholar who has worked on a variety of topics in U.S. history, from antebellum and bohemian New York City to the histories of love and human rights. She is also a good writer, having honed her style by contributing numerous essays and reviews to a variety of general-interest publications. Though dense and impeccably documented, *The Feminist Promise* is lucid, accessible, and well organized. It will be a benchmark for some time to come—although, as we shall see, it has a significant shortcoming.

Here one should pause to raise a relatively minor question of exposition and framing. Although the book's sweeping title could lead one to believe that Stansell will discuss feminist movements in a variety of countries, and although the narrative occasionally turns to developments in Europe (particularly Britain) and even, more rarely, to Japan and India, Stansell takes as her project the story of feminism in the United States. Yet she should not be understood as claiming that the United States was the sole or even the primary cradle of feminism. In her final and excellent chapter on global feminism, Stansell rightly resists the idea that feminism is an American export to developing nations. We learn, for example, that India had its own indigenous feminist movement, inspired more by local struggles than by ideas from abroad. (Although Stansell does not trace the earlier history of that movement, its roots are in the eighteenth century, like those of its U.S. counterpart.) So the book does not mislead, ultimately. Yet I wish Stansell had explained the scope of her project more emphatically at the outset—granting in the process that feminism has multiple roots and branches, few of them being the outgrowth of democratic revolutions, and that her book is going to ignore most of them in order to focus on the story of the United States.

The material Stansell has organized is diffuse, since feminism has indeed been a diverse set of movements, reflecting pronounced differences of race, class, and region. Nonetheless, she wisely coordinates the welter of facts around a single, clear narrative thesis about two basic types of feminists, whom she calls "mothers" and "daughters." "Mothers" are rather conservative feminists. They love the traditional family and are fond of exalting the virtues of caring and compassion that women allegedly cultivate more than men. When mothers advocate for certain social changes, they do so in the name of these female virtues. Often their feminism has a religious dimension. Their demands are strong but not profoundly radical: they want women to be granted political equality so that they can put their virtues to work ameliorating the public sphere, but they leave unchallenged the status quo as to the nature of marriage, sexuality, and the family. "Daughters," by contrast, are radical and boisterous. They want to shake up everything. They demand a wholesale reconsideration of women's role in the world, of the entire distinction between male and female gender, and of the nature of marriage and sexuality.

The essence of Stansell's argument is that American feminism has proceeded in a lurching and uneven series of stages, alternating between periods of ascendancy for mothers and daughters. Nonetheless, even during times like the 1950s, when it seemed that mothers were securely entrenched, feminism continued to forge ahead, often in quieter ways but with a clear record of achievement nonetheless. Mothers and daughters agree about one facet of the "feminist promise": it is the struggle to achieve justice and equality in the public sphere. Daughters, however, insist rebelliously that this "promise" cannot be fulfilled without sweeping changes in the domestic realm that are not just strategic but fundamental matters of justice as well. Mothers and daughters differ about strategies but also, more profoundly, about goals.

Stansell begins with the American Revolution, which always presupposed, and only rarely questioned, the subordination of women. Nonetheless, Stansell argues that over time the abstract promises of the new American democracy "offered sanctuary to the aspirations of women," laying a foundation on which later feminists would build. A more radical strain of feminism emerged during the antislavery movement, as female abolitionists made bold claims about ending women's servitude. The abolitionist movement was heterogeneous, and some of its Christian feminists were conservative; but ultimately abolitionism prompted, Stansell claims, a thoroughgoing rethinking of women's position in society. The radical side of abolitionist feminism was strengthened by alliances with a variety of utopian movements, including Fourierist and Owenite socialism and New England Transcendentalism; and the epoch-making Seneca Falls convention of 1848 drew more on radical notions of natural rights than on Christian doctrine.

After the Civil War, radicals such as Elizabeth Cady Stanton became increasingly isolated, as a group of mothers, including the Women's Christian Temperance Union and its leader, Frances Willard, gained influence by insisting that women should progress by disciplining and shaming men within traditional marriage rather than by altering the terms and nature of marriage itself. Willard sentimentalized marriage and idealized femininity; Stanton protested that "the real woman is not up in the clouds nor among the stars, but down here upon earth . . . striving and working to support herself." But Stanton's remonstrations proved ineffectual, and in due time the mothers were leading the battle for women's suffrage, emphasizing that the alleged special virtues of women equipped them for the vote.

Yet by 1900 a younger generation of women had transformed the suffrage movement, "turning a polite, ladylike movement into a confrontational, contentious one." These daughters differed most obviously from the mothers in tactics and style, favoring street protests and a defiant anti-Victorian style of dress; they differed ideologically too, making common cause with the labor movement and demanding far more equality than simply the vote. (Exemplary in this regard was Margaret Sanger, who launched the birth-control movement.) For the suffragette daughters, "Feminism meant headlong flight from your mother's life," Stansell writes.

The struggle for the vote united feminists across many regional and class divisions. After that great battle was won in 1920, unity dissipated, and it has never been fully restored. Nonetheless, the story of alternating mother and daughter stages has continued, with the period after World War II signaling a return to domesticity and ushering in the infamous quietism of the '50s. Even here, though, Stansell shows that progress could still be made on some issues: the Equal Rights Amendment, framed in the 1920s, was championed during the '50s, and the National Organization for Women, established in 1966, made major contributions to women's progress on a wide range of issues, even while remaining a somewhat conservative organization of mothers. Daughters returned to the forefront in the '60s and '70s, and Stansell discusses the feminist ferment of these years effectively. The struggle over contraception and abortion rights, the struggle to redefine marriage, and the battle for adequate legal treatment of sex discrimination are her focus. (She devotes scant attention to the question of sexual orientation or the connection between feminism and the struggle for justice for gays and lesbians.) "The gains were remarkable, and they were also shaky," Stansell writes. The defeat of the ERA sapped the movement of energy, and many of its achievements remain profoundly contested, as antifeminism has gained political power. Nonetheless, Stansell is optimistic about feminism's prospects: many paths have been blazed, and all that's required is the courage to follow them in the teeth of adversity and to continue drawing on the legacy of the past, taking up "the task of making good on feminism's democratic promise."

One disturbing thread running through Stansell's narrative is the racism of many white feminists. Repeatedly, the cause of women was defended by claiming that it was absurd to give African-American men the vote but to deny it to women, so much more intelligent and cultivated. Even some of the greatest feminists, such as Stanton, were not free from the taint of racism. Stansell shows that African-American feminists typically held themselves aloof from white feminists for such reasons, determined to defend both racial and gender equality. Stansell indicates that any adequate feminism for the future must be attentive to and respectful of differences of race and class and the struggles of other minorities. She is hardly the first to say this, but she says it well.

In the final chapter, on global feminism, Stansell shows that similar difficulties threaten the growing engagements of American women with feminist movements in developing nations. She gives disturbing examples of condescension and bias, of American feminists preaching enlightenment to women elsewhere as if they were mere victims and dupes. On the whole, though, as Stansell persuasively and correctly shows, global feminism has become a two-way street, with advice and knowledge traveling in both directions. Crucial human rights documents such as the Convention on the Elimination of All Forms of Discrimination Against Women (CEDAW) have been worked out in full cooperation by women in the West and developing nations from many different backgrounds, and certainly with no help from the United States, which, along with Iran, Sudan, Somalia, and a handful of small and island states, has failed to ratify CEDAW. Stansell also shows how decisive progress on issues such as improving women's access to credit and education and eliminating sex-selective abortion has been made by indigenous women's movements acting at the local level in a wide range of countries, with no "access to Western sympathizers." Like the rest of the book, the chapter on global feminism is nuanced, judicious, and edifying.

The way Stansell packages feminism's complex history is clarifying, but it also distorts. For example, by suggesting that the early twentieth century was an era when radical daughters took the lead, she downplays the contin-ued leadership of the mothers in the temperance movement, which ultimately led to Prohibition. Her account of the media in the '50s, though largely accurate, is too monolithically grim. "The workingwomen on television who left flickering imprints on the collective subconscious were inevitably single and comically lonely," she writes, singling out Eve Arden's Miss Brooks as an example but omitting Mr. Boynton, her clueless yet extremely nice boyfriend. She doesn't mention my favorite show of the period, *Perry Mason* (1957–66), which featured a long-term nonmarital sexual relationship between Raymond Burr's Perry and Barbara Hale's Della Street, a secretary, to be sure, but a very high-powered one who participated in the detecting, and who always wore stylish and sexy clothes. The show itself stood, ahead of its time, for '60s values. (Burr, for one, was a not-very-closeted gay man living with a long-term male partner.) In 1960, when William Talman, the actor who played District Attorney Hamilton Burger, was arrested and charged with smoking marijuana at a nude swimming party, Burr came to his defense and made sure he didn't lose his job. (My consternation over the words "morals charge" in the reticent newspapers of the day was swept aside when I learned that Talman had not done anything really immoral.) The show was quietly subversive on account of its dramatic allure: it was the only program that my attorney father, highly conservative, allowed us to watch at the dinner table, and while he pointed out all the legal errors, I couldn't help but notice Barbara Hale's flirtatious yet classy conduct. Still active at 88, she is certainly in my feminist pantheon.

Another distortion that cuts close to my heart is Stansell's depiction of major U.S. law schools. According to Stansell, it took post-'50s daughters to open the gates of the leading schools to women. While Stansell is correct in her depiction of Harvard Law School, which didn't admit women until 1950, and kept their numbers small until at least the 1970s (thirty-two out of 565 in the entering class of 1967), she doesn't mention that the University of Chicago Law School admitted women from its inception in 1902. The well-known social activist Sophonisba Breckinridge, who graduated from Wellesley College in 1888, was in that law school's first graduating class of 1904. Breckinridge had already become a member of the Kentucky bar in 1894, and had received a PhD in political science from the University of Chicago in 1901.

Breckinridge's time at the University of Chicago is a reminder that in many ways, though surely not in all, the Midwest was more egalitarian than the snooty East. The first female lawyer in the United States was Arabella Mansfield, admitted to the Iowa bar in 1869. In its recent opinion legalizing same-sex marriage, the Iowa Supreme Court reminded Iowans that the state has been consistently at the forefront of unpopular movements for social justice. And the court was right, even about Iowa's standing in the field of law in the Midwest. Although Missouri joined Iowa in admitting women to the bar in 1870, and a group of other Midwestern states quickly followed suit, the U.S. Supreme Court upheld the exclusion of women from the Illinois bar in 1873; Myra Bradwell, the original plaintiff in the case, was admitted to the Illinois bar in 1890 and the bar of the Supreme Court in 1892. The District of Columbia and Maine admitted women to the bar in 1872, with the rest of the states on the East Coast doing the same by the early 1890s. Such regional differences barely figure in Stansell's account, but they are fascinating, and someone should investigate them further.

A book of this sort, capacious as it is, cannot do everything, and the criticism of it that follows is no doubt colored by my own work in philosophy, law, and public policy. Nonetheless, it seems clear to me that Stansell is indifferent to the role that ideas, particularly philosophical and economic ideas, have played in feminism's history. Many of her protagonists are writers and theorists, yet she devotes scant attention to their theories. Mary Wollstonecraft is given at least some consideration for her ideas about human rights in *A Vindication of the Rights of Woman*; but the compelling arguments with which she advanced them are omitted, so it is left entirely unclear why people ought to have listened to her. John Stuart Mill's *The Subjection of Women* is mentioned as a feminist landmark, but the arguments at its core are left unexamined. Simone de Beauvoir's *The Second Sex* is the only theoretical work of the modern era that merits a reading, albeit a cursory one that ignores its roots in existentialist ideas of freedom and self-fashioning. Catharine MacKinnon, the major intellectual architect of modern legal feminism, who reoriented thinking about equality and discrimination, is discussed in a couple of sentences, and strictly as an anti-pornography activist. The ideas that led MacKinnon to her theory of pornography and to her far more influential theory of sexual harassment are ignored. Indeed, in a very odd oversight, Stansell doesn't address the topic of sexual harassment in the workplace, an ongoing concern of feminists in the late twentieth century. My legal colleagues, whatever their political persuasion, routinely cite MacKinnon's *Sexual Harassment of Working Women* as one the most influential books in U.S. legal scholarship. Around the time of its publication in 1979, political theorist Susan Moller Okin and economist Nancy Folbre were reorienting much influential thinking and policy-making about justice inside the family; Stansell does not mention either woman.

What do we miss when these ideas are overlooked? The ideas are important in themselves; but they also have immense importance for the practice of feminism and for the success of its efforts at social change. Let's take just three examples. In *The Subjection of Women*, Mill is at pains to show us that male domination has shaped not only women's opportunities but also their desires and emotional habits (a theme already broached by Wollstonecraft and that would prove central for MacKinnon and Andrea Dworkin). Thus the deference and timidity that women display toward men are not indicative of an immutable female nature, as many alleged in Mill's time. Rather, these characteristics are proof that gender hierarchy, like feudal hierarchy, leaves deep marks on the human spirit.

This insight has enormous consequences for theories of social development and measurements of "quality of life." Modern feminist economists such as Amartya Sen (winner of the Nobel Prize in 1998 for his development work) have argued that no theory of development based on the satisfaction of people's preferences could ever be normatively adequate: such a theory would always be an unwitting accomplice of an unjust status quo. The struggle to find a replacement for preference-based theories is no idle matter, since such theories are used throughout the world to measure social welfare. If women report that they are satisfied by the amount of education they have managed to attain, so the thinking goes, then they are doing fine— even though in many cases their preferences have been formed by social norms about proper female occupations. Thus Mill's insight, years later, determines the course of millions of women's lives—or, more often, fails to do so.

My second example concerns equality. Until the postwar era it was common in American law to think that equal treatment meant similar treatment, and that the "equal protection of the laws" could not possibly be violated by any symmetrical arrangement bearing on either race or sex. The principle of equal treatment was used by lower court judges, and some legal theorists, to defend laws against miscegenation: blacks can't marry whites, and whites can't marry blacks. How could such laws possibly involve a constitutional violation? The fact that African-Americans obviously bore the brunt of these laws, and that the laws were inspired by racial disgust, was left out of account. Similarly, laws that were symmetrical for women and men were also taken to be unproblematic, even when they imposed special burdens on women. If insurers denied coverage for pregnancy leave, they were not guilty of sex discrimination, so the argument went, because all "non-pregnant persons" were covered, and all pregnant ones were not covered—without regard to their sex! Sexual harassment, too, was taken to be an equal-opportunity matter, involving no illicit discrimination: after all, women could approach men for sexual favors, just as men could approach women. The hierarchy of power in the workplace was utterly ignored.

With her *Sexual Harassment of Working Women*, MacKinnon offered a new and more adequate theory. She powerfully argued that sexual harassment (and other denials of equal opportunity) should be viewed through the lens of what she called a "dominance theory" of equality rather than through the old "difference theory." That is, the right question to ask of a problematic policy is whether it creates or perpetuates a hierarchy of power that defines classes of people as higher or lower, dominant or subservient. The "equal protection of the laws" requires resisting such hierarchies. In effect, MacKinnon's is an antifeudal account of political equality. The Supreme Court had already drawn on the principle at the heart of MacKinnon's dominance theory in the area of race when, in the 1967 case *Loving v. Virginia*, it invalidated anti-miscegenation laws on the grounds that they were "designed to maintain White Supremacy." The fact that the laws were symmetrical on their face was immaterial. (The earlier invalidation of "separate but equal" schools, in *Brown v. Board of Education*, in 1954, rested on a similar analysis.) MacKinnon, however, articulated the contrasting theories with unprecedented clarity and applied them to the area of gender, where it had not previously been acknowledged in the law that an illicit hierarchy of power existed. (In *Sexual Harassment of Working Women*, MacKinnon cannily demonstrates that you can arrive at her conclusion that sexual harassment is discrimination even if you don't accept her controversial dominance theory of equality; nevertheless, it was her theory that eventually entered the judicial mind and reshaped legal doctrine.)

My final example concerns the family. For a long time in economics, the reigning concept of the family was that it was a unit held together by love and altruism, without cooperative conflicts that needed to be taken into account. Mill had long ago subjected that idea to withering criticism, arguing that the family as constituted in his time was a bastion of feudal privilege in the midst of the allegedly liberal state. But nobody took Mill's ideas seriously. In *A Treatise on the Family*, for which (among other contributions) he won the Nobel Prize in 1992, economist Gary Becker held that for analytical purposes we can assume that the "head of the household" is a beneficent altruist who always takes adequate account of the interests of all family members—an assumption that Becker, with his keen interest in reality, later criticized by acknowledging that motives such as envy and malice often shape the distribution of resources within the family.

Becker's determination, in his *Treatise*, to bring economic theory to the domain of family life was important and salutary. Nonetheless, the theory did some harm. Because development economists were highly swayed by Becker's theory, they assumed that the household can be treated as a single unit and so ignored internal distributional issues; consequently, it has been almost impossible until recently to get data about the resources and opportunities available to individual family members. Yet over the past thirty years, the dominant view of the family in economics has shifted to one in which ideas of competition and of a socially shaped bargaining position dominate. This change is due to the work of such feminist economists as Sen, Bina Agarwal, and Robert Pollak; feminist political theorist Okin; and the important journal *Feminist Economics*, which provides a venue for the exploration of such ideas. The new ideas have reshaped data-gathering, as have, simultaneously, the ideas of Nancy Folbre and others about how to ascribe a monetary value to women's unpaid household labor (a very practical matter, as anyone will know who has sought compensation for the injury or death of a partner mainly occupied in domestic labor).

Such insights are gradually making their way into national policy, as demonstrated in the recent report on the measurement of a nation's quality of life commissioned by French President Nicolas Sarkozy and chaired by Sen and Joseph Stiglitz, with both Agarwal and Folbre as commission members. The key finding was that a nation's quality of life should not be measured by gross national product per capita but instead by assessing people's "capabilities," or substantial opportunities for choice. One sphere it emphasized was the family, where opportunities are often unequally distributed along lines of sex. The newer economic theories of the family have long been accepted working paradigms in India, a nation somewhat more progressive, in terms of economic theory, than the United States and even Europe, and that has a sophisticated economist, Manmohan Singh, as prime minister and, in Kaushik Basu, a chief economic adviser who is a strong feminist and the current president of the Human Development and Capability Association (founded by Sen and me). Maybe someday the ideas of the new feminist economics will even surface in the corridors of power in the United States, though I'm not making any bets on when.

These cases show that political history written with an aversion to theoretical ideas is incomplete even as history. Ideas matter for people, and they make things happen in the world. Feminism should not be wedded to a type of historical materialism that denies this insight. Many feminists have been historical materialists; Stansell is not. But she lacks interest in philosophy and economics, and she apparently believes that telling the story of feminist ideas is a job for another book. I believe, however, that the story she eloquently tells is woefully incomplete without them. If feminists today are to make good on the promises of their predecessors, mothers and daughters alike, they need to study the arguments, testing their cogency and tracing the ways they were linked to practical struggles to achieve justice and equality for women. Feminism has succeeded, to the extent that it has, partly by dint of its bold ideas; to overlook these ideas is to diminish feminism.

# CHAPTER THIRTY-FIVE

# American Civil War

STEFAN COLLINI (2010), That's Offensive! Criticism, Identity, Respect

While I was working on a book on gay rights and law, I presented several chapters at a work-in-progress workshop at the University of Chicago Law School. As I've come to expect, my colleagues assailed me with criticisms of all sorts, tough and thoughtful, from all sides of the political spectrum. For, unlike virtually all other law schools, we have that rare thing—an open, broad-spectrum, undefensive yet rigorous intellectual community, and it is very precious.

Afterwards my most conservative colleague wrote me an email, saying that he hoped nothing in his trenchant challenges to my position had caused offence. Actually, his manner had been extremely civil, but since he's capable of intemperate and sarcastic utterance, and (like most of us) does not have perfect self-knowledge, I thought it was well-advised that he asked. He was showing the sort of care about personal civility that sustains our community and makes it so different from the ugly free-for-all that sadly characterizes much of American political life.

This story illustrates both the great virtue of Stefan Collini's eloquent argument—its ringing defense of rigorous criticism—and its most glaring gap: its failure to appreciate the virtue of civility and the special demands it makes when a majority is discussing traditionally stigmatized groups. Collini values, as I do, the no-holds-barred give-and-take of argument, and he believes, as I do, that open debate of this sort is a valuable ingredient in the political life.

His brief manifesto says that we have entered an era in which people shrink from challenge and want to be surrounded only by the like-minded; or those who will not subject the cherished beliefs others hold to searching criticism.

Particularly when beliefs are bound up with a religious, ethnic, or other group identity, people expect to be able to shield them from criticism, and would-be critics have learned to silence themselves. We are all the worse for this self-censorship, Collini argues.

All of this is right on target. Even more so is Collini's insistence that the threat of violence should never be used as a device to stifle debate: a climate in which people fear violence if they give offence is incompatible with an open political culture in which all receive equal respect.

As a historical claim this has some problems, since the founders of the United States were also inordinately fond of dueling, and this bizarre ritual of male pride did not actually stifle the growing democracy (though it did rob it of one of its greatest rational arguers, Alexander Hamilton). But we can certainly agree that it is best if people do not resort to violence when honor is outraged, or use the implicit threat of violence to stop others from criticizing them. So far, so good.

Beyond this, however, lie many questions. What forms of argumentative speech should be illegal? Collini doesn't really face this one, but it is tough, because many forms of speech are currently illegal—bribery, threats, unlicensed medical advice, fraudulent offers, defamation and many more; and any one of these could be given the superficial form of a rational argument in order to shield it from the law if the legal standard were that all rational argument is protected. I assume that Collini is not challenging the traditional torts of defamation, invasion of privacy, intentional infliction of emotional distress, or even (a case he does briefly consider) the legally defined offences of racial or sexual harassment. But then his position is less extreme than its rhetoric at times suggests, though he does make a welcome objection to Britain's archaic blasphemy law.

Next, which offensive speakers should be protected by law from violence and the threat of violence? That's not the same question, because in offering a bribe or making a fraudulent offer, one does not forfeit the law's protection against violence. Some forms of speech, however, do remove that protection: the credible threat of death or gross bodily injury. Again, this would have been useful to discuss, but it lies beyond the scope of Collini's manifesto.

The real gap, however, is where I began: civility. A robust critical culture is not easy to maintain and it is rather like a garden, which must be carefully pruned of various weeds, such as contemptuousness, vanity, intemperance and snarkiness. Collini says that in arguing one should always respect the opponent as a rational being, first and foremost. But what does that mean? Sarcasm, eye-rolling, audible sighing, jokey asides when someone is giving a paper, these things do seem to me to undermine that respect.

But now comes the real problem. The duties of civility turn out to impose asymmetrical demands on members of the majority when they are dealing with one another and, by contrast, when they are dealing with previously or currently stigmatized minority groups. Because women and African Americans, for example, have for centuries been treated as if they have no right to be in the public assembly room or the academy, special care has to be used when addressing them with critical arguments.

If I give a feminist paper and a colleague rolls his eyes, or speaks in a snarky manner, that conduct is continuous with centuries during which women were just assumed to be incapable of rational performance, and with a more recent era during which women's studies and normative feminism were assumed by most academic men not to be genuine fields of academic inquiry.

Given that context, it is good to be particularly careful. And with this virtue, as with all, context is everything. Colleagues who are trusted friends know they can tease me about my feminism and my left-wing politics (a stigmatized minority position in America), but that is not the recommended modus operandi for those same people when confronting a female or African-American job candidate, or, indeed, for anyone who is not a trusted friend of the person being teased.

Sometimes I get the feeling that Collini is hearing people urging others to be civil, and misinterpreting it as a demand that they stop arguing. The two demands, however, are utterly different and, indeed, one can't sustain a rational dialogue without the virtue of civility. A demand for delicacy and caution is not a demand for silence, it's a necessary aspect of making speech flourish.

Because Collini is right about the goal for which we should strive—a community of rigorous and open argument—it seems unfortunate that he is not attuned to the problems of civility often faced by unpopular minorities who are making new demands. Arguments are not abstract propositions in the air. They are human performances toward other particular humans, in which the specific choice of vocabulary, the tone of voice, and the look in the eyes all matter for whether the performance is virtuous or vicious. So we should seek the goal to which Collini points us, but pursue it with all our ethical and emotional wits about us.

# Index